Foundations of Library and Information Science

THIRD EDITION

RICHARD E. RUBIN

Neal-Schuman Publishers, Inc.

New York   London

Published by Neal-Schuman Publishers, Inc.
100 William St., Suite 2004
New York, NY 10038

Printed and bound in the United States of America.

The paper used in this publication meets the minimum requirements of American National
Standard for Information Sciences—Permanence of Paper for Printed Library Materials,
ANSI Z39.48-1992.

Library of Congress Cataloging-in-Publication Data

Rubin, Richard, 1949-
    Foundations of library and information science / Richard E. Rubin. — 3rd ed.
        p. cm.
    Includes bibliographical references and index.
    ISBN 978-1-55570-690-6 (alk. paper)
        1. Library science—United States. 2. Information science—United States. I. Title.

Z665.2.U6R83 2010
020'.0973—dc22

                                                                                2010009302

Contents

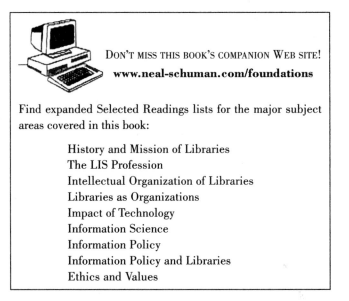

DON'T MISS THIS BOOK'S COMPANION WEB SITE!

www.neal-schuman.com/foundations

Find expanded Selected Readings lists for the major subject
areas covered in this book:

History and Mission of Libraries
The LIS Profession
Intellectual Organization of Libraries
Libraries as Organizations
Impact of Technology
Information Science
Information Policy
Information Policy and Libraries
Ethics and Values

Figures

Foreword

Textbooks are unique. We normally think of them, naturally, as instructional aids, sources that can be read or consulted when needed (or perhaps just highlighted as part of some mystically osmotic process of learning), usually accompanying a formal, structured course. They serve both as frameworks for those courses and as a kind of repository to be dipped into on demand; in some ways they're like narrative books and in others more like reference materials.

They also have a secondary function—they make great milestones, marking the path that a topic or discipline takes as it evolves. This is particularly true when you look at them over time. Reading, for example, Margaret Hutchins's *Introduction to Reference Work* from 1944, you can see just how far our knowledge and practice of reference services has come—and how much remains the same.

So writing a good textbook isn't easy, but it is important. The really fine ones leave a mark, and that's what Rick Rubin has done with this latest edition of his foundations textbook. It's staggering to think about how much effort and thought must go into a book like this; trying to distill decades (centuries, really) of theory, practice, opinion, and experience in a field that is broad and expanding and evolving on a daily basis.

It's also particularly challenging because of the audience. Many people come to the library and information professions after work in the field for a while, but many don't, so there's no common language or experience to draw upon. For some of you, this will be your first exposure to our world and professional culture. Let me reassure you that you're in very capable hands.

For those of you who are joining us, regardless of your background, this book may appear at first glance to be a straightforward exposition of the literature, history, and traditions of the library and information work, and that it is.

It is also the story of humanity. Look at the sweep of human history and what you will find is the records and traces: cave drawings, scrolls, clay tablets, manuscripts, books, newspapers, pamphlets, journals, diaries, letters, paintings, sound recordings, moving images, blogs, and on and on and on. From Lascaux to YouTube, the message is the same: I was here, and I have a story to tell.

That cultural heritage, and the human record that tells those stories, is entrusted to us to preserve, collect, organize, manage, search, and help people to use, and that's what we do. So as you read this, learning about the rich heritage and traditions of your new professional domain, once in a while I want you to stop and take a deep breath and remember that while the fine details of AACR or CIPA or OCLC or the *OED* are important, there's more going on.

We make humanity more human. We grease the wheels of knowledge, so that the people we serve can consult that human record more easily and effectively, and use what they find to learn and better themselves and their communities. The only thing I can guarantee you is that almost everything important in our world will change . . . yet much endures and you'll find a lot to help you along here.

One final word, on behalf of the long line of those who have gone before, and the thousands of colleagues eagerly awaiting your arrival. There is nothing better you can do with your life. You're entering a profession that we cherish deeply and hold dear and we can't wait to see the wonderful things you do. All the best as you start on your way.

Joseph Janes
Associate Professor, The Information School
University of Washington
Seattle, Washington

Preface

Keeping up is hard to do. Much has happened since the second edition of *Foundations of Library and Information Science* was published six years ago. The boundaries of library and information science (LIS) continue to expand, the issues proliferate and grow in complexity, and the challenges we face are serious and relentless. It is daunting and delightful. Our profession demands constant growth, continuous learning, and open minds. We know that next year something new will again force us to reexamine our thinking and reassess our practices, policies, and sometimes even our purpose. We are fortunate that we have a firm foundation on which to make changes: a distinguished history, strong values, and an active professional and academic community ready to address our challenges.

As with its predecessors, this new edition has been designed to respond to the many changes occurring in the field and the society at large. It preserves much of the content of the second edition but has been reorganized, rewritten, and extensively updated. Most important, new or enhanced discussions have been added including (1) the growing impact of the World Wide Web; (2) blogs, wikis, and other forms of social networking on services; (3) electronic publishing, including e-books, digital libraries, digital preservation, mass digitization, and digital repositories; (4) new efforts to organize knowledge such as the development of Functional Requirements for Bibliographic Records (FRBR); (5) the significance of the digital divide and policy issues related to broadband access and network neutrality; (6) changes in library services such as roving reference, e-government, and gaming; (7) legal developments such as new applications and impacts of the U.S.A. PATRIOT Act; and (8) the increasing tensions in LIS education between information science and library science.

Regarding this last point, there remains an ongoing debate as to whether library science and information science are separate disciplines. There are also arguments about what constitutes the domains of each. *Foundations of Library and Information Science* is focused on the complementary nature of these disciplines using Boyd Rayward's 1983 description of the relationship between library and information science as "a disciplinary continuum ... with no easily identifiable boundary separating them though the difference between the extreme ends of the continuum are clear and even dramatic" (p. 344). This book focuses on the points of convergence.

PURPOSE

The primary purpose of *Foundations of Library and Information Science* remains to describe the current library and information science environment and examine some of the ever-changing forces that shape that environment and the larger society. My intent is to help prepare LIS professionals to cope with and effectively manage their many complex responsibilities. Bearing this emphasis in mind, this text is designed to accomplish six objectives:

1. To provide an introduction to the field for individuals intending to work in libraries or library-like institutions, related settings, or the information field in general.

2. To identify and discuss major topics and issues in library and information science that are current in the United States and that will continue to affect the profession for years to come.

3. To provide librarians and information professionals with an opportunity to refresh their knowledge through a systematic review of major issues and topics that have changed the field.

4. To introduce the profession to interested individuals or those undecided about entering the library and information science field and to show its multifaceted character and possibilities.

5. To place library and information science in a larger social, economic, and political context. It is too easy to view the work of LIS professionals purely within an institutional setting. Increasingly, librarians and other information professionals must negotiate and respond to a variety of political, economic, technological, and social forces.

6. To invite the interested reader to further explore topics raised in this book. Many of these topics are part of an ongoing discussion in our field that requires further reading, research, and exchange.

ORGANIZATION

Although many of the original chapter headings remain, the arrangement of chapters in this edition has been altered in response to feedback from faculty members and our editorial advisory board.

The Introduction and Chapter 1 provide a broad overview and context for the ensuing chapters. The Introduction identifies and discusses four major forces shaping the broader society and concomitantly the world of LIS professionals and institutions. Chapter 1, "The Educational, Recreational, and Informational Infrastructure," provides an important context by describing and discussing critical institutions that support libraries and other information-disseminating institutions.

Chapters 2 and 3 provide the historical foundations of libraries as institutions and of library and information science as a profession. "From Past to Present: The History and Mission of Libraries" examines the character of libraries through time with specific emphasis on their many and varied purposes. Chapter 3, "Library and Information Science: An Evolving Profession," reviews the evolution and development of the profession. The contemporary American library and information professional is a product of more than a hundred years of growth and change. The current role of LIS professionals and the professional tensions that they experience are best understood when placed in the context of the historical development of library and information science education and the profession.

Chapter 4 examines the intellectual organization of libraries. "The Organization of Information: Techniques and Issues" discusses the organizational systems that make information, in all its myriad forms, available. In spite of the vast quantities of disparate materials, our classification systems, subject headings, thesauri, databases, and powerful catalogs enable LIS professionals to offer information retrieval on demand. Organizing information is one of the touchstones of our profession.

Chapters 5 and 6 explore libraries as institutions; first from a general perspective, and then focusing on the specific effects of technology. Chapter 5, "The Library as an Institution: An Organizational Perspective," examines contemporary libraries, their types, and internal functions, as well as the major organizational issues that they face. Chapter 6, "Redefining the Library: The Impacts and Implications of Technological Change," deals with one of the biggest areas of change in our field, the growth of information technologies, especially those that have affected the organization and delivery of information in libraries and information centers. Information technologies have altered the way information providers in all types of organizations interact with their users. Issues arising from these changes are addressed.

Chapter 7, "Information Science: A Service Perspective," focuses on the nature of information science as a field of study, calling special attention to those aspects of the discipline that inform the work of LIS professionals.

Chapters 8, 9, and 10 deal with philosophical and policy issues affecting library and information science. These include the policies, laws, values, and ethics that define our work. Chapter 8, "Information Policy: Stakeholders and Agendas," discusses the more general aspects of information policy and the legal environment in which libraries and other information institutions operate. Government, business, industry, public institutions, LIS professionals, and citizens all are stakeholders in trying to shape how information will be disseminated and who will disseminate it. Chapter 9, "Information Policy as Library Policy: Intellectual Freedom," focuses on libraries and examines key information policies, such as those related to intellectual freedom and equitable access to information. Chapter 10, "The Values and Ethics of Library and Information Science," examines the many ethical ramifications of working in the field. Ethical principles, codes, and situations are reviewed and the values that undergird our profession are examined.

To permit an examination of the same topic from different vantage points, *Foundations of Library and Information Science* addresses most topics primarily in one chapter, but some important issues are raised anew in a different context in other chapters. For example, censorship and intellectual freedom issues are discussed most thoroughly in Chapter 9, but they also arise in Chapter 8, on information policy, and "The Library as an Institution," Chapter 5. The Internet and Web, because they undergird most information transmission today, are covered in multiple chapters as well. Similarly, because of the tremendous breadth of our field, some complementary areas are mentioned but not explored in depth, including such fields as publishing and book arts, archives, and computer science.

A list of highly selected readings follows each chapter. These selections provide sources of additional information and stimulate thought on the basic issues raised in this text. See this book's companion Web site (www.neal-schuman.com/foundations) for expanded lists of selected readings for the major subject areas covered in this book:

- History and Mission of Libraries
- The LIS Profession
- Intellectual Organization of Libraries
- Libraries as Organizations
- Impact of Technology
- Information Science
- Information Policy
- Information Policy and Libraries
- Ethics and Values

Readers should understand that continuous consultation with the most recently published material is essential if one is to stay current.

Rounding out the book, two appendixes provide supplemental information on LIS associations and accredited schools of library and information science in the United States and Canada.

No LIS professional can function unless he or she understands the importance of information, how libraries are organized intellectually and administratively, the effects of information policies, and the values and ethics of librarians and the profession. The challenge of all professionals is to stay current in a world in flux. The library is a special place; library and information science is a special profession. The roles of the former and latter, as well as the broader forces that shape those roles, constitute the major focus of *Foundations of Library and Information Science*. Its goal is to be a valuable resource for those entering the profession and those who have already taken their place within it.

REFERENCE

Rayward, Boyd. 1983. "Library and Information Sciences." In *The Study of Information: Interdisciplinary Messages*. Edited by Fritz Machlup and Una Mansfield. New York: Wiley, 343–363.

Acknowledgments

The third edition of this book would not have been possible without the considerable help and support of many individuals. Thanks go to Carolyn Brodie, Greg Byerly, Athena Salaba, Yin Zhang, and Marcia Zeng for contributing their thoughts and carefully reviewing and commenting on drafts of various chapters. Thanks also to graduate assistants Mary Bohn, Brittany Harnisch, and Kornella Bogdanowicz, who provided invaluable assistance locating, verifying, and preparing information collected for the book. Thanks must also go to the outside readers of the manuscript, whose valuable criticisms improved the work substantially. Special thanks to my wife, Marcia, and daughter, Rachel, for their incredible patience.

Introduction

Not long ago an introductory text to the field would have been about libraries and librarians; a review of the history, basic services, organizational structure, and library classification systems would have sufficed. This is no longer a possibility. Today's library and information science (LIS) professionals are experiencing both excitement and trepidation as sweeping societal changes affect our users and institutions and transform our discipline. The library is now a part of a complex and dynamic educational, recreational, and informational infrastructure. It is also an integral part of a social infrastructure that demands that we understand how knowledge and information are created, organized, accessed, disseminated, and used. To provide a broad context for the ensuing material, this introduction explores four trends shaping some of the basic institutions in our society. These trends affect all of us, in our work life as well as our personal life. We will need to respond with adaptability, creativity, and resolve.

> **Current Trends Shaping Our Institutions**
>
> 1. The Internet is changing everything.
> 2. The population is becoming increasingly diverse.
> 3. The fiscal environment is and will remain uncertain.
> 4. Expectations of privacy are changing.

TREND 1: THE INTERNET IS CHANGING EVERYTHING

Times have changed. Millions of Americans, from all economic and social strata, now use the Internet on a daily basis. This is a remarkable development given that few people even knew what the Internet was in 1990. Although books, magazines, and other traditional media are likely to be around for many years to come, their continued presence does not diminish the immense impact of the Internet and the World Wide Web. From finding telephone numbers to exploring complex topics, from learning how to repair an automobile to viewing collections of art, from exchanging e-mails to finding a life partner, from buying a dress to downloading an e-book, the Internet has opened a vast expanse of knowledge and communication to millions of Americans.

The influence of the Web has become even more dramatic as access has moved from desktop computers to "mobiles." Hand-held devices such as iPods and Black-Berries bring the power of the Web literally into the hands of users. Such devices, according to Anderson and Rainie (2008), are likely to be "the primary connection tool to the Internet for most people in the world in 2020" (p. 2). Similarly, with the advent of widespread broadband access and increasing wireless connectivity, one can be connected almost anytime, anyplace, and anywhere. And as we move from Web 1.0 to Web 2.0, to 3.0 and beyond, the ability to learn, to be informed, to enjoy and interact with the world of information will increase and be enriched.

The Internet, of course, has also opened many doors for libraries. Local collections are now supplemented and dramatically expanded through access to world-wide digital collections. Access to authoritative knowledge (as well as not so authoritative knowledge) is now available almost instantaneously at a cost much lower than the cost of acquiring this knowledge in physical forms. People have access to the library collection and its staff remotely and interactively.

The Internet certainly has its fascination and usefulness for those of us who grew up when television was the primary source of information and entertainment, but its greater significance will be for those who are part of the "Net generation": those for whom the digital world has been a part of the natural world and their daily lives from birth. Their expectations are different. They demand the ability to perform many critical functions by themselves that traditionally were performed by others (self-service); they want to perform a variety of disparate functions, moving easily from task to task in the same virtual space (seamlessness); and they want all of this conveniently—right at their fingertips (satisfaction) (De Rosa et al. 2004). In the Internet age, people expect ever more customized service, service highly tailored to their particular wants and needs, and they want the processes that they encounter to be simpler and more effective. It is a new world—one in which public institutions must adapt or lose their users' trust and participation.

Yet, at the same time, we must pause and remain critical of the problems and issues that arise as the digital world expands—the "digital divide" is real and persistent. The electronic age requires that we be responsible citizens protecting people's privacy and confidentiality and ensuring equality of access whenever possible. The Internet is here to stay—we must use it wisely.

TREND 2: THE POPULATION IS BECOMING INCREASINGLY DIVERSE

The United States is undergoing a major transformation in the demographic character of its population. Increasing life expectancy, immigration, and childbearing patterns are changing the social, political, economic, and educational infrastructure of the nation. Passell and Cohn (2008) report on some of the demographic trends that should affect us through 2050:

1. In 2005, the U.S. population was 296 million; in 2050 it is projected to be 440 million. Immigrants or the children of immigrants will account for a significant proportion of this increase, nearly one in five Americans. In 2005 the proportion was only one in eight.

2. From 2005 to 2050, the population of elderly (the baby boomers) will increase from 37 million to 81 million, 19 percent of the population, while the population of children will increase from 73 million to 102 million. Ironically, the proportion of working-age Americans—those supporting the young and old—will grow more slowly and will decline as a percentage of the population.

3. The Latino population will triple in size, from 42 to 128 million by 2050, or 29 percent of the population. Children of Hispanic origin will increase from 20 percent to 35 percent of the population. The Asian population will grow nearly as quickly, tripling from 14 to 41 million. African Americans will increase from 38 million to 59 million while remaining 13 percent of the population. The population of people of European descent will decline, dropping from 67 percent of the population to 47 percent in 2050.

These demographic shifts require careful monitoring. Reaching out to diverse communities will be essential but will also require additional resources and new expertise. For public institutions like libraries that serve a broad spectrum of the population, these shifts will be particularly demanding, especially in an age when money is scarce.

TREND 3: THE FISCAL ENVIRONMENT IS AND WILL REMAIN UNCERTAIN

Even before the rapid deterioration of the economic infrastructure in 2008 and 2009, a variety of indicators suggested that public institutions would be fiscally challenged. For example, government funding was flat or even declining. Citizens were reluctant to increase taxes while the costs of public agencies continued to rise. In particular, costs for health care, energy, and technology put significant strains on institutional budgets. At the same time, citizens expected high performance and increasing accountability. All of these issues create serious challenges today. A report sponsored by Cisco Systems (Economist Intelligence Unit 2006) on trends to 2020 made the following observation:

> Public agencies will struggle with an array of profound challenges over the next 15 years, made worse by funding constraints and rising citizen expectations....

> Budget constraints and swelling demand mean that agencies will be expected to do more with less. There will be greater emphasis on technology deployment, on performance management and measurement, and on outsourcing of non-core services as a result.... Government services will be designed and delivered to meet the needs of citizens and businesses. Effective collaboration with other agencies and private-sector organizations will be critical in enabling public-service organizations both to deliver better service and control expenditure. (p. 62)

The complexity of the financial environment—rising health care costs, increasing strains on natural resources, and the costs of maintaining a strong technological infrastructure—are but a few of the major cost concerns that public institutions will continue to confront. There is no doubt that demonstrable productivity, no matter how it is measured and defined by public institutions, will be critical for their fiscal survival. Success will require a careful assessment of how services are structured and simplified; what types of employee skills and training will be needed to maintain and improve their public performance; and how other private and public organizations can help support their productivity. The simple fact is: money is going to be a problem.

TREND 4: EXPECTATIONS OF PRIVACY ARE CHANGING

We are living in a world where expectations of privacy are evolving. With the growth of interconnected computer networks, people's privacy is becoming increasingly vulnerable to exposure. No matter how diligently security features are addressed, there are countless stories of individuals, groups, or even nations hacking into these systems and extracting information of the most personal nature. In some cases, vendors who store the information sell it or make it available to others without consent.

The vulnerability of computer networks is only one part of a deteriorating privacy environment. The events of September 11, 2001, raised national security concerns that led to changes in laws that now allow the government to gather information on citizens that previously had been protected. There might be good reasons for some of these activities, but the result is a decrease in our privacy. As privacy is eroded, so is trust in government, at least for some. Interestingly, not everyone has the same expectation of privacy. The "millennial" generation, those born between 1977 and 1990, are now a substantial part of the population and will increase as the baby boomer population shrinks. Millennials grew up knowing that computer networks process and disseminate personal information. In fact they are likely to post their own personal information and pictures on social networking sites with the expectation that "friends" can access them. Although there are options to control access to this information, it is clear that millennials and those who come after them are less concerned about privacy.

For years, librarians assumed that a fundamental value of the profession was to protect an individual's privacy. This deeply held conviction was based on the assumption that people will avoid seeking knowledge that is controversial or sensitive if they are subject to public exposure. However, in a world where individuals assume that information sought using a search engine or a database can inevitably be tracked to a particular person, telephone, or computer, they might no longer assume that such activities are private and no longer believe that libraries need to protect them.

SUMMARY

Many more trends could be identified, but by exploring these four we begin to place our professional work in a broader social context and develop an appreciation for the complexity that surrounds and influences librarians and information scientists in the twenty-first century. It is the obligation of LIS professionals to stay current not only on techniques and issues within their own profession but also on the external forces that shape our field. It is simply not possible to plan for the future, develop essential programs and services, build collections, and staff our organizations with qualified people if we do not appreciate these broader societal changes and trends. As the reader learns about the many facets of LIS presented in this book, placing the profession within this broader context provides us with a framework to understand the complexities and challenges facing us in the years ahead.

REFERENCES

Anderson, Janna Quitney, and Lee Rainie. 2008. "The Future of the Internet III." Pew Internet and American Life Project. December 14. Available: www.pewinternet.org/~/media//files/Reports/2008/PIP_FutureInternet3.pdf (accessed June 29, 2009).

De Rosa, Cathy, Lorcan Dempsey, and Alane Wilson. 2004. *The 2003 OCLC Environmental Scan: Pattern Recognition.* Dublin, OH: OCLC.

Economist Intelligence Unit. 2006. *Foresight 2020: Economic, Industry, and Corporate Trends.* New York: EIU.

Passell, Jeffrey S., and D'Vera Cohn. 2008. *U.S. Population Projections: 2005–2050.* Washington, DC: Pew Research Center, February 11. Available: www.pewresearch.org (accessed June 4, 2009).

1

The Educational, Recreational, and Informational Infrastructure

I. INTRODUCTION

Since the nineteenth century, American libraries have served the educational, recreational, and information (ERI) needs of their users. Libraries have served educational needs either by assisting schools and colleges directly in the formal education process or by providing individuals with an opportunity to educate themselves. Similarly, few would question the entertainment value that libraries have provided through recreational fiction, newspapers, popular magazines, and, more recently, entertainment DVDs, CDs, computer games, and access to the Internet. In the twentieth century, meeting informational needs has also become prominent and the information or reference desk is a familiar and integral part of library service. While some special libraries and information centers might focus only on information needs, many libraries with broader scope, such as public, academic, or school libraries, attempt to serve several or all of the ERI needs of their users.

The amount of ERI resources now available and the speed at which they are being produced are daunting and prodigious. Information once obtained primarily through traditional media such as books and periodicals is now available in many additional formats, including microfilm, DVD, Blu-ray, and MP3, as well as Web-based formats such as PDF, GIF, and HTML. No group is more aware of this plethora of information than LIS professionals, who have been trying to collect, organize, and disseminate recorded knowledge for centuries.

To function effectively, libraries and library-like organizations rely on an extensive infrastructure that supports their activities. This infrastructure is both a foundation and a framework, much like the infrastructure of a house. Without such a structure the house would collapse. Societies have a variety of infrastructures, such as a transportation infrastructure that includes highways, train tracks, air routes, and waterways that allow people and goods to travel efficiently. It also includes the governmental agencies that regulate transportation. The ERI infrastructure is similar, except that

7

Perceptions of Information Growth

The uneasiness stemming from the ever-growing amount of knowledge and information is evidenced by some of the metaphors we use to describe this phenomenon:

Information explosion: An explosion is dangerous, terrifying, and unanticipated; it suggests a world out of control. To come near it is to risk being destroyed; to ignore it does not mean it does not exist or that its effects can be avoided.

The flood of information: A flood conveys an image of being overwhelmed and of victims helplessly being swept away. There is lack of control over the raging tide of information. In its wake are left ruins.

Bombarded by information: This is yet another image of destruction, this time by repetitive bursts of information crashing on the heads of its victims and destroying them. It is descriptive of warfare with an enemy that produces a firestorm of chaos.

Information overload: This description conveys an image of a brain malfunctioning because it can't keep up. It reflects the dissonance arising from our awareness that we need information to live and function in today's society, just as a machine needs electricity to function, but too much information, too quickly, can be destructive, resulting in short-circuited networks and brain cells.

All of these images suggest fear and trepidation. One seldom hears an optimistic phrase like "cornucopia" of information or knowledge, reflecting pleasure at its abundance, although "wealth of information or knowledge" is sometimes used. Many people seem to be in a state of information anxiety. LIS professionals can help by providing effective access to the abundance of information, but also by helping individuals make selective and appropriate judgments regarding the credibility of the information they obtain.

---

the traffic is information rather than moving objects. This infrastructure exists with or without libraries, but it is greatly enhanced by their presence.

The ERI infrastructure integrates a variety of elements. For example, primarily educational materials can be recreational as well, and some recreational resources also have substantial educational and informational value. Understanding the components of the ERI infrastructure highlights the interdependence of libraries with educational institutions and information-producing and information-providing agencies and channels, and supplies an important context for understanding the place and function of libraries in the greater society.

II. ERI INFRASTRUCTURE

Five possible ways to characterize the ERI infrastructure are described in this section.

A. ERI Infrastructure as Process

The ERI infrastructure can be viewed as a process by which knowledge and information are created, disseminated, and used in a society. The traditional process consists of five components:

1. **Creators**—for example, authors, artists, and musicians who embody their ideas in a physical form or a product

2. **Products**—traditionally books, articles, paintings, or sheet music and, more recently, multimedia presentations, databases, or Web sites—which are made available by someone other than the creator, such as a distributor

3. **Distributors**—for example, publishers or vendors who make the products of many creators available , sometimes through other agencies who might serve as disseminators

4. **Disseminators**—similar to wholesalers in that they acquire significant amounts of ERI materials from distributors and disseminate them to individual users

5. **Users**—those who consume and use the knowledge or information

The library's role has traditionally been as a disseminator, an intermediary between the users, distributors, and creators.

The linear nature of this process, however, has changed dramatically. The World Wide Web blurs the relationship between creators, products, distributors, disseminators, and users. In the Web environment, creators can be distributors and disseminators. Distributors such as publishers and disseminators such as schools and libraries can also be creators (for example, through e-sites, blogs, Twitter accounts, and wikis). Novelists can write a novel, put it on the Web, and distribute it directly to the users, for a fee or free. Well-known musicians, such as Radiohead, have distributed entire albums online. Sites such as Wikipedia are prime examples of users as creators. The impact of electronic media on creators, distributors, and disseminators will no doubt continue to be considerable.

> ### ERI Infrastructure Types
>
> 1. ERI infrastructure as a **process** by which knowledge and information is created, disseminated, and used
> 2. ERI infrastructure as **devices** used to transmit information and knowledge
> 3. ERI infrastructure as **networks** that serve as major channels for communication of information and knowledge
> 4. ERI infrastructure as **media industries** that produce and distribute knowledge and information
> 5. ERI infrastructure as **institutions** that provide the foundation for knowledge creation and dissemination

B. ERI Infrastructure as Devices

Another way to view the ERI infrastructure is in terms of the devices used to transmit information and knowledge. These devices include books, periodicals, and newspapers as well as televisions, radios, DVD recorders, players, and discs, MP3 players, e-reading devices, podcasting devices, and I-phones, as well as desktop and laptop computers. Movie theaters might also be included in this list. Many of the most recently developed devices are expected to continue to evolve in functionality. Although the utility of these devices is manifest, their constant alteration and the predictable creation of new, competing technologies create challenges for institutions attempting to organize and disseminate the information and knowledge created and stored in device-specific formats. The problem is confounded by the need in many cases to preserve the information contained in these devices over time and in a stable and usable manner.

C. ERI Infrastructure as Networks

Viewing the ERI infrastructure from a network perspective highlights the extent to which libraries depend on much larger systems. These networks serve as major communication channels and include telephone, radio, and television networks; ground-based and wireless utilities; digital/satellite links; and the network of all networks, the Internet.

> *Telephone, radio, and television networks; ground-based and wireless utilities; digital/satellite links; and, of course, the Internet are all major communication channels within society.*

The Internet connects many information networks on a global as well as local scale. The first years of the Web, sometimes called "Web 1.0," consisted of essentially passive Web sites—waiting to be discovered by the search engine or user. By intent, the content was created and controlled by the developer. New innovative applications, however, such as RSS feeds, wikis, blogs, and other social networking software spawned an Internet evolution sometimes called "Web 2.0." At its most basic level, the Web 2.0 environment permits site users to interact with and participate in the content development of that site. Such sites have become important places to exchange ideas and obtain news and other information, especially among the young. Users can also contribute text, audio, and video and create information. Wikipedia is a good exemplar. Social networking and the proliferation of information sources enabled by it have created an entirely new definition of what constitutes valid and pertinent sources of information. As such, Web 2.0 has changed the way many find information. It is therefore essential that librarians closely follow and, whenever possible, exploit these developments.

In 2000, there were approximately 108 million Internet users in the United States; by 2008, that number reached 246 million. Worldwide, there are more than 1.5 billion users, with 41 percent in Asia, 25 percent in Europe, and 15 percent in North America (Internet World Stats 2009).

There are, of course, many reasons to use the Internet. Among adults, the most common uses of the Internet included e-mail (91 percent), search engines (89 percent), maps or driving directions (86 percent), information on a hobby or interest (83 percent), and information on a product or service (81 percent). Other reasons included buying a product (71 percent), surfing for fun (62 percent), seeking health information (58 percent), watching a video on a video-sharing site (52 percent), and research for school (57 percent) (Pew 2008).

Internet use is fluid, and it varies over time based on such factors as economic conditions, availability of technology, and level of interest. Pew (2008) Internet studies revealed that approximately 72 percent of the U.S. adult population uses the Internet daily. Men and women use the Internet at the same rate; however, Internet use increases by age, income, and formal educational level. White non-Hispanics are the heaviest users (77 percent), followed by black non-Hispanics (64 percent). Geographically, 74 percent of suburban dwellers use the Internet, followed closely by urban dwellers (71 percent). Ninety-five percent of those earning more than $75,000 use the Internet, in contrast to only 57 percent of those who earn less than 30,000 a year (Pew 2008; Jones 2009).

Generational patterns also reveal that Web use is dominated by younger populations between 18 and 44, although use by older groups, including those 70 years old or older, is increasing. Nonetheless, teen use is the greatest; 93 percent of individuals between 12 and 17 are connected to the Net. The generational use patterns are predictable: younger individuals focus on social networking, using the Web for entertainment or communicating with friends and family. Younger users are also more likely to play online games, watch videos, and send instant messages than are older individuals. Older generations are more likely to use the Web for shopping, banking, or searching for health information. They are also heavy e-mail users (Jones 2009).

Networks are a double-edged sword for libraries—they allow librarians to access vast amounts of information but provide users with the same access, thus potentially reducing the users' need for a library's services.

Estabrook and Rainie (2007) described the Internet as a "go-to-source" (p. iii)—becoming the most popular source to turn to for information. Networks, however, are a double-edged sword for libraries. On the one hand, they allow librarians to access vast amounts of information. On the other hand, as more and more knowledge is created and transmitted in electronic form across networks to which users have direct access, they might rely less on libraries and librarians. The impact of all these networks on libraries is discussed in more detail in Chapter 6.

D. ERI Infrastructure as Media Industries

Libraries are dependent on the media industries that produce and distribute the knowledge and information they provide. As such, understanding the characteristics of these industries is vital to developing library collections and services.

1. Characteristics of Various Media Industries

a. Print Industry

Records (on stone, clay, vellum, papyrus, and paper) have been around since the invention of written language and print materials have been around since printing.

Printing in China predates printing in the West by many centuries. After the printing press was developed in Germany in the mid-1400s, the influence of print materials increased significantly. (Martin Luther used the printing press quite effectively in stimulating what was to become the Protestant Reformation.)

Despite predictions that print materials will disappear in the onslaught of electronic media, the data do not suggest this. Book sales have grown slowly but steadily over the past few years, reaching nearly 25 billion in 2007—a 3 percent increase over the previous year, and a compound rate of 2.5 percent since 2002. U.S. publishers printed more than 173,000 titles in 2007, compared to 160,000 in 2004. In addition, a significant percentage of increases in book title output was found among audiobooks, rising 18 percent from 2006 to 2007, and graphic novels increased nearly 40 percent. Although juvenile book sales have flattened, their compound growth rates since 2002 have been healthy at 4.6 percent (*Bowker Annual* 2008).

It is worth noting that after a slow start, the e-book is rapidly growing. The term *e-book* is not precise. It can refer to a device on which the contents of a print book are converted into electronic format and read, or it can be construed more broadly as any monograph that is available electronically. Certainly, as the e-book market expands and becomes more sophisticated, revenues are likely to increase. In fact, sales revenues have been growing substantially, with an increase of nearly 20 percent from 2006 to 2007 and a compound growth rate of nearly 56 percent since 2002. Total sales of e-books were $67 million in 2007, compared to $19 million in 2003 (*Bowker Annual* 2008).

Periodicals are also a healthy part of the print industry. More than 75,000 periodicals are published in the United States and Canada each year including general interest magazines, trade publications, and scientific and other scholarly journals. Of these, 20,000 are consumer magazines (Serials and Government Publications Division 2009). There are more than 8,300 periodical publishers in the United States, exceeding $46 billion in revenue (U.S. Census Bureau 2010). About 60 percent of the periodicals industry revenue comes from general interest magazines and another 15 percent from trade publications. The industry is heavily concentrated, with the 50 largest companies comprising 70 percent of the market (First Research 2009). Although periodicals are still widely read, scholarly publishing has experienced serious challenges in recent decades as the costs of publication have grown while demand has not.

Historically, newspapers were a popular source of information. However, recent years have seen dramatic changes in the newspaper industry. For example, daily newspaper circulation has declined steadily, from 62 million in 1990 to 52 million in 2006, particularly among some of the major U.S. newspapers. For example, by the first quarter of 2009, the *New York Times* circulation declined 3.5 percent from the previous year, the *Washington Post* 1.2 percent, the *Chicago Tribune* 7.5 percent, the *Los Angeles Times* 6.6 percent, and the *Houston Chronicle* 14 percent (Ovide and Adams 2009). Consumer spending on newspapers also declined from $52 per capita in 2000 to $50 in 2006, with a projected drop to $45 by 2010 (U.S. Census Bureau 2008).

One reason for this decline might be that other sources of information, such as the Internet, are more interesting, timely, or appealing to a visually oriented society. The combination of timely information with well-edited pictures and sound is certainly strong competition compared to the more sedate quality of the written word. Newspapers also suffer from lack of spontaneity; a paper delivered in the morning will be outdated and supplanted by its continuously updated competition online or on television. Although e-newspapers are growing in number and have developed considerable market penetration, the intense competition from cable news services such as CNN and MSNBC will make survival difficult.

Even more disturbing for the newspaper industry are the future prospects for newspaper reading among the young. Only 19 percent of people aged 18–34 read a daily newspaper; 44 percent of these younger adults visit a Web portal to obtain the news (Brown 2005). In a typical day, approximately 50 million Americans now access their news on the Internet and more than 70 percent of heavy Internet users get their news online, primarily from CNN and MSNBC (Horrigan 2006). In addition, the credibility of news on the Internet appears to be high, with two-thirds of Internet users indicating that they believe almost all or most of what they see on frequently visited news sites (Consumer Reports WebWatch 2005). Mohr (2006) suggested that with greater and greater broadband access and an ever-increasing blogosphere, user-generated content and peer-to-peer networks will represent an entirely new model for what constitutes authority and content in the media.

In addition to computers, Internet access via mobile telephones is becoming ubiquitous. The use of mobile devices to access news more than doubled from January 2008 to January 2009, and more than a third of those individuals (22.4 million people) used this medium daily (Podcasting News 2009).

b. Telephone/Mobile Phone Industry

In the history of communications, the importance of the telephone cannot be overestimated. More than 93 percent of all households in the United States have telephones. Land-based telephones provided the crucial foundation for the computer information revolution since initial computer communication was carried over telephone lines. Today, much of this communication occurs through cable and digital networks. Ground-based telephone networks are expected to remain a basic service, although their importance will likely decline as mobile telephones and use of the Internet to make telephone calls increases.

The advent of the cell phone and smartphone has had a tremendous effect on the way people receive and transmit information. Horrigan (2008c) reported that 62 percent of American adults used wireless communication devices. By mid-2008, there were more than 262 million wireless subscribers, comprising 84 percent of U.S. households; 17 percent of such households were "wireless only" (CITA 2009). There are more than 3.2 billion cellular connections worldwide (Inc.com 2008).

In addition to oral communication, smartphones can send and receive text messages, take pictures, record videos, play games, and access the Internet (Rainie 2006). Fifty-eight percent of adult Americans have used a cell phone or personal digital assistant (PDA) to send text messages, e-mail, or take a picture and 41 percent have logged onto the Internet away from home or work using a wireless laptop or handheld device. New uses include accessing financial and business information, or finding information about restaurants, movies, and other entertainment options (Podcasting News 2009). The digital measurement company ComScore (2009) reported that 9.3 million daily users of mobile devices used them for social networking and blogging in January 2009. These mobile devices will continue to evolve as more and more people use them; a Pew study reported that 39 percent of Americans had a positive and improving attitude toward mobile communication devices (Horrigan 2009).

Libraries have responded to these developments by offering services using Web sites that function both technically and aesthetically on handheld devices. IM reference (instant messaging) and SMS (short message service) applications via texting are more commonplace. Such services are likely to evolve in conjunction with enabling communication technologies.

c. Radio Industry
Nearly 110 million people, 99 percent of American households, have radios, and not just one; the average household has more than eight radios (U.S. Census Bureau 2010). The number of radio stations, particularly FM stations, has increased by 94 percent, from about 3,200 in 1980 to more than 6,200 in 2005 (U.S. Census Bureau 2008). These stations, both profit and nonprofit, offer a wide variety of programming, from traditional news broadcasts to talk shows spanning the political spectrum, to educational programs informing us about issues in the community and the nation. The ubiquitous radio not only sits on our bedside tables and kitchen counters, it is affixed to our head when we walk, run, and drive. It is broadcast in restaurants, automobiles, and other public places. It can be accessed on our computers. It is tailored to our taste and delivered to us by satellite.

d. Television Industry
The number of households owning televisions is only slightly lower than those with radios. There are more than 310 million television sets in 113 million homes (the average home owns 2.8 sets), accounting for more than 98 percent of all U.S. households. Sales in 2007 were nearly 26 million dollars for digital TVs and 14 million for LCD TVs (*Broadcasting & Cable Yearbook 2009* 2008; Quigley 2008).

Television, like radio, provides a variety of programming including news, specials, talk shows, movies, sitcoms, and reality shows. One might debate the quality of some of this programming, but one cannot ignore that Americans remain drawn to their television sets. In 2006, each person watched approximately 1,937 hours, including 989 hours on cable or satellite TV and 684 hours of broadcast TV (Quigley 2008).

The television industry also is diversifying its delivery mechanisms. For example, in the 1960s, cable television was new and not well received. By 1980 only 15 million households (20 percent) had cable television. In the past decade this has changed dramatically. By 2000, 69 million households had cable television, accounting for 68 percent of all households in the United States, and by 2007, 71 million households had cable. The number of cable systems also increased steadily from 7,500 in 1985 to more than 10,000 in 2000; however, probably due to competition from a variety of sectors, that number dropped significantly to 7,090 in 2006, but the number of subscribers has not dropped (U.S. Census Bureau 2010). Similarly, the number of commercial television stations has risen rapidly over the past few decades, from 734 in 1980 to 1,373 in 2006, although the number has been relatively stable since 2000.

In addition, those umbrella-shaped satellite antennae once thought to be the domain of astronomers at observatories and universities now adorn the roofs and yards of many American homes. There were no home satellite stations in 1980, but by 2006 there were more than 27 million satellite subscribers. Overall, the viewing of network TV stations has diminished while the consumption of cable and satellite television has increased (Quigley 2008).

The advent of the digital video recorder (DVR) has also changed the way people use their television: viewers can now fast-forward, rewind, and otherwise customize and manipulate what was before a static experience. Additionally, many people now watch television shows on their computers using sites like www.hulu.com; major networks like Comedy Central, ABC, and NBC make full episodes available for free viewing. These new services and technologies mean that people can view what they want when they want. Similarly, the combination of Congress's mandate that all television signals must be broadcast in digital form, and the development of DVD and Blu-ray technologies will no doubt stimulate new content and means of delivering it. By 2006, more than 95 million households (more than 85 percent) had DVD players. The number of DVD video titles rose from 20,000 in 2002 to 60,000 in 2006. More than 25 million DVD players were in operation in 2002, rising to more than 32 million in 2006. Of course, new competition is now coming from on-demand programming and instantly downloadable content, which will put constant pressure on the DVD and movie theater markets.

e. The Database Industry

Over the past decade, the number of databases, producers, vendors, and entries have all increased steadily. An excellent summary of their character and growth was provided by Williams (2006) in the *Gale Directory of Databases*. Unless otherwise noted, the following data have been taken from this source.

The number of databases has grown from 301 in 1975 to more than 17,000 in 2005. By 2006, there were more than 16,000 unique databases, compared to 6,000 in 1990. The number of database producers grew from 200 in 1975 to more than 4,000 in 2003, with a slight decrease to 2005. The number of vendors has grown substantially, from 105 in 1975 to 2,800 in 2005. The number of vendors continued to rise but has flattened in the first decade of the twenty-first century. Predictably, as the amount of information increased and the number of vendors and producers remained high, the number of electronically stored records has increased significantly, from 52 million records in 1975 to 21 billion in 2005—a factor of 403.

In 1977, 56 percent of all databases were government-only access; 22 percent were commercial. Over the years, this relationship has reversed. In 2006, 84 percent of all databases were commercial or industrial in nature and 10 percent were governmental. Most of the databases are business oriented (24 percent); followed by science, technology, and engineering (16 percent); multidisciplinary (14 percent); life sciences (12 percent); law (11 percent); social sciences (8 percent); general (7 percent); humanities (6 percent); and news (2 percent). Only 8 percent are not-for-profit (mostly academic). A significant majority of databases (78 percent) is produced in North America, although 19 percent are produced in Western Europe.

In terms of the types of databases available, Williams (2006) reported that the majority (67 percent) are word oriented. The trend is toward full-text databases, that is, those in which the entire text is available for viewing, not just the abstract or bibliographic citation. In 2006 there were nearly 11,000 word-oriented databases, 78 percent of which were full text, compared to only 42 percent in 1990. Bibliographic databases, on the other hand, have dropped from 32 percent in 1990 to 18 percent in 2006. Today, there are nearly four times as many full-text word-oriented databases as there are bibliographic databases. This shift is testimony to the fact that computer databases as information channels are expanding substantially. Far fewer databases (22 percent) are number oriented. The number of image- or audio-oriented databases is still small (16 percent and 5 percent respectively) but they've increased more than twenty-three-fold since 1990.

With the increasing sophistication of digitization and the ubiquity of the Web, full-text and image-based databases continue to grow, including those available at no cost on popular providers such as Google, YouTube, and Flickr. These popular databases are very different from the ones we typically encounter in academic or special libraries. Of course, access to great amounts of information in these databases does not necessarily mean that people get the right information. In fact, one can easily foresee that most citizens, awash in information, will drown in it, or at the least lose their bearings. Perhaps that is why the term *navigation* has become so popular in referring to the Web.

2. Patterns of Media Use

When examining the industries that comprise the ERI infrastructure, it is revealing to look more closely at how people are using these various media. For example, a study by the Kaiser Family Foundation (Rideout et al. 2006) found that in a typical day, 75 percent of children age 6 and under watched TV; 82 percent listened to music; and

---

Patterns of Media Consumption by Adults

Consumer and Educational Books
- Consumer book use declined at an annual rate of 1.1 percent and is expected to remain flat through 2012. However, educational book use increased at an annual rate of 1.4 percent through 2007 and is predicted to continue rising annually at a rate of 1 percent or above through 2012.
- Consumer magazine use increased at slightly less than a 1 percent annual rate through 2007, but is now beginning to decline and is expected to fall at a .3 percent rate through 2012.

Newspapers
- Newspaper use declined from 2002 to 2007 at an annual rate of 1.8 percent and is expected to decline even faster (2.6 percent annually) through 2012.

Radio
- The time spent listening to the radio declined at an annual rate of 1 percent from 2002 to 2007 and is expected to continue declining through 2012 at a 1.4 percent annual rate.

Television
- The time spent watching all types of television increased at an annual compounded growth rate of 1.2 percent from 2002 to 2007 but is expected to remain flat through 2012.
- The time spent watching broadcast television networks is steadily declining, dropping at a 2.3 percent annual compounded rate from 2002 to 2007. It is expected that the decline will end and remain flat through from 2007 to 2012.
- Watching cable television continued to increase at a 3.9 percent annual rate to 2007. However, use is expected to flatten and decline slightly by 2012.

Theaters
- Attendance at commercial movie theaters represents a very small proportion of total media consumption, less than 1 percent, and is not expected to increase.

Videos and DVDs
- Viewing home videos and DVDs grew steadily until 2004 but is now declining and should remain flat between 2007 and 2012.

Video Games
- Video game use, on the other hand, increased at a 3.8 percent annual rate from 2002 to 2007 and is expected to increase at a 10.7 percent annual rate from 2007 to 2012.

Internet
- Internet use increased at a 6 percent annual rate from 2002 to 2007, but is expected to increase more slowly (less than 1 percent annually) from 2007 to 2012. (This does not include use of traditional media on the Net such as newspaper, downloaded music, e-books, and Internet radio.)
- "Pure-play" Internet (includes communications access such as DSL, pure-play content such as eHarmony, and mobile instant message and e-mail alerts) increased at a 6 percent annual rate from 2002 to 2007 and will increase at about a 1 percent annual rate through 2012.

16 percent used a computer. In all, 83 percent used some form of screen media (e.g., watched TV, videos, or DVDs, played video games, or used a computer). This is the same percentage who either read something or were read to. However, those looking at screens did so for just under two hours a day, compared to 40 minutes of reading or being read to. Media channel use is reported annually by Veronis, Suhler, and Stevenson (2009) and recent data and projects are summarized in Figure 1.1 (see pp. 20–25).

A variety of patterns emerge. For example, individual media consumption increased from 3,388 hours in 2002 to 3,496 hours in 2007. However, total media consumption flattened and is expected to remain flat through 2012. Television viewing comprised the largest percentage of media use (46 percent), including network affiliated, independent, broadcast, and cable delivery. Cable comprised 60 percent of all television use. Broadcast and satellite radio continued to play a major role, comprising 22 percent of all media use.

E. ERI Infrastructure as Institutions

1. Libraries

Libraries have been a constant source of education, recreation, and information in the United States since the settlement of America, although the number and sophistication of these libraries were quite limited until the nineteenth century. Figure 1.2 illustrates the number and growth of libraries since 1980 (see p. 26).

Today, there are more than 115,000 libraries in the United States: 9,757 public libraries (excluding branches), 3,768 academic libraries, 7,609 special libraries, and 94,342 school or media center libraries (*American Library Directory 2007–08* 2008; *Digest of Education Statistics 2002* 2002). These various libraries play a significant role in the ERI infrastructure by providing a wealth of materials and services for educational, informational, and recreational purposes. Historically, libraries have been an especially important channel for introducing children and adults to books, and promoting reading, literacy, and self-development.

In addition, the contemporary library integrates many other information channels in its continuing mission to meet the needs of its users. Most libraries are actively engaged in developing information links to Web sites on the Internet and introducing new information technologies to their users. In this sense, libraries are continually evolving, becoming part of the larger national information infrastructure.

2. Schools and Academic Institutions

Educational institutions are a critical part of the ERI infrastructure; they serve as the foundation of knowledge creation and dissemination in our society. The United States boasts one of the largest universal education systems in the world, characterized by "its large size, organizational structure, marked decentralization, and increasing diversity" (U.S. Department of State 2008, p. 2). Figure 1.3 represents the basic structure of formal education in the United States. Primary and secondary education is offered in preschools, kindergartens, elementary schools, middle or junior high schools, and high schools (see p. 27). Postsecondary education is offered through trade schools, and undergraduate and graduate programs offering bachelor's, master's, and doctoral degrees. Academic and school libraries are embedded as subunits within these educational agencies. In terms of educational attainment, approximately 31 percent of the U.S. adult population has a high school education, 18 percent possess a bachelor's degree, 7 percent have a master's, and 1 percent achieve a PhD (U.S. Census Bureau 2008).

There are more than 97,000 public schools in the United States including 67,000 elementary schools, nearly 24,000 secondary schools, and 3,600 charter schools. There were more than 3.7 million classroom teachers serving 56 million students in 2009, and enrollments are expected to grow slowly through 2013 (NCES Table 213). There are more than 4,300 degree-granting, postsecondary institutions in the United States: 2,500 four-year institutions and 1,700 two-year institutions (NCES Table 265), with more than 991,000 faculty in the former and 381,000 in the latter (NCES Table 286). Enrollment in higher education was projected to exceed 19 million in 2010 (NCES Table 214). In 2007 the majority of post secondary students were white, non-Hispanic (66%) and female (56 percent) (NCES Table 274).

In addition to formal postsecondary education, in 2004–2005 nearly 44 percent of the adult population was engaged in some type of structured adult education, including part-time postsecondary programs; English as a second language programs; and technical, vocational, and apprenticeship programs. Seventy-three percent of these adult learners were over the age of thirty; 16 percent were unemployed; 56 percent were female; 71 percent were white; 10 percent were Hispanic; and 12 percent were African American (NCES Table 294).

3. Nonformal Educational Units

Finally, there is nonformal education (NFE) or "information learning," defined as "any organized, intentional, and explicit effort to promote learning to enhance the quality of life through non-school settings" (Heimlich 1993, p. 292). Examples of NFE can include "nature hikes, self-help clinics at home improvement stores, museums and historical site tours, and/or craft workshops at community centers" (Taylor 2006, p. 291). NFE usually focuses on individual needs, is less structured than formal education, and is learner centered. NFE accommodates many different learning styles and is self-paced (e.g., a guided tour through museum exhibits using a pre-recorded program). It is also characterized by voluntary participation, a less formal teacher-student relationship, and teachers who are subject experts though not necessarily trained teachers. Generally, NFE is not directly associated with formal educational systems and takes place outside traditional classrooms. It might be

Figure 1.1. Average Time Spent with Consumer Media per User per Year[*][†]						
	Year					
	2002	**2003**	**2004**	**2005**	**2006**	**2007**
TELEVISION						
Network-Affiliated Stations						
Hours per year	624	601	584	561	577	577
Growth (%)		–3.6%	–2.8	–4.1	3.0	–0.1
Independent & Public Stations						
Hours per year	95	96	95	94	73	63
Growth (%)		0.8%	–0.6	–1.2	–22.3	–14.0
Total Broadcast Television						
Hours per year	718	697	679	655	650	639
Growth (%)		-3.0%	-2.5	-3.7	-0.6	-1.7
Basic Cable Networks						
Hours per year	663	696	719	778	805	824
Growth (%)		4.9%	3.3	8.2	3.5	2.3
Premium Cable Networks						
Hours per year	140	147	152	164	157	149
Growth (%)		5.7%	3.1	7.9	–4.3	–4.8
Total Cable Networks						
Hours per year	803	843	871	942	962	973
Growth (%)		5.0%	3.3	8.2	2.1	1.1
Total TV						
Hours per year	1,521	1,540	1,550	1,596	1,612	1,613
Growth (%)		1.2%	0.7	3.0	1.0	0.0
OTHER MEDIA						
Broadcast & Satellite Radio						
Hours per year	824	835	821	807	791	782
Growth (%)		1.3%	–1.6	–1.7	–2.0	–1.1

(Columns continued on facing page)

Figure 1.1. *(Columns Continued)*						
Forecast					Compound Annual Growth	
2008	**2009**	**2010**	**2011**	**2012**	**2002–2007**	**2007–2012**
577	582	583	584	585		
0.1	0.8	0.2	0.2	0.1	−1.5	0.3
62	60	60	60	59		
−1.1	−3.4	0.0	0.0	−0.9	−7.9	−1.1
639	642	643	644	644		
0.0	0.4	0.2	0.2	0.0	−2.3	0.2
817	822	827	832	831		
−0.8	0.5	0.6	0.7	−0.2	4.4	0.2
147	142	137	126	122		
−1.9	−3.1	−3.6	−8.3	−3.1	1.4	−4.0
964	964	964	958	952		
−0.9	0.0	0.0	−0.6	−0.6	3.9	−0.4
1,603	1,606	1,607	1,602	1,597		
−0.6	0.2	0.1	−0.3	−0.4	1.2	−0.2
777	758	751	735	729		
−0.7	−2.5	−0.8	−2.2	−0.8	−1.0	−1.4

(Table continued on next page)

Figure 1.1. Average Time Spent with Consumer Media per User per Year*† (Continued)

	Year					
	2002	2003	2004	2005	2006	2007
OTHER MEDIA *(Continued)*						
*Pure-Play Internet**						
Hours per year	141	154	166	173	182	189
Growth (%)		9.4%	7.7	4.3	4.7	4.2
Recorded Music						
Hours per year	205	192	199	197	187	177
Growth (%)		−6.2%	3.4	−0.9	−5.3	−5.4
Newspapers						
Hours per year	188	195	192	187	178	171
Growth (%)		3.7%	−1.4	−2.5	−5.2	−3.5
Out-of-Home						
Hours per year	121	123	125	128	131	135
Growth (%)		1.6%	2.2	2.0	2.6	2.8
Consumer Magazines						
Hours per year	120	122	125	124	125	125
Growth (%)		2.0%	2.3	−1.1	1.3	−0.6
Consumer Books						
Hours per year	106	111	110	109	110	109
Growth (%)		4.5%	−0.8	−0.7	0.6	−1.1
Videogames						
Hours per year	71	76	79	73	76	85
Growth (%)		7.9%	3.0	−6.6	3.1	12.9
Home Video§						
Hours per year	55	60	67	63	62	61
Growth (%)		9.7%	12.2	−6.6	−1.8	−1.5
*Pure-Play Mobile**						
Hours per year	2	4	7	9	12	15
Growth (%)		123.2%	51.5	43.9	25.6	29.2

(Columns continued on facing page)

Figure 1.1. *(Columns Continued)*						
Forecast					**Compound Annual Growth**	
2008	**2009**	**2010**	**2011**	**2012**	**2002–2007**	**2007–2012**
193	195	197	197	197		
1.9	1.1	1.0	0.1	0.2	6.0	0.8
173	177	184	192	200		
−1.9	2.2	4.1	4.0	4.3	−2.9	2.5
164	159	155	152	150		
−4.2	−3.2	−2.5	−1.8	−1.3	−1.8	−2.6
135	135	136	138	140		
−0.3	0.2	0.8	1.3	1.9	2.2	0.8
126	124	124	122	123		
0.8	−1.6	0.3	−1.8	0.7	0.8	−0.3
109	108	108	108	107		
−0.1	−0.6	−0.2	0.0	−0.4	0.5	−0.2
101	116	125	131	142		
18.2	15.2	7.4	4.5	8.7	3.8	10.7
60	59	59	60	59		
−1.5	−1.2	0.5	0.1	−0.6	2.1	−0.6
19	24	29	32	36		
26.9	22.8	20.6	12.7	11.5	51.2	18.7

(Table continued on next page)

Figure 1.1. Average Time Spent with Consumer Media per User per Year*† *(Continued)*						
	Year					
	2002	**2003**	**2004**	**2005**	**2006**	**2007**
OTHER MEDIA *(Continued)*						
Yellow Pages						
Hours per year	11	12	12	12	12	13
Growth (%)		6.7%	1.3	1.0	0.7	0.5
Box Office						
Hours per year	14	13	13	12	12	12
Growth (%)		−5.1%	−2.6	−7.1	1.4	0.7
Educational Books±						
Hours per year	8	8	8	8	8	8
Growth (%)		0.9%	−1.0	8.2	−1.2	0.2
In-Flight Entertainment						
Hours per year	1	2	1	1	1	1
Growth (%)		7.4%	−29.4	13.1	8.4	7.2
TOTAL†						
Hours per year	3,388	3,447	3,475	3,501	3,499	3,496
Growth (%)		1.7%	0.8	0.7	−0.1	−0.1

Sources: Veronis Suhler Stevenson, PQ Media.

Note: Estimates for time spent were derived using rating data for television and cable television, survey research for radio, mobile, out-of-home and yellow pages, and consumer purchase data (units, admissions, access) for books, home video, in-flight entertainment, internet, magazines, box office, newspapers, recorded music and videogames. Adults 18 and older were the basis for estimates for newspapers, consumer books, consumer magazines, in-flight entertainment, out-of-home yellow pages and home video. Persons 12 and older were the basis for estimates for box office, broadcast TV, cable TV, Internet, mobile, radio, recorded music, and videogames.

(Notes continued bottom of next page)

viewed as complementing or supplementing formal education, or as an alternative to formal education (Taylor 2006).

Although there are no data on the number of individuals engaged in NFE, the potential involvement is substantial. For example, nearly 6.7 million adults participate in book clubs in the United States (U.S. Census Bureau Table 1203). There are nearly 13,000 museums, historical sites, and similar institutions (U.S Census

Figure 1.1. *(Columns Continued)*						
Forecast					Compound Annual Growth	
2008	2009	2010	2011	2012	2002–2007	2007–2012
13	13	12	12	12		
0.2	−0.3	−0.6	−0.6	−0.8	2.0	−0.4
12	12	12	12	12		
−0.8	−1.9	1.9	1.0	0.7	−2.6	0.2
8	8	8	9	9		
0.7	0.2	1.5	1.7	2.0	1.4	1.2
1	1	1	1	1		
−7.4	−7.1	4.0	4.7	4.9	−0.1	−0.3
3,493	3,493	3,509	3,502	3,515		
−0.1	0.0	0.5	−0.2	0.4	0.6	0.1

* Internet and mobile use of traditional media, such as downloaded music, newspaper Web sites or info alerts, e-books, cable modems, online video of TV programs and internet radio, was included in the traditional media segment, not in pure-play Internet or mobile content. Pure-play Internet and mobile services includes telecommunications access, such as DSL and dial-up, but not cable modems, pure-play content, such as eHarmony, GameSpy and MobiTV, and mobile instant messaging and e-mail alerts.

† Can include concurrent use of media, such as watching television and reading e-mail simultaneously. Does not include media use at work.

‖ Telemundo and Univision affiliates included in independent and public stations. Pay-per-view, interactive TV, home shopping, and audio-only feeds included with premium cable TV.

§ Playback of recorded VHS cassettes and DVDs only.

± Grades 9–12 and college only. Not included in consumer end-user spending.

Bureau Table 1191), which generated nearly 13 billion dollars in revenue in 2007 (U.S. Census Bureau 2010). In 2008, more than 29 million people visited a zoo or museum; more than 8 million visited art galleries or art exhibits (U.S. Census Bureau Table 1203). In that same year, the national park system had 275 million visitors (U.S. National Park Service 2007). All in all, these venues contribute considerable educational, recreational, and informational value to the society as a whole.

Figure 1.2. Number of Public, Academic, Government, and Special Libraries 1980–2009 (Excludes Branches and Community Colleges)

Year	Public	Academic	Government	Special	Total
1980	8,717	4,618	1,260	8,609	28,665
1981	8,782	4,796	1,615	8,571	29,278
1982	8,768	4,924	1,565	8,453	28,949
1983	8,822	4,900	1,591	8,387	29,044
1984	8,796	4,989	1,551	8,574	29,465
1985	8,849	5,034	1,574	8,955	29,843
1986	8,865	5,592	1,237	9,704	32,995
1987–1988	9,170	4,824	1,760	9,147	31,524
1989–1990	9,068	4,607	1,676	8,990	30,751
1990–1991	9,060	4,593	1,735	9,051	30,761
1991–1992	9,075	4,613	1,773	9,348	31,127
1992–1993	9,076	4,620	1,776	9,811	31,850
1993–1994	9,097	4,619	1,871	10,149	32,414
1994–1995	9,101	4,684	1,864	11,280	32,441
1995–1996	9,165	4,730	1,875	11,340	32,666
1997–1998	9,767	4,707	1,837	11,044	33,004
1999–2000	9,837	4,723	1,874	10,808	32,852
2000–2001	9,480	3,491	1,411	9,993	31,628
2001–2002	9,415	3,406	1,376	11,017	31,392
2002–2003	9,445	3,480	1,326	10,452	30,903
2003–2004	9,567	3,597	1,261	9,814	30,446
2004–2005	9,603	3,617	1,249	9,781	30,486
2005–2006	9,734	3,698	1,225	9,526	30,416
2006–2007	9,785	3,755	1,193	9,247	30,241
2007–2008	9,765	3,749	1,174	9,181	30,111
2008–2009	9,763	3,772	1,159	9,066	30,022
2009–2010	9,757	3,768	1 150	10,537	29,880

Source: American Library Directory. New Providence, NJ: R.R. Bowker, 1979–2010.

Figure 1.3. The Structure of Education in the United States

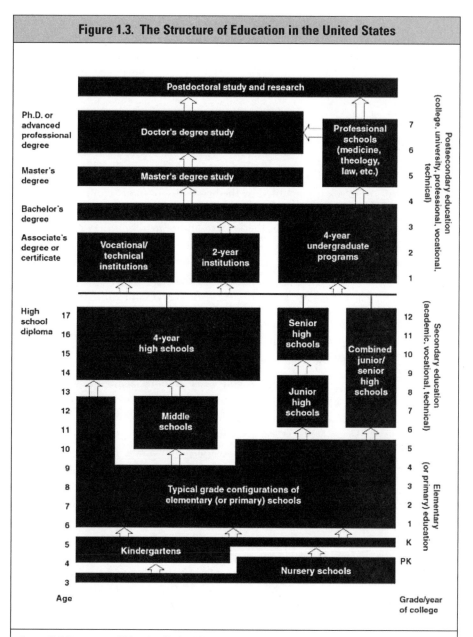

Source: U.S. Department of Education, National Center for Education Statistics, Annual Reports Program. Available: http://nces.ed.gov/programs/digest/d07/figures/fig_01.asp.

Note: Figure is not intended to show relative number of institutions nor relative size of enrollment for the different levels of education. Figure reflects typical patterns of progression rather than all possible variations. Adult education programs, while not separately delineated above, may provide instruction at the adult basic, adult secondary, or postsecondary education levels.

Libraries supplement and support these informal education experiences in a variety of ways. Many museums, for example, often have their own libraries. Educators who provide NFE often rely on libraries for their supporting materials as well as a place to offer their programs; and no doubt thousands of Americans check out their book club selections from the library.

III. SUMMARY

The role of libraries is defined by the needs of the societies that create them. Their ability to fulfill these roles is enabled by the capacities of the ERI infrastructure to supply the necessary knowledge and information to provide those services. LIS professionals must be cognizant of the larger context in which they operate. The increasingly sophisticated ERI infrastructure will continue to challenge LIS professionals as information technologies expand and become a daily part of our lives. Business and industry, the communications industry (cable, telephone, and Internet service providers), electronic database producers, Web content providers, the federal government, the military, researchers, academic institutions, and citizens all are eager to influence developments related to the ERI infrastructure. Libraries and LIS professionals must also play a role.

Revolutionary new technologies provide people with new and rich opportunities to become educated, entertained, and informed. Information consumers growing up in this digital environment have new expectations. OCLC suggested, for example, that such consumers will expect to exercise more self-sufficiency in locating information, and they will expect various technologies such as music, television, computers, and the Internet to be integrated into one seamless "infosphere" (De Rosa, Dempsey, and Wilson 2004). LIS professionals must be at the forefront of exploring and exploiting these technologies.

Important Questions to Consider

1. What are the role and mission of the library and LIS professionals in our society?
2. Where do libraries and library-like organizations fit in the ever-changing ERI infrastructure?
3. What are our citizens' rights to information and how do we protect those rights?
4. What barriers do citizens face in getting information?
5. What ethical responsibilities and dilemmas do we face in accomplishing our missions?
6. How can we ensure that our LIS institutions survive and prosper?
7. How does the growth of knowledge and information in electronic formats change the way we develop our collections and services?
8. What will happen to the library as a physical place as more and more access is provided online?
9. What kinds of LIS professionals do we need today and how are they different from the past?
10. What does the future hold for libraries, librarians, and other LIS professionals?

Some of the issues LIS professionals should expect to encounter will arise from the creation of an infosphere: open access, copyright protection, appropriate security, individual privacy, the cost of access, necessary professional training, the library's role related to literacy and reading, and the importance of the library as a place in the community. These issues, when addressed together, reveal how important it will be for LIS professionals to assess how well their libraries continue to reflect the public interest and meet their missions. It is a tremendous responsibility, and it becomes increasingly challenging as the social, economic, educational, political, and technological environment grows more complex. There are no simple answers to the important questions facing us. Yet it is hoped that this book will improve the reader's understanding of the issues involved in addressing them.

NOTE

I wish to acknowledge Dr. Brett Sutton, who first proposed the use of metaphors to understand the growth of information. This is not to say that he would necessarily interpret the significance of these metaphors in the manner that I have interpreted them.

REFERENCES

American Library Directory 2007–08. 2008. 60th ed. Medford, NJ: Information Today.

The Bowker Annual: Library and Book Trade Almanac. 2008. 53rd ed. Medford, NJ: Information Today.

Broadcasting & Cable Yearbook 2009. 2008. New Providence, NJ: ProQuest.

Brown, Merrill. 2005. "What's the Future of the News Business?" *Carnegie Reporter* 3 (Spring). Available: www.carnegie.org/reporter/10/news/index.html (accessed December 4, 2009).

CITA. 2009. "100 Wireless Facts." Available: www.cita.org/media/industry_info/index .cfm/AID/10323 (accessed March 18, 2009).

ComScore. 2009. "Mobile Internet Becoming a Daily Activity for Many." Available: www .comscore.com/Press_Events/Press_Releases/2009/3/Daily_Mobile_Internet_Usage_ Grows (accessed January 22, 2010).

Consumer Reports WebWatch. 2005. *Leap of Faith: Using the Internet Despite the Dangers.* New York: Consumer Reports WebWatch, October 26.

De Rosa, Cathy, Lorcan Dempsey, and Alane Wilson. 2004. *The 2003 OCLC Environmental Scan: Pattern Recognition: A Report to the OCLC Membership.* Dublin, OH: OCLC.

Digest of Education Statistics 2002. 2002. Washington, DC: U.S. Department of Education.

Estabrook, Leigh, and Lee Rainie. 2007. *Information Searches That Solve Problems.* Pew Internet and American Life Project. Urbana: GSLIS, University of Illinois, December 30.

First Research. 2009. "Magazine Publishers." Available: www.firstresearch.com/industry-research/Magazine-Publishers.html (accessed June 29, 2009).

Heimlich, J. E. 1993. "Nonformal Environmental Education: Toward a Working Definition." As cited in Taylor, Edward W. "Making Meaning of Local Nonformal Education: Practitioner's Perspective." *Adult Education Quarterly* 56 (August 2006): 291–307.

Horrigan, John B. 2006. *Online News*. Washington, DC: Pew Internet and American Life Project, March 23.

———. 2008a. *Home Broadband Adoption 2008*. Washington, DC: Pew Internet and American Life Project, July.

———. 2008b. "Seeding the Cloud: What Mobile Access Means for Usage Patterns and Online Content." Washington, DC: Pew Internet and American Life Project, March.

———. 2008c. "62% of All Americans Are Part of a Wireless, Mobile Population That Participates in Digital Activities Away from Home or Work." Washington, DC: Pew Internet and American Life Project, March.

———. 2009. "The Mobile Difference." Available: www.pewinternet.org/Reports/2009/5-The-Mobile-Difference-Typology.aspx (accessed April 22, 2009).

Inc.com. 2008. "Mobile Phones: A Pocketful of Marketing." Available: www.inc.com/magazine/20080201/a-pocketful-of-marketing.html?partner=newsletter_News (accessed January 22, 2010).

Internet World Stats. 2009. "Internet Usage Statistics." Available: http://internetworldstats.com/stats.htm (accessed March 18, 2009).

Jones, Sydney. 2009. "Generation Online in 2009." Pew Internet Project Data Memo. Washington, DC: Pew Internet and American Life Project, January 28.

Mohr, Tom. 2006. "Winning Online—A Manifesto." *Editor & Publisher* (September 4). Available: http://www.integratedmedia.org/files/Media/022207_457_0015592.pdf (accessed January 22, 2010).

National Center for Education Statistics. 2009. *Digest of Education Statistics: 2008*. Tables 26 and 28. Washington, DC: U.S. Department of Education, March.

———. "Table 211. School Enrollment: 1980–2017." Available: www.census.gov/compendia/statab/tables/09s0211.pdf (accessed January 22, 2010).

———. "Table 213. School Enrollment, Faculty, Graduates, and Finances—Projections: 2007–2013." Available: www.census.gov/compendia/statab/tables/09s0213.pdf (accessed January 22, 2010).

———. "Table 214. School Enrollment: 1980–2018." Available: www.census.gov/compendia/statab/tables/10s0214.pdf (accessed January 22, 2010).

———. "Table 231. Public Elementary and Secondary Schools by Type and Size of School: 2005–2006." Digest of Education Statistics. Available: www.census.gov/compendia/statab/tables/09s0231.pdf (accessed January 20, 2010).

———. "Table 233. Public Elementary and Secondary School Enrollment by Grade: 1980 to 2005." Digest of Education Statistics. Available: www.census.gov/compendia/statab/tables/09s0233.pdf (accessed January 20, 2010).

———. "Table 234. Public Elementary and Secondary Schools and Enrollment—States: 2005–2006." Numbers and Types of Public Elementary and Secondary Schools from the

Common Core of Data: School Years 2005–2006. Available: www.census.gov/compendia/statab/tables/09s0234.pdf (accessed January 20, 2010).

———. "Table 265. Degree-Granting Institutions by Control and Type of Institution: Selected Years 1949–50 through 2007–08." Available: http://nces.gov/programs/pubs 2009/2009020_3a.pdf (accessed March 19, 2010).

———. "Table 271. Degree-Granting Institutions, Number and Enrollment by State: 2006." Available: www.census.gov/compendia/statab/2010/tables/10s0271.xls (accessed January 20, 2010).

———. "Table 274. College Enrollment-Summary by Race, Sex, and Hispanic Origin: 2007." Available: www.consus.gov/compendia/statab/2010/tables/10s0274.pdf (accessed January 20, 2010).

———. "Table 286. Faculty in Institutions of Higher Education: 1970–2007." Available: www.census.govcompendia/statab/2010/tables/10s0286.xls (accessed January 20, 2010).

———. "Table 294. Participation in Adult Education: 2004–2005." Available: www.census .gov /compendia/statab/tables/10s0294.pdf. Accessed (accessed January 22, 2010).

Ovide, Shira, and Russell Adams. 2009. "Slide in Newspaper Circulation Quickens." *Wall Street Journal*, April 28: B2.

Pew. 2008. "Demographics of Internet Users." Available: www.pewinternet.org/Data-Tools/ Download-Data/~/media/Infographics/Trend%20 (accessed March 18, 2009).

Podcasting News. 2009. "Daily Mobile Internet Use Soars." Available: www.podcastingnews .com/2009/16/mobile-internet-use-soars/ (accessed March 31, 2009).

Quigley, Eileen S., ed. 2008. *International Television and Video Almanac*. 53rd ed. Groton, MA: Quigley.

Rainie, Lee. 2006. Pew Internet Project Data Memo. Pew Internet and American Life Project. AP Press Release, April.

Rideout, Victoria, Elizabeth Hamel, and Kaiser Family Foundation. 2006. *The Media Family: Electronic Media in the Lives of Infants, Toddlers, Preschoolers and Their Parents*. Menlo Park, CA: Henry J. Kaiser Family Foundation.

Serials and Government Publications Division. 2009. "Periodicals." Available: http://memory .loc .gov/ammem/awhhtml/awser2/periodicals.html (accessed June 29, 2009).

Taylor, Edward W. 2006. "Making Meaning of Local Nonformal Education: Practitioner's Perspective." *Adult Education Quarterly* 56 (August): 291–307.

U.S. Census Bureau. 2008. "Table 1. Educational Attainment of the Population 18 Years and Over, by Age, Sex, Race, and Hispanic Origin: 2008." Available: www.census.gov/population/ socdemo/education/cps2008/Table1-01.xls (accessed January 22, 2010).

———. "Table 1189: Arts, Entertainment, and Recreation—Establishments, Revenue, Payroll, and Employees by Kind of Business 1997–2007. Available: www.census.gov/ compendia/statab/2010/tables/10s1189.xls (accessed January 22, 2010).

———. "Table 1191: Arts, Entertainment, and Recreation—Establishments, Employees, and Payroll by Kind of Business: 2000 and 2005." Available: www.census.gov/prod/ 2008pubs/ 09statab/arts.pdf (accessed January 22, 2010).

———. "Table 1203: Adult Participation in Selected Leisure Activities by Frequency: 2008." Available: www.census.gov/compendia/statab/2010/tables/109s1203.pdf (accessed January 22, 2010).

U.S. Census Bureau. 2010. *Statistical Abstracts of the United States*. "Table 1191: Arts, Entertainment and Recreation Services—Estimated Revenue 2000–2007." Available: www.census.gov/compendia/statab/2010/tables/10s1191.xls (accessed January 22, 2010).

U.S. Department of State. 2008. Bureau of International Information Programs. Available: www.america.gov/publications/books/education-in-brief.html (accessed January 22, 2010).

U.S. National Park Service. 2007. "Table 1212: National Park System—Summary: 1990–2007." Available: www.docstoc.com/docs/10783025/national-park-system—summary (accessed January 22, 2010).

Veronis, Suhler, and Stevenson. 2009. *Communications Industry Forecast*. New York: Veronis, Suhler, and Stevenson.

Williams, Martha E. 2006. "The State of Databases Today: 2006." In *Gale Directory of Databases*. Detroit: Gale.

SELECTED READINGS

Books

The Bowker Annual: Library and Book Trade Almanac (Annual). Medford, NJ: Information Today.

Broadcasting & Cable Yearbook (Annual). New Providence, NJ: ProQuest.

De Rosa, Cathy, Lorcan Dempsey, and Alane Wilson. *The 2003 OCLC Environmental Scan: Pattern Recognition: A Report to the OCLC Membership*. Dublin, OH: OCLC, 2004.

Digest of Education Statistics (Annual). Washington, DC: U.S. Department of Education.

Estabrook, Leigh, and Lee Rainie. *Information Searches That Solve Problems*. Pew Internet and American Life Project. Urbana: GSLIS, University of Illinois, December 30, 2007.

Horrigan, John B. *Home Broadband Adoption 2008*. Washington, DC: Pew Internet and American Life Project, July 2008.

———. "Seeding the Cloud: What Mobile Access Means for Usage Patterns and Online Content." Washington, DC: Pew Internet and American Life Project, March 2008.

International Television and Video Almanac (Annual). Groton, MA: Quigley.

Lenhart, Amanda. *The Ever-Shifting Internet Population*. Washington, DC: Pew Internet and American Life Project, April 2003.

Mossberger, Karen, Caroline J. Tolbert, and Mary Stansbury. *Virtual Inequality: Beyond the Digital Divide*. Washington, DC: Georgetown University, 2003.

National Center for Education Statistics. *Digest of Education Statistics* (Annual). Washington, DC: U.S. Department of Education.

Rideout, Victoria, Elizabeth Hamel, and the Kaiser Family Foundation. *The Media Family: Electronic Media in the Lives of Infants, Toddlers, Preschoolers and Their Parents*. Menlo Park, CA: Henry J. Kaiser Family Foundation, 2006.

University College London and the Joint Information System Committee. "Information Behaviour of the Researcher of the Future." Available: www.jisc.ac.uk/media/documents/programmes/reppres/ggworkpackageii.pdf (accessed January 22, 2010).

Articles

Castro, Kimberly. "The Future of E-books." *Business Week* (October 29, 2007). Available: www.businessweek.com/investor/content/oct2007/pi20071026_777647.thm (accessed January 22, 2010).

Consumer Reports WebWatch. *Leap of Faith: Using the Internet Despite the Dangers.* New York: Consumer Reports WebWatch, October 26, 2005.

Mohr, Tom. "Winning Online—A Manifesto." *Editor & Publisher* (September 4, 2006). Available: www.integratedmedia.org/files/Media/022207_457_0015592.pdf (accessed January 22, 2010).

Ormes, Sarah. "An E-book Primer." Available: www.ukoln.ac.uk/public/earl/issuepapers/ebook.htm (accessed January 22, 2010).

Sottong, Stephen. "The Elusive E-book." *American Libraries* 39 (May 2008): 44–48.

Taylor, Edward W. "Making Meaning of Local Nonformal Education: Practitioner's Perspective." *Adult Education Quarterly* 56 (August 2006): 291–307.

vanKappen, Philip-Jan. "Study Shows Migration to Online Books Saves Libraries Money and Increases Usage." *Library Connect Newsletter* 6 (January 2008): 11.

2

From Past to Present: The History and Mission of Libraries

I. THE EARLY MISSIONS OF LIBRARIES

Not all societies can have libraries. Libraries require at least three conditions: a centralized population, economic development, and political stability (Harris and Johnson 1984). Libraries do not prosper in nomadic conditions; there must be a stable location for the materials. The centralization of population in cities and towns is particularly important. However, even a small stable population such as a university or monastery can serve as a sufficient concentration to produce a library. Similarly, libraries cannot prosper when the primary energies and resources of the community are devoted to subsistence; the development of libraries requires a certain level of wealth and leisure to read. Finally, libraries cannot flourish in times of revolt and political chaos. Many great libraries have been destroyed when empires fell or in times of war or other armed conflicts. Understanding how libraries emerged and the functions they served throughout history provides a basic context for understanding the current mission of American libraries and helps frame the discussion of the role of the library in the future. The discussion that follows is not a history of libraries per se, but a historical overview of the various missions of libraries with special attention to the development of libraries in the United States.

A. The Earliest Mission: Maintaining a Records Archive

No one knows when the first libraries were established, but at least two significant factors provided impetus for their creation: the invention of writing and the rise of commerce. The earliest written records come from Sumeria in Mesopotamia around 3000 B.C. They were written in cuneiform, which involved pressing a square or triangular-tipped stylus on wet clay tablets.

Temples were the social and economic center of Sumerian communities. There people conducted business, managed estates, and lent money. Temple records included "commercial accounts, grammatical exercises for young scribes, mathematical texts, treatises on medicine and astrology, and collections of hymns, prayers and incantations" (Dunlap 1972, p. 2). Some historical and literary works, as well as early codifications of law, have also been found (Harris and Johnson 1984). There is evidence that some of the temples had schools that taught cuneiform and trained clerks to keep records of accounts (Dunlap 1972). Thus, it appears that writing evolved primarily for administrative and practical business purposes (Childe 1965). In addition to temple libraries, municipal and government libraries held business records as well as deeds, contracts, tax lists, and marriage records (Harris and Johnson 1984).

Because of the volume and complexity of these records, Harris and Johnson (1984) speculated that there must have been an organized system for storing and retrieving these materials. We do know that the Sumerians had "masters of the books" or "keepers of the tablets," well-educated scribes or priests who served in this capacity. Their specific duties, however, are unknown.

B. The Religious and Practical Missions of Egyptian Libraries

Egyptian temples were cultural centers: they stored food, educated scribes, and dispensed justice. Egyptian temple records were written on rolled scrolls made from flattened papyrus reeds using a pictorial language known as hieroglyphics (Jackson 1974). The earliest Egyptian libraries were associated with these temples and probably emerged around 2400 B.C. They served as historical archives and places for learning. The library at Edfu, known as the House of Papyrus, had a collection of practical and spiritual materials that included writings on administration, magic, astronomy, astrology, and medicine (Thompson 1962; Shera 1976). Egyptian libraries were particularly notable for their medical collections, which included pharmacological information as well as materials on diagnosis and treatment of diseases and surgery (Harris and Johnson 1984).

Egyptian librarians were scribes—priests held in high esteem because the ability to read and write was so rare. Writing itself might well have been considered a sacred activity, thus giving the scribes considerably more power than today's librarian (Harris and Johnson 1984).

In addition to the temple libraries, there were also extensive private collections among royalty and individual wealthy Egyptians. Perhaps the most notable royal library was that of Pharaoh Ramses II in Thebes between 1200 and 1300 B.C. This library might have had as many as 20,000 scrolls (Nichols 1964). According to the Greco-Roman historian Diodorus Siculus, the portal to the library at Thebes was inscribed with the words "Healer of the Soul," suggesting it contained both spiritual and medicinal materials, but we do not know the actual contents (Jackson 1974).

C. The Mission of Scholarship and Research

Around the eighth century B.C., the Assyrian King Ashurbanipal expanded a library at his palace in Nineveh, Mesopotamia, begun by his great-grandfather, Sargon II. Ashurbanipal believed that a library should not only maintain archival records, but should also serve as a source of current reference materials and contribute to the education of future generations (Dunlap 1972). To this end, Ashurbanipal directed scholars and assistants to collect clay tablets produced from other lands. The library soon had thousands of tablets on a wide variety of subjects. Many were translated from their original language into Assyrian. The collection contained Sumerian and Babylonian materials, including literary texts, history, omens, astronomical calculations, mathematical tables, grammatical and linguistic tables, and dictionaries, as well as commercial records and laws. There is evidence that the collection was organized with the titles arranged by subject and listed in registers. Some of the tablets had markers to help in locating and shelving them. There is also evidence of a "keeper of the books," suggesting a librarian, but nothing else is known (Jackson 1974).

The library of Ashurbanipal was the greatest library of its time, providing a rich collection of materials and information on Mesopotamia and its culture. At its height, it was estimated to have as many as 30,000 clay tablets, two-thirds of which were collected during Ashurbanipal's reign (Dunlap 1972). Taken as a whole, the Royal Library at Nineveh was a remarkable achievement:

- the collection was a concerted effort to acquire a vast amount of material on a variety of subjects;
- the holdings were developed, at least in part, for future generations;
- many of the materials were translated to increase accessibility;
- they were systematically organized, marked, and arranged; and
- a "librarian" played a significant role in the library's activities.

No doubt part of the reason for the library's existence was to glorify Ashurbanipal's greatness, but all of the characteristics noted above also suggest that the Royal Library was the first attempt to build a library for reference and research.

Advancing the scholarly mission of libraries was also one of the notable contributions of the Greeks. Prior to the fifth century B.C., Greece had been an oral culture, and consequently there was little need for libraries. But by the fifth century B.C. some evidence suggests that scholars and young aristocrats were developing private libraries that might help them obtain social and political success (Jacob 2002). A hundred years later, in the fourth century B.C., reading and written records became more commonplace, primarily due to the rise of the philosophical schools of Socrates, Plato, and Aristotle (Dunlap 1972). In addition, as Alexander the Great extended his empire, the Greek values of reading and learning were also spread, although Alexander himself was not directly responsible for the building of libraries.

Following Alexander's death in 323 B.C., his conquered lands were divided among five Macedonian generals, one of whom, Ptolemy Soter (Ptolemy I), was given Egypt. Ptolemy had great respect for learning and he encouraged scholars to immigrate to Alexandria, which became a center of culture and learning. Ptolemy and his son Ptolemy Philadelphus (Ptolemy II), with the help and encouragement of Demetrios of Phaleron, founded the Alexandrian Museum and Library. The mission of the library was ambitious—to collect the entirety of Greek literature. To accomplish this, the founders went to great and sometimes questionable lengths. The Alexandrian, like the library of Ashurbanipal before it, aggressively collected materials throughout the known world (Harris and Johnson 1984). In addition, Ptolemy frequently confiscated cargoes of books in ships that came to Alexandria (Hessel 1955). Copies were made of the originals and the copies were returned to the ships (Thompson 1962).

The collected items were subsequently organized and edited, and many were translated into Greek. The collection was stored in two buildings: a major structure called the Brucheion, which was used for research, and a smaller library called the Serapeum, which might have provided some service to students and the public (Harris and Johnson 1984). The Brucheion was divided into ten great halls, each hall representing a separate area of learning. There were also some smaller rooms for individuals involved in special studies (Parsons 1952).

The Alexandrian was also notable for its librarians, many of whom achieved great personal fame, such as the scholar Callimachus. According to some historians, under Callimachus's guidance, the library exceeded more than a half-million items (Blackburn 2003), although the actual size of the collection relies on various accounts of questionable authenticity (Parsons 1952; Jochum 1999). Callimachus is especially known for his subject catalog of the library holdings, called the Pinakes, which contained 120 scrolls arranged into ten subject classes. Within each class, there were subdivisions listing authors alphabetically with titles. Because some entries included historical or critical remarks, some historians regard the Pinakes as more than a catalog, suggesting that it might have also served as a history of Greek literature (Jackson 1974).

The Alexandrian possessed the characteristics of any great research institution: a comprehensive collection of materials and scholars to collect them and maintain the library. In addition, the Alexandrian became a community of scholars that attracted other notable scholars including Euclid, Archimedes, and Galen (Battles 2003).

> By bringing scholars to Alexandria and inviting them to live and work, at royal expense, among an enormous store of books, the Ptolemies made the library into a think tank under the control of the royal house. The strategic implications of a monopoly on knowledge—especially in medicine, engineering, and theology, all among Alexandria's strengths—were not lost on the Ptolemies. (Battles 2003, p. 29)

It is unclear when and how the Alexandrian was destroyed. Some historians claimed that at least part of it was set afire when Caesar invaded Alexandria in 48 B.C., but there is some reason to doubt that account (Jochum 1999). Blackburn (2003) argued that the scrolls which supposedly had been destroyed had actually been removed by the librarian to protect them and still await discovery. Nevertheless, the Alexandrian deteriorated with the decline of the Greek Empire and by the third century A.D. suffered badly from pillaging and destruction.

D. The Missions of Personal Status and Public Use: The Roman Libraries

With the rise of the Roman Empire, the mission of libraries appeared to shift. During the early days of Rome, the Romans possessed few, if any, libraries. Following the conquest of Greece, however, Greek libraries were plundered, and possessing a library became a symbol of status and rank, as well as personal pride, for many generals and the aristocracy.

By the first century A.D. there were a large number of books and private libraries in Rome and in Roman country houses. Aristotle's library, for example, was brought to Rome in the first century B.C. by the Roman general Sulla (Thompson 1962). Cicero made his library "the heart of his home" (Hessel 1955, p. 6), and had a library in each of his villas (Dunlap 1972). Lucullus opened his libraries to others who lacked the means to have their own collections, and it was not uncommon for fellow aristocrats of similar literary interests to loan materials from their private libraries to each other (Dix 1994). Julius Caesar's library contained major works in Greek and Latin along with busts of their authors (Barker 2001).

During the time of Julius Caesar, there was an increasing belief that works of literature were to some extent public property that should be available to all citizens, although it is likely that less than 10 percent of the Roman citizenry could read (Harris, 1989). Julius Caesar planned to build the first "public" library in Rome, but died before it was completed. His consul, Asinius Pollio, is given credit for this accomplishment. The emperor Augustus built two additional public libraries and by the fourth century A.D. there were as many as twenty-nine public libraries in Rome (Boyd 1915). These libraries were usually associated with Roman temples but in addition to religious items they included public records and general literature, which might have been available for borrowing under rare circumstances (Harris and Johnson 1984). They also often contained rooms or audience halls that provided a public forum for authors to recite their works, which was considered a form of publication during those times (Dix 1994; Harris 1989).

> The evidence for general access to Rome's public libraries may be considered inconclusive. While those who mentioned the libraries and said they used them

come from the narrow worlds of literature and the imperial court, other evidence points to at least the expectation of general access. The presence of libraries in the great public baths, in particular, would suggest that many citizens had access to at least a few texts in a public collection. At the same time, given the economic, social, and cultural restrictions which bound most individuals in the ancient world, it seems safe to say that only a very small number are likely ever to have availed themselves of the opportunity to peruse the volumes in a public library. (Dix 1994, p. 290)

During most of the Roman Empire period, the Romans recorded their history and accounts using papyrus scrolls, like the Greeks before them. There were some obvious disadvantages to the scrolls; they were bulky and it was more difficult to find one's place because there were no pages. During the first century A.D., due to persecution and the need to record religious text quickly and in readily transportable form, the early Christians abandoned the scroll and replaced it with the parchment codex (book). The early Christians were the first to publish biblical manuscripts in codex form with bound pages and a wood covering (Boser 2006).

The format was a radical one because bound books were considered second class; almost all lengthy texts at the time were published on scrolls. But with its hard cover and compact size, the codex traveled better than a scroll and could be opened flat and have page numbers, which made for easier reading. (Boser 2006, p. 28)

By the fourth century A.D., the codex was in widespread use and had replaced papyrus scrolls (Thompson 1962). By the fourth century A.D., the Roman Empire and its libraries were in decline. As most of Western Europe plunged into political, economic, and social chaos, the archival and scholarly missions of libraries were sustained by Byzantine and Moslem libraries in the East, and in the monastic libraries of Western Europe.

E. Maintaining the Scholarly Mission: The Byzantine and Moslem Libraries

While the Western Empire was declining, the Eastern Empire under the leadership of the Christian emperor Constantine was flourishing. The center of the Byzantine Empire was Constantinople, where Constantine's son, Emperor Constantius, founded the Imperial Library in 353 A.D. (Jackson 1974). Although the Eastern Empire was more influenced by Greek culture and traditions than Rome, the Imperial Library contained both Christian and Latin works in addition to Greek materials (Harris and Johnson 1984). By 450 A.D. the library held 100,000 items.

Constantinople was also home to a large university library and the library of the leader of the Eastern Church, the Patriarch. The mission of these libraries was scholarly as well as religious, and their existence sustained the roots of Western society. As Harris and Johnson (1984) noted, "of the Greek classics known today, at least seventy-five percent are known through Byzantine copies" (p. 83). Without the preservation of these materials, the Renaissance would not have been possible.

The same can be said concerning the achievements of the Moslem Empire, which flourished from 650 A.D. until 1000 A.D. Because of the respect afforded reading and learning in this culture, libraries were commonplace in private homes, royal palaces, and universities throughout the Moslem world. The caliphs in many of the major cities were scholars and literati (Thompson 1962). Spain had seventy libraries, Baghdad thirty-six, and "every important city in Persia had its library" (Thompson 1962, p. 353).

The earliest major library was the Royal Library in Damascus, which contained materials from throughout the world on a wide variety of topics, including medicine, philosophy, history, and literature (Harris and Johnson 1984). Later, during the eighth and ninth centuries, Baghdad became the cultural center for the study of Greek medical, scientific, and philosophical works and "abounded with libraries" (Thompson 1962, p. 351).

In addition, research and learning were furthered by large university libraries located in Baghdad, Cairo, and Cordoba. The Cairo library might have held more than 200,000 volumes and the library at Cordoba was reported to contain between 400,000 and 600,000 volumes—larger than the Alexandrian (Harris and Johnson 1984; Thompson 1962). Like the Byzantine libraries, Moslem libraries contained not only Arabic works, but Persian literature as well as Greek and Latin philosophy and science. As such, Moslem libraries made a substantial contribution to Western culture by preserving the central works of Western thought. The Western world owes a particular debt to the Moslems for preserving the works of Aristotle, which were quite popular. Many of his writings were translated into Arabic for use by scholars (Harris and Johnson 1984). With the decline of the Moslem Empire, however, libraries also declined.

F. The Religious Mission: Monastic Libraries of the Middle Ages

With the fall of the Roman Empire, social and political chaos led to economic instability throughout Western Europe. Inevitably, the libraries also declined. Only one major Western institution was able to sustain the critical preconditions for library development—the Christian monastery. Monasteries, which were well established by 500–550 A.D., provided a means of isolating Christian adherents, both geographically and spiritually, from the disorder spreading across Europe. The mission of the monastic library was threefold: to provide a place for spiritual reflection, to archive religious texts, and to reproduce religious and sometimes secular texts.

Perhaps the best exemplar of the religious mission of the monastic library comes from the Benedictine Order, established in 529 A.D. in Monte Casino, Italy. According to St. Benedict, the purpose of monastic life was to concentrate on spiritual matters and to avoid secular thoughts. To this end, books were often read to monks during meals to keep their minds from straying to frivolous or worldly matters, not to enlighten them. Similarly, each monk was provided one book for study each year (Clanchy 1979). Other rules included copying books in a special room called the scriptorium. The purpose of copying was not to create more useful and instructive texts, however, but to keep the monks busy (Thompson 1962). Unfortunately, sometimes copying was also used as a punishment for a recalcitrant monk, and the quality of the copy often left much to be desired (Shera 1976).

Other monasteries founded in Ireland, Switzerland, Scotland, France, and Great Britain regarded copying in a different vein. They saw the copying of religious texts as a means to derive inspiration. Many of these monasteries produced fine, illuminated manuscripts intended to reveal the beauty of God. These works of art reflected the copyist's realization that he was representing sacred words from Scripture. Their physical beauty, however, might also have been inspirational to the laity and might even have served as an early incentive to literacy (Clanchy 1979).

> One other debt is due the monks, the Dominicans in particular. The Dominican friars created written rules related to locating the best site for a library, providing adequate shelving, organizing the library by subjects, marking the spines of books with their titles, replenishing and weeding the collection, establishing hours of operation, and selling duplicate titles (Clanchy 1979).

Regardless of whether the purpose of reading and copying books was to learn, to inspire, or to achieve an ascetic life, the monasteries helped preserve some of the writings of antiquity. However, as Thompson (1962) observed, "it is equally true their preservation was as often due to neglect and mere chance as it was to conscious intent ... the medieval scriptorium was more often a treadmill for meaningless labor than it was a shrine where the expiring flame of literary culture was sedulously preserved" (pp. 30–31).

G. The Educational Mission of Libraries: Cathedral and University Libraries of the Late Middle Ages

The educational mission of libraries reemerged in Western Europe in the late Middle Ages (800–1200 A.D.). With the growth of cities and towns, improved trade and other economic and social conditions, there was a concomitant improvement in the intellectual climate. The increasing respect for learning made fertile conditions for libraries once again.

By 1100, the cathedrals in major cities served as the administrative centers for bishops and archbishops and as training centers for priests and other religious functionaries (Harris and Johnson 1984). The cathedral libraries were larger than those in monasteries and were less dominated by religious works (Shera 1976). In fact, the mission of the cathedral libraries, unlike the monastic libraries, was to support the educational program of the cathedral and encourage study. Although some of the cathedral libraries were substantial, such as those in Verona and Monte Casino, Italy, and at Rheims and Chartres in France, they still could not rival the larger libraries of the Moslem Empire (Dunlap 1972).

Although the church continued to be a vital part of the life of the late Middle Ages, it was also a period of transition. The cities were producing a middle class, and there were those among the laity and intellectual aristocracy who did not rely on church teaching to guide their intellectual pursuits (Hessel 1955). These developments, coupled with the dominance of less contemplative and more secularly involved religious sects such as the Dominicans and Franciscans, spawned academic centers in Bologna, Paris, and Oxford. These institutions supported not only theological studies, but also classical and professional instruction in law, medicine, and philosophy. Initially, the first Western universities did not have libraries; rather, students bought their books from booksellers. The University of Paris established the first university library in the mid-thirteenth century, and Oxford and Cambridge soon followed, among others (Shera 1976). These libraries were often small, well under 1,000 items, but their mission to support and expand the educational mission of the university served as a bridge from the domination of the medieval church to the birth of the Renaissance (Harris and Johnson 1984; Shera 1976).

H. The Humanistic Mission and the Reemergence of the Library for Personal Status

The period following the Middle Ages was a time of considerable economic, social, and political ferment, much of it centered in Italy, most notably Venice and Florence. Contributing factors included the rise of secular monarchies, an increased sense of nationalism, a decline in the power of the church, an increase in literacy, interest in natural sciences, and secular politics, and a reawakening of the philosophical traditions of ancient Greek and Roman thinkers. This fervor for the knowledge of the ancients and for new secular knowledge, rather than spiritual enlightenment, characterizes much of what is referred to as Renaissance Humanism.

The Renaissance was primarily an aristocratic enthusiasm and great private libraries were developed by leading literary figures such as Petrarch and Boccaccio, who themselves were sponsored by popes or Renaissance princes such as the dukes of Urbino and the Medici. These sponsors were passionate book collectors as both a matter of personal vanity and a genuine interest in secular learning. They sent agents throughout Western Europe to locate manuscripts in deteriorating monastic libraries. Sometimes the manuscripts were copied but as often enthusiastic agents confiscated (or saved) these items for their sponsors. As a result, Renaissance libraries were richly appointed and filled with beautifully illuminated texts. They served as places for scholarship, but also as places where aristocrats could "display their sensitivity to classical Latin" (Jackson 1974, p. 107).

Although the Renaissance princes might have taken the notion of the private library as personal aggrandizement to its highest form of ostentatious display, it was hardly a new concept or new mission (remember Ashurbanipal and the wealthy Romans). One might reasonably contend, as Dunlap (1972) did, "Had it not been for the enthusiasm of a few collectors of that age . . . we should certainly possess only a small part of the literature, especially that of the Greeks, which is now in our hands" (pp. 106–107).

I. Promoting National Pride: The Mission of the National Libraries

The growth of secular monarchies and nationalism is consistent with the emergence of a new type of library—the national library. Early examples of such libraries arose in the seventeenth century in England, France, Germany, Denmark, and Scotland. The eighteenth and nineteenth centuries saw additional national libraries in Austria, Italy, Sweden, Norway, Greece, Spain, and Ireland, among others (Gates 1976). What distinguished these libraries was not simply their large collections, but rather their special mission to preserve the cultural heritage of their countries. This meant developing a comprehensive collection of materials by and about the country, including books, manuscripts, documents, and other records.

To meet this mission, a unique collection development technique arose: the creation of a depository right. That is, some nations passed laws requiring that at least one copy of each item published within the country be sent to the national library. This was accomplished, for example, in England in 1610, when an agreement was made between the Stationers' Company (which licensed publications in England) and the Bodleian Library of Oxford University. This agreement stipulated that one copy of each book published would be given to the Bodleian in return for limited borrowing privileges (Jackson 1974). In essence, this meant that all items, or nearly all items, published would become part of the national collection. In the United States, this depository right is held by the Library of Congress and although it is not officially our national library, it is a very close approximation.

II. MAKING MODERN MISSIONS POSSIBLE: THE PRINTING PRESS

If one can identify a single historical development that profoundly affected all libraries, it would be the revolutionary invention of the printing press in 1454 in

Mainz, Germany, which affected much more than libraries. The printing press made books available to the masses for the first time and thus increased a desire for learning. By 1468, the church in Rome referred to printing as the "divine art." Others referred to it as the "art which preserves all other arts" (Eisenstein 1995, p. 2). It is impossible to consider the modern mission of libraries without considering the changes wrought by the printing press (Eisenstein 1979):

- **The ability to produce exact copies**: Before printing, all copies were made by hand. This laborious process sometimes produced extraordinary works of art. More often, however, copying resulted in less-than-perfect versions; copiers made mistakes or even intentionally omitted or amended text. The printing press could produce identical copies.

- **The ability to produce more titles and more copies**: The sheer volume of printed materials increased dramatically. By the sixteenth century, more than 100,000 different books were printed in Europe alone (Harris and Johnson 1984).

- **The ability to cover more subjects**: In the first decade of printing, ending in 1460, most of the books printed were in one of four medieval categories: (1) sacred literature (Bibles and prayer books); (2) learned literature (grammatical and scholastic works such as those of Thomas Aquinas); (3) bureaucratic literature (official documents such as papal bulls and indulgence certificates); and (4) vernacular literature (works in the language of the people, notably German readers) (Clanchy 1983). During the second decade of the press, the breadth of subjects increased and spread beyond medieval categories. Obviously, the mass communication of new ideas can have a profound effect on society. For example, Martin Luther effectively disseminated his religious tracts throughout Europe using the press. The effect of the subsequent Protestant Reformation can hardly be overestimated.

- **The creation of new techniques for the organization of published materials**: Given the growth in size and subject diversity of library collections, new techniques for organizing and classifying materials became necessary. This eventually led to the complex systems we have today.

- **The stimulation of literacy and education for the general population**: When books were scarce, only a few could have access to them. As more books became available, it was inevitable that more people would learn to read. This, in turn, generated a new audience for libraries.

In sum, the invention of the printing press, coupled with the reawakening of secular and scientific interests during the Renaissance, ultimately formed the foundation for the growth in number and in the size of libraries and consequently broadened and widened the missions of libraries.

III. LIBRARIES IN THE UNITED STATES: NEW MISSIONS

The seventeenth and eighteenth centuries were formative periods for American libraries. During the early part of the seventeenth century there were few libraries because the social preconditions were not yet in place; people were struggling for subsistence. Other than Boston there were few urban settings, and there was limited economic development or individual wealth. As an agrarian society that depended on manual labor, literacy rates in the general population were low. A few ministers, doctors, and other prominent citizens had private libraries in their homes that served as a resource for dealing with the practical or spiritual problems confronting settlers in the New World. Most of these collections were quite small.

There were also a few modest college libraries. Harvard University, founded in 1636, hired its first librarian in 1667 and by the mid-eighteenth century possessed a small library of approximately 5,000 volumes. Yale University, founded in 1700, held around 2,500 volumes by 1750 (Harris and Johnson 1984). The paucity of college libraries was a reflection of the dearth of college-educated citizens. By 1775 less than one in a thousand attended any college (Hanson 1989). By 1792, only nine colonial colleges had libraries. The size of the typical college collection was small for several reasons: the low number of book titles produced in the United States, lack of fiscal resources, and lack of recognition of the library's role in academic life. If a college had a library, it was usually open infrequently and had no librarian. When assistance was available, it was usually a faculty member who served only secondarily as a librarian (Harwell 1968). The growth of the collection depended primarily on donations. Additional book selection was accomplished usually by a committee of trustees or faculty members (Hamlin 1981; Shiflett 1994).

The religious mission of libraries was also preserved. In England near the end of the seventeenth century an Anglican clergyman, Thomas Bray, created the Society for the Propagation of the Gospel, which advocated for establishing libraries devoted solely to religious purposes (McMullen 2000). Numerous parish libraries were established throughout England, and his teachings soon spread to America. By the early 1700s, seventy parish libraries were established, many in the south Atlantic region (Harris and Johnson 1984).

By 1876, there were more than 10,000 libraries of over eighty different types (McMullen 2000). Their variety was impressive: agricultural libraries, antiquarian society libraries, art society libraries, church libraries, county libraries, government libraries, historical society libraries, hotel reading rooms, ladies' libraries, law libraries, mechanics' libraries, medical libraries, prison libraries, public libraries, railroad libraries, saloon reading rooms, scientific and engineering libraries, sewing circle libraries, state libraries, university libraries, and YMCA libraries. Obviously, discussion of all these different types of libraries lies outside the scope of this book, but it is important to reflect on the character and purposes of some of the major types that formed the foundation of American libraries today.

A. The Mission of Self-Improvement: The Social Libraries of the Eighteenth Century

Advances in mechanical technologies during the eighteenth century led to the Industrial Revolution which, in turn, soon led to the growth of the economy with concomitant growth in individual and community wealth. This meant that some of the more fortunate citizens had more leisure time, time that could be spent pursuing self-development. These were fertile conditions for the emergence of new libraries and missions.

The social library emerged during the first half of the eighteenth century. According to Shera (1965), "the social library was nothing more than a voluntary association of individuals who had contributed money toward a common fund to be used for the purchase of books" (p. 57). There were two types of social libraries: proprietary libraries and subscription (association) libraries. Proprietary libraries operated on the principle that those who contributed money for the library actually owned the material purchased; in essence, they were stockholders. In subscription libraries, individuals paid a fee to use and circulate the collection, but they did not own the items (Shera 1965). Some social libraries were hybrids of the two models, with some members owning shares while others participated by annual subscription. Most social libraries had fewer than fifty members and consequently, the collections were often quite small, often less than 300 books.

The mission of the social library was to assist individuals' self-improvement and the search for truth. Many of the members had a genuine love of literature and believed that the sharing of books and information led to character improvement. They also believed that the members gained knowledge by discussing the ideas they found in books and newspapers. One of the earliest proponents of this mission was Benjamin Franklin, who is credited with establishing the first social library, called the Junto, in Philadelphia in 1728. The Junto was short lived, but he soon founded a second library, which he called a subscription library, in 1731. It survives today as the Philadelphia Library Company.

The social library became quite popular throughout New England in the latter half of the eighteenth century and well into the nineteenth, with its apex between 1825 and 1835. Although they were particularly popular among white, middle- and upper-class aspiring businessmen, the mission of self-improvement was not restricted to the relatively aristocratic and well-educated. As individuals migrated West, they took the social library model with them, which resulted in a wide variety of libraries—YMCA libraries, agricultural libraries, "ladies' clubs," mechanics, and mercantile libraries—all developed to meet the special interests of their particular constituencies (Arenson 2006). There were also many general interest social libraries that did not focus on one particular subject area. These collections often contained religious materials, history, travel, and literature (not to be confused with popular fiction, of which there was little). Although these social libraries might have contained materials of a more diverting nature, their purpose was still to appeal to one's "better angels."

Another important aspect of these social libraries was that although they required individuals to pay money, as institutions they had a distinctly public character. The majority was created for the general citizenry; anyone who could afford the modest fee could partake of the collection. Because there were few places other than work or home where one could occupy one's time productively, social libraries became a third place. There an individual could spend time conversing with friends, developing a sense of community, and reading newspapers or books (Arenson 2006).

However, given the voluntary nature of social libraries, their mission was deeply affected by the ability of members to sustain their library. Often these libraries relied on one or a few benefactors, and shifting economic times, depressions, wars, and social unrest led to the relatively quick demise of many. Similarly, the rise of the public library in urban areas significantly diminished the desirability and economic soundness of social libraries. After all, why pay taxes to support a public library and provide additional funding for a private agency? Nonetheless, the legacy of the social library is significant, especially as it relates to the social nature of such institutions and the role they played as "parlors" in the public sphere (Arenson 2006). Similarly, the idea that libraries were a place to go for self-improvement became ingrained in the American psyche, and subsequently when social libraries foundered, many of these collections formed the core of new public library collections.

B. The Mission of Providing Entertainment: The Circulating Library

While the social library was attempting to meet the need for self-improvement, the mission of the circulating library (sometimes called a rental library) was to satisfy public demand for fiction and popular material intended for entertainment rather than education. Circulating libraries were well established in England and first appeared in America in the 1760s. Although there were some selections from literature, history, and theology, the majority of the collection was fiction. The popular novels of the time consisted mostly of romances (much like today), which were fairly well established in America by 1790. Although there were few romances by American authors, there was ample supply of popular foreign novels printed by American presses. As many as 350 foreign titles may have been published in America from 1789 to 1800, compared to thirty-five titles by American authors (Shera 1965).

It is worth noting that circulating libraries often incurred the wrath of certain segments of society who were concerned with the immoral effects of popular reading. As sometimes happens today in public libraries, circulating libraries were suspected of corrupting youth, usually because of the corrupting effects of popular novels—especially the French ones (Shera 1965).

> *The distinguishing feature of circulating libraries was their profit-making character. Usually associated with a printer or bookstore, the books were rented or individuals were charged a membership fee that allowed them to borrow a designated number of materials over a specified period of time. Serving mass tastes appears to have been as profitable in colonial times as it is today; many of these libraries prospered and spread throughout New England.*

The circulating library also made several contributions to contemporary public library philosophy and service. For example, despite its profit motive, its mission to appeal to popular taste has echoes in contemporary public library service. In addition, Kaser (1980) noted, circulating libraries were the first to provide (1) service to women, (2) newspapers and magazines, (3) extended hours of service, (4) reading areas in the library itself, and (5) outreach services, including the home delivery of books. These are substantive contributions. The circulating library's survival, however, was ultimately threatened by its low status and competition from tax-supported public libraries (Kaser 1980).

C. The Mission of Providing Information: The Rise of Special Libraries

Although the circulating library as a money-making venture failed to survive, its spirit of free enterprise was certainly consistent with a capitalistic economy. Shortly after the start of the Industrial Revolution, public libraries and a few businesses started collections for factory workers, technical workers, craftsmen, and managers (Kruzas 1965). Most libraries associated with business and commerce were used for information and education, consultation with expert sources, or diversion. However, at the beginning of the twentieth century, American business and industry discovered the instrumentality of the library, and there emerged a new library whose purpose was the "direct application of recorded information to the practical goals of profit-seeking business enterprises" (Kruzas 1965, p. 109). The purpose of the commercial library was to promote the profitability of the company. The librarian's job was to provide reference service to the organization rather than build a collection per se. Providing information to an individual was much more important than instructing that person on where to find the information. This remains a fundamental characteristic of special libraries to this day. These libraries collected only materials that focused on the direct needs of the enterprise, many of which, such as technical records, industrial and market reports, proprietary documents, and business conference papers, were unfamiliar to many public librarians.

The unique concerns of these types of libraries led to the creation of the Special Libraries Association in 1909. Special libraries also fostered new technologies such as microfilm, which became available in the 1920s. Most significantly, the mission of special libraries to provide specific information rather than documents was an important factor in the rise of information science and the exploitation of information technologies in libraries.

D. The Mission to Support Teaching and Research: The American Academic Library

Although the educational mission of libraries emerged as early as the Alexandrian library, the mission of the library as a full partner in American academic institutions did not evolve until the latter part of the nineteenth century (Hamlin 1981). There are historical reasons for this late development. From the colonial period to the Civil War, the American university curriculum followed a classical model emphasizing theology, philosophy, history, and the trivium of the liberal arts—grammar, rhetoric, and logic (Hanson 1989). The faculty taught from a single text or, at best, a few books. Classroom recitation was strongly emphasized (Hamlin 1981). Such methods produced little need for libraries, and academic collections remained small throughout this period. However, four significant events in the mid-nineteenth century substantially changed academic institutions and shifted the role of the academic libraries: changes in the academic curriculum, the rise of the research model, passage of the Morrill Land Grant Act of 1862, and the professionalization of librarians.

1. Changes in the Curriculum

With the dawn of the Industrial Revolution came a need for college graduates with a practical education rather than an understanding of the classics (Hanson 1989). By the 1840s, universities began offering courses in the natural sciences. In 1850 Brown University began the first elective system including courses in the sciences and languages (Shiflett 1994). Teaching methods also changed. Seminars, laboratories, and independent study emerged as an alternative to the recitation techniques of the past (Hanson 1989). As the breadth of the curriculum expanded, access to more diverse materials became an increasingly important issue, concomitantly increasing the importance of the library. The evolution of the academic curriculum and its implication for librarianship were recognized early by Melvil Dewey (1978):

> The colleges are waking to the fact that the work of every professor and every department is necessarily based on the library; text books constantly yield their exalted places to wiser and broader methods; professor after professor sends his classes, or goes with them, to the library and teaches them to investigate for themselves, and to use books, getting beyond the method of the primary school with its parrot-like recitations from a single text. (p. 136)

2. The Rise of the Research Model

At the turn of the eighteenth century at the University of Berlin in Germany, a new model of the modern university emerged. This model envisioned faculty members as independent researchers. Objective scholarship was promoted, and an expansive faculty research agenda was encouraged (Shiflett 1994). Given the obvious need for published resources for research, the academic library played an increasingly critical role. The reforms in German higher education did not go unnoticed at some of the more prestigious academic institutions in the United States, many of which sent American students to study in Germany. Returning individuals, many of whom became professors themselves, brought the concept of research, coupled with teaching, back with them (Shiflett 1994).

Although these ideas had some effect on American higher education throughout the nineteenth century, it was not until 1876 that this model was explicitly adopted with the founding of Johns Hopkins University. Johns Hopkins placed research as a central function of the university. The seminar model of teaching was emphasized and students were encouraged to consult a wide variety of published sources. Soon thereafter, Harvard, Cornell, and Columbia adopted this teaching approach (Jones 1989). The need for a library with current and deep collections was essential to fulfill this function, and the result was to increase substantially the importance and centrality of the academic library. Although the mission of academic libraries continues to evolve, the need to support the academic curriculum and provide research support for faculty remains the academic library's primary function.

3. The Passage of the Morrill Land Grant Act of 1862

Most colleges founded before the Civil War were private and sectarian. By the nineteenth century, however, it became clear that higher education for the citizenry was also a matter for the state. Beginning in the East and South, state universities were founded in Vermont, Maine, North Carolina, Georgia, New York, Pennsylvania, Massachusetts, and Kentucky. By midcentury, the federal government recognized that it could play an important role in promoting education by providing land to states for establishing universities. This led to the passage of the Morrill Land Grant Act in 1862, which allocated 30,000 acres of public land to establish state universities promoting agriculture and the mechanical arts. The universities founded as a result of the act, including the Ohio State University and the University of Illinois, emphasized applied sciences and technology (Hamlin 1981).

4. Professional Education for Librarians

Fortunately, the growth of the academic library coincided with the development of professional education for librarians. The American Library Association (ALA) was founded in 1876 and established the first library school in 1887 (Jones 1989). As the demands for collection development, materials selection, and library service grew, increasing numbers of trained librarians were available to nurture a fertile environment for scholarship and teaching.

E. Supporting Primary and Secondary Education: The Mission of the School Library

During the colonial period, there were few publicly supported schools, although in the mid-Atlantic states and the South there were some parochial and private schools (Hanson 1989). What schools there were provided elementary-level education, considered sufficient to create an efficient pool of agrarian labor. The few secondary schools available prepared elite students for a limited number of colleges (Hanson 1989). It was not until the second half of the nineteenth century that public schools began to emerge. In 1852 Massachusetts passed the first compulsory school attendance laws. By 1890, half of the states had such laws. At the same time, more and more schools, including secondary schools with libraries, were being built.

The earliest attempt to support public school libraries occurred in New York in 1835 when the state legislature passed a law that permitted school districts to apply some of their tax receipts to create and maintain school libraries. By 1875, twenty states had passed similar legislation (Knight and Nourse 1969). In 1892, New York again passed legislation that provided matching funds to purchase library books for school districts as long as the books were first approved by the Department of Public Instruction. Approved materials consisted of "reference books, supplementary reading books, books related to the curriculum, and pedagogical books for use by teachers" (Gillespie and Spirt 1983, p. 3). Some of them could even be taken out of the library. Unfortunately, many of these legislative efforts proved unsuccessful, often allocating money for books but not for administration and maintenance. Sometimes money allocated for books went to teachers' salaries. The result was poorly developed, poorly maintained libraries that were seldom used (Knight and Nourse 1969; Cecil and Heaps 1940). Although these libraries had great potential, they did not perform their central mission. Gillespie and Spirt (1983) have suggested, however, that these early efforts to create and maintain public school libraries established the idea that public funds were an appropriate means to support school libraries, and that school libraries could play a useful role in public school education. By the last decade of the nineteenth century, the number of school libraries, especially in high schools, increased substantially, and by 1895 it was estimated that there were from 2,500 to 4,000 school libraries (Knight and Nourse 1969).

Several groups were concerned with the development of school libraries, including the National Council of Teachers of English (NCTE), the National Education Association (NEA), and ALA. In 1914 the NCTE formed a standing committee on school libraries and ALA formed a School Library Section (Cecil and Heaps 1940). In 1915 the NCTE conducted a national survey, and the findings expressed serious concern about the adequacy of school libraries. This prompted the NEA and ALA to appoint a joint committee headed by Charles Certain to study the condition of school libraries and to develop standards. Certain's first report, published in 1920, focused on high schools; the second, in 1925, focused on elementary schools. Both reports concluded that school libraries were seriously deficient.

The standards prepared by Certain's committee described the library as "an integral part of the daily life of the school" and included several significant recommendations (Certain 1925, p. 5):

1. They emphasized the centrality of "materials of instruction," that is, curricular support.
2. They advocated for a centralized collection. The centralization of materials in the school had been an issue for some years, with some arguing for small library collections in each classroom and others arguing for centralized location and control of library materials.
3. They promoted library instruction as a duty of school libraries.
4. They recognized the integral character of the school library within the total setting of school life.

Certain's reports were significant in that they proposed the first national standards for school libraries which were endorsed by both ALA and NEA (Gillespie and Spirt 1983).

One should not assume, however, that Certain's reports led to the quick development of centralized, modern school libraries, though they certainly made a major contribution. Fortunately, in addition to the reports, other significant factors contributed to progress in that direction. Among them was the educational reform movement looming on the horizon, which Certain (1925) recognized early:

> Modern demands upon the public school presuppose adequate library service. Significant changes in methods of teaching require that the school library supplement the single textbook course of instruction and provide for the enrichment of the school curriculum. (p. 1)

The decade of the 1920s was indeed an era of reform in public education. John Dewey and the progressive education movement introduced a variety of new educational theories:

1. A child's growth and development, rather than subject matter, should be the central focus of the school.
2. Education should involve children learning through a variety of experiences and exploring a variety of subjects.
3. Children learn best when they are exploring subjects of interest to them.
4. School should be a social experience that teaches children how to be self-directed. (Fargo 1930)

These "radical" ideas resulted in a more varied school curriculum requiring access to a much wider range of materials. Responding to children's interests, encouraging exploration, and providing a broad range of experiences could only increase the importance of a school library:

> With such a program, it is obvious that the library stands in a far more vital relationship to the school than before. Under the older tradition, books other than texts were desirable; in the new school they are indispensable. They are not the accompaniment of the school's activities; they are its warp and woof. (Fargo 1930, pp. 31–32)

Other influences that contributed to the emergence of the modern school library included new studies and the support of the U.S. Office of Education, NEA, ALA, the Carnegie Corporation, and the North Central Association of Colleges and Secondary Schools (Cecil and Heaps 1940; Gillespie and Spirt 1983). The combination of changing teaching philosophies and the evaluations and standards developed by NEA and ALA had a substantial impact on establishing the foundations of the school library and its mission—to support the primary and secondary curriculum by providing current and appropriate materials for students and teachers.

F. The Mission of Serving the Public: The American Public Library

The social library and the circulating library each performed a unique mission: the former to educate and enlighten, and the latter to satisfy popular taste. Both of these libraries contributed to the development of the modern public library and its very special mission—to serve the public. The term public library refers generically to libraries supported by public funds. Using this broad definition, by 1876 there were approximately 3,600 public libraries in the United States. Most of these, however, were associated with academic institutions, public schools, or social libraries. As we apply the term today, there were actually very few public libraries. By 1880 only seven of the sixteen largest cities in the United States had municipally supported libraries.

The debate as to when and where the first public library in the United States was established will continue. Some have suggested that the honor belongs to Peterborough, New Hampshire, because in 1834 "there for the first time an institution was founded by a town with the deliberate purpose of creating a free library that would be open without restriction to all classes of the community—a library supported from the beginning by public funds" (Shera 1965, p. 169).

However, there is no dispute as to where and when the first major public library was established. In March 1848, the Massachusetts legislature authorized the city of Boston to provide municipal support for a public library. The Boston Public Library, founded in 1854, receives credit for being the first major public library.

Fundamental Characteristics Shared by All American Public Libraries

1. **Supported by Taxes**: Public libraries are usually supported by local taxes, although over the years there have been exceptions. The notion of public support through taxation is rare before the nineteenth century. As noted earlier, prior to that time, libraries were most often sponsored or subsidized by private citizens, religious orders, or royal families.

2. **Governed by a Board**: This board usually consisted of prominent citizens appointed, or sometimes elected, to serve the public interest.

3. **Open to All**: A fundamental tenet of public libraries is that everyone in the community can access the collection. This is not to say that every group has been made to feel welcome. At different times, various subsets of the population have not found public libraries friendly or accommodating to their needs. But in principle, the libraries are open to all.

4. **Voluntary**: People are not forced to come; the use of the library is entirely voluntary. This distinguishes it from other educational institutions, such as public schools. Its voluntary nature is also part of the underlying social philosophy of the nineteenth century in which self-improvement was considered an important value.

5. **Established by State Law**: This point is not generally well understood. During the early development of public libraries, serious questions arose concerning whether a town could create a library and tax its citizens for its maintenance without the state's approval. As a consequence, a key aspect of the creation of public libraries was the passage of enabling legislation on the part of the states that permitted towns and communities to establish public libraries. In rare instances, public libraries were not only enabled by state legislation, they were financed by state monies. Such is the case in Ohio today, where a small percentage (less than 3 percent) of the state's general revenue fund is earmarked for funding public libraries.

6. **Provide Services without Charge**: Although some public libraries charge a small fee for special services, most of the services are provided without fees.

---

1. The Founding of the Boston Public Library

The creation of the Boston Public library is generally viewed as the result of two major factors: first, it was a natural outgrowth of urban developments in the mid-nineteenth century; and second, it was the result of prevailing social attitudes held by a small group of individuals who concluded, for a variety of reasons, that a public library was needed for the citizens of Boston.

By the middle of the nineteenth century, urbanization in America had reached a tipping point. As cities matured and prospered economically, their political and bureaucratic infrastructure, including basic services such as water, sanitation, public health, fire protection, and education, also matured. Boston was typical of a prospering and stable urban environment. Therefore, when the issue of a public library was first raised, many perceived it from an administrative point of view as a logical extension of city services.

The concept of a public library for Boston was first advanced more than a decade before its founding by a noted French actor and ventriloquist, Nicholas Marie Alexandre Vattemare. Vattemare was a highly successful and wealthy entertainer who also loved books and collected art. He abandoned his theatrical career and became a global philanthropist with a special interest in developing an international, reciprocal exchange of duplicate copies of books traded among major cultural institutions. He established a significant reputation among U.S. politicians with particular connections in Boston (Havens 2007). In the 1840s he proposed that several of the major private libraries in Boston combine into one public institution to facilitate this exchange. This proposal met with some favor from local officials, but the libraries resisted, and Vattemare's proposal failed. Nonetheless, numerous individuals in Boston had both the wealth and the power to generate a civic interest in libraries. Public discussion on this issue continued for some time and helped maintain the necessary political and social momentum that would ultimately produce the desired result more than a decade later. Particularly notable were the efforts of Charles Ticknor and Edward Everett. Ticknor was the educated son of a wealthy Boston merchant. He assumed that social change was possible if accomplished gradually, and he believed that public schools and libraries could improve social and political stability by promoting the education of the general population (Ditzion 1947). Everett was a Unitarian clergyman, teacher, scholar, and, at one point, governor of Massachusetts. A strong advocate of the public schools, Everett's beliefs were less populist and more academic than Ticknor's. He saw in the public library an opportunity for those no longer attending schools to continue their studies. He believed the public library could extend one's education by providing educational materials, not just for scholars, but for professionals and merchants. The efforts of Ticknor, Everett, and others finally convinced the Boston city fathers to appoint a Joint Standing Committee on the Library, which in turn recommended the appointment of a board of trustees. The Boston Public Library opened in the spring of 1854. Its mission was to serve the educational convictions of Everett and the popular needs espoused by Ticknor.

Everett and Ticknor were part of the educated elite of Boston. They believed that the responsibility to improve people lay not only with social institutions. Many members of the upper classes still believed in noblesse oblige and assumed that they, too, bore responsibility to provide the means by which others could improve themselves. This implied a duty on the part of the wealthy and better educated to improve the poor and uneducated insofar as they wanted to be improved. American philanthropy thus became one of the critical foundations for the growth of the public library for years to come. Libraries were seen as an ideal institution to help those less fortunate. This was, ostensibly, an underlying reason for the philanthropy of Andrew Carnegie, who asserted in his 1889 "Gospel of Wealth":

> This, then, is held to be the duty of the man of wealth: To set an example of modest, unostentatious living, shunning display or extravagance; to provide moderately for the legitimate wants of those dependent upon him; and, after doing so, to consider all surplus revenues which come to him simply as trust

funds, which he is called upon to administer, and strictly bound as a matter of duty to administer in the manner which, in his judgment, is best calculated to produce the most beneficial results for the community—the man of wealth thus becoming the mere trustee and agent for his poorer brethren, bringing to their service his superior wisdom, experience, and ability to administer, doing for them better than they would or could do for themselves. (1962, p. 25)

The growth of libraries and librarianship during the nineteenth century was deeply rooted in these beliefs (Nielson 1989).

What can we deduce about the mission of the public library from the history of the Boston Public Library? Clearly, it shares an educational mission with American public schools. In 1876, Melvil Dewey stated that popular education was actually divided into two parts: "the free school and the free public library" (Dewey 1978, p. 5). He thought of the library as a school and of the librarian as a teacher. But in what way was the mission of the public library distinct from the public schools? First, the public library could satisfy the interest in reading and learning for all ages, not just for those who were in school; second, it was a means to self-improvement in an age when self-education was still a vital means for improving one's chances in society. Third, it was intended to produce more thoughtful people, individuals capable of making balanced and well-reasoned judgments in a democratic society that depended on their judgments at the voting booth. Such citizens would serve as a strong and stabilizing force to the democratic society. Finally, libraries were perceived as "cultural agencies." Indeed, librarians of the latter half of the nineteenth century saw themselves as agents of social improvement.

It is easy to see how many could view these objectives as noble, and those who advocated for the founding of public libraries often saw them, like museums and world's fairs, as a means to advance the cultural goals of the country. They envisioned the public library as "one cathedral more" to advance the cause of learning (McCrossen 2006, pp. 169–170). In addition, McCrossen (2006) noted that nineteenth-century public libraries provided a rare public space to use free time in healthy pursuits. Much of this same rationale is used to defend libraries today from attacks of various kinds, both fiscal and philosophical.

However, for others the library was also seen as a tool for social control. This aspect of the founding of the Boston Public Library has been examined most notably by Michael Harris (1973), whose "revisionist" interpretation provides a different perspective on the motivations of the founders. Although few of the facts are disputed, Harris challenged the notion that the founding of the public library was humanitarian, idealistic, or democratic. Rather, he reminded us that the founders were among the Boston Brahmins, a highly privileged, politically conservative, and aristocratic class that dominated the social, economic, and political life of the city. He argued that the founders were far less concerned with making educated democrats than with socializing the unruly immigrants who were subject to undue influence by political demagogues and other unscrupulous politicians who could foment political and social instability. In other words, Harris suggested that the creation of the Boston Public Library was another strategy of elitist aristocrats to maintain class stratification and ensure the social order that benefited them. If the aristocrats controlled what was taught about the social and political institutions of American society, the immigrants would accept those institutions, which were controlled and shaped by the elites. In this conceptualization, the library and librarians were seen as agents of authority and social control, implementing restrictive rules, and generally unfriendly to the hoi polloi. How could they be otherwise, run by board members appointed by elites, who were themselves elites? Further, Harris suggested that the public library collection was not designed for the common person, but catered to the educated and upper classes. He argued that this pattern has been repeated time and again, as evidenced by the fact that public libraries then and today are run by elites and attended by a disproportionately large number of upper- and middle-class patrons.

Harris's position has been challenged by other library historians. Dain (1975), for example, noted that there is insufficient historical evidence for some of Harris's strongest assertions. Further, she pointed out that just because elites created the first public library does not mean that other classes were not well served by them. She noted that the authoritarian nature of early public libraries reflected all public institutions of the time. She argued that public libraries made earnest efforts to attract a variety of users. Today, such efforts are evident in extended hours of operation on Sundays and evenings, information services, open stacks, classification systems, branches, children's rooms and services, meeting rooms for community groups, cooperative activities with schools, interlibrary loan, and special services for immigrants.

Although Harris's position is controversial, it reminds us that history is shaped most often by the victors and that historical interpretation varies by the position of the teller. It is true that the history of public libraries has multiple philosophical underpinnings, some of them countervailing and incompatible. Certainly, a consciousness of class was very much a part of the era from which the Boston Public Library emerged. For example, in an 1874 article titled, "Public Libraries and Fiction," the author begins with the observation: "It is worth considering that, practically, public libraries are for the benefit of and directly influence the least cultivated classes, who do not possess private collections of books" (p. 169). Consistent with Harris' notion of control, the author goes on to observe:

> [Public libraries] operate upon the very part of society where improvement is most needed.... The legitimate office of public libraries seems to be to aid directly in the intellectual improvement of these masses, to help them to approach the standard that is fixed above and beyond them. (p. 169)

Today, many might find such language offensive, although it was not intended as such. It reflects both a notion of noblesse oblige and a sincere belief in the improvability of one's intellectual condition.

2. The Historical Struggle over Popular Materials

If public libraries were viewed as part of a "cultural hierarchy" (McCrossen 2006, p. 173) whose primary function was the diffusion of knowledge and learning, they also were seen as purveyors of a wide range of materials, many of which were clearly not learned. From the beginning, the public library was challenged by the mission of satisfying popular tastes. Their holdings of popular novels, newspapers, and magazines were of concern to some because these materials tended to attract a clientele who were more inclined to lounge than to read—the "loafers and bummers" (McCrossen 2006). Newspapers and magazines were particularly troublesome because they potentially diverted the attention of readers away from books. Nonetheless, from the beginning, Charles Ticknor advocated that popular materials should be part of the Boston Public Library's collection for the entertainment of readers. Interestingly, the library put its newspapers and light fiction in its lower hall, with more serious reading placed in its upper hall (McCrossen 2006). The pattern of separating reading rooms in this manner still exists today. It also remains a concern that reading rooms are sometimes the source of lounging, rather than reading.

Popular fiction has a long tradition of raising concerns about lowering morals. Wiegand (1989) called this the "ideology of reading" (p. 100), the idea that there was good reading and bad reading; the former led to good conduct, the latter to unacceptable behaviors. The implication, of course, was that librarians were to buy only the "good" reading materials. It was even suggested by some that reading too much bad fiction might cause insanity. These concerns were raised soon after the creation of the Boston Public Library. In an article titled "Free Fiction" that appeared in *The Nation* in 1866, the writer expressed concern over the "light literature" available at the Boston Public Library and other circulating libraries. He admitted that there was a demand for this type of material and noted that the "leading idea of those who manage these institutions seems to be that any reading is better than no reading at all—an axiom at once false and full of mischief. . . . The value of lending libraries, if we might indulge in a truism, depends very much on the quality of the books which are lent" ("Free Fiction," p. 139). His chief concern seemed to be that such materials would deleteriously affect young minds. This is an excellent example of a certain way of thinking that seems to persist through the ages:

> Read at an age when the taste is unformed, when the passions are just developing, when the will is feeble, principles are unfixed, and resistance to temptation is difficult, if they do not utterly spoil the inquisitive minds which are attracted by their glittering mediocrity, it will be because nature is stronger

than education, and original vigor more than a match for enfeebling moral influences. (p. 139)

Should library collections include such diversions? What is their effect on young people? Some early public librarians felt that popular fiction might bring less-educated readers into the library where they would then be exposed to a better quality of literature. Even among librarians with serious misgivings, most had at least some popular novels on their shelves. They realized that if they wanted library users, they would need popular fiction. Generally, their collections were not overly stocked with "cheap" novels, but offered works by Flaubert, Zola, Fielding, and Balzac. This did not protect libraries, however, from censorship attacks as the works of these masters were perceived as scandalous at the time. McCrossen (2006) nicely summarized the double edge of public library service:

> Public Libraries thus stood in the middle ground between the serious and popular—their mandate was to meet the public's demands, but their goal was to improve, indeed to shape, its tastes....Due to their inclusion of fiction, newspapers, and marginalized members of the public, public libraries occupied an ambiguous place with the hierarchy of cultural institutions. (pp. 174, 178)

The need to preserve and promote the values of literary culture while at the same time recognizing the genuine and legitimate interests of those who enjoy more common fare remains a contemporary tension with roots firmly planted in the nineteenth century.

3. Andrew Carnegie

In many ways Andrew Carnegie personified this tension. Carnegie was a Scottish immigrant who, through hard work and ingenuity, prospered in the iron and steel industry. He amassed a fortune exceeding $330 million, 90 percent of which went into charitable trusts. Carnegie's philosophy of stewardship certainly marked him as a prominent exponent of noblesse oblige, but his philanthropy served many.

From 1886 to 1919 Carnegie donated $56 million to construct more than 2,000 library buildings, many of them public libraries, in more than 1,400 communities, large and small. The communities that requested Carnegie's money viewed a library as a source of civic pride. The libraries built with Carnegie's largesse were their libraries, not his, and their shelves were stocked with materials of local interest, not his.

In fact, the specifically local character of today's public library collections and services might be a direct result of the special conditions and restrictions that Carnegie required with every donation. First, the money was for building construction only, not for the purchase and maintenance of library materials or for staff. This, in essence, guaranteed the local character of library collections. Second, all recipients had to contribute an annual sum equal to 10 percent of the money donated to build collections and hire staff. This created a tradition of shared government support of public libraries and defined local governance. The town, through its appointed board, was in control, not Carnegie. The inevitable result was that the Carnegie public library was shaped by local interest: library collections reflected the local community and popular taste. Thus one of the fundamental missions of public libraries, to meet the needs of the local community, was promoted by the Carnegie model of local taxation and local governmental control. Indeed, Carnegie might well have done more to establish this model than the Boston Public Library.

4. The Role of Women's Clubs

One cannot leave the discussion of the forces that shaped American public libraries without noting the significant contributions of women's volunteer organizations, most notably women's clubs. Such clubs became commonplace following the Civil War when it became more acceptable for women to seek an education, especially self-education. Some of these clubs were local, while others were affiliated nationally with the General Federation of Women's Clubs. Like similar organizations devoted to education, "the members were imbued with the idea of the importance of books in improving the quality of life" (Watson 1994, p. 235). Their support for improving women's education extended to developing libraries for use by members of their local community. Watson (1994) suggested that women's clubs contributed in significant ways to the development of more than 470 public libraries between 1870 and 1930. Although the exact percentage of public libraries established through the efforts of women's clubs in the early part of the twentieth century is unclear, Watson estimates that it might have ranged between 50 and 75 percent of the total. In some instances the clubs provided support for additional materials and club members volunteered as librarians. Some women's clubs were influential at the state level, lobbying for library legislation and the need for state library commissions (Watson 1994). Although many of the club members were aristocrats, or at least middle class, and therefore potentially subject to Harris's criticisms, their contributions to advancing the public library are substantial. Their stated mission of self-education and improvement is firmly in line with the history and values of their era, and the results were salutary.

5. A Mission of Inclusiveness

Throughout the nineteenth century American cities and towns experienced major immigrations of people from many countries, particularly from Europe. Amid this influx of polyglot peoples, there were legitimate concerns regarding education and socialization. The progressive philosophy of the times viewed the function of educational institutions, including libraries, as improving society and advancing the democratic tradition (Du Mont et al. 1994). For many, this meant that immigrant groups needed to be assimilated into the American mainstream. Because of their numbers, Europeans were considered to be a particularly difficult challenge (Stern 1991). Libraries were "to furnish fuel for the fires beneath the great melting pot" (Roberts 1912, p. 169). What better group to serve this function than libraries? Many librarians took this responsibility quite seriously and numerous articles in professional periodicals offered advice on providing services and understanding the needs of immigrants. Some librarians exhibited an almost missionary zeal in their efforts to bring the benefits of reading to the general public.

Nonetheless, it is true that the public library of the nineteenth century was used primarily by white middle and upper classes. Ethnic minorities were largely excluded from the benefits of library service (Trujillo and Cuesta 1989). Aside from the segregationist practices related to African Americans, there is relatively limited evidence to determine whether public libraries intentionally excluded other ethnic groups, or whether librarians and trustees were simply uninformed as to how to serve them effectively.

It was not until the turn of the century that libraries began a systematic effort to serve ethnic groups. Immigration continued, with more than 20 million arriving in the first quarter of the twentieth century (Stern 1991). Although a few librarians recognized that each ethnic group had its own literature and culture worth preserving and transmitting, the primary emphasis was on integration and assimilation. Nonetheless, library collections and services included books and newspapers written in native languages; programs on U.S. citizenship; classes in English; story hours in native languages; programs on American history and culture; supplementary materials to support school curricula; and help for immigrants in reading letters, sending messages to social service agencies, writing checks, and completing citizenship forms (Stern 1991; Du Mont et al. 1994). In 1917 ALA created a Committee on Work with the Foreign Born that collected and disseminated information on how to help educate immigrants about American values and the English language (Stern 1991). The committee produced numerous guides to assist in this process.

Perhaps the most notable service to ethnic groups and minorities was the creation of branch libraries in urban areas. Branches provided extension services that could reach special populations, especially industrial workers and those who did not speak English (Ditzion 1947). These branches also offered special services to children. By 1900 many public libraries had a separate room for children's books and services. What better place to educate the first generation of immigrant children in the ways of American life (Du Mont et al. 1994)?

Sadly, some minorities and ethnic groups did not receive much attention from librarians, most notably African Americans and Hispanics. Although Pura Belpre provided services to Hispanics at the New York Public Library as early as 1921, this was clearly an exception (Guerena and Erazo 2000). In his study of library services to Hispanics, Haro (1981) found that libraries were often perceived as one of many Anglo institutions designed and controlled by Anglos to serve Anglos:

> While most Mexican Americans, even the poor and illiterate, aspire to better education, the public library is not seen as a vehicle to attain it. The public library is viewed by far too many Mexican Americans, particularly within the lower classes, as an Anglo institution which has never cared about their needs, which does not hire their people, and which engages in the disproportionate distribution of resources to satisfy first the demands of an Anglo society. (p. 86)

Before the Civil War, blacks in the South were forbidden to read and it was unlawful to teach them. Illiteracy was a means to maintain the subordination of slaves; those who could read did it in secret. Nonetheless, there was, even before the Civil War, a class of well-educated African Americans including merchants, ministers, printers, shipbuilders, physicians, and others who placed great value on education and possessed strong literary interests, living mostly in the North. In the absence of access to libraries or formal education, they created literary societies in the first part of the nineteenth century, which served as "important entry points to a literary and intellectual world otherwise inaccessible to their membership" (McHenry 1998, p. 152). Pre–Civil War societies included the Philadelphia Library Company of Colored Persons, founded by Robert Purvis, and the Female Library Association of Philadelphia (Wheeler and Johnson-Houston 2004; McHenry 1998). McHenry (1998) observed, "These societies offered a protected, collective environment in which to develop a literary background as well as the oral and written skills needed to represent themselves with confidence" (p. 157).

Throughout the nineteenth century, these societies played a vital role, especially for black women. They could read fine literature and discuss ideas that promoted eloquence and critical thinking. The societies represented a source of both intellectual challenge and emotional support (McHenry 1998).

After the Civil War, although there was a concerted push for public schooling in the South, the development of public libraries for both blacks and whites lagged by about fifty years (Fultz 2006). What libraries there were provided severely restricted or no service to African Americans (Trujillo and Cuesta 1989). By 1900, it is estimated that 90 percent of African Americans in the South still could not read. The first two public libraries for African Americans followed a combined school/library pattern. In 1903, the LeMoyne Institute, a black normal school, provided space for a library and made the collection available to the citizens as well as the students. In 1904, Galveston, Texas, opened a branch of the Rosenberg Library for African Americans as an addition to a local black high school. In 1905, two segregated reading rooms for blacks were established in the public libraries of Lexington, Kentucky, and Jacksonville, Florida.

Other early efforts by public libraries to serve African Americans began in rented spaces in private homes or churches. For example, in 1905 the Western Colored

Branch in Louisville, Kentucky, opened in three rented rooms in a private home (Fultz 2006). This branch served the new, growing black middle class and was headed by a critical figure in the development of libraries for African Americans, Thomas Fountain Blue. Blue was a graduate of the prestigious Hampton Institute and Richmond Theological Seminary. The Louisville branch was the first public library branch serving African Americans in any American city (Josey 1994). Blue's services and library training programs for African Americans were considered a national model (Josey 1970). His Colored Department in Louisville not only provided direct service, but also established "deposit stations" and classroom collections at various sites throughout the city and surrounding counties (Fultz 2006). Similarly, the Negro Public Library in Nashville, Tennessee, which opened in 1916 as a branch of Nashville's Carnegie Library, focused on service to children. Under the leadership of the African-American branch librarian, Marian Hadley, who studied under Blue, and the librarian of the Carnegie Library, Margaret Kercheval, a solid children's collection was developed and services such as story hours were also offered (Malone 2000).

Despite these notable exceptions, in general, public library service to people of color was poor or nonexistent. Under the "separate but equal" doctrine in operation throughout the first half of the twentieth century, services for African Americans remained seriously deficient. In the South, there was considerable evidence that funding for library services to African Americans was not commensurate to the proportion of African Americans in the community (Gleason 1941).

By 1926, nationally there were perhaps forty-five public libraries providing segregated library services to African Americans; by 1935 the number had increased to seventy-five (Du Mont et al. 1994). The establishment of branches to serve African Americans was usually funded by the philanthropy of whites, the Carnegie Corporation, or the activities of churches or civic organizations (both black and white) (Cresswell 1996; Wheeler and Johnson-Houston 2004).

By the late 1930s, the main libraries of sixteen southern cities claimed to provide services to African Americans. However, in reality there were few services, often offered only in segregated circumstances: separate branches, poorly funded school libraries, and restricted hours of operation, bookmobile service, and privileges at main libraries. Sometimes the same library served both blacks and whites but had separate entrances, collections, and reading areas. By the late 1940s, there were no more than seventeen independent black libraries in the South (Fultz 2006).

Prior to the 1960s, library service to ethnic groups and minorities was based on the perception of these communities as disadvantaged. The 1960s brought significant changes, a time of ethnic self-determination (Stern 1991). Many African Americans and Hispanics argued for equal opportunity and equal access to the advantages that American society had to offer. The concept of a melting pot was replaced by the concept of a multicultural society.

It was during the 1960s when activist movements sponsored demonstrations, sit-ins, and "read-ins" that library services became widely available to African Americans, especially in the South (Graham 2001). The first sit-in in Mississippi took place at the Jackson Public Library in 1961. Even then, African Americans often paid a high price, including being beaten for attempting to apply for a library card (Wheeler and Johnson-Houston 2004). In 1963, two black ministers in Anniston, Alabama, were brutally beaten for attempting to desegregate the city's library. Nonetheless, by 1963, seventy-one of seventy-six cities in the South with populations of 50,000 or more had integrated main library facilities. Yet, the existence of integrated facilities did not mean that blacks received equal treatment. Separate restrooms, checkout desks, entrances, and age restrictions were still commonplace (Fultz 2006).

Interestingly, the desegregation of public libraries came more quickly than that of the schools, and the process began prior to the 1960s. Fultz (2006) argued that this might be because "some southerners during this period held that racial interactions in libraries were less threatening than the possibilities of social contact among children in schools or even, seemingly among strangers on buses" (p. 348). He also noted that African American library users were perceived as predominantly middle class and therefore more acceptable.

Graham (2001) observed that even in the 1960s, white librarians in the South were ambivalent about the segregation of public libraries; they were attempting to balance their professional ethos of service to all with the powerful mores of racial segregation that permeated their communities. The end of segregated libraries in the South was much more attributable to black activists than to librarians.

This is not to say that there weren't some notable heroes among librarians. Juliette Hampton Morgan, for example, was a white reference librarian at the Montgomery, Alabama Carnegie Library, who vocally supported the Montgomery Bus Boycott of 1955. The community reaction was so intense and vituperative that it probably contributed to her subsequent suicide. Similarly, Emily Wheelock Reed, director of Alabama's Public Library Service Division, in 1957 courageously defended the children's book, *The Rabbits' Wedding*, which had illustrations depicting the marriage of a black rabbit to a white rabbit. Notable politicians accused Reed of promoting anti-segregationist literature and race mixing. She kept the book on the shelves and was subjected to intense questioning and scrutiny by state politicians. Later, Reed was again criticized for pro-integrationist attitudes because she included the works of Martin Luther King in her collection (Graham 2001). Although Reed left public service in 1960, her fortitude was a measure of the conviction of some librarians to overcome the prejudices of the times. There was, in fact, a segment of southern librarians who endorsed the concept of racial accommodation, but who seldom confronted the powerful segregationist forces directly (Carmichael 2005).

These problems, of course, did not exist only in the South. Evidence that northern libraries also discriminated was generally overlooked. For example, communities that received Carnegie dollars often spent the money on the provision of service to whites but not to African Americans; or far less money was spent, resulting in inferior service. As the historian John Hope Franklin (1977) observed, "one searches in vain for an indignant outcry on the part of the professional librarians against this profanation of their sacred profession and this subversion of their cherished institutions" (p. 13).

Regrettably, ALA was not outspoken on the issue of library service to African Americans until the 1960s, when the civil rights movement made it impossible to ignore (Du Mont et al. 1994). Generally, until the 1960s the association viewed itself as representing a national constituency of librarians, including those in the South who favored segregation. ALA did not want to be perceived as judging the political or social beliefs of its members. It viewed segregationist policies as a local matter. There was also concern that too much agitation would create more resistance in the South and bring unfavorable publicity to those public libraries that were desegregating quietly (Cresswell 1996; Josey 1994). By the 1960s, a considerable number of ALA members expressed concern that the association had done little to secure open access for all citizens and to address issues of equality and social justice. In 1961 the ALA took a firm stand regarding service to African Americans as well as all other citizens, advocating equal library service to all.

At its midwinter meeting, the association passed an amendment to the Library Bill of Rights that made clear that an individual's library use "should not be denied or abridged because of his race, religion, national origins or political views." Regrettably, many communities mounted disappointingly strong opposition. In Virginia, for example, the citizens of Danville and Petersburg voted to close their public libraries rather than to desegregate them (Cresswell 1996).

Nonetheless, the civil rights movement of the 1960s was a critical turning point in ensuring minority access. It also produced several pieces of progressive legislation affecting libraries. Most notable was the passage of the Library Services and Construction Act in 1964, a major force in developing library services and collections for ethnic, disadvantaged, and underserved groups. Similar funding was provided with the passage of the Higher Education Act for Colleges and Universities (Trujillo and Cuesta 1989). Libraries responded to these initiatives by hiring individuals from ethnic groups, collecting reference resources on ethnic cultures and experiences, creating criteria to make library collections inclusive of all members of the community, developing outreach programs to attract minorities, offering information and referral programs for minorities, and building collections that were more responsive to the needs of various ethnic groups.

In 1970 the ALA created the Social Responsibilities Round Table (SRRT). Among SRRT's purposes was "to act as a stimulus to the association and its various units in making libraries more responsive to current social needs" (American Library Association [ALA] 2009, p. 149). SRRT has been very active over the years in addressing a variety of issues, including advocating for international human rights, racial minorities and gays, and the poor and homeless, as well as promoting equal rights for women. Their focus has been both on the library profession and on policies and practices of society as a whole.

Additional organizations were established as a result of the turmoil and activities of the 1960s. One such ALA-affiliated advocacy group was REFORMA (The National Association to Promote Library & Information Services to Latinos and the Spanish Speaking), which was established in 1971. REFORMA's purpose was to foster the development of library collections that included materials written in Spanish as well as materials of interest to Hispanics, to encourage the recruitment of bilingual librarians and staff, to develop services and programs for Hispanics, to educate Hispanics about libraries, and to advocate for the information needs of the Latino community (REFORMA 2009).

Similar to REFORMA, the Black Caucus of ALA has worked since 1970 on behalf of African-American librarians and the African-American community. Among its purposes are to encourage ALA to focus on the information needs of the African-American community, to promote services to that community, and to encourage the creation of information resources about African Americans for dissemination to the wider community (Black Caucus 2009). During the 1980s, members of various ethnic communities were recruited "as equal partners with nonethnic residents in the fight to improve the quality of their lives and the communities in which they reside" (Stern 1991, p. 96). Some of the resulting library collections were developed less for self-improvement than to empower.

The public library mission to serve all members of the community continues to grow and evolve. The 1991 White House Conference on Library and Information Services reaffirmed the need to respond to the needs of an increasingly multicultural society. Its recommendations included providing financial and technical assistance to promote service to multicultural populations and populations with disabilities, promoting outreach services to traditionally underserved populations, and encouraging support for training professionals to serve multicultural needs (White House Conference 1991). Today, ALA has a variety of committees and round tables that monitor minority issues in addition to the ones noted above. These include the Minority Concerns and Cultural Diversity Committee, the ALA Office for Literacy and Outreach Services, the LITA (Library and Information Technology Association)/LSSI (Library Systems & Services) Minority Scholarship in Library and Information Technology Subcommittee; LITA/OCLC Minority Scholarship Subcommittee, and the Minorities Recruitment Committee of the New Members Round Table (ALA 1997).

Despite these efforts, few would argue that the problems of unequal service have vanished. Prominent issues remain, including the need for recruitment and retention of a diverse library workforce, concern for the reduction in federal funding for library services to ethnic communities, and the need for good research on the impact of the programs and services that have been developed to serve these communities (Trujillo and Cuesta 1989).

IV. SUMMARY: SHAPING NEW MISSIONS

Exploring the many missions of libraries since ancient times provides a rich historical foundation for the profession. Today's libraries reflect their past: they serve as archives of commercial and historical records; they contain religious and liturgical works and interpretations; they offer a place for students, scholars, and academics to conduct research; and they provide a place for edifying reading and entertainment. Some even serve as monuments to honor the rich and powerful. This chapter should also make clear that libraries were shaped by their societies; the attitudes and social, economic, and political forces that evolve within a given society are the self-same forces that shape its institutions. What will be the mission of libraries in the future? As we close this chapter, let's take a look at some of the societal factors that might play a role.

A. Attitude Toward Government Agencies

A society's confidence, or lack thereof, in government agencies to perform their tasks will have a direct effect on the society's willingness to continue providing fiscal resources. Lack of confidence will diminish funding, which in turn will result in shrinking services, a situation that has been demonstrated in several states. Of course, other factors play a role, including the general health of the economy and individuals' personal finances. Nonetheless, as the public demands greater accountability from its public institutions, libraries will be forced to demonstrate their contribution to the community. Failing to do so might well affect both the quality of services provided and their delivery.

B. Attitude Toward Education

Because libraries are so closely linked with education, society's attitude toward education is a critical factor in their survival. Where learning is highly valued and libraries are perceived as positive contributors to education, libraries are likely to receive considerable support. It is safe to say, however, that confidence in public education has declined among the general public. This is a substantial change from the 1950s, when Americans were much more confident in their public schools.

Two alternative scenarios for libraries are possible. A loss of confidence in the public schools could lead to decline in support for all agencies perceived as primarily educational. In this case, public library funding and support are likely to suffer. Or if the public schools are perceived as failing, citizens might expect the library to strengthen its role in education to make up for those deficiencies. Libraries might assume greater status and responsibility for encouraging young people to read, developing their collections to support curricula, and providing increased educational programming.

C. Attitude Toward Serving All Segments of Society

There is considerable contemporary debate over the role of government agencies in helping various groups in our society. Libraries have mirrored this ambivalence, periodically recruiting new groups of people, and at other times focusing on the library's traditional clientele. Bernard Berelson (1949), in a major study of library use, concluded that the library should focus on its natural constituency—the better educated, middle-class individual who represented the typical user of public libraries at that time. This group constituted 10 percent of the adult population. Certainly, there are librarians today who feel that the energies and resources of libraries should be devoted to those individuals who are its most likely users. Underlying this belief is the essentially voluntary and passive nature of libraries; if people want to use a library, they do so. Others have argued that the library should be reaching out to those groups, who, for whatever reason, have not taken advantage of this tax-supported resource. These individuals might have not received adequate education to develop literacy skills or might have been victims of discrimination. The extent to which society sends a clear message as to how public institutions should meet the needs of various groups will help shape the library's direction. Surely, if the library directs its attention to frequent users, it is likely to devote resources to materials and services quite different from those it would use to meet the needs of other users.

D. Attitude Toward the Importance of Reading

If the society believes that reading and literacy are important, then it is likely that libraries will have great support. The materials and services of libraries will reflect this value. This might include strong print collections and considerable emphasis on children's reading programs, adult literacy programs, and support for school reading programs. If reading is undervalued, or if other values are placed above it (for example, visual or digital entertainment), then emphasis might be placed on different services.

E. Attitude Toward Literature

Throughout history, libraries have archived the great literature of the world. Yet today, many libraries appear to offer more popular materials and less literature. One might well argue that this is because most people neither value fine literature nor desire to read it. One study conducted by the National Endowment for the Arts found that literature reading was declining among all segments of the American population, particularly among young people. Others have argued that this concern has been overstated, and that, in fact, reading scores have remained relatively stable since 1971 (Kaplan 2008), and adult book circulation per public library user has remained relatively flat since 1978 (Galbi 2008). Nonetheless, a society that does not value literature is not likely to expect its libraries to devote many resources to its collection and preservation, especially if other types of materials or services are valued more highly.

F. Attitude Toward Technology

New information technologies influence almost every aspect of our lives and specifically alter the way we create, organize, store, and disseminate information. The enthusiasm or reservations a society may have about these technologies will profoundly affect institutions of education and information access. Ironically, libraries are also experiencing many pressures regarding control over access to these technologies, especially for the young.

V. SOME FINAL THOUGHTS

The dramatic changes that have occurred in the past twenty-five years have led some to speculate that the new technologies have totally revolutionized our society, so much so that traditional library missions might be obsolete. Enthusiasts of this view see books and print on paper being replaced by the virtual electronic library, where information seekers will simply go online from their homes or offices to find what they need. The "library without walls" becomes a reality without libraries (Harris and Hannah 1992). Although such predictions might be hyperbole, it is clear that the introduction of new technologies has exacerbated and magnified many of the problems and challenges that libraries face.

Today's LIS professionals confront a host of destabilizing factors: the flood of information, constant innovations in technology, and economic, educational, and political demands and stresses, as well as numerous social problems. The traditional notions of the library, collection, patron, and archive have changed and continue to evolve. The relationships among LIS professionals, users, and the content have also changed (De Rosa et al. 2004). What will be the missions of the library in the future? Sometimes platitudes are true: Only time will tell.

NOTE

I am indebted to Professor Donald Krummel, whose example in teaching library history at the University of Illinois first suggested to me addressing issues in library history from the perspective of the missions of libraries.

REFERENCES

American Library Association. 2009. *ALA Handbook of Organization*, 2008-2009. Chicago: ALA.

Arenson, Adam. 2006. "Libraries in Public before the Age of Public Libraries: Interpreting the Furnishings and Design of Athenaeums and Other 'Social Libraries' 1800–1860." In *The Library as Place*. Edited by John E. Buschman and Gloria J. Leckie. Westport, CT: Libraries Unlimited, 41–60.

Barker, Nicolas. 2001. "Libraries and the Mind of Man." In *A Potencie of Life: Books in Society* (The Clark Lectures 1986–1987). British Library: Oak Knoll Press.

Battles, Matthew. 2003. *Library: An Unquiet History*. New York: Norton.

Berelson, Bernard. 1949. *The Library's Public: A Report of the Public Library Inquiry*. New York: Columbia University.

Blackburn, Robert H. 2003. "The Ancient Alexandrian Library: Part of It Might Survive!" *Library History* 19 (March): 23–34.

Black Caucus of the American Library Association. 2009. "BCALA Mission & Purposes." Available: www.bcala.org/association/mission.htm (accessed January 22, 2010).

Boser, Ulrich. 2006. "Genesis." *Smithsonian* 37 (October): 27–28.

Boyd, Charence Eugene. 1915. *Public Libraries and Literary Culture in Ancient Rome*. Chicago: University of Chicago Press.

Carmichael, James V. Jr. 2005. "Southern Librarianship and the Culture of Resentment." *Libraries and Culture* 40 (summer): 324–351.

Carnegie, Andrew. 1962. "The Gospel of Wealth." In *The Gospel of Wealth and Other Timely Essays*. Edited by Edward C. Kirkland. Cambridge, MA: Harvard University Press. Originally published in the *North American Review* 148 (June 1889): 653–664.

Cecil, Henry L., and Willard A. Heaps. 1940. *School Library Service in the United States: An Interpretive Survey*. New York: H.W. Wilson.

Certain, Charles C. 1920. *Standard Library Organization and Equipment for Secondary Schools of Different Sizes*. Chicago: ALA.

———. 1925. *Elementary School Library Standards*. N.p.: National Education Association.

Childe, V. Gordon. 1965. *Man Makes Himself*. London: Watts.

Clanchy, Michael. 1979. *From Memory to Written Record*. Cambridge, MA: Harvard University Press.

———. 1983. "Looking Back from the Invention of Printing." In *Literacy in Historical Perspective*. Edited by D. P. Resnick. Washington, DC: Library of Congress.

Cresswell, Stephen. 1996. "The Last Days of Jim Crow in Southern Libraries." *Libraries and Culture* 31 (summer/fall): 557–573.

Dain, Phyllis. 1975. "Ambivalence and Paradox: The Social Bonds of the Public Library." *Library Journal* 100 (February 1): 261–266.

De Rosa, Cathy, Lorcan Dempsey, and Alane Wilson. 2004. *The 2003 OCLC Environmental Scan: Pattern Recognition: A Report to the OCLC Membership*. Dublin, OH: OCLC.

Dewey, Melvil. 1978. "Libraries as Related to the Educational Work of the State." In *Melvil Dewey: His Enduring Presence in Librarianship*. Edited by Sarah K. Vann. Littleton, CO: Libraries Unlimited, 136. (Original work published 1888.)

Ditzion, Sydney H. 1947. *Arsenals of a Democratic Culture*. Chicago: ALA.

Dix, T. Keith. 1994. "'Public Libraries' in Ancient Rome: Ideology and Reality." *Libraries and Culture* 29 (summer): 282–296.

Du Mont, Rosemary Ruhig, Lois Buttlar, and William Caynon. 1994. *Multiculturalism in Libraries*. Westport, CT: Greenwood.

Dunlap, Leslie W. 1972. *Readings in Library History*. New York: R.R. Bowker.

Eisenstein, Elizabeth L. 1979. *The Printing Press as an Agent of Change: Communications and Cultural Transformations in Early Modern Europe*. Cambridge: Cambridge University Press.

———. 1995. *Printing as Divine Art: Celebrating Western Technology in the Age of the Hand Press*. Oberlin, OH: Oberlin College, November 4.

Fargo, Lucile F. 1930. *The Program for Elementary Library Service*. Chicago: ALA.

Franklin, John Hope. 1977. "Libraries in a Pluralistic Society." In *Libraries and the Life of the Mind in America*. Chicago: ALA.

"Free Fiction." 1866. *The Nation* 31 (February 1): 138–139.

Fultz, Michael. 2006. "Black Public Libraries in the South in the Era of De Jure Segregation." *Libraries and the Cultural Record* 41 (summer): 337–359.

Galbi, Douglas A. 2008. "Book Circulation Per U.S. Public Library User Since 1856." *Public Library Quarterly* 27: 351–371.

Gates, Jean Key. 1976. *Introduction to Librarianship*. New York: McGraw-Hill.

Gillespie, John T., and Diana L. Spirt. 1983. "School Library to Media Center." In *Administering the School Library Media Center*. New York: Bowker.

Gleason, Eliza Atkins. 1941. *The Southern Negro and the Public Library*. Chicago: University of Chicago Press.

Graham, Patterson Toby. 2001. "Public Librarians and the Civil Rights Movement: Alabama, 1955– 1965." *Library Quarterly* 71 (January): 1–27.

Guerena, Salvador, and Edward Erazo. 2000. "Latinos and Librarianship." *Library Trends* 49 (summer): 138–181.

Hamlin, Arthur T. 1981. *The University Library in the United States: Its Origins and Development*. Philadelphia: University of Pennsylvania Press.

Hanson, Eugene R. 1989. "College Libraries: The Colonial Period to the Twentieth Century." In *Advances in Library Administration and Organization*. Vol. 8. Greenwich, CT: JAI, 171–199.

Haro, Roberto P. 1981. *Developing Library and Information Services for Americans of Hispanic Origin*. Metuchen, NJ: Scarecrow.

Harris, Michael. 1973. "The Purpose of the American Public Library." *Library Journal* 98 (September 15): 2509–2514.

Harris, Michael H., and Stanley Hannah. 1992. "Why Do We Study the History of Libraries? A Meditation on the Perils of Ahistoricism in the Information Era." *LISR* 14: 123–130.

Harris, Michael, and Elmer D. Johnson. 1984. *History of Libraries in the Western World*. Metuchen, NJ: Scarecrow.

Harris, William V. 1989. *Ancient Literacy*. Cambridge, MA: Harvard University Press.

Harwell, Richard. 1968. "College Libraries." In *Encyclopedia of Library and Information Science*. Edited by Allen Kent, Harold Lancour, and William Z. Nasri. New York: Marcel Dekker, 269–281.

Havens, Earle. 2007. "The Ventriloquist Who Changed the World." *American Libraries* (August): 54–57.

Hessel, Alfred. 1955. *A History of Libraries*. New Brunswick, NJ: Scarecrow.

Jackson, Sydney L. 1974. *Libraries and Librarianship in the West: A Brief History*. New York: McGraw-Hill.

Jacob, Christian. 2002. "Gathering Memory: Thoughts on the History of Libraries." *Diogenes* 49 (April): 41–57.

Jochum, Uwe. 1999. "The Alexandrian Library and Its Aftermath." *Library History* 15 (May): 5–12.

Jones, Plummer Alston Jr. 1989. "The History and Development of Libraries in American Higher Education." *College and Research Libraries News* 50 (July/August): 561–565.

Josey, E. J. 1970. *The Black Librarian in America*. Metuchen, NJ: Scarecrow.

———. 1994. "Race Issues in Library History." In *Encyclopedia of Library History*. Edited by Wayne A. Wiegand and Donald G. Davis Jr. New York: Garland, 533–537.

Kaplan, Nancy. 2008. "To Read, Responsibly." *Public Library Quarterly* 27: 193–201.

Kaser, David. 1980. *A Book for a Sixpence: The Circulating Library in America*. Pittsburgh: Beta Phi Mu.

Knight, Douglas M., and E. Shepley Nourse. 1969. *Libraries at Large: Tradition, Innovation, and the National Interest*. New York: R.R. Bowker.

Kruzas, Anthony Thomas. 1965. *Business and Industrial Libraries in the United States, 1820–1940*. New York: SLA.

Malone, Cheryl Knott. 2000. "Books for Black Children: Public Library Collections in Louisville and Nashville, 1915–1925." *Library Quarterly* 70 (April): 179–200.

McCrossen, Alexis. 2006. "'One Cathedral More' or 'Mere Lounging Places for Bummers'? The Cultural Politics of Leisure and the Public Library in Gilded Age America." *Libraries and Culture* 41 (spring): 169–188.

McHenry, Elizabeth. 1998. "Forgotten Readers: African-American Literary Societies and the American Scene." In *Print Culture in a Diverse America*. Edited by James P. Danky and Wayne A. Wiegand. Urbana: University of Illinois Press, 149–172.

McMullen, Haynes. 2000. *American Libraries Before 1876*. Westport, CT: Greenwood.

Nichols, Charles L. 1964. *The Library of Ramses the Great*. Berkeley, CA: Peacock.

Nielson, Brian. 1989. "The Role of the Public Services Librarian: The New Revolution." In *Rethinking the Library in the Information Age*. Washington, DC: GPO, 179–200.

Parsons, Edward A. 1952. *The Alexandrian Library*. Amsterdam, NY: Elsevier, 1952.

"Public Libraries and Fiction." 1874. *The Literary World: A Monthly Review of Current Literature*.

REFORMA. 2009. The National Association to Promote Library & Information Services to Latinos and the Spanish Speaking. Available: www.reforma.org/who.html (accessed January 22, 2010).

Roberts, F. B. 1912. "The Library and the Foreign Citizen." *Public Libraries* 17: 166–169.

Shera, Jesse. 1965. *Foundations of the Public Library*. Chicago: Shoestring.

———. 1976. *Introduction to Library Science: Basic Elements of Library Service*. Littleton, CO: Libraries Unlimited.

Shiflett, O. Lee. 1994. "Academic Libraries." In *Encyclopedia of Library History*. Edited by Wayne A. Wiegand and Donald G. Davis Jr. New York: Garland, 5–15.

Stern, Stephen. 1991. "Ethnic Libraries and Librarianship in the United States: Models and Prospects." In *Advances in Librarianship*. Vol. 15. Edited by Irene P. Godden. San Diego: Academic Press, 77–102.

Thompson, James Westfall. 1962. *Ancient Libraries*. Hamden, CT: Archon.

Trujillo, Roberto G., and Yolanda J. Cuesta. 1989. "Service to Diverse Populations." In *ALA Yearbook of Library and Information Science*. Vol. 14. Chicago: ALA, 7–11.

Watson, Paula. 1994. "Founding Mothers: The Contribution of Women's Organizations to Public Library Development in the United States." *Library Quarterly* 64 (July): 233–269.

Wheeler, Maurice, and Debbie Johnson-Houston. 2004. "A Brief History of Library Service to African Americans." *American Libraries* 35 (February): 42–45.

White House Conference on Library and Information Services. 1991. *Information 2000: Library and Information Services for the 21st Century*. Washington, DC: Superintendent of Documents, 1991.

Wiegand, Wayne A. 1989. "The Development of Librarianship in the United States." *Libraries and Culture* 24 (winter): 99–109.

SELECTED READINGS: HISTORY AND MISSION OF LIBRARIES

Books

Battles, Matthew. *Library: An Unquiet History*. New York: W.W. Norton, 2003.

Ditzion, Sidney H. *Arsenals of a Democratic Culture*. Chicago: ALA, 1947.

Maxwell, Nancy Kalikow. *Sacred Stacks: The Higher Purpose of Libraries and Librarianship*. Chicago: American Library Association, 2006.

McCabe, Ronald B. *Civic Librarianship: Renewing the Social Mission of the Public Library*. Lanham, MD: Scarecrow, 2001.

Ranganathan, S. R. *The Five Laws of Library Science*. New York: Asia, 1963. First published 1931.

Articles

Burger, Leslie. "All Seasons and All Reasons." *American Libraries* 39 (March 2008): 44–48.

Chodorow, Stanley. "To Represent Us Truly: The Job and Context of Preserving the Cultural Record." *Libraries and the Cultural Record* 41 (summer 2006): 372–380.

Cresswell, Stephen. "The Last Days of Jim Crow in Southern Libraries." *Libraries and Culture* 31 (summer/fall 1996): 557–573.

Graham, Patterson Toby. "Public Librarians and the Civil Rights Movement: Alabama, 1955–1965." *Library Quarterly* 71 (January 2001): 1–27.

Havens, Earle. "The Ventriloquist Who Changed the World: How America's French Connection Propelled the Modern Free Library Movement." *American Libraries* 38 (August 2007): 54–57.

Koontz, Christie M. "A History of Location of U.S. Public Libraries within Community Place and Space: Evolving Implications for the Library's Mission of Equitable Service." *Public Library Quarterly* 26 (2007): 75–100.

Leckie, Gloria J. "Three Perspectives on Libraries." *Feliciter* 6 (2004): 233–236.

Lor, P. J., and J. J. Britz. "Challenges of the Approaching Knowledge Society: Major International Issues Facing LIS Professionals." *Libri* 57 (September 2007): 111–122.

McCrossen, Alexis. "'One Cathedral More' or 'Mere Lounging Places for Bummers'? The Cultural Politics of Leisure and the Public Library in Gilded Age America." *Libraries and Culture* 41 (spring 2006): 169–188.

Pennavaria, Katherine. "Representation of Books and Libraries in Depictions of the Future." *Libraries and Culture* 37 (summer 2002): 229–247.

Watson, Paula D. "Founding Mothers: The Contributions of Women's Organizations to Public Library Development in the United States." *Library Quarterly* 64 (1994): 233–269.

Wheeler, Maurice, and Debbie Johnson-Houston. "A Brief History of Library Service to African Americans." *American Libraries* 35 (February 2004): 42–45.

3

Library and Information Science: An Evolving Profession

I. INTRODUCTION

Since the late nineteenth century, librarians in the United States have established a solid professional identity and important values to guide their actions and goals. Changes in the profession occurred incrementally and consequently the role of the librarian remained relatively constant. One of the most stable elements, historically, was the association of the librarian with the physical library; one does not usually think of librarians without also thinking of the place where they ply their trade. But is the identity of today's LIS professional inextricably linked to this physical entity? The profession is now in the midst of a revolutionary—and for some, a disconcerting—change. The stable condition of the past is being replaced by a dynamic environment in which the content and function of libraries are being revised and modified by technological, political, and economic change. In the new world of electronic access to information, will the library disappear? Will there be librarians without libraries? Will the term *librarian* disappear like the passenger pigeon, to be replaced with information consultant, information specialist, information manager, or knowledge manager?

Despite some distress, there is no evidence that libraries will vanish in the near future. The library might have its quiet spaces for contemplation and study, but the modern American library is not a sedate place. Consequently, those considering library and information science as a career will need to be adaptable, patient, constant in times of uncertainty, and amenable to learning new skills in a dynamic environment. How the profession evolves in the next decades will be determined by the essential worth of our foundational values, by our capacity to adapt, and the new missions required by society. This chapter focuses on three aspects of the profession: the historical forces that shaped education for librarianship; contemporary issues facing the field; and the challenges facing LIS professionals in the future.

II. HISTORY OF LIBRARY EDUCATION AND THE PREPARATION OF LIBRARIANS

As noted in Chapter 2, American libraries in the eighteenth century were small; if librarians existed, they functioned primarily in a custodial capacity. By the middle of the nineteenth century, a few librarians, invariably male, could be found in more sophisticated academic institutions. These individuals were described as "Bookmen" by Pierce Butler (1951) because they were scholars, not custodians. Before 1850, there was no training to speak of for those who worked in a library except trial and error. Librarians were self-taught or followed the example of others; a novice librarian often contacted other librarians for advice and counsel. Between 1850 and 1875, a more formal apprenticeship emerged. Sometimes a librarian would recruit an interested individual and train that person under close observation.

During the 1870s, another route for training began to emerge with the appearance of instructional publications from private publishers and the U.S. government. *Publishers Weekly* began in 1872 and although it focused on the publishing industry, there were small sections devoted to librarians. Another significant source of information was the U.S. Office of Education, which produced publications for educators. The most significant publication affecting library education was the landmark study issued in 1876, *Public Libraries in the United States of America: Their History, Condition, and Management*, which presented substantial statistical data on more than 3,600 public libraries, and data on other types of libraries as well. As part of this work, the bureau issued a manual including articles written by noted authorities on librarianship. The topics included such areas as management, administration, history, cataloging, popular reading, and library buildings. In essence, it was the first authoritative library reader (U.S. Office of Education 1876).

The period from 1876 to 1923 marked a critical time in the development of library education. A variety of forces created the foundations for the professionalization of librarianship, discussed in the sections that follow.

A. The Decline of the Classical English and Apprenticeship Models and the Rise of the Technical Education Model

American education during the nineteenth century was generally shaped by the dominant immigrant population: the British. The British model of education emphasized study of the classical languages, religion, literature, and grammar. The traditional apprenticeship model was designed for training an individual for a craft; only a few individuals could be trained at a time for a specialized, narrowly defined job. With industrialization, many people had to be trained for positions that might be quite similar from factory to factory. A classical education was inappropriate, and apprenticeship was too inefficient. It was during this period that many educators and some library leaders were exposed to the European technical education model at various international fairs and expositions in Europe and the United States. The resulting rise of technical schools in the United States and the vocational emphasis of these educational institutions fit well with the needs of libraries (White 1976).

B. The Influence of Andrew Carnegie

The latter half of the nineteenth century saw tremendous growth in the number of libraries. Between 1825 and 1850, 551 public libraries were founded; in the next twenty-five years, more than 2,200 were established (U.S. Office of Education 1876, p. xvi). There were many reasons for this rapid increase, including an increased recognition of the important role of libraries in research and teaching. But it was Andrew Carnegie who, from the end of the nineteenth century to the first two decades of the twentieth, financed the construction of nearly 3,000 libraries throughout the world, a large proportion of them public libraries built in the United States. This proliferation had the inevitable effect of increasing the demand for library workers and establishing a permanent workforce.

C. Melvil Dewey and the Professionalization of Librarianship

There is little dispute that Melvil Dewey was a prime force in the professionalization of American librarianship and in library education during the latter part of the nineteenth century. His energy and passion significantly advanced the profession. He believed that books have considerable power to shape a community's thinking, a power that can be used for good or evil. He also believed that a librarian's duty is to provide the public with "better" books that could improve people.

Four of Dewey's accomplishments are noted here that were clearly important in establishing the professional foundations of the field: his decimal classification system, his role in establishing the American Library Association, his role in creating *Library Journal*, and his influence on library education.

1. The Dewey Decimal Classification System

While a student at Amherst College, Dewey worked in the college library. After graduation, he remained at Amherst and served as the librarian. He was excited by the possibilities arising from the Industrial Revolution and

For Dewey librarianship was a profession with a serious moral and prescriptive purpose to make people better:

He must see that his library contains, as far as possible, the best books on the best subjects, regarding carefully the wants of his special community. Then, having the best books, he must create among his people, his pupils, a desire to read those books. He must put every facility in the way of readers, so that they shall be led on from good to better.... Such a librarian will find enough who are ready to put themselves under his influence and direction, and, if competent and enthusiastic, he might soon largely shape the reading, and through it the thought, of his whole community. (Dewey 1989, p. 5) was fascinated with labor-saving routines and devices. He belonged to a number of organizations promoting the use of metrics and simplified spelling (hence, Melvil rather than Melville). As the Amherst librarian, he quickly recognized that the existing classification system was inflexible and he set about to find a new, more efficient way to organize materials. He heavily promoted his new classification system, and it grew in popularity over the years. In terms of the profession, the Dewey decimal system provided a fundamental and important theoretical principle by which professional skills and responsibilities could be organized.

2. The American Library Association

Although discussions of the need for a professional association for librarians began as early as the 1850s, it took time to bring the idea to fruition. During that time, Dewey was a guiding force. In 1876 he organized a national meeting of librarians in Philadelphia. On the final day, the American Library Association (ALA) was founded with Dewey as its secretary. The creation of a national professional association is an important benchmark. It substantially increases professional identity among the practitioners, helps identify important issues, and establishes standards of service and conduct. The first national conferences, for example, provided a common forum for the discussion of ideas and issues such as classification, indexing, and protecting materials from abuse. The founding of ALA elevated librarianship and provided national visibility and recognition to the field.

3. *American Library Journal*

Dewey was also instrumental in creating the *American Library Journal*, the first major professional publication devoted solely to the interests of librarians. Dewey and the other editors intended the journal to assist librarians in their daily work. For example, in the first issue, Justin Windsor (1876), associate editor and director of the Boston Public Library, advised new librarians on management:

1. Locate whatever printed materials on librarianship are available.
2. Locate similar libraries and ask for their rules and reports.
3. Study the materials received.
4. Evaluate the extent to which other libraries are good comparisons to the library in question.
5. Contact an experienced librarian.
6. Do what seems to come naturally. (p. 2)

He also warned the novice who did not have time to do this research and analysis to "resign your trust to someone who has" (p. 2).

The value of such a publication was not lost on the ALA, which in 1877 adopted the journal as its official organ and shortened the name to *Library Journal*. Subsequent issues included articles, summaries of ALA conference proceedings, and a section titled "Notes and Queries" that responded to questions and comments from librarians, many of which concerned cataloging and classification, circulation, library buildings, equipment, and funds.

4. Library Education

Until the latter part of the nineteenth century, institutions such as the Boston Athenaeum, Amherst, and Harvard University offered traditional apprenticeships, as did major public libraries in Boston, Los Angeles, Denver, and Cleveland. Some academic or technical institutes offered special classes in library techniques. All of this training, however, was usually of short duration and idiosyncratic in terms of curriculum.

In 1879, Dewey promoted systematic training for librarianship. He envisioned that the faculty would be knowledgeable, experienced librarians in major libraries who would advise the apprentices on library matters, suggest readings, and identify areas of study worth investigating (Vann 1961). It is important to note that Dewey did not believe that just anyone could be a librarian. Rather, he thought that only people with the appropriate "character" should be accepted for training; character in this nineteenth-century sense meant a "moral potential" for self-refinement and improvement (Wiegand 1999). This proposal, however, was not well received at ALA.

Then a fortuitous event occurred in 1883. By this time, Dewey's reputation had grown considerably and he was recruited for the head librarian's position at Columbia University. During his interview with the president, F. A. P. Barnard, he discussed his desire to establish a school for formal training. President Barnard was enthusiastic and the trustees were sufficiently supportive, although perhaps naive about what would be involved. Dewey accepted the appointment in 1884, and the first library school, the School of Library Economy, opened on January 1, 1887, with a class of twenty students: three men and seventeen women (Vann 1961). The course of study was pragmatic, including selection, reader's aids, bibliography, repair of materials, administration, and cataloging. The training took three months and required an internship that could take as long as two years, so that the students were exposed to their professional tasks (Vann 1961).

Unfortunately, Dewey's relations with the university officials were tense. Some of the trustees felt that he had not been completely forthcoming, especially in regard to the problematic presence of women. Indeed, when the trustees discovered that women were accepted, they voted to deny Dewey the use of Columbia's classrooms. The students met across the street from the Columbia campus in a converted storeroom, which Wiegand (1999) called a "bootleg operation" (p. 18). By 1888 it was clear that Columbia would close the school.

Dewey, anticipating this event, accepted a position as head of the New York State Library in Albany, which agreed to have the school transferred there, thus preserving the only formal education program for librarians in the country. Dewey remained as director, but the daily operations became the responsibility of Mary Salome Cutler Fairchild, who served as its vice director and taught there for sixteen years (Maack 1986). Fairchild had worked both as a cataloger and a cataloging instructor under Dewey at Columbia.

Fairchild's view of library education differed in some significant ways from Dewey's. As a student of the Industrial Revolution, Dewey saw libraries as businesses and he emphasized the practical aspects of running an institution. Fairchild broadened this perspective by emphasizing more theoretical and cultural aspects. For example, Dewey recommended book selection using standard reviews, while Fairchild believed that a librarian should have personal knowledge of books and an under-standing of people's tastes (Wiegand 1996). Fairchild gave "form and substance to the Dewey dream" through her able administration and inspiring pedagogy (Gambee 1978, p. 168). Gambee also noted that she commanded considerable loyalty from her students and alumnae, and she was credited with establishing selective admission criteria and maintaining a quality education that made Albany the standard of library education.

D. The Growth of Library Schools

The success of the Albany program inspired additional programs. By 1900 there were four major library schools: Albany, Pratt Institute, Drexel University, and the Armour Institute, which became the Library School at the University of Illinois in 1897 (Vann 1961). Among the directors of these schools were some of the future leaders of the library profession—women who helped to shape library education and librarianship for years to come.

1. Pratt Institute

Pratt's school was established in 1890, originally to train staff for the Pratt Institute library. Mary Wright Plummer, a member of the first class at Columbia and one of its best students, became the director in 1895. She was an ardent advocate for professional training. Under her leadership, the school broadened its purpose, extended the program from six months to two years, and enriched the curriculum, making the education equivalent to the best training available (Brand 1996; Vann 1961). In 1896, Plummer offered a specialization in scholarly libraries, adding special courses in bibliography, advanced cataloging, and courses on the history of books, bindings, and engravings. Three years later, she launched a specialization in children's librarianship (Karlowich and Sharify 1978; Maack 1986). Despite the difficulties women encountered as leaders and administrators, Plummer became the second female president of ALA and director of the library school of the New York Public Library (Weibel and Heim 1979).

2. Drexel

Alice Kroeger, another Dewey protégé of the Albany school, directed the Drexel library and their training program. Kroeger's program mirrored Dewey and Fairchild's, including course work in cataloging, literature, bibliography, the history of books, and library management (Vann 1961; Grotzinger 1978a). In addition to serving as faculty, Kroeger was a prolific author and presented at numerous ALA conferences. At a time when there were few texts for the library student, she published the first major text on reference materials as well as a work on book selection.

3. Armour Institute/University of Illinois

The Armour Institute, established in Chicago in 1893, was the first library school in the Midwest. Under the leadership of Katharine Lucinda Sharp, another Dewey graduate, the basic program took one year, with the possibility of a second year of advanced work. The advanced training included courses in bibliography in specialized areas, the history of printing and libraries, or a specialized children's program (Vann 1961).

Sharp adopted Dewey's view that librarians were powerful because they could influence people's access to ideas (Grotzinger 1966). She was not satisfied with the existing admission requirements for the program and wanted to award a degree, rather than a certificate, for library training. She established such a notable program that both the University of Wisconsin and the University of Illinois courted her. She successfully negotiated a transfer of the Armour program to the University of Illinois, where she served as director of the University Library, head of the school, and a full professor. This unique position allowed the library students to use the university library as a laboratory (Grotzinger 1978b; Maack 1986).

In terms of academic requirements, the Illinois program was comparable to the Albany training (Vann 1961). Sharp was an innovative curriculum designer, adding courses on documents, extension work, and research methods (Grotzinger 1978b). She also involved students in the life of the community; they created traveling collections, conducted public story hours, and organized collections (Grotzinger 1966). Sharp did much to advance the academic credibility of library education and, although the Illinois program was a four-year program leading to a bachelor's degree, she was an early proponent of graduate-level library education. During her tenure, the school at Illinois was "constantly the center of experimentation and innovation" (Grotzinger 1966, p. 304). As a consequence, Sharp was highly respected as both a library educator and a librarian and was twice elected ALA vice president.

4. Continued Expansion of Schools

By 1919, there were fifteen programs, ten of them founded by women (Maack 1986). They varied by length of program, type of degree or certificate awarded, and requirements for admission. Most of the schools awarded a bachelor's of library science (BLS) degree after one year of library education following the regular baccalaureate degree, sometimes referred to as a fifth-year degree (Robbins-Carter and Seavey 1986). The MLS was not awarded, except at Albany, until the 1920s. The master's at Albany was given after two years of education beyond the baccalaureate (sometimes referred to as a sixth-year degree).

E. The Role and Influence of the ALA Committee on Library Training

As the number of library schools grew, ALA took a greater interest. The other methods of library training coexisted uneasily with the emerging library schools up until the end of the nineteenth century. By that time, the library schools wanted ALA to recognize and endorse them as the only appropriate forum for library training. Instead, the association created the ALA Committee on Library Training and asked the members in 1902 to review the various library training programs. This led to ALA's "Standards for Library Education" in 1903. These standards reflected no commitment to any particular source of professional preparation but established separate standards for the different types of training programs. Subsequent standards issued in 1905 and 1906 again equivocated. Tensions between academic institutions and "practical" schools became acute between 1910 and 1920. During this period, ALA established a Section on Professional Training that conducted additional reviews of the programs being offered by various organizations.

From the perspective of the academic programs, ALA failed to make a commitment and kept them at arm's length. ALA's reluctance to endorse the academic schools as the only appropriate form of library education pushed the schools to create their own organization, the Association of American Library Schools, in 1916. Establishing the association unified the schools and helped them establish a separate identity. As a result, library school educators were no longer concerned about the political value of ALA endorsement. Instead, they focused on administrative and curricular issues such as establishing consistent admission standards, faculty requirements, course content and program length, the types of degrees awarded, the proper balance between practical and theoretical approaches, and developing a system for transferring credits from one school to another (Vann 1961).

F. The Williamson Report

In the end, it was neither ALA nor the American Association of Library Schools that most profoundly influenced the direction of library education. Rather, it was the Carnegie Corporation, established by Andrew Carnegie to administer his philanthropic activities after his death. The corporation continued to fund library construction but suspected that the libraries were often inadequately staffed and supported. In 1915, the corporation appointed Alvin Saunders Johnson to investigate the status of Carnegie libraries. Johnson's 1916 report revealed serious problems; in particular, he found that library staff were often poorly trained. The corporation, concerned about Johnson's report, subsidized a major study directed solely toward library education, and investigating library schools in particular.

The corporation appointed C. C. Williamson to undertake this study. Williamson was ideally suited for the task; he was a political economist, a graduate of Columbia, and a professor of economics at Bryn Mawr. He had served as head of the Economics and Sociology Division at the New York Public Library, and at the time of his appointment was head of the Municipal Reference Library in New York. Williamson conducted a close examination of fifteen library schools and issued a final report in 1923. Referred to as the Williamson Report, its historic importance to library education is unquestioned (see p. 86).

The Williamson Report represented a breakthrough and turning point for library education. Although many of the issues raised were not original with Williamson, his report represented a culmination of the historical forces working to define library education. The imprimatur of the Carnegie Corporation could not be ignored. He criticized the quality of many programs and suggested that the corporation assist by offering scholarships to recruit better-qualified individuals, and by providing financial assistance to library schools and summer school programs. As a result, the corporation shifted its emphasis from construction to library service (Vann 1961).

The Williamson Report articulated the theoretical and professional nature of the discipline and designated the university as the appropriate provider of professional preparation. Other forms of library education did not immediately disappear, nor did the profession uncritically accept all of the recommendations, most notably the certification of librarians. Likewise, only a few library schools adopted a two-year program of study. In addition, some felt the report would adversely affected the proportion of female library educators because at the time, most academic institutions did not consider women appropriate for faculty positions (Maack 1986). But the report

> *The Williamson Report articulated the theoretical and professional nature of the discipline and designated the university as the appropriate provider of professional preparation.*

marked the eventual death knell of all other forms of professional education. Because Williamson regarded a college degree as an entrance requirement, he advocated professional preparation in librarianship as a graduate degree (Williamson 1923). In a broader sense, the Williamson Report affirmed that a substantial part of librarianship was, or should be, advanced education rather than simply training. Further, it forced the profession to consider the importance of consistency and high quality in the curricula, administration, and teaching.

The Williamson Report: Major Findings and Recommendations

1. There is a difference between clerical and professional work. Professional work deals with theory and the application of clear principles. It requires a broad education including four years of college. Clerical work requires following rules and thus far less education. Library schools should provide professional, rather than clerical, instruction.

2. The library schools did not agree on which subjects should be taught or emphasized; certain schools devoted much more time to particular subjects than to others.

3. The curricula must undergo constant reexamination so that the most current and relevant practices can be taught rather than traditional practices.

4. The breadth of content required for adequate professional preparation cannot be realized in only one year of education.

5. There was considerable inconsistency in entrance requirements. Library schools should require a college education (or its equivalent) for admission.

6. Many library school instructors lacked college degrees themselves and were therefore not adequately prepared to teach college graduates. Many lacked experience in teaching, and nearly one third had no library experience.

7. Instruction relied too much on lectures and there were too few good textbooks.

8. Faculty salaries were too low and must be adjusted to recruit teachers of better quality.

9. Schools must provide financial incentives for faculty to produce texts.

10. To recruit students, schools should maintain high educational standards and provide fellowships and scholarships to make library training more attractive.

11. Library schools should be part of a university, conforming with the model followed by other professional schools. Universities are better situated to maintain academic standards and increase the status of the graduates; public libraries cannot devote the resources necessary to maintain these standards.

12. Professional preparation should consist of two years of schooling. The first year should follow a general program of study; the second year should be highly specialized. This might involve cooperative efforts with other local educational institutions.

13. There was little incentive for employed librarians to seek continuing education. Generally, the focus was on clerical workers. Schools should redirect their attention to the enrichment of professional education. Correspondence schools should be considered.

14. There were no standards for professional preparation. Librarians should establish the standards, which, once established, should eventually be made part of the law.

15. The American Library Association should create a system of voluntary certification of librarians regulated by a national certification board, which should also accredit library schools.

(*Source:* Williamson 1923.)

G. Response to and Effects of the Williamson Report

ALA responded to the Williamson Report by creating the Temporary Library Training Board in 1924, which soon became the Board of Education for Librarianship (BEL). The BEL established additional standards for library education in 1925 and 1933, including the need for one year of postgraduate education in librarianship (Robbins-Carter and Seavey 1986). By the early 1950s, most library schools granted the fifth-year master's degree.

The Carnegie Corporation's response to the report was even more dramatic. There was obviously a considerable need for library schools to improve. In the ensuing fifteen years, the Carnegie Corporation gave nearly $2 million to seventeen library schools to that end. One of the corporation's most notable achievements was its special attention to the lack of research and quality instructional texts. The corporation determined that the best solution was to support a doctoral program for librarians. In response, the Graduate Library School was established at the University of Chicago in 1926 and a doctoral program began in 1928. The doctoral degree was granted for "library science" as opposed to librarianship, because the course work emphasized theoretical approaches and the application of the scientific and research tools of other disciplines to library work (Rayward 1983).

In addition to establishing the notion of library science, the Graduate Library School made many other contributions. First, its faculty was diverse, drawing instructors with expertise from a variety of fields including sociology and history. Second, because the faculty were primarily scholars rather than practitioners, they produced a considerable body of research, which formed the foundation for further research. Finally, the school sponsored many conferences and programs on major issues in the profession, which drew practitioners and other library school faculty together and resulted in numerous publications, which also served as texts.

Another notable Carnegie achievement following the Williamson Report was the establishment in 1925 of the Hampton Institute Library School, the first school specifically established to train African-American librarians. Prior to that time, Emory University in Atlanta was the only accredited library school in the South, but it did not admit African Americans until 1962 (Campbell 1977; McPheeters 1988). Professional preparation available to African Americans was primarily through training programs in libraries, education supported by organizations such as the Julius Rosenwald Fund, which focused on library services in the South (Campbell 1977).

In very rare instances, a few African Americans were able to attend a library school in the North. Edward Christopher Williams, a graduate of the New York State Library School, became director of the library at Howard University in 1916 (Campbell 1977). The founder and first director of the Hampton Institute Library School, Florence Rising Curtis, also played a significant role in advancing professional librarianship for African Americans. Curtis was also a graduate of Dewey's school in Albany. Before coming to Hampton, she had a distinguished career, teaching at the University of Illinois for twelve years, and serving as vice director at Drexel. She played a major role in establishing the Association of American Library Schools and served as its first secretary (Davis 1978). At Hampton, she was not only largely responsible for developing a quality library school program, but was devoted to improving library service for African Americans throughout the South.

The Hampton Institute produced some notable graduates including Virginia Lacy Jones, who became dean of the Atlanta University School of Library Service, and

Wallace Van Jackson, library director at Virginia State College and a teacher at Hampton Institute, who made substantial contributions to academic library service for African Americans (Campbell 1977). Unfortunately, the Depression led to a decline in philanthropic resources, and the Hampton Institute Library School closed in 1939. However, two years later its mission was revived at Atlanta University under the urging of its president, John Hope (Davis 1978).

H. Modern Library Education

The Depression and World War II placed severe burdens both on the development of libraries and on librarianship. Library educators were especially concerned that many schools' curricula still emphasized routines rather than theory, and there was considerable variation in quality among the schools. In 1951 the ALA Board of Education for Librarianship issued a new set of standards that finally required five years of post–high school education (in other words, a master's degree) as the standard for professional education. This ended once and for all the alternative forms of library education. In 1956 the ALA Committee on Accreditation was formed and given the responsibility of reviewing and accrediting library school programs, a task it holds to this day.

The 1950s and 1960s might be considered the heyday of library schools. The expanding economy, the baby boom, and the important federal legislation supporting the development of elementary, secondary, and higher education institutions and their libraries all led to a significant expansion of libraries and collections. This concomitantly resulted in an increased need for librarians, which, in turn, spawned new library schools. By the 1970s there were more than seventy accredited library schools with master's programs in the United States and Canada.

The next two decades, however, produced a considerable ebb, including closures of several library schools with substantial reputations, including those at the University of Chicago and Columbia. By 1999 there were only fifty-six ALA-accredited library school programs in the United States and Canada (see Appendix B).

There were many reasons for this decline. The recession of the 1980s resulted in deliberate efforts to reduce costs at universities. Taxpayers, politicians, and trustees became more reluctant to finance higher education. Library schools were never high-profile departments; they were rarely mentioned when speaking of the reputation of an academic institution, nor did they produce many major donors in comparison with law or medical schools. Many of these schools failed to develop an energetic alumni network to defend them. The result was that library schools were vulnerable targets for closing (Paris 1988).

Some library educators recognized the lessons inherent in the closings and saw the need to improve the quality of their academic programs and set higher standards (Boyce 1994). Boyce suspected that an additional one third to one half of the remaining library schools might close. It appears, however, that the precipitous decline has ended, and it is hoped that the remaining library schools have learned from this experience.

III. CONTEMPORARY ISSUES

A. The Library vs. Information Debate

The debate over the role of the library in the new information environment is complex and intricately bound up in the historical roots of the field, beliefs about the purpose of libraries, and convictions about the centrality of information provision as a mission of libraries. These issues can only be addressed superficially here.

In 1995 Cronin noted that "library and information science is certainly not a marriage made in heaven" (p. 897) and that the removal of the word *library* from many LIS programs "is a clear indication of mounting dissatisfaction with what the label connotes" (p. 898). Cronin argued that "library science" is an oxymoron; what is referred to as library science is really librarianship—a profession associated with a particular physical structure. Information science, on the other hand, is a developing academic field with emerging methodologies and models that attempt prediction. Cronin's comments illustrate some of the sticky issues in the discussion about the relationship between library science, libraries, information scientists, and information science.

This debate is not new, as evidenced by the changing names of programs. In 1964, for example, the University of Pittsburgh's program became the Graduate School of Library and Information Sciences. In 1974, Syracuse University renamed its school the School of Information Studies. In 1996, the University of Pittsburgh again renamed its program as the School of Information Sciences. Also in that year, the University of Michigan's program became the School of Information (Olson and Grudin 2009). What seems to cause so much consternation over these changes is not so much the removal of the word *library* from the names, but the suspected underlying changes in philosophical perspective and therefore curriculum content and faculty composition.

1. i-Schools

An i-school has a core vision that information, technology, and people interact with roughly equal significance (Olson and Grudin 2009). The faculties of i-schools are generally drawn from many disciplines including computer science, library and information science, business, engineering, and behavioral sciences. The increasing number of i-schools gradually led to the creation of an organization called the iSchool Caucus which sponsors conferences devoted to i-school issues. Although the interdisciplinary nature of the faculty shows great promise, it also creates problems of academic focus that can be quite challenging within the traditional academic culture (King 2006). King (2006) observed, "I-Schools have been born in a state of flux, and in most cases have added to that flux through ongoing innovation" (p. 13). He calls the movement emergent and its identity elusive but with great prospects if they can demonstrate superior academic performance and make substantial contributions both to academics and to society as a whole.

2. Two Paradigms

Some people characterize the library versus information debate as a collision of two paradigms. The library service paradigm stems from the historical roots of the library as an educational institution. As Apostle and Raymond (1997) commented, "In terms of larger social purpose, libraries perform such socially necessary functions as encouraging reading, literacy, and the diffusion of commonly-held cultural values" (p. 5). These functions coupled with the obligation to conserve the graphic record represent a primary purpose of libraries. If one accepts the library service paradigm, it then follows that the LIS curriculum should reflect an emphasis on educational theory, library service, literacy, and reading.

On the other hand, Apostle and Raymond (1997) noted, the twentieth century introduced increased industrialization, major scientific and technological advances, and the growth of both business and government, which in turn required significantly more information. This need spawned special libraries. By the second half of the century, with the rise of computer technologies, the importance of information provision as a vital societal function was manifest. By the 1970s, most libraries had, at least in part, begun to reposition themselves as information centers.

Wiegand (2001, 2005) agreed that one function of libraries was to make information accessible. However, he expressed concern that some library educators appeared to define libraries and librarianship solely in terms of technological capabilities, which resulted in curricula that ignored a central and essential purpose of libraries: to serve as a "cultural agency in the everyday life experience of ordinary people" (Wiegand

---

Nature of the Information Paradigm

Apostle and Raymond characterized the nature of the information paradigm based on several assumptions:

- Postindustrial societies are information societies.
- A merger of library and information sciences is taking place.
- Information technology is the driving force and the determiner of the future functions of libraries and of the information profession.
- The needs of library users and the functions of libraries need to be reformulated in terms of information needs.
- The concepts of information industry and information profession are interdependent.
- A convergence of library and information science education is necessary and inevitable.
- Employment prospects for LIS graduates in the emerging information market are optimistic.

2005, p. 58). According to Wiegand (2001), an information orientation produces an emphasis on information seeking while a significant body of research on the importance of reading and its significance in everyday life is ignored. He argued that much of the activity in libraries deals directly with reading and that the LIS curriculum should emphasize the importance of reading and the library as place, rather than information that can be gained from a computer. He advocated for a curriculum that included research in reading such as literacy studies, the social history of books and reading, reader-response theory, and the ethnography of reading (Wiegand 1997).

The library versus information debate led Gorman (2004) to contend that there was a crisis in library education:

- What we used to call library schools have become hosts to information science and information studies faculty and curricula. These disciplines (if they exist at all) are, at best, peripheral to professional library work.

- Some prestigious universities in the United States have given up on LIS education. This has led to a diminution of research (in quality if not quantity) into library topics.

- Many of the topics regarded as central to a library education (cataloguing, reference, collection development, etc.) by would-be employers are no longer central to, or even required by, today's LIS curricula.

- Many library educators (whether librarians or information scientists, but especially the latter) have lost faith in and regard for the traditional mission, policies, programs, and value of libraries and are more interested in research in their areas of interest (outside librarianship) or in equipping their students to take jobs in other areas of work.

- There is a dearth of research in U.S. LIS schools that is dedicated to the real needs of real libraries. (p. 99)

In response to these observations, Gorman (2004) advocated for a nationally recognized core curriculum that dealt with collection development, cataloguing, reference and library instruction, circulation, systems, management, and types of libraries. He also recommended substantial reform of the ALA accreditation process to ensure national standards for curriculum and an emphasis on research and practice that relates directly to libraries and librarianship. He also speculated that as information science faculty, which has been predominantly male, increased in dominance, the gender composition of the professorate would shift in favor of males.

More recently, Crowley (2008) noted that the adoption of the information paradigm has led to a dominance of information scientists and a delivery model that sees libraries as information providers and librarians as intermediaries rather than educators. He expressed concern that as schools embraced an information orientation, the traditional values of library education—to promote lifelong learning, reading, and education—were subjugated and diluted. He advocated for a reorientation of LIS programs to ensure that LIS education continued to emphasize learning theory, programming and education—that literacy and reading return as a central focus. Crowley's argument was not based on quaint nostalgia for the past, but on the substantive conviction that adopting an information perspective threatens the very survival of libraries and librarians. By focusing on information access, the library must compete with the ever-increasing sophistication of technologies and information providers such as Google, a competition he believes libraries will have great difficulty winning. On the other hand, by focusing on the socially critical cultural values and activities of reading, literacy, and lifelong learning, libraries and librarians can continue to make valued contributions to individuals and to the society as a whole, a concept Cowley refers to as "life-cycle librarianship." These contributions cannot be made easily by technologies whose primary purpose is to provide information.

In contrast, Van House and Sutton (2000) argued that LIS education needs to change from a traditional orientation to an information focus:

> The LIS profession's focus on libraries has been challenged by a fundamental shift from the Ptolemaic information universe with the library at its center, to a dynamic, Copernican universe with information at its center and libraries playing a significant, but not necessarily central, role. (p. 55)

Van House and Sutton saw two broad forces shaping the future of LIS education: the rapidly changing information landscape and the shifting university environment in which LIS programs are housed. In particular, they argued that as the value of information becomes increasingly clear, other disciplines, such as computer science and business administration, will become powerful competitors with LIS schools, threatening the traditional jurisdiction of library and information science. This competition, in turn, will produce an unstable university climate, with various disciplines competing for students and university resources. They warned that LIS schools must make substantial adaptations to survive and suggested that, while not abandoning a focus on libraries, LIS education must broaden its niche, making the curriculum less library centered and more information centered.

Another view, expressed by Dillon and Norris (2005), challenged the notion that there are two competing paradigms. They noted that the entire LIS community recognizes the important responsibilities of libraries as stewards of the cultural record of human knowledge. At the same time, they pointed out that LIS educators must recognize that libraries are but "one part of the system" (p. 283) and that the introduction of information technologies has, in fact, radically changed not only how people seek information, but how libraries provide their services. They challenged the claims that there was a dearth of research on library issues and cited numerous journals and a substantial body of research—including award-winning doctoral dissertations. They also found that although there were significant variations in coursework offered by LIS programs, there was actually fairly close agreement concerning requirements. In addition, they examined concerns about the gender of faculty by analyzing teaching assignments and found that "females are contributing to the development of LIS education by teaching both library science-oriented courses and information science-oriented courses" (p. 291). In sum, they argued that the term *crisis* overstates the situation, although they acknowledged some legitimate concerns about the impact of emerging information technologies on recorded knowledge and hence, on libraries:

> When the Internet has given rise to easy access to previously unimaginable amounts of information from one's own location; when cheap, widely available information and communication technologies are used by everyone across multiple task domains; and when students arrive in LIS programs familiar with and skilled in the use of such routine technologies, it would seem difficult to justify any other response from LIS programs than one of embracing the tools and opportunities for study and use they enable. That LIS programs seem to have managed this transition gracefully speaks volumes. (p. 294)

The notion of a crisis was also challenged by King (2005), who observed that such a claim has been a persistent theme at least since the Williamson Report of 1923. He noted that the elements that cause anxiety in LIS education are similar in other fields: lack of funding, lack of respect, and disagreements between practitioners and educators about what should be taught. King noted that the L-school/i-school debate "has all the markings of a Hatfields and McCoys cartoon" (p. 15). He argued that whether a school has the word *Library* in its title says little about what goes on inside and observed that the deans of the various schools appear to work quite well together. Both information and library schools belong to the Association for Library and Information Science Educators (ALISE) and there is little evidence that i-schools are abandoning LIS traditions.

Estabrook (2005) suggested that those who claim there is a crisis are crying wolf, although she exhorted LIS programs to make clear the reasons for any changes in their programs. She noted that LIS education needs both an understanding of technology and core library principles and felt that "the beauty of our LIS programs is the way in which many of them have been able to marry the two" (p. 299). Further, she argued that faculty research cannot strictly be confined to solving immediate, practical library problems—that would reduce scholarship to consultancy.

Stoffle and Leeder (2005) suggested that misunderstandings between practitioners and LIS educators exacerbate the situation:

> The greatest problem with LIS programs is the fact that many practitioners do not understand the goals of library education, the demands under which these programs operate, or the standards to which they are held. Practitioners want to

dictate a curriculum based on their interests or the hiring needs of their particular libraries, without acknowledging the tremendous range of subject matter
that these schools must address in only 36 to 42 hours of coursework. (p. 315)

3. Finding Common Ground

It is not likely that the library versus information debate will dissipate soon. However, the notion of two competing paradigms is more likely to confuse, rather than
facilitate, the discussion. Miksa (1992) analyzed the debate from the perspectives of
"library as a social institution" versus the "information movement as a system of
human communication" and found significant conceptual defects in both. He argued
that what is needed is "a more essential approach to what is involved in the work of
the field, one that conceptualizes the processes in a more thoroughgoing but unitary manner" (p. 243).

An attempt to unify, rather than divide, seems desirable since it has been hard to
determine what constructive end the debate over competing paradigms has achieved.
The notion of a paradigm as it is generally used today is taken from the work of
Thomas S. Kuhn (1970) in his groundbreaking treatise on the history of science, *The
Structure of Scientific Revolutions*. Kuhn illustrated a paradigm shift in science using
the example of the change from the Ptolemaic view of the universe with the earth at
its center to the Copernican conception with the sun at its center. Kuhn's notion of
paradigm shift is not merely an adjustment in perspective or emphasis; it is a change
so great that one paradigm cannot be held at the same time as the other. As he stated,
"scientific revolutions are here taken to be those non-cumulative developmental
episodes in which an older paradigm is replaced in whole or in part by an *incompatible* new one" (p. 92, italics added). Although Kuhn offered numerous examples
in the sciences, he questioned whether there are any social science paradigms.

In terms of LIS education, isn't it reasonable to believe that both information and
education are critical? Indeed, don't our everyday conceptions of information and
education assume that they are closely related—that information is a necessary part
of learning? Isn't the promotion of reading as a central function of libraries quite
compatible with and complementary to finding information for people? Certainly,
over the years, the mission statements of public libraries have declared a desire to
meet the educational, recreational, and informational needs of their communities.
Shouldn't LIS programs reflect these same multiple goals? Exploring the potentialities of a unitary vision, as Miksa (1992) suggested, would seem to have many happy
prospects.

B. Continuing Education

Continuing education (CE) has been a part of LIS education since the turn of the
twentieth century when a small number of public libraries and some academic

institutions offered "institutes" for library workers. The Higher Education Act of 1965 offered funding for CE, which led to the founding of the Continuing Library Education Network and Exchange (CLENE), whose purpose was to improve the quality of CE. CLENE assessed the needs of practicing librarians around the country and provided opportunities for CE. In 1983, CLENE became a Roundtable of the American Library Association (Roberts and Konn 1991). CLENE recently changed its name to Learning RT. Other professional associations, state libraries, larger libraries, and regional library systems also provide a substantial amount of CE for practicing LIS professionals.

Although the ALA Code of Ethics requires librarians to update their professional skills, CE remains for the most part a voluntary activity. Unlike teaching, where licensure often requires it, most library positions have no CE requirements, nor do employers offer monetary rewards as incentives. A few employers implement competency-based performance evaluation systems that provide financial rewards and job opportunities for those acquiring new skills, but these are still rare.

Today, with the rapidly changing information environment, much of the knowledge conveyed in LIS programs quickly becomes obsolete. Many LIS programs recognize the need to provide in-service education for graduates as well as training for other library employees. The challenge, however, is to develop CE opportunities for returning students without adding to the pedagogical burdens of the faculty, a daunting task.

C. Distance Education

With developments in telecommunications, it is now possible to deliver high-quality LIS education to remote sites using interactive video and Web-based instruction. As of 2010, there were sixteen accredited LIS programs offering a complete MLIS program via distance learning and twelve additional that are primarily online (ALA 2010b). The maturation of online LIS education was manifest with the creation of the Web-Based Information Science Education (WISE) Consortium in 2004 which began with a federal Institute of Museum and Library Services (IMLS) grant to Syracuse University and the University of Illinois at Urbana-Champaign. The mission of WISE is "to increase the quality, access, and diversity of online education opportunities in library and information science." It has three guiding ideals: quality, pedagogy, and collaboration (WISE 2009, pp. 1–3). As of 2009, there were fifteen consortium members. Members benefit from administrative and technical support. Students have access to online courses taught by the member schools, and faculty can participate in workshops and training through the consortium. WISE also makes some of its training available to nonmembers and has developed principles and metrics for effective online instruction.

Distance learning is appealing for a number of reasons, foremost among them the advantage of not having to travel or relocate, thus relieving stress on family and finances. In addition, students don't have to quit their job to enroll in a quality program (Wilde and Epperson 2006). Carey and Gregory (2002) found that participants in Web-based distance learning at the University of South Florida found the experience satisfying and equivalent or sometimes even superior to face-to-face classroom experiences. Logan, Augustyniak, and Rees (2002) found that some students actually appeared to take increased responsibility for their education in the online environment. Wilde and Epperson (2006), in a survey of distance learning alumni, found that 90 percent of the respondents believed that the distance program was comparable to a degree program delivered on-site, although there was a general feeling of being disconnected from other students and faculty. The specific programs chosen were selected primarily because they were ALA accredited, had a good reputation, and did not require travel (Wilde and Epperson 2006).

Despite its many benefits, distance education brings its own set of issues that, although not unique to distance education, must be addressed continuously due to ever-evolving technologies.

Distance Education: Important Questions to Consider

1. How do we ensure that the quality of distance education is equal to that provided in traditional classrooms?
2. How do we provide the variety of courses and specialties offered at the main campus?
3. How do we create a sense of community for students who might have little face-to-face contact with faculty members and other students?
4. How do we train faculty to use new technologies effectively?
5. How do we administer the programs?
6. How can we best assess academic performance in the distance-learning environment?

D. Competencies and the Evolving LIS Curriculum

Competencies generally refer to the necessary knowledge, skills, and abilities required to perform professional tasks. Various divisions within the American Library Association such as the Young Adult Library Services Association, the Association for Library Services to Children, the Reference and User Services Association, and the Public Library Association have developed numerous competency statements for their various specialties. Although over the years there has been a recognition that general competencies for librarians were needed, it was not until 2009 that the ALA approved its "Core Competencies of Librarianship" intended to define "the basic knowledge to be possessed by all persons graduating from an ALA-accredited master's program in library and information studies" (ALA 2009a).

ALA's Core Competencies of Librarianship: Knowledge Categories

1. **Foundations of the Profession**, including history, ethics and values
2. **Information Resources**, including the life cycle of recorded knowledge; acquisition, selection, and processing of materials; collection maintenance and management
3. **Organization of Recorded Knowledge and Information**, including the principles of organization of recorded knowledge and systems of cataloging, metadata, and classification
4. **Technological Knowledge and Skills**, including information and communication technologies and their application, and assessment and evaluation of technologies
5. **Reference and User Services**, including the principles and techniques of reference services, information retrieval and evaluation techniques, interpersonal skills, information literacy, and assessment of user needs
6. **Research**, including quantitative and qualitative methods and central research findings of the field
7. **Continuing Education and Lifelong Learning**, including the role of the library in lifelong learning; learning theories and their application to libraries; and principles related to teaching skills in seeking, evaluating, and using recorded knowledge
8. **Administration and Management**, including planning, budgeting, human resources, program evaluation, leadership, and collaboration

---

Additional competencies were promulgated by the Special Libraries Association, the Medical Library Association, the Music Library Association, and the Society of American Archivists. Certain states, including Arizona, California, Connecticut, and Ohio also identified competencies (Van Fleet and Lester 2008).

Ostensibly, academic coursework is the avenue to gain competence. Unfortunately, there appears to be little agreement in LIS programs on the core courses or those appropriate for specialization (Lynch 1989). For example, in 1994, Marco found that none of the forty-seven U.S. library schools required students to take courses in each of the seven major subject areas considered core at that time: "book selection, cataloguing and classification, reference work, administration and management of libraries, history of books and libraries, research methods, and libraries in society" (p. 182). In fact, he concluded that only two subjects were universally required: cataloging and reference. Markey (2004) examined the Web sites of fifty-six schools and suggested that programs should consider expanding their curriculum and offering certifications, specializations, or concentrations in such areas as knowledge organization, content creation, authoritative information, and collection preservation. Chu (2006), in an analysis of nearly 3,000 courses from forty-five accredited U.S. programs, found that a wide range of subjects was covered and that changes in the curriculum reflected not only technological developments but also social and cultural ones. For example, elective courses included digital libraries, Web site design, networks, digitization, information architecture, cyberspace law, and knowledge management. However, Chu also found that overall, the number of core courses was shrinking: the mean number of required courses among library schools was five or six, although in some cases the number was as low as two. The most common required courses were in traditional areas: organization of information, reference, foundations, and management.

The lack of clarity in LIS curricula echoes the ongoing debate over incorporating theory versus practice into course content. For example, Main (1990) suggested:

> There is no longer a need to be concerned with theoretical and philosophical issues. What we must be concerned with is what enables us to survive in a competitive world, namely information technology. And information technology is a practical discipline. (p. 228)

Such a view is quite different from that advanced by Williamson in 1923, and other academics would no doubt argue that the challenges and issues raised by information technologies make understanding the philosophical issues even more important today. Some argue that there is a need to increase theoretical understanding so that LIS professionals can perform the planning, evaluation, and decision-making functions that will be so vital in the rapidly evolving information environment. Lynch (1989), for example, believed:

> The shaping of the future of librarianship rests not on the vocational skills necessary to the time, but on the principles common to all specialization in the field. The professional expects library education to be built on a solid intellectual foundation. (p. 81)

LIS programs continuously struggle to maintain a balance between theory and practice. They provide practicums or internship programs that allow students, usually for academic credit, to perform professional work in a library or other information organization. Such experiences provide a real-life context, improve the student's self-confidence, and can supply important future contacts for employment and professional development. Ball (2008) suggested that "service learning," a related but distinct form of experiential learning, can occur when it is integrated into a course. "Service activities are tied to specific learning objectives and are reflected upon throughout the semester in order to enrich student appreciation of course content" (p. 71). There remains considerable debate as to the proper balance between theory and practice and no doubt these different perspectives will continue to generate discussion for years to come.

E. The Role of the Master's Degree in Library and Information Science

As the notion grew in the twentieth century that substantial theoretical knowledge and principles should form the foundation of professional practice, the importance of the master's of library and information science degree also grew. The American Library Association (1996) recognized the importance of graduate education in one of its policy statements:

> The American Library Association supports the provision of library services by professionally qualified personnel who have been educated in graduate programs within institutions of higher education.... The American Library Association supports the development and continuance of high quality graduate library/information science educational programs of the quality, scope and availability necessary to prepare individuals in the broad profession of information dissemination. The American Library Association supports education for the preparation of professionals in the field of library and information studies (LIS) as a university program at the master's level. (p. 137)

This supporting statement is strong but not unequivocal. It does not, for example, insist that all professional librarians possess a master's degree from an accredited program. Nonetheless, it is clear that graduate library education at the master's level is now the accepted norm for entry into the library profession.

Others asserted that the body of theoretical knowledge was insufficient to require graduate academic training. For example, Hauptman (1987) stated:

> There is not even any mandatory a priori knowledge necessary to function effectively as a librarian of any persuasion. Any intelligent college graduate can begin working in a special, public, or academic library and quickly learn the skills necessary to catalog, do reference work, manipulate overrated computer systems, or even administer. (pp. 252–253)

Hauptman described the work of a librarian as 90 percent clerical and claimed that librarians created a mystique regarding their work; that patrons could often learn to perform some library functions in only a short time. Campbell (1993) took a different view but raised the same issue. He argued that the computer revolution created the need for greater technical proficiencies and that the failure to alter library education significantly might lead to its obsolescence. He noted that "the MLS might no longer be a viable credential given the nature of the technological and practical challenges we face in everyday library work" (p. 560).

Obviously, others disagreed. For them, library and information science, like many professions, combines routine elements as well as considerable theoretical and conceptual knowledge and judgment. As a profession, it provides an essential social and political function that demands a broad understanding of the nature of knowledge, of information, of people, and of society. That understanding allows LIS professionals to evaluate, make judgments, and set future courses of action. For example, knowing the name of a particular source might be useful for answering a specific query, but understanding people's information needs and how to identify and evaluate them requires a different type of knowledge. This type of understanding helps LIS professionals design information systems, select areas of emphasis, and implement strategies that enable and encourage people to use such systems. The same might be said for understanding the principles of selection, the effects of information policy, the uses of technology, the manner by which knowledge is organized, and the principles that guide the operation of information-giving institutions. White (1986) noted that the master's degree is a qualification not so much for a particular position as for entry into the profession.

The importance of the master's degree became the focus of a significant court case when a legal challenge was lodged against its use as a criterion for hiring a librarian at Mississippi State University in the 1980s. Title VII of the Civil Rights Act protects various classes from discrimination by age, race, color, religion, or disability. The act extends to protecting individuals from being discriminated against in the hiring process, especially when an irrelevant characteristic or qualification is considered in that process. In other words, employers are obligated to use only those selection criteria that directly relate to an individual's ability to perform a job. Glenda Merwine sued Mississippi State University when she was not hired for a librarian's position at the Veterinary Medicine Library. Although the case, *Glenda Merwine v. Board of Trustees for State Institutions of Higher Education* (Holley 1984) had many complications, one of Merwine's arguments was that she was denied employment because she did not possess a master's degree from a program accredited by ALA. Interestingly, ALA did not take a stand on the issue, but several prominent library educators testified. The court found that no reasonable alternative to the master's degree had been provided and that the master's degree was both relevant and broadly accepted as the professional degree. Despite the supportive decision, it has not inoculated the profession from attacks from other sources, most notably the Office of Management and Budget of the federal government, which challenged the need for a master's degree from an accredited LIS program for some government positions that previously required it. Such actions put the profession on notice that it must be able to articulate clearly the nature of its professional responsibilities and the need for formal graduate education to meet them.

F. Standards for LIS Education

Since the 1950s, the ALA Committee on Accreditation has been the formal mechanism for ensuring quality in professional preparation. Only master's-level LIS programs are accredited. Accreditation standards, which have changed as the field has evolved, currently address six areas considered essential to a quality program: mission, goals, and objectives; curriculum; faculty; students; administration and financial support; and physical resources and facilities (ALA, 2010a). These standards place strong emphasis on a school's ability to articulate its own mission, develop planning and outcome assessment mechanisms, and evaluate its mission. In addition, reflecting the development of alternative teaching approaches, the standards acknowledge that education can be delivered through a variety of mechanisms, such as interactive video or online. The standards, however, remain the same regardless of the delivery technique.

Although support for accreditation remained strong historically, not all LIS educators have been satisfied with the standards and approaches. For example, in 1994 Saracevic suggested that allowing schools to set their own missions was illogical and focused too much attention away from developing a basic curriculum centered on essential competencies and the theoretical foundations of the field. His concern was prompted by the observation that too often, university administrators view LIS programs as vocational rather than academic. Without clarity about theoretical underpinnings, schools are vulnerable to closing.

More recently, the accreditation process has been subject to criticism from LIS educators who think that the standards should increase their emphasis on librarianship and reduce their focus on information science. In 2006, ALA appointed a President's Task Force on Library Education to identify the core knowledge that all programs should provide and make recommendations. The Final Report (ALA 2009c) identified a variety of concerns including a perceived misalignment between what was taught and what was actually needed for work in libraries, a lack of emphasis on values and ethics, and an overemphasis on information in some schools. Among the task force's recommendations were the following: the accreditation standards should be more prescriptive; the ALA statements on core values and core competencies should be incorporated into the standards; and a majority of faculty should be grounded in librarianship. The American Society for Information Science and Technology has a different perspective. In a recent white paper (ASIS&T, 2007), the authors asked: "Is ALA the appropriate agency to review for accreditation those programs that do not have a library focus?" (p. 3). The society proposed new accrediting standards in collaboration with a variety of information-related partners. No doubt the accreditation debate will continue. LIS professionals should understand the issues and follow evolving developments, as they will affect what will be required of LIS schools in the future.

G. Changing Demographics

The number of new professionals graduating with master's degrees increased from 4,877 in 2000 to 6,502 in 2005. The majority of students were female (79 percent) and white (76 percent). In 2005 nearly 18,271 students were enrolled in accredited programs in the United States and Canada compared to 15,000 in 2002. Although 41 percent were between the ages of twenty-five and thirty-four, 43 percent were over the age of thirty-five, and approximately 11 percent were fifty or older (ALISE 2009).

However, the American population is becoming increasingly heterogeneous; today, the four major minority populations—Hispanics, African Americans, Asians, and Native Americans—comprise approximately one third of the U.S. population. Currently in many large cities, minorities comprise the majority, or at least a very substantial proportion of the urban population. Current minority enrollments in MLIS programs, however, remain below 12 percent: in 2005 only 4 percent were African American, 3 percent were Asian, and 4 percent were of Hispanic descent (ALISE 2009).

ALA has been proactive in attempting to increase the diversity of the library profession. It launched the Spectrum Initiative in 1997, which annually recruited and supported as many as fifty students of color with the objective of doubling the number of librarians from minority groups. Subsequent support from ALA presidents led to the creation of a permanent scholarship fund that extended the initiative indefinitely; as of 2009, 560 Spectrum Scholars matriculated. Other groups, such as the Association of Research Libraries (ARL) and the Asian/Pacific American Library Association, also have outreach programs.

The challenge of recruiting nonwhite individuals into LIS has been recognized for decades. The dearth of African-American librarians and their lack of involvement at the higher levels of ALA were among the main reasons for the creation, in 1970, of the Black Caucus of ALA under the chairmanship of E. J. Josey. In 1993, McCook and Geist suggested a variety of ways to increase diversity including establishing cooperative partnerships between LIS schools and employers, providing greater monetary support, increasing recruitment activities in undergraduate and secondary education programs, recruiting in nontraditional settings such as military and community colleges, and improving the cultural climate of colleges and universities. Greiner (2008) argued that the largest barrier facing minorities interested in LIS programs was not discrimination but the financial burden. Clearly, the need to recruit members of minority groups into the profession will grow as the population becomes increasingly diverse.

IV. LIBRARY AND INFORMATION SCIENCE AS A PROFESSION

A. Professional Models

The first professionals were members of the clergy. Professions in their modern sense (law, medicine, nursing, teaching, librarianship) emerged in considerable numbers during the Industrial Revolution in the later nineteenth and early twentieth century. The following is a brief discussion of three of the several ways that professions can be characterized.

1. The Trait Model

One way to characterize a profession is by determining whether or not an occupation exhibits particular traits. Some of the most common professional traits are shared by library and information science:

- They are service-oriented and altruistic in its orientation rather than profit making.
- Professional associations hold conferences, produce publications, promulgate codes of ethics, and accredit educational institutions.
- Professional associations possess normative authority, including standards of conduct and work.

Librarianship does not correspond to all of these traits, however. For example, the power of the professional associations is limited; they cannot sanction practitioners whose conduct violates their professional codes. Librarianship exercises no monopoly, and a license is not required. In addition, the one year of formal graduate training is not equal to the extensive training required in other professions. Others have proposed different traits to satisfy the requirements of a profession:

- Commitment to serve the interests of clients, in particular, and the welfare of society, in general
- A body of theory or special knowledge with its own principles of growth and reorganization
- A specialized set of professional skills, practices, and performances unique to the profession
- A capacity to render judgments with integrity under conditions of both technical and ethical certainty
- An organized approach to learning from experience both individually and collectively, thus growing new knowledge from the context of practice
- A professional community responsible for the oversight and monitoring of quality in both practice and professional education (Gardner and Shulman 2005, p. 14)

Library and information science fits more easily under this characterization primarily because the concepts of enforcement and monopoly are missing.

2. The Control Model

An alternative approach for distinguishing professions was suggested by Winter (1988), who used a control model based on the work of several sociologists to characterize librarianship. In this view, the distinguishing features of a profession are based on different degrees of power and the nature of the control that each exercises. Professional control is based on higher education degrees and intellectual and theoretical knowledge in contrast to occupations that rely on work experience and manual skills. He identified three ways librarians exert control: classifying knowledge as a means of organizing it, indexing knowledge so it can be accessed, and understanding the formal and informal organization of various bodies of knowledge. Librarians, then, attempt to understand not one body of knowledge, but the organization of many bodies of knowledge and their interrelationship. On the face of it, this seems to provide some convincing evidence that librarianship is indeed a profession, for these functions cannot be accomplished without considerable knowledge and training, both theoretical and practical. Winter (1988) argued that "mediating between the user and the public record of knowledge is the special province of the librarian" (p. 6).

The control model, however, does not assume that all control is vested with the professional. There are, in Winter's conceptualization, other types of control: collegial control, client control, and mediated control. In collegial control, professional practice is controlled by those who provide the service. For example, doctors and lawyers tend to determine their practices in regard to their patients. In a client-controlled situation, the individuals who use the services determine their wants, their needs, and the means by which they are satisfied. In mediated control, there is a balance between collegial and client control. Winter suggested that almost all professions were moving toward mediated control. Even in medicine, for example, patients exercise a great deal more control over their medical treatment than in the past. Librarianship also fits in the mediated control category. Some patrons still rely heavily on librarians to both identify and meet their information needs; in other cases, the patron might ask for a specific item and the librarian merely locates the information requested. But there is a high probability that in the twenty-first century, the client-controlled model will dominate. Birdsall (1982), for example, suggested that new information technologies stimulated a trend toward deprofessionalization by making expert knowledge more widely available. He argued that professions will no longer be characterized by a monopoly over special knowledge, but will encourage and teach clients to become more self-sufficient. Birdsall's speculations appear to fit for all of today's helping professions, such as social work, education, and LIS.

3. The Values Model

In the past, librarians achieved their status partly because the library itself was unique. It was, after all, often the only publicly accessible place with a substantial collection of well-organized materials and people who knew how to locate the desired materials. This gave the librarian, if not a monopoly, at least significant control over some types of knowledge. This type of special status is sometimes referred to as asymmetry of expertise, and describes the special trust that a client or patron places in the knowledge of a professional (Abbott 1988, p. 5). Abbott (1988) labeled the type of knowledge controlled by librarians as "qualitative information"

(p. 216). Librarians "had physical custody of cultural capital" (p. 217), which they organized and disseminated to everyone for education or entertainment, but not profit.

This purpose reflects one of the fundamental values of all professions, the value of service. The original professions (clergy, lawyers, doctors, teachers, nurses, and social workers) were dedicated to the betterment of people and the improvement of society and "stood outside the new commercial and industrial heart of society" (Abbott 1988, p. 3). LIS professionals serve the public good by bringing people in contact with knowledge. In doing so, LIS professionals also support fundamental democratic values by ensuring that all people have equal access to that knowledge. Under this view, the professional foundation of library and information science is not its techniques, but its fundamental values. The significance of LIS lies not in mastery of sources, organizational skills, or technological competence, but in why LIS professionals perform the functions they do. The fact that modern library and information science encompasses all forms of knowledge (e.g., print, audiovisual, and electronic) increases the importance of these underlying values and differentiates it from other, even kindred, professions such as museum curators.

B. Perceptions about Librarians

1. Stereotypes

How are librarians currently perceived, and do the perceptions match the reality? Some female librarians believe that their image is mostly negative: they are spinsters, wear their hair in a bun, look stern (e.g., buy sensible shoes and glasses), act authoritarian and controlling, and are ready to say "shh" at the slightest disturbance. Male librarians have other concerns: they often assume that they are perceived to be working in a "woman's profession" and therefore fear being seen as ineffectual or effeminate. This concern is sufficient to inhibit many men from admitting that they are librarians; instead, they are more likely to identify themselves as information scientists (Morrisey and Case 1988). Such stereotypes about men and women in librarianship can have pernicious effects; they impede recruitment into the field and affect the status and growth of the profession as a whole.

But how accurate are these perceptions? Morrisey and Case (1988) examined college students' perceptions of male librarians and found that they were often quite positive. The most common terms used to describe male librarians were organized, approachable, logical, friendly, patient, and serious (p. 457). Their conclusion was that male librarians perceive themselves in a much more negative light than others do. Schuman (1990) observed that although there were some negative images about librarians, the supposition that all such images were negative was unfounded. She pointed out that such notable writers as Sinclair Lewis, Sherwood Anderson, Henry James, and Edith Wharton depicted librarians in positive terms. Furthermore, the media's occasional portrayal of librarians in a negative light is consistent with portrayals of other professions; lawyers and politicians certainly receive their share of disrespect.

More recent interpretations using a cultural studies approach suggested that librarians can use stereotypes to their advantage. Adams (2000) and Radford and Radford (2003) argued that rather than objecting to the persistent image of the "old maid," librarians should transform the stereotype into a positive using such techniques as parody, mimicry, and humor. For example, cultural studies theorists see the 1995 film *Party Girl*, in which a young woman is transformed from a self-centered, fun-obsessed individual into a serious-minded librarian, and Web sites such as Lipstick Librarian (www.lipsticklibrarian.com) as good examples of ways in which stereotypes can be used to librarians' advantage.

2. Personality Types

The personalities of librarians have been studied for many years. The first major study, conducted by Alice Bryan in 1948, was part of a large study called the Public Library Inquiry. She found that librarians were submissive and lacked qualities of leadership (Bryan 1952). Later studies summarized by Agada (1984, 1987) found that, in general, both male and female librarians exhibited personality traits of deference, passivity, and self-abasement. Scherdin (1994), using the Myers-Briggs Type Indicator, suggested that most librarians fell into one of two typologies: introversion, sensing, thinking, judging, or introversion, intuitive, thinking, judging. Among the characteristics associated with these types are determination and perseverance, independence, a drive to work hard, the desire to innovate, and placing a high value on competence. Interestingly, there is little evidence, despite the stereotype, that librarians are authoritarian. One should also hasten to add that none of these traits were pathological and, generally, librarians' personalities fell well within normal ranges. One should, of course, be careful about trying to apply these findings. Fisher (1988) reviewed a number of these personality studies and concluded that many of the personality tests were flawed, and overall there was no one distinct personality type for librarians.

Williamson, Pemberton, and Lounsbury (2008) attempted to analyze more than 2,000 librarians' personalities by their choice of library specialization using the Personality Style Inventory. Among the traits measured were adaptability, assertiveness, autonomy, conscientiousness, customer service orientation, emotional resilience, extraversion, openness, optimism, teamwork, tough-mindedness, work drive, and operational work style. Their findings suggested that different specialties did attract people with different personality traits. When taken together, they concluded:

> High extraversion, low tough-mindedness, and high teamwork (among other variables . . .) characterized person-oriented academic reference librarians, special librarians, public librarians, school librarians, distance education librarians and records managers. For the technique-oriented specialties, operational work

style and low customer service orientation characterized catalogers, and high assertiveness and high tough-mindedness characterized the archivists and systems librarians. (pp. 5–6)

3. The Role of Gender

The first female clerk was hired by the Boston Public Library in 1852; by 1878 two-thirds of the library workforce was female, and by 1910 more than 75 percent of library workers were women (Garrison 1972–1973). From a historical perspective, the numerical dominance of women in American librarianship, especially public librarianship, might explain the perception of passivity among librarians, since passivity was a normative expectation of women well into the twentieth century.

The rapid expansion of public libraries in the nineteenth century increased the need for library workers, but as these libraries were often poorly funded, they needed staff who were willing to work for low pay. Male library directors openly acknowledged the desirability of hiring talented women because they worked for half the pay. In addition, librarianship fit the values of work for women at the time. There was a narrow range of jobs outside the home that were considered acceptable for women, mostly related to children or caregiving, such as teaching and nursing, that capitalized on women's homemaking and child-raising skills. Because libraries were seen as civilizing and nurturing, they were acceptable places for women to work (Garrison 1972–1973). In addition, the nineteenth-century values of personal improvement and the belief that books and reading could improve morals also drew women into librarianship. Indeed, it was sometimes described as missionary work. The fact that librarianship still draws at least some individuals who share these convictions is, in part, a legacy of these historical forces and confirmation that its service aspect is still deeply ingrained.

Garrison (1972–1973) suggested that the feminization of public librarianship in the nineteenth century created an inferior image for the profession that it might not have had if it remained the domain of male scholars. In other words, an occupation that once had considerable status lost ground as it became dominated by women. Although women outnumbered men in libraries, they were not perceived as potential leaders or heads of libraries. Women were perceived as more delicate and unable to tolerate the rigors of administration. Indeed, some believed that administrative responsibilities might even lead to mental illness. This perceived passivity led Garrison to lament that librarianship failed to engage those with the necessary leadership or assertiveness (meaning men) to establish it in the pantheon of professions:

> Specifically lacking in the librarian's professional service code are a sense of commitment, a drive to lead rather than to serve and a clear-cut conception of professional rights and responsibilities. The feminization of library work is a major cause of these deficiencies. (pp. 144–145)

The legacy of this attitude persists particularly in public libraries where women occupy a disproportionately low percentage of leadership positions. There are several possible explanations. Women tend to have more career breaks due to family and marital responsibilities, although a study by Zemon and Bahr (2005) found that the choice of parenthood, which often creates additional burdens and barriers for women, did not appear to have a significant deleterious effect on library careers. Women often begin their library careers later than men and tend to remain within the same organization longer than men, effectively reducing the number of promotional opportunities. When women do move, they are more likely than their male counterparts to relocate because of a spouse. As a result, they often take the only positions available rather than positions involving promotion.

Image and status problems also persist. For example, women are more likely to serve as children's librarians or in cataloging positions; men are more likely to seek technology-oriented and managerial positions, despite the fact that male librarians have no greater motivation to manage than females (Swisher et al. 1985). The former categories reflect values of nurturance or attention to detail, while the latter reflect technical competence, leadership, or managerial skills. Male children's librarians are a rarity and raise eyebrows, no matter how undeservedly. The dominance of men in technical and managerial categories further supports the theory that many men are uneasy working in a field perceived as feminine. Some male librarians might seek technological and managerial positions within libraries to help mitigate their occupational ambivalence. Assuming that certain library positions are more suited to one gender further also serves to depress the status and pay of women. As Hildenbrand (1989) observed, librarians in children's services and cataloging generally receive lower pay than those in other basic service positions. These inequalities are yet another example of the persistent messages that women's work is of less value and status.

The underrepresentation of women in administrative positions, however, is not fully explained by the reasons noted above—sex discrimination still appears to play a role (Heim and Estabrook 1983). Hildenbrand (1996) argued that to fully understand the status and place of women in librarianship requires an appreciation of the historical, political, and social relationships between men and women, especially in terms of how power is distributed. She argued that the traditional analysis of library history is biased (Hildenbrand 1992). She believed that important women have largely been ignored while prominent males, such as Dewey, have been studied in detail. She criticized Garrison for holding women responsible for their poor status (blaming the victim), rather than attributing it to the pernicious attitudes of the times. She argued that a reanalysis of the history of women in librarianship would reveal that they were responsible for its rapid growth, the increase in the quality of library workers, and the growth of a national purpose for public libraries, as noted in Chapter 2.

Consistent with Hildenbrand's position, Harris (1992) suggested that librarians' self-consciousness about their image is counterproductive, especially when it leads to self-deprecation. Such self-criticism leads to blaming the victim and denigrating worthy "feminine" traits rather than focusing on why society gives nurturing activities such low status. For Harris, disparaging caring attitudes and lionizing management, research, and technical expertise (considered male traits) is tantamount to endorsing and perpetuating the suppression of women. That both men and women deprecate these traits is particularly disturbing.

Maack (1997) suggested that striving for a status traditionally associated with male-dominated professions such as law and medicine is misdirected. Rather, she argued that there is a need to reconceptualize the professions into three categories: high-authority professions, such as law and medicine; indirect or product-oriented professions, such as engineering and architecture; and empowering professions, such as education, social work, and library and information science. In empowering professions, "the professional shares expertise with the goal of enabling clients to use knowledge in order to take control of their own lives or their own learning" (p. 284). It is a collaborative, client-centered activity in which sharing and facilitation are fundamental activities of the professional. Such a profession contrasts clearly with high-authority professions in which "the professional offers prescriptions, directives, or strategies that the client must follow" (Maack 1997, p. 284). As noted earlier, in the client-centered model of the professions, it is not power and authority that dominate, but the desire to help others develop their own abilities and confidence so that they can deal with their own problems and challenges. Accepting library and information science as an empowering profession eliminates the need to strive to be like law or medicine and recognizes the vitality of a profession that increases the independence and abilities of others.

V. LOOKING TO THE FUTURE

Understanding the current state of LIS education and its future prospects is important. The W.K. Kellogg Foundation recognized this when it partnered with the Association for Library and Information Science Education (ALISE) to found the KALIPER Project in 1998 "to analyze the nature and extent of major curricular change in LIS education" (ALISE 2000, p. 3). Led by an advisory committee, five scholar teams were created, comprised primarily of faculty and doctoral students from schools of library and information science. Using a variety of data collection techniques, the KALIPER Advisory Committee concluded, based on studies of twenty-six schools, that library and information science is a "vibrant, dynamic, changing field that is undertaking an array of initiatives" (ALISE 2000, p. 1). The report identified six trends that aptly reflect the current and continuing issues facing LIS education:

Trend 1. In addition to library-specific operations, LIS curricula address broad-based information environments.

Trend 2. While LIS curricula continue to incorporate perspectives from other disciplines, a distinct core has taken shape that is predominantly user centered.

Trend 3. LIS schools and programs have significantly increased their investment and infusion of information technology into their curricula.

Trend 4. LIS schools and programs continue to experiment with the structure of specialization within the curriculum.

Trend 5. LIS schools and programs offer instruction in multiple formats to provide students with more flexibility.

Trend 6. LIS schools and programs have expanded their curricula by offering related degrees at the undergraduate, master's, and doctoral levels. (ALISE 2000)

Conrad and Rapp-Hanretta (2002) identified a number of internal and external forces contributing to these trends. Among the external forces were advances in technology, changing employer expectations, need for ongoing training, changing patterns of educational financing (including reduced governmental funding), and increasing corporate funding. Internal factors included changing modes of information access and dissemination, the increasing entrepreneurial culture of universities, shortages of faculty, and trends toward reorganization.

Taken together, these trends characterize a dynamic field that must respond not only the demands of the LIS environment but the greater demands placed on it by the many social, political, economic, and educational forces at work. In this environment, what roles will LIS professionals play? Two roles seem clear: the educational and the informational.

A. The Educational Role

Since the mid-nineteenth century, the library, whether public, school, or academic, has been characterized as providing critical support not only to students, but to individuals who desire to continue their education informally. The intimate relationship of libraries with learning, literacy, and reading remains strong, and the public continues to expect it. The librarian in the twenty-first century will continue to promote the fundamental values of reading and learning. Thus the LIS curriculum will still require knowledge of learning theories for young people and adults, skills to develop literacy and reading programs, and strategies for building collections and providing services that meet the learning needs of the community. People will continue to expect the library to be a place where they can find books and programming that stimulates the reading habit among the young. In many instances, it is this educational function that "sells" the library as an institution deserving public support. It also reflects one of the important societal purposes of the library. Books remain the library's "brand" for many people (De Rosa et al. 2005). At the same time, people see the library "as a provider of practical answers and information" (De Rosa and Johnson 2008, pp. 4–9). The public's perception of the librarian as an advocate for lifelong learning strongly influences their support for the library (De Rosa and Johnson 2008). In an age when many believe that schools are not performing their roles effectively, the perception of the library as a learning place can go a long way toward securing its future.

> *The intimate relationship of libraries with learning, literacy, and reading remains strong, and the public continues to expect it.*

B. The Information Role

1. Providing Access to Information

Some of the traditional roles of librarians will remain or expand while others will diminish. For example, in a survey of 1,000 librarians in 2001, *Library Journal* reported that librarians perceived their most significant roles as instructing patrons in navigating the Web, directing patrons to appropriate information resources, evaluating collections, organizing resources, creating programs, creating e-resources, and establishing digital archiving. Interestingly, although the participants believed that many of those functions would persist into the future, only creating e-resources and establishing digital archiving were seen as increasing in importance ("Projecting Librarians' Roles" 2002). Baruchson-Arbib and Bronstein (2002) conducted a survey of LIS experts that seemed to confirm that change will occur in an evolutionary, rather than revolutionary, fashion. The experts perceived that the traditional library model would not be replaced by a virtual one, but would undergo significant changes, especially in regard to accessing information outside the library. Similarly, they saw the role of LIS professionals as increasingly user centered rather than organization centered and that there was greater need to understand how individuals seek and use information. In addition, they saw a need for LIS professionals to be more aggressive in marketing and promoting their services to the community, and to develop the skills needed to accomplish these activities. In conjunction with information scientists, who explore the information needs not only of library users but of information seekers more generally, LIS professionals should play an increasingly important role in designing and using information systems in a manner that helps people solve their own information problems. In fact, LIS professionals will continue to perform the fundamental role of helping people locate information in an ever more chaotic information environment. What will be different is that this role will likely extend to finding information outside the library.

2. Evaluating Information

Some years ago, Rice (1989) observed that librarians never had difficulty in making judgments about what should be included in library collections, but they found it very difficult to make judgments about the quality and accuracy of the information they provided to patrons. He noted, "There is seldom a problem in finding information nowadays. The problem is usually in sorting through all of it and deciding which is best" (p. 59). He predicted that librarians would play a much larger role in consulting, teaching, and advising individuals in their search for information, and such activities would become an essential reason people would continue to go to libraries. This role will evolve as the library "collection" consists increasingly of information available through networks in digital format. Many patrons will feel adrift in this sea of information and expect the librarian to provide advice and counsel on the reliability and value of various sources. The librarian of the twenty-first century, according to Debons (1985), would be seen as an "information intermediary," performing at least three basic functions:

1. **Diagnosis**: Estimating the information need. The LIS professional as diagnostician employs analytical interviewing techniques to assess a patron's personal abilities, the level of information required, the appropriate type of information package, appropriate cost, and method of delivery.

2. **Prescription**: Organizing the information and processing it to meet a patron's needs.

3. **Evaluation**: Determining if the diagnosis and prescription were effective.

Although this prognosis appears rather clinical in nature and might be incomplete, it provides an important context for the LIS professional of the twenty-first century while maintaining the traditional information-giving function. The focus is on meeting a patron's special needs, solving individual problems, and seeing the library as part of a larger information system. Adopting such a model will require libraries to restructure their policies and practices to meet the needs of their various constituencies; information systems are only effective if they meet the needs of clients rather than the bureaucracy. This means that LIS professionals will need to regularly analyze the information needs of their constituencies and the organizational barriers to access. Similarly, they will need to continuously improve access to information through increased networking and by exploiting information technologies.

VI. THE TWENTY-FIRST-CENTURY LABOR FORCE: PRESENT AND FUTURE

Estimates of the librarian workforce vary, but the Bureau of Labor Statistics (2007) estimated there were approximately 158,000 librarians in the U.S. workforce in

2006. Compared to the numbers of computer scientists and systems analysts, software engineers, and computer and information systems managers, librarians are but a small fraction of information professionals. Primary, secondary, and elementary teachers currently exceed 4.4 million. Support staff in libraries (e.g., library assistants and technicians), number approximately 200,000 workers (ALA 2009b). This number is also small compared to 5.7 million information and record clerks. Combined, the size of the total library work force approaches 350,000.

Projected growth of the library workforce (see Figure 3.1, p. 114) is expected to be slow (3.6 percent through 2016) with more rapid, but still very modest, growth for library assistants (7.9 percent) and library technicians (8.5 percent), according to the Bureau of Labor Statistics (2007). This growth is substantially slower than those entering computer-related occupations. Although growth is expected to be slow, librarians as a group are aging; the median age of librarians is fifty years, with 60 percent forty-five or older (see Figure 3.2, p. 115). New employment opportunities will come from replacement rather than growth in new positions.

Matarazzo and Mika (2006) noted that librarians retire, on average, at age sixty-two, and that the number of librarians working beyond sixty-five has dramatically decreased. Based on their data, they concluded that "it is virtually impossible for the 56 ALA-accredited graduate programs in North America to replace the number of retirees, and there is no way to compensate for the over-65 librarians who retire" (p. 39). They attribute the lack of interest in librarianship as a career to a variety of factors such as noncompetitive salaries, a poor image, no bachelor's-level feeder programs, and increased interest in information science. The accuracy of their predictions, however, might be mitigated by the significant recession beginning in 2008. Its severity might affect retirement decisions and thus the actual number of openings that become available; it might also affect the decision to replace workers who retire.

A. The Persistently Low Numbers of Minority Librarians

Lack of diversity has been a consistent issue for many years (see Figure 3.3, p. 115). Diversity includes gender, age, level of education, income, religion, nationality, ethnicity, race, and types of life experiences, but a central focus has been on race and ethnicity. Most public librarians are white: less than 6 percent are African American and just over 4 percent are Hispanic (Bureau of Labor Statistics 2007). Among academic librarians, there are even fewer African Americans (4.8 percent) and Hispanics (2.7 percent) (Association of Research Libraries 2008).

Recruitment of underrepresented groups has been among the major objectives of a variety of professional associations, including the ALA, the Black Caucus of the American Library Association, REFORMA, and the Asian/Pacific American Librarians Association. The fact that underrepresentation remains suggests strongly

Figure 3.1. Employment by Occupation, 2006, and Projected 2016 Library and Information Science Occupations

Occupation	Employment		Projected Change 2006–2016 (Labor force growth)		Total Job Openings 2006–2016	Total Replacement Rate
	Number (in 000s)		Number (in 000s)	Percent	Number (in 000s)	Percent
	2006	2016				
Computer and information systems managers	264	307	43	16.4	86	16
Computer specialists	3,200	4,006	807	25.2	1,524	22
Computer programmers	435	417	−18	−4.1	91	21
Computer and information scientists, research	25	31	5	21.5	12	27
Computer systems analysts	504	650	146	29.0	280	27
Computer software engineers	857	1,181	324	37.9	449	15
Database administrators	119	154	34	28.6	47	11
Network and computer systems administrators	309	393	83	26.9	154	23
Primary, secondary, and special education teachers	4,413	4,963	550	12.5	1,578	23
Archivists, curators, and museum technicians	27	33	5	18.3	17	43
Librarians	158	164	6	3.6	49	27
Library technicians	121	132	10	8.5	69	49
Audiovisual collections specialists	7	6	−1	−13.8	1	14
Licensed practical and licensed vocational nurses	749	854	105	14.0	309	27
Information and record clerks	5,738	6,389	651	11.4	2,320	25
Library assistants, clerical	116	125	9	7.9	46	32
Printing occupations	389	343	−46	−11.9	70	18
Bookbinders and bindery workers	72	57	−15	−21.3	9	14

Source: Based on data provided by U.S. Department of Labor, Bureau of Labor Statistics, Employment Projects: Employment by Occupation, 2006 and Projected 2016.

Figure 3.2. Employed Persons by Detailed Occupation and Age, Annual Average 2007*

Occupation	Total 16+	16–19 n/%	20–24 n/%	25–34 n/%	35–44 n/%	45–54 n/%	55–64 n/%	65+ n/%	Median Age
Archivists and curators	42	0/0	2/05	10/24	9/21	10/24	9/21	3/07	46.7
Computer systems analysts and scientists	825	3/00	42/05	220/27	249/30	217/26	80/10	14/02	40.6
Receptionists and information clerks	1,441	107/07	268/18	301/21	250/17	271/19	171/12	74/05	36.7
Librarians	215	1/00	9/04	23/11	42/20	63/29	64/30	15/07	50.7
Library assistants, clerical	113	11/10	21/18	13/12	16/14	24/21	20/18	8/07	41.7
Social workers	673	9/01	46/07	159/24	15323	155/23	137/20	29/04	43.7
Teachers	8,484	106/01	641/08	1,995/24	1,988/23	2,009/24	1,466/17	281/03	42.5

Source: Bureau of Labor Statistics, Current Population Survey, 2007.
*n = numbers in thousands.

that structural aspects of the educational and employing institutions might tend to discourage minorities from applying and being retained. For example, it might be that LIS programs and employers do not devote enough energy to recruitment or there might be insufficient academic and financial support for minority students. There might, of course, be other factors as well. The master's degree requirement might disproportionately screen out minorities, who, for a variety of reasons including

Figure 3.3. Racial and Gender Characteristics of Selected Occupations, 2002

Occupation	Female (%)	Black (%)	Hispanic (%)
Librarians	83.2	6.0	4.1
Social workers	82.0	22.9	11.9
Library clerks	84.2	8.7	12.6
Teachers (excluding college)	76.0	10.1	7.1
Computer systems analysts	27.1	8.8	5.6

discrimination, have been unable to obtain higher academic degrees. Additionally, members of some ethnic and racial groups might not consider librarianship simply because they have not been introduced to it as a career option. Their experiences with libraries might have been negative, or they might have access to more highly paid career options. Demographically, the United States is increasing in its heterogeneity and the field must constantly evaluate its practices so that the library workforce reflects this heterogeneity.

B. Sex Discrimination

As noted earlier, librarians are primarily women (83 percent). An analysis of gender data in the labor force reveals a number of disturbing findings. A 2007 survey of recent library school graduates revealed that although 80 percent were women, men were paid 7.7 percent more on average. Higher salaries for male librarians were found among public, school, and academic libraries, but not special or government libraries. In addition, disproportionately fewer women were hired in academic positions, and significantly larger numbers worked in school library media centers (73 percent compared to 94 percent) (Maatta 2007).

University librarianship has traditionally been a career path with fewer women and comparatively lower salaries. The number of female librarians working in university libraries remains disproportionately low (64 percent compared to the general library workforce of approximately 83 percent). However, the proportion of female Association of Research Library (ARL) directors has risen significantly. In 2002, only 45 percent of the ARL directors were female, while today that number has risen to 57 percent (Association of Research Libraries 2002, 2008). Some salary improvement has also been observed. The overall salary for women in ARL libraries is 95.69 percent that of men; in 1980, it was 87 percent. Nonetheless, in many cases men are still paid more (ARL 2008).

C. Support Staff/Librarian Conflicts

With the proliferation of new information technologies, special competencies are needed in libraries today that were not required a decade ago. Knowledge of computer systems, mobile devices, networks, and broadband communications, including their evaluation, operation, maintenance, and replacement, has become essential for at least some library staff. Support staff, including clerical employees, paraprofessionals, bookkeepers or accountants, public relations officers, business managers, computer programmers, or systems analysts, have always played a vital role in libraries. However, the proliferation and sophistication of new technologies have increased tensions among librarians and support staff. This problem is exacerbated when library managers assign duties normally performed by librarians, such as answering reference questions, providing children's programs, and helping with the selection of materials, to support staff. When this happens, support staff understandably expect to be accorded the appropriate status and recognition. How library administrators deal with this issue can have serious implications for the morale and productivity of both their professional and support staff.

D. Generational Issues

For the first time, the library workforce includes a substantial number of workers from four generations. The potential for clashes is considerable. Downing (2006) reported that one-third of respondents in one survey reported that they had often been offended at work by someone from another generation, and that individuals in one generation believe that they are not viewed positively by individuals from other generations.

Millennials, those born since 1980, already number in the millions in today's workforce, and their influence will steadily increase. Fine (2008) noted that millennials grew up relatively sheltered by their parents. They are a relatively altruistic group who believe they can make the world better; they believe in causes. Their work style is collaborative. In addition, they are "digital natives," fluent in the use of information and communication technologies and familiar with social networking activities. They use blogs, RSS feeds, and Wikipedia. Rainie (2006) found that a typical twenty-one-year old entering the workforce today has played 5,000 hours of video games, exchanged 250,000 e-mails, instant messages, and phone text messages, and spoken on a cell phone for 10,000 hours. Millennials like to multitask, stay connected, and use technologies in a novel manner. They have grown up with

---

Motivating Millennials

1. Provide opportunities for engaging and meaningful work; millennials want to be contributors to a noble purpose.
2. De-emphasize traditional bureaucratic structure whenever possible.
3. Listen carefully; they want to be taken seriously.
4. Use communication technologies such as blogs and social networking for training and development.
5. Provide work that is project based with concrete outcomes and then reward them for the completed work.
6. Provide education and training on privacy issues. Millennials are used to posting all types of information on social networking sites and sharing information. In the organizational environment, this can have very serious and damaging consequences. Millennials must be familiar with the boundaries for sharing information in the workplace.
7. Provide opportunities for promotion, but also flexible working arrangements. Millennials tend to value a balance between home and work.

(*Source:* Downing 2006.)

third-generation video games, the World Wide Web, Palm Pilots, and i-Pods. In addition, millennials do not consider their jobs as lifetime employment, and they are not particularly comfortable in hierarchies. For each generation, certain events are defining moments. World War II defined the "matures"; for baby boomers it was the Vietnam War. The millennials are defined by 9/11 and the war on terror. In general, millennials are confident and high achieving, but under a good deal of pressure (Downing 2006). As they enter the workplace, there is great potential for a clash of cultures—the digital natives versus older "digital immigrants." The challenge for employers will be to find ways to motivate and engage millennials, while not de-motivating those from other generations.

V. SUMMARY

Information and knowledge do not organize themselves. Order must be imposed, and LIS professionals perform this valuable service using classification systems and controlled vocabularies. They also organize systems to meet information needs. The role of the LIS professional in the future will be to anticipate and satisfy the educational, recreational, and informational needs of patrons and to collect or provide access to an ever-expanding body of knowledge. The LIS professional will meet not only immediate individual needs but ensure that systems and services are effectively designed to meet future needs. The LIS professional of the future will be a needs assessor, evaluator, planner, services manager, and instructor. One might argue that this has been the role of librarians throughout history, but it is clear that the challenge and breadth of their responsibilities have grown substantially.

If LIS professionals can adapt to the changing technological and social environment, they might remain essential members of the educational, recreational, and informational (ERI) infrastructure. Although this is an exciting prospect, we must not rush to exploit this trend without considering all the consequences. There are many who see information as a commodity. From that perspective, the special knowledge and skills of LIS professionals might raise their status (at least temporarily), but Estabrook (1981) warned that this enthusiasm might be short-lived, as those with greater capital recognize the potential of information control and appropriate the information marketplace for themselves.

A more important question might be "Will the emphasis on electronic information access lead LIS professionals to neglect other obligations?" Finding information has always been part of our role but has traditionally been subsumed under larger purposes: humanistic and democratic values, and an ethic of helping or teaching people. Information provision is only one part of this function. Butler (1951) referred to these humanistic values as the "cultural motivation" of librarianship, which was "the promotion of wisdom in the individual and in the community" (p. 246). The librarian was to foster understanding and judgment within the citizenry and society. From this perspective, LIS professionals are educators, enriching the lives of others through their advice and guidance. They foster the love of reading, provide intellectual stimulation, welcome all into the world of knowledge and learning, provide instruction so that everyone can continue to grow and develop intellectually throughout their lives, and provide entertainment and diversion from an often wearying world. It is not technological competence that forms the basis of such a model; it is service to people. What makes library and information science attractive as a profession is not merely satisfying information needs but caring about people, solving human problems, and improving lives.

The LIS professional of the twenty-first century will thus be caught between needing to respond to rapidly changing modes of information access and the demands of those who require the most technologically intensive services and equipment and, at the same time, trying to satisfy the needs of traditional readers, and promoting library services among those with poor or nonexistent reading skills. But these are not incompatible obligations. Rather, the key question is whether the traditional social values of librarianship should form the context for the exploitation of information technologies, or whether the new information technologies create a new social context that changes the meaning and significance of libraries and LIS professionals.

REFERENCES

Abbott, Andrew. 1988. *The System of Professions*. Chicago: University of Chicago.

Adams, Katherine C. 2000. "Loveless Frump as Hip and Sexy Party Girl: A Reevaluation of the Old-Maid Stereotype." *Library Quarterly* 70 (July): 287–301.

Agada, John. 1984. "Studies of the Personality of Librarians." *Drexel Library Quarterly* 20 (spring): 24–45.

———. 1987. "Assertion and the Librarian Personality." In *Encyclopedia of Library and Information Science*. New York: Marcel Dekker, 128–144.

American Library Association. 1996. "ALA Policy Manual: Policy 56.1." In *ALA Handbook of Organization, 1995–96*. Chicago: ALA.

———. 2009a. *Core Competencies of Librarianship*. Chicago: ALA.

———. 2009b. "Number Employed in Libraries: Fact Sheet 2." Chicago: ALA. Available: www.ala.org/ ala/aboutala/offices/library/libraryfactsheet/alalibraryfactsheet1.cfm (accessed April 13, 2009).

———. 2009c. *President's Task Force on Library Education: Final Report*. Chicago: ALA.

———. 2010a. Office of Accreditation. "2008 Standards for Accreditation of Master's Programs in Library and Information Studies." Available: www.ala.org/ala/education careers/education/accredited programs/standards/index.cfm (accessed January 22, 2010).

———. 2010b. *Seachable Database of ALA Accredited Programs*. Available: www.ala.org/ Template.cfm?Section=lisdirb&Template=/cfapps/lisdir/index.cfm (accessed January 22, 2010).

American Society for Information Science and Technology. 2007. *ASIS&T White Paper: Accreditation of Programs for the Education of Information Professionals*. October 20.

Apostle, Richard, and Boris Raymond. 1997. *Librarianship and the Information Paradigm*. Lanham, MD: Scarecrow.

Association of Research Libraries. 2002. *ARL Statistics 2002–03*. Edited by Martha Kyrrillidou, Mark Young. Washington, DC: ARL.

———. 2008. *ARL Statistics 2007–08*. Edited by Martha Kyrrillidou, Mark Young, and Jason Barber. Washington, DC: ARL.

Association for Library and Information Science Educators. 2000. *Educating Library and Information Science Professionals for a New Century: The KALIPER Report: Executive Summary*. Reston, VA: ALISE.

———. 2009. *Library and Information Science Education Statistical Report 2006*. Edited by Jerry D. Saye. Chicago: ALISE.

Ball, Mary Alice. 2008. "Practicums and Service Learning." *Journal of Education for Library and Information Science* 49 (winter): 70–81.

Baruchson-Arbib, Shifra, and Jenny Bronstein. 2002. "A View to the Future of the Library and Information Science Profession: A Delphi Study." *Journal of the American Society for Information Science and Technology* 53 (March): 397–408.

Birdsall, William F. 1982. "Librarianship, Professionalism and Social Change." *Library Journal* 107 (February 1): 223–226.

Boyce, Bert R. 1994. "The Death of Library Education." *American Libraries* (March): 257–259.

Brand, Barbara B. 1996. "Pratt Institute Library School: The Perils of Professionalization." In *Reclaiming the American Library Past: Writing the Women In*. Edited by Suzanne Hildenbrand. Norwood, NJ: Ablex, 251–278.

Bryan, Alice. 1952. *The Public Librarian*. New York: Columbia University.

Bureau of Labor Statistics. 2007. "Employment by Occupation, 2006 and Projected 2016." *Monthly Labor Review* 9 (November). Available: www.bls.gov/emp/mlrappendix.pdf (accessed January 22, 2010).

Butler, Pierce. 1951. "Librarianship as a Profession." *Library Quarterly* 21 (October): 235–247.

Campbell, Jerry D. 1993. "Choosing to Have a Future." *American Libraries* 24 (June): 560–566.

Campbell, Lucy B. 1977. "The Hampton Institute Library School." In *Handbook of Black Librarianship*. Edited by E. J. Josey and Ann Shockley Allen. Littleton, CO: Libraries Unlimited, 35–46.

Carey, James O., and Vicki L. Gregory. 2002. "Students' Perceptions of Academic Motivation, Interactive Participation, and Selected Pedagogical and Structural Factors in Web-Based Distance Learning." *Journal of Education for Library and Information Science* 43 (winter): 6–15.

Chu, Heting. 2006. "Curricula of LIS Programs in the USA: A Content Analysis." In *Proceedings of the Asia-Pacific Conference on Library and Information Education and Practice 2006 (A-LIEP 2006), Singapore, 3–6 April 2006*. Edited by C. Khoo, D. Singh, and A. S. Chaudhry. Singapore: School of Communication and Information, Nanyang Technological University, 328–337.

Conrad, Clifton F., and Kim Rapp-Hanretta. 2002. "Positioning Master's Programs in Library and Information Science: A Template for Avoiding Pitfalls and Seizing Opportunities in Light of Key External and Internal Forces." *Journal of Education in Library and Information Science* 43 (spring): 92–104.

Cronin, Blaise. 1995. "Cutting the Gordian Knot." *Information Processing and Management* 31 (November): 897–902.

Crowley, Bill. 2008. *Renewing Professional Librarianship: A Fundamental Rethinking*. Westport, CT: Libraries Unlimited.

Davis, Donald G. Jr. 1978. "Curtis, Florence Rising." In *Dictionary of American Library Biography*. Edited by Bohdan S. Wynar. Littleton, CO: Libraries Unlimited, 108–109.

Debons, A. 1985. "The Information Professional: A Survey." In *The Information Profession. Proceedings of a Conference Held in Melbourne, Australia (November 26–28, 1984)*. Edited by James Henri and Roy Sanders. Melbourne, Australia: Centre for Library Studies.

De Rosa et al. 2005. *Perceptions of Libraries and Information Resources*. Dublin, OH: OCLC.

De Rosa, Cathy, and Jenny Johnson. 2008. *From Awareness to Funding: A Study of Library Support in America*. Dublin, OH: OCLC.

Dewey, Melvil. 1989. "The Profession." *Library Journal* 114 (June 15): 5. Reprinted from *American Library Journal* 1 (1876).

Dillon, Andrew, and April Norris. 2005. "Crying Wolf: An Examination and Reconsideration of the Perception of Crisis in LIS Education." *Journal of Education for Library and Information Science* 46 (fall): 280–298.

Downing, Kris. 2006. "Next Generation: What Leaders Need to Know about the Millennials." *Leadership in Action (LIA)* 26 (July/August): 3–6.

Estabrook, Leigh. 1981. "Productivity, Profit, and Libraries." *Library Journal* 106 (July): 1377–1380.

———. 2005. "Crying Wolf: A Response." *Journal of Education for Library and Information Science* 46 (fall): 299–303.

Fine, Allison. 2008. "It's Time to Focus on a New Generation." *Chronicle of Philanthropy* 20 (August 21): 22.

Fisher, David P. 1988. "Is the Librarian a Distinct Personality Type?" *Journal of Librarianship* 20 (January): 36–47.

Gambee, Budd L. 1978. "Fairchild, Mary Salome Cutler." In *Dictionary of American Library Biography*. Edited by Bohdan S. Wynar. Littleton, CO: Libraries Unlimited, 167–170.

Gardner, Howard, and Lee S. Shulman. 2005. "The Professions in America Today." *Daedalus* 134 (summer): 13–18.

Garrison, Dee. 1972–1973. "The Tender Technicians: The Feminization of Public Librarianship." *Journal of Social History* 6 (winter): 131–156.

Gorman, Michael. 2004. "What Ails Library Education?" *Journal of Academic Librarianship* 30 (March): 99–100.

Greiner, Tony. 2008. "Diversity and the MLS." *Library Journal* 133 (May 1): 36.

Grotzinger, Laurel A. 1966. *The Power and the Dignity: Librarianship and Katharine Sharp*. New York: Scarecrow.

———. 1978a. "Kroeger, Alice Bertha." In *Dictionary of American Library Biography*. Edited by Bohdan S. Wynar. Littleton, CO: Libraries Unlimited, 295–298.

————. 1978b. "Sharp, Katharine Lucinda." In *Dictionary of American Library Biography*. Edited by Bohdan S. Wynar. Littleton, CO: Libraries Unlimited, 470–473.

Harris, Roma M. 1992. *Librarianship: The Erosion of a Woman's Profession*. Norwood, NJ: Ablex.

Hauptman, Robert. 1987. "Iconoclastic Education: The Library Science Degree." *Catholic Library World* 58 (May–June): 252–253.

Heim, Kathleen, and Leigh Estabrook. 1983. *Career Profiles and Sex Discrimination in the Library Profession*. Chicago: ALA.

Hildenbrand, Suzanne. 1989. "'Women's Work' within Librarianship." *Library Journal* 114 (September 1): 153–155.

————. 1992. "A Historical Perspective on Gender Issues in American Librarianship." *Canadian Journal of Information Science* 17 (September): 18–28.

————. 1996. "Women in Library History: From the Politics of Library History to the History of Library Politics." In *Reclaiming the American Library Past: Writing the Women In*. Edited by Suzanne Hildenbrand. Norwood, NJ: Ablex, 1–23.

Holley, Edward G. 1984. "The Merwine Case and the MLS: Where Was ALA?" *American Libraries* 15 (May 1984): 327–330.

Karlowich, Robert A., and Nasser Sharify. 1978. "Plummer, Mary Wright." In *Dictionary of American Library Biography*. Edited by Bohdan S. Wynar. Littleton, CO: Libraries Unlimited, 399–402.

King, John Leslie. 2005. "Stepping Up: Shaping the Future of the Field." Plenary Address, Association for Library and Information Science Education Conference, Boston, MA, January 11–14, 2005. Available: http://dlist.sir.arizona.edu/739/ (accessed January 22, 2010).

————. 2006. "Identity in the I-School Movement." *Bulletin of the American Society for Information Science and Technology* 32 (April/May): 13–15.

Kuhn, Thomas S. 1970. *The Structure of Scientific Revolutions*. 2nd ed. Chicago: University of Chicago Press.

Logan, Elisabeth, Rebecca Augustyniak, and Alison Rees. 2002. "Distance Education as Different Education: A Student-Centered Investigation of Distance Learning Experience." *Journal of Education for Library and Information Science* 43 (winter): 32–42.

Lynch, Beverly P. 1989. "Education and Training of Librarians." In *Rethinking the Library in the Information Age*. Washington, DC: U.S. GPO, 75–92.

Maack, Mary Niles. 1986. "Women in Library Education: Down the Up Staircase." *Library Trends* 34 (winter): 401–431.

————. 1997. "Toward a New Model of the Information Professions: Embracing Empowerment." *Journal of Education for Library and Information Science* 38 (fall): 283–302.

Maatta, Stephanie. 2007. "What's an MLIS Worth?" *Library Journal* 132 (October 15): 30–38.

Main, Linda. 1990. "Research versus Practice: A 'No' Contest." *RQ* 30 (winter): 226–228.

Marco, Guy. 1994. "The Demise of the American Core Curriculum." *Libri* 44: 175–189.

Markey, Karen. 2004. "Current Educational Trends in the Information and Library Science Curriculum." *Journal of Education for Library and Information Science* 45 (fall): 317–339.

Matarazzo, James M., and Joseph J. Mika. 2006. "How to Be Popular." *American Libraries* (September): 38–40.

McCook, Kathleen de la Peña, and Paula Geist. 1993. "Diversity Deferred: Where Are the Minority Librarians?" *Library Journal* 118 (November 1): 35–38.

McPheeters, Annie L. 1988. *Library Service in Black and White: Some Personal Recollections, 1921–1980*. Metuchen, NJ: Scarecrow.

Miksa, Francis L. 1992. "Library and Information Science: Two Paradigms." In *Conceptions of Library and Information Science: Historical, Empirical and Theoretical Perspectives*. Edited by Pertti Vakkari and Blaise Cronin. London: Taylor Graham, 229–252.

Morrisey, Locke J., and Donald O. Case. 1988. "'There Goes My Image.' The Perception of Male Librarians by Colleague, Student, and Self." *College and Research Libraries* 49 (September): 453–464.

Olson, Gary M., and Jonathan Grudin. 2009. "The Information School Phenomenon." *Interactions* (March–April): 15–19.

Paris, Marion. 1988. *Library School Closings: Four Case Studies*. Metuchen, NJ: Scarecrow.

"Projecting Librarians' Roles." 2002. *Library Journal* 127 (February 1): 48.

Radford, Marie L., and Gary P. Radford. 2003. "Librarians and Party Girls: Cultural Studies and the Meaning of the Librarian." *Library Quarterly* 73: 54–69.

Rainie, Lee. 2006. "Digital 'Natives' Invade the Workplace." Available: http://pewresearch .org/pubs/70/digital-natives-invade-the-workplace (accessed January 22, 2010).

Rayward, W. Boyd. 1983. "Library and Information Sciences: Disciplinary Differentiation, Competition, Convergence." In *The Study of Information: Disciplinary Messages*. Edited by Fritz Machlup and Una Mansfield. New York: Wiley, 343–363.

Rice, James. 1989. "The Hidden Role of Librarians." *Library Journal* 114 (January): 57–59.

Robbins-Carter, Jane, and Charles A. Seavey. 1986. "The Master's Degree: Basic Preparation for Professional Practice." *Library Trends* 34 (spring): 561–580.

Roberts, Norman, and Tania Konn. 1991. *Librarians and Professional Status: Continuing Professional Development and Academic Libraries*. London: Library Association.

Saracevic, Tefko. 1994. "Closing of Library Schools in North America: What Role Accreditation?" *Libri* 44 (November): 190–200.

Scherdin, Mary Jane. 1994. "Vive la Difference: Exploring Librarian Personality Types Using the MBTI." In *Discovering Librarians*. Edited by Mary Jane Scherdin. Chicago: ACRL, 125–156.

Schuman, Patricia Glass. 1990. "The Image of Librarians: Substance or Shadow?" *Journal of Academic Librarianship* 16: 86–89.

Stoffle, Carla J., and Kim Leeder. 2005. "Practitioners and Library Education: A Crisis of Understanding." *Journal of Education for Library and Information Science* 46 (fall): 312–318.

Swisher, Robert, Rosemary Ruhig DuMont, and Calvin J. Boyer. 1985. "The Motivation to Manage: A Study of Academic Librarians and Library Science Students." *Library Trends* 34 (fall): 219–234.

U.S. Office of Education. 1876. *Public Libraries in the United States of America: Their History, Condition, and Management: Special Report*. Washington, DC: GPO.

Van Fleet, Connie, and June Lester. 2008. "Is Anyone Listening? Use of Library Competencies Statements in State and Public Libraries." *Public Libraries* (July/August): 42–53.

Van House, Nancy, and Stuart A. Sutton. 2000. "The Panda Syndrome." *Journal of Education for Library and Information Science* 41 (winter): 52–68.

Vann, Sarah K. 1961. *Training for Librarianship before 1923*. Chicago: ALA.

Web-Based Information Science Education. 2009. *Strategic Plan*. Syracuse, NY: WISE.

Weibel, Kathleen, and Kathleen M. Heim. 1979. *The Role of Women in Librarianship 1876–1976: The Entry, Advancement, and Struggle for Equalization in One Profession.* Phoenix: Oryx.

White, Carl M. 1976. *A Historical Introduction to Library Education: Problems and Progress to 1951.* New York: Scarecrow.

White, Herbert S. 1986. "The Future of Library and Information Science Education." *Journal of Education for Library and Information Science* 26 (winter): 174–181.

Wiegand, Wayne A. 1996. *Irrepressible Reformer: A Biography of Melvil Dewey*. Chicago: ALA.

———. 1997. "Out of Sight, Out of Mind: Why Don't We Have Any Schools of Library and Reading Studies?" *Journal of Education for Library and Information Science* 38 (fall): 314–326.

———. 1999. "The Structure of Librarianship: Essay on an Information Profession." *Canadian Journal of Information and Library Science* 24 (April): 17–37.

———. 2001. "Missing the Real Story: Where Library and Information Science Fails the Library Profession." In *The Readers' Advisors' Companion*. Edited by Kenneth D. Shearer and Robert Turgin. Englewood, CO: Libraries Unlimited.

———. 2005. "Critiquing the Curriculum." *American Libraries* 36 (January): 60–61.

Wilde, Michelle L., and Annie Epperson. 2006. "A Survey of Alumni of LIS Distance Education Programs: Experiences and Implications." *Journal of Academic Librarianship* 32 (May): 238–250.

Williamson, Charles C. 1923. *Training for Library Service: A Report Prepared for the Carnegie Corporation of New York*. Boston: Updike.

Williamson, J. M., A. E. Pemberton, and J. W. Lounsbury. 2008. "Personality Traits of Individuals in Different Specialties of Librarianship." *Journal of Documentation* 64: 273–286.

Windsor, Justin. 1876. "A Word to Starters of Libraries." *American Library Journal* 1 (September): 1–3.

Winter, Michael F. 1988. *The Culture and Control of Expertise: Toward a Sociological Understanding of Librarianship*. Westport, CT: Greenwood.

Zemon, Mickey, and Alice Harrison Bahr. 2005. "Career and/or Children: Do Female Academic Librarians Pay a Price for Motherhood?" *College and Research Libraries* 66 (September): 394–405.

SELECTED READINGS: THE LIS PROFESSION

Books

Abbott, Andrew. *The System of Professions*. Chicago: University of Chicago, 1988.

Bobinski, George S. *Libraries and Librarianship: Sixty Years of Challenge and Change, 1945–2005*. Lanham, MD: Scarecrow, 2007.

Budd, John. *Self-Examination: The Present and Future of Librarianship*. Westport, CT: Libraries Unlimited, 2008.

Crowley, William A. *Renewing Professional Librarianship*. Westport, CT: Libraries Unlimited, 2008.

Greer, Roger C., Robert J. Grover, and Susan G. Fowler. *Introduction to the Library and Information Professions*. Westport, CT: Libraries Unlimited, 2007.

Harris, Michael H., Stan A. Hannah, and Pamela C. Harris. *Into the Future: The Foundations of Library and Information Services in the Post-industrial Era*. 2nd ed. Greenwich, CT: Ablex, 1998.

Harris, Roma M. *Librarianship: The Erosion of a Woman's Profession*. Norwood, NJ: Ablex, 1992.

Leckie, Gloria, and John E. Buschman, eds. *Information Technology in Librarianship: New Critical Approaches*. Westport, CT: Libraries Unlimited, 2009.

Vann, Sarah K. *Training for Librarianship before 1923*. Chicago: ALA, 1961.

Winter, Michael F. *The Culture and Control of Expertise: Toward a Sociological Understanding of Librarianship*. Westport, CT: Greenwood, 1988.

Articles

Abram, Stephen. "An Open Letter to My New Peers: You're the Profession's Future." *Information Outlook* 12 (May 2008): 46–48.

Adams, Katherine C. "Loveless Frump as Hip and Sexy Party Girl: A Reevaluation of the Old-Maid Stereotype." *Library Quarterly* 70 (July 2000): 287–301.

Bobinski, George S. "Is the Library Profession Over-Organized?" *American Libraries* 31 (October 2000): 58–61.

Cronin, Blaise. "The Sociological Turn in Information Science." *Journal of Information Science* 34 (2008): 465–475.

Crowley, Bill, and Bill Brace. "The Control and Direction of Professional Education." *Journal of the American Society for Information Science* 50 (1999): 1127–1135.

———. "Lifecycle Librarianship." *Library Journal* 133 (April 2008): 46–48.

Danner, Richard A. "Redefining a Profession." *Law Library Journal* 90 (1998): 315–356.

Dawson, Alma. "Celebrating African-American Librarians and Librarianship." *Library Trends* 49 (summer 2000): 40–87.

Dillon, Andrew, and April Norris. "Crying Wolf: An Examination and Reconsideration of the Perception of Crisis in LIS Education." *Journal of Education for Library and Information* 46 (fall 2005): 280–297.

Garrison, Dee. "The Tender Technicians: The Feminization of Public Librarianship." *Journal of Social History* 6 (winter 1972–1973): 131–159.

Gorman, Michael. "Whither Library Education?" *New Library World* 105 (2004): 376–380.

Harman, Kenneth E. "From a Distance." *American Libraries* 40 (October 2009): 48–51.

Helmick, Catherine, and Keith Swigger. "Core Competencies of Library Practitioners." *Public Libraries* 45 (March–April 2006): 54–69.

Kim, Kyung-Sun, and Sei-Ching Joanna Sin. "Increasing Ethnic Diversity in LIS: Strategies Suggested by Librarians of Color." *Library Quarterly* 78 (April 2008): 153–177.

King, John Leslie. "Identity in the I-School Movement." *Bulletin of ASIST* 32 (April/May 2006): 13–15.

Maack, Mary Niles. "Women in Library Education: Down the Up Staircase." *Library Trends* 34 (winter 1986): 401–432.

Maatta, Stephanie. "What's an MLIS Worth?" *Library Journal* 132 (October 15, 2007): 30–38.

Miksa, Francis L. "Library and Information Science: Two Paradigms." In *Conceptions of Library and Information Science: Historical, Empirical and Theoretical Perspectives.* Edited by Pertti Vakkari and Blaise Cronin. London: Taylor Graham, 1992, 229–252.

Mulvaney, John Philip, and Dan O'Connor. "The Crux of Our Crisis." *American Libraries* 37 (June/July 2006): 3840.

Nardini, Robert F. "A Search for Meaning: American Library Metaphors: 1876–1926." *Library Quarterly* 71 (April 2001): 111–149.

Seavey, Charles A. "The Coming Crisis in Education for Librarianship." *American Libraries* 36 (October 2005): 54–56.

Singer, Paula, and Jeanne Goodrich. "Retaining and Motivating High-Performance Employees." *Public Libraries* 45 (January–February 2006): 58–63.

Stoffle, Carla J., and Kim Leeder. "Practitioners and Library Education: A Crisis of Understanding." *Journal of Education for Library and Information Science* 46 (fall 2005): 312–319.

Van House, Nancy, and Stuart A. Sutton. "The Panda Syndrome." *Journal of Education for Library and Information Science* 41 (winter 2000): 52–68.

Wiegand, Wayne. "Dewey Declassified: A Revelatory Look at the 'Irrepressible Reformer.'" *American Libraries* 27 (January 1996): 54–60.

Zwadlo, Jim. "We Don't Need a Philosophy of Library and Information Science—We're Confused Enough Already." *Library Quarterly* 67 (April 1997): 103–121.

4

The Organization of Information: Techniques and Issues

I. INTRODUCTION

Considering the quantity of information available today, and the inevitable and explosive growth of information in the future, the challenge of organizing all this information and making it accessible is daunting. As we noted earlier, a library's primary purpose is to acquire, store, organize, preserve, disseminate, or otherwise provide access to materials and information already produced. The library itself is a type of retrieval system. Any retrieval system has at least two parts: a database and a system for retrieving the information in the database. A library's database includes all of its contents: the books, periodicals, audiovisual materials, and other items in the collection. The retrieval system includes the hardware, software, rules, policies, and management practices by which that content can be accessed. Systems to organize all this content can be simple and straightforward, such as organization by the type of media used to record the information (e.g., print, sound, or image); by type of user (e.g., children, adults, vision impaired); by genre (e.g., westerns, jazz, impressionism); or even by size (e.g., oversize). Obviously, except in the smallest of collections, however, such general forms of organization will not be sufficient to locate most materials effectively. A primary tool in a library's retrieval system is the library catalog, governed by a sophisticated classification scheme consisting of alphabetical and numerical rules. Although it is sometimes difficult to locate information or items in libraries, what is truly remarkable is that, despite the incredible range and diversity of information they contain, the correct information is usually located in a relatively short period of time. This is due in large part to the intricate systems and techniques that have been developed over time to organize the content of libraries.

An important aspect of information retrieval, which constitutes an important focus of this chapter, is the concept of access points. Those designing the information systems create access points that are then used to locate the desired material or information. Types of access include author, title, and subject headings in a bibliographic record, or they can be something as simple as a sign indicating subject area or the range of classification numbers located on a shelf. Access points can also be human, such as reference librarians.

Intellectual technologies are another tool important to information retrieval. LIS professionals use intellectual technologies to arrange knowledge in ways that promote its retrieval. The organizing principles must be relatively easy to apply and easy to understand by both LIS professionals and users, and they must reflect, to the greatest extent possible, the way that people ordinarily seek information. Understanding the individual information seeker is an essential variable. Individuals seek information with their own idiosyncratic mental constructs, and no system can account for all of these constructs. In other words, no particular organizing system will satisfy every information seeker's needs perfectly (Mann 1993). Nonetheless, LIS professionals, by use of their intellectual tools, provide an efficient means of retrieving a vast amount of information.

A complete discussion of knowledge organization is not practical in this chapter. The primary discussion, therefore, centers on five of the key intellectual tools used in libraries to organize information: (1) classification systems; (2) controlled vocabularies including thesauri and lists of subject headings such as the Library of Congress Subject Headings; (3) the library catalog based on the Anglo-American Cataloging Rules (AACR2); (4) indexes, abstracts, and bibliographies; and (5) electronic databases. These tools are not exclusive to libraries, nor are they mutually exclusive; indeed, some rely heavily on others. For example, the library catalog and electronic databases rely heavily on controlled vocabulary. Following a review of these tools, some of the challenges related to organizing information on the Web are discussed.

II. CLASSIFICATION SYSTEMS

Retrieval by discipline and subject is fundamental to information access. Discipline and subject are closely related but distinct concepts. Put simply, a subject is what an item is about; a discipline is a related body of knowledge that defines a particular approach. Take, for example, the subject of the origin of the human species. A book that examines that subject from scriptural text is placed within the discipline of religion; a book that focuses on physical processes and evolution is placed in the biosciences: same subject, different disciplines. Despite these differences, however, disciplines and subjects

Access by discipline and subject is fundamental to information access. A subject is what an item is about; a discipline is a related body of knowledge that defines a particular approach.

share many similarities when it comes to searching for information. Two tools that provide access to subjects and disciplines are considered here: classification systems and controlled vocabularies.

One of the primary intellectual technologies or organizing principles used by LIS professionals is called classification, "the process of organizing knowledge into some systematic order" (Chan 2007, p. 309). Classification provides "a descriptive and explanatory framework for ideas and a structure of the relationships among the ideas" (Kwasnik 1992, p. 63). Classification schemes attempt to identify knowledge and the interrelationships among knowledge. In this way, one is connected not only to a specific item, but also to other items on the same subject, or items on related subjects. Good classification systems reflect the interconnectedness of ideas; they not only help individuals locate specific material on a shelf but also help them to think about related aspects of their topic. By placing items addressing the same or related subjects in the same physical area, a concept called collocation, people can discover items of similar interest through browsing.

Two classification systems dominate in American libraries: Dewey Decimal Classification (DDC) and Library of Congress Classification (LCC). These tools were devised originally to organize books—the traditional medium for information. In more recent times they have been adapted for use with other media. Suffice it to say, these systems are quite complex, and the following discussion is meant only to highlight a few of their major characteristics.

A. Dewey Decimal Classification

The most widely used classification system in the world is DDC, which has formed the foundation of organization in American libraries since 1876, when it was first proposed by Melvil Dewey. It is used in 200,000 libraries around the globe and in 95 percent of all U.S. public and school libraries, a quarter of all college and university libraries, and one-fifth of all special libraries (OCLC 2004).

DDC arranges items and collections of items in a logical fashion using Arabic numerals. It divides knowledge into ten main classes representing traditional academic disciplines that are intended to encompass the universe of knowledge. Each class is assigned a specific numerical range. The main classes are shown in Figure 4.1 (see p. 130).

Each item that falls within the scope of a class is assigned a number within the designated numerical range, called a class number. The internal logic within a main classification is hierarchical: that is, within a main discipline or class, there are subclasses or subdivisions, and the subclasses are further subdivided with greater and greater specificity. Each subclass is assigned a range of numbers within the range of the main class. For example, items about the home and family management are classed in the 640s. Items assigned a number in the 641s deal with food and drink, while those dealing with household furnishings are classed in the 645s (Mitchell et al. 1996, pp. 363–377). The class number becomes longer as the subclass of the discipline becomes more specific. To this end, decimals are used.

Figure 4.1. Dewey Decimal Classification Main Classes
000   Generalities
100   Philosophy, Parapsychology and Occultism, Psychology
200   Religion
300   Social Sciences
400   Language
500   Natural Sciences and Mathematics
600   Technology (Applied Sciences)
700   The Arts
800   Literature (Belles Lettres) and Rhetoric
900   Geography, History, and Auxiliary Disciplines

Hence, the number 795 applies to games of chance, 795.4 to card games, 795.41 to "games in which skill is a major element," and 795.412 to poker (Mitchell et al. 1996, pp. 731–732). The length of the decimal notation can extend many digits, reflecting highly detailed subdivisions of a discipline.

DDC is a remarkable system for organizing both physical and intellectual materials and has served library users for more than a century. Interestingly, although DDC affects the physical location of items, a key feature is that it provides for a relative location rather than a fixed one. Before DDC, books in libraries were numbered based on a specific, fixed physical location. In DDC, the numbers are related not to a particular place, but to other books (Chan 2007). Hence, the physical location of materials can change as long as the books remain in appropriate relation to each other (any shelver shifting books will tell you this). In online library catalogs, the same function remains for locating and exploring library materials in virtual spaces.

This is not to say that DDC is without problems. One major problem is that the system is closed; the range of numbers is limited between 000 and 999, and the disciplines they designate have already been assigned. New disciplines must be accommodated within the existing ten classes, and in many cases this is not easy. Disciplines that were just emerging or unknown a hundred years ago today must be crowded into narrow ranges. For example, the growth of the social sciences in the twentieth century and, more recently, the introduction of computers have necessitated considerable modifications. DDC has been revised many times, but the changes entail substantial work on the part of library staff. A second problem is that DDC places heavy emphasis on knowledge created and disseminated in European and North American culture, reflecting the nineteenth-century biases from which the system emerged. There has been a concerted effort to remove Christian and Western biases from the system, and the latest edition (the twenty-second) continues this effort. Most other classification systems also share these difficulties.

\multicolumn{4}{c}{**Figure 4.2. Library of Congress Main Classes**}			

A	General Works	L	Education
B	Philosophy; Psychology and Religion	M	Music
C	Auxiliary Sciences of History	N	Fine Arts
D	General and Old World History	P	Language and Literature Tables
E–F	American History	Q	Science
G	Geography; Maps; Anthropology; Recreation	R	Medicine
		S	Agriculture
H	Social Sciences; Economics and Sociology	T	Technology
		U	Military Science
J	Political Science	V	Naval Science
K	Law (General)	Z	Bibliography; Library Science

B. Library of Congress Classification

LCC developed at the turn of the century to deal with the ever-growing collection at the Library of Congress. Other libraries that often adopt LCC tend to be academic libraries or research libraries with large collections. Although DDC and other existing classification systems influenced the development of LCC, the system is unique. LCC is an alphanumeric system. Each class number begins with one to three letters followed by one to four integers. Decimals can be used to expand the class. The letters represent the main class and subclass divisions followed by the integers that further subordinate the discipline. Hence a notation that begins with the letter P deals with language and literature, while PT stands for German literature. There are twenty main classes, as shown in Figure 4.2, with specific subclasses under the main classes. For example, under class K (law), there are specific schedules for laws of the United States, Germany, United Kingdom and Ireland, Latin America, and Canada.

C. Classification and Shelf Arrangement

The manner in which a library physically arranges its collection plays a critical role in the ability of the user to retrieve the desired information and browse related materials. The arrangements must take into account a wide variety of subjects, formats, and uses. Theoretically, a library could assign accurate and highly precise classification numbers to items but arrange the materials on the shelf randomly, ignoring the benefits of the classification system. Such randomness might promote serendipity but it is hardly efficient retrieval. Fortunately, shelf arrangement in libraries is not random and reflects a variety of organizational models, predominately alphabetical, numerical, and disciplinary.

Most library collections begin with the premise that items on the same subject or from the same discipline should be shelved together. Because disciplines are designated by numerical notations (DDC) or alphanumeric notations (LC), subject proximity is created through the alphabetical/numerical sequences arranged hierarchically from broader to narrower within disciplines or topics. Alphabetical arrangement predominates in fiction collections in public libraries, which are usually arranged in alphabetical order by author's last name and not generally classified by number. It should also be noted that discipline affects the arrangement even when the numbers for the disciplines are not sequential. For example, one might place language materials and literature together (grouping 800s and 400s in Dewey), because users of one are also frequent users of the other. Other models of knowledge organization are usually more general, but certainly quite common. For example, collections might be organized by (1) type of materials (indexes, general reference materials, periodicals); (2) format (videocassettes, audiocassettes, computer software, microforms, print materials); or (3) user (children's, young adult, adult, vision impaired).

III. CONTROLLED VOCABULARIES

A second crucial intellectual technology is controlled vocabulary, which is "a list of terms that have been enumerated explicitly. This list is controlled by and is available from a controlled vocabulary registration authority. All terms in a controlled vocabulary must have an unambiguous, non-redundant definition" (National Information Standards Organization [NISO] 2005, p. 5). Vocabulary control is "the process of organizing a list of terms (a) to indicate which of two or more synonymous terms is authorized for use; (b) to distinguish between homographs; and (c) to indicate hierarchical and associate relationships among terms in the context of a controlled vocabulary or subject heading list" (NISO 2005, p. 10).

Decisions about which terms will be used to refer to authors, titles, or subjects are referred to as authority control. With authority control, one term is selected for use. The list of accepted terms used in a controlled vocabulary is referred to as an authority list. Authority control extends beyond the words or vocabulary itself; it also includes the rules for assigning terms, methods for describing relationships among terms, and a means for changing and updating terms (Meadows 1992).

Controlled vocabularies are critical, especially when seeking subject-related information, because they provide consistency in the assignment and use of subject terms or headings, as well as name and title terms. Controlled vocabularies, such as lists of subject headings and thesauri, are vital for effective searching and for the collocation function of the library catalog. People use a controlled vocabulary when consulting subject headings in a catalog, when consulting the index terms in a periodicals index, or when searching a computerized bibliographic database. The following are some of the issues addressed by controlled vocabularies:

1. **Synonymy**: A variety of terms can mean the same thing. Organizers of information must select and consistently apply the same term so that people can retrieve information effectively. Those selecting such terms also can create additional access points by using terms synonymous with the one selected for use, such as "see" references in the catalog. For example, if the term selected is "guns" there might also be a "see firearms" reference.

2. **Hierarchical relationships**: Controlled vocabularies can reveal when a topic identified by a particular term is part of a larger concept or when it can be narrowed further, such as references to broader terms or narrower terms.

3. **Associative relationships**: Controlled vocabularies help identify related terms (concepts) that can broaden and enrich an information search.

4. **Homographs**: Sometimes terms spelled the same way might represent different concepts. Controlled vocabularies reveal this ambiguity and refer information seekers to the appropriate terms, such as "China (country)" versus "china (table setting)."

It is easy to see why controlled vocabularies are important. Consider the problem of synonymy. Suppose there was no vocabulary control for the subject headings related to entries on aircraft. Catalogers could choose any number of terms such as aircraft, airplanes, planes, or flying machines to describe the content of various items on this subject. A person would then need to look in at least four places in the catalog to find all the material, if he or she could think of each of these terms. Clearly, if different terms are assigned to describe the same content in different items, it becomes very difficult to retrieve those items. Controlled vocabularies reduce error and ambiguity and guide people to the proper place by showing relationships between terms. For example, when someone consults a given term, the controlled vocabulary might suggest additional terms that are broader or narrower, or give the equivalent term used by the controlled vocabulary. Examples of these relationships are discussed further in the context of the Library of Congress Subject Headings.

A. Thesauri

A critical tool intended to promote retrieval of information through the use of a controlled vocabulary is the thesaurus, (not to be confused with the glossary type of thesaurus such as *Roget's Thesaurus*), which is a "controlled vocabulary arranged in a known order and structured so that the various relationships among terms are displayed clearly and identified by standardized relationship indicators" (NISO 2005, p. 9). Indexers and catalogers use thesauri to determine precisely what terms to assign as access points to a record or document. Individuals can also refer to these thesauri to identify the proper terms for searching or to discover related terms and subjects prior to using indexes, catalogs, and databases. According to NISO, thesauri and other types of controlled vocabularies accomplish five purposes:

> (1) Translation: To provide a means for translating the natural language of authors, indexers, and users into a controlled vocabulary that can be used for indexing and retrieval; (2) Consistency: To promote uniformity in term format and in the assignment of terms; (3) Indication of relationships: To indicate semantic relationships among terms; (4) Label and browse: To provide consistent and clear hierarchies in a navigation system to help users locate desired content objects; (5) Retrieval: To serve as a searching aid in locating content objects. (NISO 2005, p. 11)

Thus thesauri play critical roles in structuring access as well as information retrieval.

Thesauri list core index terms, usually single words referred to as descriptors, but sometimes combinations of words, phrases, or names. The list of core terms indicates the preferred terms to represent and provide access to concepts in the catalog, index, or database. In addition, many equivalent, but non-preferred terms are also identified, which will direct a user to the preferred term. These are sometimes referred to as lead-in terms. Lead-in terms are critical because most people trying to gain access to a particular information system are often unaware of the preferred terms. They come with their own vocabulary and ideas about which terms describe the subject matter. The value of the thesaurus is also enriched by suggesting associated concepts and their relationships. Although thesauri have existed for many years, they have become especially important in conjunction with automated information retrieval systems, such as the ERIC Thesaurus and INSPEC Thesaurus.

B. Subject Heading Lists

Subject headings provide another critical access point for finding information. The list of subject headings of greatest importance for American libraries is the Library of Congress Subject Headings (LCSH). LCSH serves as an authoritative source not only for library catalogs but also for many indexes around the world. Among its significant advantages is that it controls terms for both the information organizer (e.g., cataloger or indexer) and the information seeker (the patron or librarian).

Subject headings have a special relationship to the classification system. Classification puts subjects into the context of disciplines. For example, information on horses can appear in an animal class (zoology), in sports (horse racing), and in pets. Subject headings, in contrast, list subjects outside a disciplinary context, so a search on horses retrieves items about horses regardless of disciplinary context. Subject headings act as a kind of index to the classification scheme. That is, by identifying a subject through a subject heading, one also discovers the classification number or numbers assigned to that subject.

The Library of Congress developed LCSH to provide access to its own collections, but they are widely used, in part, because they are one of the few general (nondisciplinary) controlled vocabularies in English. LC uses these headings in MARC records (discussed below), which means that any organization that uses MARC records also benefits from the LCSH.

The subject headings are arranged alphabetically. Among the types of headings used are (1) single noun or term (e.g., lifeguards), (2) adjective with a noun (e.g., life-saving apparatus), (3) prepositional phrases (e.g., lifesaving at fires), (4) compound or conjunctive phrases (e.g., lifting and carrying), and (5) phrases or sentences (see Figure 4.3, pp. 136–137). The headings can also include subheadings by time (e.g., nineteenth century), geography (e.g., France), or form of item (e.g., dictionary).

The dominance of these subject headings highlights their importance in providing effective and complete access to library collections. As with all controlled vocabularies, LCSH employ a syndetic structure that links related terms as discussed earlier in relation to thesauri. For example, for the subject heading "life-saving apparatus" there is a reference to a broader term (BT), "survival and emergency equipment," and a narrower term (NT), "emergency vehicles." If someone began a search using "life science ethics" she would learn that there is an equivalent term, bioethics, which is the preferred LCSH, indicated by the notation (USE). Indexers and catalogers use this structure to provide the helpful "see" and "see also" references in catalogs and indexes.

The LCSH are not the only subject headings in common use. Many smaller public libraries, for example, use the Sears List of Subject Headings, whose terms and structure are less complex. On the other end of the spectrum is the highly technical Medical Subject Headings (MeSH) created by the National Library of Medicine for searching Medline, a database of medical materials.

Over the years, critics have expressed concern that some of the LCSH are inadequate or that they reflect a cultural bias. Sanford Berman (1971) argued for many years that the "LC list can only 'satisfy' parochial, jingoistic Europeans and North Americans, white-hued, at least nominally Christian (and preferably Protestant) in faith . . . and heavily imbued with the transcendent, incomparable glory of Western civilization" (p. ix). Berman repeatedly exposed subject headings that suggested racial or religious prejudices and stereotypes and subsequently, LC modified some headings considered discriminatory (Menchaca 1997). Berman also suggested that many of the headings were too formal and that there weren't nearly enough "people helping descriptors" or popular terms. As a consequence, people coming to the catalog with a popular term often could not find that term, and therefore were at a loss to find the desired information. Other criticisms included the complaint that many of the headings had an academic bias that was not helpful in public libraries.

Figure 4.3. Sample Library of Congress Subject Headings

Survival swimming
Life-saving apparatus
  VK1460-VK1481
  BT Survival and emergency
    equipment
  NT Emergency vehicles
    Immersion suits
    Life-boats
    Life-preservers
    Life rafts
    Life-saving nets
    Line-throwing guns
    Line-throwing rockets
    Submarine rescue
      vehicles
  —Law and legislation *(May*
    Subd Geog)
Life-saving at fires *(May Subd*
  Geog) TH9402-TH9418
  BT Fire-escapes
    Fires
    Rescue work
Life-saving nets
  TH9418
  BT Life-saving apparatus
Life-saving stations *(May Subd*
  Geog)
  VK1460-VK1471
  BT Life-saving
  NT Lifeboat service
Life science engineering
  USE Bioengineering
Life science publishing *(May*
  Subd Geog)
  BT Life sciences
    Publishers and publishing
    Science publishing
Life sciences *(May Subd Geog)*
  UF Biosciences
    Sciences, Life
  BT Science
  NT Agriculture
    Biology
    Life science publishing
    Medical sciences
    Medicine

—Bibliography
  RT Life sciences literature
—Moral and ethical aspects
  USE Bioethics
Life sciences ethics
  USE Bioethics
Life sciences libraries *(May*
  Subd Geog)
  UF Libraries, Life sciences
  BT Scientific libraries
  NT Agricultural libraries
    Biological libraries
    Medical libraries
  —Collection development
    (May Subd Geog)
  BT Collection development
    (Libraries)
Life sciences literature *(May*
  Subd Geog)
  QH303.6
  BT Scientific literature
  RT Life sciences—
    Bibliography
  NT Agriculture literature
    Biological literature
    Medical literature
Life skills *(May Subd Geog)*
  Here are entered works that
discuss a combination of the
skills needed by an individual to
exist in modern society, including
skills related to education,
employment, finance, health,
housing, psychology, etc.
  UF Advice-for-living books
    Basic life skills
    Competencies, Functional
    Coping skills
    Everyday living skills
    Functional competencies
    Fundamental life skills
    Living skills
    Personal life skills
    Problems of everyday
    living, Skills for solving
    Skills, Life

  BT Interpersonal relations
    Social learning
    Success
  NT Conduct of life
    Self-help techniques
    Social skills
    Study skills
    Survival skills
  —Handbooks, manuals, etc.
  UF Life skills guides
  SA *subdivision* Life skills
    guides under classes of
    persons and ethnic
    groups
  —United States
  NT Hispanic Americans—
    Life skills guides
    Vietnamese Americans—
    Life skills guides
Life skills guides
  USE Life skills—
    Handbooks,
    manuals, etc.
Life span, Productive *(May*
  Subd Geog)
  UF Productive life span
    Work life
    Working life
  BT Age and employment
    Aged
    Life cycle, Human
    Mortality
    Occupations
Life span prolongation
  USE Longevity
  Information Organization
  231
Life stages, Human
  USE Life cycle, Human
Life style *(May Subd Geog)*
  HQ2042-HQ2044
  Here are entered theoretical
works on an individual's
distinctive, recognizable way
of living, and the behavior that
expresses it.

(Continued)

Figure 4.3. Sample Library of Congress Subject Headings *(Continued)*

UF Counter culture
    Lifestyle
    Social environment
    Style, Life
BT Human behavior
    Life cycle, Human
    Manners and customs
    Quality of life
NT Living alone
Life support systems
(Critical care) *(May*
Subd Geog)
RC86.7
BT Critical care
    medicine
Life support systems (Space
environment)
UF Man in space
BT Bioengineering
    Environmental
    engineering
    Human engineering
Space flight—
    Physiological effect
Space medicine
NT Closed ecological
    systems (space
    environment)
    Extraterrestrial bases
    Space cabin
    atmospheres
    Space ships
    Space suits
    Space vehicles—
    Oxygen
    equipment
    Space vehicles—
    Water supply
Life tables
    USE Mortality—Tables
Life testing, Accelerated
    USE Accelerated life
    testing
Life time light (Portrait
    sculpture)
    USE Strong, Brett-
    Livingstone, 1953–
Life time light

Life without death (Tale)
    USE Youth without age and
    life without death (Tale)
Life zones *(May Subd Geog)*
QH84
UF Biogeographic zones
    Zones, Life
BT Biogeography
    Ecology
NT Crop zones
    Hybrid zones
Lifeboat crew members *(May*
Subd Geog)
BT Life-saving
    Lifeboat service
Lifeboat service *(May Subd*
Geog)
BT Life-boats
    Life-saving stations
NT Lifeboat crew members
    Lifecare communities
    USE Life care communities
Lifecycle, Human
    USE Life cycle, Human
Lifeguards *(May Subd Geog)*
GV838.72-GV838.74
UF Life guards
BT Life-saving
    Swimmers
Lifeline earthquake
engineering *(May Subd*
Geog)
BT Earthquake engineering
Lifelong education
    USE Continuing education
Lifestyle
    USE Life style
Lifjell (Telemark fylke, Norway)
BT Mountains—Norway
Lifoma (African people)
    USE Foma (African people)
Lifou language
    USE Dehu language
Lift (Aerodynamics)
UF Aerodynamic forces
BT Aerodynamic load
    Aerodynamics
RT Drag (Aerodynamics)

NT Flaps (Airplanes)
    Ground-cushion
    phenomenon
    Stalling (Aerodynamics)
—**Computer programs**
Lift fans
UF Fans, Lift
    Lifting fans
BT Air jets
    Fans (Machinery)
RT Ground-effect machines
NT Fan-in-wing aircraft
Lift irrigation *(May Subd*
Geog)
BT Irrigation
Lift net fishing
SH344.6L5
UF Dip net fishing
    Lift nets
BT Fisheries
    Fishing nets
Lift nets
    USE Lift net fishing
Lift-off from the moon
    USE Artificial satellites—
    Lunar launching
Lift stations
    USE Pumping stations
Lifters, Vacuum
    USE Vacuum lifters
Lifthrop family
    USE Liptrap family
Lifting and carrying
T55.3L5
UF Carrying weights
BT Materials handling
NT Slings and hitches
    Vacuum lifters
    Weight lifting
Lifting and carrying
(Jewish law)
BT Jewish law
    Prohibited work
    (Jewish law)
Lifting fans
    USE Lift fans
Lifting-jacks
TJ1430-TJ1435

Another problem was that some of the headings were outdated, and therefore newer items listed under outdated terms might not be located because the user was searching for the more modern term. More recently, O'Neill and Chan (2003) observed that "LCSH's complex syntax and rules for constructing headings restrict its application by requiring highly skilled personnel and limit the effectiveness of automated authority control" (p. 1).

Despite these criticisms, the LCSH will likely serve as a foundation for new systems that can provide more flexibility for accessing information on the Web. To this end, a collaboration involving the Online Computer Library Center (OCLC), the Library of Congress, the Association for Library Collections and Technical Services of the American Library Association developed the Faceted Application of Subject Terminology (FAST), a simplified vocabulary based on LCSH. FAST was designed for use in the Web environment and was intended to meet three goals: "it should be simple in structure (easy to assign and use) and easy to maintain; it should provide optimal access points; [and] it should be flexible and interoperable across disciplines and in various knowledge discovery and access environments including the online public access catalog" (O'Neill and Chan 2003, p. 2). FAST retained over two million LCSH in an authority file, but simplified the rules for syntax, so that it can be used by individuals with little training and experience. Hopefully it will provide effective access in the Web environment.

IV. THE LIBRARY CATALOG

The library catalog, whether physical cards in a manual catalog or electronic records, is an intellectual technology that represents the knowledge contained in a library in a systematic fashion. A catalog lists all the materials that comprise a library's collection. The records are considered surrogates for the physical materials. A catalog that arranges records in one alphabetical file is called a dictionary catalog. Catalogs that have separate subject catalogs are called divided catalogs. Catalogs that arrange their records by classification number are called classified catalogs. While card catalogs might have separate physical files, one electronic catalog can provide even more search options and perform the search far more efficiently. Classification numbers on the cataloging record, combined with the classification number on the material itself, effect retrieval of the materials. The contemporary library catalog also provides access to electronic indexes and other information retrieval tools that expand a library's resources far beyond its own collection.

Charles Ami Cutter was among the earliest and most influential developers to define the purpose of the catalog. He developed what he called the "objects" of the catalog in his *Rules for a Dictionary Catalog* (Cutter 1904). As shown in Figure 4.4, Cutter's first two items describe the two basic access functions of catalogs: the finding function and the collocation function. The catalog was designed to help locate items and to bring similar identifiers together: "a library catalog should facilitate finding a desired item and should enlighten us about related items by displaying, in one place, all items that share a common characteristic, be it author, title, or subject" (Tillett 1991, p. 150).

These purposes were affirmed in 1961 by the International Federation of Library Associations (IFLA), which included fifty-three countries, at the International Conference on Cataloguing Principles. At the conference, a "Statement of Principles" (or "Paris Principles") was adopted, which established basic principles for access (see Figure 4.5).

The goal of a catalog, therefore, is not only to permit individuals to find items that they already know exist, but also to help them find items of which they were previously unaware (Layne 1989, p. 188). Some of the descriptive functions of the catalog include the following:

1. To state significant features of an item; to identify an item

2. To distinguish one from other items by describing its scope, contents, and bibliographic relation to other items

3. To present descriptive data that respond best to the interests of most catalog users

---

Figure 4.4. Cutter's Objects of the Catalog

Objects
1. To enable a person to find a book of which either
   (a) the author
   (b) the title   } is known
   (c) the subject
2. To show what the library has
   (d) by a given author
   (e) on a given subject
   (f) in a given kind of literature
3. To assist in the choice of a book
   (g) as to its edition (bibliographically)
   (h) as to its character (literary or topical)

Source: Cutter, Charles Ami. 1904. Rules for a Dictionary Catalog. Washington, DC: GPO, p. 12.

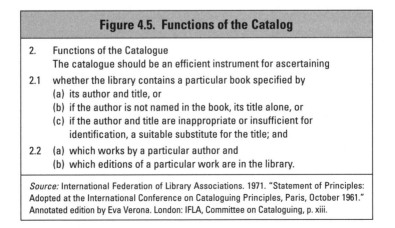

Figure 4.5. Functions of the Catalog

2. Functions of the Catalogue
   The catalogue should be an efficient instrument for ascertaining

2.1 whether the library contains a particular book specified by
   (a) its author and title, or
   (b) if the author is not named in the book, its title alone, or
   (c) if the author and title are inappropriate or insufficient for identification, a suitable substitute for the title; and

2.2 (a) which works by a particular author and
   (b) which editions of a particular work are in the library.

Source: International Federation of Library Associations. 1971. "Statement of Principles: Adopted at the International Conference on Cataloguing Principles, Paris, October 1961." Annotated edition by Eva Verona. London: IFLA, Committee on Cataloguing, p. xiii.

4. To provide justification for access points, that is, to make clear to users why they have retrieved an item; for example, to discover that a particular person authored, illustrated, or adapted a particular work (Carlyle 1996)

These descriptive functions provide valuable information about an item and ensure that the item is actually the one sought. This leads naturally to a discussion of a key element of catalogs—the bibliographic record itself.

A. Bibliographic Records
(For Print or Machine-Readable Catalogs)

An essential aspect of designing information retrieval systems is creating records that represent the items needed. The content in a record is called the bibliographic description and the entire record is the bibliographic record. Bibliographic records can be found in the library catalog, bibliographies, indexes, and abstracts. Such a record consists of a series of data elements (author, title, place and date of publication, subject heading, etc.). Elements created specifically for retrieval are called access points or index terms.

Sometimes the bibliographic record alone can provide the information needed, without the necessity of actually retrieving the object for which it is a surrogate. In this sense the record itself can be seen as part of the body of knowledge to be retrieved. Some bibliographic records contain just a little information, while others might be quite detailed, but their purpose is always the same: to represent and distinguish a unique item. For example, there are many versions of *Alice in Wonderland*. A bibliographic record must provide sufficient information to distinguish one version, or manifestation, from others and yet relate the particular item to the other related items, a concept referred to as bibliographic families. Smiraglia (2001) defined a bibliographic family as "all texts of a work that are derived from a single progenitor" (p. 75). These texts have a "derivative bibliographic relationship" to the original. To illustrate this concept, Smiraglia identified some of the possible manifestations of a novel, which include but are not limited to these:

1. The first edition of the published novel
2. Subsequent editions with changes
3. Translated editions of the first or subsequent editions of the novel
4. A screenplay of the novel
5. A motion picture

Other manifestations might include radio versions, abridgements, or adaptations including musical works or plays. Smiraglia observed that even the smallest bibliographic families are complex, but the largest families are those most often found in academic research libraries. If information retrieval systems could effectively identify common bibliographic relationships among family members, the results could be used to co-locate the family members and increase access to this complexly related group of materials. As Smiraglia and Leazer (1999) pointed out: "The development of direct and explicit control of bibliographic families would greatly enhance the user's ability to navigate the bibliographic universe" (p. 494).

Creating bibliographic records is a complex task, and there is considerable discussion as to how much and what type of information is needed to represent an item. In fact, each surrogate must reflect subtle intellectual distinctions. For example, there is a distinction between a particular book (the physical object) and the "work," which is embodied not only in a particular book but in many books. Hence, the work *Moby Dick* is embodied in many books of the same name, including many editions or translations. Creating a bibliographic record, called descriptive cataloging, requires that the physical and intellectual character of each manifestation of the work are properly described and differentiated. Lubetzky (1985) observed, "a book is not an independent entity but represents a particular edition of a particular work by a particular author" (p. 190).

The creation of bibliographic records is guided by codes that provide standards or rules. Two major factors have dramatically affected descriptive cataloging over the past two decades: the realization that shared cataloging efforts could yield significant economic advantages and the use of computer technologies (Delsey 1989). Today the National Coordinated Cataloging Program, which involves the Library of Congress, designated libraries, and bibliographic utilities such as OCLC, promote cooperative efforts for standardized cataloging. Obviously, if one standard computer-generated record can be used by all or most libraries, significant fiscal and human resources can be saved. Standardization makes it easier for individuals to use a variety of information systems and databases and makes production of bibliographic records more economical.

Momentum is building for standardization on the international level. In 1971, the IFLA promulgated the International Standard Bibliographic Description for Monographs or ISBD(M). In the years following, standards were developed for serials, the ISBD(S), printed music, maps, and other nonbook materials that identified the key components for bibliographic description, the punctuation, and the preferred order for the components. These standards were incorporated in other cataloging codes, including Anglo-American Cataloguing Rules (AACR). IFLA continues these standardization activities through its Universal Bibliographic Control program.

Similarly, major constituencies involved in the creation of cataloging records are also working to improve bibliographic access. Most notably, in 1992 the Library of Congress, OCLC, and the Research Libraries Group formed the Cooperative Cataloging Council to "facilitate an increase in the number of mutually acceptable bibliographic records available for use by the cooperative community" (Cromwell 1994, p. 415). The cooperative was succeeded by the Program for Cooperative

Cataloging in 1995. Of course, perfect standardization might not be possible, or even desirable, as variations in languages, cultural values, types of users, and purposes of institutions might be sufficiently great to create a need for variation in bibliographic description.

B. Anglo-American Cataloguing Rules

AACR is widely used to create bibliographic descriptions. AACR descends from the rules first proposed by Antonio Panizzi for the British Museum library in 1841. In 1908, the American Library Association promulgated its own rules for descriptive cataloging and revised them several times. The Library of Congress used its own internal rules for description until the 1960s, when there was a strong interest in developing international standards and in accommodating the use of computers. The first code designed specifically to respond to these needs was AACR1, promulgated in 1967 and developed following the "Paris Principles" noted earlier. AACR1 included rules for choosing access points for description and for cataloging non-book materials.

Although the intention was to create international standards, in reality the practices of American, Canadian, and British libraries varied in significant ways (a separate edition was issued for British libraries), and required constant revision and enhancement. This ultimately led an international committee comprising representatives from various national library associations and representatives from Canada, Great Britain, and the United States to undertake a major revision of AACR1 in 1974. The resulting revision is called the Anglo-American Cataloguing Rules Second Edition (AACR2), which incorporated International Standard Book Description (ISBD) standards. AACR2 set the international standard for bibliographic description and continues to be revised.

The growth of the Internet and the ever-increasing diversity of electronic resources challenged the adequacy of AACR2. In 1997, the Joint Steering Committee for Revision of AACR (JSC) sponsored a conference in Toronto to review the underlying principles of AACR2 (JSC 2009). The JSC began work on a new version, AACR3, in 2004 and in April 2005 distributed a first draft of a section. The response to the draft confirmed for the committee a need for a new approach that more closely corresponded to the emerging digital environment. The new approach, Resource Description and Access (RDA), provides a "comprehensive set of guidelines and instructions on resources description and access covering all types of content and media" (RDA 2009). RDA was developed as a cooperative effort of the American Library Association, the Canadian Library Association, and the Chartered Institute of Library and Information Professionals. RDA provides a framework to describe both analog and digital data, and adapts to database structures and existing online catalogs. It was designed primarily for libraries and uses the entity model established by the Functional Requirements for Bibliographic Records (FRBR) (see following section) as its foundation. RDA focuses on resource description only; it does not provide guidelines for subject headings.

This large-scale rethinking of AACR2 has not been without controversy. The Library of Congress Working Group on the Future of Bibliographic Control (2008) argued that "the business case for moving to RDA has not been made satisfactorily" (p. 27). Broad-based concerns included potential financial implications, impact on workflow and supporting systems, and the lack of evidence of improved navigation or enhanced description of electronic records. The Working Group recommended suspension of RDA activities until more research was conducted. Those interested in the critical area of bibliographic control will need to monitor the developments in RDA for years to come.

C. Functional Requirements for Bibliographic Records

Because the complexity of the bibliographic universe increases daily, cataloging practices and applications have been inconsistent. In an attempt to provide a more concise conceptual model, IFLA created a study group in 1992 to establish a common understanding of the aims of the information provided in the bibliographic record. The group developed an "entity relationship" model, the FRBR. Although FRBR is not associated with any particular cataloging code, it provides an opportunity for organizers of information to take a new look at cataloging rules and principles (Tillett 2004). The model is designed to help users, who can be professional organizers of information such as catalogers, consumers or library patrons, or someone involved in developing bibliographic systems. FRBR focuses on four user tasks: find, identify, select, and obtain.

FRBR shifts attention away from concerns about cataloging per se toward viewing the catalog as a whole and to its navigational aspects. Emphasis is on how the data elements function to assist the user (Riva 2007). In addition, FRBR examines these principles as they apply to three groups of entities. Group 1 comprises the products of creative or artistic endeavors and includes four,

---

FRBR User Tasks

- To *find* entities that correspond to the user's stated search criteria (i.e., to locate either a single entity or a set of entities in a file or database as the result of a search using an attribute or relationship of the entity)

- To *identify* an entity (i.e., to confirm that the entity described corresponds to the entity sought or to distinguish between two or more entities with similar characteristics)

- To *select* an entity that is appropriate to the user's needs (i.e., to choose an entity that meets the user's requirements with respect to content, physical format, etc., or to reject an entity as being inappropriate to the user's needs)

- To acquire or *obtain* access to the entity described (i.e., to acquire an entity through purchase, loans, etc., or to access an entity electronically through an online connection to a remote computer

(*Source:* IFLA Study Group, 1998, p. 82.)

often confounded, entities: work, expression, manifestation, and item. Tillett (2004) explained how these entities were related:

> When we say "book" to describe a physical object that has paper pages and a binding...FRBR calls this an "item." When we say "book" we also might mean a "publication" as when we go to a bookstore to purchase a book. We might know its ISBN but the particular copy does not matter....FRBR calls this a "manifestation." When we say "book" as in "who translated that book," we have a particular text in mind and a specific language. FRBR calls this an "expression." When we say "book" as in "who wrote that book" we could mean a higher level of abstraction, the conceptual content that underlies all of the linguistic versions....FRBR calls this a "work." (pp. 2–3)

Group 2 entities are related to Group 1 entities. They include persons or corporate bodies responsible for the creation, production, and distribution of Group 1 entities. Group 3 entities are the subjects of works. According to Tillett, "these can be concepts, objects, events, places, and any of the 'Group1' or 'Group 2' entities" (p. 3). For example, there can be works about another work or work about a person or corporate body. Subjects are related at the level of the work.

For FRBR, the concept of relationships is critical; the more people understand those relationships, the greater chance they have to encounter the entire family of works that will meet their needs. FRBR helps clarify not only the hierarchical relationships among Group 1 entities but also the complex content relationships of works. This family of works lies along a continuum. At one end of the continuum are works that are expressed in the same way, as in a reprint, facsimile edition, or copy. That same work moving along this continuum might be modified in some way to produce a new expression of the work, as in an abridgement, arrangement, revision, or translation. At some point, however, an entirely new work is created based on the original work but transformed into something new—for example, if a novel is turned into a play or movie or is parodied. Works that are very different but still members of the same family reside at the end of the continuum of new works. Examples might be reviews, criticism, or commentaries on a given work. The cataloging rules for how an item is cataloged depend, in part, on where an item fits on this continuum. This conceptual model allows catalogers to place a given expression on this continuum and provides an important tool for consistent decision making in ordering the bibliographic universe.

The potential benefits of FRBR are many: improved searching for staff and users, easier catalog navigation, more effective insertion of data into bibliographic records, and easier copy cataloging and sharing of records. Because FRBR is particularly sensitive to the many manifestations and expressions of a given work, it should be particularly useful for sophisticated collections that possess many different forms of a given work (Salaba and Zhang 2007). Dudley (2006) provided a simple example of how FRBR could be useful:

A "FRBR-ized" database (one constructed using FRBR concepts) would present results in a more hierarchical manner. For example, a search for Jane Austen... might first give us a result with two choices: works *by* Jane Austen or works *about* Jane Austen. A click on the works by Jane Austen would take us to a list of titles, without specifying particular editions. Then, a click on a title would lead us to specific editions of that work. In this example, detailed information about individual publications is hidden or kept back until needed by the searcher.

In the same hypothetical FRBR-ized database, a search for *Pride and Prejudice* might first give us a display that lists the various formats of this Jane Austen work. A click on motion pictures would lead us to a listing of all the motion pictures. And, a click on the 2005 version would result in a list of all the various editions and material types (e.g. VHS, DVD) available for last year's motion picture. (pp. 1–2)

FRBR is in the early stages of implementation and considerable room remains for interpretation and improvement. A variety of types of materials are currently being subjected to "FRBRization," including artworks, classical texts, fiction, film and video, live performing arts, music, and serials. It is also being applied in a variety of organizational settings including traditional libraries, consortia, digital libraries, institutional repositories, museums, Internet archives, and Web portals (Salaba and Zhang 2007).

Despite growing interest, Zumer (2007) identified a variety of factors that might inhibit broad acceptance, including (1) legacy data, which makes transition to a new model difficult; (2) conservative attitudes of librarians; (3) ambiguities of the model including clearly differentiating between works and expressions; (4) absence of the necessary cataloging rules, although they might be developed in the near future; and (5) the fact that only 20 percent of all works in catalogs have more than one manifestation. Nonetheless, FRBR has "provided a unifying framework and a common terminology for discussion" on cataloging standards (Riva 2007, p. 9). Zumer (2007) summed up the potential of FRBR this way:

After a relatively slow start, FRBR has recently gained some momentum. To foster further development, we have to emphasize the model's biggest potential: access to distributed bibliographic information in union catalogs and portals.... For such portals, FRBR offers meaningful clustering of search results and navigation. The same approach could then be applied to access all cultural information. (p. 29)

IFLA continues to develop this model though its review groups.

D. The Role of the Library Catalog in the Internet Age

The role and significance of the online catalog has been the subject of considerable attention in recent years. The online catalog offers many advantages, but many users struggle with the search strategies, such as Boolean searching, and have experienced particular difficulty with subject searches because of the need to match their own subject terms to the system's. Nonetheless, people tend to like online catalogs and expect them to provide additional services because of their familiarity with Web and Internet search engines (Bates 2003). As a result, many online library catalogs in public libraries are being redesigned in an attempt to offer the same flexibility and convenience as the Web environment (Calhoun et al. 2009).

These discussions have been particularly pointed among academic and research librarians. Karen Calhoun (2006), focusing on the needs of students and scholars, prepared a report on this matter for the Library of Congress titled *The Changing Nature of the Catalog and its Integration with Other Discovery Tools*, which noted:

> Today, a large and growing number of students and scholars routinely bypass library catalogs in favor of other discovery tools, and the catalog represents a shrinking proportion of the universe of scholarly information.... The online catalog is losing appeal for students and many scholars. Catalog usage, drifting downward compared to other discovery tools, might soon plummet. (p. 5)

Calhoun argued that the online catalog has had considerable value over the years but with the increasing use of search engines and the flexibility of the Web, the online catalog is reaching the "ends of its lifecycle" (p. 5). Too often, according to Calhoun, users experience "failed searches, frustrating navigation, unfamiliar subject indexing policy and vocabulary, confusing search and retrieval methods . . . and poorly organized search result sets" (pp. 25–26). She described catalogs as "hard to use and their interfaces seem increasingly out of date" (p. 26). Increasingly, the catalog contains only a small portion of the available scholarly knowledge.

The declining use of the online catalog in academic and research institutions is particularly notable because of the millions of dollars spent maintaining them. Thus the cost-benefit ratio of such expenditures becomes an important issue. Although she does not recommend their elimination, Calhoun suggested that significant innovations and cost reductions are needed. She suggested a systematic examination of the entire online catalog process including the following:

1. Defining accurately the communities being served and focusing on particular user populations

2. Reducing costs and improving turnaround time through simplifying cataloging records and reducing localized cataloging practices, substituting best practices

3. Improving finding functions by abandoning the LCSH in favor of subject keywords, and supporting new techniques including automatic classification, and development in ontologies and taxonomies

4. Streamlining workflows to encourage faster turnaround times, cooperative workflows, and collaborative development of best practices

5. Improving the user experience through features such as "more like this" or "get it" options, full text links, relevancy ratings, and extended hour services

6. Promoting catalog use with a marketing plan and publicity campaigns

7. Partnering with other organizations and training staff to work in a business environment that requires innovation, joint ventures, and effective budgeting and grant writing (Calhoun 2006)

Responding to these criticisms and suggestions, Thomas Mann (2006) argued that Calhoun employed an inappropriate business model and overemphasized turnaround time as the "gold standard in cataloging" (p. 1), with potentially destructive consequences for scholarly research. Mann noted that the attention businesses give to supply and demand is a function of their need to maintain and increase profits, but profit is not the goal of a research library: the goal is to promote scholarship. Mann did not question Calhoun's notion of creating niche markets for research libraries; however, he argued that scholars, as a market, need to be distinguished from "quick information seekers" (p. 7). He argued that search engines might be effective competitors to the online catalog for the latter but have significant deficits for the former. Mann distinguished the needs of scholars from those of quick information seekers as follows:

1. Scholars seek the most clear and extensive overview of all relevant sources.

2. They are especially concerned that they do not overlook sources that are unusually important, significant, or standard in their field of inquiry.

3. They do not wish to unnecessarily duplicate prior research.

4. They particularly wish to be aware of cross-disciplinary connections to their work.

5. They wish to find current books on a subject categorized with the prior books on the same subject, so that the newer works can be perceived in the context of the existing literature.

6. They particularly appreciate mechanisms that enable them to recognize highly relevant sources whose keywords they cannot think up in advance, to enter into Boolean combinations in a blank search box.

7. Although they are more cognizant of the need for extended effort and the need to check multiple sources beyond the "first screen" of any Internet retrievals, they also wish to avoid having to sort through huge lists or displays. (p. 8)

Mann argued that Internet search engines cannot accomplish these critical functions. He pointed out similar issues when comparing LCSH and other forms of vocabulary control to keyword searching and relevance ranking, noting the superiority of LCSH for scholars. As for designing online catalogs so that they are more like the Web, he observed that for scholars, the book remains the preeminent format, while electronic resources are more useful for background and supplementary materials (Mann

2007). The research library's catalog, therefore, needs to give highest priority to controlling book literature. By refocusing on the scholar, rather than the quick information seeker, it is also easy to see why quick turnaround time is less important. In sum, Mann was concerned that the changes suggested by Calhoun reflected an information seeker perspective, rather than a scholarly one.

Even if one accepts Mann's points, there remains the issue of the increasing costs of providing these services and whether those costs can be sustained while still providing the other critical services of research libraries. Eden (2008) suggested that "the era of the library OPAC is over" (p. 38). He contended that the budget situation is sufficiently dire that it is difficult to justify the personnel needed to control the catalog when it is used by only a small proportion of the library's clientele. Eden believed that academic libraries are in a fight for survival and that "'Good enough' is just fine for today's users" (p. 38). Taking a less draconian view, Banush and LeBlanc (2007) described the situation as the "tension between the utilitarian greatest good for the greatest number and the well-intentioned urge to do the greatest good for each individual bibliographic entity" (p. 101). They noted that if more and more funding is devoted to traditional cataloging, it will deplete resources for other initiatives. Similarly, even if search engines such as Google and its mass digitization projects do not substitute for the online catalog, what roles can they play to reduce cataloging costs so that funding can be devoted to the needs of scholars? For Marcum (2006), "the question, then, is not whether new information technologies and services from Google and other companies make cataloging dispensable, but what changes in cataloging will be necessary and at what cost, to enable librarians to take full advantage of new technologies to help information users of all kinds" (p. 11). Marcum identified four critical questions that must be addressed to determine the future of cataloging:

1. If the commonly available books and journals are accessible online, should we consider the search engines the primary means of access to them?

2. Massive digitization radically changes the nature of local libraries. Does it make sense to devote local efforts to the cataloging of unique materials only rather than the regular books and journals?

3. We have introduced our cataloging rules and the MARC format to libraries all over the world. How do we make massive changes without creating chaos?

4. And finally, a more specific question: Should we proceed with AACR3 in light of a much-changed environment? (p. 9)

V. BIBLIOGRAPHIES, INDEXES, AND ABSTRACTS

In addition to classification and bibliographic description, there are other knowledge organization tools. These tools not only help identify and locate materials in a library; they also extend retrieval capabilities beyond those of the classified collection or catalog. Among these are bibliographies, indexes, and abstracts, which can come in print, microform, and electronic formats. The effectiveness of these tools relies heavily on their ability to apply many of the intellectual technologies previously described, most notably the principles involved in controlled vocabulary, including the assignment of subject headings or descriptors.

Bibliographies, as lists with the purpose of defining the literature of a particular topic, first appeared in the Renaissance around 1500 (Krummel 1984). A bibliography usually restricts in some way, such as by subject, form (e.g., periodicals), or coverage (e.g., items published before 1900). There are basically two types of bibliographies: systematic and analytical. Systematic bibliographies generally focus on a particular subject or are designed for a particular purpose. They are sometimes further subdivided into enumerative bibliographies and subject bibliographies. The latter is self-explanatory; it is a bibliography in a particular subject area. Enumerative bibliography is designed to provide an extensive list of items, but not necessarily on a specific subject. A catalog is an enumerative bibliography, as is a national bibliography. Analytical bibliography (also known as descriptive bibliography) is a list of items that carefully focuses on the physical aspects of the item so that historical and comparative analyses can be affected. In such bibliographies, careful attention is paid to the physical characteristics of various editions, and they identify any characteristics of the item that would permit a scholar to place the item in its historical or aesthetic context (Bates 1976). As a rule, bibliographies are intended to lead the user to the sources they identify. Bibliographies centralize bibliographic information: they are another form of collocation. Some, which include a brief note or summary of the contents of each item, are referred to as annotated bibliographies.

An index is "a systematic guide designed to indicate topics or features of documents in order to facilitate retrieval of documents or parts of documents" (NISO 1997, p. 8). This very broad characterization is especially appropriate for automated indexes, which consist of five components: terms, rules for combining terms, cross-references, a method for linking headings, and a particular order of headings, or search procedure (NISO 1997). More simply, an index can be viewed as an alphabetized list of items that direct the searcher to further information. It can point to content within a given work (e.g., an index in the back of a book) or to items located outside the work (such as a periodical index). For example, when a searcher uses a book index, the index term provides the appropriate section or page numbers within the work where information denoted by the term is provided. Indexes can provide retrieval information for most types of materials, including books, periodical articles, and dissertations. Other indexes have features much the same as bibliographies, for example, periodical indexes such as the *Readers' Guide to Periodical Literature* or the *Social Sciences Citation Index*. These tools provide bibliographic citations arranged under various index terms, which might include, but are not limited to, subject terms, author names, article, or book titles. Some indexes are devoted to a specific discipline, such as *Art Index*, while other indexes are considerably more general, such as *Magazine Index*; some are devoted to a single publication, like the index for *National Geographic* or the *New York Times Index*. Given the proliferation of journals and published articles over the years, the periodical index provides an essential pathway for the location of up-to-date material.

There are two major methods of indexing: precoordinate and postcoordinate. In precoordinate indexing, the indexer coordinates all the indexing terms at the time of the indexing. That is, the control over the combining of terms or the indication of relationships between terms is done prior to the information seeker's use of the retrieval system. Postcoordinate indexing allows searchers to coordinate index terms of their own choosing (within the bounds of the controlled vocabulary) at the time of searching. This method is most common in (although not exclusively restricted to) electronic information retrieval systems in which the searcher selects combinations of search terms and connects them by logical operators, such as the Boolean terms "and," "or," or "not." Obviously, postcoordinate indexing permits great flexibility when using electronic indexes.

An abstract is "a brief and objective representation of the contents of a document or an oral presentation" (NISO 1997, p. 1). Whether prepared by the author or not, it is a type of surrogate that summarizes the contents of a document so that readers can determine if the document is appropriate for their purposes. Because of their abbreviated character, abstracts can serve many useful purposes. For example, abstracts serve as a current awareness tool, a quick way to stay up to date; they also enable information seekers to access a large body of literature that can be scanned quickly, including material in foreign languages (Pao 1989).

An abstract usually includes a bibliographic citation indicating where the entire text of an item can be located. It can be quite detailed or brief, but at a minimum it attempts to describe key aspects of the document. There are two varieties of abstracts: informative and indicative. Informative abstracts represent and summarize the content of all major aspects of the material. Indicative abstracts briefly summarize what the document is about and include results when they are significant. Abstracts, however, are neither critical nor evaluative (Pao 1989); this differentiates an abstract from an annotation, which is a "brief explanation of a document or its contents, usually added as a note to clarify a title" (NISO 1997, p. 1), or a review, which is usually a more extensive summary of a document that includes evaluation and comment. Tools that arrange abstracts so that they can be accessed by index terms are especially useful for knowledge location. Such tools often arrange the abstracts by broad classifications or subjects. The tools operate like periodical indexes except that they also contain abstracts, providing the searcher with even more information to help decide if consulting the full text would be helpful. Examples of such tools include *Psychological Abstracts* or *Library and Information Science Abstracts*.

The intention of bibliographies, abstracts, and indexes is to centralize bibliographic information for materials that might exist in a variety of physical locations, to arrange it in a systematic way, and to provide the information needed to locate the items. As such, they represent important finding tools for both the LIS professional and the library user. But it also must be kept in mind that such tools have their limitations. They often reflect the cultural or theoretical biases of their authors or, because of economic limitations, are not complete. Some tools, notably those published as books, can quickly become outdated, especially in disciplines that change or produce new information rapidly. Few periodical indexes and abstracts are comprehensive; they seldom index all periodicals that might have a relevant article. Hence, some journals might not be indexed or might be only partially indexed. This is not to underestimate the importance of these tools. Rather, it highlights the complexity of trying to control and organize large bodies of knowledge. Information professionals must understand that all intellectual technologies and tools have their deficiencies; our confidence should not be placed entirely in any one item.

> *The intention of bibliographies, abstracts, and indexes is to centralize bibliographic information for materials that might exist in a variety of physical locations, to arrange it in a systematic way, and to provide the information needed to locate the items.*

VI. THE ORGANIZATION OF KNOWLEDGE WITHIN ELECTRONIC INFORMATION RETRIEVAL SYSTEMS

Electronic information retrieval systems include a wide variety of tools. The online catalog is one example, as are online periodical indexes and other online databases. Understanding their basic structure is critical, because these systems are integral components of information access in libraries and other information centers and will continue to grow in importance.

A. Records, Fields, and Files

The foundation of electronic databases is in many ways similar to the card catalog: it is a record, the information stored, concerning a particular document. Each record refers to a document and consists of a series of fields. Fields are units of information within a record; that is, each field is a special area into which a specific attribute or characteristic is added. For example, in a bibliographic record there might be fields for an author, title, issue or volume, subject heading or descriptor, and perhaps for special comments or notes. Database designers design these records and fields, but they do not necessarily select the access points to these records. Rather, it is common that the vendors who offer the databases determine which fields will actually be searchable and which ones will simply be displayed. LIS professionals might also have influence over which fields will be searchable. In general, the searchable fields might vary depending on the vendor, but the overall effect is to increase dramatically the number of access points that a searcher can use in locating information sources.

One of the most important advances in the creation of electronic records and fields was the development of MARC (Machine-Readable Cataloging), which was developed by the Library of Congress in the mid-1960s. The intention was to create a standard machine-readable format for bibliographic description. MARC is a communications tool, designed for the creation and sharing of bibliographic information in a computerized or online environment. Today, MARC is the standard for the creation of bibliographic records.

MARC consists of various fields with three codes: tags, indicators, and subfield codes, each associated with specific information concerning a bibliographic entity (see Figures 4.6 and 4.7). There are many possible fields, including the basic ones such as author, title, subject, and publisher. Additional fields include those for series, notes, related titles, and physical description. The effect of the MARC format

---

Figure 4.6. Selected MARC Fields

010	LC card number	246	Variant form of title
020	International Standard Book Number	250	Edition statement
050	Library of Congress Classification Number	260	Publication information
		300	Physical description
082	Dewey Decimal Classification Number	440	Series
		500	General note
100	Personal name main entry	505	Contents note
245	Title proper, subtitle, and statement of responsibility	650	Subject heading
		700	Personal author added entry

Figure 4.7. Sample MARC Record with Fields*

020	ISBN 1-56308-354-X	500	Rev. ed. of: Genreflecting / Betty Rosenberg, 3rd ed. 1991.
050	PS374.P63R67 1995		
082	016.813009	504	Includes bibliographical references and indexes.
100	Herald, Diana Tixier.		
245	Genreflecting: a guide to reading interests in genre fiction / Diana Tixier Herald.	650	American fiction-Stories, plots, etc.
		650	Popular literature-Stories, plots, etc.
		650	English fiction-Stories, plots, etc.
250	4th ed.	650	Fiction genres-Bibliography.
260	Englewood, Colo.: Libraries Unlimited, 1995.	650	Fiction-Bibliography.
		650	Reading interests.
300	xxvi, 367 p.; 25 cm.	700	Rosenberg, Betty. Genreflecting.

Source: Reprinted with permission from OCLC Online Computer Library Center, Inc.
*Record modified and is not complete.

cannot be overestimated. MARC made possible the first substantive use of computer technologies for libraries—the centralized preparation of catalog cards—as well as the founding of bibliographic utilities such as OCLC. The impact on collection development and resource sharing has been tremendous.

However, the MARC format was developed primarily for cataloging, and the organization of knowledge in other types of computer databases can be quite different. Abstracting and indexing databases, for example, use a variety of formats. The fields available and the type and number of searchable fields might also be different. The situation, however, is not totally chaotic. Some database producers in common subject areas have agreed to use substantially the same formats. For example, Chemical Abstracts Services (CAS) and Biosciences Information Services (BIOSIS) use standardized record formats. Nonetheless, there is definitely a need for greater standardization.

A file is a group or collection of records that share common characteristics. A library catalog might be seen as a file of works with shared characteristics contained within the library. Of course, there are many other types of files. Electronic files are referred to as databases, and there are literally thousands of such databases. The way files are arranged in a database is referred to as file organization. Just like in a physical file, the logical organization within an electronic file determines how well the information can be retrieved. Generally, storage of files is logically organized around a key field such as a field containing the record number or the author's name.

For example, a common arrangement of files is alphabetical: hence, a database might be arranged alphabetically by author's name. This results in a linear or sequential file. The files arranged by key field make up the main file. Anything but the simplest databases must be much more flexible than being searchable by a key field. This is certainly true of online catalogs and databases that LIS professionals use. Most file searching is supplemented by the use of inverted files, which serve as indexes to the main file. An inverted file consists of particular fields associated with particular records within the database. For example, if the key field is an author field, the inverted files might contain title words or subject heading terms or descriptors. Searching on any of these terms leads to the identification of documents associated with that term. Although there are other ways to organize electronic files such as list chains and clustered files, the inverted file is the fundamental organization for searching electronic databases (Pao 1989).

B. MARC21

MARC21 is the latest version of the MARC format and should greatly improve global access and sharing of bibliographic records. In fact, MARC21 is now being used not only in the United States and Canada, but also in Australia, New Zealand, many Latin American countries, the Middle East, and Asian countries including China

(Radebaugh 2003). The British Library adopted MARC21 in June 2004. MARC 21 brings together the U.S. and Canadian MARC formats and also updates MARC to include access to Web pages in library catalogs. There are now fields to add URLs, FTP sites, and other computer addresses. In addition, hypertext links can now be embedded into the bibliographic record so that a link to a Web site can be accomplished directly from that record. Although some have questioned the applicability of the MARC21 format in the Web environment, others believe it can be used effectively in this way (Radebaugh 2003).

NISO Standards Relevant to Libraries	
Z39.2	Information Interchange Format
Z39.4	Guidelines for Indexes and Related Information Retrieval Devices
Z39.9	International Standard Serial Numbering
Z39.14	Guidelines for Abstracts
Z39.18	Scientific and Technical Reports— Organization, Elements, and Design
Z39.19	Guidelines for the Construction, Format, and Management of Monolingual Thesauri
Z39.41	Printed Information on Spines
Z39.48	Permanence of Paper for Publications and Documents in Libraries and Archives
Z39.50	Information Retrieval: Application Service Definition and Protocol Specification
Z39.63	Interlibrary Loan Data Elements
Z39.84	Syntax for the Digital Object Identifier
Z39.85	Dublin Core Metadata Element Set

C. Standardization of Records

With the ever-expanding volume of documents, the need to standardize the format and organization of records has become critical. Considerable help in this direction is provided by NISO, which is accredited by the American National Standards Institute (ANSI) to create and maintain technical standards for information organizations and others that exchange data. NISO develops standards only after a considerable process of consultation and participation by the individuals and organizations that would be affected by the standard under development. When NISO believes a consensus has been reached, a standard is issued (although sometimes not all participants agree with a standard, even when it is issued in its final form). Compliance with the standard is voluntary, but the use of standardized formats can be of considerable value, both financial and instrumental.

VII. THE INTERNET ERA AND THE SEMANTIC WEB: ORGANIZING KNOWLEDGE ON THE INTERNET AND WORLD WIDE WEB

A current and growing problem facing all seekers of information is how to deal with the deluge of information available on the Internet and World Wide Web. A major obstacle is that the Internet was developed as a decentralized system with minimal content control or organization. Such a system has great advantages from the perspective of producing and making information widely available, but offers significant disadvantages from the perspective of standardization. It should be obvious from the discussions in this chapter that the standardization of information organization can make vast amounts of information accessible. Unfortunately, this standardization is not available on the Web.

With the growth of information retrieval through online computer systems and the Web, alternative techniques for describing, organizing, and retrieving electronic documents are being developed. Most notable has been the Standard Generalized Markup Language (SGML), originally developed in 1970 as the Generalized Markup Language (GML) (Gaynor 1996). SGML provides a standardized means to describe various classes of documents and to identify the elements that comprise each class. Classes are characterized by document-type definitions or schemas, which also identify the structure of the document by identifying the necessary and optional elements. Each element for a class is assigned a code number. For example, one class of documents might be poems, and among the elements might be lines, stanzas, couplets, and an author (Gaynor 1996). SGML can describe content as well as structure. For example, it can identify phone numbers, chemical structures, and citations within a document. It also permits the addition of nonbibliographical elements that can provide evaluative and analytical information. Overall, the use of SGML permits a hierarchical structure in which the bibliographical information, analytical information, and the full text itself can be tagged for retrieval. In this environment, retrieval can be very flexible and informative: each element or combination of elements, including whole documents, can be manipulated electronically and retrieved.

The consistent application of SGML in the creation or processing of documents has substantial implications for effective retrieval not only of individual documents, but of the individual elements. SGML is now accepted as both a national and international standard (ISO 8879). In addition, items in MARC format can be translated into SGML, making the application even broader for library use.

Perhaps the most far-reaching application of SGML has been the development of Hypertext Markup Language (HTML), which is now the fundamental language used to create Web documents. It allows the designer to structure a Web page, display images, and create links to other pages or documents so that individuals can navigate the Web. HTML was described by Miller and Hillman (2002) as the "first layer or first tier" (p. 57) of a three-tiered Web. HTML assigned a simple set of tags to describe a Web document and allowed document sharing based on these tags. The extent of sharing, however, was limited, especially when the document was rich in information.

A second tier was established through the creation of XML (Extensible Markup Language) files, which allowed a greater degree of document sharing. Approved by the World Wide Web Consortium (W3C) in 1998, XML is a subset of SGML and is compatible with both SGML and HTML. Where HTML focuses on how information is displayed, XML describes the information content of an electronic document. Although it was first conceived for use on the World Wide Web, it can be used for general electronic publication as well. XML "is not a single, fixed format like HTML, nor is it a replacement for HTML. XML is a meta-language that lets users design their own markup languages to meet specific applications or industry needs. It provides a standard way for describing and exchanging data regardless of its nature, how the sending system stored it, or how the receiving system will use it" (Desmarais 2000, p. 10). A particular advantage of XML documents is that they can be created in one application but used in others without conversion; as such, XML has encouraged open-source solutions and stimulated the development of products that cross operating systems. XML is expected to be widely used and advantageous to help describe and organize Web contents. Indeed, with the development of XML, a new version of HTML, called XHTML, has been developed. XHTML is written in XML and can be viewed on current browsers and also used for XML documents (Lemight and Colburn 2003).

XML, through its linking features, can reveal that two or more documents are related to one another, but it cannot describe how one document is related to another. The tags used in XML do not have meaning in and of themselves unless linked to the XML schema that defined them. Understanding how objects on the Web are connected or related requires that the system actually understand the meaning within the tags, and by understanding the meaning within the tags, the system goes a long way to understanding the meaning of the Web pages themselves and how their meanings relate.

Establishing a World Wide Web that allows computers to relate Web sites on the basis of their meaning, referred to as the Semantic Web was a fundamental aim of the early Web creators. The Semantic Web "is not a separate Web but an extension of the current one, in which information is given well-defined meaning, better enabling computers and people to work in cooperation" (Berners-Lee et al. 2001, p. 40). The Semantic Web moves beyond the notion of "link to" relationships to richer connections such as "Works for," "is Author of," or "Depends on." The Semantic Web, according to Miller and Swick (2003), "is based on the idea of having data on the Web defined and linked such that it can be used for more effective discovery, automation, integration and reuse across various applications" (p. 11). Currently, meaning is absent except for the basic notion that one page is linked to another.

Creating the tools to develop this semantic relationship is the third layer of the Web, and much of the activity involves the World Wide Web Consortium. A key component in the development of the Semantic Web is the Resource Description Framework (RDF). RDF is an application of XML and provides a framework for creating metadata. "In RDF, a document makes assertions that particular things (people, Web pages or whatever) have properties (such as 'is a sister of,' 'is the author of") with certain values (another person, another Web page)" (Berners-Lee et al. 2001, p. 40). As Semantic Web researchers develop the necessary rules and logic to expand the potential of RDF, one might soon see new and exciting opportunities to exploit the knowledge represented on the Web.

Some, however, have suggested that the vision of a Semantic Web is unrealistic and might even be counterproductive. Morville and Rosenfeld (2006) noted that these individuals see greater potential in social networking, blogs, and so forth as the means by which individuals will meaningfully link on the Web. Whether a Semantic Web is really obtainable and functional remains an open question.

A. Metadata

Underpinning all aspects of organizing the Web is the concept of metadata. As Web sites have proliferated and digital libraries have emerged as major sources of information, metadata has become the critical means of locating and using them. As noted earlier in the chapter, LIS professionals have been dealing with the concept of metadata for many years using the intellectual technologies of cataloging: subject headings, classification numbers, indexing, and bibliographic description. Metadata performs the same function in the electronic environment by creating access points for electronic resources. It facilitates resource discovery in four ways:

1. Allowing resources to be found by relevant criteria
2. Identifying resources
3. Distinguishing dissimilar resources
4. Giving location information (NISO 2004, p. 1)

Metadata is sometimes referred to as data about data. More precisely, metadata "is structured information that describes, explains, locates, or otherwise makes it easier to retrieve, use, or manage an information resource" (NISO 2004, p. 1). Metadata can be applied to a single resource, an aggregation of resources, or parts of a single resource. Metadata can be used not only for locating current materials but for archival and preservation purposes as well. NISO describes three main types of metadata:

1. *Descriptive metadata* describes a resource for purposes such as discovery and identification. It can include elements such as title, abstract, author, and keywords.
2. *Structural metadata* indicates how compound objects are put together, for example, how pages are ordered to form chapters.
3. *Administrative metadata* provides information to help manage a resource, such as when and how it was created, file type and other technical information, and who can access it. (NISO 2004, p. 1)

Administrative metadata includes rights management information and preservation metadata deals with information needed for archival or preservation purposes.

As with traditional rules for cataloging, there are standards for using metadata. For example, the NISO Framework Working Group established six metadata principles for good metadata when building a digital collection:

Metadata Principle 1: Good metadata conforms to community standards in a way that is appropriate to the materials in the collection, users of the collection, and current and potential future uses of the collection.

Metadata Principle 2: Good metadata supports interoperability.

Metadata Principle 3: Good metadata uses authority control and content standards to describe objects and co-locate related objects.

Metadata Principle 4: Good metadata includes a clear statement of the conditions and terms of use for the digital object.

Metadata Principle 5: Good metadata supports the long-term curation and preservation of objects in collections.

Metadata Principle 6: Good metadata records are objects themselves and therefore should have the qualities of good objects, including authority, authenticity, archivability, persistence, and unique identification (NISO 2007, pp. 61–62).

There are a variety of metadata schemes created for specific purposes. The Dublin Core Metadata Element Set, developed by the Dublin Core Metadata Initiative (DCMI), is probably the most prominent example and defines a set of elements for resource description in the online environment. A metadata system with these standardized elements makes it possible for many individuals who lack the expertise of a professional cataloger to describe their Web sites and assign terms that could significantly aid others in accessing them. DCMI is an "open organization . . . engaged in the development of interoperable online metadata standards that support a broad range of purposes and business models" (DCMI 2009). Its emphasis is collaborative and international. The primary mission of DCMI is threefold:

1. Developing and maintaining international standards for describing resources
2. Supporting a worldwide community of users and developers
3. Promoting widespread use of Dublin Core solutions (DCMI 2009)

A wide variety of individuals and organizations are participating in this initiative, including the Library of Congress, National Science Foundation, OCLC, the National Center for Supercomputing Applications, the national libraries of Australia and Canada, archives and museums, educational institutions, digital libraries, governmental agencies, networks, publishers, and knowledge managers.

The Dublin Core Metadata Element Set

ELEMENT NAME	DEFINITION
Contributor	An entity responsible for making contributions to the resource.
Coverage	The spatial or temporal topic of the resources, the spatial applicability of the resources, or the jurisdiction under which the resource is relevant.
Creator	An entity primarily responsible for making the content of the resource.
Date	A point or period of time associated with an event in the life cycle of the resource.
Description	An account of the content of the resource.
Format	The file format, physical medium, or dimensions of the resource.
Identifier	An unambiguous reference to the resource within a given context.
Language	A language of the resource.
Publisher	An entity responsible for making the resource available.
Relation	A related resource.
Rights	Information about rights held in and over the resource.
Source	A related resource from which the described resource is derived.
Subject	A topic of the resource.
Title	A name given to the resource.
Type	The nature or genre of the resource.

(*Source:* DCMI 2009.)

The Dublin Core Metadata elements were formally endorsed as a NISO Standard (Z39.85–2007) and establish the basis for the international standard (ISO 15836:2009). The Dublin Core provides the basic elements for resource description in an electronic environment, as well as for specialized applications and standards for describing particular types of objects. These include, for example, the Content Standards for Digital Geospatial Metadata (CSDGM) for objects such as maps and gazetteers, Categories for the Description of Works of Art (CDWA) for describing art objects, Visual Resources Association (VRA) Core Categories for Visual Resources, and Learning Object Metadata (LOM) for learning objects such as syllabi, lecture notes, simulations, and educational kits.

As digitization becomes commonplace and digital repositories are created, additional standards are being developed. For example, under the sponsorship of the Digital Library Federation with the support of the Library of Congress, an XML schema, the Metadata Encoding and Transmission Standard (METS), was created to encode digital library materials and assist institutions in sharing the digital objects. In 2004, the new standard was registered by NISO. The METS framework allows the incorporation or linking of metadata from different resources in one structure. This means a METS record can package descriptive, administrative, and structural metadata in one XML document. METS can be particularly useful in the context of digital repositories. As the Library of Congress noted:

> The Metadata Encoding and Transmission Standard (METS) is a data encoding and transmission specification, expressed in XML, that provides the means to convey the metadata necessary for both the management of digital objects within a repository and the exchange of such objects between repositories (or between repositories and their users). . . . When a repository of digital objects intends to share metadata about a digital object, or the object itself, with another repository or with a tool meant to render the object, the use of a common data transfer syntax between repositories and between tools greatly improves the facility and efficiency with which the transactions can occur. METS was created and designed to provide a relatively easy format for these kinds of activities during the life-cycle of the digital object. (p. 5)

There are other common metadata schemes as well, including the Text Encoding Initiative devised for electronic texts such as novels, plays, and poetry; the Metadata Object Description Schema, created for use with MARC21 records; and the Encoded Archival Description to improve access through finding aids in archives and special collections.

VIII. SUMMARY

Information cannot be effectively retrieved unless it is usefully organized. New information channels, such as the Web, have produced great excitement, but as knowledge continues to expand, the challenge of providing access to this universe also increases. It might be true that everything is on the Web now but this, of course, is the problem. There is too much information without the necessary structure and organization to retrieve it. It is hoped that those who produce and make available new sources of information will call upon the expertise of librarians and information scientists and the technologies that they have developed to gain some control over this ever-expanding universe. This will continue to be a central issue for those in library and information science.

REFERENCES

Banush, David, and Jim LeBlanc. 2007. "Utility, Library Priorities, and Cataloging Policies." *Library Collections, Acquisitions, and Technical Services* 31 (June): 96–109.

Bates, Marcia. 1976. "Rigorous Systematic Bibliography." *RQ* 16 (fall): 2–26.

———. 2003. *Task Force Recommendation 2.3 Research and Design Review: Improving User Access to Library Catalog and Portal Information.* Los Angeles: UCLA, June 1.

Berman, Sanford. 1971. *Prejudices and Antipathies: A Tract on the LC Subject Heads Concerning People.* Metuchen, NJ: Scarecrow.

———. 1981. *The Joy of Cataloging: Essays, Letters, Reviews, and Other Explosions.* Phoenix: Oryx.

Berners-Lee, Tim, James Hendler, and Ora Lassila. 2001. "The Semantic Web." *Scientific American* 284: 34–43.

Calhoun, Karen. 2006. *The Changing Nature of the Catalog and Its Integration with Other Discovery Tools (Final Report)*. Ithaca, NY: Cornell University Press, March 17.

Calhoun, Karen, Joanne Cantrell, Peggy Gallagher, and Janet Hawk. 2009. *Online Catalogs: What Users and Librarians Want*. Dublin, OH: OCLC.

Carlyle, Allyson. 1996. "Descriptive Functions of the Catalog." Unpublished class materials. Kent, OH: Kent State University, SLIS.

Chan, Lois Mai. 2007. "Classification and Categorization." In *Cataloging and Classification: An Introduction*. 3rd ed. Lanham, MD: Scarecrow, 309–319.

Cromwell, Willy. 1994. "The Core Record: A New Bibliographic Standard." *Library Resources and Technical Services* 38 (October): 415–424.

Cutter, Charles Ami. 1904. *Rules for a Dictionary Catalog*. Washington, DC: GPO, 1904.

Delsey, Tom. 1989. "Standards for Descriptive Cataloguing: Two Perspectives on the Past Twenty Years." In *The Conceptual Foundations of Descriptive Cataloging*. Edited by Elaine Svenonius. San Diego: Academic Press, 51–60.

Desmarais, Norman. 2000. *The ABCs of XML: The Librarian's Guide to the eXtensible Markup Language*. Houston: New Technology.

Dublin Core Metadata Initiative. 2009. "About the Initiative." Available: http://dublin-core.org/ about/ (accessed June 30, 2009).

Dudley, Virginia. 2006. "What's All the Fuss about FRBR?" *Messenger Extra*. Minitex Library Information Network (June 30): 1–3.

Eden, Bradford Lee. 2008. "Ending the Status Quo." *American Libraries* (March): 38.

Gaynor, Edward. 1996. "From MARC to Markup: SGML and Online Library Systems." *ALCTS Newsletter* 7 (Supplement): A–D.

IFLA Study Group on the Functional Requirements for Bibliographic Records. 1998. *Functional Requirements for Bibliographic Records: Final Report*. Munich: K.G. Saur. Available: www.ifla.org/VII/s13/frbr/frbr.htm (accessed February 12, 2010).

Joint Steering Committee. 2009. "International Conference on the Principles and Future Development of AACR." Available: www.collectionscanada,gc.ca/jsc/intlconf.html (accessed June 9, 2009).

Krummel, D. W. 1984. *Bibliographies: Their Aims and Methods*. New York: Mansell.

Kwasnik, Barbara H. 1992. "The Role of Classification Structures in Reflecting and Building Theory." In *Advances in Classification Research: Proceedings of the 3rd ASIS SIG/CR Classification Research Workshop*. Vol. 3. Medford, NJ: Learned Information, 63–81.

Layne, Sara Shatford. 1989. "Integration and the Objectives of the Catalog." In *The Conceptual Foundations of Descriptive Cataloguing*. Edited by Elaine Svenious. San Diego: Academic Press, 185–195.

Lemight, Laura, and Rafe Colburn. 2003. *Web Publishing with HTML and XHTML in 21 Days*. 4th ed. Indianapolis: Sams.

Library of Congress Working Group on the Future of Bibliographic Control. 2008. On the Record. January 9. Available: www.loc.gov/bibliographic-future/news/lcwg-ontherecord-jan08-final.pdf (accessed February 12, 2010).

Lubetzky, Seymour. 1985. "The Objectives of the Catalog." In *Foundations of Cataloging: A Sourcebook*. Littleton, CO: Libraries Unlimited, 186–191.

Mann, Thomas. 1993. *Library Research Models: A Guide to Classification, Cataloging, and Computers*. New York: Oxford.

———. 2006. "The Changing Nature of the Catalog and Its Integration with Other Discovery Tools, Final Report. March 17, 2006. Prepared for the Library of Congress by Karen Calhoun: A Critical Review." April 3. Prepared for AFSCME 2910. Available: www.guild2910.org/AFSCMECalhounReviewREV.pdf (accessed January 26, 2010).

———. 2007. "More on What Is Going on at the Library of Congress." Prepared for AFSCME 2910. January 1. Available: www.guild2910.org/AFSCMEMoreOnWhatIsGoing.pdf (accessed January 26, 2010).

Marcum, Deanna B. 2006. "The Future of Cataloging." *Library Resources and Technical Services* 50 (January): 5–9.

Meadows, Charles T. 1992. *Text Information Retrieval Systems*. San Diego: Academic Press.

Menchaca, Deirdre. 1997. "Robert B. Downs Award." Available: http://lists.webjunction.org/wjlists/publib/1997-February/078039.html (accessed February 2, 2010).

Miller, Eric, and Diane Hillmann. 2002. "Libraries and the Future of the Semantic Web: RDF, XML, and Alphabet Soup." In *Cataloging the Web: Metadata, AACR, and MARC21: ALCTS Papers on Library Technical Services and Collections*. Edited by Wayne Jones, Judith R. Ahronheim, and Josephine Crawford. Lanham, MD: Scarecrow, 57–64.

Miller, Eric, and Ralph Swick. 2003. "An Overview of W3C Semantic Web Activity." *Bulletin of the American Society of Information Science and Technology* 29 (April/May): 8–11.

Mitchell, Joan S., et al., eds. 1996. *Dewey Decimal Classification and Relative Index*. 22nd ed. Albany: Forest Press.

Morville, Peter, and Louis Rosenfeld. 2006. *Information Architecture for the World Wide Web*. Third Edition. Sabastopol, CA: O'Reilly Media.

National Information Standards Organization. 1997. "Guidelines for Indexes and Related Information Retrieval Devices." [TR-02-1997.] Bethesda, MD: NISO.

———. 2004. *Understanding Metadata*. Bethesda, MD: NISO.

———. 2005. "Guidelines for the Construction, Format, and Management of Monolingual Controlled Vocabularies." [Z39.19-2005.] Bethesda, MD: NISO.

———. 2007. *A Framework of Guidance for Building Good Digital Collections*. 3rd ed. Washington, DC: IMLS, December. Available: www.niso.org/publications/rp/framework3.pdf (accessed January 26, 2010).

OCLC. 2004. "Dewey Services." Available: www.oclc.org/dewey/default.htm (accessed February, 12, 2010).

———. 2009a. "About the Initiative." Available: http://dublincore.org/about/index.shtml (accessed June 8, 2009).

———. 2009b. "Dublin Core Metadata Element Set, Version 1.1." Available: http://dublincore.org/documents/dces (accessed June 8, 2009).

O'Neill, Edward T., and Lois Mai Chan. 2003. "FAST (Faceted Application of Subject Terminology): A Simplified LCSH-Based Vocabulary." World Library and Information Congress: 69th IFLA General Conference and Council. August 1–9, 2003, Berlin, Germany.

Pao, Miranda. 1989. *Concepts of Information Retrieval*. Englewood, CO: Libraries Unlimited.

Radebaugh, Jackie. 2003. "MARC Goes Global—and Lite." *American Libraries* 34 (February): 43–44.

RDA. 2009. "RDA: Resource Description and Access." Available: www.rdaonline.org (accessed January 26, 2010).

Riva, Pat. 2007. "Introducing the Functional Requirements for Bibliographic Records and Related IFLA Developments." *Bulletin of the American Society for Information Science and Technology* 33 (August/September): 7–11.

Salaba, Athena, and Yin Zhang. 2007. "From a Conceptual Model to Application and System Development." *Bulletin of the American Society for Information Science and Technology* 33 (August/September): 17–23.

Smiraglia, Richard P. 2001. *The Nature of "A Work": Implications for the Organization of Knowledge.* Lanham, MD: Scarecrow.

Smiraglia, Richard P., and Gregory H. Leazer. 1999. "Derivative Bibliographic Relationships: The Work Relationship in a Global Bibliographic Database." *Journal of the American Society for Information Science* 50: 493–504.

Tillett, Barbara B. 1991. "A Taxonomy of Bibliographic Relationships." *Library Resources and Technical Services* 35 (April): 150–158.

———. 2004. *What Is FRBR? A Conceptual Model for the Bibliographic Universe.* Washington, DC: Library of Congress.

Zumer, Maja. 2007. "FRBR: The End of the Road or a New Beginning?" *Bulletin of the American Society for Information Science and Technology* 33 (August/September): 27–31.

SELECTED READINGS: INTELLECTUAL ORGANIZATION OF LIBRARIES

Books

Anderson, Richard L., Brian C. O'Connor, and Jodi Kearns. *Doing Things with Information: Beyond Indexing and Abstracting.* Westport, CT: Libraries Unlimited, 2008.

Calhoun, Karen, Joanne Cantrell, Peggy Gallagher, and Janet Hawk. *Online Catalogs: What Users and Librarians Want: An OCLC Report.* Dublin, OH: OCLC Online Computer Library Center, 2009.

Eden, Bradford. *More Innovative Redesign and Reorganization of Library Technical Services.* Westport, CT: Libraries Unlimited, 2008.

Kneale, Ruth. *You Don't Look Like a Librarian: Shattering Stereotypes and Creating Positive New Images in the Internet Age.* Medford, NJ: Information Today, 2009.

Taylor, Arlene. *Understanding FRBR.* Westport, CT: Libraries Unlimited, 2007.

Taylor, Arlene G., and Daniel N. Joudrey. *The Organization of Information.* 3rd ed. Westport, CT: Libraries Unlimited, 2009.

Weihs, Jean. *Metadata and Its Impact on Libraries.* Westport, CT: Libraries Unlimited, 2005.

Zeng, Marcia Lei, and Jian Qin. *Metadata.* New York: Neal-Schuman, 2008.

Zhang, Yin, and Athena Salaba. *Implementing FRBR in Libraries: Key Issues and Directions.* New York: Neal-Schuman, 2009.

Articles

Calhoun, Karen. "The Changing Nature of the Catalog and Its Integration with Other Discovery Tools." Prepared for the Library of Congress, March 17, 2006. Available: www.loc.gov/catdir/calhoun-report-final.pdf (accessed June 19, 2009).

Coyle, Karen. "Understanding Metadata and Its Purpose." *Journal of Academic Librarianship* 31 (2005): 160–163.

Dudley, Virginia. "What's All This Fuss about FRBR?" *Minitex Messenger Extra* (June 30, 2006): 1–3.

Mann, Thomas. "More on What Is Going On at the Library of Congress." AFSCME (January 1, 2007). Available: www.guild2910.org/AFSCMEMoreOnWhatIsGoing.pdf (accessed January 26, 2010).

———. "What Is Going On at the Library of Congress?" Paper prepared for AFSCME 2910, the Library of Congress Professional Guild, June 19, 2006. Available: www.guild2910.org/AFSCMEWhatIsGoingOn.pdf (accessed January 26, 2010).

Marcum, Deanna B. "Digitizing for Access and Preservation: Strategies of the Library of Congress." *First Monday* 12 (July 2007). Available: http://firstmonday.org/htbin/cgiwrap/bin/ojs/index.php/fm/article/view/1924/1806 (accessed January 26, 2010).

———. "The Library of Congress and Cataloging's Future." *Cataloging and Classification Quarterly* 45 (2008): 3–15.

Mathes, Adam. "Folksonomies: Cooperative Classification and Communication Through Shared Metadata." December 2004. Available: www.adammathes.com/academic/computer-mediated-communication/folksonomies.html (accessed January 26, 2010).

Peterson, Elaine. "Beneath the Metadata: Some Philosophical Problems with Folksonomy." *D-Lib Magazine* 12 (November 2006). Available: www.dlib.org/dlib/november06/peterson/11peterson.html (accessed January 26, 2010).

Zhang, Yin, and Athena Salaba. "Critical Issues and Challenges Facing FRBR Research and Practice." *Bulletin of the American Society for Information Science and Technology* 33 (August–September 2007): 30–31.

5

The Library as an Institution: An Organizational Perspective

I. INTRODUCTION

Libraries are not independent and self-sufficient organizations whose survival relies solely on their own internal operations. Libraries are part of the bibliographic sector of society which also includes publishers, materials retailers and wholesalers, networks, and indexing and abstracting services. This sector is "the assemblage of institutions and organizations that collectively take the output of the publishing industry and try to make it accessible for public use" (Wilson 1984, p. 389). The purpose of this sector is to provide both intellectual and physical access to information.

At the same time, as organizational theorists have noted, each organization seeks to survive through adaptation. Today's social, political, and economic climate presents a number of threats to libraries' survival. Among the many factors stressing libraries and related organizations are the rapidly increasing costs of materials and human resources, the reluctance of the public to provide funding, the increase in the diversity and quantity of published materials, the pressure to acquire computerized systems and resources, and the increasing power of publishers and other information providers to control access to the information they produce and hence control the costs of such information (Young 1994). Other challenges include lack of money, lack of political support, social controversy arising from some of the materials and services that libraries provide, information competitors, changes in how information is produced and supplied, legal constraints, personnel issues, demanding patrons who insist on both traditional and nontraditional materials and services, and rapid technological changes. Some of these stresses are new; others have been present at various times in the past. It is crucial, then, to understand the many ways in which libraries are currently organized and to assess their capacity to adapt in the future.

II. THE FUNCTIONAL ORGANIZATION OF LIBRARIES

A. Organizational Units

Libraries are generally organized to perform certain basic functions:

1. Selecting materials and developing collections
2. Ordering and acquiring materials
3. Making information available in a variety of formats and delivery mechanisms
4. Conserving and preserving materials
5. Providing educational programs

These functions are assigned to different departments which vary depending on a library's focus and size. The units discussed next pertain generally to larger public libraries, although other types of large libraries, such as university or research libraries, might also have them. Smaller libraries might combine many functions within one department. Typically, larger libraries include a governing board, administration, public service divisions, and support units.

1. Governing Boards

Most public libraries are governed by a board that has statutory authority to operate the library. The board's primary purpose is to establish policies, plan strategically, set goals and directions, and ensure fiscal accountability. The chief administrator reports to the elected or appointed board of trustees. In academic libraries, school library media centers, and special libraries, the director generally reports to other administrators, such as an academic dean, principal, or department head.

2. Library Administration

The administration includes the director and other individuals such as the treasurer, assistant or associate directors, and heads of administrative departments such as personnel, planning, and information systems. These individuals are responsible for the overall operation of the library. They contribute to policy creation, enforce those policies, administer personnel practices, conduct fiscal operations, and implement program functions.

3. Public Service Units

Depending on the size of the library, there might be several public service units, including branches, departments, or divisions. Public service units often select their own materials and provide services directly to patrons. Each unit usually has at least one individual at the management level who supervises staff, manages budgets, and participates in planning with library administrators, as well as providing direct public service in many instances. The following are some of the more common public service units.

a. Reference Department

The reference department might also be called the information division or information center. Services include answering user-initiated queries for information from print and non-print materials, as well as the Web; suggesting books (reader's advisory); helping patrons locate materials; interpreting materials; preparing guides; instructing individuals on how to use materials and services in the library (bibliographic, mediagraphic, or Web instruction); maintaining reference files; creating Web sites; conducting tours; and delivering programs. Reference staff might also select materials and electronic resources for the department and the library or offer story times and other programs for children, either in the library or in classrooms.

Depending on its size and service philosophy, a library might have a single reference department or several. Reference librarians in smaller libraries need to have a considerable breadth of knowledge to answer all the questions from diverse patrons. Larger reference departments can be subdivided by subject (history, science, business), by age (children, adults, young adults), by characteristics of the user (visually or hearing impaired), or by geography (branches or decentralized libraries).

b. Circulation Department (Access Services)

The term *circulation* suggests the flow of materials in and out of the library; more recently, the department has also been called access services. Its concern is dispensing or receiving library materials and administering fines and procedures for late or lost materials. Circulation staff might also have control over periodicals, interlibrary loans, and materials held for restricted use (e.g., reserve files in an academic library).

c. Audiovisual Department

The audiovisual (AV) department provides AV materials, equipment, and sometimes advice. Organizationally, not all AV materials are necessarily included in this division. For example, although DVDs might be found in AV, music compact discs might still be found in a music or fine arts department.

d. Archives and Special Collections

An archive deals with records of local or general historical importance or with materials that are considered rare or especially fragile. The size and scope of special collections departments vary tremendously. Research libraries (special, public, or academic) are more likely to house, manage, and preserve materials in special collections.

e. Special Services

Some libraries have departments that serve special clientele such as people with visual or hearing impairments, or people who are physically unable to come to the library such as prisoners, nursing home residents, or those who are homebound. Bookmobile service could also be considered in this category.

4. Technical Services

Technical services prepares materials, including electronic information, so library patrons can use them. Typically, the department consists of subdivisions including acquisitions, serials, and cataloging and classification. In addition, depending on the need, areas such as preservation, government publications, and integrated library systems could also be part of technical services.

The transformation of many library collections into items that are only accessible through electronic means, while also maintaining the availability of physical items, presents a number of challenges. Gorman (1998) noted that the term *collection* now includes four categories of items: (1) tangible materials (e.g., books); (2) intangible materials owned by the library (e.g., electronic resources on CD-ROMs); (3) tangible materials not owned by the library (e.g., materials available on interlibrary loan); and (4) intangible materials not owned by the library (e.g., electronic materials from the Web). Additional changes stem from the introduction of automated systems, which has led to the integration of some traditional technical service functions such as acquisitions and cataloging into the functions of other units (Younger et al. 1998). Younger et al. predicted that the future of technical services will "focus on cost and product effectiveness, a client-centered mission, and managing an accelerating rate of change. Shrinking staff size, time-saving computing applications, less complicated cataloguing rules, streamlined workflows, and outsourcing... will be among the challenges in, and proposed solution to, managing technical services in the twenty-first century" (p. 174).

Questions regarding the future of the technical services workforce have also arisen. Since the late 1980s, there has been a decline in the demand for technical services personnel, although Deeken and Thomas (2006) suggested that trend might be reversing. There are currently increases in openings for all types of technical services positions that require both strong computer skills and work experience. The following is a brief description of some of the major subdivisions within technical services.

a. Acquisitions

The acquisitions department (AD) orders and receives materials. When ordered materials do not arrive, the AD is responsible for following up. Schmidt and Ray (1998) identified the major AD tasks: bibliographic searching, order preparation and placement, online record maintenance, vendor assignment, correspondence, receiving materials, invoicing, and monitoring budgets and funds. Historically, AD also included materials selection and collection development, but these activities are now performed by bibliographers, subject specialists, or other librarians or are performed automatically using protocols created by professionals. These automated systems have improved the efficiency of acquisition processes by integrating library systems with those of vendors and publishers.

b. Serials

Magazines, journals, newsletters, and other serials require a complex and coordinated process, called serials control, to ensure availability for users. Kao (2001) defined serials control as "library tasks involved in managing serials titles and keeping them in good order and accessible to library users. Included are functions such as check-in, claiming, binding, replacement of back issues, and shelf maintenance" (p. 73). Serials staff assist in the selection and evaluation of vendors, monitor subscription costs, manage the growth of e-serials, and adapt to the decrease in serials due to the declining purchasing power of libraries. As more and more serials are acquired through electronic access en masse through vendors, the purchase of serial titles should continue to decline and the need for their individual control in many circumstances will diminish.

c. Cataloging and Classification

Cataloging and classification is responsible for bibliographic control, which includes descriptive and subject cataloging, copy cataloging, classification, and authority control (see Chapter 4). Trained catalogers perform original cataloging based on the item itself. Copy cataloging involves creating a bibliographic record for the library based on information provided through a bibliographic utility such as OCLC, usually in the MARC format created by the Library of Congress. OCLC also suggests a classification number, but the local copy cataloger might modify that depending on local needs. Obviously, the expertise of an original cataloger is substantially greater than that required of a copy cataloger, hence the critical need for librarians who specialize in this area.

d. Preservation

Substantial portions of many collections, especially in research and academic libraries, are brittle due to the acidification of the paper. Although dealing with deteriorating materials is an essential function of any library's preservation program, in fact, preservation begins with the proper handling of newly acquired materials. The better the preservation techniques used in the beginning, the longer materials are likely to survive. Preservation functions include developing and implementing disaster plans, repairing and rebinding materials, de-acidifying and/or encapsulating materials, reformatting or digitizing, and migrating materials. In many libraries, some of these functions are performed by staff located in the collection development or technical services departments; some might be in public services while others might be in independent preservation units reporting directly to the director.

Preservation units will remain critical if artifacts and the intellectual content contained in older formats are to survive. In the future, preservation specialists will be particularly challenged by the need to preserve information stored in electronic formats that are manifestly impermanent and easily altered or destroyed.

5. Support Units

Support departments in libraries provide essential functions that enable librarians to perform their services. These units include maintenance, public relations, security, and integrated systems.

a. Maintenance

Probably the least visible and least appreciated department is maintenance, which ensures that the facilities and grounds are clean and operate smoothly. Staff clean, maintain, and landscape grounds; attend to heating, plumbing, and electrical repair; and construct displays. In small libraries, the maintenance department might also perform some security functions as well.

b. Public Relations

Public relations (PR) provides an important conduit for communication to and from the public. PR staff prepare promotional materials for library programs and activities; develop PR plans for major projects; write grants; manage communication with the media, as well as political, civic, and religious leaders; and manage crises when controversies arise.

c. Security

Security needs vary with the environment and the community. Security problems can range from dealing with minor nuisances to major felonies. Security staff patrol the premises, monitor security devices, guard entrances and exits, deal with difficult or problem patrons, and contact additional safety forces as needed.

d. Integrated Systems

Given the fiscal and human resources now devoted to information technologies and the increasing integration of these technologies into all aspects of library service, there is a clear need to coordinate the acquisition and use of such technologies. Thus some libraries have created a separate department or appointed an individual to be responsible for these technologies. This person or department participates in the evaluation and selection of technologies, trains staff, troubleshoots technology problems, and provides network security to prevent viruses or inappropriate or unauthorized use of the system.

III. THE ORGANIZATION OF AUTHORITY IN LIBRARIES

A. Three Types of Authority

Organizations can also be understood in terms of how they assign authority, which is the power to command or influence others. In most organizations, including libraries, there are usually three types of authority: bureaucratic, professional, and informal.

1. Bureaucratic Authority

Most libraries are organized as bureaucracies, meaning that the organization is structured based on a number of formal positions identified to fulfill basic functions. Each bureaucratic position has at least three elements: (1) a set of clearly defined responsibilities, (2) an appropriate level of authority to meet those responsibilities, and (3) a set of clearly defined qualifications required for an individual to properly fill the position. In a bureaucracy, it is the responsibility of organizational leaders to rationally and objectively select individuals who can satisfy the needs of a particular position. Personal considerations or any considerations unrelated to the required skills are ignored.

Within a bureaucracy, positions are arranged so their relationship to each other is clear. The most common structure is pyramidal and hierarchical; positions of similar character and authority report to a smaller number of positions of higher authority. For example, reference librarians might report to the head of the reference department; the heads of various departments report to a director. This hierarchical relationship is sometimes referred to as a scalar chain of command. Higher on the pyramid of authority, the number of positions diminishes until there is a single position at the top (the director). Individuals in higher positions of authority rely on sanctions to get subordinates to obey (Lynch 1978). Bureaucratic authority rests on the location of a position within the hierarchy. Individuals who leave a particular position no longer have its authority. In smaller organizations, the pyramid has far fewer levels and is therefore "flatter."

2. Professional Authority

Examining authority solely from a bureaucratic perspective provides an incomplete picture. Within the library bureaucracy is a professional activity—librarianship. Librarians derive authority by virtue of their expertise. Lynch (1978) characterized the difference between bureaucratic authority and professional authority as a clash of ends: the purpose of bureaucracies is to increase organizational efficiency; the purpose of professionals is to provide superior service, that is, effectiveness. Winter (1988) observed, "Professionalization is a way of dealing with the more immediate challenges of bureaucratic authority, in the everyday sense of fighting off the attempts of business to invade spheres of professional practice" (p. 13). This difference inevitably leads to friction as librarians clamor for more services and materials, and bureaucrats resist on the basis of fiscal control. Bureaucratic authority also clashes with professional authority when administrators make decisions that require professional, as well as administrative, expertise. Professional staff might, in fact, reject, sabotage, or otherwise make the work situation difficult if they believe that decisions are being made that lie outside an administrator's intellectual and professional ken. This is not to suggest that all bureaucrats lack professional knowledge or care less about service.

It does suggest, however, that it is wise to consider that managerial or administrative positions involve different perspectives and concerns than professional positions.

3. Informal Authority

The third type of authority arises from informal, social relationships among staff. Informal authority is defined by the persuasiveness of an individual or group or a personal relationship to those who are more powerful. These informal relationships are referred to as the informal organization. Sometimes individuals or groups can be more powerful than the formal authority structures or than their professional expertise might warrant. Because libraries are labor intensive, a relatively complex set of social relationships defines which individuals or groups are influential and which are less so. There is no reason to presume, however, that informal authority always works against the interests of those with formal authority.

B. Is Bureaucracy the Best Way to Organize Libraries?

Hierarchical structures persist primarily for three reasons: (1) a belief that changes in the decision-making structure can lead to chaos, (2) a belief that participatory decision making results in mediocre choices, and (3) a belief that participatory decision making is an abdication of administrator responsibility (Euster 1990). Although these reasons are not entirely without merit, do they represent convincing reasons for preserving a structure that might hinder a library's ability to adapt?

Some theorists suggest that bureaucratic structures function best in stable environments where threats and demands are predictable. In these instances, bureaucratic elements such as written rules, standardized procedures and practices, and centralized decision making are appropriate. However, if the environment is unstable, or the threats less predictable, the organization requires flexibility to respond quickly and effectively. This requires that more power should be invested in those parts of the organization that deal directly with customers (patrons) or that anticipate new developments, such as new technologies or competitors. In such environments, decentralized authority seems more appropriate.

Euster (1990) argued that the increasing complexity of librarianship makes the traditional hierarchical structure obsolete, that "leadership and expertise must reside at all levels of the organization not just among designated leaders" (p. 41). No longer can one individual be expected to be sufficiently informed to make the necessary decisions; efficient exchange of information among all knowledgeable individuals is desirable. The system must be designed to coordinate and share information so that decision making can be a joint process. Euster (1990) referred to the sharing of information for decision making, usually via automated systems, as "informating" the organization (p. 43). Such systems convey critical information throughout the organization so that decisions are made by whoever has the most information.

How well a library functions is determined by its ability to adapt to the changing and increasing demands of the environment in which it operates. Given the remarkable technological transformation occurring, it is likely that only organizations that can respond rapidly and sensitively will survive and prosper in the years to come.

IV. ORGANIZATION OF LIBRARIES BY TYPE

Another approach to understanding library organization is to examine the various types of libraries: public, academic, school, and special, although within a given type there might be considerable organizational variation. The *American Library Directory 2009–2010* (Information Today 2009) categorizes the number of U.S. libraries (see Figure 5.1).

A. Public Libraries

There are approximately 9,200 public libraries in the United States housed in more than 16,000 buildings (ALA 2009b). Total collections exceed more than 815 million print materials, 41 million audio materials, and nearly 40 million video materials. Total operating income exceeds $9.1 billion, 81 percent of which comes from local funding, 10 percent from state contributions, 8 percent from gifts and other sources, and 1 percent from federal sources (National Center for Educational Statistics [NCES] 2007b).

1. Mission and Roles

The mission of a public library is exceedingly broad: to meet the educational, recreational, informational, and cultural needs of its community. The comprehensive nature of these roles (see sidebar) frequently taxes library resources.

The Public Library Association (PLA) recommends that libraries emphasize a limited number of roles. Roles are selected, generally, based on the community

Figure 5.1. Number of Libraries in the United States			
Public libraries	17,064	Special libraries	7,609
Public libraries excluding branches	9,757	Law	912
Public library branches	7,307	Medical and religious libraries	2,033
Academic libraries	3,768	School and media center libraries	~100,000
Community college libraries	1,167		
University and college libraries	2,601		

Source: American Library Directory 2009–2010; National Center for Education Statistics, "Table 43: Of Public Schools with Library Media Centers, characteristics of library media center staff, by state: 2003–04." Available: http://nces.ed .gov/surveys/sass/tables/state_2004_43.asp (accessed February 10, 2010).

ALA's Eight Roles for Public Libraries

1. **Community Center**, providing a central focus for community activities, meetings, and services
2. **Information Center**, serving as a clearinghouse for information on community organizations, issues, and services
3. **Educational Support Center**, assisting students of all ages enrolled in formal courses of study
4. **Independent Learning Center**, supporting individuals engaged in independent study
5. **Popular Materials Center**, offering current, high-demand, high-interest materials in a variety of formats
6. **Early Learning Center**, encouraging young children to develop an interest in reading and learning
7. **Reference Center**, providing timely, accurate, and useful information for community residents
8. **Research Center**, supporting scholars and researchers who conduct in-depth studies, investigate specific areas of knowledge, and create new knowledge

(*Source:* Palmour et al. 1980.)

---

served. For example, only the largest public libraries serving communities with a significant business, technological, academic, or scientific infrastructure could support a research role. Suburban or rural libraries are more likely to emphasize popular materials and education. However, these generalities are not hard and fast, and certainly libraries can and do fulfill multiple roles. With ongoing competition from other information sources, especially electronic information, it is important to remember that the public library is a unique place, and part of its essential mission is integrally related to its physical presence.

2. Usage

Americans use their public libraries. A Department of Education study (NCES 2007b) found that almost one-third of all U.S. households used a public library in the previous month, with almost half (48 percent) using it within the preceding year. Households with children were the heaviest users. Two out of three households with children used the library in the past year: 69 percent of two-parent families and 60 percent of single-parent households. A 2007 ALA study found that among adults, the heaviest users (74 percent) were aged thirty-five to forty-four years while those least likely to use the library were fifty-five and older. African Americans (64 percent) and whites (63 percent) were the heaviest users; 49 percent of Hispanics used the library.

In the NCES study, public library use varied by income; households with the highest incomes were nearly twice as likely to use the public library. A similar pattern was revealed by educational level: 66 percent of households with the highest levels of education used the public library, compared to 21 percent of those households with less than a high school diploma (NCES 2007b).

Borrowing materials (26 percent) or using the public library for enjoyment or hobbies (19 percent) were the most popular reasons for using a public library; only 9 percent came to the library to get information for personal use (NCES 2007b). A 2009 survey commissioned by the ALA reported similar findings, with 39 percent indicating they visited the library to borrow books; 12 percent took out CDs and other AV or computer materials; 10 percent used a computer; 9 percent used reference materials; and 8 percent accessed the Internet. African Americans and Hispanics were much more likely to come to the library to use computers than whites (ALA 2007a). The ability of public libraries to address the digital divide is notable; 73 percent of public libraries report that they are the only source of free computer and Internet service in their area (ALA 2008b).

3. Attitudes Toward Public Libraries

Americans generally have very positive attitudes toward public libraries. One study by the Americans for Libraries Council (ALC) (2006) concluded that Americans value public libraries highly and consider them well-run. Three in four respondents indicated that the public library was doing an excellent or good job and put them at the top of the list of well-run services when compared to public education and health care. Respondents appreciated free services, having enough books for young people, providing good reference materials, and knowledgeable, friendly librarians. The highest priority was for children's services. They also valued Internet and computer access services; two out of three respondents felt that providing adequate computer and online services should be a high priority. In the same study, the ALC interviewed numerous community leaders who expressed the hope that the public library could extend its community role in four areas: more services to teens, helping to deal with adult illiteracy, providing ready access to government documents and forms, and providing greater access to computers. Other studies show similar findings: OCLC reported that among a survey of online users aged fourteen and above, 80 percent had a favorable overall impression of the public library, with those aged twenty-five and older reporting the most favorable ratings (De Rosa et al. 2005).

4. Major Issues Confronting Public Libraries

a. The Political Climate

Public librarianship is inherently political, a fact often overlooked and greatly underestimated. Library administrators work to preserve a nonpartisan and effective working relationship with all political groups because public libraries rely almost entirely on public monies to finance their operations, and library board members are often appointed by local political powers. Balancing the various political interests is a complex and challenging task. Consider the expectations of such disparate groups as the business community, governmental agencies and legislative bodies, schools and other educational institutions, religious groups, clubs and civic organizations, and parents. These differing interests make the political complexities of running a public library considerable.

b. Financial Stresses

A number of recent economic events have made life difficult for public libraries. The economic slowdown that began in 2008 resulted in significant deficits in state and national funding. Many states, including California, New York, and Ohio, suffered serious budget shortfalls, leading to reductions in hours, staffing, and book budgets. Such reductions are particularly troublesome because public library use tends to increase during difficult economic times. The American Library Association (2009c) reported that library use was increasing dramatically; the percentage of Americans owning library cards increased 5 percent from 2006 to 68 percent in 2008 and 76 percent of Americans had visited a public library in the previous year compared to 66 percent in the preceding two years. In-person visits increased 10 percent; online visits increased from 24 percent in 2006 to 41 percent in 2008. At the same time, the association reported "significant losses of state funding for public libraries," with 41 percent of state libraries reporting declining state funding for fiscal year 2009 and a good portion of these indicating that the cuts would continue (ALA 2009c, p. 2).

Other sources of financial stress include the increasing costs of traditional library materials, especially periodicals, and new information technologies. Computer hardware and software, along with connection costs for electronic access, can be considerable. These costs, coupled with static or declining funding, create significant financial burdens on public libraries. Attempts to save money and improve operational efficiency, such as outsourcing public library services to private vendors, have had mixed results. Hennen (2003) recommended additional tactics to improve fiscal conditions such as combining individual libraries into library districts, creating library foundations, developing e-commerce initiatives, assessing "impact fees" on new homes, and introducing legislation that would set

---

Voter Attitudes Toward Funding Public Libraries

1. A large percentage of voters (75 percent) claimed they would support library funding, but for half of them, the commitment was not particularly strong.

2. Public awareness of library services was often limited to the provision of books and other materials; the public was less aware of such services as teen programming, computer training, or ESL classes.

3. The public was not aware of how libraries are funded and did not know that libraries were financially stressed.

4. Public officials had a positive attitude toward libraries but were not necessarily supportive of additional funding.

5. Not all library users supported additional funding support; those who believed that libraries transform lives were more likely to support additional funding.

6. Library funding supporters were involved in their communities, considered librarians as advocates of lifelong learning, and perceived the library as a vital part of their community.

(*Source:* De Rosa and Johnson 2008.)

aside a percentage of property taxes to finance public libraries. The effectiveness and practicality of such strategies will no doubt vary by locality, but it is clear that public libraries will need to take a more aggressive, entrepreneurial approach if they are to survive and prosper in the economically challenging years to come.

c. New Information Technologies, the Internet, and the World Wide Web

Public library services, physical structures, and organizational charts have been dramatically redesigned as information technologies and the World Wide Web have opened new ways of accessing information on a local, regional, national, and global scale. There is no doubt, for example, that the ubiquity of Web access has transformed information services provided by libraries. As of 2007, more than 99 percent of public libraries had access to the Internet and 54 percent offered wireless access. The majority of public libraries provided a variety of Internet-based services: licensed databases (85 percent); homework resources (68 percent); digital references (58 percent); podcasts and other audio content (38 percent), and e-books (38 percent). Among the most used Internet services were e-mail, job-related searching, social networking, e-commerce, genealogy research and homework, e-government, and online games (ALA 2007a). "Ask the Librarian" and e-newsletters were also very popular e-services (Hoffert 2008). The benefits of these services to libraries are significant. For example, public libraries that provided public-access computing had increases in visits, circulation, and new patrons (Jorgensen 2005). The continuing evolution of the new technologies will require public libraries to make further adaptive changes. For example, librarians' skills will need to keep pace with the technologies, and they will need to be comfortable with social networking, podcasting, and electronic publishing. Librarians will need to adapt their knowledge organization skills so they can catalog or otherwise organize, tag, and make digital material accessible. There will also be a need for entirely new staff dedicated to and trained in information technology and networking. In addition, and somewhat ironically, the public library's role as a central place to obtain access to these technologies will place additional adaptive demands on that physical place. Those demands could be challenging. As Clark and Davis noted (ALA 2007a):

> Many library buildings predate the Internet. . . . As a result, these buildings are ill-equipped to accommodate the space and electrical needs of more than a few workstations. Seventy-six percent of public libraries reported that space limitations are the top factor affecting their ability to add computers. Related to this, 31 percent of libraries reported this year that the availability of electrical outlets, cabling or other infrastructure issues limited addition computers. (p. 4)

Jaeger et al. (2006) noted additional challenges including increasing bandwidth and connectivity, training staff and patrons, increasing the number and availability of public access stations, securing additional funding to maintain infrastructure, and outreach to groups who otherwise would not have access. In particular, by making these various technologies available to all, public libraries help minimize the digital divide.

i. THE DIGITAL DIVIDE

The data are clear that access to the Internet and the utilities that make it most effective are not distributed evenly among the population. Fortunately, public libraries provide access for at least some of those who otherwise have neither the training nor resources to connect. Examples of the digital divide abound. For example, as income rises so does Internet use, and the differences are dramatic. Only 25 percent of those with incomes of less than $15,000 use the Internet, compared to 67 percent of those with incomes exceeding $75,000. Whites and Asian Americans (60 percent) use the Internet more than African Americans (40 percent) or Hispanics (32 percent). Not surprisingly, cost is one of the most common reasons for nonuse and is also a primary factor in the discontinuation of Internet use. This strongly suggests that the digital divide persists at least in part due to economic disparities. Similarly, use is more common among individuals who are younger, have higher incomes, are employed, and live in urban or suburban areas in contrast to rural ones. Rainie et al. (2003) also found that people who are socially content, feel they have control over their lives, and use other media such as newspapers, radio, and television are also more likely to use the Internet.

Among the primary reasons for nonuse are cost, concern about identity theft, lack of time, and complexity of the technology. Many nonusers assert simply that they do not want or need the Internet. Lenhart (2003) added disability as a factor: "The disabled have among the lowest levels of Internet access in America" (p. 5). Only 38 percent go online, compared to 58 percent of individuals who are not disabled and 28 percent of disabled nonusers say their disability makes it very difficult or impossible to go online.

Mossberger, Tolbert, and Stansbury (2003) suggested that the digital divide must be understood as more than unequal access; it is also a skills gap. They found that 22 percent of adults still needed assistance using a mouse and keyboard; 31 percent needed help using e-mail; and 52 percent needed assistance with word-processing or spreadsheet programs. Those most likely to need assistance were the elderly and less educated, individuals of low income, African Americans, and Latinos. Interestingly, the public library might be an excellent place to redress this gap because these groups are most likely to view the public library as a "community gathering place" (p. 51). This skills gap also applies to children who lack information literacy skills. As more and more information becomes available online, there is a tremendous need to teach effective search techniques and evaluation skills.

Examining more detailed data concerning how computers are used in public libraries is particularly revealing and suggests that public libraries can play a significant role in addressing the problem of the digital divide. For example, because

Hispanics and African Americans are less likely to have Internet access in their homes than whites, the public library can be a critical access point for online services for these populations. Similarly, a large percentage of rural libraries (82 percent) report that they are the only provider of free Internet access in their community (ALA 2009d).

Most discussions of the digital divide focus on the "have-nots." However, Horrigan (2003) focused on the "haves," concluding that there is a technology elite in the United States who are "high-end technology adopters." These individuals are consistent users of the Web, cell phones, digital videodisc players, and personal digital assistants (PDAs), and include (1) "young tech elites," usually males in their early twenties; (2) "older wired baby boomers," usually males in their mid-fifties; (3) "wired generation Xer's" who use the Web and cell phones heavily; and (4) "wired senior men" who are wealthy and average seventy years old. As a group, these adopters constitute less than one-third of the U.S. population, but have a disproportionate impact and influence on the information goods and services used and produced in the United States.

Although the digital divide might be with us for some time, there is some cause for optimism. A U.S. Department of Commerce (2002) analysis suggested that "whether measured against income, education, family type, or race/Hispanic origin, the distribution of Internet use at home has moved in the direction of lower inequality" (p. 87). In other words, the gap might be closing and schools and public libraries might be contributing.

ii. The Internet Public Library

The new technologies have the potential to create new types of libraries that are not physical structures. In 1995, the University of Michigan's School of Information created the Internet Public Library (IPL) which was described as:

> A global information community that provides in-service learning and volunteer opportunities for library and information science students and professionals, offers a collaborative research forum, and supports and enhances library services through the provision of authoritative collections, information assistance, and information instruction for the public. (IPL 2003)

Today, the IPL Consortium is composed of three managing partner universities, (Drexel, Florida State, and the University of Michigan), six partner universities, and seven participating universities. The IPL explores best practices for providing library service via the Internet, and conducts research aimed at increasing our knowledge about digital libraries and librarianship. It offers twenty-four-hour online service, with subject collections including art and humanities, business, computers, education, health, law and government, and science and social science, as well as a ready-reference service. It also provides special services to teens and children. The objective of IPL is not to replace local libraries, but to explore potential enhancement of the library through the digital world. Over the years, the reference services of IPL have grown dramatically, from 1,116 questions answered in 1995 to 71,723 in 2007 (IPL 2003).

iii. ROVING REFERENCE

The traditional reference service was a passive model in which a librarian responded to requests from patrons who approached the desk for information. In a world in which people can acquire a great deal of information simply by accessing a Web site, patrons develop high expectations for service. This has led some libraries to develop a new approach sometimes referred to as roving, proactive, or point of need reference, which de-emphasizes and sometimes eliminates reference desks. If reference desks are preserved, they are usually smaller, have less storage area, permit easy egress for the librarian, and are adjustable to accommodate both adults and children (Pitney and Slote 2007). Lipow (2003) observed, "If truth be known, as a place to get help in finding information, the reference desk was never a good idea" (p. 31). She described it as fraught with contradictory messages. Theoretically, the reference desk implies professional expertise, but it is often staffed by support personnel. When librarians are at the desk, they often appear busy, thus creating a barrier for the patron seeking service. In the roving reference model, librarians model a customer service approach, actively seeking out and greeting patrons. Roving reference emphasizes serving patrons at their point of need rather than at a desk.

Roving is not without problems and "requires a different world view" (Pitney and Slote 2007, p. 56). For example, some librarians find it difficult to approach patrons. In addition, roving can require changes in staffing patterns or additional service time on the floor which can reduce librarians' time to perform other duties (Pitney and Slote 2007). It also requires training and sensitivity so the librarian is not seen as intrusive and mobile support technology or other information-finding tools when patrons are not near the catalog. To solve this problem, some libraries have used portable wireless communication devices such as tablets. Other solutions include installing online public access catalogs in different areas of the library. Despite these issues, roving reference has the potential to serve many patrons who might otherwise leave a library without getting the materials or information they need. As such, it serves as another strategy to meet the mission of the library and concomitantly serve as an excellent public relations tool.

iv. SEARCH ENGINES AND GOOGLE

It is unclear how the World Wide Web and the rise of search engines such as Google will affect public libraries. However, there is certainly reason to believe that people will first use a search engine at home before they go to a library. OCLC, for example, reported that among Internet users, 84 percent used a search engine like Google first, and only 1 percent went to a library Web site (De Rosa et al. 2005). As might be expected, the percentage was significantly higher among those fourteen to twenty-four years of age. In addition, although public libraries got favorable ratings, search engines got higher ones. In the same study, 86 percent of respondents reported favorable impressions of search engines, compared to 80 percent for public libraries (De Rosa et al. 2005). In addition, 93 percent of the respondents believed that Google provided worthwhile information. When respondents compared search engine performance to that of a librarian, respondents were equally and highly satisfied, and trusted the information provided equally. More troubling, however, was that respondents were more satisfied with the quantity of information, speed, and overall experience provided by the search engines. They also described search engines as a much better fit with their lifestyles.

d. Perception of the Public Library: Is It Meeting Its Purpose?

Given the popularity of search engines such as Google, is the existence of the public library threatened? Will adults simply stay home or at the office and find the information they need; will students do their school or college work using Google and other databases without the need to come to the public library? The OCLC study offered some troubling findings. For example, a third of Internet users indicated that they used the library less; 26 percent reduced their book and newspaper reading, and 39 percent watched less television. Nearly one in four criticized the services they received at a library, the limited hours of operation, the library policies, and the online catalog. Substantially more respondents criticized the facility, complaining it was dirty, too noisy, too confusing, and unsafe.

On the positive side, the survey also found that people were very pleased with the books, the information provided, and the staff. This is certainly testimony to the primary functions of the public library and should help sustain its use. However, the study also revealed that books were the "brand" of the public library. That is, when asked about the first thing that comes to mind when thinking of the public library, 69 percent answered books and only 12 percent answered information. Yet as to the main purpose of the public library, 53 percent said information and only 31 percent indicated books. Does this mean that there is a misfit between people's perception of public libraries' role and their current function? Not necessarily. A significant percentage of those in the OCLC study agreed that the library was many things, including a place to learn, to read, to make information freely available, to support literacy, to provide research support, to get books and other materials, to provide homework support, and to access the Internet. To the extent that the Internet cannot perform all of these functions, the library is here to stay. But it is also important to realize that the Internet is a preferred and trusted information source; that it is often perceived as more convenient and befitting our contemporary lifestyle. In a world where individuals prefer self-service and speed, the public library will need to maintain and enhance its value to compete.

e. Planning and Evaluating Public Library Services

Over the years, ALA and especially PLA have worked to build the capacity of public library administrators to plan strategically. The first major planning resource, *A Planning Process for Public Libraries*, was published in 1980. It helped libraries identify their primary and secondary roles based on assessed community needs (Palmour et al. 1980). *Planning and Role-Setting for Public Libraries* (McClure et al. 1987), *Planning for Results* (Himmel and Wilson 1998), and *The New Planning for Results* (Nelson 2001) continued to update administrators' knowledge and skills. In the latest documents, topics such as designing and preparing for the planning process, identifying community needs, selecting service responses and activities, writing and communicating the plan, allocating resources, and monitoring plan implementation were methodically discussed.

Although few doubt that public libraries greatly benefit their communities, those benefits are sometimes hard to define or quantify. Nonetheless, in a climate of taxpayer reluctance to fund public services, it is crucial that libraries demonstrate why they make a difference. For example, a report by the Urban Libraries Council (2007) found "that the return on investment in public libraries not only benefits individuals, but also strengthens community capacity to address urgent issues related to economic development" (p. 1). According to the study, libraries provide early literacy services that contribute to long-term economic success; their employment and career resources help prepare a workforce able to deal with new technologies; library support to small business through resources and programs contributes to development and stability; and the library bolsters cultural and commercial activities and provides a stable, safe, and high-quality environment for community activities.

To some extent, a public library must be judged based on the expectations of its local community. The best-known measurements are those created by the Public Library Association. First promulgated in 1982 in *Output Measures for Public Libraries* (Zweizig 1982) and revised in 1987 (Van House et al. 1987), these measures were intended to help public libraries plan, document, and evaluate based on their own community's expectations rather than on national standards. A number of measures were suggested including per capita visits, circulation, in-library materials use, reference transactions, and program attendance. In addition, a variety of rates was proposed, including the number of times a requested title was found (fill rate), subject and author fill rate, and browsers' fill rate.

Many of these measures, however, address only traditional library services. As electronic networks play increasingly important roles in the delivery of library services, Bertot, McClure, and Ryan (2001) proposed additional measures including the number of public-access Internet workstations, virtual reference transactions, full-text titles available by subscription, database sessions, virtual visits to library networked resources, and users instructed. Casey and Stephens (2008) proposed specific measures for social networking applications including tracking hits and uses of blogs, wikis, and other Web applications; gathering comments to determine readership of library blogs and news sites; and gathering staff and users' anecdotes on how the service is working.

Other measures of public library service include national rankings. For example, Hennen's American Public Library Ratings is based on five categories of population size, and six input and nine output measures. The weighted measures, sometimes expressed per capita, include circulation, expenditures, staff size, volumes per capita, number of visits, number of hours open, and number of reference questions. More recently, these measures have been criticized as incomplete and even Hennen (2008) noted the need to introduce additional measures for electronic resources, youth services, and building size, but to date they have not been added. In 2009, *Library Journal* implemented the LJ Index of Public Library Service, which identified "star" libraries in the United States. The index, sponsored by Baker & Taylor's Bibliostat, was created by Ray Lyons and Keith Curry Lance. It rates more than 7,000 public libraries categorized by operating expenditures using four per capita output measures: circulation, visits, program attendance, and public Internet use. Highly ranked libraries receive three, four, or five stars (Miller 2009).

Libraries in the twenty-first century will emphasize quantitative evaluation, such as economic valuation. The Americans for Libraries Council (2007) identified several reasons for conducting such evaluations, including demonstrating the library's value in dollars and cents; meeting the community's need for accountability by providing quantifiable results; and providing evidence to gain support from advocates and elected officials. Certainly, public library use is not free. De Rosa, Dempsey, and Wilson (2004) estimated that the cost to visit a public library, when such factors as travel time, time in the library, and per capita library expenditures were taken into account, was $26.43 for someone with an annual income of $50,000, and $40.43 for someone with an income of $85,000.

Economic studies generally employ two basic research techniques: (1) the analysis of comparative data such as those of the National Center for Educational Statistics, and (2) economic valuation methods such as cost-benefit analysis, contingent evaluation, and studies that measure the indirect impact of libraries (secondary economic impact analysis) (Imholz and Arns 2007). Holt and Elliott (2003) suggested that with increasing accountability pressures, cost-benefit analysis will become more common, although the emphasis should shift from outputs to outcomes. That is, the focus will shift from what libraries do, to what tangible benefits they provide to their communities. Their proposed cost-benefit measures include (1) consumer surplus, which is "the value that library users place on separately-valued library services" (p. 429); and (2) contingent valuation, which measures how much an individual would be willing to pay rather than lose library service, or how much an individual would be willing to pay in taxes to maintain current services.

In general, studies of the economic benefits of public libraries have produced positive results. For example, a study of nine libraries in southwestern Ohio reported operating costs of a little more than $74 million, but the direct economic benefit exceeded $238 million or $3.81 for every $1.00 expended (Levin, Driscoll & Fleeter 2006). A study of Pennsylvania public libraries found a return on investment of $5.50 for every $1.00 of tax support (Pennsylvania Library Association 2009). A study in Suffolk County, New York, found similar results: every dollar spent on the public library yielded $3.87 in economic benefit (Americans for Libraries Council 2007). However, the study methodologies were not consistent. There is a critical need for consistent data standards and valuation techniques, greater national coordination, and greater awareness of appropriate valuation techniques (Imholz and Arns 2007). In addition, although such measures are often undertaken to maintain or secure funding, they should also be directed toward helping the library fulfill its purpose. As Rodger (2002) reminded us, the key question should not be, "How can we get more money?" but rather "How can we become more valuable to the community?"

f. Censorship Issues

Attempts to restrict access or remove materials are hardly new, but some citizens are becoming even more vocal and requests to filter access to the Internet at library terminals are increasing. With the passage of the Children's Internet Protection Act, these requests will likely be more frequent. Recent attacks extend beyond individual items in specific libraries to ALA itself, especially the ALA Library Bill of Rights. As a result, public librarians have been forced to defend not only their own libraries, but also their professional association and its tenets. Complaining patrons have led some librarians to compromise their professional standards by restricting access or eliminating controversial materials. A more detailed discussion of censorship and intellectual freedom issues is found in Chapter 9.

g. The Quality versus Demand Problem

The breadth of a public library's mission makes it difficult to determine exactly how it should be implemented. Selection and collection development have always prompted intense discussion regarding the purchase of high-circulation materials of limited or ephemeral value versus materials of lasting educational value that circulate infrequently. Arguments in support of acquiring popular materials include these:

1. They are heavily used, suggesting that the library is meeting the demand of its community.
2. They provide important diversion and entertainment.
3. High circulation is an important indicator of a library's success.
4. High circulation assists the library in obtaining popular political support.

Libraries embracing the demand perspective have been redesigned to compete with retail book stores, marketing the availability of popular items by placing them in the path of the library visitor, and directing traffic patterns accordingly.

Arguments in favor of purchasing items of more lasting value include these:

1. The library's primary role is education, not entertainment.
2. High demand is artificially created by mass-market publishers, and libraries should not succumb to these manipulations.
3. Libraries have a duty to serve individual tastes and not cater to mass-market appetites.
4. There is already too much emphasis on circulation statistics (which encourage the purchase of ephemeral popular materials), while measures of in-house use of educational or reference materials are less valued.
5. Mass-market materials have a degrading effect on the public's intellect. (Bob 1982; Rawlinson 1981)

As budgets remain tight, the allocation of scarce resources requires that libraries answer important questions about their primary functions so that they might make these allocations wisely.

h. Service to Diverse Populations

As the U.S. population becomes increasingly heterogeneous, libraries continue to diversify their services to meet the needs of various groups despite a number of barriers including shortages of resources, lack of staff diversity, insufficient understanding of diverse populations and other cultures, competing demands among ethnic and racial groups, lack of patron knowledge of libraries, and lack of time (Du Mont, Buttlar, and Caynon 1994). Overcoming these barriers requires vigorous recruitment of minority librarians, more staff development and training, improved needs assessments, targeted marketing of library services, improved dissemination of research on service to ethnic and racial groups, and participation of community members in the design and implementation of library services.

The diverse populations living in inner-city areas often regard the public library as the heart of the community. In Bernardi's (2005) view, inner-city libraries perform several key roles:

1. Provide access to computers and technology
2. Ensure safety, especially for children
3. Disseminate information from nonprofits and service organizations
4. Compile information on jobs and careers
5. Serve as an ethnic and cultural center
6. Welcome teens and young people

Service to the poor has been a matter of great concern to librarians for decades. ALA has promulgated a number of policies addressing this issue, most notably "Library Services for the Poor" (ALA 2008a), which describes the urgency of responding to the needs of "poor children, adults, and families" (p. 55). The recommendations include the removal of all barriers to library services including fees, the provision of funds for programming to people with low income, and increasing the materials and services that realistically address the issue of poverty and homelessness. In addition, ALA (2008a) advocates training library staff to deal with the poor.

Despite these encouragements, some believe that the profession has not been sufficiently aggressive in reaching out to low-income communities. For example, Gieskes (2009) reported that the poor "appear to be an invisible population among library potential constituencies" (p. 55). He found that few libraries consult with ALA divisions or resources in seeking ways to serve poor people and many are uncomfortable identifying poor people as a distinctive group due to a reluctance to label them. Nonetheless, he recommended that libraries and the ALA take a more proactive approach.

i. Service to Rural Communities

Although rural residents comprise only 17 percent of the U.S. population, they live on four-fifths of the land area. Nearly 50 million people reside in nonmetropolitan areas in the United States. The population of Hispanics has doubled in rural areas since 1980 (Economic Research Service 2004). Rural libraries serving fewer than 25,000 people average 3.5 paid, full-time staff equivalents, a book collection of 26,000 volumes, and an operating budget of $155,000 (Vavrek 2003). The smallest libraries possess even fewer resources.

Rural libraries face many challenges including these:

1. Insufficient resources
2. Utilities and connectivity issues
3. Lack of expertise to support electronic networks
4. Locating, hiring, and retaining professionally trained staff
5. Significant geographic barriers
6. Supporting schools and homeschoolers
7. Providing reading, information, and computer literacy instruction for recent immigrants
8. Serving as a community center (Vavrek 2003; Johnson 2000)

Despite these challenges, rural librarians find their work very satisfying and believe that they play a vital role in their communities, supporting economic development and making a difference to individuals' lives (Flatley and Wyman 2009).

j. Service to Individuals with Disabilities

It is estimated that more than 51 million Americans have disabilities, comprising 18 percent of the population (U.S. Bureau of the Census 2006). Native Americans have the highest rates of disability followed by African Americans. In general, increasing disability rates are associated with lower incomes and fewer years of formal education. Similarly, because disabilities increase with age, the maturing of the baby boom population will increase the numbers in the future. These factors, combined with the fact that individuals with disabilities often have increased information needs, place a special burden on libraries (Rubin 2001). Further, individuals with disabilities are often part of the digital divide; they are less likely to have Internet access in their homes, and thus have less access to information.

Public libraries' commitment to provide service to all, including individuals with disabilities, carries a number of implications such as providing physical access to the building and services in compliance with the Americans with Disabilities Act. This requires attention to ramps, curb cuts, parking availability, elevators, signage, telephones, drinking fountains, alarm systems, wider aisles, and access to assistive technologies such as page-turning devices, modified keyboards, speech input capability, machines that read print aloud, adjustable workstations, and computer hardware and software that enlarge print, speak, and produce Braille. Accessible collections include large-print books, audio books and tapes, Braille books, and closed-captioned DVDs and videos. Extended loan and reserve periods, remote access to the catalog, library cards for caregivers, and programs that include signers for the deaf are also helpful. Additional services might include programs for the homebound, books by mail, and fax and e-mail services. Staff training is also important (Klauber 1998; Rubin 2001).

k. Children's and Young Adult Services

The importance of children's and young adult (YA) or teen services are often underestimated. In fact, a substantial proportion of public library circulation comes from youth. Nearly 90 percent of public libraries offer young adult programming, with approximately 52 percent having at least one full-time equivalent staff devoted to YA services (ALA 2007b). There is cause for concern, however. A study by the National Endowment for the Arts (Bradshaw 2004) found that "over the past 20 years, young adults (18–34) have declined from being those most likely to read literature to those least likely (with the exception of those aged 65 and above" (p. xi). Similarly, a 2008 study of the reading abilities of young people found that although the reading skills and comprehension of younger children had improved, those of seventeen-year-olds were almost identical to those of seventeen-year-olds in 1971. In other words, any improvements in elementary school were lost in high school (Tomsho 2009). These findings, which suggest that the reading habit is being lost or seriously threatened among young adults, are particularly troubling because reading is strongly correlated with literacy skills and successful academic performance. The potential role of the public library is manifest. For example, Whitehead (2004) found that distributing library cards to children and taking them on field trips to the public library resulted in greater reading accuracy and comprehension compared to those without the cards or field trips. What, then, are some of the major trends and challenges facing children's and YA librarians?

i. DEMOGRAPHIC CHANGES

American communities have become more racially and ethnically diverse. Family structures have changed; nearly 18 million children in the United States live in single-parent families, including nearly 19 percent of white children, 27 percent of Hispanics, and 54 percent of African-American children (U.S. Bureau of the Census 2007). As a consequence, children's and YA services, collections, and programs must respond to these changes. Programs for latchkey or "at-risk" children and out-reach functions at local day care facilities have become more common. Tomorrow's libraries will devote considerable energy to developing a wide array of programs to accommodate our increasingly heterogeneous society.

ii. PROLIFERATION IN THE VARIETY OF CHILDREN'S AND YA MATERIALS

Books for children and young adults have been one of the healthier economic segments in publishing; 3,000–5,000 books are published each year in the United States and the number of children's authors and illustrators has increased significantly. Picture books for very young children have been written on a wide range of subjects in a variety of formats with exceptional artistic and literary merit. Many of these works, especially for young children, are brilliantly illustrated using printing technologies that make the illustrated page a visual feast for the eyes. YA fiction has grown in subject depth as well, confronting difficult situations including drug abuse, suicide, and divorce. Many of the new nonfiction titles are well researched and well written by knowledgeable authors reflecting multicultural perspectives. There are now, for example, far more biographies of minority individuals and women. Science books for children have also proliferated, including pop-up formats and some that incorporate computer chips that make sounds. All this is good news, but this bounty challenges collection development. Should children's and YA librarians purchase multiple copies of fewer materials or purchase just one of many titles? How can they order the plethora of newly published materials while maintaining the quality of their core collections?

iii. OUTREACH TO VERY YOUNG CHILDREN

The changing U.S. family structure has resulted in increased numbers of working parents and a proliferation of day care and preschool programs. Children's and YA librarians collaborate with schools, Head Start programs, day care centers, and other organizations serving very young children. Many develop special library programs for infants (lap-sit programs), toddlers, and students in preschools. Alternatively, some libraries prepare kits of print materials, AV materials, and lists of appropriate Web sites that can be borrowed by groups serving children at remote sites. Some public libraries even send their librarians into these establishments to provide programs. Although clearly important, this type of outreach is costly in terms of personnel and time. Nonetheless, children's need for library materials is critical. If children cannot come to the library, many librarians have committed to take materials and services to them.

Underlying this attention to the youngest children is the concept of emergent literacy. Historically, studies of reading tended to focus on children in the early years of schooling. We now know that a child's reading habits are affected by experiences from birth; the ability to read has its origins in a child's early nonverbal and verbal interactions with others and the environment. Early experiences with language and books build the foundation for literacy skills (Stratton 1996). Informal literacy activities, even as an observer, can have substantial effects on the development of reading skills. Justice and Kaderavek (2002) found that children acquire literacy skills at different rates. For example, it is not surprising that children with disabilities such as autism or other mental impairments experience delays in acquiring literacy skills. Others at risk are children in poverty, those with limited English proficiency, and those with limited access to literacy materials.

Byrnes, Deerr, and Kropp (2003) recommended four critical services that public libraries can provide to develop literacy skills: "age-appropriate spaces, materials, programming, and the opportunity for parents to gain skills through modeling" (p. 42). Early literacy programming requires the cooperation, and often the presence, of a parent or caregiver. In addition to modeling, librarians help them better utilize the library's resources and encourage them to read to their children at home, incorporating such activities as reciting and singing nursery rhymes together. This focus on emergent literacy is another example of how LIS professionals translate important research into programs and services to meet the needs of their communities.

iv. THE GROWTH OF ELECTRONIC MATERIALS

Computers have become an everyday part of children's experience, and the Web now provides a vast array of information for young people including encyclopedias and other reference materials. Web access, of course, creates new challenges for librarians, who must identify the best Web sites and make them available to children, parents, and teachers. An ALA Public Library Funding and Technology Access study (ALA 2009a) reported that nearly 80 percent of public librarians believed that "providing educational resources and databases for K–12 students is the Internet-based service most critical to the role of the library" (p. 2). As of 2009, 83 percent of public libraries offered online homework resources. In addition, three-quarters of homeschooling parents used the public library for educational support.

Gaming is a particularly interesting growth area in YA services. A growing number of libraries now offer services to gamers, including special events or gaming tournaments (Levine 2006). Some libraries incorporate video games into summer reading programs or community programming, while others offer dedicated gaming workstations and MMPOGs (massively multiplayer online games) (Ward-Crixell 2007; Levine 2006). Although aimed primarily at young people, gaming crosses many socioeconomic and demographic categories. For example, a large number of individuals who play games online, especially word and puzzle games, are women over the age of forty. In fact, women make up 38 percent of all gamers, a larger fraction than teenage boys, who make up 30 percent. Similarly, some libraries are attracting older adults to their libraries to play Wii or other electronic games using teens as coaches (Lipschultz 2009). Nicholson reported that 80 percent of public libraries permitted patrons to play games on library computers; 20 percent of libraries circulated games; and 40 percent used in-house gaming programs (ALA 2008b).

With the increasing sophistication and collaborative nature of electronic games, educators and sociologists have investigated the effects of gaming on young people. Numerous studies have found that games offer a variety of factors of interest to librarians, including the following (Levine 2006):

- Games test out problem-solving skills.
- Games are inclusive.
- Games create community.
- Games facilitate learning.
- Games provide fields for practice of leadership and team skills.
- Games develop identity. (p. 5)

In addition, Faris (2007) observed that gaming promotes literacy skills by helping preschool children acquire pre-reading skills and older children acquire logic skills including hypothesis testing. Because some games require teamwork and a community, some believe that gaming creates a "participatory culture." Games "break down barriers between the library and community and make the library a welcoming place for a whole new group of users" (Ward-Crixell 2007, p. 38). Although some believe that gaming diverts attention from the basic mission of libraries, there is little doubt that young people find gaming attractive and that it is likely to grow in the future:

> Playing games in today's public and school libraries is a profoundly social experience for library patrons both young and old.... What matters is the opportunity for play, a willingness to learn, the supportive presence of experts and novices, and the library as the setting for learning, playing, and gaming. (Lipschultz 2009, p. 40)

v. INTELLECTUAL FREEDOM

Censorship and intellectual freedom issues are often at the forefront of library services to children and young adults. With the passage of the Children's Internet Protection Act, children's and YA librarians face new challenges to abide by the law and still protect the information access rights of the young (see School Library Media Centers). Keep in mind, however, that in terms of intellectual freedom, the public library differs fundamentally from a school library in at least two important ways. First, public libraries contain a great quantity of materials primarily published or produced for adults; school libraries seldom have adult materials, except those for teachers. Second, unlike schools, public libraries do not serve in loco parentis, that is, in the place of the parent, although some parents and political groups want the library to act as a monitor and censor. Given ALA's policy on open access, there is considerable discussion regarding children's exposure to materials aimed at adults, which will likely increase, not only because of the increasingly graphic nature of violence and sexuality in visual and audio materials, but also because access is expanding through the Internet. The resulting political and legal tensions will require ever more vigilance on the part of librarians to protect the rights of minors. To some extent, ALA has tried to accommodate the concerns of parents and other adults by establishing Web sites that link to numerous educational and recreational sites.

vi. PUBLIC LIBRARY–SCHOOL LIBRARY MEDIA CENTER COOPERATION

Cooperative programs can include class visits by public librarians, extended borrowing periods for teachers, compiling information on Web resources for teachers, coordinating public library materials to coincide with curriculum units, providing bibliographic instruction and library tours to students, and participating on education-related committees. Despite the obvious benefits of school–public library cooperation, a number of factors tend to inhibit cooperation:

- Schools and public libraries are usually separate political subdivisions. There is often little or no administrative or board support for cooperation.
- Teachers, school librarians, and public librarians have little free time; they tend to focus their time and attention primarily on the duties within their own institutions.
- Limited fiscal resources reduce the time and staffing available for cooperation.
- Public librarians are sometimes wary that their cooperation is really being used as an inappropriate subsidy of the school budget. That is, the public library budget is being used for services that should be in the school budget.
- There is insufficient expertise to develop effective cooperation.

Perhaps the ultimate in public library–school library cooperation is the combined school–public library facility. In hard economic times, citizens want their public institutions to cooperate to maximize fiscal efficiencies. Combining libraries is, at least on the surface, attractive. There are significant advantages to students who, in one place, have librarians trained to assist them and a collection that is usually much larger than that of a typical school library. On the other hand, there are a number of challenges. For example, who will manage the library? How will use of the facility be determined? Who determines policies related to materials access? How are costs allocated? Who is expected to perform cataloging and processing functions? Who has priority during certain times of day? Are there two separate staffs? How will conflicts between school library and public library staff be handled (Owens 2002; Casey 2002; Blount 2002)? Despite these problems, the advantages of shared resources, expanded hours, increased economies, shared technologies, shared expertise, and potential community approbation make this a tempting alternative.

B. School Library Media Centers

School library media centers (SLMCs) in the United States have nineteenth-century origins, but few existed until the twentieth century when the National Education Association's Committee on Library Organization and Equipment published the first standards for junior and senior high schools in the early 1920s (Woolls 1994). In 1925 the National Education Association created standards for elementary schools. The first comprehensive standards for K–12 were published in 1945 (ALA 1998).

Major improvements in American school libraries occurred after the Soviet Union launched the Sputnik satellite in 1957. This event triggered considerable social and political upheaval as Americans feared they would fall behind their cold war adversary. In response, the federal government increased funding for elementary and secondary education, especially to improve curricula and teacher training. For example, the National Defense Education Act of 1958 was intended to strengthen mathematics and science. Title III of the act provided money for books, other print materials, and AV materials. Later changes to Title III provided funding for equipment in school libraries. Political support for education continued well into the 1960s, resulting in the passage of the Elementary and Secondary Education Act in 1965, which provided additional funding for materials for schools and libraries. At the same time, standards for SLMC were updated to emphasize the importance of a strong collection and resulted in increased materials, particularly in AV formats (Brodie 1998). A more complete discussion of legislation promoting SLMCs is found in Chapter 8.

Today, it is estimated that there are nearly 100,000 SLMCs located in 94 percent of public schools and 86 percent of private schools in the United States (NCES 2004). The size of the workforce is considerable: more than 66,000 librarians and 34,000 support staff (ALA 2009b). Unfortunately, these numbers are deceiving. For example, the average number of staff members per SLMC is one librarian and one support staff (Shontz and Farmer 2007) or one librarian for every 953 students (Minkel 2003; Shontz and Farmer 2007). A quarter of all schools have no school librarian, and 48 percent have no full-time support staff.

SLMCs are bureaucratically embedded in their school systems, and the school board's policies ultimately govern their activities. Although board members seldom supervise or control libraries, they often become involved when there are complaints about materials. The degree of autonomy and authority of SLMC librarians varies greatly. In some cases, a school librarian can exercise considerable autonomy, but general control and supervision often rest with a school principal or a district's curriculum director or district librarian who might be responsible for selecting or approving materials for all of the district's library media centers. The American Association of School Librarians (AASL) has taken a very active role in shaping the character of SLMCs. They describe the mission of a SLMC as:

> To ensure that the students and staff are effective users of ideas and information. The school library media specialist (SLMS) empowers students to be critical thinkers, enthusiastic readers, skillful researchers, and ethical users of information. (AASL 2009a)

Eisenberg (2002) summarized the role of the school library media specialist similarly:

> School librarians teach meaningful information and technology skills that can be fully integrated with the regular classroom curriculum. They advocate reading through guiding and promoting it. And they manage information services, technologies, resources and facilities. (p. 47)

In AASL's (2009a) publication *Empowering Learners: Guidelines for School Library Media Programs*, the association identified five ways that the SLMC accomplishes its mission:

> (1) collaborating with educators and students to design and teach engaging learning experiences that meet individual needs; (2) instructing students and assisting educators in using, evaluating, and producing information and ideas through active use of a broad range of appropriate tools, resources and information technologies; (3) providing access to materials in all formats, including up-to-date, high quality, varied literature to develop and strengthen a love of reading; (4) providing students and staff with instruction and resources that reflect current information needs and anticipate changes in technology and education; (5) providing leadership in the total education program and advocating for strong school library media programs as essential to meeting local, state, and national education goals. (p. 8)

As a companion to *Empowering Learners*, AASL has issued *Standards for the 21st-Century Learner* (AASL 2009b), which established specific skills needed by students to be effective learners. The standards are based on nine common beliefs:

1. Reading is a window to the world.
2. Inquiry provides a framework for learning.
3. Ethical behavior in the use of information must be taught.
4. Technology skills are crucial for future employment needs.
5. Equitable access is a key component for education.
6. The definition of information literacy has become more complex as resources and technologies have changed.
7. The continuing expansion of information demands that all individuals acquire the thinking skills that will enable them to learn on their own.
8. Learning has a social context.
9. School libraries are essential to the development of learning skills. (p. 12)

The standards themselves identify in detail the skills, responsibilities, and self-assessment strategies needed to help students develop four abilities:

(1) inquire, think critically, and gain knowledge; (2) draw conclusions, make informed decisions, apply knowledge to new situations, and create new knowledge; (3) share knowledge and participate ethically and productively as members of our democratic society; and (4) pursue personal and aesthetic growth. (p. 14)

The school library media center faces many challenges. The following sections provide a brief discussion of some of these critical issues.

1. Achieving the Educational Mission of Schools

If SLMCs are to thrive, they must be recognized for their substantial contribution to academic achievement. Too often, the library media center is considered an expensive appendage to the educational process rather than an integral part. This viewpoint is especially ironic, given the evidence. In one study, Lance, Welborn, and Hamilton-Pennell (1993) found that students who scored higher on norm-referenced tests tended to come from schools with larger library staff and collections. In addition, high academic performance was correlated with SLMCs in which librarians served in an instructional and collaborative role. The size of the library staff and the collection were, in fact, the best predictors of academic performance, with the exception of at-risk conditions such as poverty. This study was later repeated with similar findings (Lance et al. 2000). In Ohio, Todd (2003) surveyed more than 13,000 students in grades 3–12 and interviewed more than 870 teachers. More than 90 percent of the students felt that the school library had helped them at least to some extent with finding information, working on school topics, locating different sources of information, or finding different opinions about topics. Overall, the study concluded that "an effective school library, led by a credentialed school librarian who has a clearly defined role in information-centered pedagogy, plays a critical role in facilitating student learning for building knowledge" (p. 6).

Shontz and Farmer (2007) reported that 92 percent of SLM specialists communicated regularly with their principals and 42 percent served as mentors for new teachers or other SLM personnel. In addition, 60 percent served on school leadership teams or educational committees at the building, district, or state level. SLMC specialists were also active in reading motivation programs, providing book talks, storytelling, and read-aloud programs, as well as popular materials such as graphic novels. SLMC specialists played major roles in crafting board policies for selecting and reevaluating library media resources, with 84 percent indicating that their policies had been approved. These findings highlight the need for school librarians to communicate clearly and cooperate closely with teachers, principals, and administrators. By demonstrating the library's ability to contribute to the school's mission, greater political and fiscal support is more likely to follow.

2. Information Technologies

Schools are leaders in the use of educational technologies and devote considerable resources to them. For example, televisions have been used in classrooms for decades, along with CD-ROMs, DVDs, and computers. The proportion of elementary and secondary school students using computers at school rose from 70 percent in 1997 to 83.5 percent in 2005 (NCES, 2007a). School librarians have been in the forefront in identifying Web-based resources, and in training and educating both students and teachers on how to locate and evaluate Web sites. As new technologies are introduced, however, SLMCs struggle to meet increasing demand with dwindling budgets and increasing equipment costs, as well as staffing, training, and facility issues.

3. Information Literacy

With the increasing use of technologies in both the classroom and the media center, there is a clear need to teach students how to locate and evaluate information. Although students born after 1990 (Generation Z) tend to be technology savvy because they grew up with Web browsers, wireless access, video games, and multitasking cell phones, this does not mean that they know how to critically evaluate information or access it efficiently. Geck (2006) recommended that SLMC librarians collaborate with teachers to integrate the Internet into the classroom, demonstrate the most effective search strategies, and create communities of learners. School librarians are uniquely prepared for this role. The purpose of such training is not to develop skills solely for academic purposes but to prepare students to be lifelong learners:

Central to this new context is the idea of the "learning community." This phrase suggests that all of us—students, teachers, administrators, and parents as well as our local, regional, state, national, and international communities— are interconnected in a lifelong quest to understand and meet our constantly changing information needs. (AASL 2009a, p. 2)

ALA (1998) created nine information literacy standards that all students should meet, not only involving how to access, evaluate, and use information, but also defining what it means to be an independent, lifelong learner and what responsibilities we have to the learning community.

ALA's Information Literacy Standards

Standard 1: The student who is information literate accesses information efficiently and effectively.

Standard 2: The student who is information literate evaluates information critically and competently.

Standard 3: The student who is information literate uses information accurately and creatively.

Standard 4: The student who is an independent learner is information literate and pursues information related to personal interests.

Standard 5: The student who is an independent learner is information literate and appreciates literature and other creative expressions of information.

Standard 6: The student who is an independent learner is information literate and strives for excellence in information seeking and knowledge generation.

Standard 7: The student who contributes positively to the learning community and to society is information literate and recognizes the importance of information to a democratic society.

Standard 8: The student who contributes positively to the learning community and to society is information literate and practices ethical behavior in regard to information and information technology.

Standard 9: The student who contributes positively to the learning community and to society is information literate and participates effectively in groups to pursue and generate information.

(*Source:* ALA 1998, pp. 8–9.)

---

4. Declining Funds

Ninety-seven percent of SLMCs depend on local funding; only a quarter receive any supplemental or federal funds. There is little doubt that in numerous communities, as demonstrated by the repeated failure of school levies, that many citizens have limited confidence in their schools. In the face of dwindling funds, there is an understandable temptation to direct existing resources to teaching, classroom materials, and support activities. However, failure to adequately fund SLMCs significantly diminishes their ability to assist teachers and students effectively. To keep pace with the rapid changes in learning technologies and the proliferation of excellent print materials published today for young people, SLMCs need continued, if not increased, funding.

5. A Diminishing Workforce

The average age of SLMC librarians is forty-five, and approximately 68 percent will retire in the next few years (Everhart 2002). Already, this trend has resulted in severe shortages of certified school library media specialists in all types of settings nationwide. In response, schools of library and information science are offering more school library media programs, some using online and interactive video delivery systems. The Institute for Museum and Library Services offers a variety of initiatives to help alleviate the shortage. However, if professional programs do not respond quickly to this pressing need, schools will be tempted to replace certified media specialists with paraprofessionals without the necessary training. The resulting loss in quality and vitality of the media center would be disturbing.

6. Censorship

Few issues in librarianship generate so much heat and so little light as censorship, and schools are particularly vulnerable. Two factors contribute to this situation: (1) differing views regarding the purpose of schools and the role of SLMCs, and (2) the rights and powers of school boards versus the rights of students and parents. These issues have been disputed in court for years, often resulting in unclear or contradictory outcomes. This judicial ambivalence was particularly highlighted in the Supreme Court case referred to as *Island Trees* or *Pico*, one of the most important SLMC cases. Stephen Pico was the student who filed the complaint (Board of Education 1982). Some issues raised by this case are discussed in the following sections.

a. The Purpose of Schools and the Role of School Library Media Centers

How one defines the purpose of schools profoundly affects how one perceives the role of SLMCs. There are two fundamentally different viewpoints. Some people believe that schools are places to inculcate particular values. This notion is not unreasonable. However, too often these individuals believe that children should not be exposed to unorthodox points of view unless such exposure occurs under tightly controlled conditions to ensure that the views are not mistakenly understood as acceptable or reasonable. From this perspective, the SLMC represents a potential problem. Generally, students can enter the library at will and select their own materials. As a rule, there is considerably less guidance and control over exposure and interpretation of materials in the library than in a classroom. To inculcate values, a library worker would need to monitor each student's selections, a practical impossibility. The alternative is to restrict the materials in the collection or restrict access.

Another perspective views schools as places where students are exposed to many ideas, and critical thinking and the development of judgment skills are emphasized. Individuals who hold this view do not think it is a school's place to assert a particular perspective or attempt to inculcate particular values. Instead, students should be prepared to discriminate among various points of view so they can make judgments on important issues on which there are many differing opinions. From this perspective, the SLMC is quite different, containing many perspectives, some unorthodox as well as orthodox, and the librarian's role would be less supervisory and controlling. Access might be guided, but unrestricted.

These two views have been painted here as polar opposites, although there are certainly many gradations. All schools promulgate values, and all try to get students to think, more or less. But beliefs about its primary purpose are likely to affect one's attitude about the role of the SLMC, particularly when books about suicide, revolution, or sexuality are part of the collection.

A third perspective is to believe that the function of the school is different from that of the SLMC. One might argue, for example, that the school is where certain values are inculcated but still believe that the SLMC's purpose is different, a place for exposure to a wide array of ideas, even those that are unorthodox. Within this framework, the SLMC serves as a special forum, where many different, even controversial and subversive ideas might be considered. Obviously, if the library is a special forum for ideas, its collection would be more catholic in perspective, no matter what the defined purpose of the classroom.

b. The Rights of School Boards, Students, and Parents

Censorship problems often arise from conflicting authorities. In general, states have delegated considerable authority to local school boards to establish policies, hire teachers, approve curricula, and select materials. From time to time, school boards are surprised to discover that some materials in the media center are controversial or unacceptable to some parents. Problems usually arise when parents file objections to materials their children have checked out, but objections can also come from principals, teachers, students, and school board members themselves. Many boards respond to challenges by restricting or discarding the disputed material, especially when there are no formal policies regarding selection or reconsideration of disputed materials.

Although the rights of young people might be less than those of adults, the courts have recognized that minors retain First Amendment and due-process rights. This finding highlights the dynamic balance between the rights of school boards to run a community's schools and the rights of citizens, including young people, to First Amendment and due-process protection. As one court decision noted:

> A library is a storehouse of knowledge. When created for a public school it is an important privilege created by the state for the benefit of the students in the

school. That privilege is not subject to being withdrawn by succeeding school boards whose members might desire to "winnow" the library for books the content of which occasioned their displeasure or disapproval. (*Minarcini v Strongsville City School District* 1977)

In the *Island Trees* case, the Supreme Court decided that school board members "possess significant discretion to determine the content of their school libraries" but they cannot exercise that discretion in a "narrowly partisan or political manner" (*Board of Education* 1982, p. B3922). If a school board intended to deprive students of access to ideas just because the board didn't like those ideas, then the board was violating the constitutional rights of the students. Interestingly, the Supreme Court left open the possibility that a school board could remove materials that were "pervasively vulgar" or educationally unsuitable, if they followed a well-structured procedure to review and evaluate those materials.

The lack of clarity regarding the rights of boards, the role of the SLMC, and the rights of students ensures that these issues will arise again and again. These problems will be magnified as SLMCs expand Internet access. The SLMC will remain a lightning rod for this debate.

C. Academic Libraries

As noted in Chapter 2, the academic library has existed in the United States since the seventeenth century, beginning with the library at Harvard. By 1792, there were nine colonial colleges with libraries, though the collections were quite small due to the emphasis on religion, rhetoric, and the classics which required little library study (Jones 1989). Well into the nineteenth century, academic collections were too small to require a separate structure and there was little linkage between the library collection and academic instruction. In fact, professors, academic departments, and college debating societies often maintained their own collections that were superior to those of the academic library (Jones 1989). It wasn't until the latter half of the nineteenth century that academic libraries as we know them began to prosper, following a shift away from the classical model of education toward professional, technical and scientific, and social scientific education. This change was heavily influenced by industrialization and the German model of the university, which identified research as a central function. As more American universities adopted this approach, the library grew in status; it was a logical place to centralize research collections and provide a place for study.

The contemporary academic research library came into its own in the 1960s, although it had roots a decade or so earlier following the passage of the GI Bill after World War II (Churchwell 2007). This bill allowed nearly 12 million veterans to attend institutions of higher education, some of whom went on to graduate programs in the 1960s. Other factors that contributed to expansion included the use of universities to conduct military research; the reaction to Sputnik and the cold war in the 1960s; and the higher education initiatives of the Kennedy administration, which provided an infusion of funds for the necessary facilities and equipment to educate millions of baby boom students.

The combination of these factors placed considerable demand on library resources and resulted in significant growth in library collections and reference, cataloging, and acquisition departments. It also led to the development of separate graduate and undergraduate libraries, increases in subject departments, the creation of a collection development office, and the development of area studies departments specializing in specific regions such as the Middle East, Africa, Eastern Europe, and Asia. Over the years, support for academic libraries also came from the American Library Association and its divisions: the Association of College and Research Libraries and the Association of Research Libraries.

Academic libraries are found at any institution providing postsecondary education including universities, four-year colleges, and community and junior colleges. Like SLMCs, the academic library does not have an independent purpose; its functions are directly related to the larger academic institution in which it is embedded. Its primary purpose is to serve the students and faculty and to a lesser extent, the administration and staff, with perhaps limited service to the local community.

The type and sophistication of materials in the collection reflect the mission of the particular institution, generally either teaching or research. Major university libraries, for example, tend to emphasize research and graduate programs, and their collections hold research journals, special collections, rare materials, dissertations, and theses, as well as monographs. While the undergraduate program is supported, much of the library's financial resources are devoted to research materials. This might also be true for a few four-year liberal arts colleges, but less so. For the most part, the liberal arts college tends to emphasize teaching and a well-rounded undergraduate education. Hence the collection is primarily for curricular support. Insofar as the college expects research and publication from its faculty, the library provides resource materials, but the bulk of the funding supports teaching. Community and junior colleges devote almost all of their energies to teaching and continuing education, and their collections and services reflect this emphasis.

Outsell (2003a) listed several trends shaping academic libraries:

- Higher levels of administrative authority, suggesting increasing influence at the administrative level of the institution
- Broadening missions, becoming more global
- Increased emphasis on self-service and personalized services
- Flat or declining budgets
- Movement toward a digital library environment

Academic libraries also struggle with challenges including these:

1. Recruitment, education, and retention of librarians
2. Clarifying the role of the library in the academic enterprise
3. Dealing with the impact of information technologies
4. Creation, control, and preservation of digital resources
5. Chaos in scholarly publication
6. Support of new users (Albanese 2001)

1. Recruitment and Retention of Academic Librarians

There is considerable concern that there will be too few academic librarians in the near future. The Association of College and Research Libraries (ACRL 2002) identified a number of factors to explain this shortage, including an aging workforce, a poor image of academic librarians, flat or declining numbers of interested library and information science graduates, relatively low salaries, and competition from other sectors of the economy. ACRL recommended new marketing and media campaign efforts, more promotion of the field, more effort to identify and support interested students, and encouraging partnerships among academic institutions.

A relatively recent and controversial recruitment strategy has been to attract individuals from outside the profession. The Council on Library and Information Resources (CLIR), for example, recruits individuals with PhDs, offers them some LIS training, and then places them in academic libraries. Crowley (2004) criticized this type of apprenticeship training, arguing that it undermines the importance of the professionally trained academic librarian. He noted that "the aim of academic library leaders should be to enhance service by embedding librarians in the center of the academic enterprise" (p. 44). Neal (2006) also expressed concerns:

> Academic libraries now hire an increasing number of individuals to fill professional librarian positions who do not have the master's degree in library science. Instead of appointing librarians with the traditional qualifying credential, they hire staff to fill librarian positions who hold a variety of qualifications, such as advanced degrees in subject disciplines, specialized language skills, teaching experience, or technology expertise. (p. 1)

Neal pointed out that if this trend continues, many of these "feral" librarians will lack the norms and values that are instilled in LIS programs. The effect on libraries is currently unknown but will need to be monitored.

Recruiting academic librarians from various racial and ethnic backgrounds is a particular concern. To address this issue, ACRL recommended research on best practices, gathering and reporting of accurate workforce data regarding minority employment in academic libraries, and setting realistic goals for representation of racial and ethnic minorities in the profession (Neely and Peterson 2007). As part of its diversity outreach efforts, the Association of Research Libraries (ARL) developed an Initiative to Recruit a Diverse Workforce funded by an IMLS grant that provides a stipend of up to $10,000 to attract students from underrepresented groups to academic and research library careers.

ACRL is also concerned with retaining academic librarians once they enter the labor force. The association recommends creating a more stimulating environment through job rotation and job sharing, flexible work schedules, and the assignment of more interesting and challenging duties. Needless to say, salary increases would also be helpful, although there is little reason for optimism.

2. Networked Information and the World Wide Web

There is certainly no doubt that the growth of electronic resources and the World Wide Web have profoundly changed the academic library:

> The Web has revolutionized the way libraries are delivering services, enabling them to offer more value ranging from remote access to online catalogs, indexing and abstracting tools, and full-text resources delivered at the user's desktop. The delivery of new and innovative services through digitization projects and distance learning technologies is transforming the brick-and-mortar library model to a virtual model. (Kyrillidou 2000, pp. 434–435)

These changes have altered the nature of the library's collection, the means of access to that collection, and how the library assists patrons (Bailin and Grafstein 2005). The trend toward digital resources will continue. Tenopir (2003), for example, summarized more than 200 research publications on the use of electronic resources:

- Both faculty and students use and like electronic resources and most readily adopt them if the sources are perceived as convenient, relevant, and time saving to their natural workflow.
- Personal subscriptions to journals continue to decrease, so users rely more on electronic subscriptions subsidized by the library and on the Internet.
- College and high school students use the Internet more than the library for research. (pp. 3–4)

Barjak (2006) found that research productivity among scientists was correlated with use of the Internet: "the more productive scientists are, the more they use the Internet" (p. 1363). Marcum and George (2003) surveyed more than 3,200 faculty and graduate and undergraduate students and found that more than 90 percent of the respondents felt comfortable retrieving and using electronic information. Undergraduate students found electronic resources particularly valuable. Although the majority still used print journals, electronic journals were also heavily used. Reassuringly, a large percentage still recognized the library as an important way to obtain information, but more than a third indicated that they used the library significantly less than they did two years previously.

The reluctance to use a library is likely a generational issue. Students born after 1980 are extremely comfortable with technology as an integral part of their lives and are more likely to visit the Web before the library. When these students do use the library, they are less likely to check out a book and more likely to use a computer. Only one in ten asks reference questions. They also expect the library to have food and drink and be open 24/7 (Gardner and Eng 2005). Holliday and Li (2004) recommended several steps that academic libraries could take to better serve this new generation of students, including providing spaces for group activities, using peers whenever possible to assist fellow students, ensuring that there are plenty of computers, and enabling remote access to digital information. Twenty-four-hour access to reference assistance and the library facility would also enhance service.

The breadth of the cultural shift in both society at large and academic culture is great:

> The academic library, as a growing organism, exists in a dynamic relationship to a multitude of other interdependent life forms. Through this complex of relationships—the living reef grows and changes. Print and paper were the binding agents in this earlier information ecology. Deliver this bond in another format, through other delivery systems, and the library must either adapt to the changes or disappear. (Shuler 2006, p. 540)

Shuler (2006) further commented that the academic library is "on its way to being a second or third information destination for many academic communities" (p. 142). Campbell (2006) observed, "For most people, including academicians, the library—in its most basic function as a source of information—has become overwhelmingly a virtual destination" (p. 20).

There is considerable evidence that the academic library is adapting successfully to these shifts. Library space has been altered to accommodate digital technologies and services; cataloging has evolved into metadata, which in turn has been applied to new forms of digital data involving graphics, sound, and video; virtual reference services have emerged; bibliographic instruction has become information literacy; resource selection and management now consider databases. Mann (2001), however, offers a cautionary note. He advised academic libraries not to adopt the "information paradigm" uncritically and warned that infatuation with electronic information technologies creates certain "blind spots" (p. 277). He urged academic librarians to consider other factors:

- The full effects that format changes have, not just on the quickness of finding a record without physical travel, but on the ease of understanding lengthy narrative or expository texts

- The need to build new library buildings to accommodate the continuing production of books and other records in paper formats
- The quality control and selection processes of real libraries that make their collections such desirable alternatives to the clutter of the Internet
- The tacit and crippling message that students pick up when we encourage them to confine their searches to Internet sources alone
- The powerful commercial and governmental forces that are seeking to make libraries completely unnecessary as on-ramps to the Internet
- The crucial difference between searching superficial surrogate catalog records arranged in classified order versus searching the actual full texts of books themselves in classified order (pp. 277–278)

Mann noted that with each new development, there will be problems as well as advantages. Academic librarians must judiciously employ the most effective repertoire of services and products if they are to survive, prosper, and serve their users.

3. The Information Commons

Academic libraries also face significant changes in pedagogy, including greater emphasis on active learning, cooperative or collaborative learning in groups, and networked resources; and changes in learning styles, mainly stemming from increased reliance on electronic resources. In response, many academic libraries have created new spaces known as the information commons (IC), information center, learning commons, or instructional commons. The IC is a physical space configured to offer a variety of library services, emphasizing digital resources. Located in the commons are computer workstations (including multimedia workstations) with access to the Internet and local databases, the online catalog, and software to prepare assignments. Reference materials and computer and reference staff are located nearby for consultation and support. Tutoring and writing support might also be available, and spaces for group work are provided. The creation of an IC requires careful planning, significant resources, and adequate staffing, training, and funding. It also requires a productive liaison with faculty whose assignments and attitude toward the commons must encourage its use (MacWhinnie 2003).

Will the IC improve the ability of academic libraries to adapt and integrate the new approaches to teaching and learning? Beagle (2002) suggested that given the growing use of learning technologies outside the library, librarians, faculty, and students will need to find ways to shape and integrate the information space. Librarians must be able to organize and make digital content available; faculty must be able to locate and bring online resources together; and students must be able to locate and use the digital content. Beagle speculated that the IC has the potential to go beyond instructional support and allows students to exploit more effectively the expansive digital environment. It remains to be seen if ICs will help secure the survival of the academic library. There is at least some cause for optimism. Samson and Oelz (2005), for example, reported that their information commons at the University of Montana–Missoula resulted in an increase in visitors to the library as well as to the library's Web site.

4. Preservation and Conservation

Preservation and conservation are two closely related but distinct concepts. According to Cloonan (2001), conservation usually refers to the "physical treatment of individual library materials, while preservation refers to the care of library materials in the aggregate (for example, by monitoring environmental conditions)" (p. 232).

It is clear that the complexity of the preservation problem is increasing for both physical and digital collections. Teper (2005) identified eight challenges:

1. Ensuring the accessibility, integrity, and permanence of digital materials
2. Preserving circulating print collections
3. Preserving rare book collections
4. Preserving audio-visual collections
5. Dealing with the deterioration of library facilities
6. Educating and training preservation and conservation professionals
7. Sustaining and developing the necessary resources to maintain a preservation program
8. Selecting and evaluating materials for preservation

Serious deterioration of library collections is a far-reaching problem, and academic libraries are particularly vulnerable because they retain their collections for long periods of time. The primary cause is acid paper. Most books and other print materials have been printed on acid paper since the 1860s. Over a period of years, the acidity dries the paper until it is brittle. Simply touching or turning the pages can crumble the paper. Brittle books are an immense problem in research libraries. The Council of Library Resources estimated that there are more than 75 million brittle books in American research libraries alone, and to preserve just 3 million of them would cost over $200 million (Byrnes 1992). The simple fact is that few dollars are available when limited funds must be used to keep pace with the ever-expanding plethora of new knowledge available in new formats.

Other factors exacerbate the problem, including improper handling of materials, improper heating and air conditioning, improper lighting, poor plumbing, fire hazards, insects, poor security to prevent mutilation, and the lack of disaster planning. To address these threats, libraries develop preservation programs that include professional development for staff and educational programs on proper handling for students, using proper storage facilities, implementing effective environmental controls, using reformatting and migrating techniques for materials that are physically deteriorating, creating disaster recovery plans, and physically treating materials in need of repair and restoration (Cloonan 2001). Although many academic libraries provide most of these services, disaster recovery plans are often missing. One need only think of Hurricane Katrina in 2005 or Tropical Storm Allison in 2001 to realize that natural disasters can wreak havoc on valued library collections (Silverman 2006). Silverman proposed a National Disaster Center for Cultural Property that could provide immediate assistance to protect collections containing cultural artifacts.

Information stored in electronic formats brings additional problems. Digital data have tremendous flexibility; they can be easily manipulated, updated, and altered. This flexibility, however, is a double-edged sword; what can be easily altered might be difficult to preserve in its original form. It is often difficult to determine authenticity if an item has been altered or manipulated electronically. Electronic data deteriorate and information stored in electronic formats must be monitored and periodically refreshed or transferred onto new storage devices to preserve integrity. In fact, electronic formats are not particularly durable; hard drives and disks are vulnerable to many problems. Compared to some new media, print has been a highly stable format; acid-free paper can last for hundreds of years and even acid paper can last for decades. Electronic formats quickly become obsolete, as do their storage formats. Therefore it is critical that the mechanisms to read the data are also preserved (Cloonan 1993, 2001).

As a result of these serious problems, major universities and the federal government have increased their efforts to preserve materials by digitizing significant collections. Preserving important research collections has taken priority, but there have also been cooperative preservation efforts among smaller academic libraries. However, these efforts are more access initiatives than preservation efforts. Smith (1999) noted ironically that providing greater access to collections through digitization often increases demand for the original items, thus risking further deterioration. Similarly, Cloonan (2001) expressed concern that attention to digitization projects might, in fact, divert attention from important preservation initiatives.

5. Increasing Costs of Periodicals and Other Materials

Research-oriented academic libraries have always relied heavily on periodicals and serials; journals provide the most current information. In 2005, the Association of Research Libraries estimated that research libraries served 10 percent more students and 16 percent more faculty than they did in 1986. During that same period, however, serials budgets declined at an annual rate of 7.6 percent (ARL 2005). Although full-text, aggregated databases have helped control some costs, academic libraries must still purchase substantial numbers of periodicals despite significantly rising prices. For example, periodical prices increased 7.2 percent from 2006 to 2007; serials rose 7.1 percent, while books rose only 1.9 percent. Inflation was greatest in the areas of science and technology; science periodical prices rose

7.5 percent (Information Today 2008). Foreign publications are a particular problem because fluctuations in foreign currencies create substantial price differences and make it difficult to track real costs. The effects of these financial pressures are troubling; the Association of Research Libraries reported significant declines in the overall purchasing power of research libraries. This trend, combined with annual average increases of 6.4 percent for library materials in general, 2.5 percent for monographs, and 4.5 percent for salaries, places research libraries in considerable fiscal jeopardy (ARL 2006). Even prestigious universities such as Harvard, Cornell, and the University of California have announced large cuts in their serials budgets ("Harvard, Cornell Slash Journal Subscriptions" 2004).

6. Accountability

Most academic institutions struggle for fiscal security, particularly public institutions supported by tax dollars. In difficult financial times, the public is not inclined to vote for increased taxes. Whether private or public, academic libraries must compete with other academic departments for dollars. These stresses place great pressure on academic library directors to demonstrate the value that the library adds to the institution. In today's accountability climate, academic libraries must provide quantitative evidence of that value. Kaufman (2008), in a groundbreaking study, developed a model for return on investment by measuring the relationship between use of library resources and grants obtained by faculty using the University of Illinois library. Her goal was to create a "quantitative measure that recognizes the library's value in supporting the university's strategic goals, using grant income generated by faculty using library materials" (p. 424); that is, she attempted to verify the effectiveness of the library's electronic resources for faculty productivity. Kaufman found that $4.38 of grant income was generated for every dollar invested in the library. Measures of service quality have also been developed. LibQUAL+, a Web-based software program, measures service quality based on service effect, library as place, and information control (Thompson et al. 2005). LibQUAL+ has been found to be a valid and reliable measure of service quality, although some research suggests that it is more a measure of user satisfaction than of actual outcomes (Thompson et al. 2005). As fiscal pressures on academic libraries mount, more cost-benefit studies and new research methods will become more and more important.

7. Information Literacy

Owusu-Ansah (2001) observed that the changing information environment calls "for an extended role for academic libraries in the formation of the intellectual aptitude of the student. These libraries must no longer just acquire, organize, disseminate, and preserve information, but they must also instruct in the strategies for retrieving, evaluating, and using information" (p. 285). Academic librarians have been doing this for many years, but with increasing challenges, they recognize the need to capitalize on their value for information literacy. Retention in higher education has become an increasingly important issue, and information literacy is a key factor (Carr and Rockman 2003). In January 2000 the Association of College and Research Libraries approved five competency standards for higher education, each with specific performance indicators.

ACRL Competency Standards for Higher Education

Standard 1: The information-literate student determines the nature and extent of the information needed.

Standard 2: The information-literate student accesses needed information effectively and efficiently.

Standard 3: The information-literate student evaluates information and its sources critically and incorporates selected information into his or her knowledge base and value system.

Standard 4: The information-literate student, individually or as a member of a group, uses information effectively to accomplish a specific purpose.

Standard 5: The information-literate student understands many of the economic, legal, and social issues surrounding the use of information and accesses and uses information ethically and legally.

---

8. The Crisis in Scholarly Publishing

Scholarly publishing is in flux. A report by the New Media Consortium and Educause (2007) characterized the situation this way:

> The time-honored activities of academic research and scholarly activity have benefited from the explosion of access to research materials and the ability to collaborate at a distance. At the same time, the processes of research, review, publication, and tenure are challenged by the same trends. The proliferation of audience-generated content combined with open-access content models is changing the way we think about scholarship and publication—and the way these activities are conducted. (p. 21)

Important issues related to scholarly publishing include the following:

1. The continuing increases in the price of academic journals

2. Publisher and vendor control of the content on electronic databases, resulting in a shift from purchasing a physical object to purchasing access to a database, usually through a negotiated license (licensing generally provides far fewer rights to users than the Copyright Act afforded)

3. Huge profits by large journal publishers, especially in the sciences, at the expense of academic and research libraries, leaving libraries little choice but to transfer their declining budgets for monographs to serials, with an attendant narrowing of their monographic collections

4. Reduced competition among major journal publishers due to mergers and acquisitions

In March 2000 many concerned parties, including the Association for Research Libraries, Johns Hopkins University, Indiana University, Pennsylvania State University, and numerous other research and academic institutions met to discuss the crisis. Concluding that the current system was simply too costly, they produced nine Principles for Emerging Systems of Scholarly Publishing (Case 2010). These principles go beyond the fiscal issues to examine the entire process of evaluating and refereeing scholarly works, preservation issues, the assignment of publishing rights, and individual privacy rights. Only through constant vigilance can the rights of scholars and students be balanced against the economic interests of academic publishers.

ARL's Principles for Emerging Systems of Scholarly Publishing

1. The costs to the academy of published research should be contained so that access to relevant research publications for faculty and students can be maintained and even expanded. Members of the university community should collaborate to develop strategies that further this end. Faculty participation is essential to the success of this process.

2. Electronic capabilities should be used, among other things, to provide wide access to scholarship, encourage interdisciplinary research, and enhance interoperability and searchability. Development of common standards will be particularly important in the electronic environment.

3. Scholarly publications must be archived in a secure manner so as to remain permanently available, and, in the case of electronic works, a permanent identifier for citation and linking should be provided.

4. The system of scholarly publication must continue to include processes for evaluating the quality of scholarly work, and every publication should provide the reader with information about evaluation the work has undergone.

5. The academic community embraces the concepts of copyright and fair use and seeks a balance in the interest of owners and users in the digital environment. Universities, colleges, and especially their faculties should manage copyright and its limitations and exceptions in a manner that assures the faculty access to and use of their own published works in their research and teaching.

6. In negotiating publishing agreements, faculty should assign the rights to their work in a manner that promotes the ready use of their work and choose journals that support the goal of making scholarly publications available at reasonable cost.

7. The time from submission to publication should be reduced in a manner consistent with the requirements for quality control.

8. To ensure quality and reduce proliferation of publications, the evaluation of faculty should place a greater emphasis on quality of publications and a reduced emphasis on quantity.

9. In electronic as well as print environments, scholars and students should be assured privacy with regard to their use of materials.

a. Open Access

One approach taken by some members of the academic research community to obtain this balance is open access (OA), which "refers to full-text scholarly articles made completely free and unrestricted to all users to read, copy, download, and distribute over the World Wide Web" (Schmidt et al. 2005, p. 407). An underlying principle of OA is that scholarly research is a public good that should be shared unfettered by economic or intellectual property constraints. Open access is usually achieved either through alternative publishing venues or through the creation of institutional or disciplinary repositories (Lustria and Case 2005). Nicholas and Rowlands (2005) reported that although OA's visibility and importance have increased, it is still relatively limited, with only 10 percent of authors reporting publication in OA journals. Van Orsdel and Born (2007) noted that OA "stands alone as an alternative to the existing system of journal publication, which most say is unsustainable in its current form" (p. 43).

One exemplar of OA in academia was the creation of the Scholarly Publishing and Academic Resources Coalition (SPARC) in June 1998. Originally an initiative of the Association of Research Libraries, SPARC is a worldwide alliance of academic institutions, research libraries, and other organizations committed to increasing access to scholarly publications through the creation of a more competitive marketplace, with lower-cost journals publishing high-quality research. SPARC members provide financial support by subscribing to the new journals. One underlying assumption was that scientists will choose alternatives that can disseminate their findings widely (Johnson 1999). SPARC maintains partnerships with scientific societies, university publishers, and other organizations to promote alternative journals that attract authors of high reputation. The major focus has been on science, technology, and medicine titles because these are among the most expensive journals, but the organization is moving into the field of economics. SPARC also educates the academic community and others about the issues facing academic publishing today.

We might, in fact, be entering a two-tier system that accommodates both OA and traditional publication models. Zhao (2005) found that articles published on the Web were more likely to be in the forefront of research than those found in print journals. If this pattern emerges more consistently, scholarly publishing might consist of OA in real time, while the second tier would continue as more formal publications dominated by traditional journals. Whether a two-tier system emerges in a substantive way or not, it is likely that OA and traditional sources will share scholarly publication, sometimes referred to as mixed open access (MOA) (Schmidt et al. 2005). MOA presents additional challenges to academic librarians who will need to be well versed in both types, maximize the capacities of search engines to locate such materials, and catalog and update holdings. The costs of these new responsibilities are unknown.

b. Digital Repositories

As the relationship between publishers and academic libraries has eroded, faculties have begun to consider aggregating scholarly content at a university or multi-university level. These discussions have led some institutions to create digital repositories, which are "digital collections capturing and preserving the intellectual output of a single or multi-university community" (SPARC 2002, p. 4). A variety of factors have spawned these repositories, including the need for quicker access to the ever-growing volume of research:

> Institutional repositories centralize, preserve, and make accessible an institution's intellectual capital, at the same time they will form part of a global system of distributed, interoperable repositories that provides the foundation for a new disaggregated model of scholarly publishing. (SPARC 2002, p. 6)

The resulting repositories should increase institutional visibility and prestige as well as access to scholarly knowledge.

Despite the potential value of institutional repositories, it is unlikely that the current system of academic publishing, which is well integrated into existing systems of tenure and promotion, will disappear anytime soon. SPARC (2002) noted that "the purpose of a disaggregated scholarly publishing model is not to destroy the current journal system, but to weaken the monopolistic impact of that system on academic institutions and their libraries" (p. 15). Nonetheless, the stakes are high for traditional publishers with mature markets where there is little room for sales growth. Some are now offering authors the opportunity to make some of their articles open access, but with considerable intellectual property restrictions (Van Orsdel and Born 2007).

D. Special Libraries and Information Centers

No single definition can aptly accommodate the variety of special libraries and information centers, but a distinction is usually made between the two. Mount (1995) defined special libraries as "information organizations sponsored by private companies, government agencies, not-for-profit organizations or professional associations" (p. 2). This definition includes special subject units in public and academic departments, as well. Information centers are "special libraries with a very narrow scope" (Mount 1995, p. 3). For example, there might be an information center on aluminum within a special library devoted to metals manufacturing. This definition subsumes an information center under the broader notion of a special library. White (1984) identified a number of characteristics of special libraries and information centers:

1. They tend to emphasize the provision of information for practical purposes rather than instruction on how to find information or a physical document.

2. They generally involve the librarian researching and finding the answer for a client, rather than the client expecting to locate the answer with the librarian's assistance.

3. They tend to give librarians a great deal of autonomy because those requesting the information are unfamiliar with the function of information centers.

4. They tend to have a relatively small number of users and restricted access to relatively small, but highly specialized collections.

5. They are directly and narrowly related to the mission of the organization in which they are located, and must regularly demonstrate their usefulness to survive.

6. They involve management oriented to the goals of the larger organization rather than the library, and the library staff itself represents only a small fraction of the total organizational workforce.

The roots of special libraries can be traced to the ancient and medieval periods (Wiegand and Davis 1994), but Mount (1995) places their modern origin in the eighteenth century with the founding of the library at the Military Academy at West Point in 1777. The Special Library Association (SLA) was founded in 1909 when there were about a hundred special libraries. By 1920 this number had grown to about 1,000. Major growth occurred after World War II, and by the 1960s there were over 10,000 special libraries. Information centers, as defined above, arose in this period, starting primarily in scientific and technical laboratories (Mount 1995).

As individuals recognized quick access to up-to-date information as a cornerstone of a competitive intellectual and economic society, the role of special libraries and information centers became obvious. Their continuing growth is attributable to at least three factors: ever-increasing amounts of information, continued development of information technologies, and recognition of the critical role of information for organizational survival (Christianson et al. 1991). In fact, special libraries and information centers tend to operate in a more entrepreneurial environment, often within private, profit-oriented organizations—quite different from most other types of libraries. They serve only their special clients or sponsors. In addition, special libraries and information centers have been expanding their functions and image well beyond the traditional library, promoting "knowledge services" or "content management services." "Knowledge Services is about establishing social communities; about creating the social infrastructure, a foundation of trust, and a collaborative environment in which all stakeholders contribute to the successful achievement of the parent organization's mission (St. Clair et al. 2003, p. 11).

Estimates of the current number of special libraries and information centers in the United States range from 14,000 to 21,000, depending on how they are defined. There are approximately 35,000 special libraries and information centers worldwide.

The heterogeneous character of these libraries is revealed in the various divisions of the Special Libraries Association (2009): business and finance, chemistry, education, engineering, government information, knowledge management, military, museums, news, pharmaceuticals, science and technology, social sciences, solo librarians, and transportation.

Following is a brief discussion of some of the issues confronting special libraries.

1. Scarce Resources

Similar to all libraries, budget stresses are considerable. Outsell (2003b) reported, for example, that the budgets of corporate information centers declined 7 percent from 2002 to 2003 while operating costs and vendor prices rose. This creates a considerable burden, especially in host organizations that expect high performance with minimum expenditures. Thus library staffs tend to be quite small even though the profitability of the organization might depend on the timeliness and accuracy of information they provide.

2. Establishing Worth

Because a library seldom produces a product of its own, it is often viewed as a cost center rather than a profit center. This means that librarians must justify their existence or be trimmed from the budget. Therefore special libraries actively promote their product—information—as something that improves the performance of others and the organization as a whole. Benchmarking, a technique to demonstrate value, involves comparing a library's performance with the performance of others to identify the best practices and improve efficiency and effectiveness. The benchmark becomes a standard against which performance can be assessed. The Special Libraries Association considers benchmarking sufficiently important that it is incorporated as a skill among its competencies (Henczel 2002). Another technique, called a balanced scorecard, evaluates the library from four perspectives: customer, internal, innovation and learning, and financial. The organization develops targets for each area and then measures success in reaching them (Mathews 2003). Overall, particular attention is paid to "return on investment", which usually involves focusing on outcome measures:

> For the special library, there is compelling evidence that libraries provide
> information services that have real value to the larger organization. This value
> might be in the form of accomplishments, time savings, and financial impacts—
> both financial savings and increased revenues. (Matthews 2003, p. 28)

In the current economic climate there will be constant attention to units that are considered "overhead." Thus it is critical that special libraries demonstrate their tangible contributions to the bottom line and critical mission of the organizations that they serve.

3. Storage and Retrieval Issues

Given that special libraries and information centers often deal with technical, scientific, and economic information, the format of information might be less important than accuracy and delivery speed, as it might be vital now but lose its utility quickly. It is crucial that the most current information be procured, and special librarians must be able to work under considerable time pressure. Meeting this responsibility entails increased reliance on information technologies and, consequently, special librarians are generally on the cutting edge of innovation, constantly updating their knowledge. Kassell (2002) identified a variety of important skills including electronic searching, analyzing competitive intelligence, conducting market research, and intranet development.

4. Copyright

Making copies has been an extremely important method of disseminating current information, especially in research-related contexts. Copyright issues are particularly thorny in the context of special libraries in for-profit organizations, which was highlighted in the 1992 case *American Geophysical Union v. Texaco*. A research scientist at Texaco, a for-profit company, made copies of eight articles from various journals. Although copying materials for research purposes generally meets fair use criteria, the court found that the purpose was commercial rather than research. The court ruled that Texaco's action had a deleterious effect on the journal publishers. That is, the company could have taken alternative actions that would have accomplished the same purpose while respecting the copyright privilege of the journal. For example, they could have ordered more journal subscriptions, ordered copies from a document delivery service, or paid additional royalties to the Copyright Clearance Center, which reimburses publishers. These arguments led the court to find in favor of the publisher. The case was upheld on appeal and Texaco ultimately settled the suit at considerable expense ("Court Upholds Ruling" 1994; "Texaco Settles" 1995). This decision could impact academic libraries as well as special libraries and information centers, and it might require librarians to ask patrons about the purpose of the copies. Such an action would raise serious privacy and intellectual freedom issues. Of course, all the issues related to copyright in the digital environment for other libraries also apply to special libraries (see Chapter 8).

V. SUMMARY

It is not surprising that libraries are often organized in conventional bureaucratic and hierarchical fashion: using these structures, they have prospered quite nicely over the years. However, today's environment presents new challenges caused by situations and events that lie outside librarians' direct control and that require rapid and adaptive responses. Common stressors include decreasing budgets and increasing inflation, the rapid expansion and obsolescence of knowledge, and the growth of new technologies. Other challenges are unique to various types of libraries. Regardless of the source of these challenges, libraries, as organizations, will need to maintain clarity of mission and structure their functions effectively.

REFERENCES

Albanese, Andrew Richard. 2001. "Moving from Books to Bytes." *Library Journal* 126 (September 1): 52–54.

American Association of School Librarians. 2009a. *Empowering Learners: Guidelines for School Library Media Programs*. Chicago: ALA.

———. 2009b. *Standards for the 21st Century Learner*. Chicago: ALA, AASL.

American Library Association. 1998. *Information Power: Guidelines for School Library Media Programs*. Chicago: ALA.

———. 2007a. *The State of America's Libraries*. Chicago: ALA.

———. 2007b. "Youth and Library Use Studies Show Gains in Serving Young Adults." (July 2007). Available: www.ala.org/ala/newspresscenter/news/pressreleases2007/july2007/yalsastudy07.cfm (accessed February 2, 2010).

———. 2008a. *Handbook of Organization 2008–2009*. Chicago: ALA.

———. 2008b. *The State of America's Libraries*. Chicago: ALA.

———. 2009a. *Libraries Connect Community: Public Library Funding and Technology Access Study*. Chicago: ALA.

———. 2009b. "Number of Libraries in the United States: Fact Sheet 1." Chicago: ALA. Available: www.ala.org/ala/aboutala/offices/library/libraryfactsheet/alalibraryfactsheet1 .cfm (accessed January 29, 2010).

———. 2009c. *The State of America's Libraries*. Chicago: ALA.

———. 2009d. *Supporting Learners in the U.S. Public Library*. Chicago: ALA.

Americans for Libraries Council. 2006. *Long Overdue: A Fresh Look at Public and Leadership Attitudes about Libraries in the 21st Century*. Public Agenda.

———. 2007. *6 Things Every Library Needs to Know about Economic Valuation*. New York: ALC.

Association of College and Research Libraries (ACRL/ALA). 2000. "Information Literacy Competency Standards for Higher Education." Available: www.ala.org/ala/mgrps/divs/acrl/standards/standards.pdf (accessed January 29, 2010).

———. 2002. *Recruitment, Retention and Restructuring: Human Resources in Academic Libraries*. ACRL, Ad Hoc Task Force on Recruitment and Retention. Final Draft. May 20.

Association of Research Libraries (ARL). 2005. *ARL Statistics 2004–05*. Washington, DC: ARL 2006.

Bailin, Alan, and Ann Grafstein. 2005. "The Evolution of Academic Libraries: The Networked Environment." *Journal of Academic Librarianship* 31 (July): 317–323.

Barjak, Franz. 2006. "The Role of the Internet in Informal Scholarly Communication." *Journal of the American Society for Information Science and Technology* 57 (August): 1350–1367.

Beagle, Donald. 2002. "Extending the Information Commons: From Instructional Testbed to Internet2." *Journal of Academic Librarianship* 28 (September): 287–296.

Bernardi, John. 2005. "The Poor and the Public Library." *Public Libraries* (November/December): 321–323.

Bertot, John Carlo, Charles R. McClure, and Joe Ryan. 2001. *Statistics and Performance Measures for Public Library Networked Services*. Chicago: ALA.

Blount, Patti. 2002. "Double Your Fun with a Combination Public-High School Library." *Public Libraries* 41 (September/October): 254–255.

Board of Education, Island Trees Union Free School District v. Pico [42 CCH S. Ct. Bull.] (1982).

Bob, Murray C. 1982. "The Case for Quality Book Selection." *Library Journal* 107 (September 15): 1707–1710.

Bradshaw, Tom. 2004. *Reading at Risk: A Survey of Literary Reading in America*. Washington, DC: National Endowment for the Arts.

Brodie, Carolyn. 1998. "A History of School Library Media Center Collection Development." In *The Emerging School Library Media Center: Historical Issues and Perspectives*. Edited by Kathy Howard Latrobe. Englewood, CO: Libraries Unlimited, 57–73.

Byrnes, Marci, Kathleen Deerr, and Lisa G. Kropp. 2003. "Book a Play Date: The Game of Promoting Emergent Literacy." *American Libraries* 34 (September): 42–44.

Byrnes, Margaret M. 1992. "Preservation and Collection Management: Some Common Concerns." In *The Collection Building Reader*. Edited by Betty-Carol Sellen and Arthur Curley. New York: Neal-Schuman, 57–63.

Campbell, Jerry D. 2006. "Changing a Cultural Icon: The Academic Library as a Virtual Destination." *Educause Review* 41 (January/February): 16–31.

Carr, Jo Ann, and Ilene F. Rockman. 2003. "Information-Literacy Collaboration: A Shared Responsibility." *American Libraries* (September): 52–54.

Case, Mary M. 2010. "Principles for Emerging Systems of Scholarly Publishing" Available: www.arl.org/bm~doc/principles.pdf (accessed February 3, 2010).

Casey, James. 2002. "The Devil Is in the Details." *Public Libraries* 41 (September/October): 252.

Casey, Michael, and Michael Stephens. 2008. "Measuring Progress." *Library Journal* 133 (April 15): 28.

Christianson, Elin B., David E. King, and Janet L. Ahrensfeld. 1991. *Special Libraries: A Guide for Management*. 3rd ed. Washington, DC: SLA.

Churchwell, Charles D. 2007. "The Evolution of the Academic Research Library during the 1960s." *College and Research Libraries* 68 (March): 104–105.

Cloonan, Michele Valerie. 1993. "The Preservation of Knowledge." *Library Trends* 41 (spring): 594–605.

———. 2001. "W(h)ither Preservation?" *Library Quarterly* 71: 231–242.

"Court Upholds Ruling That Texaco Violated Copyright." 1994. *American Libraries* 25 (December): 974.

Crowley, Bill. 2004. "Just Another Field?" *Library Journal* 129 (November 1): 44–46.

Deeken, JoAnne, and Deborah Thomas. 2006. "Technical Services Job Ads: Changes Since 1995." *College and Research Libraries* (March): 136–145.

De Rosa, Cathy, et al. 2005. *Perceptions of Libraries and Information Resources*. Dublin, OH: OCLC.

De Rosa, Cathy, Lorcan Dempsey, and Alane Wilson. 2004. *The 2003 OCLC Environmental Scan: Pattern Recognition*. Dublin, OH: OCLC.

De Rosa, Cathy, and Jenny Johnson. 2008. *From Awareness to Funding: A Study of Library Support in America*. Dublin, OH: OCLC.

Du Mont, Rosemary Ruhig, Lois Buttlar, and William Caynon. 1994. "Multiculturalism in Public Libraries." In *Multiculturalism in Libraries*. Westport, CT: Greenwood, 37–51.

Economic Research Service, Department of Agriculture. 2004. "Briefing Room: Rural Population and Migration." Available: www.ers.usda.gov/briefing/Population (accessed January 27, 2004; April 14, 2009).

Eisenberg, Mike. 2002. "This Man Wants to Change Your Job." *School Library Journal* 48 (September): 47–49.

Euster, Joanne R. 1990. "The New Hierarchy: Where's the Boss?" *Library Journal* 115 (May 1): 41–44.

Everhart, Nancy. 2002. "Filling the Void." *School Library Journal* 48 (June): 44–49.

Faris, Crystal. 2007. "Game On! Research into Children and Gaming." *Children and Libraries* 5: 50–51.

Flatley, Robert, and Andrea Wyman. 2009. "Changes in Rural Libraries and Librarianship: A Comparative Survey." *Library Quarterly* 28: 24–39.

Gardner, Susan, and Susanna Eng. 2005. "What Students Want: Generation Y and the Changing Function of the Academic Library." *Portal: Libraries and the Academy* 5: 405–420.

Geck, Caroline. 2006. "The Generation Z Connections: Teaching Information Literacy to the Newest Net Generation." *Teacher Librarian* 33: 19–23.

Gieskes, Lisa. 2009. "Why Librarians Matter to Poor People." *Public Library Quarterly* 28: 49–57.

Gorman, Michael. 1998. "Technical Services Today." In *Technical Services Today and Tomorrow*. 2nd ed. Edited by Michael Gorman. Englewood, CO: Libraries Unlimited, 1–7.

"Harvard, Cornell Slash Journal Subscriptions." 2004. *American Libraries* 35 (January): 23–24.

Henczel, Sue. 2002. "Benchmarking Measuring and Comparing." *Information Outlook* 7 (July): 12–20.

Hennen, Thomas J. Jr. 2003. "Performing Triage on the Budgets in the Red." *American Libraries* 34 (March): 36–39.

———. 2008. "American Public Library Ratings 2008." *American Libraries* 39 (October): 57–61.

Himmel, Ethel E., and William James Wilson. 1998. *Planning for Results: A Public Library Transformation Process*. Chicago: ALA.

Hoffert, Barbara. 2008. "Pushing Circ with E-Service." *Library Journal* 133 (February 15): 36–38.

Holliday, Wendy, and Qin Li. 2004. "Understanding the Millennials: Updating Our Knowledge about Students." *Reference Services Review* 32: 356–366.

Holt, Glen E., and Donald Elliott. 2003. "Measuring Outcomes: Applying Cost-Benefit Analysis to Middle-Sized and Smaller Public Libraries." *Library Trends* 51 (winter): 424–440.

Horrigan, John B. 2003. *Consumption of Information Goods and Services in the United States.* Washington, DC: Pew Internet and American Life Project.

Imholz, Susan and Jennifer Weil Arns. 2007. *Worth Their Weight: An Assessment of the Evolving Field of Library Valuation.* New York: Americans for Libraries Council.

Information Today. 2008. *The Bowker Annual: Library and Book Trade Almanac.* New Providence, NJ: Information Today.

———. 2009. *American Library Directory 2009–2010.* Medford, NJ: Information Today.

Internet Public Library. 2003. Available: www.ipl.org/div/about (accessed December 11, 2003; April 14, 2009).

Jaeger, Paul T., John Carlo Bertot, Charles R. McClure, and Lesley A. Langa. 2006. "The Policy Implications of Internet Connectivity in Public Libraries." *Government Information Quarterly* 23: 123–141.

Johnson, Linda. 2000. "The Rural Library: Programs, Services, and Community Coalitions and Networks." *Rural Libraries* 20: 38–62.

Johnson, Richard K. 1999. "Competition: A Unifying Ideology for Change in Scholarly Communications." Available: www.arl.org/DM2dDC/Competition.pdf (accessed February 2, 2010).

Jones, Plummer Alston Jr. 1989. "The History and Development of Libraries in American Higher Education." *College and Research Libraries News* 50 (July/August): 561–564.

Jorgensen, Corinne. 2005. "The Internet and Public Library Use." In *Encyclopedia of Library and Information Science*, 2nd ed. First Update Supplement. Edited by Miriam A. Drake. New York: Taylor and Francis, 261–270.

Justice, Laura M., and Joan Kaderavek. 2002. "Using Shared Storybook Reading to Promote Emergent Literacy." *Teaching Exceptional Children* 34 (March/April): 8–13.

Kao, Mary Liu. 2001. *Introduction to Technical Services for Library Technicians.* Binghamton, NY: Haworth.

Kassell, Amelia. 2002. "Practical Tips to Help You Prove Your Value." *MLS: Marketing Library Services* 16: 1–3.

Kaufman, Paula T. 2008. "The Library as Strategic Investment: Results of the Ilinois Return on Investment Study." *Library Quarterly* 18 (December): 424–436.

Klauber, Julie. 1998. "Living Well with a Disability: How Libraries Can Help." *American Libraries* 29 (November): 52.

Kyrillidou, Martha. 2000. "Research Library Trends: ARL Statistics". *The Journal of Academic Librarianship* 26(6): 427–436.

Lance, Keith Curry, Marcia J. Rodney, and Christine Hamilton-Pennell. 2000. *How School Librarians Help Kids Achieve Standards: The Second Colorado Study.* Castle Rock, CO: Hi Willo Research and Publishing.

Lance, Keith Curry, Lynda Welborn, and Christine Hamilton-Pennell. 1993. *The Impact of School Library Media Centers on Academic Achievement.* Castle Rock, CO: Hi Willo Research and Publishing.

Lenhart, Amanda. 2003. *The Ever-Shifting Internet Population.* Washington, DC: Pew Internet & American Life Project.

Levin, Driscoll & Fleeter. 2006. *Value for Money: Southwestern Ohio's Return from Investment in Public Libraries.* Columbus, OH: Levin, Driscoll & Fleeter, June 22.

Levine, Jenny. 2006. *Gaming and Libraries: Intersection of Services. Library Technology Reports* 42 (September/October): 1–80.

Lipow, Anne Grodzins. 2003. "The Future of Reference: Point-of-Need Reference Service: No Longer an Afterthought." *Reference Services Review* 31: 31–35.

Lipschultz, Dale. 2009. "Gaming." *American Libraries* 40 (January/February): 40–43.

Lustria, Mia Liza A., and Donald O. Case. 2005. "The SPARC Initiative: A Survey of Participants and Features Analysis of Their Journals." *Journal of Academic Librarianship* 31 (May): 236–246.

Lynch, Beverly P. 1978. "Libraries as Bureaucracies." *Library Trends* 26 (winter): 259–267.

MacWhinnie, Laurie A. 2003. "The Information Commons: The Academic Library of the Future." In *Portal: Libraries and the Academy*. Vol. 3. Baltimore: Johns Hopkins University Press, 241–257.

Mann, Thomas. 2001. "The Importance of Books, Free Access, and Libraries as Places—and the Dangerous Inadequacy of the Information Science Paradigm." *Journal of Academic Librarianship* 27 (July): 268–281.

Marcum, Deanna B., and Gerald George. 2003. "Who Uses What? Report on a National Survey of Information Users in Colleges and University." D-Lib Magazine (October). Available: www.dlib.org/dlib/october03/george/10george.html (accessed February 17, 2010).

Mathews, Joseph R. 2003. "Determining and Communicating the Value of the Special Library." *Information Outlook* 7 (March): 27–31.

McClure, Charles R., et al. 1987. *Planning and Role-Setting for Public Libraries: A Manual of Options and Procedures*. Chicago: ALA.

Miller, Rebecca. 2009. "Is Your Library a Star? LJ Launches the Index of Public Library Service." Available: www.libraryjournal.com/article/CA6636953.html (accessed March 17, 2009).

Minarcini v. Strongsville City School District. 541 F 2d 577 (1977).

Minkel, Walter. 2003. "The Year in K–12 Libraries: School Librarians Redefine Themselves." In *The Bowker Annual: Library and Book Trade Almanac*. Medford, NJ: Information Today, 10–14.

Mossberger, Karen, Caroline J. Tolbert, and Mary Stansbury. 2003. *Virtual Inequality: Beyond the Digital Divide*. Washington, DC: Georgetown University.

Mount, Ellis. 1995. *Special Libraries and Information Centers: An Introductory Text*. 3rd ed. Washington, DC: SLA.

National Center for Education Statistics. 2004. "Of Public Schools with Library Media Centers (2004) Table 43." Available: www.nces.ed.gov/surveys/sass/tables/state_2004_43 .asp (accessed February 2, 2010).

———. 2007a. *Digest of Education Statistics 2007*. Washington, DC: National Center for Education Statistics.

———. 2007b. *Households' Use of Public and Other Types of Libraries: 2002*. Washington, DC: NCES.

Neal, James G. 2006. "Raised by Wolves": Integrating the New Generation of Feral Professionals into the Academic Library." *Library Journal*. Available: www.libraryjournal .com/article/ CA6304405.html (accessed April 20, 2009).

Neely, Teresa Y. and Lorna Peterson. 2007. "Achieving Racial and Ethnic Diversity Among Academic and Research Librarians: The Recruitment, Retention, and Advancement of Librarians of Color—a White Paper." *C&RL News* 68 (October). Available: www.library careers.org/ala/ mgrps/divs/acrl/publications/crlnews/2007/oct/ALA_pri (accessed April 21, 2009).

Nelson, Sandra. 2001. *The New Planning for Results: A Streamlined Approach*. Chicago: ALA.

New Media Consortium and Educause Learning Institute. 2007. *The Horizon Report 2007 Edition*. Stanford, CA: New Media Consortium.

Nicholas, David, and Ian Rowlands. 2005. "Open Access Publishing: The Evidence from the Authors." *The Journal of Academic Librarianship* 31: 179–181.

Outsell. 2003a. *The Changing Roles of Content Deployment Functions: Academic Information Professionals*. Burlingame, CA: Outsell.

———. 2003b. *The Changing Roles of Content Deployment Functions: Corporate Information Professionals*. Burlingame, CA: Outsell.

Owens, Margaret. 2002. "Get It in Writing!" *Public Libraries* 41 (September/October): 248–250.

Owusu-Ansah, Edward K. 2001. "The Academic Library in the Enterprise of Colleges and Universities: Toward a New Paradigm." *Journal of Academic Librarianship* 27 (July): 282–294.

Palmour, Vernon E., Marcia C. Bellassai, and Nancy V. DeWath. 1980. *A Planning Process for Public Libraries*. Chicago: ALA.

Pennsylvania Library Association. 2009. "Return on Investement (ROI) Materials." Available: www.palibraries.org/displaycommon.cfm?an=1&subarticlenbr=23 (accessed June 29, 2009).

Pitney, Barbara, and Nancy Slote. 2007. "Going Mobile: The KCLS Roving Reference Model." *Public Libraries* 46 (January/February): 54–68.

Rainie, Lee, Mary Madden, Angie Boyce, Amanda Lenhart, John Horrigan, Katherine Allen, and Erin Grady. 2003. *The Ever-Shifting Internet Population: A New Look at Internet Access and the Digital Divide*. Washington, DC: Pew Internet and American Life Project.

Rawlinson, Nora. 1981. "Give 'Em What They Want!" *Library Journal* (November 15): 77–79.

Rodger, Eleanor Jo. 2002. "Values & Vision." *American Libraries* (November): 50–54.

Rubin, Joyce Rhea. 2001. *Planning for Library Services to People with Disabilities*. Chicago: ALA.

Samson, Sue, and Erling Oelz. 2005. "The Academic Library as a Full-Service Information Center." *Journal of Academic Librarianship* 31 (July): 347–351.

Schmidt, Karen A., and Ron L. Ray. 1998. "The Ordering, Claiming, and Receipt of Materials." In *Technical Services Today and Tomorrow*. 2nd ed. Edited by Michael Gorman. Englewood, CO: Libraries Unlimited, 9–20.

Schmidt, Krista D., Pongracz Sennyey, and Timothy V. Carstens. 2005. "New Roles for a Changing Environment: Implications of Open Access for Libraries." *College and Research Libraries* (September): 407–416.

Shontz, Marilyn L., and Lesley S. J. Farmer. 2007. "Expenditures for Resources in School Library Media Centers, 2005." In *The Bowker Annual: Library and Book Trade Almanac 2007*. 52nd ed. Edited by Dave Bogart. Medford NJ: Information Today, 445–458.

Shuler, John. 2006. "The Revolution Will Not Be Catalogued: Gutenberg's Librarians and the 21st Century." *Journal of Academic Librarianship* 32 (September): 540–542.

Silverman, Randy. 2006. "Toward a National Disaster Response Protocol." *Libraries and the Cultural Record* 41 (fall): 497–511.

Smith, Abby. 1999. *The Future of the Past: Preservation in American Research Libraries.* Washington, DC: Council on Library and Information Resources.

SPARC. 2002. "The Case for Institutional Repositories: A SPARC Position Paper." Prepared by Raym Crow. Washington, DC: SPARC.

Special Libraries Association. 2009. "Divisions." Available: www.sla.org/content/community/units/divs/index.cfm (accessed June 25, 2009).

St. Clair, Guy, Victoria Harriston, and Thomas A. Pellizzi. 2003. "Toward World-Class Knowledge Services: Emerging Trends in Specialized Research Libraries." *Information Outlook* 7 (July): 10–16.

Stratton, J. M. 1996. "Emergent Literacy: A New Perspective." *Journal of Visual Impairment and Blindness* 90 (May/June): 177–183.

Tenopir, Carol. 2003. *Use and Users of Electronic Library Resources: An Overview and Analysis of Recent Research Studies.* Washington, DC: Council on Library and Information Resources.

Teper, Thomas H. 2005. "Current and Emerging Challenges for the Future of Library and Archival Preservation." *Library Research and Technical Services (LRTS)* 49: 32–39.

"Texaco Settles Copyright Case." 1995. *American Libraries* 26 (July/August): 632–634.

Thompson, Bruce, Colleen Cook, and Martha Kyrrillidou. 2005. "Concurrent Validity of LibQUAL+(tm) Scores: What do LibQUAL+(tm) Scores Measure?" *Journal of Academic Librarianship* 31 (November): 517–522.

Todd, Ross J. 2003. "Student Learning Through Ohio School Libraries: A Summary of the Ohio Research Study." Available: www.oelma.org/studentlearning.htm (accessed April 23, 2009).

Tomsho, Robert. 2009. "Few Gains Are Seen in High School Test." *Wall Street Journal* (National Edition) April 29: A5.

Urban Libraries Council. 2007. "Making Cities Stronger: Public Library Contributions to Local Economic Development." Available: www.urban.org/uploadedpdf/1001075_stronger_cities.pdf (accessed January 29, 2010).

U.S. Bureau of the Census. 2006. "Americans with Disabilities, 2002." Issued May 2006. Available: www.census.gov/prod/2006pubs/p70-107.pdf (accessed February 2, 2010).

———. 2007. "Children/1 by Presence and Type of Parent(s), Race, and Hispanic Origin/2: 2007." Available: www.census.gov/population/socdemo/hh-fam/cps2007/tabC9-white nohisp.xls (accessed January 29, 2010).

U.S. Department of Commerce. 2002. *A Nation On-Line: How Americans Are Expanding Their Use of the Internet.* Washington, DC: Department of Commerce.

Van House, Nancy A., et al. 1987. *Output Measures for Public Libraries.* 2nd ed. Chicago: ALA.

Van Orsdel, Lee C., and Kathleen Born. 2007. "Serial Wars." *Library Journal* 132 (April 15): 43–48.

Vavrek, Bernard. 2003. "Rural Public Library Services." In *Encyclopedia of Library and Information Science.* 2nd ed. Edited by Miriam Drake. New York: Marcel Dekker, 2550–2555.

Ward-Crixell, Kit. 2007. "Gaming Advocacy: New Ways Librarians Can Support Learning and Literacy." *School Library Journal* 53 (September): 36–38.

White, Herbert. 1984. *Managing the Special Library*. White Plains, NY: Knowledge Industry.

Whitehead, Nicole. 2004. "The Effects of Increased Access to Books on Student Reading Using the Public Library." *Reading Improvement* 41 (fall): 165–178.

Wiegand, Wayne, and Donald G. Davis, eds. 1994. "Special Libraries." In *Encyclopedia of Library History*. New York: Garland, 597–599.

Wilson, Patrick. 1984. "Bibliographical R&D." In *The Study of Information: Interdisciplinary Messages*. Edited by Fritz Machlup and Una Mansfield. New York: Wiley, 389–397.

Winter, Michael F. 1988. *The Culture and Control of Expertise: Toward a Sociological Understanding of Librarianship*. Westport, CT: Greenwood.

Woolls, Blanche. 1994. *The School Library Media Manager*. Englewood, CO: Libraries Unlimited.

Young, Peter R. 1994. "Changing Information Access Economics: New Roles for Libraries and Librarians." *Information Technology and Libraries* 13 (June): 103–114.

Younger, Jennifer A., D. Kaye Gapen, and Cecily Johns. 1998. "Technical Services Organization." In *Technical Services Today and Tomorrow*. 2nd ed. Edited by Michael Gorman. Englewood, CO: Libraries Unlimited, 165–181.

Zhao, Dangzhi. 2005. "Scholarly Communication in Transition: Evidence for the Rise of a Two-Tier System." ICCC International Conference on Electronic Publishing, Leuven-Heverlee, Belgium. June 8–10, 2005. Available: http://elpub.scix.net/data/works/att/240elpub2005.content.pdf (accessed January 29, 2010).

Zweizig, Douglas L. 1982. *Output Measures for Public Libraries*. Chicago: ALA.

SELECTED READINGS: LIBRARIES AS ORGANIZATIONS

Books

American Association of School Librarians. *Empowering Learners: Guidelines for School Library Media Programs*. Chicago: American Association of School Librarians, 2009.

American Library Association. *The State of America's Libraries*. (various years). Available: www.ala.org.

Battles, David M. *The History of Public Library Access for African Americans in the South, or, Leaving Behind the Plow*. Lanham, MD: Scarecrow, 2009.

Cassell, Kay Ann, and Uma Hiremath. *Reference and Information Services in the 21st Century: An Introduction*. 2nd ed. New York: Neal-Schuman, 2009.

De Rosa, Cathy, et al. *Perceptions of Libraries and Information Resources: A Report to the OCLC Membership*. Dublin, OH: OCLC Online Computer Library Center, 2005.

Healey, Paul D. *Professional Liability Issues for Librarians and Information Professionals*. New York: Neal-Schuman, 2008.

Hernon, Peter, Ronald R. Powell, and Arthur P. Young. *The Next Library Leadership: Attributes of Academic and Public Library Directors*. Westport, CT: Libraries Unlimited, 2003.

Imholz, Susa, and Jennifer Weil Arns. *Worth Their Weight: An Assessment of the Evolving Field of Library Valuation.* New York: Americans for Libraries Council, 2007.

Mathews, Joseph R. *Measuring for Results.* Westport, CT: Libraries Unlimited, 2004.

Rosenfeld, Esther, and David V. Loertscher. Eds. *Toward a 21st Century School Library Media Program.* Lanham, MD: Scarecrow, 2007.

Squires, Tasha. *Library Partnerships: Making Connections Between School and Public Libraries.* Medford, NJ: Information Today, 2009.

Articles

Allner, Irmin. "Managerial Leadership in Academic Libraries." *Library Administration and Management* 22 (spring 2008): 69–78.

Campbell, Jerry D. "Changing a Cultural Icon: The Academic Library as a Virtual Destination." *Educause Review* 41 (January–February 2006): 16–31.

De Rosa, Cathy, and Jenny Johnson. *From Awareness to Funding: A Study of Library Support in America: A Report to the OCLC Membership.* Dublin, OH: OCLC, 2008.

Fister, Barbara. "What If You Ran Your Bookstore Like a Library?" *Library Journal* 133 (April 15, 2008): 30–32.

Fultz, Michael. "Black Public Libraries in the South in the Era of De Jure Segregation." *Libraries and the Cultural Record* 41 (summer 2006): 337–359.

Gits, Carrie. "Second-in-Command: Creating Leadership and Management Opportunities through Organizational Structures." *Florida Libraries* 51 (spring 2008): 14–16.

Gregory, Cynthia L. "'But I Want a Real Book': An Investigation of Undergraduates' Usage and Attitudes Toward Electronic Books." *Reference and User Services Quarterly* 47 (2008): 266–273.

Hightower, Jim. "Why Libraries Matter." *American Libraries* 35 (January 2004): 50–52.

Holt, Glen E., and Donald Elliott. "Cost Benefit Analysis: A Summary of the Methodology." *The Bottom Line* 15 (2002): 154–158.

Kaser, Linda R. "A New Spin on Library Media Centers: The Hub of the School with the Help of Technology." *Library Media Connection* 24 (August/September 2005): 64–66.

Leckie, Gloria J., and Jeffrey Hopkins. "The Public Place of Central Libraries: Findings from Toronto and Vancouver." *Library Quarterly* 72 (2002): 326–372.

Matoush, Toby Leigh. "New Forms of Information Literacy." *Reference Services Review* 34 (2006): 156–163.

McClure, Charles R., Paul T. Jaeger, and John Carlo Bertot. "The Looming Infrastructure Plateau? Space, Funding, Connection Speed, and the Ability of Public Libraries to Meet the Demand for Free Internet Access." *First Monday* 12 (December 3, 2007). Available: http://firstmonday .org/htbin/cgi wrap/bin/ojs/index.php/fm/article/view/2017/1907 (accessed June 9, 2009).

McCrossen, Alexis. "One Cathedral More or 'Mere Lounging Place for Bummers'? The Cultural Politics of Leisure and the Public Library in Gilded Age America." *Libraries and Culture* 41 (spring 2006): 169–188.

Neal, James G. "Raised by Wolves: Integrating the New Generation of Feral Professionals into the Academic Library." *Library Journal* 32 (February 2006): 443.

Orange, Satia Marshall, and Robin Osborne. "From Outreach to Equity: An Introduction." *American Libraries* 35 (June/July 2004): 46–51.

Public Agenda. "Long Overdue: A Fresh Look at Public and Leadership Attitudes about Libraries in the 21st Century." (2006). Available: www.publicagenda.org/files/pdf/Long_Overdue.pdf (accessed January 29, 2010).

Rodger, Eleanor Jo. "What's a Library Worth? Piecing Together the Structure of Value." *American Libraries* 38 (September 2007): 58–60.

Schachter, Debbie. "Creative Chaos: Innovation in Special Libraries." *Information Outlook* 9 (December 2005): 10–11.

Simmons-Welburn, Janice, Georgie Donovan, and Laura Bender. "Transforming the Library: The Case for Libraries to End Incremental Measures and Solve Problems for Their Campuses Now." *Library Administration and Management* 22 (summer 2008): 130–134.

Todd, Ross. "The Evidence-Based Manifesto." *School Library Journal* 54 (April 2008): 38–43.

Urban Libraries Council. "Making Cities Stronger: Public Library Contributions to Local Economic Development." Available: www.urban.org/uploadedpdf/1001075_stronger_cities.pdf (accessed January 29, 2010).

Zemon, Michkey, and Alice Harrison Bahr. "Career and/or Children: Do Female Academic Librarians Pay a Price for Motherhood?" *College and Research Libraries* 66 (September 2005): 394–405.

6

Redefining the Library: The Impact and Implications of Technological Change

I. INTRODUCTION

The unrelenting need for information, and its increasingly electronic nature, has produced major competitors and alternatives to traditional library services. In response, libraries, sometimes referred to as "hybrid" libraries (Pinfield et al. 1998), continue to provide traditional print and AV materials, but also e-books and e-journals, remote databases, and electronic collections from outside vendors or databases developed internally but accessible from almost any place. In the midst of the considerable excitement generated by new information technologies, it is tempting to believe that they will inevitably lead to progress. In fact, one is often made to feel behind the times when doubts are raised. The alternative to uncritical acceptance, however, is not to be a Luddite, lamenting all new technologies and pining for the old days of print materials and card catalogs. Rather, LIS professionals should think critically about the need for evidence before adopting any technology purported to benefit library service (Bushman 1990). All technological developments need to be evaluated objectively and critically, in the same manner that other new techniques, devices, or practices are evaluated. The fact that new technologies can have both positive and negative consequences is not to say that they should be discouraged; only that they should be applied appropriately and their negative as well as positive effects anticipated and, when necessary, ameliorated.

II. INFORMATION TECHNOLOGIES IN THE TWENTIETH CENTURY

The term technology can be defined many ways. For the purposes of this discussion, Webster's *Third New International Dictionary* (1970) provides a sound working definition: "a technical method of achieving a practical purpose." Obviously, libraries have used technologies since their earliest days. New technologies in the nineteenth century included the introduction of electric lights in library stacks, which undoubtedly helped locate materials without burning down the library. Other developments included important intellectual technologies such as the Dewey Decimal Classification System and the card catalog. Even today, some would maintain that manual card catalogs have some distinct advantages over electronic ones (Baker 1994). The following historical overview of technology, a thumbnail sketch from 1900 forward, is intended to provide a basic framework for discussing the issues now facing our field.

Technological Change in Libraries, 1900–2010: A Timeline

1900–1960	Developments in microphotography
1960s	First applications of computers in libraries
1970s	Use of online information in reference services
1980s	Growth of CD-ROMs and integrated library systems
1990s	Growth of Internet and World Wide Web
2000s	Expansion of online information technologies such as: • Digital libraries • Web portal • Web 2.0 • Social networking

---

A. Developments in Microphotography: 1900–1960

The first half of the twentieth century was a fruitful period for technological development. Major improvements in communications and transportation were especially notable, including the growth and expansion of telephone services, improvements in airplanes and automobiles, development of the cathode ray tube, diode, triode, and photoelectric cell, and the development of photo technologies.

Perhaps the most notable developments were related to the new photographic technologies, especially microphotography, which permitted the reproduction of print documents (reprography) onto film (microforms). The physical format was usually a roll of film, the microfilm, or a rectangular card, the microcard. As an alternative to paper, microphotography had many advantages: it provided much more information in a more compact medium and it was lighter and easier to store. In addition, it proved to be an exceptional medium for the preservation of materials that were likely to deteriorate over time, such as newspapers, magazines, and documents. By the 1920s, there were tremendous successes in reducing print to microform as well as in developing equipment to read the microforms. The potential of microphotography for the library led at least one enthusiast to suggest that the actual book could be photographed and attached to the back of the catalog card. Hence, once the user found the right catalog card, the item was literally on the back of the card (Rider 1944).

Reprography saw additional advances in the 1960s with the development of duplicating machines, most notably the photocopier. Photocopying had a profound effect on the dissemination of knowledge (as well as paper consumption). Although not as dramatic as the invention of the printing press, photocopying revolutionized communications because it permitted greater flexibility in the distribution of published materials. In essence, "Libraries became publishers of single copies on demand" (De Gennaro 1989, p. 42). Interestingly, photocopying sometimes saved time for patrons, who no longer needed to copy material out of texts by hand.

B. First Application of Computers to Libraries: The 1960s

Although punch cards that could be used for mechanical sorting were present in the nineteenth century (Buckland 1996), our contemporary sense of technology deals primarily with electronic devices, especially computers. Computer use in libraries did not begin in earnest until the 1960s. It was then that the concept of library automation originated, although it was first known as "library mechanization." Bierman (1991) defined it as "the application of computer and communication technologies to traditional library processes and services" (p. 67). The rationale for using these technologies was simple: computerization would increase efficiency, produce costs savings, and reduce the size of staff.

The first significant application of computer technologies in libraries was the creation of Machine Readable Cataloging (MARC), which became the standard for the creation of bibliographic records. MARC allowed bibliographic data to be entered, stored, and disseminated electronically on computer tapes (see Chapter 4). Once records were centralized, the tapes were used to generate catalog cards. Their potential was quickly grasped by support agencies known as bibliographic utilities, such as the Ohio College Library Center (OCLC), which was incorporated as a not-for-profit corporation in 1967. OCLC loaded the MARC tapes, which were supplemented by the cataloging efforts of the OCLC member libraries, and made these records available to member libraries. The member libraries could examine the bibliographic record, make needed changes for their local institutions (which were entered into the database), and then electronically order the tailored cards which quickly arrived, ready for filing. In effect, this created an online shared cataloging network. The advantages quickly became clear, and in 1972, OCLC opened its membership to nonacademic libraries as well (Grosch 1995). This led to tremendous growth in membership and increased cooperation among different types of libraries and among regional library networks. Consequently, in 1981 OCLC changed its name to the Online Computing Library Center. Over the decades, OCLC services grew, offering interlibrary loan and document delivery, acquisition systems, serials control, electronic publishing, and access to electronic databases.

Other bibliographic utilities appeared. For example, major research libraries formed a group called the Research Libraries Group (RLG). This group created the Research Libraries Information Network (RLIN), offering access to bibliographic databases containing thousands of research records. (RLG is now part of OCLC.) It is difficult to underestimate the major changes created by these utilities. The impact on cataloging departments, for example, was substantial, resulting in a significant reduction in the number of catalogers.

The first applications of online information retrieval also developed in the early 1960s. These were prototype systems, usually consisting of a small database and one terminal. One of the early developers was the System Development Corporation (SDC) in California, which produced some of the earliest computers for simple, full-text searching and document retrieval (Hahn 1996). The Lockheed Missiles and Space Company, working primarily with government agencies such as NASA, developed the DIALOG system around 1964 and in 1972 created the Lockheed Retrieval Service to make DIALOG available for commercial use.

Other developments included the computerizing of specialized bodies of knowledge for scientific and medical purposes. The National Library of Medicine (NLM), one of the great special libraries in the world, was confronted with a rapid expansion of scientific and technical knowledge during this period. For years NLM had been indexing the medical literature manually, but this was becoming extremely cumbersome and costly. The decision to input bibliographic citations on computer tapes led to a computerized version of its medical index, Index Medicus. At first, the computer tapes were used to produce a paper copy of the index, but soon became obvious that the tapes themselves could be searched, creating a searchable database that is one of the great achievements of the decade.

Other events in the 1960s had even greater impact. In 1969 the Defense Advanced Research Projects Research Agency within the Department of Defense developed a computer network called ARPANET at the University of California at Los Angeles. The network was developed to improve government-sponsored research by electronically linking organizations at different sites and allowing them to share research and data (Tennant 1992). One of the fundamental innovations of this system was the first practical use of a new technology to break information messages into discrete packets, which could be sent independently of one another across "packet-switching" networks. These packets could be reassembled at the receiving computer, increasing reliability and speed and substantially improving the transmission of research data and analysis. Although ARPANET membership was restricted to institutions with defense-related contracts, this network was the genesis of what would become the Internet, and it significantly advanced development of key features such as file transfer, remote access of data, and electronic mail (Bishop 1990).

Most of these advances had little effect on libraries in the 1960s. Although MARC records were rapidly adopted and some advances occurred in automating basic functions like creating catalogs and generating purchase orders, there remained considerable skepticism that automation could be applied practically to most library functions and services (Grosch 1995). Nonetheless, the knowledge base was expanding and the application of computers was inevitable.

C. Use of Online Information Technologies for Reference: The 1970s

The increasing sophistication of computer technologies, including the development of the minicomputer, made online interactive capabilities a reality (Grosch 1995). Major information-dependent institutions, such as the military, and business and industry, quickly recognized their potential and commercial vendors rapidly developed a variety of databases that could be accessed through telephone lines.

Although these vendors did not necessarily design their services for libraries, it was clear that libraries would be substantial users. However, due to the technical and scientific nature of the available databases, academic and public libraries often created separate facilities and assigned a specially trained librarian to conduct online searches because the cost of a search was calculated based on the time it took to perform it. Even then, libraries often had to pass on at least part of the costs to the individual for whom the search was conducted—a disconcerting practice that ran counter to the normal practice of providing free services.

Online access also required search strategies that could exploit the unique flexibility of computerized systems.

The application of online computer access for information retrieval, replacing card files and print indexes, represented one of the most significant breaks from the past.

Perhaps the most prominent development in this area was Boolean searching, based on the nineteenth-century logic theory of George Boole. Its application in the online environment permitted searching using logical connectors such as "and," "or," and "not," which narrowed the search and yielded more precise access to large bodies of knowledge in a much shorter period of time. Another strategy involved searching for a particular key word or phrase anywhere in the bibliographic record, including an abstract. This strategy differed significantly from traditional searches using subject terms, titles or authors.

The 1970s also saw the beginning of early attempts to automate library circulation, serials control, cataloging, and acquisition systems. However, these systems were far more complex than anticipated, and they did not reach maturity until a decade later.

D. The Growth of the CD-ROM and Integrated Library Systems: The 1980s

1. The CD-ROM

The 1980s saw a remarkable revolution in information access with the development of the Compact Disk–Read Only Memory (CD-ROM). One 4½" disk could contain all, or most, of the contents of standard reference tools, such as the *Reader's Guide to Periodical Literature*. Information vendors sent the disks, along with updates and the software to load onto library computers.

CD-ROMs had several distinct advantages over online searching. First, the CD-ROM was locally held in the library; there was no need for a telephone line. All the user had to do was come to the library. Second, the disks could hold a tremendous amount of searchable information. Third, CD-ROMs allowed the flexibility of Boolean searching using one term or multiple terms, similar to online access, as well as by author, title, and subject. Fourth, libraries subscribed to vender services that provided the CD-ROMs, thus offering a fixed-cost alternative to the variable online computing costs.

2. Integrated Library Systems

The 1980s also saw substantial developments in automating basic library functions such as acquisitions, serials, cataloging, online catalog, circulation, and collection management. These integrated library systems reduced duplication of effort and allowed more efficient information sharing. These advances would not have been possible without developments in online catalogs and automated systems.

a. The Development of Online Public Access Catalogs

Online public access catalogs (OPACs) were an early example of end-user search systems. OPACs allowed patrons to access the library's bibliographic records much as they had using the manual card catalog, with little or no mediation by the librarian. In addition, OPACs offered more flexible search capabilities, including remote search—by author, title, subject, keywords, and sometimes combinations of these terms. Some systems could also be searched using call numbers or ISBNs. There was no longer any need to buy catalog cards or hire individuals to file them; however, these savings were offset by major investments in hardware, software, and computer maintenance. In addition, the removal of the card catalog often required changes in the library's physical environment.

Although OPACs were helpful, Borgman (1996) noted that much of the improvement in user interfaces was superficial. Patrons experienced persistent problems related to their lack of knowledge of (1) the conceptual and semantic framework of OPACs' specific terminology; (2) basic search strategies such as "browse" or "keyword" searching; (3) how to search fields other than author, title, or subject; and

(4) Boolean searching. Today, as more people become familiar with the functionalities of search engines and the Internet, they will demand the same flexibility from the online catalog (Novotny 2004). Markey (2007) noted that although online catalogs used to be where people started searching for information, Google now takes precedence. He suggested that online catalogs need to be redesigned with similar retrieval capabilities, with improved subject searching and metadata, and with the ability to return precise search results.

b. The Linked System Project/Linked Systems Protocol

As online catalogs proliferated, the advantages of linking computers in various libraries and organizations became obvious. Unfortunately, at the time, computers could not "talk" to each other because different developers had created systems that were incompatible with each other. Efforts to solve this problem led to the creation of the Linked System Project, funded by the Council on Library Resources, which involved the American Library Association, OCLC, the Research Libraries Information Network, the Western Library Network, and the Library of Congress. The Project produced the linked systems protocol (LSP), also known as the Z39.50 standard (National Information Standards Organization [NISO] 1994) which became a national standard for bibliographic information retrieval. By allowing different automated systems to be linked together electronically, authorized users could consult the online catalogs of countless libraries and information organizations (Buckland and Lynch 1987, 1988). Although there were concerted efforts to realize this goal in the 1980s, it wasn't until the 1990s, with major improvements in telecommunications technologies, when significant gains occurred.

c. The Maturation of Online Circulation Systems

Once materials could be accessed electronically, the next logical step was automating circulation. Although the 1970s saw early developments, it wasn't until the 1980s that commercial vendors developed automated circulation systems in earnest. Referred to as "turnkey" systems, they were introduced with little modification from one library to another. Although they were relatively inexpensive, it took considerable time for staff to prepare the materials, bar-coding them and converting records into machine-readable format (retrospective conversion). Additional time was needed to weed the collection to avoid spending money to input old, unused materials.

While most public library systems were designed so that staff continued to check out the materials, some academic libraries enabled patrons to check out their own books. These latter systems, known as self-initiated services, could track overdue items, send out recall notices, and produce circulation reports. They also helped analyze how the library collection was being used and, therefore, could assist in planning.

d. Automated Acquisitions and Serials Systems

The 1980s also saw the burgeoning of systems designed to help libraries acquire materials. Some of the larger book vendors, such as Blackwell North America and Baker and Taylor, were quite active in developing these systems. Other vendors such as Innovative Interface developed acquisitions systems for serials. All of these systems were directly linked to the vendors and the library ordered its materials online. The system could set limits so that a particular department could not exceed its budget, and produced reports for analysis and evaluation. Some systems included a serials check-in system to save labor on the cumbersome tasks of checking in magazines and other periodicals. They could also create an electronic profile of the library based on its purchases. The vendor could then automatically send materials that matched the profile without the library ordering each item, saving time for both the library and the vendor.

E. The Growth of the Internet and the World Wide Web: The 1990s

The Internet is, in essence, a network of many networks. The Internet uses a standardized communication protocol, the Transmission Control Protocol/Internet Protocol (TCP/IP), originally developed by the Department of Defense (DoD) as part of the ARPANET project, to transmit messages and data. Every computer (known as a host) linked to the Internet has a numeric address (for example, 121.123.46.22) based on the Internet Protocol (IP). Because most people are better at remembering names than numbers, a service called DNS (Domain Name Service) translates the numeric IP address into a name (e.g., www.slis.kent.edu).

The birth of the "public" Internet was the product of a mutually beneficial arrangement between DoD and the National Science Foundation (NSF). In 1984 NSF was establishing supercomputing centers at major research centers, including several universities, to provide high-speed computing for national research purposes, some of the most advanced research in the world. NSF needed a "high-speed telecommunications backbone" to facilitate communication among the centers. At the same time, funding for ARPANET was beginning to decline. NSF negotiated an agreement with DoD to use the ARPANET technology to establish a civilian network. This network formed the foundation of the Internet. Once developed, the NSF invited other universities to join the network for a flat, reasonable fee and encouraged faculty and students to participate. As more people used the Internet, the need for speed increased exponentially.

During this same period, increased attention to national productivity issues and international competitiveness brought heightened awareness of the importance of research and computer technologies. The George H. W. Bush administration (with strong support from then Democratic Senator Al Gore) introduced legislation to develop a national "information highway" that could significantly advance access to information. The National High Performance Computing Act of 1991 not only provided for the development and maintenance of an extremely efficient electronic highway, but also mandated the creation of the National Research and Education Network (NREN). NREN's purpose was to increase electronic access to federal agencies, industry and business, libraries, and educational institutions, and to the information resources contained within them. If achieved, the result would be a virtual library, where countless documents could be consulted from a multitude of sources at tremendous speed.

While moving toward this goal, however, a significant shift in political attitudes occurred during the Clinton administration which advocated for greater privatization and less reliance on government support. Private groups with a significant stake in the Internet's development and use became more involved, with the government providing limited financial assistance and some regulatory relief (Gomery 1994). The telecommunications industry (e.g., telephone, television, and cable industries) and private enterprises, as well as literally thousands of interested individuals and organizations, became the primary developers of the Internet, resulting in an open architecture. In an open-architecture structure, individual networks might be designed and developed with their own unique interface which could then be offered to users and/or other Internet providers (Leiner, et al. 2010). Each network could be designed for specific environments and user requirements, resulting in tremendous flexibility, a concept Zittrain (2006) referred to as "generative capacity."

> Generativity denotes a technology's overall capacity to produce unprompted change driven by large, varied, and uncoordinated audiences.... The Internet is built to be open to any sort of device: any computer or other information processor could be part of the new network as long as it was properly inter-faced, an exercise requiring minimal technical effort. (pp. 1974–1976)

The Internet is an especially generative technology because it is highly adaptable, relatively easy to use, makes a variety of difficult tasks easier, and is accessible to a wide audience using many applications. The fact that developments and innovations were not controlled by a small number of proprietary interests or governed by a centralized unit created tremendous potential for growth and creativity:

> The design of the Internet also reflects both the resource limitations and intellectual interests of its creators, who were primarily academic researchers and moonlighting corporate engineers. These individuals did not command the vast resources needed to implement a global network and had little interest in exercising control over the network or its users' behavior.... The resulting Internet is a network that no one in particular owns and that anyone can join. (Zittrain 2006, pp. 1989, 1993)

1. Early Features of the Internet

a. E-mail

First introduced in October 1972, electronic mail (e-mail) allowed fast communication between individuals and organizations; messages could be sent locally or worldwide. The benefits were immense as ideas could be quickly and easily exchanged. Another model of e-communication was a listserv to which individuals could subscribe and post information, usually on a particular topic or area of interest. Some listservs were open; others had restricted membership and there was usually an administrator who handled the membership and other administrative functions. A listserv allowed a common message to be sent to thousands of individuals, promoting further discussion and responses from listserv members.

b. Remote Login

Remote login allowed an individual to access thousands of computer systems including databases and library catalogs located anywhere in the world, using standardized protocols referred to as "telnet" that connected computers using IP addresses. Today, remote login is also accomplished by Web access. Tennant (1992) identified the significant advantage of remote login:

> What makes this application truly remarkable is that ease and speed of access are not dependent upon proximity. An Internet user can connect to a system on the other side of the globe as easily as . . . he can connect to a system in the next building. In addition, since many Internet users are not at present charged for their network use by their institutions, or at least are not charged by the level of their use, cost is often not a significant inhibitor of usage. Therefore the barriers of distance, time and costs, which are often significant when using other forms of electronic communication, can be reduced in the Internet environment. (p. 2)

c. File Transfer

The File Transfer Protocol (FTP) allowed the transfer of files, including reports, numerical data, sounds, and images, from one computer to another. FTP could transfer or make available large numbers of electronic files, sometimes referred to as archives, for access or download on demand. This function is still offered today, but usually incorporated into other, more sophisticated, services.

2. The World Wide Web

The Web is not the same as the Internet; it is an interface that provides a means of structuring Internet documents and relating them to other documents to maximize use of Internet resources (December and Randall 1995). Librarians quickly recognized the advantages of the Web. Kuttner (2006) observed, perhaps somewhat romantically, "In some respects the Internet is just an extension of the physical library, the Enlightenment dream of a universal encyclopedia" (p. 13). Given the utility of the Web, it is not surprising that nearly 99 percent of all public libraries now connect to the Internet, with 98 percent connectivity in both urban and rural areas, regardless of poverty level. In addition, public libraries have significantly increased the numbers of computer workstations, wireless connectivity, and training in the use of these technologies (Jaeger, Bertot, and McClure 2007).

Using a variety of protocols including HTML (hypertext markup language) and HTTP (hypertext transfer protocol), Web designers can embed sound, video, graphics, and illustrations in documents. When the document is accessed, the embedded images and sound are also available. In a hypertext environment, these documents have visible (highlighted) links to other documents, which allow ideas or terms to be connected. A user can move from one part of a text or document to another merely by clicking on the highlighted term. Navigation between documents is accomplished by graphical Web browsers such as Netscape and Internet Explorer which display the Web documents and enable the hyperlinks (December and Randall 1995).

Search engines seek the desired documents on the Web. Fielden and Kuntz (2002) described a search engine as "an automated software that matches a searcher's topic terms (keywords) with an indexed list of documents found on the Web...arranges that list according to some order of relevancy, and provides hyperlinks to those documents so that they might be visited" (p. 13). Search engines do not search the entire Web, but rather a particular database or specific collection of documents, which can be composed of millions of Web sites and documents. Google, for example, indexes billions of Web documents.

Search engines compile collections of sites by sending out what are called spiders, robots, bots, or crawlers to locate as many seemingly relevant documents as possible. Located documents are then scanned by software that creates an index based on the keywords in each document. Some crawlers might scan entire documents, or just the title and certain segments. When someone types a query, the search engine relates the search terms to the index and produces the relevant documents. Each search engine is unique and therefore the results might vary substantially. Some search engines rank the contents from most relevant to least relevant. Ranking might be influenced by the tags assigned to a particular Web document, or the frequency of keywords or phrases contained in the document. Individuals can choose from a number of search engines including Google, Yahoo, Mozilla, and Bing.

Approximately the same number of people who use e-mail daily also use search engines on a daily basis (Rainie 2005), a number that has grown substantially. In 2002, one-third of Internet users used search engines daily compared to 49 percent in 2008 (Fallows 2008). Most people use simple search strategies; 29 percent use two-word phrases and 28 percent use three-word phrases (OneStat 2006).

Despite their tremendous capacity, search engines are not perfect. For example, Rose (2006) pointed out that there is little variation in the search engine interfaces and therefore they cannot be tailored to the various types of information-seeking needs. Rose contended that search engines fail to recognize that the search process is often iterative; that is, the search strategy and goals often change as the searcher begins to get results. Rose noted a need for new interfaces that could respond to different search goals and could adapt to the iterative process common to searching.

Regardless of their weaknesses, it is obvious that search engines compete with the library as an information service. De Rosa et al. (2005), for example, found that search engines and the physical library were both preferred information sources and that people were equally satisfied with both. However, people ranked Google ahead of a library Web site for worthwhile information and considered search engines to be more accessible, cost effective, easier to use, and more convenient. In general, search engines were considered as trustworthy as library sources, and by a considerable margin were seen as fitting better into people's lifestyle. As might be expected, young people tended to be more satisfied with search engines, particularly with their speed.

Today, the proliferation of Web sites and the popularity of the Web is a mixed blessing. Of particular concern is the quality, or lack thereof, of the information retrieved. Traditionally, librarians select materials, particularly reference materials, using criteria that help establish the items' authority and accuracy. This is not the case, however, with Web. The Pew Internet and American Life Project reported that one in six adult users could not tell the difference between unbiased search results and paid advertisements. Thirty-eight percent of adults searching the Web did not know the difference between sponsored links and regular ones and less than half could indicate which links had been paid for (Associated Press 2005).

Librarians have begun to address this issue by establishing their own Web pages that guide patrons to specific sites that have been vetted like other library materials. This is not to say that access to other sites is prohibited; rather, this service exemplifies LIS professionals' tradition of guiding patrons to timely and accurate information.

Establishing standards and consistency on the Web was one of the goals of its early developers. The World Wide Web Consortium (W3C) was created in 1994 to develop common protocols and guidelines that would enable long-term growth of the Web (World Wide Web Consortium 2010). Over the years, W3C working groups have produced technical reports and open source software and promoted standardization by making recommendations regarding the architecture of the Web. It has also addressed features that affect interaction with Web users including social, legal, and public policy concerns; and accessibility issues related to usability for people with disabilities.

III. INFORMATION TECHNOLOGIES IN THE TWENTY-FIRST CENTURY

A. Digital Libraries

The original purpose of digital libraries was to promote scientific and technical research (Bearman 2007). Their development was further spurred by the growth of distance learning opportunities at universities, which required students to be able to access a virtual library in the absence of a local one (Fox and Urs 2002; Wright 2002).

The twentieth-century advances in electronic technologies gave birth to digital libraries.

The Digital Libraries Federation (2009) defined digital libraries as:

> organizations that provide the resources, including the specialized staff, to select, structure, offer intellectual access to, interpret, distribute, preserve the integrity of, and ensure the persistence over time of collections of digital works so that they are readily and economically available for use by a defined community or set of communities. (n.p.)

Arms (2000) described them as "a managed collection of information, with associated services, where the information is stored in digital formats and accessible over a network" (p. 2). Sun Microsystems defined a digital library "as the electronic extension of functions users typically perform and the resources they access in a traditional library" (Wright 2002, p. 3). The manipulation of the resources might be electronic or intermediated by an information professional, but a key concept is that they are managed, not simply a static collection of data. In sum, digital libraries are organized on computers, accessible over a network, and employ procedures to select, organize, make available, and archive information (Arms 2000). Greenstein (2000) observed that digital libraries create a "'digital library service environment,' that is, a networked online information space in which users can discover, locate, acquire access to and, increasingly, use information" (pp. 290–291). Since the environment is electronic, the format of the information is relatively unimportant and extends well beyond text, including graphic, video, audio, images, data sets, and software (Fox and Urs 2002).

Because many digital libraries remain rooted in their academic beginnings, however, they often have a disciplinary or subject-based focus. Bearman (2007) argued that "digital library content will increasingly encompass all kinds of information. The proportion of past information in digital form will grow exponentially over the coming decade, until nearly everything in print is available online" (p. 253). In fact, digital libraries have proliferated as increasing amounts of information originate in electronic format (were "born digital"). As digital libraries evolved, there was increased emphasis on making them accessible not just to academicians but to everyone, which the Web has now accomplished.

Digital libraries have clear advantages: large amounts of information in digital formats can be consulted, shared by multiple users simultaneously, updated quickly, and available twenty-four hours a day. With the increasing capacities and portability of computers and the growth of high-speed networks, digital libraries are becoming commonplace (Fox and Urs 2002; Arms 2000; Wright 2002). Nonetheless, they still require a number of value-added services such as searching, user profiling, authentication services, and user interfaces. Patrons of digital libraries still expect these systems to be easy to use and reliable in terms of the search results (Kani-Zabihi, Ghinea, and Chen 2006).

Although digital libraries have many advantages, there are also some potential problems. Postman (1992) observed, "Every technology is both a burden and a blessing" (pp. 4–5). Levy (1997) expressed concern, for example, that reading, especially in-depth reading, within digital libraries might be quite different. He noted that concentrated attention is required for careful and reflective reading. Attention is not an unlimited resource, and the process of searching and choosing sources of information expends a great deal of it. Levy argued that digital libraries encourage "hyper-extensive reading...characterized as a frenzy of short bursts of shallow attending to information fragments" (p. 208). This type of reading is encouraged by hyperlinks and the hypertext environment, which, ironically, is perceived as a strength of digital libraries. Although digital libraries can locate and display a great deal of information, Levy argued that the sustained reading needed for true reflection and scholarship might be sacrificed. Kuttner (2006) warned that "the Internet itself leads to attention deficit disorder. There is so much stuff just a click away that it's hard to concentrate and stay focused—it's so much more intoxicating to click and see what else is out there" (p. 14). Carr (2008) expressed similar misgivings, noting that deep reading was becoming more and more difficult for him as the Net "seems to be chipping away my capacity for concentration and contemplation. My mind now expects to take in information the way the Net distributes it: in a swiftly moving stream of particles" (p. 57).

At the same time, Shuler (2002) reminded us that we must not simply resist changes because they do not resemble the traditional print culture of the past:

> It is this idea of "understanding" that is most confounding to traditional literacy advocates and their institutional fellow travelers. To their way of thinking, literacy is a fixed element...the same for everyone in a society. There are "great books," thinking is done "critically," you read books because "they are good for you." The Internet, along with its poor cousins, films, television, and video games, provides a different form of narrative, something much more episodic and disjointed than the linear nature of reading. It is drenched with dramatic shifts in perspective and logic, more interested in keeping one entertained first, informed second. (p. 159)

Shuler suggested that reading advocates might need to shift their language, at least in part, from traditional literacy to a "multifaceted and multitasking literacy" more appropriate to the Internet than the print culture (p. 159). Consistent with Shuler's point of view, Cascio (2009) saw Google and anticipated breakthroughs in genetic engineering and artificial intelligence as a form of "intelligence augmentation" (p. 96). He argued that the new multi-faceted media and complex information have actually made us smarter, stimulating the ability to make new connections and observe new patterns, sometimes referred to as "fluid intelligence":

> In any case, there's no going back. The information sea isn't going to dry up, and relying on cognitive habits evolved and perfected in an era of limited information flow—and limited information access—is futile. Strengthening our fluid intelligence is the only viable approach to navigating the age of constant connectivity. (Cascio 2009, p. 96)

Information technologies are already well integrated into contemporary library service. Bearman (2007) noted that acquisitions, cataloging, reference, and circulation have changed significantly. In addition, many academic libraries have become institutional repositories of unique digital data or documents, giving them a particular cachet and identity and an alternative means of controlling and accessing scholarly content without the involvement of publishers (Bearman 2007). With these repositories, it becomes clear that the future holds not one all-encompassing digital library, but thousands of distributed digital libraries linked together by metadata and mined by federated search engines.

In 2007, the NISO Framework Working Group, under the sponsorship of the Institute for Museum and Library Services, developed guidelines for creating good digital library collections:

> When digitization first began, a collection was considered "good" if it provided proof of concept or resulted in new institutional capabilities—even if the resulting collection itself was short-lived or of minimal usefulness to the organization's users. As the digital environment matured, the focus of digital collection-building efforts shifted toward the creation of useful and relevant collections that served the needs of one or more communities of users. The bar of "goodness" was raised to include levels of usability, accessibility, and fitness for use appropriate to the anticipated user group(s). Digital collection development has now evolved and matured to a third stage, where simply serving useful digital collections effectively to a known constituency is not sufficient. Issues of cost/value, sustainability, and trust have emerged as critical success criteria for good digital collections. Objects, metadata, and collections must now be viewed not only within the context of the projects that created them, but as building blocks that others can reuse, repackage, repurpose, and

build services upon. "Goodness" now demands interoperability, reusability, persistence, verification, documentation, and support for intellectual property rights. (p. 1)

The *Framework of Guidance* provides criteria for goodness organized around four core types of entities: collections (organized groups of objects), objects (digital materials), metadata (information about objects and collections), and initiatives (programs or projects to create and manage collections).

Nine Principles for Building a Digital Collection

1. A good digital collection is created according to an explicit collection development policy.
2. Collections should be described so that a user can discover characteristics of the collection, including scope, format, restrictions on access, ownership, and any information significant for determining the collection's authenticity, integrity, and interpretation.
3. A good collection is curated, which is to say, its resources are actively managed during their entire life cycle.
4. A good collection is broadly available and avoids unnecessary impediments to use. Collections should be accessible to persons with disabilities, and usable effectively in conjunction with adaptive technologies.
5. A good collection respects intellectual property rights.
6. A good collection has mechanisms to supply usage data and other data that allow standardized measures of usefulness to be recorded.
7. A good collection is interoperable.
8. A good collection integrates into the user's own workflow.
9. A good collection is sustainable over time.

(*Source:* NISO Framework Working Group 2007, p. 4.)

The guidelines specifically excluded services as a core type on the assumption that if quality collections, objects, and metadata were created, it would be possible to create high-quality services to take advantage of them. Cloonan and Dove (2005), adapting principles from the twentieth-century library philosopher S. R. Ranganathan, suggested five additional laws for digital library service:

1. Make sure online resources are available where and when they're needed.
2. Eliminate the obstacles that prevent users from making effective use of electronic resources.
3. Integrate electronic resources into virtual learning environments and other Web pages of the institution.
4. Provide meta-searching capabilities so that users can search entire sets of electronic resources.
5. Offer 24/7 anytime, anywhere, access to libraries. (p. 3)

A digital collection conforming to these principles should form a solid foundation for strong library service.

B. Web Portals

As the number of Web pages proliferates, it becomes increasingly difficult to retrieve exactly what is wanted. Search engines like Google are easy to use, but they often locate incorrect sites, or find many more sites than are needed. When the Internet was first introduced, libraries attempted to manage this chaos by compiling lists of favorite Web sites and bookmarking them (Franco 2003), a strategy that is no longer feasible. A more recent approach is the Web portal. There is no one definition, but suffice it to say that a portal assembles a variety of information resources, including Web sites, catalogs, online journals, and digitized resources, and links them to library-like services, such as online reference and interlibrary loan. Rather than randomly searching the Web, a portal permits a patron to go to one location, perform high-quality searches of high-quality resources, and receive other value-added services as well. Jackson (2002) described the ideal portal:

> Imagine one web site that can combine the powerful searching of web resources with the searching of local catalogs, online journals, or locally digitized resources. Add to this the ability to initiate a reference question, submit an interlibrary loan (ILL) request, and transfer into course management systems a citation or portion of a journal article, all without leaving that web site. (p. 36)

Although, to date, the potential of portals has been exploited primarily in scholarly work environments and academic libraries, the concept has wide-ranging applications:

1. Portals can be personalized to limit the resources that are consulted. Limitations can be by many factors, including date, journal title, and whether a source is full text. They can also be configured to display results in certain formats and possibly to rank results by relevancy.

2. Portals can offer access to both generally accessible and restricted sites.

3. Portals can provide value-added delivery services by providing full-text material or interlibrary loan access.

4. Portals can provide online reference services which might require contact with a human intermediary or interaction with an online reference tool.

5. Portals can provide alert services. Once the portal is personalized, the system might notify the user when pertinent material has been added to the portal. (Schottlaender and Jackson 2003, pp. 281–283)

For public libraries, portals offer opportunities well beyond a library home page. With a portal, the library provides a customizable electronic gateway into a wide variety of resources and searching tools that can be linked to delivery systems such as interlibrary loan, as well as online reference services. Both local and remote sources can be provided, including e-books and e-journals, licensed databases, abstracting and indexing services, online catalogs, and other Web resources. Further, the portal can store information about a particular searcher, so that subsequent searches can be customized. In essence, a portal becomes a powerful, personalized, and integrated library system for the patron. The advantage is obvious: if a library can provide easy, one-stop, personalized access to the world of information, it can remain competitive with a World Wide Web that remains unorganized and unselective:

> Portals serve library patrons by highlighting high-quality online information sources and streamlining access to frequently used Web sites and library resources, thereby reducing the phenomenon of information overload that can distract and confuse library patrons. (Brantley et al. 2006, p. 146)

C. Internet2

Although originally designed for research and development, the Internet was diverted in the 1990s to popular and commercial purposes that have served the general public's needs well. Nonetheless, the original purpose remains critical for academics and scholars. Consequently, the Internet2 Consortium was founded in 1996 for the purpose of promoting "leading-edge network capabilities and unique partnership opportunities that together facilitate the development, deployment and use of revolutionary Internet technologies" (Internet2 2009, p. 1). It began with more than 200 U.S. universities and other institutions of higher learning, seventy corporate partners, and forty-five government agencies and laboratories as well as fifty international partner organizations. Through their collaborative efforts, the Internet2 Consortium is "enabling a new generation of network applications, creating a leading edge network capability for research and education, and fostering the transfer of technology and experience to the global Internet" (Internet2 2009, p. 1). Its goal is not to replace the Internet but to enhance and improve it and share new developments with others in the educational community. Nearly $175 million was devoted to this effort by the end of 2009 (Internet2 2009).

More than 500 four-year colleges and 550 community colleges have access to the Internet2 backbone called Abilene (Olsen 2003). The speed of this backbone is remarkable: data that would normally take thirty minutes to transfer over a T1 line takes about one second on Abilene (Mutch and Ventura 2003). The consortium has working groups focused on such areas as network infrastructure, middleware (software that performs intermediate functions like authentication, authorization, and security), engineering, and applications (e.g., digital libraries, digital video, virtual laboratories). In addition, the consortium sponsors discussion groups on special topics and advisory groups that provide expertise to the various working groups (Internet2 2008). For example, its Science and Engineering Initiative works to connect members of the international community and provide them with relevant network applications; the Internet2 Health Sciences and Health Network Initiative "supports and facilitates the use of advanced networking applications in clinical practice, medical and related biological research, education, and health awareness" (Internet2 2009, p. 5).

Already the developments of Internet2 have transformed higher education, permitting greater quantities of data to be transferred quickly. Similarly, video-conferencing and distance education have significantly advanced. Internet2 can benefit libraries by opening these new communication channels to library users and allowing the library to continue to fulfill its educational mission.

D. Social Networking: Web 2.0 and Beyond

As the Internet evolved in the first decade of the twenty-first century, dramatic improvements in applications increased the potential for social interaction and the creation of online communities. The Internet became a dynamic network where the users added to the online content—in effect creating an "architecture of participation" (O'Reilly 2005, p. 7). This phenomenon is sometimes referred to as Web 2.0.

A distinctive characteristic of Web 2.0 is the social networking site, "an online place where a user can create a profile and build a personal network that connects him or her to other users" (Lenhart 2007, p. 1). Examples include MySpace and Facebook, both launched in 2004, and LinkedIn, a site that connects businesspeople and professionals. On these sites, individuals can submit personal profiles, music, videos, and photographs, interact with friends, and maintain contacts with countless individuals. The popularity of MySpace and Facebook is revealed by the fact that by 2008, each site had approximately 115 million unique monthly visitors (Arrington 2008). Interestingly, Facebook has a larger international audience than MySpace, with about 70 percent of its users located outside the United State (Facebook 2009). From the start, social networking sites have attracted young people, and this demographic remains dominant. Approximately 55 percent of online teens use social networks, primarily to maintain communication with friends (Lenhart 2007). Nonetheless, Facebook reported that its most rapidly growing demographic was individuals over the age of thirty-five. Adolescents are a declining proportion of MySpace users, while the number of individuals between thirty-five and fifty-four has significantly increased, comprising more than 40 percent of the visitor base (O'Malley 2006). Other common manifestations of social networks include blogs, wikis, and RSS feeds.

1. Blogs

A blog or weblog "refers to a category of website where the content is presented in a continuing sequence of dated entries. Put simply, 'a blog is an online diary'"

(Kajewski 2006, p. 157). Blogs permit an individual or a group to post their ideas on a Web site, permit others to respond and link to other Web sites. Users can react to the content, contribute their own content, and see what others post as well. Blogs can be highly personal—of interest primarily to one's family or friends— or they can disseminate information on a broad scale; some report or analyze current news or political events. During national or international crises, blogs have been a major source of news when traditional sources were either unavailable or suppressed by authorities. Blog use is increasing steadily, with one-third of Internet users indicating they read blogs; 11 percent read them daily. Forty-two percent of Internet users have read a blog at one time or another. More than one in ten Internet users have created their own blog (Smith 2008).

Libraries have used blogs to communicate news or information to the public about new services, new books and AV materials, and to stimulate discussion, as well as to promote the library and its services (Kajewski 2006). In addition, blogs can be professional awareness tools and can provide links to reviews, book awards, and book discussions.

2. Wikis

Wikis, derived from the Hawaiian word for "quick," were intentionally designed for collaborative development by Ward Cunningham, an Oregon-based computer programmer in 1994 (Stephens 2006). Chawner and Lewis (2006) described a wiki as "a server-based collaborative tool that allows any authorized user to edit Web pages and create new ones using nothing more than a Web browser and a text entry form on a Web page" (p. 33). Wiki can refer to a Web site or the software that runs it. Wikis do not require knowledge of coding or programming languages; rather they use a "simple text-based markup language that is easy to learn" and allow any user with a Web browser to insert new pages, enter new content in existing pages, or delete information (Cochenour 2006, p. 34).

Librarians were among the first to make use of wikis as a form of professional information sharing. Meredith Farkas's wiki, Library Success: A Best Practices Wiki, was launched in 2005 and collects resources about technology issues like podcasting, social networking, and IM reference in libraries. It also gathers links related to more traditional library services like collection maintenance, programming, and readers' advisory ("Playing with Technology" 2006). Wikis can have many uses in libraries, including enhancing user services by updating a library's Web site, serving as a communication tool with the public, linking library resources, developing subject guides, providing library instruction, serving as a resource for best practices, providing information services to patrons, and providing a forum for a book club. Wikis can also serve as a means for internal organizational activities including committee and meeting work, planning activities, and a suggestion box (Kajewski 2006; Chawner and Lewis 2006).

A particularly interesting use of the wiki was in the development of reference tools, the most prominent example being Wikipedia. Binkley (2006) noted that Wikipedia has editors and several hundred experienced users, designated as administrators who have special powers to regulate content and users, although the content is created almost entirely by the users. O'Reilly (2005) referred to this as the harnessing of "collective intelligence" (p. 9). Underlying the creation of this revolutionary reference work was the belief that the community of users could also be creators and contributors to the content. Rather than relying on a limited number of "experts" to create the tool, thousands of contributors and reviewers have collaboratively contributed to this massive, dynamic, ever-expanding and changing work that is vetted in large part by the users themselves. Critics argued that Wikipedia's open-source content management system and anonymity made it susceptible to vandalism and fraud since non-expert members of the public can write and edit articles, increasing the possibility of inaccuracies (Miller 2007). But in theory, errors are caught by those reading the articles or by groups with a specific interest in a particular topic area and they become more and more accurate over time, a phenomenon known as "eventualism" (Crovitz 2009). In fact, the journal *Nature* performed a side-by-side comparison of forty-two science-related articles in the *Encyclopaedia Britannica* and Wikipedia:

> The exercise revealed numerous errors in both encyclopedias, but among 42 entries tested, the difference in accuracy was not particularly great: the average science entry in Wikipedia contained around four inaccuracies; Britannica, about three. (Giles 2005, p. 900)

On the other hand, Giles reported that many reviewers found Wikipedia articles to be "poorly structured and confusing" (p. 900). Eiffert (2006) cautioned that no single source should be used when exploring a topic, but also concluded:

> Bottom line: Subject to ongoing critical review, Wikipedia articles are generally well-researched and substantiated by footnoting and linking to sources, allowing readers to judge the quality of information being used. Moreover, Wikipedia entries often have more and more current information. (p. 83)

Although the collaborative model of publication might have its deficiencies, it is clearly working. Wikipedia is one of the top Web sites accessed by Internet users, one of the most consulted sites on Google searches, and received 97 percent of the traffic for online encyclopedias (Crovitz 2009). A 2006 study by the Pew Internet and American Life Project found that over one-third of American homes with Internet access used Wikipedia and that 50 percent of Wikipedia users were college students (Harris 2007). Among its obvious advantages is that it is constantly being updated and expanded. O'Reilly (2005) called Wikipedia "a profound change in the dynamics of content creation!" (p. 9). Although Wikipedia has been met with skepticism by some librarians, it is likely that many find it a good place for patrons (and librarians themselves) to start a basic background research. Additionally, using the citations at the end of Wikipedia articles, librarians can help patrons locate additional materials and teach them about issues related to accuracy and authority at the same time.

3. Really Simple Syndication

Really Simple Syndication (RSS) is "an XML-based document format for the syndication of web content so that it can be republished on other sites or downloaded periodically and presented to users" (RSS Advisory Board 2010, p. 2). The stream of content from an RSS account is called a "feed." Feeds allow online sources to send information to users in real time once the user subscribes to the feed and possesses the necessary software (Wikipedia 2009). This is a highly valuable medium to maintain current awareness. Users might receive messages about news, events, and activities sent to their designated communication devices. Commercial enterprises can inform customers about sales and new product developments; libraries can push announcements out to patrons about upcoming activities, the latest services, or newest materials being acquired by the library. O'Reilly (2005) contends that "RSS is the most significant advance in the fundamental architecture of the web. . . . [It] allows someone to link not just to a page, but to subscribe to it, with notification every time that page changes" (p. 7).

RSS technology formed the basis of podcasting. Originally, podcasts were "audio files that [could] be downloaded and played either through a computer or an MP3 player such as an iPod" (Balas 2005, p. 29). It is the syndication aspect that makes podcasts unique. In other words, people no longer have to access the Web each time they want certain information; rather, once they have subscribed to a particular feed, new files are downloaded automatically. Podcasts became quite popular for news updates and music downloads. Today, podcasts contain video as well as audio content and can be sent to phones and other communication devices as well as computers. In 2008, 19 percent of Internet users indicated that they had downloaded a podcast, compared to 7 percent in 2006 (Pew Internet and American Life Project 2008). Obviously, as a current awareness resource for the librarian, podcasting can be used in a variety of ways, such as training and development for patrons and staff, book reviewing, updates on the library, a source of presentations or lectures, and library tours. The library not only becomes a place to access podcasts (some libraries loan iPods; (Stephens 2005; Kajewski 2006) but can become a content creator.

Although it has taken time to embrace the potential of social media, a number of libraries now have MySpace pages and Facebook accounts. They use Twitter, post pictures on Flickr and videos on YouTube, and host podcasts on their own Web pages. Some have even set up residence on Info Island in Second Life. All of these media allow libraries to interact with their patrons in virtual spaces. Additionally, a number of academic and public libraries are now offering IM reference services by using services like Meebo and Pidgin that allow patrons to use their own IM chat clients to IM a librarian. Some have even employed Skype to provide virtual service.

Web 2.0 is still in its infancy, and its application to libraries will continue to grow. Among the many potential contributions are the following:

1. Providing training and education in information literacy to ensure safe and effective use of these types of sites

2. Employing IM Twitter, and other applications for reference and current awareness services for patrons

3. Creating affinity group wikis on a variety of topics such as e-government or book clubs

4. As an internal means of communication for staff, librarians, and administrators

On the other hand, some people have expressed concern that making social networking sites available at the library could place young people in jeopardy. The ALA recognizes the serious problem of online predators, but notes that the preferred course of action is to teach children about using social network sites properly. Similarly, the ALA notes that many wikis and blogs have substantial educational value and benefit to young people.

IV. TECHNOLOGY-RELATED ISSUES FOR THE TWENTY-FIRST-CENTURY LIBRARY

The last decade of the twentieth century and the first decade of the twenty-first have seen the most dramatic changes in libraries in their many centuries of evolution. As political walls have fallen, statues have tumbled, the currencies of many nations exchanged for a common unit, and the globe enveloped in an electronic web, libraries, too, have been subjected to economic, social, technological, and other transformative forces (Billings 2002). De Rosa, Dempsey, and Wilson (2004) characterized the transformation succinctly:

> The library itself has long been a metaphor for order and rationality. The process of searching for information within a library is done within highly structured systems and information is exposed and knowledge gained as a result of successfully navigating these preexisting structures. Because this is a complicated process, the librarian helps guide and navigate a system where every piece of content has a preordained place. Contrast this world with the anarchy of the Web. The Web is free-associating, unrestricted and disorderly. Searching is secondary to finding and the process by which things are found is unimportant. "Collections" are temporary and subjective where a blog entry might be as valuable to the individual as an "unpublished" paper.... The

individual searches alone without expert help and, not knowing what is undiscovered, is satisfied. (p. ix)

Morville (2005), following the work of Theodore Nelson, described this new searching and finding process as "intertwingling" as Web users discovered the "potential of nonsequential text to transform how we organize and share ideas" (p. 64). There is little doubt that the rise of electronic information technologies and the digital age have wrought radical changes.

Five Great Challenges of the Digital Age

1. **Malleability**—digital information invites constant change and manipulation.

2. **Selectivity**—if those who have grown up in a digital environment consider pre-digital forms of information, such as print books and articles, as "prehistoric" and not worth using, they might never be exposed to important knowledge.

3. **Exclusivity**—the digital age is likely to create a new class of haves and have-nots.

4. **Vulnerability**—the digital environment will increasingly be susceptible to viruses, security violations, unscrupulous e-commerce transactions, e-mail attacks, and scams.

5. **Superficiality**—the ability to network with many more people and to access so much more information does not mean that the relationships established or the information obtained are particularly substantive or reliable. In addition, we might be more inclined to make judgments quickly, less reflectively, and superficially.

(*Source:* Rutenbeck 2000.)

On the other hand, D'Elia, Jorgensen, and Woelfel (2002) argued that use of the Internet and the public library are, in fact, complementary. Based on a national sample, they observed that "75 percent of Internet users are public library users and 60 percent of public library users are Internet users" (p. 818). In addition, the frequency of Internet use did not affect frequency of library use. Nonetheless, it is important to reflect on the more profound effects of these transformations.

A. Impact on the Library as a Physical Place

The physical library has clearly been challenged by the virtual environment. The new technologies have forced a major redesign of library buildings, particularly wiring and the placement of electrical outlets and lighting. It can be quite expensive and complicated to make such modifications in buildings that were built 50 or 100 years ago, and many libraries have made an uneasy accommodation. Other changes are more superficial but nonetheless costly, such as new ergonomically designed furniture to avert potential health concerns associated with using electronic devices for long periods.

As early as 1994, Whitney and Glogoff described a "library without walls ... using technologies to expand services, resources, and relationships between libraries and resources around the world" (p. 321). For some, this notion conjures an exciting image of breaking down physical barriers, permitting total freedom of access to all information throughout the world. To be sure, electronic information access resolves some of the liabilities of the physical library such as duplications in collections or unequal access due to economic disparities in certain communities.

For others, however, the idea that more and more information can be accessed remotely or provided through telecommunication lines and electronic databases raises apprehensions about the eventual demise of libraries (Birdsall 1994). Birdsall suggested that those who envision the end of physical libraries might be thinking more about research and academic libraries than American public libraries.

So do information technologies presage the end of the library as a physical place? Will "real" libraries be replaced by the digital library? As noted elsewhere, the answer to these questions depends on how we perceive the purpose of libraries. For centuries, libraries have served as a symbol of cultural and educational values. In addition, Simon (2002) noted that "the public library is a communications center where people interact not only with the library's resources but also with other people" (p. 104). He noted that the library serves as a play space, study hall, economic asset, lifelong learning center, museum and cultural center, and marketing research center. The importance of the library as place is integrally bound up in the notion of the library as a central focus of community life. Obtaining information is but one function of a public library, but information technologies might erode other aspects of the library as place:

> What once took place in the town square, the neighborhood tavern, in the marketplace, or the library now occurs more often in the study or in the bedroom. The locus of communication and participation is shifting from the public sphere to the private sphere.... The shift from public space to private space threatens older forms of community. (Schement 1997, pp. 1–2)

Schement worried that the role of the library as a "pivotal community institution" might end if people do not perceive it as the place to get the information they need. Leckie (2004), in contrast, argued that public libraries will remain a critical public space but only if they ensure that they are welcoming to all and maintain a focus on their educational function rather than their entertainment function. She argued that the unique contribution of public libraries is that they provide public spaces "where citizens can engage in quiet reflection and study, able to pursue their own intellectual projects and personal growth" (p. 236). It is unclear how electronic networks could serve in these social capacities.

B. The Impact on Library Services

One of the most profound impacts of technology has been the expansion of libraries' ability to access information remotely and to cooperate with other libraries in an electronic environment. In addition, libraries exploit electronic networking in many other ways including online catalogs, collection development, circulating materials from other libraries, and cooperative reference services. In some cases, these networks have saved money by reducing duplication of materials and human resources. At the same time they have increased staff such as network liaisons and interlibrary loan and document-delivery personnel, and created new departments. Some of the major consequences of these developments are discussed in the sections that follow.

1. The Next Generation Catalog

The term *online catalog* is probably no longer accurate, for the catalog has become a portal to a universe of information far beyond the walls of the library. The next-generation catalog has become a one-stop shop for accessing the physical holdings of the library, allowing a patron to assess their availability and reserve them, and in some cases, triggering a delivery system. The next-generation catalog can also link the user directly to the Web, to sites and databases with thousands of resources including periodicals with full text. The next-generation catalog can also provide access to Web sites selected by the library on topics of special interest, and to specialists in various fields, to interlibrary loan, and to reference librarians.

2. Impact on Selection and Acquisitions

Traditional library collection development has always involved the selection and acquisition of materials through publishers and vendors. Vendors have created new electronic systems that permit selectors to consult tables of contents, access their databases and identify items, read reviews, place orders, and download essential bibliographic material for cataloging purposes. These electronic processes not only streamline acquisition and selection processes but also provide fiscal control and financial reports. In addition, electronic technologies have increased the number of information resources for selectors such as listservs that provide advice and information on material selection.

3. Impact on Circulation

Radio Frequency Identification (RFID) technology improves security and control of the collection:

> [RFID] uses the frequency spectrum (e.g. radio waves) to transfer data on an item or product that is stored in a small microchip that is usually physically attached to the item or product.... RFID tabs are activated by an electronic reader and the transponder on the tag then sends the reader its data. (Adams et al. 2002, p. 35)

RFID tags are easier to use than bar codes because they don't need to be aligned, and can be read from considerable distances. There are two types of RFID tags: active and passive. Passive tags "have no power source and no on-tag transmitter" (Book

Industry Study Group 2004, p. 3). They are relatively inexpensive and rely on an external reader to activate them. Active tags have "both an on-tag power source and an active transmitter. . . . They are usually used in manufacturing, such as tracking equipment and other high value assets, toll collections systems" (Book Industry Study Group 2004, p. 3). Libraries generally employ passive tags, which are particularly useful in inventory control, security, and circulation processes including self check-out.

Despite their usefulness, some have expressed concern that important privacy rights could be threatened through the use of RFID. Morville (2005) described RFID as a "disruptive technology poised to shift paradigms by transforming our ability to identify and locate physical objects" (p. 81). Warfield (2005) explained that "RFID's fundamental privacy threat comes from the fact that the tags reveal their information to any compatible reader" (p. II). For example, a borrower's name could be revealed, connected to a particular book title. The concern was sufficiently great that the ALA (2006) created *RFID in Libraries: Privacy and Confidentiality Guidelines*, which were adopted by the Intellectual Freedom Committee (IFC) in June 2006:

> Because RFID tags might be read by unauthorized individuals using tab readers, there are concerns that the improper implementation of RFID technology will compromise users' privacy in the library. . . . Libraries implementing RFID should use and configure the technology to maintain the privacy of library users. (ALA 2006, p. 1)

The IFC also advised libraries to make sure that information stored on RFID tabs was kept to a minimum and that the library's privacy and confidentiality policies were reviewed and updated regularly to ensure that the rights of their patrons were protected. Similarly, the IFC recommends that patrons should be clearly informed regarding the RIFD technologies used by the library.

4. Digital Reference Service

Traditional reference service was synchronous; that is, a question was asked and answered at the same time. In a digital environment, reference can be asynchronous, permitting a patron to ask a question at any time and receive an answer later. Digital Reference Service (DRS) is not simply an additional service; it is a transformative activity. In the digital environment, the reference librarian functions more like an information broker than an intermediary who simply places a library user in contact with a resource (Lankes, 2000). The DRS librarian links people to the entire world of information rather than just to items in the local collection:

> The widespread reach and use of the Internet has presented a twofold challenge to the familiar reference paradigm: the rise of resources, both free and licensed, available via the Internet, and the use of a number of Internet-based technologies as potential ways of interacting with people with information needs and questions. (Janes 2002a, p. 549)

There are a number of challenges in building digital reference collections, including selection, financing, acquiring, licensing, and maintaining such collections as well as developing Web techniques and design to present and use digital holdings effectively (Farmer 2009). Nonetheless, Digital Reference Service (DRS) offers benefits to both the patrons and the library. Patrons benefit by the potential availability of service 24/7, or well beyond typical library hours. DRS increases accessibility for individuals who prefer anonymous communication, who are homebound, or who possess disabilities that make travel difficult. Young people who use electronic technologies every day, in particular, find DRS more user-friendly, as indicated by the fact that student use of the reference desk has been steadily declining (Bradford et al. 2005). The library benefits by gaining access to experts who are not part of the regular staff or who might be geographically remote (Clapp and Pfeil 2005).

In the future it is likely that collaborative digital reference services will provide service at off hours through regional, national, or even global networks. As McClure (2000) observed, "Digital reference can no longer be considered the future of librarianship. Digital reference is now" (p. xiii). Embracing this concept, the Reference and User Services Association (RUSA) of ALA created its "Guidelines for Implementing and Maintaining Virtual Reference Services" in 2004. RUSA uses the synonymous term "virtual reference" and defines it as:

> reference service initiated electronically, often in real-time, where patrons employ computers or other Internet technology to communicate with reference staff without being physically present. Communication channels used frequently in virtual reference include chat, videoconferencing, Voice over IP, co-browsing, e-mail, and instant messaging. (RUSA 2004, p. 9)

Although these standards are useful, there is little evidence that the guidelines are actually being used to evaluate DRS in libraries (Shachaf and Horowitz 2008).

C. Impact on the Library Collection

One of the major challenges of new technologies will be the need to redefine the library collection. Traditionally, the collection was the physical objects. Today, vast amounts of information reside in computer databases or on the Web, and it is difficult to know where the library collection begins and ends. How does the library effectively control such a collection? To what extent can the library apply its traditional notions of selection? If the traditional tools no longer apply, we will need to develop new ones.

Similarly, the library has the opportunity not just to offer individual Web sites, but to build substantial electronic collections. Kovacs (2000) suggested that e-libraries can save patrons time, create an organized environment of accurate and credible resources, and increase access to new users. The potential range of such collections

---

Important Questions to Consider

- What are the selection criteria for information available on the Web?
- To what extent does the library staff control access to Web content? What policies are needed to balance intellectual freedom issues with protection of vulnerable clientele such as children?
- To what extent does the library staff create interfaces that guide patrons to particular Web sites?
- How does the library staff decide if a particular information resource should be accessible in print, AV, or electronic format? When should the same information be available in multiple formats?
- What responsibility does the library staff have to make available only information that they feel is accurate or reliable?
- To what extent are librarians responsible for evaluating information for the patron?
- To what extent should libraries or information centers warn patrons that information might be inaccurate, biased, or incomplete?
- Under what conditions does a library decide to order a physical item, even when it can be obtained from another library easily?

---

is considerable, including core reference materials as well as collections on business, health, law, social and physical sciences, and education.

Remote access also creates new issues regarding collection evaluation. It is no longer enough to determine if the local collection is meeting users' needs. Rather, more attention must be paid to whether the library provides adequate access. As De Gennaro (1989) presciently observed two decades ago, "In the future, the size of a library's collection of conventional materials will matter far less than it does now. The question is no longer how many volumes a library has, but how effectively the library can deliver needed resources from a wide variety of sources to users via the new technology" (p. 42). As digital collections increase in number, breadth, and use, evaluating their effectiveness grows in importance. Chowdhury et al. (2006) found few studies but noted that future evaluations will need to be user-centered and tailored for the specific content and target audiences of a given digital library.

1. Financial Implications

Making information available costs money. Vendors provide access to vast amounts of information, including data from statistical databases and articles from hundreds of periodicals in full text but often at considerable expense. In efforts to economize, some libraries form networks to negotiate costs. Similarly, DRS might incur additional expenses for contracting with outside reference firms. Digital information requires telecommunication upgrades, access to databases, downloading fees, and copyright compensation, as well as the costs of the hardware and software. Obviously, the new collection requires new perspectives on the allocation of resources and which items will be collected locally or remotely accessed. Janes (2002b) noted that

LIS professionals must determine the value of introducing new systems or devices before rushing to adopt them. He asks librarians: "Is there a benefit to the user? Is it accessible, affordable, and worth the cost? Does it help uphold the values of the profession? Does it play to our strengths? Is it likely to endure? and Does it feel right?" (p. 52). Dugan (2002) proposed a "costs structure model" in assessing the overall fiscal burden of a new technology. The eight components or stages of the model included the following:

1. **Investigation**: Researching what is needed and what choices are available in the marketplace.

2. **Negotiation**: Leveraging economic and legal advantages into an agreement to acquire or lease.

3. **Acquisition**: Turning a negotiation into a purchase or lease (although this might require approval from other parts of a hierarchy).

4. **Installation**: Preparing the library and/or the technology for use.

5. **Training**: Educating staff and patrons on how to use the technology.

6. **Maintenance**: Keeping the technology functional.

7. **Evaluation**: Determining whether the acquisition continues to serve a purpose and making a recommendation based on the findings.

8. **Upgrade, Migrate, Replace, or Abandon**: Implementing the evaluative recommendation.

LIS professionals should also consider the benefits or cost savings that might result from new technology. For example, networks that benefit many libraries yield a much broader access to materials at very reasonable costs. Some statewide networks such as OhioLINK, which serves academic libraries in Ohio, and the Ohio Public Library Information Network negotiated with vendors like EBSCO to provide access to thousands of periodicals, including full text. The costs were borne significantly by the state rather than by individual libraries. Similarly, interlibrary loan was a relatively cumbersome, time-consuming, and staff-intensive process. OhioLINK provides highly effective resource sharing and therefore libraries can limit purchases because their patrons can obtain the desired copies quickly, with a significant savings for monograph budgets.

2. Mass Digitalization

Libraries and other institutions have digitized materials for years, but recently the scale of such efforts has grown dramatically. In December 2004, Google entered into a partnership with five major research libraries: the University of Michigan, Harvard, Stanford, Oxford, and the New York Public Library, known as the G5, to digitize and index more than 10 million unique titles. This project was intended to "create a comprehensive, searchable, virtual card catalog of all books in all languages, while respecting copyright" (U.S. National Commission on Libraries and Information Science 2006, pp. 8–9).

> The Google proposal seemed to offer a way to make all book learning available to all people, or at least those privileged enough to have access to the World Wide Web. It promised to be the ultimate state in the democratization of knowledge set in motion by the invention of writing, the codex, movable type, and the Internet. (Darnton 2008, n.p.)

The amount of content available will be determined by whether the books are out of print and in the public domain (15–20 percent). For materials still protected by copyright, if publishers wanted to opt in Google would reveal a few pages of a book and then provide links to booksellers. If they wanted to opt out, they would need to notify Google (Hahn 2006). In any case, Google is assuring publishers that, except for a few pages, the digitized versions of copyrighted books would not be available; they would be retained in a "dark archive." Other libraries that wished to partner with Google could have various proportions of their collections scanned and receive digital copies in return.

Many parties including publishers and librarians have expressed concern over this project's impact and implications. The U.S. National Commission on Libraries and Information Science (NCLIS) held a conference at the University of Michigan in March 2006. Librarians, scholars, publishers, and government leaders met and identified nine issues that have an impact on national information policy:

1. How should important aspects of copyright—fair use, orphan works, opt-in vs. opt-out models—be handled in digitization projects?
2. Quality: When is the quality of OCR (optical character readers) good enough? What about quality of content and authentication?
3. What are the roles and priorities for libraries in the digital age?
4. Who will assume long-term ownership of books and journals and other media? Who will take responsibility for long-term preservation of books and journals and other media, and preserving the public record?
5. Standardization and interoperability: How can the silos of digital initiatives communicate with each other?
6. What are the roles of publishers and booksellers in the digital age?
7. What business models are needed in the era of mass digitization? How will the open access movement affect the economics of digitization?
8. Information literacy: What should be done about information illiteracy?
9. Assessment: What types of assessment are being used? How will we know if digitization and electronic access are meeting people's needs? (NCLIS 2006, pp. 3–5)

Some of these complex issues will be resolved through legal agreements and settlements between the publishers, other copyright holders, and Google. There has been some success in defining the rights of U.S. parties through an Amended Settlement Agreement signed on November 13, 2009, by Google, the Author's Guild, and the Association of American Publishers. But as of this date, copyright infringement questions concerning foreign publishers and books in foreign languages remain an open area of dispute (Band 2009).

Nonetheless, book collections may soon be shared electronically on a national and international level with far greater efficiency than in the past. The implications of these developments are yet to be fully known and this is not the end of Google's forays into the digital domain.

> Keep an eye on Google, whose stated mission is "to organize the world's information and make it universally accessible and useful." . . . You see, the tricky thing about Google is they keep changing their definition of information. First, it was just web sites. Then images, online discussions, blogs, news, and products entered the fold. Then phone numbers, addresses, street maps, and FedEx tracking data. Then the contents of your desktop computer. Then, the contents of the world's largest research libraries. . . . Google has big plans for information, plans that reach far beyond what we normally think of as the Web. (Morville 2005, p. 62)

3. Rise of the E-book

Large companies such as Amazon.com, AOL Time Warner Book Group, Barnes and Noble, Dell, HarperCollins, Houghton Mifflin, and Simon and Schuster are all involved in either the publication or distribution of e-books. Castro (2007) noted that e-books have several advantages:

1. The text is quickly searchable and cross-referenced through hyperlinks.
2. E-books require little physical space.
3. The hardware can store hundreds of books
4. Text size and fonts can be adjusted.

Connaway (2001) noted five key trends that will increase demand for e-books:

1. The e-book market is growing.
2. There is a growing commitment among publishers to provide e-book content.
3. There is an increasing demand for access to electronic "knowledge that matters."
4. There is an increasing number of remote/distributed learning programs and a need for the electronic resources to support this type of teaching and learning.
5. There is a growing demand for increased functionality and more advanced technology for utilizing electronic content. (p. 27)

The importance of e-books for libraries will increase for several reasons. First, e-books are becoming more widely available due to digitization. Second, many best-selling authors such as Stephen King and John Grisham are now being published as e-books, some exclusively. Third, academic libraries have discovered that e-books have distinct advantages; titles made available online in academic libraries were at least six times more likely to be used than print titles (van Kappen 2008). A study by University College London et al. (2008) predicted that by 2017, "Electronic books, driven by consumer demand, will finally become established as the primary format for educational textbooks and scholarly books and monographs, as well as reference formats" (p. 26).

The economics of e-book publication are not completely clear. E-book titles are currently sold either as individual titles or through a subscription service such as NetLibrary, with considerable potential for cost savings for libraries. Ormes (n.d.) noted that savings were derived from lower costs per title: no need to buy both hard-back and paperback of the same title, no repair or replacement costs, no large-print versions needed, little processing or acquisition, storage, or space costs. In addition, the collection can expand without the need for additional shelving. All of these could be substantial benefits.

Some of the limitations of e-books are the need for a reader device, the quality of the reader displays, and issues related to flicker and glare. There are three hardware options: a device designed strictly to read e-books, a personal digital assistant (PDA) that can be used for a variety of purposes, and a desktop or laptop computer (Long 2003). The Amazon Kindle, launched in 2007, the Sony Reader, and other readers are becoming increasingly popular. Much of e-books' potential success will rely on these readers being easy to use, inexpensive, and commonplace. One of the criticisms of the early Kindle, for example, was that it could not display newspapers or textbooks. A new larger Kindle with this capacity was offered in 2009, but at a price approaching $500. In 2010, at a similar price, Apple introduced the iPad which integrated the capacities of e-readers with many other functions including e-mail, Web access, and the ability to view movies and photos. We should expect the competition to be intense with new versions and innovations continuously emerging. Similarly, as major Internet content providers such as Google pursue the mass digitization of books, e-books will become more and more available. In fact, Sony Electronics entered into a nonexclusive partnership with Google to make available half a million copyright-free titles through the online Sony e-Bookstore. Many more such partnerships should be expected in the future.

Sottong (2008) identified several potential problems with e-books. For example, there is some evidence that reading lengthy texts on e-books is not comfortable for our normal visual processes. This suggests that people might be more likely to read shorter texts such as articles, but less likely to view books (Sottong 2008). In one study, students preferred electronic to print resources when conducting research or reference functions but not when reading for pleasure (Safley 2006). Comparing e-book readers to the iPod, Sottong argued that similar growth should not be expected because (1) there is no open format such as MP3 that leads to competition and price reductions; (2) books are usually read only once, unlike repeated playing of music on the iPod; (3) books are read only one or two at a time, so the large storage in an e-book reader is unnecessary; and (4) reading requires full attention, unlike listening to music, which permits multitasking. Given the relatively high costs of e-book readers, these might be significant deterrents.

In 2007 the International Digital Publishing Forum accepted the Open Publication Structure (OPS) 2.0, creating industry standard specifications so that publishers could create one digital book file instead of multiple formats. The stated goal of the OPS is in part:

> to define a standard means of content description for use by purveyors of electronic books (publishers, agents, authors et al.) allowing such content to be provided to multiple Reading Systems and to insure maximum presentational equivalence across Reading Systems. (International Digital Publishing Forum 2007, p. 3)

Constantly improving and enhancing features to e-book readers combined with ever-increasing access to e-books should increase usage. Librarians will need to monitor this situation regularly and carefully adapt as needed.

4. Digital Preservation and Archiving

Historically, the focus of preservation was to protect an item. Use of the item, in fact, was often perceived as one of the threats to preservation. For example, using rare and fragile paper documents might cause them to deteriorate further. In contrast, preserving information in a digital format increases access; fragile documents can be converted to a digital format so that millions can use them. Digitization can take many forms, including making a "digital double" of a paper document or a physical object. In such circumstances, the digital copy is not identical to the original but a representation of it.

Candidates for digital preservation and archiving include cultural objects such as artworks that are difficult to access due to their remote location or fragility; scientific data both current and historical; and books, journals, and other paper records for education, business, and governmental purposes. Digital preservation also includes objects such as Web pages that were born digital; that is, they were originally created digitally and might not have a representation outside the digital environment. Digital information originally created and stored in an obsolete format can be migrated to a new format, thus restoring access.

Caplan (2008) identified at least three functions of digital preservation: (1) protecting materials against unauthorized alterations, (2) conserving storage media to avoid deterioration, and (3) maintaining digital materials so they can be used over time. The third concept implies a larger notion that Caplan referred to as "digital curation," which takes a "life-cycle approach focusing on the ongoing use and re-use of digital materials" (p. 38). In this light, preservation takes on a new purpose: preservation of access (Zeng 2008):

> The survival of a document is not dependent on how long the medium carrying
> it will last, but on the capacity of that document to be transferred from one
> medium to another as often as possible. . . . The most significant threats to digi-
> tal continuity concern loss of the means of access. (p. 8)

Access and preservation are related but distinct activities. In our rush to provide access, we must remember that the media we use must be stable:

> The next century's major preservation challenge will be to cope with the fragile
> media of the present [twentieth] century from magnetic tape to digital files. The
> record of the twentieth century exists on many media that are far more fragile
> than paper. (Smith 1999, p. 13)

The problem is referred to as fixity. That is, print materials have some permanence, but electronic text is impermanent. Ironically, the ease with which digital material can be altered raises serious questions about its capacity to serve as a preservation technique. In many instances modifications or damage can be done inadvertently as well as intentionally. But with so many possible iterations, which versions are to be preserved and how? Similarly, electronic information is vulnerable to damage, tampering, and deterioration over time. For more than a decade, some information has been stored on CD-ROMs. As they become an outdated information storage format, what do we do with valuable information stored on them? How can we migrate that material onto more contemporary media? Electronic information has also been stored on floppy or zip disks. Such data will need to be refreshed or transferred to a different medium; otherwise, the data might be corrupted. How can this vast amount of information be effectively preserved? Also, retaining CD-ROMs or floppy disks is of little use if the software and hardware to use them are not available. As more and more information appears on Web sites, how do we preserve them? A significant proportion of sites disappear from the Web in just a few years, and it is estimated that there are more than a billion Web pages with average life spans of forty-four days (Zeng 2008; Abdelaziz 2004). It is common to search for a Web site and see the familiar message: "File Not Found."

> The fundamental problem is that important data have been placed and will
> continue to be placed on storage systems (Web servers, e-mail servers, file
> systems, legacy database systems) that were not designed with data archiving as
> the primary goal. The designers of these legacy data stores focused on other
> design goals such as efficiency, ease-of-use, or reduced costs, usually to the

> detriment of the long-term reliability of the system. (Cooper and Garcia-Molina 2005, p. 106)

Storage media are often fragile and vulnerable to viruses and other external attack. Similarly, new storage hardware and software are constantly introduced so that digital material must be refreshed and migrated often. Smith (1999) observed that although digitization is often seen as a means of reducing costs and greatly expanding access, it is, in fact, expensive and it does not have the permanence of microfilm. Sannett (2003) identified a variety of such costs including capital costs (e.g., software development, hardware, facilities, interface design), direct costs (e.g., identifying and acquiring records, producing metadata, selecting preservation strategies, storage, maintenance, evaluation, and deletion), and indirect costs (e.g., staff supervision, clerical support, facilities rental, off-site storage, amortization of capital costs, and administrative activities). Nonetheless, as new digital storage technologies are developed, digital preservation will become increasingly common. Recently, for example, a microholographic disc was developed using holograms. This disc can store the content of 100 standard DVDs on a single disk (Glader 2009).

If the marketplace determines what is preserved and archived, then probably only material of commercial value will remain (Coyle 1994). Similarly, if the e-mail of government officials is not preserved, considerable historical documentation will be lost. These are just a couple of the challenges that will face the digital preservation and archives officers of today and tomorrow as their electronic collections increase.

D. Impact of Technology on Staffing and Organizational Structure

During the 1960s and 1970s, when automation was first introduced, little attention was paid to the effect on staff. Indeed, a major argument for its desirability was that it would reduce dependence on library staff. However, experience has made it clear that the reaction of the staff to new technologies plays an important role in its effective use and the retention of valued employees. Introducing new technologies generally creates considerable perturbation from two perspectives: the effects on staffing and changes in the library's organizational structure.

Whenever new technologies are introduced, new people with different knowledge and skills are often needed. For example, libraries have hired systems and network experts to maintain and enhance computer systems, to train others, to report on the system's operation, and to make recommendations for new systems as needed. The individuals hired for these positions are often quite different from library staff in terms of both knowledge and disposition. The organizational culture from which they come might also be different. The result is potential estrangement of certain staff or conflict within the organization, which in turn can affect organizational productivity. In addition, these new positions often require new job descriptions, new classifications, and new reporting lines, which can lead to resentment or concern. For example, the head of a systems department might report directly to the library director or other high-level administrative position. These seemingly privileged lines of communication might make other managers uneasy or suspicious. Similarly, compensation is often problematic because the marketplace for individuals with computer expertise is often substantially more lucrative than that for librarians. To recruit and retain talented individuals, it might be necessary to pay them more than librarians, which can affect morale. Support staff who provide electronic reference services or who develop desktop publishing or information management skills are also likely to demand greater status and pay.

Libraries are affected in other ways as well. Automated acquisitions allow vendors to supply some materials already processed and cataloged, and even rebound to specification. This outsourcing effectively reduces the need for library departments devoted to these activities. Finally, the new technologies allow patrons to do for themselves what librarians used to do. These are sometimes referred to as patron-initiated service systems. Examples include self-checkout, direct interlibrary loan and document delivery, and electronic systems that permit renewal, recalls, and holds on materials or access to databases or the Web.

E. Impact on the Physical and Psychological Condition of Workers

The effect of technologies on people can be profound. One concern is the physical impact of electronic technologies. Experience with employees working with computers has revealed that a variety of physical symptoms, some quite serious, can arise: carpal tunnel syndrome, repetitive motion disorders, headaches, neck aches, vision problems, joint pain, numbness in limbs, and fatigue. Ergonomics, which studies the fit between people and machines, has revealed the need for carefully redesigning workspaces so that lighting is appropriate for video display terminals; chairs provide proper support for arms, legs, neck, and back; and keyboards and desks are designed and placed at appropriate heights to minimize injury. Employers are also discovering that employees working on computers need frequent breaks to maintain their productivity.

Similarly, employers are concerned about "technostress," defined as "a condition resulting from the inability of an individual or organization to adapt to the introduction and operation of new technology" (Brod 1984, p. 30). New technologies sometimes create irrational fears, but many of the concerns are justified and need to be anticipated and dealt with. There are, for example, natural fears of job loss, of being unable to master new training, of technical jargon, and of physical harm, as well as fear that computers will be used to inappropriately monitor work. Regrettably, the symptoms of technostress can be quite serious, including mental fatigue, combativeness, depression, increased errors and bad judgments, panic, resistance to change, and feelings of helplessness. These undesirable responses can result in loss of productivity and poor morale, not only among the workers experiencing the problem, but also among those who work with or rely on those employees. The causes of technostress include poorly designed or inadequate computer hardware and software, poor lighting or wiring, noisy equipment, poor training, poor organizational communication, and existing feelings of job insecurity and fragmentation.

Steps to Alleviate Technostress

1. Involving staff from the beginning in the planning and acquisition of new technologies. Keeping secrets only leads to the proliferation of rumors and a feeling of being left out. Ideas should emerge from the staff itself, which increases commitment and reduces the feeling that the technology is being imposed.

2. Demonstrating that there are direct beneficial consequences from the change. Self-interest is a strong motivator: if a change helps employees do their work, it is more likely to be greeted positively.

3. Communicating to staff the progress of technological changes and providing time to adjust. This should include plenty of time for learning how to operate and use new technologies, opportunities to make mistakes without penalties, and chances to receive and provide feedback on effectiveness or any problems with new systems. For technological change to work well, there must be open communications in both directions.

4. Refraining from ridiculing critics. There are bound to be people who will resist change. Although they sometimes can be difficult, they also can serve a vital purpose by revealing inadequacies that should be remedied. Criticizing these individuals might simply build resentment and fear on the part of others.

5. Ensuring staff they will not lose their job or be reduced in rank or pay following the change.

V. SUMMARY

As new information technologies provide increasing access to information, LIS professionals must acknowledge that continuous change is an inherent part of this process. In such a dynamic environment, many questions need to be answered:

- How will new technologies affect the future mission of libraries?
- How will electronic publications and information be evaluated and selected?
- How will access to electronic information be provided, controlled, and paid for?
- How does technology affect the employees of the organization?
- How can technology be implemented for maximum productivity?

Some say that libraries are in transition from "collection to connection." It is not yet clear what the ultimate impact will be. There is no doubt that LIS professionals in the future will require new skills and abilities, and will need to emphasize continuing education and training. There are many unknowns. What we do know is that libraries have adapted for hundreds of years to meet the changing needs of their communities and constituencies. There is no reason to assume that they have lost any of those resiliencies.

REFERENCES

Abdelaziz, Abid. 2004. "Preserving Our Digital Heritage: A UNESCO Perspective." Available: http://xdams.fondazionefeltrinelli.it/dm_0/FF/FeltrinelliCmsPortale/0086.pdf (accessed February 5, 2010).

Adams, Helen R., Robert F. Bocher, and Carol A. Gordon. 2002. *Privacy in the 21st Century*. Westport, CT: Libraries Unlimited.

American Library Association. 2006. *RFID in Libraries: Privacy and Confidentiality Guidelines*. Chicago: ALA. Available: www.ala.org/ala/aboutala/offices/oif/statementspols/other policies/ rfidguidelines.cfm (accessed February 18, 2010).

Arms, William Y. 2000. *Digital Libraries*. Cambridge, MA: MIT Press.

Arrington, Michael. 2008. "Facebook No Longer the Second Largest Social Network." Available: www.techcrunch.com/2008/06/12/facebook-no-longer-the-second-largest-social-network/ (accessed February 1, 2010).

Associated Press. 2005. "Users Confuse Search Results and Ads." Available: www.msnbc.msn.com/id/6861158/ (accessed February 1, 2010).

Baker, Nicholson. 1994. "Discards." *The New Yorker* (April 4): 64–86.

Balas, Janet L. 2005. "Blogging Is So Last Year—Now Podcasting Is Hot." *Computers in Libraries* (November/December): 29–32.

Band, Jonathan. 2009. "A Guide for the Perplexed: Part III: The Amended Settlement Agreement." Available: www.arl.org/bm~doc/guide_for_the_perplexed_part3_final.pdf (accessed December 10, 2009).

Bearman, David. 2007. "Digital Libraries." In *Annual Review of Information Science and Technology*. Edited by Blaise Cronin. Medford, NJ: Information Today, 223–272.

Bierman, Kenneth J. 1991. "How Will Libraries Pay for Electronic Information?" *Journal of Library Administration* 15 (1991): 67–84.

Billings, Harold. 2002. *Magic and Hypersystems: Constructing the Information-Sharing Library*. Chicago: ALA.

Binkley, Peter. 2006. "Wikipedia Grows Up." *Feliciter* 52: 59–61.

Birdsall, William F. 1994. "Breaking the Myth of the Library as Place." In *The Myth of the Electronic Library: Librarianship and Social Change in America*. Westport, CT: Greenwood, 7–29.

Bishop, Ann P. 1990. "The National Research and Education Network (NREN): Promise of a New Information Environment." *ERIC Digest* (November): EDOIR–90–4.

Book Industry Study Group. 2004. *BISG Policy Statement POL-002: Radio Frequency Identification*. New York: BISG.

Borgman, Christine L. 1996. "Why Are Online Catalogs Still Hard to Use?" *Journal of the American Society for Information Science* 47: 493–503.

Bradford, Jane T., Barbara Costello, and Robert Lenholt. 2005. "Reference Service in the Digital Age: An Analysis of Sources Used to Answer Reference Questions." *Journal of Academic Librarianship* 31 (May): 263–272.

Brantley, Steve, Annie Armstrong, and Krystal M. Lewis. 2006. "Usability Testing of a Customizable Library Web Portal." *College and Research Libraries* (March): 146–163.

Brod, Craig. 1984. "How to Deal with 'Technostress.'" *Office Administration and Automation* 45 (August): 28–47.

Buckland, Michael K. 1996. "Documentation, Information Science, and Library Science in the U.S.A." *Information Processing and Management* 32: 63–76.

Buckland, Michael K., and Clifford A. Lynch. 1987. "The Linked Systems Protocol and the Future of Bibliographic Networks and Systems." *Information Technology and Libraries* 6: 83–88.

———. 1988. "National and Linked Systems Protocol for Online Bibliographic Systems." *Cataloging & Classification Quarterly* 8: 15–31.

Bushman, John. 1990. "Asking the Right Questions about Information Technology." *American Libraries* 21 (December): 1026–1030.

Caplan, Priscilla. 2008. "Digital Defense: A Primer for the Preservation of Digital Materials." *American Libraries* (May): 38.

Carr, Nicholas. 2008. "Is Google Making Us Stupid?" *Atlantic Monthly* 302 (July/August): 56–63.

Cascio, Jamais. 2009. "Get Smart." *The Atlantic* 304 (July/August): 94–100.

Castro, Kimberly. 2007. "The Future of E-books." *Business Week Online* (October 29). Available: www.businessweek.com/investor/content/Oct2007/pi20071026_777647.htm (accessed February 4, 2010).

Chawner, Brenda, and Paul H. Lewis. 2006. "WikiWikiWebs: New Ways to Communicate in a Web Environment." *Young Adult Library Services* 4 (March): 33–43.

Chowdhury, Sudatta, Monica Landoni, and Forbes Gibb. 2006. "Usability and Impact of Digital Libraries: A Review." *Online Information Review* 30: 656–680.

Clapp, Janet, and Angela Pfeil. 2005. "Virtually Seamless: Exploring the Role of Virtual Public Librarians." *Public Libraries* 44 (March/April): 95–100.

Cloonan, Michelle, and John Dove. 2005. "Ranganathan Online: Do Digital Libraries Violate the Third Law?" *Library Journal* 130 (April 1): 58–60.

Cochenour, Donnice. 2006. "Is There a Wiki in Your (Library) Future?" *Colorado Libraries* 32 (winter): 34–36.

Connaway, Lynn Sillipigni. 2001. "eBook Trends in Public Libraries." *Public Libraries* (Supplement) (September/October): 27–29.

Cooper, Brian F., and Hector Garcia-Molina. 2005. "InfoMonitor: Unobtrusively Archiving a World Wide Web Server." *International Journal of Digital Libraries* 5: 106–119.

Coyle, Karen. 1994. "Access: Not Just Wires." Paper presented at the annual meeting of the Computer Professionals for Social Responsibility (CPSR). San Diego, October 1994.

Crovitz, L. Gordon. 2009. "Wikipedia's Old-Fashioned Revolution." *Wall Street Journal* (National Edition) 258 (April 6): A13.

Darnton, Robert. 2008. "The Library in the New Age." *New York Review of Books* 55 (June 12): 5. Available: www.nybooks.com/articles/21514 (accessed March 13, 2009).

December, John, and Neil Randall. 1995. *The World Wide Web Unleashed 1996*. Indianapolis: Sams.

De Gennaro, Richard D. 1989. "Technology and Access in an Enterprise Society." *Library Journal* 114 (October 1): 40–43.

D'Elia, George, Corinne Jorgensen, and Joseph Woelfel. 2002. "The Impact of the Internet on Public Library Use: An Analysis of the Current Consumer Market for Library and Internet Services." *Journal of the American Society for Information Science and Technology* 53: 802–820.

De Rosa, Cathy, et al. 2005. *Perceptions of Libraries and Information Resources*. Dublin, OH: OCLC.

De Rosa, Cathy, Lorcan Dempsey, and Alane Wilson. 2004. *The 2003 OCLC Environmental Scan: Pattern Recognition: A Report to the OCLC Membership*. Dublin, OH: OCLC.

Digital Libraries Federation. 2009. Available: www.diglib.org/about/dldefinition.htm (accessed August 8, 2009).

Dugan, Robert E. 2002. "Information Technology Budgets and Costs: Do You Know What Your Information Technology Costs Each Year?" *Journal of Academic Librarianship* 28 (July): 238–243.

Eiffert, Robert. 2006. "Wikipedia, the Review." *School Library Journal* 52 (March): 82–83.

Facebook. 2009. "Press Room—Statistics." Available: www.facebook.com/home.php?ref= logo (accessed April 2, 2009).

Fallows, Deborah. 2008. "Search Engine Use." Pew Internet and American Life Project. Available: www.pewinternet.org/Reports/2008/Search-Engine-Use.aspx (accessed February 1, 2010).

Farmer, Lesley S. J. 2009. "The Life Cycle of Digital Reference Sources." *Reference Librarian* 50: 117–136.

Fielden, Ned L., and Lucy Kuntz. 2002. *Search Engines Handbook*. Jefferson, NC: McFarland.

Fox, Edward A., and Shalini R. Urs. 2002. "Digital Libraries." In *Annual Review of Information Science and Technology*. Vol. 36. Medford, NJ: Information Today, 503–590.

Franco, Adrienne. 2003. "To the Internet: Finding Quality Information on the Internet." *Library Trends* (fall): 229–246.

Giles, Jim. 2005. "Internet Encyclopedia Goes Head to Head." *Nature* 438 (December 15): 900–901.

Glader, Paul. 2009. "GE Disk Can Store 100 DVDs." *Wall Street Journal* (National Edition) (April 28): B5.

Gomery, Douglas. 1994. "In Search of the Cybermarket." *Wilson Quarterly* (summer): 9–17.

Greenstein, Daniel. 2000. "Digital Libraries and Their Challenges." *Library Trends* 49 (fall): 290–303.

Grosch, Audrey N. 1995. *Library Information Technology and Networks*. New York: Marcel Dekker.

Hahn, Trudi. 1996. "Pioneers of the Online Age." *Information Processing and Management* 32: 33–48.

———. 2006. "Impacts of Mass Digitization Projects on Libraries and Information Policy." *Bulletin of the American Society for Information Science and Technology* (October/November). Available: www.asis.org/Bulletin/Oct-06/hahn.html (accessed February 5, 2010).

Harris, Chris. 2007. "Can We Make Peace with Wikipedia?" *School Library Journal* 53 (June): 26.

International Digital Publishing Forum. 2007. "Open Publication Structure (OPS) 2.0." Available: www.openebook.org/doc_library/informationaldocs/OPS/OPS_2.0_0.7_draft.htm (accessed February 1, 2010).

Internet2. 2008. "Internet2 2008 Member Report." Available: www.internet2.edu/pubs/2008MemberReport.pdf (accessed August 5, 2009).

———. 2009. "About Internet2." Available: www.internet2.edu/resources/AboutInternet2.pdf (accessed August 5, 2009).

Jackson, Mary E. 2002. "The Advent of Portals." *Library Journal* 127 (September 15): 36–39.

Jaeger, Paul T., John Carlo Bertot, and Charles McClure. 2007. "Public Libraries and the Internet 2006: Issues, Funding, and Challenges." *Public Libraries* 46 (September–October): 71-75.

Janes, Joe. 2002a. "Digital Reference: Reference Librarians' Experiences and Attitudes." *Journal of the American Society for Information Science and Technology* 53: 549–566.

———. 2002b. "How to Think about Technology." *Library Journal* 127 (February 1): 50–52.

Kajewski, Mary Ann. 2006. "Emerging Technologies Changing Public Library Service Delivery Models." *Aplis* 19 (December): 157–163.

Kani-Zabihi, Gheorghita Ghinea, and Sherry Y. Chen. 2006. "Digital Libraries: What Do Users Want?" *Online Information Review* 30: 395–412.

Kovacs, Diane. 2000. *Building Electronic Library Collections*. New York: Neal-Schuman.

Kuttner, Robert. 2006. "In Defense of Books." *Oberlin Alumni Magazine* (spring): 13–15.

Lankes, R. David. 2000. "The Foundations of Digital Reference." In *Digital Reference Service in the New Millennium: Planning, Management, and Evaluation*, edited by R. David Lankes, John W. Collins III, and Abby S. Kasowitz. New York: Neal-Schuman.

Leckie, Gloria J. 2004. "Three Perspectives on Libraries as Public Space." *Feliciter* 233–236.

Leiner, Barry M., et al. 2010. "A Brief History of the Internet." Available: www.isoc.org/internet/history/brief.shtml (accessed February 4, 2010).

Lenhart, Amanda. 2007. "Social Networking Websites and Teens: An Overview." Pew Internet Project Memo. Washington, DC: Pew Internet and American Life Project, January 7.

Levy, David M. 1997. "I Read the News Today, Oh Boy: Reading and Attention in Digital Libraries." In *Proceedings of the 2nd ACM International Conference on Digital Libraries*. Philadelphia: 2-2-211.

Long, Sarah Ann. 2003. "The Case for e-Books: An Introduction." *New Library World* 104: 29–32.

Markey, Karen. 2007. "The Online Library Catalog: Paradise Lost and Paradise Regained?" *D-Lib* 13 (January/February). Available: http://dlib.org/dlib/january07/markey/01markey.html (accessed February 1, 2010).

McClure, Charles R. 2000. "Foreword." In *Digital Reference Service in the New Millennium: Planning, Management, and Evaluation*. Edited by David R. Lankes, John W. Collins III, and Abby S. Kasowitz. New York: Neal-Schuman, xiii–xiv.

Miller, Nora. 2007. "Wikipedia Revisited." *ETC* 64: 147–150.

Morville, Peter. 2005. *Ambient Findability: What We Find Changes Who We Become*. Sabastapol, CA: O'Reilly.

Mutch, Andrew, and Karen Ventura. 2003. "The Promise of Internet2." *Library Journal* 128 (summer): 14–16.

National Information Standards Organization. 1994. *Information Retrieval: Application Service Definition and Protocol Specification*. Bethesda, MD: NISO.

NISO Framework Working Group. 2007. *A Framework of Guidance for Building Good Digital Collections*. 3rd ed. NISO.

Novotny, Eric. 2004. "I Don't Think I Click: A Protocol Analysis Study of Use of a Library Online Catalog in the Internet Age." *College and Research Libraries* (November): 525–537.

Olsen, Florence. 2003. "Internet2 at a Crossroads." *Chronicle of Higher Education* 49 (May 16, 2003).

O'Malley, Gavin. 2006. "MySpace Is Getting Older, and That's Not a Good Thing." *ifthen* (December 19). Available: www.ifthen.biz/market-news-article/117 (accessed February 4, 2010).

OneStat.com. 2006. "Less People Use 1 Word Phrase in Search Engine Engines According to OneStat.com." Available: www.onestat.com/html/aboutus_pressbox45-search-phrases .html (accessed February 1, 2010).

O'Reilly, Tim. 2005. "What Is Web 2.0." Available: www.oreilly.com/lpt/a/6228 (accessed February 1, 2010).

Ormes, Sarah. n.d. "An E-book Primer." Networked Services Policy Taskgroup Issue Paper. The Library Association. Available: www.ukoln.ac.uk/public/earl/issuepapers/ebook.htm (accessed May 22, 2009).

Pew Internet and American Life Project. 2008. "Podcast Downloading 2008." Available: www.pewinternet.org/PPF/r/261/report_display.asp (accessed February 1, 2010).

Pinfield, Stephen, et al. 1998. "Realizing the Hybrid Library." *D-Lib Magazine* (October). Available: www.dlib.org/dlib/october98/10pinfield.html (accessed February 1, 2010).

"Playing with Technology—Meredith Farkas." 2006. *Library Journal* (March 15). Available: www.libraryjournal.com/article/CA6312495.html (accessed February 1, 2010).

Postman, Neil. 1992. *Technopoly: The Surrender of Culture to Technology*. New York: Random House.

Rainie, Lee. 2005. "Big Jump in Search Engine Use." Pew Internet and American Life Project. November 20, 2005. Available: www.pewinternet.org/Reports/2005/Big-jump-in-search-engine-use.aspx (accessed May 21, 2009).

Reference and Users Services Association. 2004. "Guidelines for Implementing and Maintaining Virtual Reference Services." *Reference and User Services Quarterly* 44 (fall): 9.

Rider, Freemont. 1944. *The Scholar and the Future of the Research Library: A Problem and Its Solution*. New York: Hadham, 99.

Rose, Daniel E. 2006. "Reconciling Information-Seeking Behavior with Search User Interfaces for the Web." *Journal of the American Society for Information Science and Technology* 57: 797–799.

RSS Advisory Board. 2010. "Really Simple Syndication Best Practices Profile." Available: www.rssboard.org/rss-profile (accessed February 4, 2010).

Rutenbeck, Jeff. 2000. "The 5 Great Challenges of the Digital Age." *Netconnect* (fall): 30–33.

Safley, Ellen. 2006. "Demand for E-books in an Academic Library." *Journal of Library Administration* 45: 445–457.

Sannett, Shelby. 2003. "The Costs to Preserve Authentic Electronic Records in Perpetuity: Comparing Costs across Cost Models and Cost Frameworks." *RLG DigiNews* 7 (August 15): 1–9.

Schement, Jorge Reina. 1997. "Preface: Of Libraries and Communities." In *Local Place, Global Connections: Libraries in the Digital Age.* Available: www.benton.org/archive/ publibrary/libraries/preface.html (accessed February 4, 2010).

Schottlaender, Brian E. C., and Mary E. Jackson. 2003. "The Current State and Future Promise of Portal Applications." In *The Bowker Annual: Library and Book Trade Almanac.* 48th ed. Edited by Dave Bogart. Medford, NJ: Information Today, 279–290.

Shachaf, Pnina, and Sarah M. Horowitz. 2008. "Virtual Reference Service Evaluation: Adherence to RUSA Behavioral Guidelines and IFLA Digital Reference Guidelines." *Library and Information Science Research* 30: 122–137.

Shuler, John A. 2002. "Freedom of Public Information versus the Right to Public Information: The Future Possibilities of Library Advocacy." *Journal of Academic Librarianship* 28 (May): 157–159.

Simon, Matthew. 2002. "Will the Library Survive the Internet? What Patrons Value in Public Libraries." *Public Libraries* 41 (March/April): 104–106.

Smith, Aaron. 2008. "New Numbers for Blogging and Blog Readership." Washington, DC: Pew Internet and American Life Project, July 22.

Smith, Abby. 1999. "The Future of the Past: In American Research Libraries." Available: www.clir.org/pubs/reports/pub82/pub82text.html (accessed February 1, 2010).

Sottong, Stephen. 2008. "The Elusive E-book." *American Libraries* (May): 44–48.

Stephens, Michael. 2005. "The iPod Experiments." *Netconnect* (spring): 22–25.

———. 2006. "Web 2.0 & Libraries: Best Practices for Social Software." *Library Technology Reports.* Available: https:publications.techsource.ala.org/products/archive.pl?article= 2580. (accessed February 5, 2010).

Tennant, Roy. 1992. "Internet Basics." *Eric Digest* 18: EDO-IR-92-7.

University College London, et al. 2008. "Information Behaviour of the Researcher of the Future." London: UCL. Available: www.bl.uk/news/pdf/googlegen.pdf (accessed February 1, 2010).

U.S. National Commission on Libraries and Information Science. 2006. *Mass Digitization: Implications for Information Policy.* Washington, DC: NCLIS.

Van Kappen, Philip-Jan. 2008. "Study Shows Migration to Online Books Saves Libraries Money and Increases Usage." *Library Connect* 6 (January): 1–4. Available: http://libraryconnect.elsevier .com/lcn/0601/lcn060110.html (accessed May 21, 2009).

Warfield, Peter. 2005. "RFID: More Worrisome Than You Think." *Public Libraries* 44: II.

Webster's Third New International Dictionary. 1970. Springfield, MA: G & C Merriam.

Whitney, Gretchen, and Stuart Glogoff. 1994. "Automation for the Nineties: A Review Article." *Library Quarterly* 64 (July): 319–331.

Wikipedia. 2009. "RSS." Available: http://en.wikipedia.org/wiui/Rss (accessed April 6, 2009).

World Wide Web Consortium. 2010. "Mission." Available: www.w3.org/Consortium/Mission (accessed February 4, 2010).

Wright, Cheryl D. 2002. "Introduction." In *Digital Library Technology Trends.* Available: www .lib/buu.ac.th/webnew/libtech/digital_library_trends.pdf (accessed February 4, 2010).

Zeng, Marcia Lei. 2008. "Digital Preservation: For the Future of the Past." [Unpublished Presentation Overheads]. Kent State University.

Zittrain, Jonathan L. 2006. "The Generative Internet." *Harvard Law Review* 119 (May): 1974–2040.

SELECTED READINGS: IMPACT OF TECHNOLOGY

Books

Bertot, John Carlo, and Denise M. Davis. *Planning and Evaluating Library Networked Services and Resources*. Westport, CT: Libraries Unlimited, 2004.

Bushman, John. *Information Technology in Librarianship*. Westport, CT: Libraries Unlimited, 2008.

Courtney, Nancy. *Library 2.0 and Beyond: Innovative Technologies and Tomorrow's User*. Westport, CT: Libraries Unlimited, 2007.

De Rosa, Cathy, Lorcan Dempsey, and Alane Wilson. *The 2003 OCLC Environmental Scan: Pattern Recognition: A Report to the OCLC Membership*. Dublin, OH: OCLC, 2004.

Farkas, Meredith G. *Social Software in Libraries: Building Collaboration, Communication, and Community Online*. Medford, NJ: Informaton Today, 2007.

Haley, Connie, Lynne Jacobsen, and Shai Robkin. *Radio Frequency Identification Handbook for Librarians*. Westport, CT: Libraries Unlimited, 2007.

Lankes, R. David, John W. Collins III, and Abby S. Kasowitz, eds. *Digital Reference Service in the New Millennium: Planning, Management, and Evaluation*. New York: Neal-Schuman, 2000.

Leckie, Gloria J., and John E. Buschman, eds. *Information Technology in Librarianship: New Critical Approaches*. Westport, CT: Libraries Unlimited, 2009.

Miller, Joseph B. *Internet Technologies and Information Services*. Westport, CT: Libraries Unlimited, 2009.

Articles

Barjak, Franz. "The Role of the Internet in Informal Scholarly Communication." *Journal of the American Society for Information Science and Technology* 57 (August 2006): 1350–1367.

Bearman, David. "Digital Libraries." *Annual Review of Information Science and Technology* 41 (2007): 223–272.

Bell, Steven J. "Technology Killed the Reference Desk Librarian." *Reference Librarian* 48 (2007): 105–107.

Burke, Leslie, and Stephanie McConnell. "Technical Services Departments in the Digital Age: The Four R's of Adapting to New Technology." *Against the Grain* 19 (November 2007): 58–64.

Caplan, Priscilla. "Digital Defense: A Primer for the Preservation of Digital Materials." *American Libraries* 39 (May 2008): 38.

Carr, Nicholas. "Is Google Making Us Stupid?" *Atlantic Monthly* 302 (July/August 2008): 56–63.

Eisenberg, Mike. "The Parallel Information Universe." *Library Journal* 133 (May 2008): 22–25.

Griffey, Jason. "Podcast 1-2-3." *Library Journal* 132 (June 15, 2007): 32–34.

Kajewski, Mary Ann. "Emerging Technologies Changing Public Library Service Delivery Models." *APLIS* 19 (December 2006): 157–163.

Kani-Zabihi, Elahe, Gheorghita Ghinea, and Sherry Y. Chen. "Digital Libraries: What Do Users Want?" *Online Information Review* 30 (2006): 395–412.

Kolbitsch, Josef, and Hermann Maurer. "The Transformation of the Web: How Emerging Communities Shape the Information We Consume." *Journal of Universal Computer Science* 12 (2006): 187–213.

Kuzyk, Raya. "Reference into the Future." *Library Journal* 132 (November 16, 2007): 8–11.

Levine, Jenny. "The Gaming Generation." *Library Technology Reports* 42 (September–October 2006): 18–23.

O'Leary, Mick. "Wikipedia: Encyclopedia or Not?" *Information Today* 22 (September 2005): 49–53.

Phillips, Angus. "Does the Book Have a Future?" *LOGOS: The Journal of the World Book Community* 19 (March 2008): 26–33.

Poe, Marshall. "The Hive." *Atlantic Monthly* 298 (September 2006): 86–94.

Rosenzweig, Roy. "Can History Be Open Source? Wikipedia and the Future of the Past." *Journal of American History* 93 (June 2006): 117–146.

Schneiderman, R. Anders. "A Non-Librarian Explains 'Why Librarians Should Rule the Net.'" *Information Outlook* 1 (April 1997): 34–35.

Sottong, Stephen. "The Elusive E-book." *American Libraries* 39 (May 2008): 44–48.

Zittrain, Jonathan L. "The Generative Internet." *Harvard Law Review* 119 (May 2006): 1974–2006.

7

Information Science:
A Service Perspective

I. INTRODUCTION

If information is a critical aspect of life in the twenty-first century, LIS professionals must develop information systems that can acquire, organize, maintain, and disseminate information with minimum effort and cost to users. To provide the best service in this rapidly changing information environment, LIS professionals must also understand how and why people use information. Studies of current information-seeking behavior and information needs suggest that some traditional perspectives of librarians might require substantial adjustment. For example, historically, librarians built collections as the primary means of meeting the education, recreation, and information needs of their communities. Proliferating information technologies today make that a woefully inadequate approach. LIS professionals will need to decide what role the library will play in this new environment and how they will accomplish that role.

II. THE CHARACTER OF INFORMATION SCIENCE

Over the centuries, librarians systematically organized knowledge, primarily contained in books, so that people could obtain information and meet their needs. Innovations such as the Dewey Decimal System greatly increased efficiency. However, with the proliferation of scientific and technical information in the twentieth century, often stored in media other than books, came considerable interest in the theoretical and practical aspects of how to organize nonprint information and improve access to the new media. The package containing the information was far less important and from this realization, a new field emerged. Developed first in Europe and known originally as "documentalism," it focused on the creation, organization, and dissemination of information in all formats. Organizations to promote the field were established, most notably the Federation Internationale de Documentation (FID) and its U.S.

counterpart, the American Documentation Institute, which continues today as the American Society for Information Science and Technology (ASIS&T). Library schools quickly recognized the value of documentalism, and Case Western Reserve University in Ohio and Columbia in New York offered the first two courses in 1950 and 1951 respectively (Taylor 1966).

Defining Information Science

Information science (IS) has many definitions, but Taylor (1966, p. 19) captured the essential elements:

Information Science: The science that investigates the properties and behavior of information, the forces governing the flow of information, and the means of processing information for optimum accessibility and usability. The processes include the origination, dissemination, collection, organization, storage, retrieval, interpretation, and use of information. The field is derived from or related to mathematics, logic, linguistics, psychology, computer technology, operations research, the graphic arts, communications, library science, management, and some other fields.

Three features of this definition stand out:

1. a focus on the phenomenon of information regardless of the format (e.g., a book or database) or context (e.g., government, business, or personal);
2. attention to the entire information cycle from creation to use; and
3. recognition of the interdisciplinary nature of the field, drawing from scientific, social scientific, and psychological disciplines as well as library science.

The foundation of contemporary information science also rests on the development of computers, which increase the capacity to store information without the need for a physical object. Early articles on the potential of computers following World War II predicted great things. Vannevar Bush's (1945) seminal article "As We Might Think," in which he forecast a machine for the storage and retrieval of documents that he dubbed "Memex," was a prominent exemplar of the hopes raised by computerized information technologies. Only five years later, the phrase "information retrieval" was first used (Wellisch 1972, p. 161). Interestingly, Veith (2006) noted that, with some modification, the iPod is the realization of Memex.

Some have described the period 1950–1970 as the "golden age" of information science in the United States (Burke 2007, p. 13). The growth of computers combined with technology needs stemming from the cold war, an increased number of well-funded applied research projects at large universities, and the resulting need for sophisticated indexing and information retrieval tools provided a fertile ground for the growth and development of the field. Given the broad-based needs of business, government, military, and research demands for information properly organized and stored, the evolution of documentalists (pre–World War II) into information scientists (post–World War II) focusing on indexing and retrieving information was inevitable. One might argue that this period reified the professional identity of information science (Burke 2007).

Not explicit in Taylor's definition above is the notion that IS is not institution based. Information science comprises a library without walls; its collection is the entire world of information and the information scientist, a term attributed to Farradane in the early 1950s (Summers et al. 1999), is the agent who acquires, organizes, and disseminates that information to help people meet their needs, whether practical, theoretical, religious, or aesthetic. In fact, this purpose can be seen as a defining characteristic of both librarianship and IS. Brittain (1980) observed: "It might be that information science is a different way of looking at many of the problems and tasks that have confronted librarians for many decades" (p. 37).

Indeed, IS has sometimes been characterized as deinstitutionalized library science.

Summers et al. (1999) identified three core concerns of information science: "storage (digital libraries);

> *Information science comprises a library without walls; its "collection" is the entire world of information and the "information scientist" acquires, organizes, and disseminates that information to help people meet their needs.*

communication (information retrieval and intelligent agent interaction), and use (knowledge management) of information" (p. 1159). For them, IS exhibited scientific, social scientific, and humanistic characteristics:

> it is not surprising that information science, which is dependent upon human activities such as writing articles, having information needs, creating search strategies, and making relevance judgments, shows itself to have a mixture of science-like and nonscience-like characteristics. (p. 1156)

Bates (2007) speculated that IS might be different from many traditional disciplines. While the traditional spectrum of disciplines is often characterized with the arts and humanities on one end and the social and natural sciences on the other, information science might be orthogonal to the conventional disciplines—that is, its concerns cut across them. Orthogonal disciplines focus on a particular social purpose and draw from the various traditional disciplines as needed. Bates identified these special disciplines as information disciplines (including information science and librarianship), communication/journalism, and education (see Figure 7.1, p. 274).

In Bates's (2007) characterization, information science is more related to scientific disciplines while library science is associated more with the use and preservation of the cultural record, even though both fields share a concern for recorded information. Bates (1999) identified three "Big Questions" addressed by information science:

1. The physical question: What are the features and laws of the recorded-information universe?

2. The social question: How do people relate to, seek, and use information?

3. The design question: How can access to recorded information be made most rapid and effective? (p. 1048)

Figure 7.1. The Spectrum of the Information Disciplines

THE SPECTRUM OF THE INFORMATION DISCIPLINES

Disciplines of the Cultural Record

The Sciences of Information

Library Science   Information Science

Records Management   Information Systems
Archives
                          Knowledge Management
Museum Studies

Social Studies of Information

Bibliography   Document and Genre Studies   Informatics

Arts   Humanities   Social and Behavioral Sciences   Natural Sciences and Math

THE SPECTRUM OF THE TRADITIONAL DISCIPLINES

Source: Bates 2007. Reprinted with permission.

The breadth and variety of fields explored by information science is considerable. *Information Science and Technology Abstracts*, for example, identified eleven major categories including information science research, knowledge organization, the information profession, societal issues, the information industry, publishing and distribution, information technologies, electronic information systems and services, subject-specific sources and applications, libraries and library services, and government and legal information issues (Hawkins et al. 2003).

III. FEATURES OF INFORMATION SCIENCE

The following is a more detailed discussion of some major areas explored by information science and their implications for libraries. Additional aspects of information technology and information policy are explored in Chapters 6 and 8.

A. Understanding Information Needs, Seeking, Use, and Users

The concept of an information need can be understood generally as an uncertainty that arises in an individual and which the individual believes can be satisfied by information (Krikelas 1983). Case (2002) described an information need as "a recognition that your knowledge is inadequate to satisfy a goal that you have" (p. 5). But the concept can also be separated into information wants (or desires) and information needs. An information want is a desire for information to satisfy an uncertainty; an information need is the condition, whether recognized by an individual or not, in which information is required to resolve a problem. Such a distinction is especially important for LIS professionals if they intend to satisfy both their patrons' wants and needs. Merely answering a patron's question might not be enough; the individual might want a particular piece of information, only to discover that something different is needed. If LIS professionals are to perform their jobs well, they must find out what is wanted and needed. Interestingly, they must also be careful not to find too much information. Studies reveal, for example, that there is "an inverted-U relationship between the volume of information and decision quality" (Morville 2005, p. 165). In other words, too much information reduces decision quality as does too little.

Approaches to studying information needs vary considerably. Some focus on individuals; others on institutions, often libraries; still others specifically on the information needs of various disciplines, such as business, science, nursing, and engineering. Information systems cannot be well designed without a clear understanding of what the intended users want or need to know, how they seek information, and how they evaluate it.

Seeking and gathering information is a highly complex process that requires considerable explanation and refinement. How someone seeks information can vary by age, level of education, intelligence, and discipline. Scientists, for example, need current information and tend to rely on informal communications with their colleagues, conferences, journal references and articles, and electronic sources. Humanities scholars, on the other hand, like to browse and rely more heavily on references in books, subject catalogs, and printed indexes and bibliographies (Broadbent 1986; Van Styvendaele 1977; Meadows 1974). These differences persist in an online environment. Humanities scholars used more named individuals, geographical terms, chronological terms, and discipline terms (Bates et al. 1993). As Durrance (1989) observed, "What people do drives their need for information" (p. 161).

Effectively assessing information wants and needs requires knowledge of how people search for information and how they learn, as well as how to interview effectively, how to evaluate the person's need, and how to evaluate the degree to which the proffered information satisfied the need. It also requires thorough and current knowledge of the available electronic, print, and human resources and how to access these sources. This places a serious responsibility on LIS professionals, beyond merely getting requested pieces of information.

Chen and Hernon (1982) found that among the general population, the primary reason for seeking information was personal. That is, more than half of their subjects (52 percent) sought information to solve day-to-day problems and nearly three-quarters

(73 percent) described their information need as personal. Among information of greatest interest were the following:

1. Job-related issues such as performing specific tasks or establishing businesses, getting or changing jobs, advancing careers, or obtaining promotions
2. Consumer issues relating to the quality or availability of a product or obtaining product information
3. Housing and household maintenance issues relating to dealing with landlords, obtaining loans and mortgages, or performing repairs on the car or home
4. Adult education, parenting, and obtaining support for education

These findings are of great value to LIS professionals, especially those in public libraries, in building their collections and services.

Emphasis on use was central to an important model of information seeking called the sense-making approach, developed by Brenda Dervin (1983). According to Spink and Cole (2006), in this model, "the information user is conceptualized as constructing information based on the values and specific environment of the 'small world' in which the user exists concurrently apart from and as a member of the larger society" (p. 27). The more we understand the person, the better we can determine what to provide for that individual. Many other studies provide useful knowledge for LIS professionals. Indeed, the wide-ranging body of research in this area is stimulating the development of an emerging field, human information behavior (Spink and Cole 2006). A highly selected summary of some of the findings follows.

1. There Is a Difference between Information Seeking and Information Gathering

Krikelas (1983) defined information seeking as "an attempt to satisfy an *immediate* need by searching for relevant information. Information gathering is an attempt to satisfy a *deferred* need" (p. 8, emphasis added). In information gathering there is no immediate need, but a search is expected to yield useful information for future use. This distinction might profoundly affect how a library is used. An information seeker might be looking for a specific item, ask a reference librarian a specific query, or have a specific time requirement. Alternatively, the patron might browse a collection without need for specific information or time pressure. Similarly, newspaper and magazine collections might be most often consulted, albeit not exclusively, by information gatherers, while reference materials might be most often consulted by information seekers.

2. People Usually Search for Information in Some Context

As Case (2002) noted, "information needs do not arise in a vacuum, but rather owe their existence to some history, purpose, and influence" (p. 226). People seldom seek information as an end in itself; it is usually needed within a particular context or "problem environment" (Durrance 1989, p. 162). For example, a scientist might seek information on a technical procedure; an English teacher might look for a particular essay; an electrician might need directions for repairing a refrigerator; or a minister might want quotations for a sermon.

People ask questions for a purpose. Historically, reference librarians were taught not to probe why a particular question was asked for fear of violating a patron's privacy and thus deterring someone from seeking help. Today we know that this practice is not consistent with research on information seeking. Some patrons have a problem that needs to be solved and librarians can only help if they distinguish between wants and needs. The issue is not only, "What do you want to know?" but "How and why is the information needed? How is it likely to help? What does the user know already? What is expected? What are the parameters of the problem?" (Durrance 1989, p. 163). This is not to suggest that librarians should pry, but merely answering questions without understanding the underlying issues can be problematic. Wilson (1986) offered an approach that he called the "face value rule," which emphasized "clarifying the question" rather than inquiring into the purposes of the questions (p. 469). Nonetheless, research suggests that librarians should not be too hesitant to ask questions.

3. People Prefer Personal Rather Than Institutional Sources

When an information need arises, people first scan their memory for ready solutions. If this fails, they attempt to use their powers of observation (Krikelas 1983). Failing this, they seek information from external sources: first from nearby individuals, then institutions (Chen and Hernon 1982). This means that people are more likely to contact their family, friends, coworkers, neighbors, doctors, or clergy, before coming to a library. In a large study of information seekers in New England, Chen and Hernon (1982) found that only 3 percent of people with a recent information need identified the library as a possible source for resolving that need. Although people do, in general, prefer other people to institutions as sources of information, popular search engines like Google and Bing provide a new means of obtaining information. This choice is particularly popular among young people and will remain highly competitive as an alternative information source.

4. People Seldom See Librarians as a Source of Information

When individuals have an information need, they think of the library, not the librarian, as the primary source. Durrance (1989) noted that we speak of "library users" rather than a "librarian's clients" (p. 165). This is something LIS professionals should consider seriously—how do we make ourselves more visible? A lack of visibility contributes to perceptions that librarians are not important in the information transfer process. If people really prefer human sources of information, emphasizing the librarian rather than the library might increase library use.

5. Information Seeking Proceeds in Stages

The search for information generally begins with an undefined notion of the need, sometimes referred to as an "anomalous state of knowledge" (Belkin et al. 1982, p. 62). As the process proceeds, the search becomes more and more defined, and the area to be explored narrows. The search strategy will vary depending on the nature of the inquiry itself, and as the query becomes narrowed, the strategy and type of information sought will vary (Rouse 1984). Bates (1989) described the process as "berrypicking"; berries are usually scattered on bushes, not found in one clump. Kuhlthau (1991) described six stages that she referred to as the information search process (ISP).

Kuhlthau's Six Stages of the Information Search Process

Stage 1: Initiation. Characterized by uncertainty, as the individual realizes an unfocused need for some knowledge or understanding. The topic and the search approach are undefined. Alternative courses of action might be discussed with others.

Stage 2: Selection. The topic comes into focus and various search strategies are considered; tentative searching begins.

Stage 3: Exploration. The seeker obtains preliminary information on the topic to provide an orientation for further searching. Considerable confusion or doubt might remain if the information appears contradictory or provides little direction. At this point, the seeker still might not be able to articulate precisely the type of information required.

Stage 4: Formulation. The seeker begins to establish a clear focus and feelings of uncertainty diminish. Rather than just collecting information, the seeker begins to evaluate critically the information obtained, accepting some and discarding what appears to be irrelevant. The seeker experiences increased confidence both in the direction of the search and in the methods used.

Stage 5: Collection. The focus is now clear, and the seeker collects only information related to the defined topic. The seeker can articulate clearly the type of information needed; the search process becomes more effective, uncertainty is reduced, and the seeker's confidence is increased further.

Stage 6: Presentation. The search is complete. Its success might vary depending on factors such as the availability of information, the effectiveness of the information system used, and the skills of the searcher. Some of the information might duplicate previous results, so attention is turned to summary, synthesis, and reporting of the information gathered.

Search processes, like Kuhlthau's, reveal the essentially personal nature of information seeking. The problem context provides its own frame of reference, and the meaning and relevance of the information is largely dictated by this frame rather than some objective measure. Kuhlthau (1993) suggested that the ISP can help librarians and other information intermediaries identify the appropriate "zone of intervention" when "a user can do with guidance and assistance" (p. 176). Kalbach (2006) suggested that Kuhlthau's incorporation of feelings into her model might also be useful for studying information seeking on the Web, which has a strong emotive component.

6. Search Abilities Vary among Individuals

Although information-seeking ability improves with age, information technologies tend to be less friendly to older individuals. Other differences include intelligence, analytical ability, manual dexterity, or marginalization. Chatman (1996) found that marginalized individuals often see information seeking as a trade-off between giving and receiving. For example, if they have to report income, family problems, or health condition in order to get information, some might find the risk greater than the potential benefit, and not seek information at all. These differences substantially shape library services. The more varied the users' abilities, the more flexible the systems must be to accommodate those variations. For example, public libraries serve patrons ranging from the highly educated to those who are barely literate. On the other hand, in a specialized library where the users are highly educated, familiar with the organization of the literature, and the appropriate search technologies, the system requires little flexibility.

7. The Principle of Least Effort

People seek the most convenient source to meet their needs, even when they know that this source might produce information of lower quality than other sources. This is referred to as the principle of least effort. Such a finding, although not surprising, can be disconcerting when considering the amount of time and energy LIS professionals devote to building collections that yield the highest quality information. One hopes that people prefer authoritative to nonauthoritative sources. In fact, one would hope that as the importance of a task increases, individuals would insist on quality information. Research by Xu, Tan, and Yang (2006), however, belies this point. Although they found a positive relationship between the quality of a personal source and its use, they also noted that "as the task becomes more important, seekers pay less attention to source quality, and they look for closer rather than more remote sources.... They resort to the local network for problem solving" (p. 1675). It is certainly more convenient to ask a neighbor or friend than to drive to the library. However, a library collection and services must be designed so that convenience and quality are one and the same (Mann 1993).

Many people view libraries as complicated places. Factors that impair or prevent information seeking at a library include the following:

- **Physical aspects**: A library's location affects its use. Libraries that are geographically remote or difficult to reach are bound to have use problems. Similarly, libraries that are difficult to enter or negotiate, especially for those with physical disabilities, will have limited use. No doubt, collections with a poor physical arrangement or poor signage will also exacerbate user difficulties.

- **Policy and procedural aspects**: Libraries often create well-meaning rules, regulations, and procedures that inhibit the use of materials and services.

Restrictive circulation or reference policies, inadequate operating hours, limited use of meeting rooms, inadequate staff training, or poor scheduling of library staff all can frustrate information seeking.

- **Legal aspects**: Laws and regulations governing the flow of information, such as copyright law or the recently passed Children's Internet Protection Act, inevitably affect the ability of libraries to provide access to some information.

- **Social aspects**: A troubling but common finding is that those most likely to use libraries have more formal education, tend to have higher incomes, and are white. Some reasons for this might relate to the way members of minority groups perceive the library or are treated by library staff. If libraries are perceived as aristocratic, authoritarian institutions, unfriendly and unresponsive to minorities, then these groups are bound to have diminished enthusiasm for libraries as sources of information.

8. People's Search Behavior on the Web Varies Widely

Bilal (2002) identified at least three ways the Web differs from traditional sources: (1) it is an extraordinarily large system that often produces information overload and disorientation; (2) it is constantly changing; and (3) it is not indexed. Rose (2006), citing the work of Broder (2002), identified three types of Web-based searches: (1) navigational searches to locate a specific Web site; (2) information searches to obtain specific information; and (3) transactional searches to locate an online service that allows additional interaction, such as a map database. Approximately 30 percent of all Web searches are unsuccessful and people frequently stop looking after the first page of hits. Alternatively, many people use a "spoke-and-hub" approach to searching; that is, they begin at a certain point, search, return to the original point, and start a search again. This style relies heavily on the Back button and is sometimes called "backtracking" (Slone 2002). Because it is easy to lose one's place on the Web, returning to an original page provides a stable point of reference.

a. Personal Attributes

Personal attributes that influence adult Web searching include cognitive style, level of anxiety related to searching, previous experience with Web searching, gender, and domain (subject) expertise. Research on adults, sometimes called digital immigrants, revealed that many depend on hyperlinks to find documents, seldom use Boolean search strategies, rely heavily on keyword searching, limit their explorations to specific sections within a site, use a few pages frequently, and spend considerable time scrolling, reading Web pages, and waiting for Web pages to load (Hsieh-Yee 2001). Novice users made more errors, retrieved irrelevant hits, avoided the use of advanced features, or quickly became frustrated and stopped the search (Slone 2002). On the other hand, despite these problems, novice searchers sometimes exhibited very high and even "frenetic levels of effort throughout the process"

(Debowski 2001, p. 378). Historically women tended to encounter more difficulty than men, believed they were less competent in searching, used the Internet less frequently, and used fewer Internet applications (Hsieh-Yee 2001). However, new evidence suggests that the gender gap has narrowed. Dresang (2005) noted that "studies consistently used to find males were more interested and involved with technology than females; this is often no longer the case" (p. 182). She further noted that a 2004 study revealed that "girls and boys, ages nine to thirteen, were equally positive about computers and their ability to use them" (p. 182). Searchers with domain expertise had significantly greater success and were faster (Lazonder et al. 2000). One would assume that academics have domain expertise. However, the British Library (2008) found that academic user behavior was diverse and included the following:

- **Horizontal information seeking**: A skimming activity where people viewed just one or two pages from an academic site and then bounced out, perhaps never to return.
- **Navigators**: People spent as much time finding their way around a digital environment as they did actually viewing what they found.
- **Viewers**: The average time spent on e-book and e-journal sites was very short: typically four and eight minutes respectively.
- **Squirreling behavior**: Academics saved information for future use by downloading content, especially when downloads were free.
- **Checkers**: Users assessed authority and trust in a matter of seconds by dipping and cross-checking across different sites, and by relying on favored brands (e.g., Google).

b. Web Use and Youth

Adolescents and young adults search quite differently than their parents. Known variously as millennials, the Net generation, or digital natives, these individuals have grown up with the Internet and are adept at its use. Griffiths and Brophy (2005) summarized the research of Cmor and Lippold, who found:

1. Students use the Web for everything.
2. They might spend hours searching or just a few minutes.
3. Searching skills vary and students will often assess themselves as being more skilled than they actually are.
4. They will give discussion list comments the same academic weight as peer-reviewed journal articles. (p. 541)

Griffiths and Brophy also noted that students (1) prefer search engines, especially Google, over other means of locating materials; (2) use few academic resources and find it difficult to locate resources; (3) will sacrifice quality to save time and effort; and (4) set their expectations of other electronic resources according to their experience with search engines. These findings are consonant with the principle of least effort discussed above.

The research behavior of the "Google generation" was a special focus of a study by the British Library (2008). Among their findings was that young people (1) spent little time evaluating information for accuracy or authority; (2) employed poor search strategies because they did not have a good grasp of their own information needs; (3) preferred natural language rather than using keywords; (4) had difficulty discriminating relevant hits from a long list of sites; and (5) had a poor conception of the Internet and therefore relied on search engines such as Google and Yahoo. Heinstrom (2006) studied the search strategies of master's-level students and found three patterns: (1) fast surfing dominated by minimal effort, easy access, and easily digestible material; (2) broad scanning, employing an exploratory search pattern and spontaneous planning, using wide searches among many types of information sources; and (3) deep diving, involving substantial efforts, structured searches, and a preference for high-quality information sources. Interestingly, Heinstrom used a standardized personality measure with each group and found that fast surfing was associated with a lack of conscientiousness and positive associations with openness to experience and sensitivity. Extroversion was positively associated with broad scanning. Personality traits had little effect on deep diving.

Younger children have fewer problem-solving and mechanical skills as well as less developed cognitive abilities than adults. They prefer to browse the Web and do not search systematically (Hsieh-Yee 2001). They have difficulty evaluating the quality of Web sites, developing search strategies, using correct search syntax, typing in the proper search terms, and locating relevant hits. Despite these handicaps, children felt confident about their Web searches. Dresang (2005) noted that children preferred sites that were high in visual content and possessed animation and interactivity and simple text. Dresang also found some exploratory studies suggesting that children prefer to do their searching collaboratively with other children. This might explain the roots of older children's heavy use of social networks and computer games that involve group activity, which dominate many young peoples' lives today.

B. Information Storage and Retrieval

Research into information retrieval systems in the 1960s constituted the "first flowering of information science as a science" (Rayward 1983, p. 353). Harter (1986) defined an information retrieval system as "a device interposed between a potential end-user of an information collection and the information collection itself. For a given information program, the purpose of the system is to capture wanted items and filter out unwanted items from the information collection" (p. 2). This definition highlights a central concept of information retrieval: relevance. Much has been written on the subject (Saracevic 1975). There are at least two aspects of relevance: relevant to the user and relevant to the topic. In the former, the user defines the context for relevance; an item is relevant if the user believes it helps meet the information need. In the latter case, an item is relevant if it is about the subject regardless of a given user (Pao 1989). Relevance is a critical variable in much of the evaluation of information systems. Systems that retrieve relevant items and avoid irrelevant items, also called false hits or false drops, naturally are considered more effective.

1. Evaluating Information Retrieval Systems

By what criteria should information retrieval systems be evaluated? Two frequently used criteria are recall and precision. Within any given system, it is critical to know if all the available items relevant to a particular search were found; the degree of success is a measure of recall. With poor recall, many items that might have been useful were not located. On the other hand, it is also important to weed irrelevant items from relevant ones. This weeding is difficult and time consuming if the

searcher has to read through all of the items to identify the useful information. The degree to which a system finds only relevant items is a measure of precision.

These measures, however, are somewhat controversial because they emphasize only quantity. Froehlich (1994) observed that rele-

> *Recall = Total number of documents retrieved ÷ Total number of documents in the file*
>
> *Precision = Total number of relevant documents ÷ Total number of documents retrieved*

vance judgments are made dynamically and often involve multiple criteria, not just one. More recent approaches to evaluation place greater emphasis on a searcher's knowledge, cognitive process, and the problem to be solved.

2. Search Models

Information storage and retrieval systems are not useful unless information can be quickly and effectively retrieved. The search approach can make a big difference. The most common search strategy in library settings is Boolean logic. In the Boolean model, an individual combines search terms with various operators such as *and*, *or*, or *not*. Multiple terms can be used simultaneously, permitting highly flexible search strategies compared to manual searching operations. Other operators can further limit searches. For example, retrieval models might permit searching by author, title, year of publication, and journal title. LIS professionals must be adept at using these search models.

3. Database and File Structure

Database design, the structure of the information, and how it is presented significantly affect the user's ability to retrieve information. For example, what types of information are available (numerical, textual, video, audio)? What vocabulary must be used in the search process, highly restricted or relatively open? What fields and subfields can be searched—by author, by title or keyword, by subject? Can the search be narrowed by date, language, or publisher? Do the records contain abstracts, full text, or images? The answers to these questions determine the usefulness of a database.

4. Human-Computer Interface

Libraries must take steps to make the user comfortable and make the searching process as easy as possible. This means that designers of information storage and retrieval systems must understand the way people use computers and search for information to create "user-friendly front ends" that allow users to satisfy their needs with a minimum of jargon, confusion, or technical knowledge. The point of contact between the individual and the computer is called the human-computer interface. Issues include screen display features such as color and windows, speed of response, interaction functions such as commands and menus, postprocessing functions such as downloading, help systems and messages, graphics capabilities, training time required, user satisfaction, and error rates (Shaw 1991). Other factors might be font type and size, screen brightness, screen layout, spatial arrangement, organization of text and graphic organization. Individual factors such as age, gender, cognitive ability, level of education, motivation, and attitude must also be considered (Chalmers 2003).

One important area of research explored how user knowledge and the knowledge contained in the systems can be matched effectively. These studies examined how users judged the relevance of information, how memory affected users, how they learned to use information systems, and the relationship between cognitive ability and the ability to use an information system. Allen (1991) formulated four categories of knowledge that interact with each other to affect the use of information systems:

1. **World knowledge**: Users' world knowledge might affect the information they search for and their search strategies. Factors such as ethnicity, gender, and nationality have all been shown to influence use.

2. **Systems knowledge**: The extent and type of knowledge about information systems and user expectations of the systems affect their ability and manner of use.

3. **Task knowledge**: The users' particular information goals or needs affect their use of the systems: how users define the information problem to be solved, how to apply problem-solving techniques, and how to search.

4. **Domain knowledge**: The amount and depth of knowledge a user possesses affects how they search. Experts use information systems differently than naive users.

Understanding how people think, what they know, and how they approach information problems helps designers create knowledge models that more closely match the methods and data by which users can meet their needs. This knowledge helps designers create user-friendly systems or effective gateways for information access.

How people communicate with computers is a related area of study that draws upon the field of linguistics. A crucial issue is natural language processing (NLP), which attempts to develop user interfaces that allow people to search using their natural language. In other words, using NLP, they should be able to ask a computer a question in the same way they would ask a reference librarian. This capability eliminates the need for the user to know terms selected by the database developers. Lee and Olsgaard (1989) observed that four areas must be considered in developing NLP:

1. **Speech recognition**: A computer needs a voice recognition system that allows it to hear and understand a question.

2. **Command recognition**: A computer should be able to understand the command without use of an artificial language or vocabulary.

3. **Content analysis and representation**: To respond to a question, a computer must first interpret the question's meaning, which requires understanding its context. Given the subtleties and ambiguities of language, content analysis represents a major challenge in NLP.

4. **System interaction**: The system has to be able to take the natural language query and relate it to the database so that correct information can be retrieved.

The need to better understand how users and computers interact has spawned a new field, usability engineering or usability studies, which focuses on the experience of users primarily in the Web environment. This field is discussed in more detail later in the chapter.

5. Artificial Intelligence and Expert Systems

Artificial intelligence (AI) is an extremely broad field that includes machine translation, robotics, expert systems, natural language interfaces, knowledge acquisition and representation, and pattern matching. One of the most intriguing areas of study is the continuing attempt to create computers that mimic human thought processes, judgments, and sometimes actions in the hope that they can provide needed information, perform valuable services, and even render judgments that can assist people. Applications of this research can be found in industrial production (robotics for manufacturing), gaming, and expert systems assisting physicians and lawyers. Expert systems are "computer programs which inform, make recommendations, or solve problems in a manner and at a level of performance comparable to that displayed by a human expert in the field" (Vedder 1990, p. 4). Although much of the

AI research and its application lie outside the realm of librarianship, AI might be applied to reference functions such as identification and retrieval of documents or data, cataloguing and authority control, and patron education through computer-assisted instruction (Smith 1987). In addition, work in developing "expert search intermediaries" could assist users in searching online systems without the need for human intermediaries (Smith 1987, p. 55).

C. Defining the Nature of Information

Perhaps the most conspicuous debate in information science deals with distinguishing among three basic constructs: data, information, and knowledge. From time to time, a fourth construct, wisdom, is added. The discussion that follows is intended to provide a brief overview.

1. Data

Data are the building blocks of information and knowledge. In this sense, data are numbers, letters, or symbols. Some data are more readily processed by a computer than others. The term often implies that meaning is as yet absent, or unassigned, as in raw data. The numbers stored in a computer file are referred to as a data set. Although the terms *data* and *information* are often used synonymously, a greater understanding can be gained by noting their distinctive characteristics.

2. Information

Information has a very long etymological history. Early senses of the term suggested that information involved a "forming" or "moulding of the mind" (*Oxford English Dictionary* 1989, p. 944). In this early sense, the soul might be "informed." Although not a current usage of the term, it is suggestive of the power of information. The verb form of the term, "the action of informing" or the "communication of the knowledge or 'news' of some fact or occurrence" (*OED*, p. 944) suggests both an active process and the object being communicated. It is the "knowledge communicated concerning some particular fact, subject, or event; that which one is apprised of or told; intelligence, news" (*OED*, p. 944). Libraries both inform their users and provide them with information.

In fact, there are numerous definitions of information, many of them highly technical. Summers et al. (1999) noted that information "sometimes seems to be the prototypical 'weasel' word: one, the dictionary tells us, that is intentionally ambiguous or misleading" (p. 1153). Bates (2006) identified eighteen types or forms of information, the most general of which was "the pattern of organization of matter and energy" (p. 1036). Other definitions were highly specific, relating to such things as genetics, expressed information including speech, and recorded information, including information in durable media.

LIS professionals commonly see information as an aggregation, organization, or classification of data, and perhaps more importantly, as data that has been assigned meaning. This also seems to imply that some type of human understanding and processing has occurred. Somewhat more restrictive definitions hold not only that information must contain meaning, but that the meaning must be previously unknown to the recipient; in other words, it is something new. Some argue that the information must also be true or accurate, or that it must be conveyed from one person to another. One might argue that libraries and information centers hold data which are then processed either by staff or patrons, creating information—in this sense, meaning arises within the walls of the library or information center.

3. Knowledge (and Wisdom)

Knowledge is defined as a cohesive body of information or information that is integrated into a larger body of knowledge. Knowledge is applied or potentially applicable to some end. From our perspective, one presumes that knowledge as well as information is gained through libraries—that users can gain an understanding of the interrelationship of the information obtained and its applicability to a particular setting. Such a view recognizes the potential of libraries and librarians to help make connections whenever possible so that users can translate information into knowledge.

Wisdom, although not always part of the discussion, is also an important notion. Wisdom can be appreciated as knowledge applied to human ends to benefit the world. In this sense, wisdom is the only one of these terms imbued with values. One can apply knowledge to immoral ends, but there is a beneficial end to the application of wisdom. The goal of libraries as a social institution is to provide the data that becomes information that increases knowledge that results in wisdom to benefit society. In summary, there appears to be a conceptual ladder: data are raw and unprocessed; information is processed data from which meaning arises and is communicated; and knowledge is further processed information that is organized and interrelated and more broadly understood and applied. Wisdom is knowledge applied to the benefit of humanity.

Despite the seeming simplicity of this hierarchy, one should accept these distinctions with great caution. For LIS professionals, the question of what constitutes knowledge is very important, because they rely on bodies of knowledge, or knowledgeable works, to perform many of their question-answering functions. That is, although libraries are full of information, when LIS professionals attempt to respond to a query, the knowledgeable or authoritative work is the one that is preferred. In this sense, LIS professionals rely on a canon of authorities and authoritative literature to provide the most dependable responses.

But how does something come to be accepted as knowledge that we put on a shelf to refer to and transmit to others? Wilson (1983) observed that most of the knowledge people acquire does not come from direct experience (firsthand knowledge), but from secondhand knowledge: "We mostly depend on others for ideas, as well as for information about things outside the range of direct experience. . . . Much of what we think about the world is what we have second hand from others" (p. 10).

What leads us to infer that one item is more authoritative than another is referred to as cognitive authority. We trust those sources we think have greater cognitive authority. What sources have the greatest cognitive authority for LIS professionals? Do librarians censor materials because they regard some authors or publishers as low in cognitive authority (although other groups might not agree)? Are there new cognitive authorities on the Web? Can we assess the cognitive authority of a Web site in the same way we do other publications? Savolainen (2007) observed that although people are aware of the Web's many credibility issues, it is still seen as a "relatively credible source of information. . . . In particular, factual information was perceived to be equally credible in the Internet and in the printed newspaper" (p. 9). Morville (2005) cautioned that authority on the Web can be based as much on popularity as other characteristics; he noted that search engines rank Web sites by the number of hits they receive. The fact is that what people identify as authoritative is being redefined because of the Web. For example, persons with a medical condition are likely to visit the Web to learn about their condition, whether they see a doctor or not. In the end, this places greater responsibility on the individual to discern high-quality information and less reliance on a particular authority such as the doctor. As Morville noted, "As we take responsibility for our own decisions, our relationship with authority changes" (p. 163). This presents a dilemma for LIS professionals who, on the one hand, are acutely aware of the importance of assessing authority, but at the same time recognize that the Web presents many opportunities for helping people find the information they need.

D. The Value of Information and Value-Added Processes

Part of understanding the nature of information is appreciating its value. Over the centuries, attempts to determine its monetary value have increased. With the industrial society evolving into an information-based society, the concept of information as a product, a commodity with its own value, has emerged. As a consequence those people, organizations, and countries that possess the highest-quality information are likely to prosper economically, socially, and politically. Investigations into the economics of information encompass a variety of categories including the costs of information and information services; the effects of information on decision making; the savings from effective information acquisition; the effects of information on productivity, sometimes referred to as "downstream productivity"; and the effects of specific agencies (such as corporate, technical, or medical libraries) on the productivity of organizations. Obviously many of these areas overlap, but it is clear that information has taken on a life of its own outside the medium in which it is contained. Information has become a recognized entity to be measured, evaluated, and priced.

Value-added functions are those performed by LIS professionals to increase the value of the information by making it more accessible. Much of the early research in this area was conducted by Robert Taylor (1986), who viewed libraries as document-based systems within broader information systems. He identified a variety of value-added functions related to information systems in general and to libraries in particular.

Taylor's Value-Added Functions

Access processes narrow the search for information and include classification systems, indexes, and subject headings. Additional processes reduce larger amounts of information into manageable quantities for summary and review such as abstracts, summaries, and graphs.

Accuracy processes decrease the possibility of error in the data or information provided. These processes include the use of standards to ensure consistency, completeness, and accuracy of bibliographic records; the use of high-quality sources to select materials; and weeding processes to remove inaccurate materials.

Browsing processes permit the patron to browse a "neighborhood" of information. Such processes include classification systems that group items of a similar subject or author together. Physical book arrangements can also foster browsing, as do book displays or special exhibitions of materials. These processes also encourage the serendipitous discovery of related information.

Currency processes ensure that the materials are up to date and include weeding and ordering later editions, using the most recent indexing and abstracting terms, and subject headings that reflect current thinking.

Flexibility (adaptability) processes provide a variety of methods or techniques, adapted to the needs and abilities of users, to help them find reliable information and analyze, interpret, and evaluate it.

Formatting processes affect the physical arrangement and presentation of information, including the arrangement of a particular electronic record on a computer screen, as well as signs and graphics to guide patrons to the appropriate information or services.

Interfacing processes provide assistance to the user in understanding and using the system. Computer-based systems have screens and navigation systems that facilitate users' access. In libraries, the fundamental interpreter of the system is the librarian, who conducts reference interviews and provides orientations.

Ordering processes organize the collection by subject area, format, or type of user and separates encyclopedias and other reference works from the rest of the collection.

Physical access processes improve access to library collections or computer databases and include circulation systems, checkout desks, study areas, shelving and shelf-reading, and computers that permit searching remote databases and other library collections throughout the nation and world.

Despite the importance of these value-added services in libraries, they are often underestimated. The reason might well be, at least in part, that by making access to information easier, these processes become invisible. The patron doesn't necessarily struggle to find information and, therefore, underestimates the complex design of the system that makes the search so easy. Librarians need to find ways to increase the user's understanding of these processes. Perhaps the status of LIS professionals would increase if these value-added processes were more obvious.

E. Bibliometrics and Citation Analysis

Wallace (1989) defined bibliometrics as "the application of quantitative methods to the study of information resources" (p. 10). The field explores patterns in the production of knowledge as well as its use. In libraries, bibliometrics includes but is not limited to:

1. **Analysis of circulation patterns**: Studies of which items circulate or fail to circulate provide valuable information for future purchases or reveal deficiencies in the library's organization or practices.

2. **Studies of in-house use**: How materials are used inside libraries provides valuable insights into the information-seeking behavior of patrons and the use of reference materials.

3. **Aging studies**: Review of the obsolescence (aging) of library materials can reveal the currency of library collections and the patterns that govern the use of aging materials.

4. **Collection overlap**: Studies comparing the collections of two or more libraries reveal duplications and can help in planning cooperative collection development, reveal unique features of different library collections, and reduce unnecessary expenditures for materials.

Bibliometric studies can also provide a broader understanding of entire disciplines, revealing which authors are most productive or which countries or languages produce greater amounts of material. Sometimes these studies reveal consistent patterns to the extent that bibliometric laws can be established. One of the most common of these is Lotka's law, named after Alfred Lotka (1926), who observed that there are a few authors who contribute a large number of publications, a larger number of authors who contribute smaller numbers of publications, and many authors who contribute a few or only one. He expressed this relationship as $1/n^2$, where n is the number of contributions. Hence, the number of authors making three contributions in a field would be one-ninth ($1/3^2$) of the total number of authors. The number of authors making four contributions would be one-sixteenth ($1/4^2$). Lotka's law is not a perfect description of how authors and publications are related within a discipline, but generally it is a good estimate.

Another frequently mentioned bibliometric law is Bradford's law or the Bradford distribution, based on the work of Samuel Bradford (1934). Bradford's law deals with the concept of scatter, which describes in a quantitative manner how articles within a particular field are distributed among periodical titles. Bradford found that given a body of journal literature in a particular area (such as engineering), the distribution throughout the various journals is not even, nor is the literature consulted equally. Although the distribution is not even, it is predictable. Most notably, he found that the spread of journal articles could be placed into three zones. The first zone was the nucleus of the field in which most articles appeared, generally in a relatively small number of journal titles. A second zone contained the same number of articles spread out in a substantially larger number of journals. The third zone contained the same number of articles but scattered among even more titles. This relationship was expressed as $1:n:n^2$. That is, if there were a total of 1,500 articles, the first 500 might be found in ten journals (Zone 1); the next 500 might be found in 50 journals (Zone 2). This produced a ratio of Zone 1 to Zone 2 of 1:5. The next 500 articles should therefore be of a ratio of 1:25. This means that Bradford's law would predict that the 500 articles of Zone 3 would be scattered among (10×25) or 250 journal titles. This regularity suggests a predictable scatter. Therefore, in selecting materials for library collections, the crucial selections would be those found in the nucleus, or Zone 1. As with Lotka's law, Bradford's law has its exceptions, but nonetheless it holds for many disciplines and represents an important bibliometric contribution to the field.

A related area of bibliometrics is citation analysis, which deals with the frequency and pattern of citations in articles and books. Among the various ways to analyze citations are direct citation, bibliographic coupling, and co-citation. Direct citation analyzes the items cited by authors. Bibliographic coupling and co-citation are closely related but distinct concepts:

> Two documents are bibliographically coupled if their reference lists share one or more of the same cited documents. Two documents are co-cited when they are jointly cited in one or more subsequently published documents. Thus in co-citation earlier documents become linked because they are later cited together; in bibliographic coupling later documents become linked because they cite the same earlier documents. The difference is that bibliographic coupling is an association intrinsic to the documents (static) while co-citation is a linkage extrinsic to the documents, and one that is valid only so long as they continue to be co-cited (dynamic). (Smith 1981, p. 85)

Citation studies can identify which works and authors are most often cited within a given discipline and why items are cited. This tool can be very useful for collection development or selection because it helps identify influential works or authors who are likely to be requested. Citation analysis can also help explain which ideas and thinkers influence conceptual development within a discipline or which disciplines appear to be active and whose work is playing a central role.

F. Management and Administrative Issues

LIS managers and administrators must carefully consider which information technologies to purchase because making the wrong decisions can be expensive in terms of time, money, productivity, and human resources. The following are some of the issues that should be considered.

1. Identifying and Selecting Information Technologies

It is often assumed, erroneously, that introducing technology always results in increased productivity. Administrators must first determine which processes and tasks lend themselves to technology and which do not. Once those processes are selected, the appropriate technology must be identified and installed using these steps:

1. Identify appropriate vendors.
2. Develop criteria and establish decision-making structures for comparing and evaluating vendors.
3. Develop timetables for implementing automation.
4. Plan on-site visits and demonstrations.
5. Develop and implement training and orientation on automated systems for staff.
6. Conduct post-implementation evaluation to determine if the technologies are performing effectively.

2. Dealing with Human Factors in Technology

The application of new technologies usually requires the involvement of people. Over the last three decades, it has become increasingly obvious that how well people deal with computers can have a significant effect on how useful they are, and that technologies can significantly affect the people who use them regularly. For this reason, information science examines implementation issues: what factors generate resistance or acceptance of technologies, and what aspects of technologies have the potential to create physical problems for people. This latter area has spawned a field called ergonomics, which explores the fit between people and machines.

3. Developing Information Systems to Manage Organizations

Complex organizations increasingly rely on information systems to perform a variety of tasks such as records maintenance and oversight (which has created a subfield called records management), day-to-day decision making, and strategic and tactical planning. Making the best management decisions relies, in part, on an organization's ability to acquire, access, and evaluate information in a timely fashion. Managing the various formats, ranging from raw data to text, images, sound, or multimedia, is addressed by the field known as information resources management (IRM) or information management. Managing information has become a task with the same significance as managing the fiscal and human resources of an organization.

IRM is much more than file maintenance. Each aspect of the organization needs to be considered in terms of how it produces, organizes, selects, and disseminates information for use by its members. Among the major objectives of IRM are the following:

- Ensuring that relevant information is available for decision making
- Analyzing the cost/benefit of information provision
- Ensuring that management and administration recognize that IRM and the information manager are major contributors to the organization
- Assisting in the evaluation and implementation of information management technologies
- Defining responsibility and accountability for information management, preservation, and disposal
- Promoting awareness by corporate managers that properly organized and accessible information is critical for corporate decisions (Levitan 1982)

The creation of new positions such as chief information officer is testimony to the increasing recognition of how important IRM is to the survival of organizations.

4. Measuring and Evaluating Information Services

LIS administrators need to determine whether their systems are accomplishing what they were designed to do. Among the most common measures for evaluating information services are studies that focus on some aspect of the collection or services and users' satisfaction with them. These studies are usually conducted through questionnaires, focus groups, interviews, or analysis of data such as circulation or interlibrary loan data. A user study examines a particular population by such variables as age, income, sex, and level of education and analyzes them in relation to library use. It might focus on the reasons individuals use a particular service or where they sought information before coming to the library. Such studies attempt to answer the question: who is using the library and why? Alternatively, nonuser studies investigate why some people do not use particular services. These studies can reveal organizational inadequacies. For example, perhaps certain groups do not know about a particular service, believe that it does not have what they need, or consider the service staff unfriendly.

Use studies, on the other hand, focus on what is used. They might look at the subjects consulted (e.g., fiction or nonfiction, specialized subject areas), the number of items used, where they were used (e.g., in-house or checked out), the types of materials used (e.g., AV, print, Internet Web sites), types of services used (e.g., reference, children's, the Web), the types of programming used, or whether a librarian was consulted. Such information can provide valuable planning information. As might be expected, because of the close connection between users and uses of libraries, it is common that both are studied and cross-analyzed.

Perhaps the best-known measures of library performance, output measures, were developed by the Public Library Association (1987). In addition, the Public Library Association worked with the Young Adult Library Services Association (YALSA) to create output measures for young adult services (Walter 1995), and with the Association for Library Service to Children to create output measures for children's services (Walter 1992). Unfortunately, the more generalized the activities and purposes of a library, the more difficult it is to measure its effectiveness, which is why public libraries are more difficult to assess than special libraries. This difficulty is especially apparent when trying to measure productivity and cost effectiveness or develop cost-benefit ratios (Koenig 1990). A more detailed discussion of measurement and evaluation is found in Chapter 5.

IV. EMERGING FIELDS IN INFORMATION SCIENCE

A. Informatics

The growth of the Internet, the ubiquity of computers, and the ever-expanding quantities of information stored in the digital environment have challenged our ability to organize, locate, evaluate, and use information in a timely and effective manner. A number of disciplines including library and information science, cognitive sciences, business, computer sciences, medicine, nursing, and communications contribute insights, research, and methods for resolving this challenge—giving rise to a new interdisciplinary field called informatics. Etymologically, informatics is a combination of the science of information and automated information processing (Wikipedia 2009). Still not clearly defined, informatics has been variously described as "the art, science, and human dimensions of information technology" or "the study, application, and social consequences of technology" (Wikipedia 2009). In its broadest sense, its focus is on "information and how it is represented in, processed by, and communicated between a variety of systems" (Fourman 2002, p. 2). Informatics emphasizes aspects of computerization and technology and its relationship to information creation, processing, organization, and transfer. Indeed, informatics has become a subspecialty in a number of disciplines. For example, Hersh (2008) defined medical informatics as "the integrative discipline that arises from the synergistic application of computational, information, cognitive, organizational, and other sciences whose primary focus is the acquisition, storage, and use of information in the health/biomedical domain" (p. 1). Kling (1999) defined social informatics as "the interdisciplinary study of the design, uses and consequences of information technologies that take into account their interaction with institutional and cultural contexts" (p. 1). Sawyer (2005) viewed social informatics as "the trans-disciplinary study of the design, deployment and uses of information and communication technology (ICT) that account for their interaction with institutional and cultural contexts, including organizations and society" (p. 9). Several LIS schools in the United States and internationally currently offer both degrees and specializations in informatics, and the number is expected to grow.

B. User Experience Design

As Web sites proliferate and their applicability extends to nearly every aspect of people's lives, it is clear that how information is organized and presented on a Web site has substantial impact on people's ability to get the information they need. Lindgaard and colleagues (2006) found that people form their first impressions of a Web site in as little as 50 milliseconds. Today, "post-Web information system design" has seen the emergence of a number of new fields including knowledge management, experience design, content management, interaction design, information design, customer relationship management, and information architecture (Rosenfeld 2002). Although the boundaries are not yet clearly delineated, the developing field of "user experience design" (UX) is increasing in prominence. UX integrates various aspects from interaction design, information architecture, usability, human computer inter-action, human factors engineering, and user interface design (Paluch 2006). At the heart of UX is the user's experience. Morville (2005) described this as "the vital importance of empathy for the users" (p. 31). As Garrett (2003) observed:

> The user experience development process is all about ensuring that no aspect of the user's experience with your site happens without your conscious, explicit intent. This means taking into account every possibility of every action the user is likely to take and understanding the user's expectations at every step of the way through that process. (p. 21)

The ultimate goal of UX is to create Web sites that will create a highly fruitful experience for the user; for example, the site is useful, usable, desirable, findable, accessible, credible, and valuable (Morville 2005). To broaden understanding of this emerging field, we examine two areas in greater detail: information architecture (IA) and usability engineering, keeping in mind that there might be some overlap with other related and still-emerging fields.

1. Information Architecture

IA focuses on two distinct but closely related areas: the use of graphic or multimedia design to facilitate communication, and the use of intellectual technologies, such as site and content organization, needs analysis, usability studies, metadata application, and programming to make an information interface or source easy to locate, comprehend, navigate, and use (Froehlich, 2003). Attention is paid both to the mission of the site and the anticipated needs of those who use it. Froehlich (2003) defined IA as:

> the art and science of organizing information and interfaces to help information seekers solve their information needs efficiently and effectively.... The information architect designs and implements a specific system and interface, based on organizational requirements and aesthetic and functional considerations, similar to the ways an architect deploys a building in physical space, focusing on aesthetic, functional and use goals. (n.p.)

Farnum (2002) described information architects as those who "help build Web sites by organizing them to make it easier for people to find what they want.... Much like an architect for physical buildings, information architects design information spaces by considering the ways they will be used and then create blueprints and detailed plans for that use" (p. 34). He identified four design components: (1) visual design, concerned with the graphic design and layout of the information on the site; (2) interaction design, designing the dynamic components of the sites; (3) user experience design, tailoring the site to users needs; and (4) usability, evaluating the site to make sure it can be used easily, efficiently, and effectively. Because of the newness of the field, the precise disciplinary tasks that information architects perform are still evolving. Rosenfeld and Morville (1998) identifed four:

- Clarifies the mission and vision for the site, balancing the needs of its sponsoring organization and the needs of its audiences.
- Determines what content and functionality the site will contain.
- Specifies how users will find information in the site by defining its organization, navigation, labeling, and searching systems.
- Maps out how the site will accommodate change and growth over time. (p. 11)

Information architects should not be confused with graphic designers, who focus only on the graphical aspects of the Web site. Aesthetic concerns are important to the information architect as well, but their primary emphasis is the underlying structure of the site. Among the issues they consider are the following:

- Creating effective navigation techniques so that users can move easily throughout the site (e.g., menus, hyperlinks, guided tours, site maps, and indexes)
- Providing effective orientation for users within the site
- Making the site usable in terms of language and terminology employed
- Developing an aesthetically pleasing site

- Maintaining portability, a consistent look and feel across different platforms, different browsers, and different screen resolutions
- Employing effective search systems, such as Boolean or natural language
- Establishing a logical site structure that is easily understood by the user
- Using effective hyperlinks that anticipate user information needs
- Labeling for improved information access (links, terms in indexes, choices in drop-down lists, product names)
- Linking to related information on other Web sites
- Enabling users to personalize or customize their own preferences for a site, or provide filters for site content
- Using metadata effectively to improve access
- Ensuring that the Web site is scalable—that it can grow and retain its effectiveness and usability

With the increasing reliance on Web sites for education, business, and government, their effective design is critical. For this reason, it is expected that the field will continue to grow and represent an important new aspect of organizational life.

2. Usability Engineering

Usability engineering assesses satisfaction with a Web site, and its efficiency and effectiveness, from the user's perspective. The International Standards Organization (1998) defined usability as "the extent to which a product can be used by specified users to achieve specified goals with effectiveness, efficiency and satisfaction in a specified context of use" (p. 2). To address these issues, individuals are given a set of tasks while trained observers collect information on how a site is used. A variety of research methods are employed: questionnaires, surveys, interviews, focus groups, and intrusive and unobtrusive observation. Occasionally ethnographic and field studies, journals, eye tracking, and "think aloud" protocols might be used. In think aloud studies, a user is observed or videotaped while engaged in a particular task and is asked to talk aloud, expressing his or her feelings, thoughts, opinions, and

> **Web Site Evaluation Criteria**
>
> **Effectiveness**: Does the site satisfy the needs of the user? Is it accurate and complete for the intended use? Can users readily find and navigate to the needed information?
>
> **Efficiency**: To what extent are the resources readily used to meet the need?
>
> **Satisfaction**: What are the feelings of the user toward the site? Is there freedom from discomfort in using the site? Does the user have a positive attitude toward its use?
>
> **Learnability**: How easy is it to learn how to use the site?

strategies through the process. The responses are recorded for subsequent analysis. Another technique employs a question-asking protocol. In this case, the researcher asks questions of the user to get feedback while he or she is using a Web site (Norlin and Winters 2002). Software packages, including site usage logs that collect information on the sites visited and search strategies employed, are also helpful. Although usability testing is not perfect—the studies frequently use small samples that might or might not represent the many users who might visit a particular Web site—the field is establishing some valid and reliable criteria for evaluation. As the number of Web sites proliferates, usability testing will play an increasing role in ensuring that users are prominent participants in their design, maintenance, and improvement.

C. Knowledge Management

Knowledge is dynamic because it evolves as it is influenced by people's thoughts, feelings, and experience (McInerney 2002). Some knowledge can be explicit, such as knowledge contained within a database or document; but a vast quantity of organizational knowledge is tacit, consisting of the values, beliefs, and perspectives of the individuals within an organization who create the context for the explicit knowledge. Organizations themselves can have values, history, unwritten laws, and ways of doing things that also constitute tacit knowledge. Effectively managing both explicit and tacit knowledge in an organization is likely to achieve the best results. When important knowledge is not accessible or unused, it degrades decision processes, reduces decision quality, and impairs organizational effectiveness.

Similarly, organizations rely on inventiveness and innovation to survive and prosper. This means that they rely on their employees' knowledge, skills, and ideas (sometimes referred to as human capital, one of the main components of the organization's intellectual capital) to create new services and products. Innovation and inventive thinking often require collaboration and the sharing of information, and a work environment that encourages both activities on a formal and informal level. Individuals engaged in these activities or in similar work often form "communities of practice." These communities define authority and work goals within them based on the expertise of the participants rather than formal assignments. Organizations structured to facilitate collaborative activities, information sharing, and communities of practice are likely to progress more quickly and leverage the talents of their people effectively. In the for-profit environment this can mean a competitive advantage and increased profitability. In the nonprofit environment it can mean better service and stronger political support.

The field of knowledge management (KM) emerged to help build human and intellectual capital and diminish the impact of poor knowledge use within organizations. KM focuses specifically on understanding and structuring organizations so that knowledge can be best accessed, communicated, and used. Although information and information technologies remain important, KM places considerable emphasis on people. As Blair (2002) noted, "knowledge management is largely the management and support of expertise.... It is primarily the management of individuals with specific abilities, rather than the management of repositories of data and information" (p. 1022). For Blair, people are the repositories of the knowledge. Davenport, De Long, and Beers (1997) identified four objectives of KM: creating repositories, improving access, enhancing the environment, and managing knowledge as an asset. Overall, KM is concerned with planning, capturing, organizing, interconnecting, and providing access to organizational knowledge through both intellectual and information technologies. It is an interdisciplinary field drawing from a variety of disciplines including psychology, sociology, business, economics, information science, and computer science.

Brief Overview of Knowledge Management Tools and Approaches

Strategies for Managing the People Who Have Knowledge

1. Create an environment to stimulate knowledge growth and identify barriers to knowledge creation.
2. Create an organizational culture that facilitates the sharing of knowledge and collaborative processes, both formal and informal.
3. Develop and manage people as knowledge assets.
4. Ensure that useful (tacit) knowledge is accessible when decisions are being made.
5. Create a corporate culture and values that encourage knowledge building and sharing.
6. Identify, develop, and use effectively the expertise of staff (human capital).
7. Develop competent individuals who manage and supervise the knowledge processes and expertise of the organization.
8. Develop and maintain processes that enable the knowledge of individuals to be used effectively.

Strategies for Managing the Knowledge Itself

1. Organize knowledge so that it can be accessed and used through effective search and document management.
2. Represent knowledge in ways that improve its use (documents, databases).
3. Facilitate use of knowledge from outside sources.
4. Facilitate processes that develop and exploit the intellectual capital and assets of the organization, including individual expertise, corporate memory, and organizational research.
5. Develop effective document management techniques throughout the life cycle of a document, that is, from authorship to archiving and disposal.
6. Identify the nature of the knowledge and where it is stored in the organization so that it can be exploited.
7. Evaluate, maintain, and improve the information technology infrastructure to encourage knowledge building and sharing.
8. Develop effective techniques for competitive intelligence.
9. Facilitate effective publishing and dissemination of information, for example, through e-mail or word processing.

Given the tremendous range of functions involved in KM and its inherent value, McInerney (2002) suggested that organizations should spend less time trying to extract "knowledge artifacts" from workers and spend more time developing a "knowledge culture" in which opportunities for knowledge creation are optimized and there is encouragement for learning and sharing. To achieve this end, St. Clair and Stanley (2008) proposed:

> Information management, knowledge management and strategic learning converge in knowledge services, enabling the highest levels of service delivery by those information professionals who lead the effort. Indeed, it is through knowledge services that the business value of knowledge is established within the company or organization, resulting in higher-level research, strengthened contextual decision making, and accelerated innovation. (p. 36)

D. Competitive Intelligence

Competitive intelligence (CI) is a subunit of information management sometimes called business intelligence or social intelligence. CI serves as the scout to determine the nature and magnitude of threats to the organization and to uncover opportunities. The Society of Competitive Intelligence Professionals (SCIP 2010) defined CI as "a necessary, ethical business discipline for decision making based on understanding the competitive environment" (p. 1). The goal of CI is "actionable intelligence that will provide a competitive edge" (Miller 2003, p. 1). Bergeron and Hiller (2002) outlined four phases of the CI process: planning and identifying CI needs, data collection, organization and analysis, and dissemination. The analysis stage is particularly important, and a variety of techniques such as SWOT analysis (strength, weaknesses, opportunities, and threats), benchmarking, environmental analysis, scenario planning, patent analysis, and bibliometrics have been used. The value of CI in the entrepreneurial environment has been well documented; organizations with CI units tend to outperform their competitors when comparing average sales, market share, and profitability (Cappel and Boone 1995). It is estimated that the market value of business intelligence is $2 billion a year and companies large and small have undertaken formal CI programs (SCIP 2010).

Another function of CI is counterintelligence, which involves developing systems that prevent access to organizational information that could threaten competitiveness. To be clear, CI is not the same as industrial espionage, which involves unlawful and unethical tactics and actions. CI is governed by ethical standards and generally relies on sources that are open to inspection. The SCIP Code of Ethics for CI Professionals promulgated by SCIP explicitly identified such responsibilities as complying with all laws and disclosing truthfully one's identity prior to seeking information.

A related and growing area of CI is information warfare (IW), which was first conceived in a military context and concerned such areas as disinformation, psychological warfare, and propaganda. In the post-9/11 era, however, there is considerable concern regarding terrorist attacks that could disrupt the national information grid. Cronin (2000) identified at least three categories of IW threats to information assets: (1) the ability to destroy, damage, or otherwise make these assets inaccessible; (2) the ability to alter, falsify, or otherwise change information; and (3) the ability to penetrate security to steal information assets. IW is particularly attractive because it uses low-cost electronic techniques anonymously and in areas remote from the actual point of disruption or penetration. As the United States becomes increasingly reliant on information technologies, CI and IW will likely be a significant focus of the information science community for years to come.

V. SUMMARY

Cronin and Meho (2008) reported major information science contributions to a number of disciplines including computer science, artificial intelligence, medical informatics, computer support systems, and management information systems in addition to library science. Research has contributed much to our understanding of how information is generated, organized, disseminated, and used. Librarians and information science professionals share numerous common values related to making information accessible and usable, and satisfying individuals' information needs. In particular, we share a need to understand how to distinguish information needs and wants, how to understand individuals' behavior when they search for information, and how information systems can best be designed and used to satisfy needs. To a large extent, librarians depend on information scientists for this understanding. As the field of information science grows, librarians can only benefit from strong partnerships with information scientists.

REFERENCES

Allen, Bryce L. 1991. "Cognitive Research in Information Science: Implications for Design." *Annual Review of Information Science and Technology* (ARIST) 26: 3–37.

Bates, Marcia J. 1989. "The Design of Browsing and Berrypicking Techniques for the Online Search Interface." *Online Review* 13 (October): 407–424.

———. 1999. "The Invisible Substrate of Information Science." *Journal of the American Society for Information Science* 50: 1043–1050.

———. 2006. "Fundamental Forms of Information." *Journal of the American Society for Information Science and Technology* 57: 1033–1045.

———. 2007. "Defining the Information Disciplines in Encyclopedia Development." *Information Research* 12 (October). Available: http://informationr.net/ir/12-4/colis/colis29 .html (accessed August 31, 2009).

Bates, Marcia J., Deborah N. Wilde, and Susan Siegfried. 1993. "An Analysis of Search Terminology Used by Humanities Scholars: The Getty Online Searching Project Report Number 1." *Library Quarterly* 63 (January): 1–39.

Belkin, Nicholas J., Helen M. Brooks, and Robert N. Oddy. 1982. "ASK for Information Retrieval." *Journal of Documentation* 38: 61–71.

Bergeron, Pierrette, and Christine A. Hiller. 2002. "Competitive Intelligence." In *Annual Review of Information Science and Technology*. Vol. 36. Edited by Blaise Cronin. Medford, NJ: Information Today, 353–390.

Bilal, Dania. 2002. "Children's Use of the Yahooligans! Web Search Engine." *Journal of the American Society for Information Science and Technology* 53: 1170–1183.

Blair, David C. 2002. "Knowledge Management: Hype, Hope, or Help?" *Journal of the American Society of Information Science and Technology* 53: 1019–1028.

Bradford, Samuel C. 1934. "Sources of Information on Specific Subjects." *Engineering* 85–86.

British Library. 2008. *Information Behaviour of the Researcher of the Future*. London: University College London. Available: www.jisc.ac.uk/media/documents/programmes/reppres/gg_final_ keynote_11012008.pdf (accessed February 6, 2010).

Brittain, J. M. 1980. "The Distinctive Characteristics of Information Science." In *Theory and Application of Information Research: Proceedings of the Second International Research Forum on Information Science*. Edited by Ole Harbo and Leif Kajberg. London: Mansell.

Broadbent, Elaine. 1986. "A Study of Humanities Faculty Library Information Seeking Behavior." *Cataloguing and Classification Quarterly* 6 (spring): 23–37.

Burke, Colin. 2007. "History of Information Science." In *Annual Review of Information Science and Technology*. Vol. 41. Edited by Blaise Cronin. Medford, NJ: Information Today, 3–53.

Bush, Vannevar. 1945. "As We Might Think." *Atlantic Monthly* 176 (July): 101–108.

Cappel, James J., and Jeffrey P. Boone. 1995. "A Look at the Link between Competitive Intelligence and Performance." *Competitive Intelligence Review* 6 (summer): 15–23.

Case, Donald O. 2002. *Looking for Information: A Survey of Research on Information Seeking, Needs, and Behavior*. San Diego: Academic Press.

Chalmers, Patricia A. 2003. "The Role of Cognitive Theory in Human-Computer Interface." *Computers in Human Behavior* 19: 593–607.

Chatman, Elfreda A. 1996. "The Impoverished Life-World of Outsiders." *Journal of the American Society for Information Science* 47: 193–206.

Chen, Ching-Chih, and Peter Hernon. 1982. *Information Seeking: Assessing and Anticipating User Needs*. New York: Neal-Schuman.

Cronin, Blaise. 2000. "Strategic Intelligence and Networked Business." *Journal of Information Science* 26: 133–138.

Cronin, Blaise, and Lokman I. Meho. 2008. "The Shifting Balance of Intellectual Trade in Information Studies." *Journal of the American Society for Information Science and Technology* 59: 551–564.

Davenport, Thomas, David De Long, and Michael Beers. 1997. "Building Successful Knowledge Management Projects." Center for Business Innovation Working Paper, Ernst & Young.

Debowski, Shelda. 2001. "Wrong Way: Go Back! An Exploration of Novice Search Behaviors While Conducting an Information Search." *The Electronic Library* 19: 371–382.

Dervin, Brenda. 1983. "An Overview of Sense-Making: Concepts, Methods, and Results to Date." Paper presented at the International Communication Association Annual Meeting, May 1983, Dallas, Texas.

Dresang, Eliza T. 2005. "The Information-Seeking Behavior of Youth in the Digital Environment." *Library Trends* 54 (fall): 178–196.

Durrance, Joan C. 1989. "Information Needs: Old Song, New Tune." In *Rethinking the Library*. Washington, DC: GPO, 159–178.

Farnum, Chris. 2002. "Information Architecture: Five Things Information Managers Need to Know." *Information Management Journal* (September/October): 33–40.

Fourman, Michael. 2002. "Informatics." July. Available: www.infomatics.ed.ac.uk/ (accessed February 9, 2009).

Froehlich, Thomas J. 1994. "Relevance Reconsidered—Towards an Agenda for the 21st Century." *Journal of the American Society of Information Science* 45 (April): 124–134.

———. 2003. PowerPoint presentation on information architecture. Kent State University, Ohio.

Garrett, Jesse James. 2003. *The Elements of User Experience: User-Centered Design for the Web*. Indianapolis, IN: AIGA, New Riders.

Griffiths, Jillian R., and Peter Brophy. 2005. "Student Searching Behavior and the Web: Use of Academic Resources and Google." *Library Trends* 53 (spring): 539–554.

Harter, Stephen. 1986. *Online Information Retrieval*. Orlando, FL: Academic Press.

Hawkins, Donald T., Signe E. Larson, and Bari Q. Cato. 2003. "Information Science Abstracts: Tracking the Literature of Information Science. Part 2: A New Taxonomy for Information Science." *Journal of the American Society for Information Science and Technology* 54: 771–781.

Heinstrom, Jannica. 2006. "Broad Exploration or Precise Specificity: Two Basic Information Seeking Patterns among Students." *Journal of the American Society for Information Science and Technology* 57: 1440–1450.

Hersh, William. 2008. "What Is Medical Informatics?" Available: www.ohsu.edu/ohsuedu/academic/som/dmice/about/whatis.cfm (accessed February 9, 2009).

Hsieh-Yee, Ingrid. 2001. "Research on Web Search Behavior." *Library and Information Science Research* 53: 167–185.

International Standards Organization. 1998. *ISO 9241–11: Ergonomic Requirements for Office Work with Visual Display Terminals (VDTs)—Part 11: Guidance on Usability*. London: International Standards Organization.

Kalbach, James. 2006. "'I'm Feeling Lucky': The Role of Emotions in Seeking Information on the Web." *Journal of the American Society for Information Science and Technology* 57: 813–818.

Kling, Rob. 1999. "What Is Social Informatics and Why Does It Matter?" *D-Lib Magazine* 5 (January): 1.

Koenig, Michael E. D. 1990. "Information Services and Downstream Productivity." *Annual Review of Information Science and Technology* 25: 74–76.

Krikelas, James. 1983. "Information-Seeking Behavior: Patterns and Concepts." *Drexel Library Quarterly* 19 (spring): 5–20.

Kuhlthau, Carol C. 1991. "Inside the Search Process: Information Seeking from the User's Perspective." *Journal of the American Society of Information Science* 361–371.

————. 1993. *Seeking Meaning: A Process Approach to Library and Information Services*. Westport, CT: Libraries Unlimited.

Lazonder, Ard W., Harm J. A. Biemans, and Iwans G. J. H. Wopereis. 2000. "Differences between Novice and Experienced Users in Searching Information on the World Wide Web." *Journal of the American Society for Information Science* 51: 576–581.

Lee, Chingkwei Adrienne, and John N. Olsgaard. 1989. "Linguistics and Information Science." In *Principles and Applications of Information Science for Library Professionals*. Edited by John N. Olsgaard. Chicago: ALA, 27–36.

Levitan, Karen B. 1982. "Information Resources Management." *Annual Review of Information Science and Technology (ARIST)* 17: 227–266.

Lindgaard, Gitte, Gary Fernandes, Cathy Dudek, and J. Brown. 2006. "Attention Web Designers: You Have 50 Milliseconds to Make a Good First Impression!" *Behavior and Information Technology* 25 (March–April): 115–126.

Lotka, Alfred J. 1926. "The Frequency Distribution of Scientific Productivity." *Journal of the Washington Academy of Sciences* 16: 317–323.

Mann, Thomas. 1993. "The Principle of Least Effort." In *Library Research Models: Guide to Classification, Cataloging, and Computers*. New York: Oxford University Press, 91–101.

McInerney, Claire. 2002. "Knowledge Management and the Dynamic Nature of Knowledge." *Journal of the American Society for Information Science and Technology* 53: 1009–1018.

Meadows, A. J. 1974. *Communication in Science*. London: Butterworths.

Miller, Stephen H. 2003. "Competitive Intelligence—An Overview." Available: www.ipo .org/AM/Template.cfm?Section=Home&Template=/CM/ContentDisplay.cfm_Content ID=15904 (accessed February 6, 2010).

Morville, Peter. 2005. *Ambient Findability: What We Find Changes Who We Become*. Sabastopol, CA: O'Reilly.

Norlin, Elaina, and C. M. Winters. 2002. *Usability Testing for Library Web Sites: A Hands On Guide*. Chicago: ALA.

Oxford English Dictionary. 1989. 2nd ed. Oxford: Clarendon Press.

Paluch, Kimmy. 2006. "What Is User Experience Design." Available: www.montparnas.com/ articles/what-is-user-experience-design/ (accessed February 4, 2010).

Pao, Miranda Lee. 1989. *Concepts of Information Retrieval*. Englewood, CO: Libraries Unlimited, 54–55.

Public Library Association. 1987. *Output Measures for Public Libraries*. 2nd ed. Chicago: ALA.

Rayward, Boyd. 1983. "Library and Information Sciences." In *The Study of Information: Interdisciplinary Messages*. Edited by Fritz Machlup and Una Mansfield. New York: Wiley, 343–363.

Rose, Daniel E. 2006. "Reconciling Information-Seeking Behavior with Search User Interfaces for the Web." *Journal of the American Society for Information Science and Technology* 57: 797–799.

Rosenfeld, Louis. 2002. "Information Architecture: Looking Ahead." *Journal of the American Society for Information Science and Technology* 53: 874–876.

Rosenfeld, Louis, and Peter Morville. 1998. *Information Architecture for the World Wide Web*. Sebastopol, CA: O'Reilly.

Rouse, William B. 1984. "Human Information Seeking and Design of Information Systems." *Information Processing and Management* 20.

Saracevic, T. 1975. "Relevance: A Review of and a Framework for the Thinking on the Notion in Information Science." *Journal of the American Society for Information Science* 26: 321–343.

Savolainen, Reijo. 2007. "Media Credibility and Cognitive Authority. The Case of Seeking Orienting Information." *Information Research* 12 (April). Available: http://informationr .net/ir/12-3/paper319.html (accessed February 6, 2010).

Sawyer, Steve. 2005. "Social Informatics: Overview, Principles, and Opportunities." *Bulletin of the American Society for Information Science and Technology* 31 (June/July): 9–12.

Shaw, Debora. 1991. "The Human-Computer Interface for Information Retrieval." *Annual Review of Information Science and Technology (ARIST)* 26: 155–195.

Slone, Debra J. 2002. "The Influence of Mental Models and Goals on Search Patterns during Web Interaction." *Journal of the American Society for Information Science and Technology* 53: 1152–1169.

Smith, Linda C. 1981. "Citation Analysis." *Library Trends* 30 (summer): 83–106.

———. 1987. "Artificial Intelligence and Information Retrieval." *Annual Review of Information Science and Technology (ARIST)* 22: 41–77.

Society of Competitive Intelligence Professionals. 2010. "FAQ." Available: www.scip.org/ resources/content.cfm?itemnumber=601&navitemNumber=533 (accessed February 6, 2010).

Spink, Amanda, and Charles Cole. 2006. "Human Information Behavior: Integrating Diverse Approaches and Information Use." *Journal of the American Society for Information Science and Technology* 57: 25–35.

St. Clair, Guy, and Dale Stanley. 2008. "Knowledge Services: The Practical Side of Knowledge. Part I." *Information Outlook* 12 (June): 55–61.

Summers, Ron, Charles Oppenheim, Jack Meadows, Cliff McKnight, and Margaret Kinnell. 1999. "Information Science in 2010: A Loughborough University View." *Journal of the American Society for Information Science* 50: 1153–1162.

Taylor, Robert S. 1966. "Professional Aspects of Information Science and Technology." In *Annual Review of Information Science and Technology*. Vol. 1. Edited by Carlos A. Cuadra. New York: Wiley, 15–40.

———. 1986. *Value-Added Processes in Information Systems*. Norwood, NJ: Ablex.

Van Styvendaele, J. H. 1977. "University Scientists as Seekers of Information: Sources of References to Periodical Literature." *Journal of Librarianship* 9 (October): 270–277.

Vedder, Richard G. 1990. "An Overview of Expert Systems." In *Expert Systems in Libraries*. Edited by Rao Aluri and Donald E. Riggs. Norwood, NJ: Ablex.

Veith, Richard H. 2006. "Memex at 60: Internet or iPod?" *Journal of the American Society for Information Science and Technology* 57: 1233–1242.

Wallace, Danny P. 1989. "Bibliometrics and Citation Analysis." In *Principles and Applications of Information Science for Library Professionals*. Edited by John N. Olsgaard. Chicago: ALA, 10–26.

Walter, Virginia A. 1992. *Output Measures for Public Library Services to Children: A Manual of Standardized Procedures*. Chicago: ALA.

————. 1995. *Output Measures and More: Planning and Evaluating Public Library Services for Young Adults*. Chicago: ALA.

Wellisch, Hans. 1972. "From Information Science to Informatics: A Terminological Investigation." *Journal of Librarianship* 4 (July): 157–187.

Wikipedia. 2009. "Informatics." Available: http://en.wikipedia.org/wiki/Informatics (accessed February 9, 2009).

Wilson, Patrick. 1983. *Second-Hand Knowledge*. Westport, CT: Greenwood.

————. 1986. "The Face Value Rule in Reference Work." *RQ* 25 (summer): 468–475.

Xu, Yunjie, Bernard Cheng-Yian Tan, and Li Yang. 2006. "Who Will You Ask? An Empirical Study of Interpersonal Task Information Seeking." *Journal of the American Society for Information Science and Technology* 57: 1666–1677.

SELECTED READINGS: INFORMATION SCIENCE

Books

Case, Donald Owen. *Looking for Information: A Survey of Research on Information Seeking, Needs, and Behavior*. 2nd ed. Amsterdam: Elsevier/Academic Press, 2007.

Garrett, Jesse James. *The Elements of User Experience: User-Centered Design for the Web*. Indianapolis, IN: New Riders, 2003.

Lester, June, and Wallace C. Koehler Jr. *Fundamentals of Information Studies*. New York: Neal-Schuman, 2003.

Machlup, Fritz, and Una Mansfield, eds. *The Study of Information: Interdisciplinary Messages*. New York: Wiley, 1983.

Srikantaiah, Kanti T., and Michael E. D. Koenig. *Knowledge Management in Practice: Connections and Context*. Medford, NJ: Information Today, 2008.

Articles

Alfino, Mark, and Linda Pierce. "The Social Nature of Information." *Library Trends* 49 (winter 2001): 471–485.

Bates, Marcia. "Defining the Information Disciplines in Encyclopedia Development." *Information Research* 12 (October 2007). Paper from the Sixth International Conference on Conceptions of Library and Information Science, Borås, Sweden, August 13–16, 2007. Available: http:// informationr.net/ir/12-4/colis/colis29.html (accessed February 4, 2010).

Borko, H. "Information Science: What Is It?" *American Documentation* 19 (December 1968): 3–5.

Bush, Vannevar. "As We May Think." *Atlantic Monthly* 176 (July 1945): 101–108.

Case, Donald O. "Information Behavior." Annual Review of Information Science and Technology (ARIST) 40 (2006): 327.

Courtright, Christina. "Context in Information Behavior Research." *Annual Review of Information Science and Technology (ARIST)* 41 (2007): 273–306.

Dresang, Eliza T. "The Information-Seeking Behavior of Youth in the Digital Environment." *Library Trends* 54 (fall 2005): 178–196.

Drott, M. Carl. "Open Access." *Annual Review of Information Science and Technology (ARIST)* 40 (2006): 79–109.

Farnum, Chris. "Information Architecture: Five Things Information Managers Need to Know." *Information Management Journal* 36 (September–October 2002): 33–40.

Herner, Saul. "Brief History of Information Science." *Journal of the American Society for Information Science* 35 (May 1984): 157–163.

Hupfer, Maureen, and Brian Detlor. "Gender and Web Information Seeking: A Self-Concept Orientation Model." *Journal of the American Society for Information Science and Technology* 57 (2006): 1105–1115.

Kalbach, James. "I'm Feeling Lucky": The Role of Emotions in Seeking Information on the Web." *Journal of the American Society for Information Science and Technology* 57 (2006): 813–818.

Lindgaard, Gitte, Gary Fernandes, Cathy Dudek, and J. Brown. "Attention Web Designers: You Have 50 Milliseconds to Make a Good First Impression!" *Behaviour and Information Technology* 25 (March–April 2006): 115–126.

McInerney, Claire. "Knowledge Management and the Dynamic Nature of Knowledge." *Journal of the American Society for Information Science and Technology* 53 (2002): 1009–1018.

Reih, Soo Young, and David R. Danielson. "Credibility: A Multidisciplinary Framework." *Annual Review of Information Science and Technology (ARIST)* 41 (2007): 307–364.

Spink, Amanda, and Charles Cole. "Human Information Behavior: Integrating Diverse Approaches and Information Use." *Journal of the American Society for Information Science and Technology* 57 (2006): 25–35.

Veith, Richard H. "Memex at 60: Internet or iPod?" *Journal of the American Society for Information Science and Technology* 57 (2006): 1233–1242.

Warner, Julian. "W(h)ither Information Science." *Library Quarterly* 71 (2001): 243–255.

8

Information Policy: Stakeholders and Agendas

I. INTRODUCTION

> As printed and electronic information have become the lifeblood of government, commerce, education, and many other daily activities, information policy has come to influence most interactions in society. Further, the importance of information means that information policy now has considerable impact on other forms of public policy. (Jaeger and Fleischmann 2007, p. 843)

Information policy is any law, regulation, rule, or practice (written or unwritten) that affects the creation, acquisition, organization, dissemination, or evaluation of information. Information policy can be discussed from the perspective of information technologies for educational and industrial uses, telecommunications, privacy issues, computer regulations and crimes, copyright and intellectual property, and government information systems (Burger 1993). Not surprisingly, a variety of stakeholders in the information policy process are deeply concerned about information from both legal and political perspectives. These stakeholders include business and industry, government, and information producers and disseminators, as well as individual citizens and various organizations that represent their interests.

Major Information Policy Questions

Jaeger and Fleischmann (2007, p. 844) noted that information policy and access are closely connected and their relationship raises a number of important questions:

- What information cannot be accessed
- What information individuals can access
- What information social groups can access
- What information organizations can provide access to
- What information the government must provide access to
- What information the government does not have to provide access to
- What information the government can access about citizens

A. Business and Industry

In American society, the discussion of information policy highlights a fundamental tension between entrepreneurship and democracy. Under capitalism, information can be viewed as a form of private property that can provide a competitive edge. Insofar as it can be held privately, there is a strong incentive for individuals to discover information and use it to create new products and services. On the other hand, the democratic values of American society promote the free flow of information and access to it both as a right and as essential to a free society. This is not to say that capitalism and democracy are incompatible; it is to suggest that information policy in a democratic society requires a balancing of social, economic, and political interests. Because information is critical to competition, business and industry actively lobby to influence policies that will affect its dissemination and restriction. Business and industry have special interests in both protecting new knowledge, and accessing and organizing current knowledge.

1. Protecting New Knowledge to Improve Productivity and Profits

Business and industry invest considerable sums in pursuit of new inventions or discoveries and have legitimate needs to protect their proprietary information. Patent, copyright, and trademark laws offer protection, as do laws that restrict an employee's use of protected knowledge even after separation from employment. Employers can use a no competition clause in contracts and prevent former employees from working for a competitor so that they cannot reveal information about the employer's processes or inventions. Such restrictions allow businesses to maintain a competitive edge with domestic and foreign competitors and help ensure organizational survival. Similarly, laws governing and regulating computer programs and codes that modify an organization's products are important protections for software designers.

2. Access to Information and Its Organization

The extent to which government policies permit easy and inexpensive access to technical and scientific information can have a substantial effect on a company's ability to function effectively in competitive national and international environments. Similarly, the way information is organized and made accessible within a company, such as the manner of indexing and storage, can affect the ability to use it efficiently and effectively.

B. Government

Local, state, and federal governments collect, organize, and evaluate vast quantities of information. The federal government holds numerous hearings, departments generate volumes of data, and agencies like the FBI or the CIA are constantly acquiring information. The federal government controls how that information is disseminated by promulgating regulations. These regulations specify what information is restricted, such as information affecting national security, or released to the public (or the press). Laws such as the Freedom of Information Act, the National Security Act, and the U.S.A. PATRIOT Act form part of the policy framework that defines the dissemination and control of information from government sources.

C. Information Producers and Disseminators

Stakeholders in information policy include members of the business community such as the telecommunications industry, including the telephone, television, cable, and radio industry; producers of DVDs; publishers; computer manufacturers including database producers and vendors; and technology giants such as Microsoft and Google. All of these stakeholders have a special interest in information policy because of its direct and profound effect on their operations. For example, a number of laws and regulations either promote or diminish their effectiveness, such as laws affecting competition, pricing of services, taxation, postal rates, royalties, and laws concerning libel or privacy rights.

A particular subgroup of information producers and disseminators is known as the "digerati." According to West (2001), the digerati form "the broad group of individuals who invent, create, develop, manage, and sell a wide spectrum of information technologies. They have job titles like 'chief technology officer,' 'chief information officer,' 'manager of information systems,' 'software developer,' 'software engineer,' 'programmer,' 'vice president of sales,' and 'director of marketing.'" Because these individuals have special knowledge and control of technology companies and research, they can be particularly influential in the policymaking arena.

This sector also includes libraries. Libraries have a special role and exercise a special interest because they are among the few stakeholders in this group whose motivations are not profit oriented.

D. American Citizens and Organizations That Represent Their Interests

Every citizen in a democratic society is a major stakeholder in laws and policies dealing with information. The way information flows in a society directly affects each person's ability to make informed decisions. The subtlest shift in policy can affect the extent to which the public receives accurate, up-to-date, and sufficient information, as well as who receives

A fundamental cornerstone of a democratic society is the right of individuals to obtain information and an expectation that national policies will support that right.

this information. For Americans, defining rights to information is a critical responsibility. Individual citizens, however, seldom have the ability to influence these policies. Consequently, a variety of organizations try to represent the public's interests, including the American Library Association (ALA), the American Civil Liberties Union, and Computer Professionals for Social Responsibility.

II. THE POLITICAL AND ECONOMIC CHARACTER OF INFORMATION

Information is being reconceptualized from something useful for improving understanding to a commodity—something to be bought, sold, or controlled—a transformation that could potentially threaten the existence and purpose of libraries. This phenomenon has been fostered, in large part, by two factors: computers with the capacity to store and process vast amounts of information, and the increasing sophistication of telecommunications that enable computers to transmit data throughout the world almost instantaneously. The benefit of having the right information at the right time, or having the ability to deprive others of information to gain an advantage, quickly became obvious, and it was inevitable that some individuals would realize the economic and political value of information.

The notion of information as a commodity is reflected in the common metaphor "information marketplace." Those who are economically advantaged by the creation, dissemination, use, and control of information might seek to limit the ability of others to obtain social, cultural, and creative knowledge that has traditionally been available at no cost to library users. Such a prospect creates significant concerns for LIS professionals, both professionally and as advocates for citizens. The more others perceive that information has less to do with libraries and more to do with technology and telecommunications, the less libraries might be perceived as important. Similarly, as information technologies spawn an increasing variety of information channels such as electronic networks and the Internet, the temptation to think of information as a commodity, rather than a right, intensifies. What, then, are some of the major information policy issues facing librarians and citizens today?

III. INFORMATION POLICY ISSUES

A. Protecting the Privacy of Citizens

Judith Krug (2005), in the foreword of *Privacy in the 21st Century*, described the issues facing LIS professionals today:

> Privacy is the issue of the moment in librarianship, brought forward by relentless changes in technology, law, and social attitudes. Whether it is the question of adopting Radio Frequency Identification Devices (RFIDs) to track book

inventory, devising policy to deal with law enforcement inquiries under the USA PATRIOT Act, or addressing a library user's concerns about the use of her personal information, each day finds librarians confronting new questions and new challenges concerning privacy and confidentiality. (p. ix)

Although there is no expressed right to privacy in the U.S. Constitution, the Supreme Court recognized that the amendments in the Bill of Rights have "penumbras." In common usage, a penumbra is "a space of partial illumination between the perfect shadow (as in an eclipse) on all sides and the full light" (*Merriam-Webster's Collegiate Dictionary* 1996). However, in a legal sense, a penumbra is doctrine that refers to implied powers of the federal government. This concept is best known from the Supreme Court decision *Griswold v. Connecticut* (1965). In this opinion, given by Justice William O. Douglas, *penumbra* was used to describe an individual's constitutional right of privacy. In the *Griswold* case, appellants Estelle Griswold, executive director of the Planned Parenthood League (PPL) of Connecticut, and Dr. C. Lee Buxton, a professor at Yale Medical School and director of the New Haven PPL office, were convicted for prescribing contraceptive devices and giving contraceptive advice to married persons in violation of a Connecticut statute that made it unlawful to use any drug or medicinal article for the purpose of preventing conception. They challenged the constitutionality of the statute on behalf of the married persons with whom they had a professional relationship. The Supreme Court held that the statute was unconstitutional because it was a violation of a person's right to privacy. In his opinion, Douglas stated that the specific guarantees of the Bill of Rights have penumbras "formed by emanations from those guarantees that help give them life and substance," and that the right to privacy exists within this area (Gale Group 1998).

Maintaining individuals' privacy rights has many dimensions. Solove (2008) identified several including the following:

1. Ensuring that information is kept entirely secret
2. Maintaining appropriate norms of confidentiality of information
3. Establishing and implementing rigorous standards maintaining confidentiality and the grounds for disclosure
4. Maintaining security in information systems
5. Allowing individuals to decide for themselves when information can be released or the conditions of release

Solove (2008) observed, "Privacy thus involves more than keeping secrets—it is about how we regulate information flow, how we ensure that others use our information responsibly, how we exercise control over our information, and how we should limit the way others can use our data" (p. 59).

The ubiquity of information technologies raises growing concerns that unauthorized individuals can gain access too easily to personally identifiable information on citizens' health, financial affairs, or buying habits. Federal and state governments have passed legislation broadly referred to as privacy acts and public records acts that define a citizen's right of access to files and the rights of others to access those files. Some acts were designed to protect privacy in specific areas, such as the Right to Financial Privacy Act of 1978, which protects financial records; the Electronic Communications Privacy Act of 1986, which deals with the privacy of cellular phones; and the Communications Assistance for Law Enforcement Act of 1994, which in part deals with the privacy of cellular phones and data communications (Science Applications International Corporation 1995). Other acts, such as the Health Insurance Portability and Accountability Act (HIPAA) and the Family Educational Rights and Privacy Act (FERPA), deal with the confidentiality of health and education records.

Internet communication involves many different activities, including sending and receiving e-mail messages, transmitting and downloading files, participating in social networking, and the purchase and sale of goods and services. Although these activities usually take place in the privacy of one's home or work setting, the ability of Web sites to attach "cookies" to the hard drives of personal computers, or the involuntary installation of spyware or adware to track an individual's use, raise serious privacy concerns. Many Internet users are under the impression that their identities are private; in reality, they can usually be discovered easily. Consequently, users should assume that their e-mail is a public communication (Adams et al. 2005). Marc Rotenberg (1994), of Computer Professionals for Social Responsibility, observed that "protection of personal privacy might be the single greatest challenge facing the developers of the National Information Infrastructure" (p. 50).

Although it would be useful if librarians could assert a "privilege" during librarian-patron transactions much the same as doctor-patient or lawyer-client privilege, it is unlikely that this would be recognized by a court. Austin (2004), although sympathetic to the desirability of such a privilege, cited eight reasons why it would not be supported:

1. The client does not directly pay for the service.
2. No permanent records are maintained.
3. Patrons can perform many of the functions themselves.
4. The relationship is usually ephemeral.
5. In general, the importance of the transaction is minimal.
6. In general, disclosure of the information would have minimal impact.
7. Most reference queries are of minor significance.
8. Much of the transaction takes place in public.

Nonetheless, libraries take seriously the need to protect a citizen's privacy from third-party intrusions—from individuals or governments. The ALA has taken a strong stance on privacy in the Internet environment and in 2002 adopted "Privacy:

An Interpretation of the Library Bill of Rights," which is discussed further below. In addition, many states have passed statutes on the confidentiality of circulation records that provide fairly complete protection against third-party access to borrowers' records, while still providing limited access by governmental agencies for specific reasons. For example, the U.S.A. PATRIOT Act can compel libraries to provide information about their patrons.

B. Promoting Access to and Freedom of Information

Openness of information is basic to American democracy. As James Madison wrote in 1822, "A popular government without popular information, or the means of acquiring it, is but a Prologue to a Farce or a Tragedy or perhaps both" (Madison 1973). Protecting privacy is vital, but it is equally important that citizens have a right to information regarding governmental activities. This balance between privacy and public records is constantly being tested and redefined. Ironically, some of the same acts that protect an individual's privacy are also ones that ensure rights of access when legitimate interests arise. The most prominent of these acts is the federal Freedom of Information Act (FOIA) of 1966, which applies to "all records held by all executive branch agencies, creates a presumption in favor of release, permits only defined reasons for withholding information, and authorizes a requester to invoke judicial review" (Strickland 2005, p. 548). The act was meant to ensure that government records that were not specifically protected for national security or other valid reasons would be available for inspection by members of the public. The intent was to prevent government officials from withholding information because they thought it might be embarrassing or a political liability. The federal act was followed by many state acts defining which records the public could access. Restricted records may include law enforcement investigation records, adoptions, and personnel or medical records.

1. Internet (Network) Neutrality

On the Internet, participation and access are open; that is, if someone wanted to create a Web site or an application, once certain protocols were observed, the developer could make that product available to all. Similarly, individuals can move throughout the Internet without barriers or restrictions from the Internet service provider (ISP), such as AT&T. In fact, "The sine qua non of the Internet is the ability for everyone to connect and have their traffic routed to the desired location" (Weitzner 2006, p. 10). This concept is known as network neutrality:

> "Net neutrality" is the term used to describe the concept of keeping the Internet open to all lawful content, information, applications, and equipment. There is increasing concern that the owners of the local broadband connections (usually either the cable or telephone company) might block or discriminate against

> certain Internet users or applications in order to give an advantage to their own services. While the owners of the local network have a legitimate right to manage traffic on their network to prevent congestion, viruses, and so forth, network owners should not be able to block or degrade traffic based on the identity of the user or the type of application solely to favor their interests. (Educause 2009, p. 1)

The ISP provides the "pipes" for Internet use and should be neutral. The ISP should not discriminate based on the content of the message or character of the user. The notion of ISP neutrality has been essential in promoting rapid development and innovation on the Internet. In fact, companies such as Google and Yahoo! depend in large part on Internet neutrality to preserve the value of their search engines.

Internet neutrality is also grounded in legislative history. Early Internet transmission was carried by telephone lines, which were governed by the Communications Act of 1934. This act had a nondiscrimination requirement for "common carriers" such as telephone companies and cable operators:

> It shall be unlawful for any common carrier to make any unjust or unreasonable discrimination in charges, practices, classifications, regulations, facilities, or services for or in connection with like communication service, directly or indirectly, by any means or device, or to make or give any undue or unreasonable preference or advantage to any particular person, class of person, or locality, or to subject any particular person, class of person, or locality to any undue or unreasonable prejudice or disadvantage.

However, as Internet access moved away from its dependence on telephone lines toward broadband and other forms of access, the courts were less inclined to apply the common carrier provisions. In March 2002, the Federal Communications Commission (FCC) ruled that broadband Internet services provided by cable companies were to be treated as "information services," not "telecommunication services," a decision upheld by the U.S. Supreme Court in 2005. Hence, telephone or cable companies that provide broadband services do not need to comply with the common carrier provision (Gilroy 2006; Windhausen 2009).

However, because of this decision, some have argued that there is a need to craft new legislation that preserves the neutrality of ISPs and reestablishes the common carrier approach to broadband Internet services. As might be expected, those who believed that such legislation would stifle entrepreneurial activities and impose excessive costs on ISP providers were opposed to that idea. They argued that the forces of the marketplace should price Internet use. Ed Whitacre of AT&T made the following case:

> Now what they would like to do is use my pipes free, but I ain't going to let them do that because we have spent this capital and we have to have a return

on it. So there's going to have to be some mechanisms for these people who use these pipes to pay for the portion they're using. Why should they be allowed to use my pipes? The Internet can't be free in that sense, because we and the cable companies have made an investment and for a Google or Yahoo! or Vonage or anybody to expect to use these pipes free is nuts! (Weitzner 2006)

These comments conjure a world in which ISPs block or otherwise obstruct some content. If network providers were allowed to prioritize traffic, the results might be chilling. The ALA (2007) noted, "'Pipe' owners (carriers) should not be allowed to charge some information providers more money for the same pipes, or establish exclusive deals that relegate everyone else...to an Internet 'slow lane'" (p. 1). Gilroy (2006) observed that the "consolidation and diversification of broadband providers into content providers has the potential to lead to discriminatory behaviors which conflict with net neutrality principles" (p. 2). An ISP might, for example, make its own content more readily available. Similarly, the ability to move throughout the Internet might be restricted since some links might not be available. This could produce serious and adverse effects on social networking activities. Access to a blog, for example, might be substantially limited if a poster's network operators did not have an agreement with a particular ISP (Weitzner 2006). This defeats one of the most important aspects of the Internet—open access. The stakes are high.

Although the courts have been reluctant to apply the common carrier provisions of the current Communications Act, they have also expressed a desire to maintain the remarkable opportunities that the Internet affords to society as a whole. In the U.S. Supreme Court case *Janet Reno v. American Civil Liberties Union et al.* (1997), the court clarified four signal attributes of the Internet:

1. The Internet presents very low barriers to entry.
2. These barriers to entry are identical for both speakers and listeners.
3. As a result of these low barriers, astoundingly diverse content is available on the Internet.
4. The Internet provides significant access to all who wish to speak in the medium, and even creates a relative parity among speakers.

Similarly, the FCC, which has authority over information services, identified four principles for promoting broadband and also ensuring openness on the Internet (Gilroy 2006). Consumers are entitled to:

1. Access the lawful Internet content of their choice
2. Run applications and services of their choice
3. Connect their choice of legal devices that do no harm to the network
4. Competition among network providers, application and service providers, and content providers

Weitzner (2006) suggested a need to distinguish between the related but distinct concepts of Internet neutrality and network neutrality—the former remaining critical if the Internet is to conserve its value; the latter deserving further scrutiny to ensure that discriminatory practices do not arise, but which does not demand legislative regulation at this time. The Center for Democracy and Technology (2006) recommended that "the focus of the debate today should be squarely on preserving the openness of the Internet—as opposed to other, non-Internet services that also might be carried over broadband networks" (p. 1). This focus is consistent with the 2006 ALA "Resolution Affirming 'Network Neutrality,'" which stated in part that the association "affirms the right of all library users to enjoy equal and equitable internet access free from commercial bias, whether provided in the library, or through remote access to library resources" (ALA 2010).

2. Broadband Access

Broadband access was an issue of particular interest to President George W. Bush and on October 10, 2008, he signed the Broadband Data Improvement Act. Among the act's provisions was a requirement to identify geographical areas not yet served by broadband access and to conduct periodic surveys in urban, suburban, and rural areas to determine current levels of broadband capability. Availability of broadband service is critical to the information infrastructure, and overall access is increasing rapidly primarily using DSL or cable connections. According to a Pew Internet and American Life Project study, by April 2009, 63 percent of adult Americans had broadband connections at home, a significant increase from 55 percent in just one year (Horrigan 2009). Usage was increasing among groups that previously had been slow to acquire broadband, including senior citizens and low-income Americans.

Not surprisingly, however, as with access to the Internet, there appears to be a significant digital divide. For example, the percentage of white households with broadband connections was considerably greater than black households (65 percent compared to 46 percent). Access rose steadily with household income. The differences were dramatic in some cases: only 35 percent of households with annual salaries of $20,000 or less had broadband connections, compared to 88 percent of households with an income of $100,000 or more. Education levels were also correlated, with only 30 percent of adults with less than a high school education having broadband access compared to 83 percent of those with a college education. Although age and access were also related, a severe drop did not occur until after age sixty-five: 61–77 percent of individuals between the ages of eighteen and sixty-four had broadband access; only 30 percent of individuals over sixty-five had such access (Horrigan 2009). The divide was also international, with the United States slipping in rank from third per 100 people in 1999 to twenty-second in 2007 (Windhausen 2009).

Windhausen (2009) argued that there needs to be substantially greater involvement of the federal government in overseeing the development of broadband services. He recommended that federal policy should (1) provide seed money to create high-capacity broadband networks across the county; (2) promote investment by the public and private sectors, including the use of tax incentives; (3) promote regulatory reform and federal-state cooperation to encourage openness and accessibility; and (4) promote adoption and use of broadband services through financial assistance to low-income families, promotion of network openness and accessibility, and providing education to individuals on the advantages of online access.

As more information services are provided through broadband access, librarians will have to increase their involvement in the political discourse. Certainly, the new technologies are opening up the real possibility of universal and affordable access to digital information for millions of Americans. Yet, despite the potential value of broadband networks to aid in economic, social, and educational development, to date there has been minimal federal regulation, legislation, or guidance (Wind-hausen 2009).

C. The Production and Control of Government Information

The well-informed citizen lies at the heart of good government, and librarians have for many years supported this principle through their collections of government documents. Historically, government publication through the Government Printing Office and the Federal Depository Library Program (FDLP) was based on print materials and the production of physical products that were collected and organized by decentralized physical libraries (depositories). In the last decades, however, as the government became more vigilant following the events of 9/11 and more sensitive to economic concerns, two issues emerged that significantly affected libraries: privatization and digitization of government information.

1. The Privatization of Government Documents

The Office of Management and Budget's "Circular A–130, Management of Federal Information Resources" requires a cost-benefit analysis of government information activities, and new reliance on the private sector to disseminate government information or to recover costs by charging users (ALA 1991). The ALA's greatest concern with this directive was that it reflected an orientation toward information dissemination strictly based on costs, and therefore the philosophical, pedagogical, and social benefits of information dissemination were less likely to be considered. The fear was that the end result would be the publication of material that made a profit, not necessarily that of most value to the public. Even if an item with poor sales potential was published, the price was bound to be high, making access or acquisition prohibitive. Furthermore, private publishers are permitted to copyright their version of the material even though the Government Printing Office (GPO) cannot. An additional concern was that information produced privately was also exempt from the FOIA. These concerns remain.

2. Digitization of Government Information

By the 1990s, ever-increasing amounts of government information were available either directly on the Web or through CD-ROMs. This included GPO Access, which was "a collection of online searchable databases of government information" (Mason 2008). As Jorgensen (2006) noted:

> Electronic dissemination methods allowed government agencies to load information directly on their own Web sites, bypassing any government body responsible for standardizing, indexing, or archiving government information products. This method of distribution saved a great deal of time and money, but the documents were not easy to find or use. (p. 154)

By the end of 1998, "about 34 percent of the titles received by the Federal Depository Library at the end of the fiscal year were in electronic format" (Jorgensen 2006, p. 153). Although 9/11 moderated the amount of government information freely available on the Web, the general trend to increase digitally produced government information continued through the first decade of the twenty-first century.

Jacobs et al. (2005) noted that as the GPO produced more materials in digital format, fewer print items were available for deposit. The result was that some depository libraries had to build their own documents collections because materials were no longer provided by the GPO. In addition, FDLPs had to access the material by other means, raising their costs. They proposed five criteria for the future of the FDLP:

- Information is available and fully functional to all without charge.
- Information is easy to find and use.
- Information is verifiably authentic.
- Information is preserved for future access and use in a distributed system of digital depository libraries.
- Privacy of information users is ensured so that citizens can freely use government information without concern that what they read will be subject to disclosure or examination. (p. 201)

On the other hand, Shuler (2005) pointed out that as more and more information is digitized and made available through GPO Access and searchable databases, the need for physical collections is substantially reduced. Although it is highly unlikely that FDLPs will disappear, Shuler contended that librarians must move beyond the "collection" to understanding how government information is accessed and used by individuals:

> Imagine, in the not too distant future, a national library collective that draws upon (and is supported by) an aggressive use of the freedom of information and open meetings laws. Instead of waiting for the documents to be "published," these libraries could establish a system of tools, digital spaces, and/or portals to open up the public digital space in such a way that makes users aware of what is happening in their government. The goal would not be the "collection" of information, but a discursive tool that enables people to navigate and understand how and why governments do what they do. (p. 382)

For Shuler this requires less focus on technical expertise and collections and more on how government works, how people seek and use information, and how this information influences the lives of citizens and their communities.

3. The Rise of E-government and the Library's Role

In one study of adults seeking information to solve problems, more than half of the respondents reported some contact with a branch of government in the past year, usually by visiting or phoning a government agency or office (Estabrook and Rainie 2007). In the future, more of that contact will occur electronically. The federal government recognized the centrality of e-government when it passed the E-Government Act of 2002 (reauthorized in 2007). The original act defined electronic government as:

> the use by the Government of web-based Internet applications and other information technologies, combined with the processes that implement these technologies, to—(A) enhance the access to and delivery of Government information and services to the public, other agencies, and other Government entities; or (B) bring about improvements in Government operations that might include effectiveness, efficiency, service quality, or transformation. (U.S. Congress 2002)

The act's definition emphasizes the more mechanical aspects of e-government. Alternatively, Bertot, Jaeger, and McClure (2008) characterized e-government with a more political orientation:

> The promise of E-Government (and its more recent spin-offs of E-Democracy, E-Participation, E-Procurement, and a range of other "E's") is to engage citizenry in government in a citizen-centered manner, but also to develop quality government services and delivery systems that are efficient and effective. (p. 137)

La Porte (2005) identified three "threads" of e-government:

- Development of bureaucratic processes to provide greater administrative convenience, transparency, interactivity and openness

- Efforts to improve management processes to achieve costs savings and efficiencies

- Development of means to increase public participation in both electoral and regulatory processes to respond better to expressions of popular will and increase government legitimacy and support (p. 23)

Oder (2008), summarizing an ALA study on computer use in public libraries, reported that "some 74 percent of libraries report their staffers help patrons understand and use e-government services, including enrolling in Medicare, and applying for unemployment" (p. 14). Estabrook and Rainie (2007) studied how people use information sources to answer questions related to government agencies and programs. These questions often dealt with serious health problems, decisions about enrolling and financing education, tax issues, increasing work skills, changing a job or starting a business, or obtaining information on major programs such as Medicare and Medicaid. Among their findings was that with rare exceptions, people relied on the Internet more other than any other source of information including experts and family members. "Fifty-eight percent of those who had recently experienced one of those problems said they used the Internet (at home, work, a public library or some other place) to get help" (p. v). The researchers concluded, "E-government is not an option, it's a necessity" (p. iii).

The Estabrook and Rainie study also confirmed the importance of the library in e-government. They found that a majority of the people who turned to public libraries found them helpful, with 65 percent indicating that Internet access was particularly useful. Somewhat surprisingly, individuals between the ages of eighteen and thirty (Generation Y) were the most likely to turn to libraries for problem-solving information.

Although the federal government increasingly relies on the Web to deliver information, agencies seldom involve citizens when developing their e-services, nor do they solicit feedback or engage in systematic analysis of service quality (Bertot et al. 2008a). As a result, many people continue to rely on public libraries to help them locate and understand electronic government information. Bertot et al. reported that individuals access e-government in libraries for four reasons: "(1) lack of computer and Internet technology access; (2) lack of technology skills; (3) inability to understand government services and resources; and (4) the need to ask for assistance from an individual rather than a website or seldom answered phone help service" (Bertot et al. 2008a, p. 138). The public library is often perceived as a place to get assistance from staff in navigating the maze of sites and completing complicated government forms such as Medicare, immigration and tax forms, among others (Jaeger 2008; Jaeger and Fleischmann 2007).

Despite the obvious need for LIS professionals to assist in e-government activities, libraries receive little if any financial assistance to provide these new services

(Bertot et al. 2006b). The ALA, in a 2007 statement to the U.S. Senate Committee on Homeland Security and Governmental Affairs, noted that the federal Library Services and Technology Act (LSTA) provided only 1 percent of all public library operating budget funding, and explicitly urged greater support, noting:

> When government moves to save costs by E-Government, they pass the costs to public libraries, yet the library community has seen little collaboration or support from federal agencies for the significant increase in services public libraries provide on their behalf. (ALA 2007, p. 1)

In addition, Bertot et al. (2006b) made a number of policy recommendations aimed at increasing the importance of libraries in e-government:

1. Recognize public libraries as outlets for e-government services in legislation, policy initiatives, and program literature
2. Provide training for state library and public library staff regarding e-government service provision in a public library context
3. Provide direct support from federal, state, and local agencies to public libraries for the services that libraries offer on behalf of the agencies
4. Educate government officials regarding the roles public libraries play in relation to e-government, the effect of agency referrals to public libraries, and the need to support the public library
5. Coordinate and update federal, state, and local information policies to support better the role of public libraries as agents of e-government
6. Expand the responsibilities and funding of state library agencies to assist and support public libraries in their e-government role
7. Develop, through a collaborative process that includes key library professional associations, public librarians, policymakers, and LIS researchers, a set of best practices and practical guides that provide public libraries with insight into how to serve as providers of e-government services, issues associated with serving as e-government providers, and ways in which libraries can develop e-government services and resources (p. 4)

D. National Security Issues

As a matter of policy, the government wants to restrict information that could threaten national security. This is a complex issue, requiring a balance between the nation's interest and the rights of citizens to obtain information. This issue was brought into bold relief by the events occurring on September 11, 2001.

1. Homeland Security

The events of 9/11 clearly demonstrated that the United States was vulnerable to attack and precipitated a re-evaluation of the nation's security systems. The critical infrastructure of the United States was defined in the U.S.A. PATRIOT Act as "systems and assets, whether physical or virtual, so vital to the United States that the incapacity or destruction of such systems, and assets would have a debilitating impact on security, national economic security, national public health or safety, or any combination of those matters" (the PATRIOT Act is discussed in more detail later). The information and telecommunications sector was identified as part of that vital infrastructure. Among the major information-related initiatives proposed were:

- Quick and efficient sharing of information regarding the cyber-infrastructure (with concomitant limitations of the same information to the public)
- Improving information sharing among intelligence and law enforcement (Office of Homeland Security [OHS] 2002, p. 48)
- Integrating information sharing across the federal government
- Integrating information sharing among federal, state, and local government and law enforcement
- Adopting common metadata standards for data related to homeland security (OHS 2002, pp. 55–58)

President Bush also created a Critical Infrastructure Protection Board (CIPB) composed of representatives from government and the private sector. The CIPB was charged with creating a national strategy to secure the "critical information infrastructure." The CIPB issued its report in February 2003, viewing cyberspace as the "nervous system" of our infrastructure (CIPB 2003, p. vii). "Without a great deal of thought about security, the Nation shifted the control of essential processes in manufacturing, utilities, banking, and communication to networked computers" (CIPB 2003, p. 5). This shift left the U.S. cyber-infrastructure vulnerable despite concerted efforts to install virus protections, firewalls, and intrusion detection devices. Therefore, the strategic objectives of a national strategy to secure cyberspace were to "prevent cyber attacks against America's critical infrastructures; reduce national vulnerability to cyber attacks; and, minimize damage and recovery time from cyber attacks that do occur" (CIPB 2003, p. viii). To accomplish these objectives, the CIPB recommended a comprehensive national plan for securing information technology and telecommunications systems, providing crisis management support when and where threats exist, providing technical assistance to the private sector, improving coordination of federal agencies to provide warning and advice about protective measures, and conducting and funding research and development to help secure the technological infrastructure (CIPB 2003).

In a democratic society, a considerable amount of scientific, technical, and economic information is generally available either directly from the federal government on its Web sites or through government documents in local libraries. The OHS was concerned that this information could be used by terrorists to damage essential governmental facilities. For this reason, the federal government recalled or removed information from public access including Department of Energy reports and risk management plans from the Environmental Protection Agency (ALA 2003a). In October 2001 the GPO and the U.S. Geological Survey requested government depository libraries to destroy a CD-ROM on U.S. water supplies. Since depository documents remain the property of the U.S. government, compliance was expected (Smith 2002). Similarly, in March 2003, local Homeland Security agents removed Haz-Mat and emergency plan documents from local libraries without prior consultation with the libraries (ALA 2003a).

The ALA and other organizations were deeply concerned about the withdrawal or restriction of government information and the effects of broad and indiscriminate application of a protected status to a wide range of material that would otherwise be available to the public. The "Resolution on Withdrawn Electronic Government Information" and the "Resolution on Security and Access to Government Information" speak to these issues. In addition, the ALA appointed a task force on Restrictions on Access to Government Information (RAGI) to review government policy on dissemination of government information (ALA 2003b). The task force's report expressed serious reservations:

> While acknowledging the need on the part of government to consider potential security risks when making public information available for access, it is the conclusion of the Task Force that recent federal government actions limiting access promote a climate of secrecy tending to upset the delicate balance between the public's need to access government information and perceived national security concerns. (ALA 2003b, p. 4)

The RAGI task force issued ten recommendations that exhorted ALA to oppose vigorously any attempts to restrict access to government information on the basis of national security assertions, to monitor activities that lead to restrictions, and to stimulate advocacy on the part of librarians to protect the rights of patrons to government information (ALA 2003b).

In particular, the RAGI task force expressed concern about two memoranda. The first, issued by Attorney General Ashcroft, instructed executive agencies to interpret narrowly the FOIA, and its emphasis on the legal authority to withhold. The second memo, issued to all agency and department heads by White House Chief of Staff Andrew Card in March 2002, was titled "Action to Safeguard Information Regarding Weapons of Mass Destruction and Other Sensitive Documents Related to Homeland Security." The memo instructed agency administrators to review their records management procedures with an eye to protecting information that could be misused to harm national security such as unclassified documents that should be classified and other information that should be treated as sensitive, even if not classified. He attached to his request a memorandum from the government's top FOIA classification officers that said agencies should proceed on a case-by-case basis to evaluate sensitivity and the benefits of information sharing. Card's memo stated that this "sensitive but unclassified" (SBU) homeland security information could include records that dealt with the agency, public infrastructure that the agency might regulate or monitor, some internal databases (reports, data the agency collected, maps, etc.), vulnerability assessments, and information provided to the government by private firms such as chemical companies. It said that SBU information could be withheld using exemptions that protected personnel rules and practices (b)(2) and involving proprietary information (b)(4). It also suggested that some classifications should be extended beyond their ten- or twenty-five-year limits, and that some sensitive information should be classified.

> In making decisions about this category of information—such as whether to make it available on agency web sites—agencies must weigh the benefits of certain information to their customers against the risks that freely available sensitive homeland security information might pose to the interests of the Nation. (OHS 2002, p. 56)

One effect of the memo was that a number of agencies reviewed their Web site postings and by one estimate, more than 6,000 pages were withdrawn (Coalition of Journalists for Open Government 2009). The Federal Aviation Administration removed several databases from public access; the Office of Pipeline Safety discontinued access to its National Pipeline Mapping System; and the U.S. Geological Survey requested that depository libraries destroy information on CD-ROMs dealing with surface water (Hammitt 2005). In some cases, the information removed had little or no clear relationship to terrorism (Jaeger and Fleischmann 2007). It is likely that little of this information was archived or saved.

Another effect of the Card memo was the government's claim that it could restrict information requested under the FOIA if agency administrators believed that it might be used in a manner that "could," although not necessarily "would," be harmful to the American people (Feinberg 2004). These FOIA exemptions were used with increasing frequency by the military. For example, use of the executive privilege exemption by the Department of Defense increased 42 percent from 2000 to 2005 (Cochran and Davenport 2006). Although the military claims it used the exemption primarily to protect employees, others argued that the exemption privileges were abused. At the same time, the percentage of approved FOIA requests declined significantly, dropping from 54 percent in 2000 to 44 percent in 2004 (Cochran and Davenport 2006). The reliance on administrative discretion, rather than statutory guidance, significantly undermined the intent of FOIA. One review of SBU activity by the Information Sharing Environment Program Office of the GAO revealed that 81 percent of the SBU assignments were based on department or agency policies, rather than on formal regulations (OpenTheGovernment 2007).

Of course, federal agencies have a responsibility to safeguard information that might be damaging to national security, but, as Hammit (2005) observed:

> Part of the dismantling of electronic information sources after 9/11, was because agencies had made too much information available without much thought about the potential consequences. However, in taking down large chunks of information, there was never any sense that agencies were going through a thoughtful process in analyzing whether information should be taken down and balancing the legitimate societal value of the information against the heightened sensitivity of some information after 9/11. (p. 431)

Feinberg (2004) noted that categories such as SBU or "for official use only" or "sensitive security information" sometimes collided with other important ideals such as the right of the public to be informed. In addition, she observed that access to government information is now in a "nether world" (p. 439), with each agency adopting its own definitions for these categories, resulting in a lack of consistency in their application. Such ad hoc directives of various executive administrations have complicated the policies on information protection (Strickland 2005). These actions bring into relief the larger issue: a significant lack of an underlying theory that balances openness and secrecy within a consistent U.S. information policy. Fortunately, there is some evidence that access to government information might increase under the Obama administration. Attorney General Eric Holder promulgated new rules for government officials related to FOIA that emphasized the importance of transparency in government and encouraged openness in the provision of government information, even if there might be a plausible rationale for exemption (Sanchez 2009).

2. The U.S.A. PATRIOT Act (P.L. 107-56)

One of the direct consequences of the terrorist attack on September 11, 2001, was the passing of the Uniting and Strengthening America by Providing Appropriate Tools Required to Intercept and Obstruct Terrorism Act, better known as the PATRIOT Act. The act, signed by President George W. Bush on October 26, 2001, amended at least fifteen different statutes dealing with tracking and intercepting communications, conducting foreign intelligence investigations, money laundering, and dealing with alien terrorists and victims. The law created a broadly defined new crime of "domestic terrorism," expanded the authority of domestic investigative agencies (such as the FBI) and broadened powers related to wiretaps, search warrants, and subpoenas.

The ALA and other library organizations quickly expressed serious concerns about potential violations of First Amendment and privacy rights. Although the PATRIOT Act contained no provisions specifically directed at libraries or their patrons, it had several that might apply, particularly the provisions that amended the

Foreign Intelligence Surveillance Act (FISA). FISA created a Foreign Intelligence Surveillance Court, composed of selected federal judges, which had the power to authorize FBI agents involved in foreign intelligence investigations to wiretap, search, or use pen/trap devices that could secretly identify the source of telephone calls to and from a particular phone. It also authorized "roving wiretaps" that could trace an individual's communication on a variety of devices, regardless of place. This provision allowed FBI agents to track an individual's communication from a public phone or an e-mail to a friend's computer, or track that individual's activity on a public library computer. In other words, it focused on the person, not the place. Not surprisingly, this raised serious Fourth Amendment search and seizure concerns.

The PATRIOT Act significantly expanded the power of FISA. For example, it broadened FISA's definition of business records that can be searched. Originally, the covered records included common transportation carriers such as airlines or bus companies, vehicle rental agencies, or businesses that provided public accommodations such as hotels. The PATRIOT Act (Section 215) expanded this definition to "any relevant tangible item," which could include books, circulation records, or electronic records of Internet searches in libraries. If a request for such a record was made under the PATRIOT Act, librarians were required to keep the request secret. Further, because of this gag, the individuals who were the subject of the request could not be informed, and there could be no discussion of the incident with other librarians. Similarly, there was concern that requests for library records authorized under the PATRIOT Act were not subject to the traditional requirement of probable cause. Rather, the FBI merely needed to assert to the Foreign Intelligence Surveillance Court that the information was needed as part of an ongoing investigation into terrorism. Such an assertion could be made in a secret proceeding.

Although chilling in its potential, the actual impact of the PATRIOT Act on libraries is unclear. In May 2003 the House Judiciary Committee reported that the FBI had visited about fifty libraries ("FBI Has Visited" 2003), although Attorney General Ashcroft stated that no Section 215 requests were made. The Justice Department confirmed that as of March 2005, the authority had been used on thirty-five occasions, but not to acquire library, bookstore, gun sale, or medical records (Doyle 2005). The ALA and other organizations remain vigilant.

The overall fear concerning the PATRIOT Act was that the normal checks and balances that protect individual rights had been seriously eroded, significantly violating public trust in libraries. Of primary concern was that (1) innocent patrons might be subjected to surveillance regarding their reading habits, their use of electronic resources, or program attendance; (2) librarians might be unduly tempted to monitor patrons; and (3) libraries might be reluctant to collect and maintain data that were traditionally used for planning and management purposes for fear the data might be used as part of an investigation (Jaeger et al. 2004). In addition to the Resolution on the USA PATRIOT Act and Related Measures that Infringe on the Rights of

Library Users, the ALA developed a series of resolutions and procedures to deal with the PATRIOT Act including Resolution Reaffirming the Principles of Intellectual Freedom in the Aftermath of Terrorist Attacks, and Privacy: An Interpretation of the Library Bill of Rights. These resolutions condemned the use of governmental power to suppress the free and open exchange of information and free inquiry, and exhorted librarians to support open access and user privacy.

Following vigorous efforts on the part of ALA and others, the PATRIOT Act was reauthorized in 2006 with significantly strengthened civil liberties protections:

1. The FBI must show "reasonable grounds" that the requested records were relevant to an authorized investigation.

2. More specific description of the requested records was required to prevent "fishing expeditions."

3. Requests for library records as well as those from bookstores required additional administrative approval.

4. The gag order rules were loosened to permit consultation with legal counsel prior to providing the records.

5. Section 215 orders could be challenged using a special petition process.

6. In addition, greater reporting requirements were added so that information on the number of orders related to library records as well as other records could be determined. (ALA 2009b)

3. Library Awareness Program

Librarians' strong reactions to the PATRIOT Act were grounded in a previous experience. Beginning in the early 1960s, Soviet intelligence systematically collected unclassified information in U.S. libraries using Soviet agents as well as innocent university students. When this activity became known to the FBI, they recruited staff in the scientific and other technical libraries that were the likely Soviet targets in the New York area. The initiative was called the Library Awareness Program.

Librarians became aware of the program in June 1987, when two FBI agents came to the Math and Science Library at Columbia University and asked a clerk about foreigners using the library (Schmidt 1989). A librarian who overheard the conversation referred the agents to the library director, who reported this exchange to the New York Library Association's Intellectual Freedom Committee, who in turn reported it to the ALA. This led to an ALA investigation and subsequent congressional hearings. The FBI agreed to discontinue the program but did not guarantee that it would not be started again. National security is an important issue, but so is the concern that it not be used as a rationale to suppress embarrassing information or to impede the free flow of ideas unnecessarily. Balancing these important interests will remain a challenge for all.

E. Transmission and Control of Information across National Boundaries

In a world in which satellites instantaneously transmit information around the globe, and in which substantial electronic computer storage is both practical and economical, the globalization of information raises a number of issues. The international exchange of information is sometimes referred to as transborder data flow (TDF). At present, TDF primarily concerns storage or processing of information in foreign computers. Although there might be many reasons to control international dissemination of information, the United Nations asserted an underlying principle familiar to all Americans. In its Universal Declaration of Human Rights, Article 19, it stated:

> Everyone has the right to freedom of expression and opinion. This right includes freedom to hold opinions without interference and to seek, receive, and impart information and ideas through any media regardless of frontiers. (United Nations 1948)

The impact of TDF can occur on at least four levels—personal, economic, national, and sociocultural.

1. Personally Identifiable Information

Because great quantities of personal information are stored on computer systems, organizations can now transmit personally identifiable information across state and national borders to various groups, both private and governmental. Europe, especially, has made attempts to control the unnecessary transmission of personal information so that individual rights are protected while permitting approved information to be transmitted (Bortnick 1985).

2. Economic

The information industry is worth billions of dollars, and nations naturally compete for this market. As a result, some countries have imposed tariffs and trade regulations that restrict or encourage the flow of information and information technologies. Other countries have imposed special standards based on the type of information or the equipment needed to use it, or insist on a particular pricing structure (Bortnick 1985).

3. National

Some countries attempt to jump ahead of their neighbors by importing technologies, software, and information. Such actions often come at a price. For example, to use the hardware, software, and language of a borrowed technology, the borrowing country might sacrifice some of its own culture. Many people within such countries express serious concerns about foreign nationals or multinational corporations dominating their information resources. When nations become increasingly dependent on the technologies of other nations, sovereignty is often threatened and efforts to create an indigenous information infrastructure are inhibited. In addition, not all countries define public and private information the same. Information readily and legally available in one country might not be legally available in another (such as information on drugs or sexuality). A related issue is protecting national security information from electronic intrusion. Electronic storage of highly sensitive government information is now common, and the fear that this information might be accessed and transmitted across international borders is an important consideration.

4. Sociocultural

Technologies can transform values, fundamental assumptions, and traditional activities within a society. Xue (2005) noted that countries with well-developed policies regarding information technology were more likely to have access to the Web, which in turn resulted in a free flow of information, expanded education and training, and the ability to diffuse the benefits of the Internet in the general population. He cautioned, however:

> While the Internet brings visible economic, social, and cultural benefits to nations, it also brings quick idea diffusion, and therefore has a huge impact on social values and political ideology in developing and non-democratic countries. (p. 238)

The introduction of technologies that are not consistent with national values and assumptions can create social and cultural dislocations. From a cynical perspective, could information technologies increase the capacity of government leaders to control their populations? Could such technologies change the economic basis of a society from rural to urban? Could devoting fiscal and human resources to building a technological infrastructure divert needed resources from other vital activities such as agriculture or education?

F. Attempts to Control Artistic and Other Individual Expression

Many governments attempt, in a variety of ways, to control information assumed to be harmful to national security, libelous or slanderous, or that could incite individuals to violence. Among the many categories of information the U.S. government has tried to control, at one time or another, are various forms of artistic expression, expression of opposition to the U.S. government, and sexually explicit materials.

1. Artistic Expression

There is a long history in the United States of attempts to censor books, plays, and works of art. Such suppression has been of great concern to LIS professionals.

Although some suppressed works were of questionable artistic merit, many others are now considered literary classics, including James Joyce's *Ulysses* and J. D. Salinger's *Catcher in the Rye*. Historically, the government used obscenity statutes, postal regulations, or the withholding of funding to regulate this type of information. For example, the National Endowment of the Arts has withheld funding because certain staff members objected to the content of some citizen-approved projects.

2. Expression of Opposition to the U.S. Government

A variety of State Department, postal, and import regulations have been used to bar individuals and information from entering the country when the information or the person was considered contrary to the interests of the U.S. government. Foreign nationals, such as members of certain ethnic or political groups, for example, have been prevented from speaking at conferences. Similarly, films considered to be propaganda have been prohibited.

3. Sexually Explicit Material

Federal, state, and local laws prohibit the production, importation, and mailing of "obscene" materials. These laws have created a complex, often opaque, de facto national policy. It is clear, for example, that child pornography is not permitted in our society. On the other hand, books that depict nude children but that are clearly intended to educate minors about puberty might also be construed as obscene under these laws. Policy on sexual information remains confused because court interpretations of obscenity laws are often based on community standards. It is hard to know what materials can be restricted and what cannot. What is clear is that laws are used to try to define and restrict such material.

IV. COPYRIGHT LEGISLATION AND ISSUES

A. Characteristics of the Copyright Law

The U.S. Constitution grants to the federal government the power to "promote the Progress of Science and useful Arts, by securing for limited Times to Authors and Inventors the exclusive Right to their respective Writings and Discoveries" (U.S. Constitution, Article I, Section 8, Clause 8). The underlying foundation of this right is the idea that by rewarding individuals for their creative efforts, the whole society benefits. The original intent of copyright focused on its application as a social good and not on protecting creative property (Bailey 2006).

1. What Is Protected?

The most recent version of the Copyright Act, reauthorized in 1976, does not focus on ideas themselves, but on ideas once they are fixed in some form. Generally, copyright ownership resides with the author of a particular work, unless it is transferred by contract to another individual or organization, such as a publisher.

Copyright interpretation is complicated because so many works are now available electronically. Central to these issues for LIS professionals is determining to what extent the creator or publisher of information can control copying and use by others. This dilemma has been further complicated by the Internet, which has changed our notion of publication. Does something become

---

Categories of Works Protected by the Copyright Act

1. Literary works
2. Musical works, including any accompanying words
3. Dramatic works, including any accompanying music
4. Pantomimes and choreographic works
5. Pictorial, graphic, and sculptural works
6. Motion pictures and other audiovisual works
7. Sound recordings
8. Architectural works

(*Source:* 17 U.S.C. Section 102[a] [1988 & Supp V 1993].)

---

a publication once it is available on the Internet? Given the ease with which electronic material can be changed, which version is copyrighted and how can it be protected? ALA considers this such a serious issue that one provision of its code of ethics is specifically devoted to respect for intellectual property rights, and the Association of Research Libraries has its own statement on this issue as well.

From a constitutional perspective, information policies must consider a balance among several interests—individuals who deserve to profit from their ideas and creations, the rights of individuals to access and use information, and the benefit to society as a whole. This balance can be very difficult to obtain, especially given the political power of the for-profit sector. The predominant attitude seems to be that copyright law protects the economic interests of publishers and producers. This tension creates considerable controversy, and LIS professionals often find themselves caught in the center. LIS professionals depend on authors and producers of information to maintain the reservoir of knowledge so critical to library functions. On the other hand, LIS professionals also have a strong conviction that information access, either physical or electronic, should be available at minimal or no cost to the user. Hence LIS professionals favor very generous copying privileges, and producers favor restricted ones:

> Librarians face a dilemma when it comes to copyright. On the one hand, if content providers disappeared, libraries and our patrons would suffer. By doing our part to eliminate copyright violations, we help keep publishers in business. On the other hand, we understand that "information wants to be free." We resent license agreements that prevent us from sharing information. Who hasn't bent the rules or seen others do so? We became librarians in order to help people find information; we don't want to be gatekeepers or copyright cops. (Skala et al. 2008, p. 28)

The 1976 Copyright Act does not explicitly identify electronic works as being protected by copyright legislation and therefore legal interpretation has been complicated because so many documents are now available electronically. However, the act does state:

> Copyright protection subsists, in accordance with this title, in original works of authorship fixed in any tangible medium of expression, now known or later developed, from which they can be perceived, reproduced, or otherwise communicated, either directly or with the aid of a machine or device. (17 U.S.C. 102)

In addition, a 1976 House report on the Copyright Act revealed that a broad meaning was to be given to the concept of a literary work, including "computer databases and computer programs to the extent that they incorporate authorship in a programmer's expression of original ideas" (House Report 1976, p. 566). This language suggests that ideas fixed in media such as DVDs or on a Web site are covered by copyright protections. Once a creative work is in a fixed form, the individual who created the work does not have to do anything to obtain the copyright; it resides with the creator, who can affix a copyright notice without registering the work with the Copyright Office.

The length of time the work is protected is determined by a variety of factors. In general, works published in the United States before 1923 are now in the public domain; they can no longer be privately owned. Works created after January 1, 1978, are protected from the point of creation until the creator dies plus seventy additional years. During those years, copyright protection varies based on whether the material was registered with the Copyright Office or otherwise claimed.

2. What Are the Rights and Limitations of the Copyright Owner?

Exclusive Rights of the Copyright Owner

Owners' rights are considerable, including the right to:

1. Reproduce the copyrighted work in copies or phonorecords
2. Prepare derivative works based upon the copyrighted work
3. Distribute copies or phonorecords of the copyrighted work to the public by sale or other transfer of ownership, or by rental, lease, or lending
4. Perform publicly: literary, musical, dramatic, and choreographic works, pantomimes, motion pictures and other audiovisual works
5. Display publicly: literary, musical, dramatic, and choreographic works, pantomimes, and pictorial, graphic, or sculptural works, including the individual images of a motion picture or other audiovisual work

(*Source:* 17 U.S.C. Section 106 [1988 & Supp. V 1993].)

As might be expected, those who produce original works, or who purchase rights to reproduce them, want to restrict copying privileges. LIS professionals, on the other hand, seek to disseminate information as freely as possible. Librarians do this by loaning a copy of the work, making additional copies, or permitting others to make copies. The right to perform these functions is defined under two doctrines in the copyright law: the first sale doctrine and the doctrine of fair use.

a. First Sale Doctrine

The first sale doctrine (codified at 17 U.S.C. §109 [a]) permits libraries and others to loan copyrighted materials. Under the doctrine, the holder of a lawfully owned copy is authorized "without the authority of the copyright owner, to sell or otherwise dispose of the possession of that copy." Libraries exercise this right when they purchase an item (first sale) and then subsequently loan the book, periodical, or film without remunerating the copyright owner further. The first sale doctrine supports the notion of subsidized browsing, a critical concept in librarianship. That is, libraries spend public dollars to purchase an item, essentially subsidizing its use by members of the community. It is critical to keep this in mind, because electronic dissemination of information substantially alters this notion. The implications of this change are discussed below.

b. Fair Use Doctrine

The doctrine of fair use evolved over many years and as a result of a substantial number of court decisions. It was codified in section 107 of the copyright law, which contains a list of the various purposes for which reproduction of a particular work may be considered fair, such as criticism, comment, news reporting, teaching, scholarship, and research. When an individual makes a copy under the fair use doctrine, he or she is not required to get permission from the copyright owner. However, Section 107 sets out four criteria that should be considered in determining whether or not a particular use is fair (see sidebar). The complexity and subtleties involved in interpreting fair use are considerable, and the issue becomes even more complicated with the introduction of electronic access. As a rule, the fair use doctrine is more likely to apply when the use is noncommercial (educational or research purposes) and would have little effect on the profits of the copyright owner. There are many restrictions, however. For example, films, videocassettes, and sheet music have more severe restrictions.

Librarians depend heavily on the fair use doctrine in making copies for patrons or permitting them to make copies for themselves. It is natural, however, that publishers are concerned with loss of subscription income. Not surprisingly, they often take issue with librarians making liberal numbers of copies for interlibrary loan purposes, especially copies of periodical articles. The librarian does not want to

> **Criteria for Determining Fair Use**
> - The purpose and character of the use, including whether such use commercial or for nonprofit educational purposes
> - The nature of the copyrighted work
> - The amount and substantiality of the portion used in relation to the copyrighted work as a whole
> - The effect of the use upon the potential market for, or value of, the copyrighted work
>
> (*Source:* 17 U.S.C. § 107.)

risk "contributory copyright infringement," which in one court case was described as "one who, with knowledge of the infringing activity, induces or causes, or materially contributes to the infringement of another" (*Gershwin Publishing Corp* 1971; Lipinski 2005, p. 2). Nor does the library want to be liable for encouraging others to violate the Copyright Act. The copyright law permits libraries to make individual copies of most copyrighted works, but not "in such aggregate quantities as to substitute for a subscription to or purchase of" a copyrighted item (17 U.S.C. § 108 [g][2]). Russell (2005a) characterized the conditions for making copies under Section 108:

> If the following three things are true—your library is open to the public, and you do not make a copy (of an article or a portion of a copyright work) in order to see "commercial advantage," and you include the copyright notice on the copy or a legend that states the work might be protected by copyright—you can make reproductions without the prior authorization of the copyright holder. (p. 275)

Russell warned, however, that "these allowances do not apply to musical works; pictorial, graphic, or sculptural works; motion pictures; and other audiovisual works" (p. 275). Although copyright for digital materials remains somewhat unclear, Russell suggested that libraries should consider digital works as covered by copyright law, keeping in mind that databases and online sources are often purchased with licensing agreements that might limit copying (see discussion below). If patrons copy excessively, libraries might consider time restrictions for computer use or charging for printing. By the same token, Russell (2005b) cautioned libraries not to serve as "copyright police" (p. 339), which might ultimately increase the library's liability and violate the basic notions of privacy and confidentiality that form the foundation of library service.

Also, the law does not clearly identify how much copying is too much. Fortunately, this issue was addressed by the National Commission on New Technological Uses of Copyrighted Works (CONTU), a group created when the 1976 Copyright Act was being drafted, comprised of representatives from the legal profession, librarians, journalists and writers, consumer organizations, publishers, business executives, and officials of the Library of Congress and the Copyright Office. The commission was formed primarily to deal with the effects of computers on copyrighted works but it agreed to address the issue of photocopying as well (CONTU 1978). The result of their deliberations is known as the "CONTU Guidelines on Photocopying under Interlibrary Loan Arrangements" (CONTU 1978, p. 54). CONTU attempted to balance the interest of periodical publishers with those of libraries, and to clarify what was meant by "aggregate quantities as to substitute for a subscription" (17 U.S.C. § 108 [g][2]) The guidelines apply to requests for periodical articles published within the past five years and permit libraries to make as many as five copies of a given periodical in a given calendar year (CONTU 1978). The guidelines were subsequently incorporated as part of the legislative history of the 1976 Copyright Act

(CONTU 1978). They continue to play an important role in guiding library photo-copying practices for interlibrary loans.

For copying of print materials that might exceed fair use, the Copyright Clearance Center (CCC) was created to help pay royalties to publishers. The CCC creates agreements with a wide variety of journal publishers. Royalty payments are made to the CCC, which then grants the right to copy material to corporations and other institutions.

The growth of electronic publication on the Web brought new concerns about interpreting fair use. In 1994, the Working Group on Intellectual Property Rights, a committee of the Information Infrastructure Task Force (1995) created by President Clinton, published a report called the Green Paper that suggested that the traditional interpretations of fair use were difficult to apply in the digital environment. Consequently, the working group convened a Conference on Fair Use, which brought together information users and copyright owners to review and discuss how fair use might be applied in the digital environment and to determine what new guidelines might be needed. These deliberations lasted over four years but regrettably produced mixed success. Guidelines for educational multimedia were developed, and guidelines related to digital images and some aspects of distance learning were proposed. Many other issues were deferred. The group also considered it premature to draft guidelines for digital transmission of documents for interlibrary loan (U.S. Patent and Trademark Office 1998). Academic libraries, in particular, were concerned that the proposals regarding digital images and e-reserves lacked balance between copyright owners and users, narrowed inappropriately the concept of fair use, overly restricted access to e-materials, placed unreasonable restrictions on course materials that could be included in reserves, and limited electronic access to too short a term (Jackson 1997).

In response to these concerns, fourteen organizations including the ALA, the American Association of Law Librarians, the Association of American Universities, the American Council on Education, the Medical Library Association, and the Association of Research Libraries developed a statement enunciating important precepts and goals related to protecting fair use and liberal access to ideas:

> We will work to extend the application of fair use into digital networked environments in libraries and educational institutions by relying on it responsibly to lawfully make creative use of information. . . . We will encourage our members to reject any licensing agreement clause that implicitly or explicitly limits or abrogates fair use or any other legally conveyed user privilege. (Association of Research Libraries 1997a, p. 2)

B. File Sharing

Today's technologies allow all types of information, visual, audio, and print, to be digitized and stored electronically. It can then be uploaded, downloaded, and otherwise made available on electronic networks. It can be copied many times without loss of quality and sent to literally hundreds or thousands of individuals. However, copying and sharing files with MP3 technology was particularly problematic when it was first introduced. MP3 stands for MPEG Audio Layer III, a file format that compresses audio files to less than one-tenth of their original size by removing parts of the sound inaudible to human hearing. MP3 technology permits audio files (speech or music) to be uploaded and downloaded on the Internet with minimal compromise to the quality of the recording. It also permits the transfer of music on CD into computer files. MP3 players have a download interface and a variety of control features that permit the downloading, playback, and manipulation of the digitized audio file. This technology allows millions of (mostly young) people to share music files without purchasing a copy from the recording producers. For them, "MP3 is more than an algorithm, a format, and software—MP3 is a culture, a movement, a religion, almost" (Stevens 2000, p. 115). Today, MP3 files can be downloaded from thousands of sites, and there are many software and hardware products that support the MP3 format. Not surprisingly, the recording industry was very vocal about the sharing of audio files, which they argued was a violation of copyright law. Several court decisions supported this position, and the recording industry successfully applied pressure where individuals were likely to share MP3 files, such as universities. In addition, the Recording Industry Association of America began suing individuals who shared large collections of digital music.

With increasing broadband access and the rise of YouTube, similar issues have been raised with video productions on both the national and international level. Madden (2009) reported that 57 percent of online video viewers share links, and 75 percent of viewers indicate they receive links to watch videos that others have seen. In addition, 48 percent of Internet users have been to a video-sharing site and the percentage is expected to rise (Rainie 2008).

C. Digital Rights Management

Historically, fair use was determined by the user; that is, the copyright holder placed faith in the individuals using the material to ask for copyright permission when it was required. In reality, it was nearly impossible to monitor how people used copyrighted material. Such vulnerability is especially problematic in the digital environment where copies can be quickly created, disseminated widely, and altered by anyone with access. As digitized information became "commoditized," its producers and distributors have increasingly attempted to control use of their digital products.

Digital rights management (DRM) was defined as "the documentation and administration of rights for the access to and use of digital works" (Agnew and Martin 2003, p. 267). DRM controls access to digital information unless special permissions or fees have been obtained. DRM covers a broad spectrum including access, viewing, copying, printing, editing, or transferring digital data. It involves a variety of technological efforts to render digital information difficult to access, manipulate, distribute, and copy. Among these efforts has been the creation of "trusted systems," which generally focus on two areas: authentication and authorization. Authentication deals with making sure that a user is in fact a valid user of the system—for example, a faculty member at a university. Authorization deals with ensuring that a user has the right to access the system and determines the degree of access—for example, has the user paid a required fee, and is access limited or can the user manipulate or alter the digital data?

One trusted system is the Digital Object Identifier (DOI). The DOI identifies content objects in the digital environment and assigns names to any entity for use on digital networks (DOI Foundation 2009). Although information about a digital object might change over time, including where to find it, its DOI name does not change. The system is managed by the International DOI Foundation, an open-membership consortium including both commercial and noncommercial partners. DOI was recently accepted for standardization within ISO. Approximately 40 million DOI names were assigned in the United States, Australasia, and Europe by 2009. Using DOI names as identifiers makes managing intellectual property in a networked environment much easier and more convenient, and allows the construction of automated services and transactions. Although DOI was developed as a digital rights system, it has much broader potential to assist in organizing objects on the Web. The DOI identifies the digital object itself, not its address, and is therefore independent of location and can be searched independently. It is sometimes compared to a bar code for physical objects. However, the extent to which will be used beyond rights management remains to be seen.

Those who produce digital information certainly have rights to protect the fruits of their labors. The problem resides in the controls that inhibit what would normally be considered fair use of such material. In other words, the digital technologies can subvert types of access normally considered beneficial and permitted. In fact, such technologies are intended to inhibit sharing of digital information, thus controverting the underlying principle of the first sale doctrine. If there is a cost every time digital information is shared, the costs will become prohibitive for libraries:

> The protections afforded by these systems need not bear any particular relationship to the rights granted under, say, U.S. copyright law. Rather, the possible technological restrictions on what a user might do are determined by the architects themselves and thus might (and often do) prohibit many other legal uses.... Libraries that subscribe to electronic material delivered through copyright management systems might find themselves technologically incapable of lending out that material the way a traditional library lends out a book, even though the act of lending is a privilege—a defense to copyright infringement for unlawful distribution—under the first sale doctrine. (Zittrain 2006, p. 1998)

LIS professionals clearly have a stake in DRM. As they increasingly digitize their own collections and provide access to digital information, they, too, become engaged in DRM. Academic libraries routinely restrict access to their databases, requiring special passwords or other controls to authenticate the user. Public libraries have a long history of protecting the privacy and confidentiality of users; yet the need to control access to certain materials will also mean that users might be identifiable and the nature of their use might be recorded. Such record keeping undermines some of the fundamental principles of librarianship.

D. The Open Source Initiative

A countervailing force to the proprietary interests protected by copyright is the open source movement. This movement, begun in the mid–1980s, relates to the development of software products, including the source code, which are made available at little or no cost through a license. The defining characteristic of open source software is that the license encourages people to modify and improve the software and make the resulting improvements available to others for further enhancement. Traditionally, when a software company creates a product, they closely scrutinize for copyright violations products produced by others who claim that they have enhanced the original product or created a product that can be used with the original product. Open source products become public rather than private property. This is in many ways how the Internet and Web developed so rapidly. As the Open Source Initiative (2003), a nonprofit corporation, explains it:

> The basic idea behind open source is very simple: When programmers can read, redistribute, and modify the source code of a piece of software, the software evolves. People improve it, people adapt it, people fix bugs. And this can happen at a speed that, if one is used to the slow pace of conventional software development, seems astonishing.

Open source software has grown rapidly since the 1980s, and some major products use it, most notably Linux, a server operating system. Other important examples of open source operating systems include:

- Apache, a program that runs over 50 percent of the Web servers in the world
- Perl, a widely used language for implementing interactive Webpages
- BIND, a program that supports the Domain Name Service

Dorman (2002) predicted that open source software might well become a significant computing trend because it has strong ethical, economic, and technical foundations. Certainly, any movement that welcomes open access to critical technical information and that, in turn, could lead to significant progress for all rather than serving proprietary interests, is consonant with librarianship's values. In fact, libraries have significant potential to employ open source systems, especially given the high costs of online systems purchased from traditional vendors. Several groups have been working on open system software for library management, document delivery, circulation, cataloging, and e-mail (Mickey 2001). For example, Evergreen (2009), which first launched in September 2006 in Georgia's PINES consortium, is used in over 300 libraries in over a dozen countries worldwide. Other products include Koha, originally developed in New Zealand and deployed in 2000, and Emilda. It will take some time, however, to assess the potential influence of open source software in the library world.

E. Creative Commons Movement

Like the open source movement, the creative commons movement offers an alternative to the "all rights reserved" perspective. Creative Commons, a nonprofit organization established in 2001 with funding from the Center for the Public Domain, provides copyright licenses at no cost to the public. Using a Web application platform, these licenses allow creators to protect their works based on four options (see sidebar; Creative Commons 2009).

Creative Commons Options

Attribution: Others can copy, distribute, display, and perform the copyrighted work—and derivative works based upon it—but only if they give credit as stipulated by the author.

Share Alike: Others can distribute derivative works only under a license identical to the license that governs the creator's work as long as the creator is credited.

Noncommercial: Others can copy, distribute, display, and perform the original work—and derivative works based upon it—but for noncommercial purposes only. The creator must be credited.

No Derivative Works: Others can copy, distribute, display, and perform only verbatim copies of the original work, not derivative works based upon it. The creator must be credited.

Creative Commons licenses have gained considerable support; as of March 2009, an estimated 130 million licenses were issued. The Creative Commons (2009) developed new approaches to reducing the barriers to the free flow of knowledge and has focused on increasing the availability of scientific information on the Internet.

In summary, the issues related to copyright are numerous and complex. The many stakeholders involved, as well as the constant emergence of new technologies and digital content, create continuing challenges for LIS professionals. Bailey (2006) summarized the basic copyright trends from a historical perspective, noting that copyright has moved from:

- Promoting progress to protecting intellectual property owners' rights
- From covering limited types of works to covering virtually all types of works

- From granting only basic reproduction and distribution rights to granting a much wider range of rights
- From offering a relatively short duration of protection to a relatively long (potentially perpetual) one
- From requiring registration to providing automatic copyright
- From drafting laws in Congress to drafting laws in work groups of interested parties dominated by commercial representatives
- From making infrequent extensions of copyright duration to frequent ones
- From selling works to licensing them
- From relatively modest civil penalties to severe civil and criminal penalties
- From ignoring ordinary citizens' typical use of copyrighted works to branding them as pirates and prosecuting them with lawsuits (p. 119)

Constant monitoring of the policy environment is necessary to ensure that LIS professionals maximize their ability to make the intellectual products of our world available to the greatest number of people.

F. Contract and Licensing Law versus Fair Use

Today, online access to intellectual property in electronic format is regulated as much, if not more, by licensing and leasing agreements as by copyright. Libraries negotiate contracts with vendors that set forth the conditions under which a library may disseminate the information. Because these agreements are mutual, they are governed by state contract laws rather than copyright law. Unlike copyright law, which had idealistic motives to advance social progress, contract law has no such objective. Once a contract is signed, copyright law does not apply if it conflicts with the contract. Contracts are written to benefit the parties to them; benefits to society at large are incidental. For the producers and distributors of information, there is no need to consider social issues at all—merely economic ones. Because libraries must sign a licensing agreement before they can gain access to information, they have less control over the material's dissemination than under the doctrine of first sale. In fact, if a library discontinues its lease on an information product, it can lose access to both current and retrospective information files. Bailey (2006) described these developments as moving from a "permissive culture" to a "permission culture."

More recently, librarians and publishers have sought to avoid the burdensome, costly, and time-consuming complexities of licensing with individual libraries, especially in the area of e-resources, through what is referred to as shared e-resource understandings (SERUs). SERUs eliminate the need to negotiate a separate contract for each library. The National Information Standards Organization (NISO) identified best practices in the implementation of such agreements (NISO RP-7-2008). These guidelines outline commonly accepted practices and expectations for use of e-resources and rely on existing copyright law as a foundation. A SERU is based on a sense of trust, goodwill, and mutuality, but in some circumstances a license may remain the best practice (NISO 2009).

The extent to which information producers control access to electronic information in the future will depend on the policies and practices regarding use of information on electronic networks. In the absence of such policies, six library associations—the ALA, the Association of Research Libraries, the American Association of Law Libraries, the Association of Academic Health Sciences Libraries, the Medical Library Association, and the Special Libraries Association—developed fifteen principles when negotiating licenses for electronic resources (Association of Research Libraries 1997b). Among the issues addressed were the need for clear statements concerning the nature of the access rights obtained, liability or lack thereof for unauthorized use, protection of users' privacy and confidentiality, rights to make archival copies, and protection of rights under the current copyright law.

G. International Copyright Issues

Control over intellectual property was recognized as an international issue in early international treaties such as the Rome Convention for the Protection of Performers, Producers of Phonograms and Broadcasting Organizations (1961) and the Berne Convention for the Protection of Literary and Artistic Works (1971). But developments in networked communication technologies made it clear that these treaties were inadequate for the dramatically changed information environment. Thus, in December 1996, members of the World Intellectual Property Organization (WIPO), an agency of the United Nations, adopted a new copyright treaty for literary and artistic works, including electronic works. Among its central features was the extension of copyright protection to computer programs, including their copying, distribution, and rental (WIPO 1996). Interestingly, a major issue debated at the conference was whether accessing a Web page, which requires a computer to store data in RAM on a temporary basis, constituted making a copy—hence requiring permission from the copyright owner. After much debate and controversy, the treaty did not grant copyright to this type of use. In other words, the copy still must be fixed or distributable in a tangible form (Blum 1997).

Copyright issues in the international, digital environment have become so complicated that various library associations including the American Association of Law Libraries, the American Library Association, the Association of Research Libraries, the Medical Library Association, and the Special Library Association, have joined together to create the Library Copyright Alliance (LCA) (Wiant 2008). The LCA has four goals:

- A robust and growing public domain to provide new opportunities for creativity, research, and scholarship
- Effective library programs and services as a means of advancing knowledge
- High levels of creativity and technological process resulting from individual research and study
- Harmonization of copyright (p. 46)

H. Recent Copyright Legislation

Three recent legislative initiatives are particularly noteworthy: the Uniform Computer Information Transaction Act (UCITA), the Digital Millennium Copyright Act (DMCA), and the Technology, Education and Copyright Harmonization Act (TEACH).

1. The Uniform Computer Information Transaction Act

UCITA was originally introduced as an amendment to the federal Uniform Commercial Code, which was intended to make commercial state contract laws consistent regarding the licensing of software, databases, and Web sites throughout the United States. UCITA covered only electronic products such as software or electronically distributed materials. Although increasing uniformity among state licensing laws would be helpful, UCITA contained a number of provisions that would affect free expression and use of software that have become quite controversial, and attempts to pass it as a federal law have not been successful. Among the major concerns were the following:

1. UCITA made the conditions set forth in "shrink-wrap" licenses binding. Shrink-wrap licenses are usually included with software products, but the buyer is not aware of the conditions when the product is purchased. In effect, sellers can hide the terms of purchase until after the purchase has occurred. Similarly, UCITA also made binding "click-through" licenses, which are similar agreements that are discovered only after the product is loaded and the purchaser is trying to use it. Traditionally, when two parties enter into a contract, negotiating the terms is part of the process. There was no possibility for negotiation with such licenses under UCITA, and courts have been skeptical about their binding character.

2. Because the terms in shrink-wrap or click-through licenses tend to be quite restrictive, the right of fair use normally provided under the Copyright Act was subverted. Similarly, the terms and conditions in a license might permit the monitoring of use, which might, in turn, violate traditional privacy rights afforded to patrons by libraries.

3. The act, through licensing terms, might have prevented reverse engineering, which permits examination of a program or product for such purposes as

debugging, adding value. Reverse engineering might also be needed to evaluate a product critically.

4. The act stifled protections for free expression by permitting software producers to create nondisclosure terms in their licenses and thus take legal action against individuals who criticize their products. This provision could substantially limit the ability of individuals to prepare and publish critical reviews of a software product.

5. The act limited the rights of users to sell or transfer licensed software, which subverts the first sale doctrine under the Copyright Act.

6. The act permitted software distributors to avoid liability for damage caused by defects in their software, even if those defects were known to the seller but unknown to the buyer.

7. The application of UCITA was unclear if a particular product was a combination of print and electronic, such as a book with an accompanying CD.

8. The act allowed a software seller to determine the forum in which state legal actions could be considered. Obviously, sellers would likely select states where the laws were most amenable to them.

UCITA was a clear attempt by software producers to gain legal support for their proprietary interests. From the perspective of LIS professionals, there is general concern that the bill would seriously disturb the balance that protects both sellers and consumers.

Not to be deterred, however, several large software developers and sellers began introducing the tenets of UCITA on a state-by-state basis. Their arguments for passage have generally been economic: the state will benefit if software developers and producers are able to control their products and benefit financially. Opponents, however, point out that the evidence that such a law really would promote substantive economic growth is very weak. In addition, they argued that the Copyright Act is adaptable and applicable to electronic products, and, with the Digital Millennium Copyright Act and the No Electronic Theft Act, there is no need for additional regulation in this area. To date, UCITA has been passed in Maryland and Virginia. A coalition of libraries, industry, and businesses was formed to resist its passage in other states, and the library community remains vigilant.

2. Digital Millennium Copyright Act

DMCA, signed into law on October 28, 1998, was designed to make copyright protections more consistent around the world. Section 1201 of the DMCA provides protections against circumventions of technological measures of copyright owners to protect their materials. Section 1202 protects copyrighted management information systems. DMCA prevents both unauthorized access to a copyrighted work and unauthorized copying. The manufacture, sale, or distribution of devices or services that would circumvent these copyright protections is unlawful. These provisions effectively prevent the piracy of copyrighted material and prohibit the dissemination of information that might help others violate copyright restrictions.

Although the act does provide some exemptions for law enforcement and for libraries under very limited conditions (U.S. Copyright Office 1998), DMCA has significant implications for librarians, scientific researchers, and other academics. It appears to favor information owners over users (Adler 2001) and there are some substantial negative consequences.

- Making a single copy of an article is a common practice in libraries and other educational agencies and is protected under fair use provisions. Yet this type of copying might be impossible because of software protections on electronic products. If a library should attempt to disable the copyright protections, it would violate the DMCA. These technological protections will present serious barriers to libraries' efforts to disseminate new knowledge.

- Some large corporations have used the law to hinder competitors who, by breaking computer protection codes, were able to engineer products that could be used with the corporation's product. This form of reverse engineering is generally lawful, but the ability to bring lawsuits under the DMCA creates a burdensome expense to smaller companies. The end result might be a reduction of marketplace innovations. This issue was highlighted in 2009 when some independent software developers created unauthorized applications for the Apple iPhone that required modifying the iPhone software. Apple argued in a statement to the U.S. Copyright Office that this was a violation of the DMCA (Kane 2009).

- Concern about civil and criminal liability for disseminating information on copyright protection devices has led researchers and others to delimit both their investigations of copyright protection systems and their publications of research on current security protocols. The result is a serious erosion of research related to encryption technologies and a stifling of innovation.

3. The Technology, Education, and Copyright Harmonization Act

Section 110(1) of the Copyright Act extended to educators the right to display and perform others' works in the classroom. This right applied to any work, regardless of the medium. However, when a remote classroom was linked through a distance education program, the law's generous terms shrank dramatically (Section 110[2]). These severe limitations on what could be performed in distance education prompted Congress in 1998 to ask the Copyright Office to suggest how to facilitate the use of digital technologies in distance education. The Copyright Office recommended significant changes, which were incorporated into a bill passed in November 2002.

The TEACH Act expanded the scope of educators' rights to perform and display works and to make the copies integral to distance education. However, significant inequities remained between face-to-face teaching and distance education. For example, an educator could show or perform any work related to the curriculum, regardless of the medium, face to face in the classroom—still images and music of every kind, as well as movies; there were no limits and no permission required. Under 110(2), however, even as revised and expanded, the same educator would have to limit what could be shown to distant students. In particular, only "reasonable and limited portions" of audiovisual works and dramatic musical works could be shown. In addition, the act dealt only with materials provided as part of "mediated instructional activities"; that is, materials that an instructor used or played in a classroom. It does not cover digital dissemination of supplemental reading materials.

The traditional concept of fair use remains under consideration (Harper 2002). Overall, the act liberalized the opportunities to use and distribute copyrighted material but also set substantive restrictions. It also required educational institutions to take a more active role in controlling access and developing and enforcing the necessary copyright policies. As Crews (2002) observed:

> Much of the law is built around permitting uses of copyright works in the context of "mediated instructional activities" that are akin in many respects to the conduct of traditional classroom sessions. The law anticipates that students will access each "session" within a prescribed time period and will not necessarily be able to store the materials or review them later in the academic term; faculty will be able to include copyrighted materials, but usually only in portions or under conditions that are analogous to conventional teaching and lecture formats. (p. 3)

The pertinent provisions of the TEACH Act include the following: only accredited, nonprofit institutions are included; an institution must develop and enforce appropriate copyright policies; the institution must provide information on copyright responsibilities to faculty, students, and staff; special notification must be provided to students regarding copyright protections; and only enrolled students may receive copyrighted materials. This last point places special responsibilities on the technology officers of an educational institution to ensure that access is limited only to appropriate parties and that the storage and dissemination of digital materials are available only to authenticated individuals and only for a designated period of time. Educational institutions must also ensure that DRM safeguards are protected from interference. Faculty can only disseminate materials that are an integral part of the course content, and they must control or supervise the dissemination of the material.

Librarians are not specifically mentioned in the act, but the role of libraries in assisting faculty and students in distance learning is substantial. Functions such as digital reserves and services that deliver electronic information to students are closely related concerns. Crews (2002) observed that librarians might be involved in a number of areas:

1. Active participation in developing copyright policies
2. Locating and preparing electronic materials for dissemination
3. Locating alternative materials when copyright restrictions prohibit some materials
4. Assisting others in the interpretation of fair use in the digital environment
5. Monitoring enforcement and interpretation of the TEACH Act

The Association of College and Research Libraries (ACRL) noted that TEACH did not, nor was it intended to, cover e-reserves. Consequently, ACRL (2003) issued a "Statement on Fair Use and Electronic Reserves" identifying important considerations when determining fair use for digitally stored documents. In effect, the ACRL policy interpreted the four basic criteria for fair use: the character of the use, the nature of the work, the amount used, and the effect of the use on the market in the e-reserve environment. For example, fair use of e-reserves is more likely to be appropriate when the use is nonprofit, when it serves the interests of faculty and students, where there is a clear relationship of the amount used to the course objectives, and when access is restricted to registered students and materials are unavailable after the course is completed. Taking another tack, the Association of American Publishers and several universities including Cornell, Hofstra, Marquette, and Syracuse, reached an independent agreement establishing fair use guidelines of their electronic reserves. The universities agreed to apply the four traditional factors in determining fair use and conceded that simply because something was published on the Internet did not free the university from obtaining permission from the publisher (Wiant 2008).

The relationship of e-reserves and copyright law remains unclear. Band (2008) suggested that insofar as instructors use digital material in a transformative manner, that is, repurposing it by integrating it into the course in a special way, recent court decisions on fair use would support them.

V. TELECOMMUNICATIONS LEGISLATION

A. Telecommunications Act of 1996/Communications Decency Act

The Telecommunications Act of 1996, signed by President Clinton on February 8, 1996, contained two provisions that directly affected libraries. First, the Snowe-Rockefeller-Exon-Kerry provision authorized reduced rates to access the Internet for libraries, schools, and health care providers. The E-rate—more precisely, the Schools and Libraries Universal Service Support Mechanism—provides discounts that enable most U.S. schools and libraries to obtain affordable access. Four service categories were funded: telecommunications services, Internet access, internal connections other than basic maintenance, and basic maintenance of internal connections. Discounts ranged from 20 percent to 90 percent of the costs of these services, depending on the urban or rural status of the population served and its level of poverty. Eligible schools, school districts, and libraries could apply individually or as part of a consortium. The E-rate supported connectivity—the conduit or pipeline for communications; the school or library was responsible for providing the end-user equipment (computers, telephones, etc.), software, professional development, and other necessary elements. The Universal Service Administrative Company administers the program under the direction of the FCC. Disbursements to schools and libraries in funding year 2009 were in excess of the annual $2.25 billion cap (Universal Service Administrative Company 2009).

The second provision, the Communications Decency Act (CDA), subjected a person who knowingly transmitted or displayed materials that might be construed as indecent to minors, to fines and criminal penalties. Indecency was construed very broadly to include words as well as images. This provision was challenged by the ACLU, the ALA, and other organizations. The Supreme Court declared this section of the law unconstitutional and a violation of the First Amendment. Justice John Paul Stevens, writing for the majority of the Court, noted that

> the CDA lacks the precision that the First Amendment requires when a statute regulates the content of speech.... As a matter of constitutional tradition, in the absence of evidence to the contrary, we presume that governmental regulation of the content of speech is more likely to interfere with the free exchange of ideas than to encourage it. The interest in encouraging freedom of expression in a democratic society outweighs any theoretical but unproven benefit of censorship. (*Janet Reno v. American Civil Liberties Union et al.* 1997)

B. Child Online Protection Act

The Supreme Court ruling on the CDA delayed, but did not deter, Congress from attempting to control content on the Internet that it deemed inappropriate. In 1998, it passed the Child Online Privacy Protection Act. In part, the act stated:

> Whoever knowingly and with knowledge of the character of the material, in interstate or foreign commerce by means of the World Wide Web, makes any communication for commercial purposes that is available to any minor and that includes any material that is harmful to minors shall be fined not more than $50,000, imprisoned not more than 6 months, or both. (Section 231)

The law attempted to restrict the viewing of sexually explicit or other adult materials to adults only by requiring commercial distributors to obtain credit card certifications and adult access codes or pin numbers. The law was again challenged on constitutional grounds. The federal district court determined that the law was unconstitutional and issued a permanent injunction against its enforcement. Eventually, the Supreme Court heard the case and sent the case back. As of 2009, the law remained unconstitutional and unenforced.

C. Children's Internet Protection Act

The Children's Internet Protection Act (CIPA) was enacted by Congress to address concerns about access to offensive content over the Internet on school and library computers. In early 2001, the FCC issued rules implementing CIPA for schools and libraries receiving E-rate discounts. CIPA imposed the following requirements:

- Schools and libraries may not receive the discounts offered by the E-rate program unless they certify that they have an Internet safety policy and technology protection measures in place. An Internet safety policy must include technology protection measures on computers that are available for use by minors that block or filter Internet access to pictures that are: (a) obscene, (b) child pornography, or (c) harmful to minors.

- Schools and libraries must also certify that they educate minors about appropriate online behavior, including cyber bullying awareness and response, and using social networking sites and chat rooms.

- Schools were also required to adopt and enforce a policy to monitor online activities of minors.

A complementary piece of legislation, the Neighborhood Children's Internet Protection Act (NCIPA), was passed at the same time as CIPA. NCIPA provisions required the Internet safety policy to address the following five components:

1. Access by minors to inappropriate matter on the Internet and Web
2. The safety and security of minors when using e-mail, chat rooms, and other forms of direct electronic communications (including instant messaging)
3. Unauthorized access, including so-called hacking and other unlawful activities by minors online
4. Unauthorized disclosure, use, and dissemination of personal identification information regarding minors
5. Measures designed to restrict minors' access to materials harmful to minors (not just visual depictions) (E-Rate Central, 2009)

Schools and libraries were required to certify that their safety policies and technology were in place before receiving E-rate funding. CIPA did not affect E-rate funding for schools and libraries receiving discounts only for telecommunications, such as telephone service. An authorized person could disable the blocking or filtering measures during any use by an adult to enable access for bona fide research or other lawful purposes. CIPA did not require the tracking of Internet use by minors or adults

In 2002, responding to First Amendment concerns, the ACLU, ALA, and other organizations challenged CIPA on constitutional grounds, focusing on the fact that filters are imperfect tools for at least two reasons. First, filters block constitutionally protected sites as well as those that might be considered obscene. Second, filters block sites that might be considered obscene for young people but not adults, thus reducing Internet access to only materials available to children. Although a federal district court agreed that the CIPA provisions for filtering were unconstitutional, on June 23, 2003, the Supreme Court reversed the federal district court decision in a 5–4 vote. The majority, recognizing a compelling state interest in protecting young people from inappropriate materials, held that CIPA did not impose an unconstitutional condition on libraries, and that Congress has broad powers to define limits on how its funds might be used. In fact, the Court held that Congress, in making such limitations, was actually aiding the selection activities of libraries in their "traditional role of obtaining materials of requisite and appropriate quality for educational and informational purposes" (*United States et al. v. American Library Association* 2002, p. 3). It is notable, however, that the Supreme Court did not deny that filters remove constitutionally protected speech as well as obscenity, but the majority argued that the filters could easily be removed at the request of an adult. The Court left open the possibility of a subsequent challenge if libraries were unable to disable filters easily or if Internet access to constitutionally protected speech was otherwise burdened in a substantial way. This decision raised numerous intellectual freedom concerns for libraries:

- Although the intent of CIPA was to block materials deemed harmful to minors, the filters inevitably block sites that contain material that is constitutionally protected when viewed by adults, a concept known as "overblocking." The blocking of constitutionally protected speech is anathema to the ALA Library Bill of Rights.

- The Supreme Court did not deny that filters overblock; rather, the justices argued that as long as a filter could easily be disabled, there was little or no constitutional problem. The assumption that filters can easily be disabled does not diminish the intellectual freedom issue—the need to request that a filter be disabled places a barrier between the patron and the information. Such barriers are specifically proscribed in the ALA document "Restricting Access to Library Materials." Although a request to disable a filter might be innocent, many patrons would be reluctant to make such a request because it might imply that they wish to see sexual or otherwise sensitive material. This situation is analogous to the time when individuals had to ask a librarian for sexual materials that were stored in closed stacks.

- Filters block access to speech that is constitutionally protected, even for minors. The Supreme Court was silent on the rights of minors and instead emphasized the compelling interest of the state to protect them from harmful materials. The ALA Library Bill of Rights affirms that age is not to be considered when access to information is involved. There is substantial evidence that filters block sites that are totally unrelated to harmful material and the blocking of sites that are constitutionally protected for minors is a violation of our profession's intellectual freedom principles.

Although the Supreme Court's ruling on CIPA was decided by a narrow margin, it might still encourage states to pass new laws modeled on CIPA that might be written even more broadly and further erode the intellectual freedom rights of library users.

VI. EDUCATION LEGISLATION

A. Elementary and Secondary Education Act of 1965, Improving America's Schools Act of 1994, and the No Child Left Behind Act of 2001

The Elementary and Secondary Education Act of 1965 (ESEA) was created to supplement state and local funding to improve the quality of education in both public and private schools. Much of the act was devoted to supporting programs for low-income children (Title I) or those with special needs. Title II was designed to enhance school library collections. At the time the law was passed, nearly one-third of the nation's students attended schools without libraries. ESEA helped address this problem by providing monies for textbooks, library resources including monographs, periodicals, and AV materials; staff training and development; and media demonstration programs, special education programs, programming for at-risk children, materials for bilingual studies, and support for the acquisition of materials in areas of social problems (Krettek 1975).

In 1994, ESEA was reauthorized as the Improving America's Schools Act. It contained a variety of provisions focused on issues such as equal access to a quality education, especially for children in poverty; parental participation in schooling; and professional development programs for teachers, administrators, and other school staff (U.S. Department of Education 1994).

On June 8, 2002, the law was reauthorized as the No Child Left Behind Act (NCLB), a sweeping revision of the ESEA that redefined the role of the federal government in K–12 education. Then Secretary of Education, Margaret Spellings noted:

> The law...signaled a fundamental and common-sense change to American education. Academic standards would be set by states, schools would be held accountable for results, and the federal government would support both with increased resources and flexibility. (U.S. Department of Education 2007)

According to the U.S. Department of Education (2010), NCLB is based on four pillars: stronger accountability for results, more freedom for states and communities, proven education methods, and more choices for parents.

> Under NCLB, states must work to insure that all students, including those who are disadvantaged, achieve academic proficiency. Parents and communities receive annual state and school district report cards about progress. Schools that do not make progress must provide supplemental services, such as free tutoring or after-school assistance; take corrective actions; and, if still not making adequate yearly progress after five years, make dramatic changes to the way the school is run.
>
> NCLB allows increased flexibility in how states and schools use federal education funds. For example, it is possible for most school districts to transfer up to 50 percent of the total federal formula grant funds they receive into one of those programs, or to their Title I program, without separate approval. This allows districts to use funds for their particular needs, such as hiring new teachers, increasing teacher pay, and improving teacher training and professional development.
>
> NCLB puts emphasis on determining which educational programs and practices have been proven effective through rigorous scientific research. Federal funding is targeted to support those programs and teaching methods. In reading, NCLB supports scientifically based instruction programs in the early grades under the Reading First program and in preschool under the Early Reading First program.
>
> Parents of children in low-performing schools (schools that do not meet state standards for at least two consecutive years) can transfer their children to a better-performing public school, including a public charter school, within their district. The district must provide transportation, using Title I funds if necessary. Students from low-income families in schools that fail to meet state standards for at least three years are eligible to receive supplemental educational services, including tutoring, after-school services, and summer school. (U.S. Department of Education 2010)

Because NCLB emphasized reading, student achievement, and testing, it highlighted not only the critical role of teachers, but also that of school library media specialists. Whelan (2004) described NCLB as a golden opportunity and recommended that school librarians become experts on their state curriculum standards and then partner with classroom teachers to meet those standards. Given the strong emphasis on reading, Whelan argued that librarians could also obtain funding for library materials. If school library media specialists can demonstrate that they help meet their state curricular standards, they can become substantial beneficiaries of the act.

B. Higher Education Act of 1965/1992/1998/2008

The Higher Education Act of 1965 (HEA) supported colleges and universities. It focused on four areas: improving student financial assistance; supporting services and activities that would help students, especially disadvantaged students, to graduate from high school, enter a postsecondary institution, and complete its program; providing aid to academic institutions; and improving K–12 teacher training at a postsecondary institution (Almanac of Policy Issues 2003). HEA was reauthorized in 1986, 1992, 1998, and 2008. The current law (PL 110-315) was enacted on August 14, 2008, and includes titles and sections dealing with a variety of issues in higher education including:

- Improving teacher quality through grants for professional development coupled with increased accountability and evaluation of teachers
- Promoting international education
- Improving financial aid and student assistance processes
- Monitoring tuition costs and the total costs of a higher education

In addition, the act has specific provisions regarding peer-to-peer file sharing and protection of student speech and association rights. Recent amendments encourage the development of distance learning programs at the postsecondary level and create new reporting requirements for academic institutions on the costs of higher education.

VII. LIBRARY LEGISLATION

A. The Library of Congress

The Library of Congress (LC) was established in 1800 when President John Adams signed a bill transferring the seat of government from Philadelphia to the new capital city of Washington. The legislation also created a reference library for Congress; the closest thing the United States has to a national library (especially in conjunction with the National Library of Medicine, the National Agricultural Library, and the National Archives). Its mission is "to make its resources available and useful to the Congress and the American people and to sustain and preserve a universal collection of knowledge and creativity for future generations" (LC 2009). LC is one of the great repositories of the world, with more than 141 million items, an operating budget exceeding $600 million, and staff of more than 3,600 individuals. The use and collections of the LC for 2008 are summarized in Figure 8.1.

The programs funded by Congress and implemented by the LC are many and varied. Historically, some of its programs have had a profound influence on librarianship. For example, as developers of MARC, LC transformed and made uniform the bibliographic record, which in turn greatly accelerated the development of bibliographic utilities. Similarly, the Copyright Office which is part of the

Figure 8.1. Library of Congress Year 2008 at a Glance

Welcomed more than 1.6 million on-site visitors.

Provided reference services to 545,084 individuals in person, by telephone, and through written and electronic correspondence.

Total of 141,847,810 items in the collections, including:

- 21,218,408 cataloged books in the Library of Congress classification system
- 11,599,606 books in large type and raised characters, incunabula (books printed before 1501), monographs and serials, music, bound newspapers, pamphlets, technical reports, and other printed material
- 109,029,796 items in the nonclassified (special) collections, including:
  - o 3,005,028 audio materials, such as discs, tapes, talking books, and other recorded formats
  - o 62,778,118 total manuscripts
  - o 5,357,385 maps
  - o 16,086,572 microforms
  - o 5,674,956 pieces of sheet music
  - o 14,388,175 visual materials, including:
    - 1,207,776 moving images
    - 12,536,764 photographs
    - 98,288 posters
    - 545,347 prints and drawings

Circulated nearly 22 million disc, cassette, and Braille items to more than 500,000 blind and physically handicapped patrons.

Registered 232,907 claims to copyright.

Completed 871,287 research assignments for the Congress through the Congressional Research Service.

Prepared 1,529 legal research reports for Congress and other federal agencies through the Law Library.

Recorded more than 85 million visits and 610 million page-views on the Library's Web site. At year's end, the Library's American Memory online historical collections contained 15.3 million digital files.

Employed a permanent staff of 3,637 employees.

Operated with a total fiscal 2008 appropriation of $613,496,414, including authority to spend $50,447,565 in receipts.

Source: "About the Library." Available: www.loc.gov/about/generalinfo.html#2007_at_a_glance (last updated May 2009).

Library of Congress, requires that publishers deposit two copies of each item published. Although LC is not required to retain material sent to it, the law created a central repository for much of the material printed in the United States. The historical and research implications are manifest.

The LC's highest priority is service to Congress through its Congressional Research Service (CRS), which was created in 1914 under President Woodrow Wilson. CRS "serves as a shared staff to congressional committees and Members of Congress" (LC 2009). The reports of CRS are intended to be confidential, authoritative, objective, and nonpartisan. CRS has nearly 700 employees, including 450 analysts, attorneys, information professionals, and experts from a variety of disciplines.

LC provides services to the public through its reading rooms and Web site. In cooperation with the Online Computer Library Center (OCLC), it provides an online reference service called Question-Point, which is a collaborative network of reference librarians throughout the United States, available twenty-four hours a day. A less immediate online reference service, the Ask a Librarian Service, provides responses to queries submitted online within five business days. It also provides limited services to the general citizenry; for example, it provides materials to the blind and physically handicapped.

LC has also placed considerable emphasis on U.S. history through its American Memory Project. Originally begun as a CD-ROM project in 1990, the American Memory Project is now an online resource created by LC as part of the National Digital Library Program. The purpose of the project is to provide "free and open access through the Internet to written and spoken words, sound recordings, still and moving images, prints, maps, and sheet music that document the American experience" (LC 2009). The project now involves a partnership with a variety of collecting institutions, includes primary source and archival materials. These collections represent a critical contribution to a national digital library. Photographs and documents can be searched full text by keyword. To date, over 15 million items have been scanned, representing access to more than 100 thematic historical collections. In a related area, LC has also partnered with a variety of organizations including the Pew Internet and American Life Project to create the September 11 Web Archive. The archive is intended to "identify and preserve expressions on the Web by individuals, organizations, and the press about the historic attack" (Marcum 2007, p. 90). More than 30,000 Web sites have been preserved and 2,300 Web resources cataloged.

A related program is the National Digital Information Infrastructure and Preservation Program (NDIIPP). For some time LC recognized that digital technologies produce information that is often impermanent and fragile but nonetheless of significant historical value. Consequently, LC has been aggressive in preserving it. Created in 2000 by Congress with approximately $100 million in funding, NDIIPP's mission is to "develop a national strategy to collect, archive and preserve the burgeoning amounts of digital content, especially materials that are created only in digital formats, for current and future generations" (LC 2009). Currently, NDIIPP focuses on three areas:

> (1) Capturing, preserving, and making available significant digital content [including]...geospatial information, web sites, audio visual productions, images and text, and materials related to critical public policy issues.
> (2) Building and strengthening a network of partners. The NDIIPP national network currently has more than 130 partners drawn from federal agencies, state and local governments, academic, professional and nonprofit organizations, and commercial entities.
> (3) Developing a technical infrastructure of tools and services. (LC 2009)

The NDIIPP has also been exploring the relationship of the current Copyright Act to the preservation and scholarly use of digital materials in libraries and archives. In April 2005, the NDIIPP convened a nineteen-member committee of experts in libraries, archives, museums, and the publishing industry, known as the Section 108 Study Group, to explore how to interpret the law in the light of digitally produced documents and information. Section 108 of the Copyright Act (as noted above) refers to a section known as the "library exception." It states in part:

> Section 108 Limitations on exclusive rights: Reproduction by libraries and archives
>
> > (A) Except as otherwise provided in this title...it is not an infringement of copyright for a library or archives...to reproduce no more than one copy or phonorecord of a work...or to distribute such copy or phonorecord under the conditions specified by this section.

The conditions stipulated that reproduction and distribution must be for noncommercial purposes; that the copying institution was open to the public and served outside researchers; and that the distributed work included a copyright notice. In addition, the right to reproduce and distribute applied to only three copies that must be available only on the premises. For preservation purposes, the original item must also be in a deteriorated state or lost, and a replacement not available at a fair price (Wiant 2008). Obviously, the implications are significant, particularly in the digital environment. For example, if an item must be shared within the library, the flexibility of digital documents is greatly diminished and the ability to serve remote patrons removed. Similarly, as Wiant (2008) noted:

> Because libraries devote significant resources and expertise to developing a collection of electronic information and often that information is unstable and subject to risks of corruption and loss, libraries and archives believe that they should be able to preserve at-risk portions of the collection, both print and electronic. Currently, Section 108 is too limiting. Often by the time libraries are aware of damage to electronic information, it's too late to preserve it. (p. 47)

The committee submitted its report in March 2008 with suggestions for increasing flexibility in relation to the preservation and use of digital copies (U.S. Copyright Office 2008). It is hoped that the current act will be appropriately amended to reduce some of the constraints libraries and archives experience and increase access to academic and scholars throughout the world.

B. The Federal Depository Library Program

The FDLP makes substantial information available to the citizenry by providing approximately 1,250 libraries with government documents. About half of these libraries are academic and 20 percent are public, with the remaining consisting of community colleges and state, federal, and special libraries. Some receive more complete sets of these documents than others. Nonetheless, the program makes vast quantities of information available. For example, in December 2009 more than 100,000 copies of materials were distributed (FDLP 2010). Recent attempts to reduce funding for this program have concerned many people. In addition, as mentioned previously, with the movement toward privatization of government information, such materials might not find their way to depository libraries in the future, which would result in a significant reduction of information available to the citizenry.

C. The Library Services Act and the Library Services and Construction Act

Since 1956 the federal government has passed legislation to foster improved library services in the United States. Originally this legislation was meant to redress the considerable inequalities evident in cities compared to rural areas. The original Library Services Act funneled monies through state library agencies to address the needs of public libraries serving fewer than 10,000 people. This restriction was removed in 1964 and the legislation's name was changed to the Library Services and Construction Act (LSCA). Administered by the Department of Education, LSCA was the largest single provider of federal assistance to libraries for many years (Molz 1990). As the title change reflected, the funding was expanded to include not only improving library services, but also library construction. Over the years, other titles (sections) were added: Title I, funding for public library services; Title II, funding for construction; Title III, funding for interlibrary cooperation; Title IV, services for Indian tribes; Title V, foreign-language materials acquisition; and Title VI, library literacy programs.

D. The Museum and Library Service Act of 1996 and the Library Services and Technology Act

President Clinton signed the Museum and Library Services Act (MLSA) of 1996, which established the Institute of Museum and Library Services (IMLS) within the

National Foundation on the Arts and Humanities. The new law repealed LSCA. The new agency combined the Institute of Museum Services, which had been in existence since 1976, and the Library Programs Office, which had been part of the Department of Education since 1956. IMLS operates through two offices: the Office of Library Services and the Office of Museum Services. The LSTA, a subtitle of MLSA, directed the institute to support library services and technology, with an emphasis on access and literacy programs for underserved communities. LSTA authorized appropriations for grants to states for the purpose of improving information access through technology and information empowerment through special services. It also authorized other federal library grant programs, including grants to Indian tribes, and a program of national leadership and evaluation activities (IMLS, 2009). MLSA specified the National Commission on Libraries and Information Science to advise the Office of Library Services. The Museum Services Act, the law's other subtitle, continued to authorize grants to museums to increase and improve museum services.

The MLSA was reauthorized in 2003 and IMLS continues to emphasize lifelong learning by providing grants to 17,500 museums and 123,000 libraries throughout the United States. President Obama requested over $265 million for libraries for fiscal year 2010 (IMLS 2009). IMLS encourages leadership and innovation in libraries and museums by emphasizing their education role. IMLS provides grants to

---

Current Lifelong Learning Initiatives

- **21st Century Skills**: The institute's Museums, Libraries, and 21st Century Skills initiative underscores the critical role our nation's museums and libraries play in helping citizens build such twenty-first-century skills as information, communications and technology literacy, critical thinking, problem solving, creativity, civic literacy, and global awareness.

- **Connection to Collections**: a national initiative to raise public awareness of the importance of caring for our treasures, and to underscore the fact that these collections are essential to the American story.

- **Engaging America's Youth** looks at the contributions IMLS grants have made to positive outcomes for youth aged nine to nineteen, with four key goals: to examine what works, to share best practices, to encourage effective programming, and to build bridges with policymakers.

- **The International Strategic Partnership Initiative** is intended to strengthen cross-cultural connections between U.S. museums and libraries and their global counterparts.

- **The National Medal** honors outstanding institutions that make significant and exceptional contributions to their communities. Selected institutions demonstrate extraordinary and innovative approaches to public service, exceeding the expected levels of community outreach.

- **The WebWise Conference** annually brings together representatives of museums, libraries, archives, systems science, education, and other fields interested in the future of high-quality online content for inquiry and learning.

(*Source:* IMLS 2009.)

all types of libraries, with an aim toward improving access to information, especially through technology, promoting equal access, and assisting the underserved. IMLS also sponsors research and convenes forums and conferences that emphasize best practices.

E. National Commission on Libraries and Information Science Act of 1970 (P.L. 94-345)

The National Commission on Libraries and Information Science Act created the U.S. National Commission on Libraries and Information Science (NCLIS), a nonpartisan, independent agency charged by Congress to assess continuously the problems that face libraries and to find ways to harness their potential. According to NCLIS (2008), the commission's primary historical statutory functions were to:

- Discover the needs of U.S. residents for library and information services
- Translate those needs into recommended national policy to meet the needs of Americans for library and information services
- Advise the president, the Congress, state and local governments, and others on implementation of national policy

The commission was authorized to conduct studies, appraise the state of library resources and services and evaluate their effectiveness, develop national plans for library services, and promote research and development activities that would improve the nation's libraries. It was responsible for sponsoring influential major conferences involving multiple national constituencies on library services. The commission's activities and concerns were quite varied including the creation, dissemination, and access to government information on the part of the public, particularly information in electronic form; the role of school library media centers in educational achievement and literacy, and advocacy for more certified media specialists; mass digitization and its implications for the Copyright Act; and advocacy for health information distribution centers. Following September 11, 2001, the commission also examined the potential role that libraries could play after a terrorist attack or natural disaster.

In addition, the commission developed a Library Statistics Program in cooperation with the National Center for Education Statistics (NCES), the IMLS, and NISO. The program encouraged national collection of library data and helped develop models of data collection, particularly in the area of network statistics and performance measures for public libraries.

Because national information policy was a major focus of the commission, it advocated for the value of public information as a foundation for a free society. Public information was defined by NCLIS as "information created, compiled and/or maintained by the Federal Government." In 1990, the commission promulgated eight principles of public information that it hoped would serve as a foundation for information policy in the federal government:

1. The public has a right of access to public information.
2. The Federal Government should guarantee the integrity and preservation of public information, regardless of its format.
3. The Federal Government should guarantee the dissemination, reproduction, and redistribution of public information.
4. The Federal Government should safeguard the privacy of persons who use or request information, as well as persons about whom information exists in government records.
5. The Federal Government should ensure a wide diversity of sources of access, private as well as governmental, to public information.
6. The Federal Government should not allow costs to obstruct the people's access to public information.
7. The Federal Government should ensure that information about government information is easily available and in a single index accessible in a variety of formats.
8. The Federal Government should guarantee the public's access to public information, regardless of where they live and work, through national networks and programs like the Depository Library Program. (NCLIS 2008, p. 21)

Pursuant to instructions in House Report 110-231 and Senate Report 110-107, the commission was integrated into the IMLS.

VIII. OTHER LEGISLATION: THE AMERICAN RECOVERY AND REINVESTMENT ACT OF 2009

The American Recovery and Reinvestment Act of 2009 was signed into law on February 13, 2009, in response to considerable economic dislocations during the latter half of 2008. By February 2009, approximately 3.6 million jobs had been lost since the beginning of the recession in December 2007. The legislation was intended to improve the job market, fund substantial improvements in the national transportation and communication infrastructure, improve educational systems, invest in efforts to develop alternative energy resources, and provide additional support for scientific and technological innovation and research. The ALA (2009a) identified several of the act's programs from which libraries might benefit:

1. $7.2 billion for broadband support: This included $200 million in grants for increasing computer access in public and community college libraries. Additional funding was available for broadband outreach to vulnerable populations.

2. $53.6 billion for the State Fiscal Stabilization Fund: Included substantial funds earmarked for education including funding for critical needs in public and school libraries.

3. $120 million for the Senior Community Service Employment Program: Included funding for community service jobs in nonprofit agencies including public libraries.

4. $130 million for the rural Community Facilities Program: Included funding to assist in the development of critical community facilities for public use including libraries.

IX. SUMMARY

As the value of information increases, more and more stakeholders attempt to shape information policies to serve their needs. Because LIS professionals generally serve the public interest, value service rather than profit, and uphold fundamental democratic principles, they serve as critical advocates for an open, free exchange of ideas and information. A long legislative tradition has supported this role. But the growth of electronic technologies has created competitors—many more interested in gain than in universal access. This might be both just and natural in an entrepreneurial society, but it makes it doubly important that LIS professionals have a place in the information policy debate. LIS professionals must actively monitor the information policy climate and aggressively make the case for their values.

REFERENCES

Adams, Helen R., Robert F. Bocher, Carol A. Gordon, and Elizabeth Barry-Kessler. 2005. *Privacy in the 21st Century*. Westport, CT: Libraries Unlimited.

Adler, Prudence. 2001. "Copyright and Intellectual Property Legislation and Related Activities: New Challenges for Libraries." In *Impact of Digital Technology on Library Collections and Resource Sharing*. Edited by Sul H. Lee. Binghamton, NY: Haworth Press, 107–118.

Agnew, Grace, and Mairead Martin. 2003. "Digital Rights Management: Why Libraries Should Be Major Players." In *The Bowker Annual: Library and Book Trade Almanac*. 48th ed. Edited by Dave Bogart. Medford, NJ: Information Today, 267–278.

Almanac of Policy Issues. 2003. "Higher Education Act: Reauthorization Status and Issues." Available: www.policyalmanac.org/education/archive/crs_higher_education.shtml (accessed February 5, 2010).

American Library Association. 1991. *Less Access to Less Information by and about the U.S. Government: XVII:A 1991 Chronology: June–December*. Washington, DC: ALA.

———. 2003a. "Homeland Security Agents Pull Ohio Libraries' Haz-Mat Documents." American Libraries. Available: www.ala.org/ala/alonline/currentnews/newsarchive/2003/april2003/homelandsecurity.htm (accessed February 5, 2010).

———. 2003b. *Restrictions on Access to Government Information (RAGI) Report*. Chicago: ALA.

———. 2006. "Resolution Affirming 'Network Neutrality.'" Chicago: ALA.

———. 2007. "E-government 2.0: Improving Innovation, Collaboration and Access." Available: www.ala.org/ala/aboutala/offices/wo/woissues/governmentinfo/egovernment/ALAE-Government Statem.pdf (accessed February 7, 2010).

———. 2009a. "American Recovery and Reinvestment Act 101." Available: www.bespacific .com/ mt/archives/020773.html (accessed February 7, 2010).

———. 2009b. *The U.S.A. PATRIOT Act*. Chicago: ALA. Available: www.ala.org/ala/issues advocacy/advocacy/federalegislation/theusapatriotact/index.cfm (accessed March 5, 2009).

———. 2010. "Network Neutrality." Chicago: ALA. Available: www.ala.org/ala/issuesadvocacy/ telecom/netneutrality/index.cfm (accessed February 7, 2010).

Association of College and Research Libraries. 2003. "Statement on Fair Use and Electronic Reserves." November. Available: www.ala.org/ala/mgrps/divs/acrl/publications/white papers/statementfair.cfm (accessed February 7, 2010).

Association of Research Libraries. 1997a. "Conference on Fair Use Joint Statement." Available: www.arl.org/pp/ppcopyright/copyresources/confu.shtml (accessed Febraruy 7, 2010).

———. 1997b. "Principles for Licensing Electronic Resources." Available: www.arl.org/sc/ marketplace/license/licprinciples.shtml (accessed March 19, 2010).

Austin, Brice. 2004. "Should There Be 'Privilege' in the Relationship between Reference Librarian and Patron?" *Reference Librarian* 42: 301–311.

Bailey, Charles W. Jr. 2006. "Strong Copyright + DRM + Weak Net Neutrality = Digital Dystopia?" *Information Technology and Libraries* 25 (September): 116–127.

Band, Jonathan. 2008. "Educational Fair Use Today." In *Library and Book Trade Almanac: The Bowker Annual, 2008*. 53rd ed. Edited by Dave Bogart. Medford, NJ: Information Today.

Bertot, John Carlo, Paul T. Jaeger, Lesley A. Langa, and Charles R. McClure. 2006a. "Drafted: I Want You to Deliver E-government." *Library Journal* 131 (August 1): 34–37. Available: www.libraryjournal.com/index.asp?layout=articlePrint&articleID=CA6359866 (accessed April 23, 2009).

———. 2006b. "Public Access Computing and Internet Access in Public Libraries: The Role of Public Libraries in E-government and Emergency Situations." *First Monday* 11 (September 4). Available: www.uic.edu/htbin/cgiwrap/bin/ojs/index.php/fm/rt/printer Friendly/1392/1313/ (accessed February 5, 2010).

Bertot, John Carlo, Paul T. Jaeger, and Charles R. McClure. 2008. "Citizen-Centered E-government Services: Benefits, Costs, and Research Needs." Proceedings of the 9th Annual International Digital Government Research Conference, Montreal, Canada, May 18–21, 2008, pp. 137–142.

Blum, Oliver. 1997. "The New WIPO Treaties on Copyright and Performers' and Phonogram Producers' Rights." Available: www.educause.edu/Resources/ThenewWIPOTreatieson Copyrighta/153941 (accessed February 7, 2010).

Bortnick, Jane. 1985. "National and International Information Policy." *Journal of the American Society for Information Science* 36: 164–168.

Burger, Robert H. 1993. *Information Policy: A Framework for Evaluation and Policy Research*. Norwood, NJ: Ablex.

Center for Democracy and Technology. 2006. *Preserving the Essential Internet*. June. Available: www.cat.org/speech/200660620neutrality/pdf (accessed February 6, 2010).

Coalition of Journalists for Open Government. 2009. "The Card Memo." Available: www.cjog.net/ background_the_card_memo.html (accessed August 24, 2009).

Cochran, Wendell, and Coral Davenport. 2006. "'Executive Privilege' Used by More Federal Agencies to Withhold Information." *The IRE Journal* 29 (October): 9–10.

Communications Act of 1934, 47U.S.C., Section 202(a).

CONTU (National Commission on New Technological Uses of Copyrighted Works). 1978. *Final Report*. July 31, 1978. Washington, DC: GPO.

Creative Commons. 2009. "About Licenses." Available: http://creativecommons.org/about/history (accessed March 18, 2009).

Crews, Kenneth D. 2002. "New Copyright Law for Distance Education: The Meaning and Importance of the TEACH Act." Available: www.ala.org/Template.cfm?Section=Distance_Education_and_the_TEACH-Act&Template=contentManagement/ContentDisplay.cfm &Content ID=25939#newc. (accessed February 7, 2010).

Critical Infrastructure Protection Board. 2003. *National Strategy to Secure Cyberspace*. Washington, DC: White House.

DOI Foundation. 2009. "Welcome to the DOI System." Available: www.doi.org (accessed August 27, 2009).

Dorman, David. 2002. "Open Source Software and the Intellectual Commons." *American Libraries* 33 (December): 51–54.

Doyle, Charles. 2005. *Libraries and the USA PATRIOT Act*. CRS Report for Congress. Updated July 6, 2005. Available: www.fas.org/sgp/crs/intel/RS21441.pdf (accessed August 25, 2009).

Educause. 2009. "Net Neutrality." Available: www.connect.educause.edu/term_view/Net% 2BNeutrality (accessed March 6, 2009).

E-Rate Central. 2009. "Internet Safety Policies and CIPA: An E-Rate Primer for Schools and Libraries." Available: www.e-ratecentral.com/CIPA/cipa_policy_primer.pdf (accessed August 27, 2009).

Estabrook, Leigh, and Lee Rainie. 2007. *Information Searches That Solve Problems*. Pew Internet and American Life Project. December 20, 2007.

Evergreen. 2009. "Growing Evergreen 2010 International Conference." Available: www.open-ils.org (accessed August 27, 2009).

"FBI Has Visited about 50 Libraries." 2003. Available: http://libraryjournal.com/article/CA302414.html (accessed February 7, 2010).

Federal Depository Library Program. 2010. "Library Services and Content Management Performance Metrics: Executive Summary: December 2009." Washington, DC: FDLP, 2010. Available: www.google.com/search?q=Library+Services+and+Content+Management+Performance+Metrics%3A+Executive+Summary%3A+December+2010&rls=com.microsoft: en-us:IE-SearchBox&ie=UTF-8&oe=UTF-8&sourceid=ie7&client=&rlz=1I7GGLL_en (accessed February 7, 2010).

Feinberg, Lotte. 2004. "FOIA, Federal Information Policy, and Information Availability in a Post-9/11 World." *Government Information Quarterly* 21: 439–460. Available: www.sciencedirect.com/science?_ob=ArticleURL&_udi=B6W4G-4DN9TWB-1&_user=

10&_coverDate=12%2F31%2F2004&_rdoc=1&_fmt=high&_orig=search&_sort=
d&_docanchor=&view=c&_searchStrId=1196870977&_rerunOrigin=google&_acct=C0
00050221&_version =1&_urlVersion=0&_userid=10&md5=69dde0c1100bc283437b
04869773d5bf (accessed February 7, 2010).

Gale Group. 1998. "Penumbra" *West's Encyclopedia of American Law*. Available: www
.answers.com/topic/penumbra (accessed December 10, 2009).

Gershwin Publishing Corp. v. Columbia Artists Management, Inc., 443F.2d 11 59, 1162 (2d Cir.
1971).

Gilroy, Angela A. 2006. *Net Neutrality: Background and Issues*. Washington, DC: Library of
Congress, Congressional Research Service, May 18, 2006.

Griswold v. Connecticut, 381 U.S. 479, 85 S. Ct. 1678, 14 L. Ed. 2d 510 (1965).

Hammitt, Harry. 2005. "Less Safe—The Dismantling of Public Information Systems after
9/11. *Social Science Computer Review* 23 (Winter): 429–438.

Harper, Georgia. 2002. "The TEACH Act Finally Becomes Law." Available: www.utsystem
.edu/ogc/intellectualproperty/teachact.htm (accessed February 6, 2010).

Horrigan, John B. 2009. "Home Broadband Adoption 2009." Pew Internet and American
Life Project, July. Available: www.pewinternet.org/~/media/Files/Reports/2009/Home-
Broadband-Adoption-2009.pdf (accessed June 25, 2009).

House Report. 1976. "House Report No. 94-1476, Copyright Act." In *United States Code:
Congressional and Administrative News. 94th Congress-Second Session 1976*. St. Paul,
MN: West, 5659–5823.

IMLS. 2009. "Institute of Museum and Library Services." Available: www.imls.gov/about/
services1996.shtm (accessed August 28, 2009).

Information Infrastructure Task Force. 1995. *Intellectual Property and the National Information
Infrastructure*. Washington, DC: IITF.

Jackson, Mary E. 1997. "CONFU Concludes; ARL Rejects Guidelines" Available: www
.umsl.edu/ services/summer/1997/copyright/confu.html (accessed February 7, 2010).

Jacobs, James A., James R. Jacobs, and Shinjoung Yeo. 2005. "Government Information in
the Digital Age: The Once and Future Federal Depository Library Program." *Journal of
Academic Librarianship* 31 (May): 198–208.

Jaeger, Paul T. 2008. "Building E-government into the Library and Information Science
Curriculum: The Future of Government Information and Services." *Journal of Education
for Library and Information Science* 49 (summer): 167–179.

Jaeger, Paul T., and Kenneth R. Fleischmann. 2007. "Public Libraries, Values, Trust, and
E-government." *Information Technology and Libraries* 26 (December): 34–43.

Jaeger, Paul T., Charles R. McClure, John Carlo Bertot, and John T. Snead. 2004. "The USA
PATRIOT Act, the Foreign Intelligence Surveillance Act, and Information Policy
Research in Libraries: Issues, Impacts, and Questions for Libraries and Researchers."
Library Quarterly 74: 99–121.

Janet Reno v. American Civil Liberties Union et al. 1997. "Supreme Court Opinion." Cited in
Citizen Internet Empowerment Coalition. Available: www.ciec.org/SC_appeal/opinion
.shtml (accessed February 5, 2010).

Jorgensen, Jan. 2006. "The Online Government Information Movement: Retracing the Route to
DigiGov Through the Federal Documents Collection." *Reference Librarian* 45: 139–162.

Kane, Yukari Iwatani. 2009. "Breaking Apple's Grip on the iPhone." *Wall Street Journal* (March 6): B1.

Krettek, Germaine. 1975. "Library Legislation, Federal." In *Encyclopedia of Library and Information Science*. Vol. 15. New York: Marcel Dekker, 337–354.

Krug, Judith. 2005. "Foreword." In *Privacy in the 21st Century*. By Helen R. Adams, Robert F. Bocher, Carol A. Gordon, and Elizabeth Barry-Kessler. Westport, CT: Libraries Unlimited, ix–x.

La Porte, Todd M. 2005. "Being Good and Doing Well: Organizational Openness and Government Effectiveness on the World Wide Web." *Bulletin of the American Society for Information Science and Technology* (February/March): 23–27.

Library of Congress. 2009. "About the Library." Available: www.loc.gov/about (accessed March 2, 2009).

Lipinski, Tomas A. 2005. "The Legal Landscape after *MGM v. Grokster*: Is It the Beginning of the End or the End of the Beginning?" *Bulletin of the American Society for Information Science and Technology* 32 (October/November). Available: www.asis.org/Bulletin/Oct-05/lipinski.html (accessed February 5, 2010).

Madden, Mary. 2009. "Online Video: 57% of Internet Users Have Watched NISO. Shared E-Resource Understanding (SERU)." Available: www.niso.org/workrooms/seru (accessed April 27, 2009).

Madison, James. 1973. "Letter to W.T. Barry, August 4, 1822." In *The Mind of the Founder: Sources of the Political Thought of James Madison*. Indianapolis: Brandeis, 437.

Marcum, Deanna B. 2007. "United States Library of Congress: Expanding in Three Directions." *Alexandria* 19: 83–93.

Mason, Marianne. 2008. "Providing Access to Electronic Government Information to Diverse Populations." In *Managing Electronic Government Information in Libraries: Issues and Practices*. Edited by Andrea M. Morrison. Chicago: ALA, 44–59.

Merriam-Webster's Collegiate Dictionary. 1996. Springfield, MA: Merriam-Webster, Inc.

Mickey, Bill. 2001. "Open Source and Libraries: An Interview with Dan Chudnov." *Online* (January). Available: www.onlinemag.net/OL2001/mickey1_01.html (accessed February 5, 2010).

Molz, R. Kathleen. 1990. *The Federal Roles in Support of Public Library Services: An Overview*. Chicago: ALA.

National Commission on Libraries and Information Science. 2008. *Meeting the Information Needs of the American People: Past Actions and Future Initiatives*. Washington, DC: NCLIS, March.

National Information Standards Organization. 2009. "Shared E-Resource Understanding (SERU)." Available: www.niso.org/workrooms/seru (accessed April 27, 2009).

Oder, Norman. 2008. "ALA: Computer Demand Increases." *Library Journal* 133 (September 15): 14–15.

Office of Homeland Security. 2002. *National Strategy for Homeland Security*. Washington, DC: White House.

Open Source Initiative. 2003. "Open Source Initiative." Available: www.opensource.org (accessed February 7, 2010).

OpenTheGovernment.org. 2007. "Secrecy Report Card 2007." Washington, DC: OpenThe Government. Available: www.openthegovernment.org/otg/SRC2007.pdf (accessed February 7, 2010).

Rainie, Lee. 2008. "Increased Use of Video-Sharing Sites." Pew Internet and American Life Project. Available: www.pewinternet.org/Reports/2008/Increased-Use-of-Videosharing-Sites.aspx (accessed February 5, 2010).

Rotenberg, Marc. 1994. "Privacy and the National Information Infrastructure." *Educom Review* 29 (March/April): 50–51.

Russell, Carrie. 2005a. "Copyright Concerns: Photocopies, Scanners, and Downloads: Is the Library Liable? (Part 1)." *Public Libraries* 44 (September/October): 275–276.

———. 2005b. "Copyright Concerns: Photocopies, Scanners, and Downloads: Is the Library Liable? (Part 2)." *Public Libraries* 44 (November/December): 339.

Sanchez, Jullian. 2009. "New FOIA Rules Official—Let the Data Flood Begin." Available: http://arstechnica.com/tech-policy/news/2009/03/will-new-foia-rules-yield-a-data-flood.ars (accessed March 26, 2009).

Science Applications International Corporation (SAIC). 1995. *Information Warfare: Legal, Regulatory, Policy and Organizational Considerations for Assurance.* Washington, DC: Pentagon.

Schmidt, James C. 1989. "Rights for Users of Information: Conflicts and Balances among Privacy, Professional Ethics, Law, National Security." *Bowker Annual: Library and Book Trade Almanac 1989–90.* 34th ed. Medford, NJ: Information Today, 83–90.

Shuler, John. 2005. "The Political and Economic Future of Federal Depository Libraries." *Journal of Academic Librarianship* 31 (July): 377–382.

Skala, Matthew, Brett Bonfield, and Mary Fran Torpey. 2008. "Enforcing Copyright." *Library Journal* 133 (February 15): 28–30.

Smith, Ted D. 2002. "Security versus Freedom of Information: An Enduring Conflict in Federal Information Policy." *OLA Quarterly* 8 (winter): 2–6.

Solove, Daniel J. 2008. "The Future of Privacy." *American Libraries* 39 (September): 56–59.

Stevens, Al. 2000. "Into the World of MP3." *Dr. Dobb's Journal* (September): 115–120.

Strickland, Lee S. 2005. "The Information Gulag: Rethinking Openness in Times of National Danger." *Government Information Quarterly* 22: 546–572.

United Nations. 1948. "Universal Declaration of Human Rights." Available: www.un.org/en/documents/udhr/ (accessed February 7, 2010).

United States et al. v. American Library Association, Inc. et al. "Syllabus." Supreme Court of the United States. October Term, 2002.

Universal Service Administrative Company. 2009. "Overview of E-Rates." Available: www.usac.org/_res/documents/sl/pdf/E-rate-Overview.pdf (accessed August 27, 2009).

U.S. Congress. 2002. E-government Act of 2002 (Public Law 107-347). 107th Congress. Available: www.archives.gov/about/laws/egov-act-section-207.html (accessed February 7, 2010).

U.S. Copyright Office. 1998. *The Digital Millennium Copyright Act of 1998: U.S. Copyright Office Summary.* Washington, DC: Copyright Office, December.

———. 2008. *The Section 108 Study Group Report.* Washington, DC: Copyright Office, March.

U.S. Department of Education. 1994. "HR 6: Improving America's Schools Act of 1994." Available: www.ed.gov/legislation/ESEA/toc.html (accessed June 22, 1997; February 10, 2010).

————. 2007. *Building on Results: A Blueprint for Strengthening the No Child Left Behind Act*. Washington, DC: U.S. Department of Education.

————. 2010. "Overview: Four Pillars of NCLB." Available: http://ed.gov/nclb/overview/intro/4pillars.html (accessed February 7, 2010).

U.S. Patent and Trademark Office. 1998. "The Conference on Fair Use: Final Report to the Commissioner on the Conclusion of the Conference on Fair Use." Available: www .uspto.gov/web/ offices/dcom/olia/confu/confurep.pdf (accessed February 18, 2010).

Weitzner, Daniel J. 2006. "The Neutral Internet: An Information Architecture for Open Societies." Available: http://dig.csail.mit.edu/2006/06/neutralnet.html (accessed February 5, 2010).

West, Cynthia K. 2001. *Techno-Human Mesh: The Growing Power of Information Technologies*. Westport, CT: Quorum.

Whelan, Debra Lau. 2004. "A Golden Opportunity." *School Library Journal* (January): 40–42.

Wiant, Sarah K. 2008. "Developments in Copyright Law: The Search for Balance Goes On." In *Library and Book Trade Almanac: The Bowker Annual 2008*, 53rd ed. Edited by Dave Bogart. Medford, NJ: Information Today, 46–55.

Windhausen, John Jr. 2009. *A Plan to Extend Super-Fast Broadband Connections to All Americans*. New York: Century Foundation.

World Intellectual Property Organization. 1996. "WIPO Copyright Treaty." Available: www.wipo.int/ treaties/en/ip/wct/trtdocs_wo033.html (accessed February 7, 2010).

Xue, Susan. 2005. "Internet Policy and Diffusion in China, Malaysia and Singapore." *Journal of Information Science* 31: 238–250.

Zittrain, Jonathan L. 2006. "The Generative Internet." *Harvard Law Review* 119 (May): 1974–2040.

SELECTED READINGS: INFORMATION POLICY

Books

Mossberger, Karen, Caroline Tolbert, and Mary Stansbury. *Virtual Inequality: Beyond the Digital Divide*. Washington, DC: Georgetown University Press, 2003.

National Digital Information Infrastructure and Preservation Program. *Preserving Our Digital Heritage: Plan for the National Digital Information Infrastructure and Preservation Program*. Washington, DC: Library of Congress. Available: www.digitalpreservation.gov/ library/resources/pubs/docs/ndiipp_plan.pdf (accessed June 15, 2009).

U.S. Department of Commerce. *Falling Through the Net II: New Data on the Digital Divide*. Available: www.ntia.doc.gov/ntiahome/net2 (accessed February 5, 2010).

Articles

Bailey, Charles W. Jr. "Strong Copyright + DRM + Weak Net Neutrality = Digital Dystopia?" *Information Technology and Libraries* 25 (September 2006): 116–127, 139.

Band, Jonathan. "Educational Fair Use Today." In *The Bowker Annual*. 53rd ed. Medford, NJ: Information Today, 2008, 56–65.

Bertot, John Carlo, Paul T. Jaeger, and Charles R. McClure. "Citizen-Centered E-government Services: Benefits, Costs, and Research Needs." From *Proceedings of the 9th Annual International Digital Government Research Conference*. Montreal, Canada, May 18–21, 2008, 137–142. Available: www.ala.org/ala/aboutala/offices/wo/woissues/government info/egovernment/citizencenteredegov.pdf (accessed June 15, 2009).

Choemprayong, Songphan. "Closing Digital Divides: The United States' Policies." *Libri* 56 (2006): 201–212.

Cloonan, Michèle V., and John G. Dove. "Ranganathan Online: Do Digital Libraries Violate the Third Law?" *Library Journal* (April 1, 2005). Available: www.libraryjournal.com/article/ CA512179.html?q=do+digital+libraries+violate+the+third+law (accessed June 17, 2009).

Gilroy, Angele A. "Net Neutrality: Background and Issues." CRS Report for Congress. Washington, DC: Congressional Research Service, Library of Congress, May 16, 2006.

Hammitt, Harry. "Less Safe—The Dismantling of Public Information Systems After 9/11." *Social Science Computer Review* 23 (winter 2005): 429–438.

Jaeger, Paul T. "Information Policy, Information Access, and Democratic Participation: The National and International Implications of the Bush Administration's Information Politics." *Government Information Quarterly* 24 (2007): 840–859.

Jaeger, Paul T., and Kenneth R. Fleischmann. "Public Libraries, Values, Trust, and E-government." *Information Technology and Libraries* 26 (December 2007): 34–43.

Maxwell, Terrence A. "Parsing the Public Domain." *Journal of the American Society for Information Science and Technology* 56 (2005): 1130–1139.

McCain, Roger A. "Information as Property and as a Public Good: Perspectives from the Economic Theory of Property Rights." *Library Quarterly* 58 (1988): 265–282.

Neal, James G. "Copyright Is Dead . . . Long Live Copyright." *American Libraries* 33 (December 2002): 48–51.

Shuler, John. "The Political and Economic Future of Federal Depository Libraries." *Journal of Academic Librarianship* 31 (July 2005): 377–382.

Solove, Daniel J. "The Future of Privacy." *American Libraries* 39 (September 2009): 56–59.

Weitzner, Daniel J. "The Neutral Internet: An Information Architecture for Open Societies." Available: http://dig.csail.mit.edu/2006/06/neutralnet.pdf (accessed June 15, 2009).

Wiant, Sarah K. "Developments in Copyright Law: The Search for Balance Goes On." In *The Bowker Annual*. 53rd ed. Medford, NJ: Information Today, 2008.

Windhausen, John Jr. "A Plan to Extend Super-Fast Broadband Connections to All Americans." A Century Foundation Report. January 27, 2009. Available: www.tcf.org/Publications/ mediapolitics/windhausen.pdf (accessed June 15, 2009).

9

Information Policy as Library Policy: Intellectual Freedom

I. INTRODUCTION

Information policy affects the field of library and information science in multiple ways. In addition to the influence of federal and state legislation, the policies and practices of libraries themselves have considerable impact on accessibility. Such policies address the creation, organization, use, and dissemination of the knowledge in their collections as well as larger issues like intellectual freedom. Because intellectual freedom plays such a central role in our profession, it is treated in a separate section in this chapter.

A. Policies Related to the Organization of Materials and Collections

A primary function of libraries is organizing collections for easy access by patrons and librarians. The policies affecting this process are, therefore, some of the most important that a library establishes. Generally, libraries use one of two basic organization systems: the Dewey Decimal Classification (DDC) or the Library of Congress Classification (LCC) system. These tools and related systems such as the Library of Congress Subject Headings and the Anglo-American Cataloguing Rules are discussed in detail in Chapter 4.

B. Collection Development Policies and Selection Criteria

Collection development policies and selection criteria determine the nature and type of information that a library provides. A collection development policy takes a broad view and answers such questions as these:

- What is the fundamental mission of the library?
- What subjects should be collected and in what depth?

- What types of formats should be included in the collection and what should be the balance among these formats?
- Who are the library users and what types of materials and services should be provided to meet their needs?
- What cooperative relationships should be established with other libraries and other information providers?

Other development policy issues that libraries might consider include answers to such questions as "Does the library have a responsibility to control access to some types of information that would not otherwise be selected by the library?" or "Should the library restrict certain electronic files, such as sexually explicit sites, or impose age restrictions on users?"

Policies based on the answers to these questions provide considerable direction for the library and serve additional purposes:

1. As a planning tool to determine the use of monetary resources and staff
2. As a guide to selectors in developing their collections
3. As a means to ensure that collections are developed consistently over time and through changes of staff
4. As a means to train new library staff
5. As a statement of philosophy
6. As a defense in case of challenges to library materials (which are not uncommon)

Development policies and selection criteria are closely related but distinct. Selection criteria are used to choose individual items or groups within the broader framework established by the development policy. The selection criteria help to determine if items are of sufficient quality. The criteria might vary in complexity, but there are some conventionally used criteria.

Common Selection Criteria

Authority: Knowledge and reputation of the author or of the organization producing the item.

Appropriateness: Match of the item to the intended users. For example, is the age level appropriate?

Accuracy or timeliness: The accuracy of the content and its currency.

Physical characteristics: The quality of the binding, paper, or material on which the information is stored, and the size and quality of the print.

Collection fit: The contribution the item makes to the collection, the appropriateness of a particular item in relation to the collection development plan, and the balance it provides to other points of view.

Demand: The popularity of an item and the likelihood of use by library patrons.

Content: The quality of the information or narrative and the clarity of its organization.

Special characteristics: The availability of such features as indexes, bibliography, notes, prefaces, introductions, teacher guides, and interpretive material.

Other selection criteria might be applied depending on the nature of the work and the format. For example, a library's decision to provide access to information electronically through the Web raises additional issues that require guidance through policy. The Web is growing rapidly and therefore in constant flux; individual sites might change daily. In addition, the large volume of items produced by a search makes selecting the most credible items difficult because the Web lacks the selection filters traditionally used to assure reliability in print sources (Doyle and Hammond 2006). Further, the Web is a "self-sustaining reference system"; that is, sources are often verified by reference to other Web sources (Burbules 2001, p. 443). All of these factors represent significant challenges to identifying credible sources.

> **Web Site Evaluation Criteria**
>
> • What does the domain name indicate; that is, is the Web site authored by an individual or an educational institution, commercial enterprise, or organization?
> • Are there additional links that are useful?
> • Over time, are the links updated?
> • Can the information be corroborated?
> • What Web sites link to this Web site?
> • Can you get into the site easily?
> • Does the site download information quickly?
> • Can you navigate on the site easily?
> • Is there an effective internal search engine to search the site?
> • Is the Web site accessible to those with disabilities, such as visual or aural impairments?

When individuals evaluate information on the Web, they tend to make credibility judgments on at least three levels: "valuation of the Web itself; evaluation of Web sites, and evaluation of Web information" (Rieh and Danielson 2007, p. 334). Based on a survey of information researchers in business, academia, and government, Norman (2006) identified several factors that tended to generate the greatest trust in a particular Web site:

1. The content could be corroborated.
2. The site was recommended by a subject matter expert.
3. The author was reputable.
4. The viewer perceived the site as accurate.
5. The information on the site was reviewed by an editor or peer.
6. The author was associated with a reputable organization.
7. The publisher of the site was reputable.

C. Service Policies

Even the simplest policies can impact information access. For example, the library's hours of operation can be seen as an information policy because they affect when individuals can use the collection. Other service-related information policies include the following:

- **Circulation policies**: include the length of loan periods and renewal practices. They might also include the designation of non-circulating materials.

- **Reference policies**: stipulate the types of services provided and any restrictions. For example, time limits for the provision of reference service to an individual patron or a restriction based on the type of assistance, such as helping students with their homework or answering test questions. They might also include the library's philosophical orientation on issues such as whether reference service should be primarily instructional; that is, teaching a patron how to obtain information (quite common in academic and school libraries), or fulfillment-oriented; that is, providing the answers (more common in public library adult reference service or special libraries).

- **Personnel and staffing policies**: Library service remains a labor-intensive activity. Therefore, the type and size of the staff have a direct effect on the quantity and quality of information services provided. If a library hires subject experts in a particular field (e.g., business or genealogy), this will affect the use and depth of service provided. The same might be said if knowledgeable children's librarians are hired to develop in-depth children's services.

D. Preservation Policies

One of the oldest purposes of libraries is the preservation of the human record. If libraries are to develop comprehensive preservation policies, it will be necessary to make a stronger case to administrators for the societal value of preservation in general:

> Without clarifying to the public why it is important to society in general and to individuals in particular to make long-term commitments of resources to the collection and preservation of cultural content, it is unlikely to happen. (Smith 2007, p. 5)

In particular, as more and more records are produced in digital form, some exclusively, preservation issues have grown increasingly complex. In many libraries their policies related to digital information tend to focus exclusively on providing access to the most current information (Smith 2007) with considerably less attention to the historical significance of the digital record and preserving that information for future generations. However, given the increasing amount of critical information now stored in digital form, there is a serious need for explicit policies on preserving it. This issue is not insignificant for in many ways, such policies will decide what ideas or materials will continue to exist in local communities in the future.

Issues to consider in digital preservation include criteria for selecting which materials will be microfilmed, repaired, or digitized. What measures are in place to protect digital information in case of unpredictable natural events like fires or floods, or intentional events such as computer hacking or terrorist acts?

II. INTELLECTUAL FREEDOM AS INFORMATION POLICY

A need to preserve intellectual freedom and a responsibility to resist censorship are two fundamental values of LIS professionals. Dresang (2006) defined intellectual freedom as "freedom to think or believe what one will, freedom to express one's thoughts and beliefs in unrestricted manners and means, and freedom to access information and ideas regardless of the content or viewpoints of the author(s) or the age, background, or beliefs of the receiver" (p. 169). Intellectual freedom is based on a fundamental belief that the health of a democratic society is maintained and improved when ideas can be created and disseminated without governmental, political, or social impediment.

Such a belief can have far-reaching implications. For example, in some cases, it could lead to the propagation of heinous ideas with deleterious results; think of Hitler's *Mein Kampf*. Such a view presumes, however, that the best way to combat a bad idea is not to suppress it, but to produce a better idea, and that the only alternative to censorship is free expression. It also presumes that the generation of good ideas increases when there is unimpaired freedom to produce them.

Individuals who fear that some ideas might be so harmful that they should be suppressed or restricted are prone to acts of censorship. Censorship is an act or set of acts by government, groups, or individuals (including librarians) to restrict the flow of information or ideas, usually because the content is considered offensive for political, religious, or moral reasons. Attempts to censor library materials are most often based on sexual explicitness, religious viewpoints, offensive language, homosexuality, or racism. For example, among the most challenged books in 2008 were *And Tango Makes Three* by Justin Richardson and Peter Parnell on the grounds of being antiethnic, antifamily, and unsuited to the intended age group; Philip Pullman's *His Dark Materials Trilogy* for its political and religious perspectives, and *The Kite Runner* by Khaled Hosseini for its language, sexual explicitness, and unsuitability for the intended age group. Interestingly, based on American Library Association (ALA) data, the number of book challenges has dropped in the past decade. Dresang (2006) suggested that this might be partly because so many materials are now easily available on the Internet that attempting to restrict access is futile. She also suggested that it might signify a shift in emphasis from censoring books to censoring the Net. Books are just one target for censors; sex and violence in movies are also frequent complaints. Some of the censorship targets have been surprising, such as *Snow White*, *The Little Mermaid*, and *My Friend Flicka*. In addition, there have been broad-based attempts to limit the range of materials and services that could be provided in libraries using legislative means.

On its surface, it seems obvious that censorship should be inhibited and intellectual freedom promoted. However, the protection of intellectual freedom is, in fact, one of the most difficult aspects of library work and the focus of considerable professional debate. Although perhaps not intuitively obvious, intellectual freedom issues relate to multiple library activities such as selecting, weeding, or classifying materials, physically locating materials in the library, and establishing reference service, confidentiality, and access policies. At the root of the problem is what individual LIS professionals often perceive as conflicting moral, ethical, personal, social, and legal obligations. Some of these obligations form powerful motivators to restrict access to some materials, while other obligations serve as countervailing forces, encouraging unrestricted access. By making these forces more explicit, it becomes clear why libraries sometimes have difficulty making policy decisions on this issue.

A. Factors That Tend to Restrict or Encourage Access

1. Factors That Tend to Restrict Access

a. The Obligation to Act in Accordance with One's Personal Values

Each of us, through childhood training and experience, develops certain moral precepts. LIS professionals do not surrender these precepts when they go to work. This is not to say that information providers should impose values, but certain circumstances in libraries are more likely to evoke an interest in applying them than others. A common example would be materials that might promote bigotry. Librarians might be tempted to restrict access to such material, especially to young people. The conflict between being responsive to certain social values and the advocacy of open access to ideas that might be inimical to those values is a constant tension that some might feel is professionally irreconcilable (Dresang 2006).

b. The Obligation to Protect, Preserve, and Maintain the Values of One's Community

Quite naturally, LIS professionals perceive themselves as part of the community. Many live, as well as work, in the community and participate in its many social, political, recreational, and cultural activities. Similarly, most libraries, public and school libraries in particular, depend on their local communities for dollars and local boosters. If the LIS professional values the community, then it is reasonable that the library's collection and services should reflect its needs and desires. Indeed, the LIS professional might feel that the promotion of such values is both necessary and worthwhile. Thus, purchasing materials that represent values substantially different from the community's or that might offend a significant number of community members might seem inappropriate and a source of unnecessary conflict.

c. The Obligation to Protect Children from Harm

Few obligations are as indisputable as the obligation of all members of a society (no matter what their profession or job) to protect from exploitation those who are defenseless or vulnerable. What group falls more clearly into this category than children? Society even recognizes that many groups dealing with children—teachers, health care workers, social workers, university researchers—are obligated to monitor potential harm to children and to report suspected harm to authorities. Although most LIS professionals are not required by law to monitor such harm, it is unreasonable to presume that they have no stake in caring for and protecting children. Indeed, a central tenet of librarianship, historically, has been nurturing children and developing their minds through exposure to books and other materials. Can one reasonably believe that books and information can improve children, but that they cannot also harm them? This is a common argument by those who wish to restrict materials for young people, and it can be persuasive.

d. The Obligation to Protect the Survival of the Library

Few obligations are dearer to librarians than the preservation of the library as an institution. The survival of a major cultural and social institution is an important factor in ethical decisions. Therefore, the selection, organization, and dissemination of particular materials that might threaten the fiscal and political support of the community gives librarians pause. Those who wish to restrict materials often threaten to campaign against funding for library services, thus threatening the survival of the library itself.

2. Factors That Tend to Increase Access

The obligations that tend to restrict access are not trivial; in fact, they enlighten us about the realistic pressures that many LIS professionals face. But there are other counterbalancing obligations that help them to resist the temptation to restrict access.

a. The Obligation to Educate Children

Public libraries educate children through careful collection development, responsive reference services, entertaining and educational programming, and cooperation with outside agencies such as schools and social service agencies. Although some might feel that public libraries should prevent children from being exposed to certain ideas, others would argue that children who are free to explore ideas become healthy adults and better-educated citizens. Many LIS professionals in public libraries think that the choice to restrict access rests with the parents alone

School library media centers, on the other hand, are more subject to the views and beliefs of the educational community in which they are embedded. Some educators see the library as a means of inculcating the young with only particular values and behaviors. Others contend that a comprehensive education involves exposing the young to many different points of view and teaching them the critical thinking skills necessary to make well-reasoned decisions. This argument was a fundamental issue in one of the most important Supreme Court cases on school censorship, *Island Trees v. Pico* (1982).

The perspective of the ALA generally has been that access to information should be unrestricted and this has been supported by a variety of formal statements. ALA's social marketing campaign, Kids Need Libraries, outlined a variety of factors that contribute to healthy child development, including the following:

- The belief in a worthwhile future and their responsibility and desire to contribute to that future
- A positive sense of self-worth
- The ability to locate and use information and the awareness that this ability is an essential key to self-realization in the information age
- Preparation to use present-day technology and to adapt to a changing technological world
- Equal access to the marketplace of ideas and information
- The ability to think critically in order to solve problems
- The ability to communicate effectively—to listen, to speak, to read, and to write
- Preparation to live in a multicultural world and to respect the rights and dignity of all people
- The desire and ability to become lifelong learners
- Creative ability to dream a better world (Mathews et al. 1990, pp. 33–37)

These factors strongly support unimpeded access to library materials, but they also suggest that LIS professionals play a critical role in helping guide children to become thoughtful, well-informed citizens with abilities to discover the information they need for themselves.

b. The Obligation to Preserve the Values of One's Profession

Through formal education and on-the-job training, LIS professionals assimilate the professional standards of behavior and service best expressed in the ALA's Library Bill of Rights and the Code of Ethics of both the ALA and the American Society for Information Science and Technology. Another obligation is to select materials based on objective criteria, such as those previously discussed in the section on Collection Development Policies, rather than personal interest. LIS professionals can certainly have personal preferences, but what distinguishes professional judgment from personal bias are reasonably objective criteria on which selection judgments are based. Lester Asheim (1954) characterized the difference between selection and censorship in the following way:

> To the selector, the important thing is to find reasons to keep the book. Given such a guiding principle, the selector looks for values, for virtues, for strengths, which will overshadow minor objections. For the censor, on the other hand, the

important thing is to find reasons to reject the book. His guiding principle leads him to seek out the objectionable features, the weaknesses, the possibilities for misinterpretation.... The selector says, if there is anything good in this book let us try to keep it; the censor says, if there is anything bad in this book, let us reject it. And since there is seldom a flawless work in any form, the censor's approach can destroy much that is worth saving. (pp. 95–96)

Adherence to these values is demonstrated by the breadth of a library's collection. For some librarians, these professional values are so meaningful and powerful that they have preferred to lose their positions rather than sacrifice them.

c. The Obligation to Protect the Rights of Citizens in a Democratic Society

The First Amendment of the U.S. Constitution plays a central role in the establishment, maintenance, and protection of libraries and their patrons. The First Amendment not only provides Americans with the right to express themselves, it establishes a corollary right to receive the ideas of others.

A value held dear by many LIS professionals, both personally and professionally, is the importance of providing information to all those who seek it. This view corresponds with a number of beliefs about democracy: it is the most effective form of government; citizens should be able to obtain information about a variety of viewpoints in order to make informed choices; opposing points of view are aired, not suppressed; and the untrue should be heard as well as the true because falsehoods can often be quite useful in the learning process. Indeed, sometimes what is considered false in one generation becomes the truth of another. LIS professionals have a commitment to protect the flow of information, whether true or false (Swan 1986). Therefore, materials with conflicting points of view, even if considered heinous or patently false, should be a part of a library's collection. Restricting access to materials contravenes the letter and spirit of the First Amendment and diminishes its authority and effect.

B. Research on Censorship and Intellectual Freedom

Intellectual freedom is a strong value within library and information science professions, upheld by the majority of LIS professionals. Nonetheless some librarians respect the principles of intellectual freedom but find it difficult to practice them in the real world or they express ambivalence about the competing obligations noted above. This ambivalence is not without historical roots. In the nineteenth and well into the twentieth century, many librarians felt it was their duty to limit patrons' exposure to materials (such as romances) that might have unfortunate effects. The library literature is replete with admonitions to librarians to obtain only the most "wholesome" materials. As Dewey (1989) noted, "only the best books on the best subjects" were to be collected (p. 5). Women who were hired as librarians at the end of the nineteenth century were expected to represent the values of polite middle-class society and to steer individuals to "better" books (Garrison 1972–1973).

In the 1950s, Serebnick (1979) found that censorship in schools and public libraries was not just due to the complaints of principals and parents, but largely from the librarians themselves, often without prompting, and based on a belief that certain books could harm children. In many cases, the librarians simply did not buy books they thought might be controversial, or they restricted access to them (Eakin 1948; Fiske 1959). In other words, a considerable amount of censorship was self-imposed. Subsequent research confirmed this conclusion. Studies of librarians in high schools and public libraries in the Midwest in the 1960s and 1970s revealed that a significant proportion of them had weak or wavering views about censorship and that there was little correlation between asserting a belief in intellectual freedom and censoring materials (Farley 1964; Busha 1971). Again, much of the censorship was self-imposed and occurred more often with materials that had pictures than with those that were not illustrated. In general, throughout this period, the propensity to restrict materials was greatest among school librarians, followed by public librarians, and then academic librarians. Librarians with the strongest educational backgrounds were least likely to restrict materials (Pope 1973).

Subsequent research often focused on censorship schools. One study, titled Limiting What Students Shall Read, sampled 1,891 librarians in public elementary and secondary schools, library supervisors, principals, and district superintendents using mail and telephone surveys. Nearly one-third of the librarians reported at least one challenge in the previous year, and in 30 percent of the cases the material was altered, restricted, or removed. More than 50 percent of the challenges came from parents, about 10 percent from teachers, and 6 percent from school-board members (Association of American Publishers 1981). In a subsequent study, Hopkins (1993) sampled more than 6,500 U.S. school systems and found that challenges came from both within and outside the libraries. Challenges from within, especially by principals, were the most problematic because the item was least likely to be retained in this circumstance. In addition, the political aspect of protecting library materials was also highlighted as Hopkins noted that support from media and outside groups played a significant role in protecting materials from removal. Librarians were found to be most supportive of intellectual freedom when they had a high level of confidence in their own abilities. Dresang (2006), in reviewing the censorship literature between 2000 and 2004, found that 75 percent of all book challenges reported to the ALA were in schools, with 44 percent involving the school library.

Aiken (2007) examined the commitment of public library directors to the Library Bill of Rights. He surveyed 400 directors nationally, asking about any restrictions the library imposed that might be considered a violation of the age discrimination prohibitions in the Library Bill of Rights. He found that more than 50 percent of the 110 respondents failed to conform to the open access policies prescribed by the

Library Bill of Rights. Nearly 20 percent did not permit access to social networking sites. Aiken concluded that the ALA was out of touch with the library community and suggested that it was not responding to the changes in family structure that make it difficult for parents to accompany their children to the library. It might be time to revisit the potential role librarians might play in serving in loco parentis. At the least, he suggested that the ALA needed to communicate more effectively with library directors and increase public awareness of the Library Bill of Rights.

C. Major Concerns of Those Who Wish to Censor Materials

What is it that bothers people so much that they believe people, especially children, should not be able to obtain certain materials in libraries? The most common reasons are offensive language and offensive subjects, particularly sexual content and violence. Other vulnerable subjects include those that appear to undermine the "traditional family," seem antireligious, challenge authority, appear antidemocratic, or offend certain racial or ethnic groups. Sometimes religious works are censored. For example, in 2007 the Bureau of Prisons, in an effort to prevent terrorism, wanted to remove religious works from prison collections, including nine titles by C. S. Lewis (Goodstein 2007). The following is a discussion of some of the most common concerns.

1. Sexual Content

Some individuals believe that sexual subject matter of any type should not be in libraries, especially if it is available to minors. Such people often believe that sexuality education should be provided only by parents, and children's access to sexually related materials in the library should be restricted. Similarly, some argue that certain materials promote "perverse" sexual behaviors and adversely affect the attitudes of young people. This was the central focus of the debate over *Daddy's Roommate* and *Heather Has Two Mommies*, two books for children that dealt with the family life of homosexual couples. Clearly, sexuality is a topic that triggers strong passions. Sometimes even a single word might cause a problem. For example, the 2007 Newbery Medal award winner, *The Higher Power of Lucky*, was challenged by both patrons and some librarians because the word *scrotum* appeared in the book (Schultz 2007).

2. Violent Content

A second content issue is violence. Does exposure to violent themes in books, music, and films promote unacceptable behavior? Some evidence suggests a relationship between exposure to violence and subsequent aggressive behavior. Kunkel and Zwarun (2006), reviewing the literature on TV violence and youth behavior, noted:

> It is well established by a compelling body of scientific evidence that television violence is harmful to children. These harmful effects include (1) children's learning of aggressive attitudes and behaviors; (2) desensitization, or an increased callousness toward victims of violence; and (3) increased or exaggerated fear of being victimized by violence. (p. 203)

At the same time, the researchers point out that the relationship is complex; not all children are negatively affected by what they see or read. In addition, they note that although television violence might be pervasive, it is not necessarily the most potent factor in subsequent violent behavior. Evidence on the relationship of violent lyrics in music and subsequent aggressive behavior is modest, but a few studies confirm a relationship between exposure to rap and heavy metal music and aggressive attitudes and behavior (Wilson and Martin 2006). Other research suggests that exposure to violent themes in music, linked with sexual content, can affect the behavior of young people. Martino et al. (2006), for example, conducted a three-year study of 12–17-year-olds that examined the association between exposure to certain music lyrics and sexual experience. The researchers noted that young people in the United States listen to music 1.5 to 2.5 hours a day, not including music videos. They found a complex relationship between certain types of music and subsequent sexual activity:

> Youth who listened to more degrading sexual content . . . were more likely to subsequently initiate intercourse and to progress to more advanced levels of non-coital sexual activity, even after controlling for 18 respondent characteristics that might otherwise explain these relationships. In contrast, exposure to non-degrading sexual content was unrelated to changes in participants' sexual behavior. (p. 431)

It does seem obvious that constantly watching people get shot, stabbed, and brutalized, or listening to music that promotes violence of one kind or another diminishes the shock of these disturbing actions. Clearly, as a society, we are less shocked by such explicit violence than we were in the past. Are libraries promoting this insensitivity or contributing to the violence by making available materials with violent themes?

Libraries, as noted before, are imbedded in their communities and the larger society. As American society grows ever more concerned about the violence within it, people search for factors that might promote or foster this violence. Some people believe that certain materials in libraries contribute to this problem. On the other hand, freedom of expression, even violent speech, is protected by the First Amendment. Efforts to limit exposure to violence might rest more effectively on educational efforts by parents and the media industry than attempts to control it by legal means (Ross 2006). Nonetheless, concerns over censorship were sufficient that the ALA, along with eight other national organizations including the American Society of Journalists and Authors and the Association of American Publishers, adopted "Violence in the Media: A Joint Statement" (ALA 2001). This statement acknowledged that the community has legitimate reasons to be concerned about violence in the media, including the Internet, but that some of the proposed solutions had a deleterious effect on freedom of expression. It noted that "concern for our children and fundamental speech freedoms are not mutually exclusive." The statement identified six principles:

1. Censorship is not the answer to violence in society.
2. The First Amendment protects the widest range of expression.
3. It is not properly the role of government to evaluate the merits of expression.
4. Evaluating the worth of expression is subjective.
5. Portrayals of violence in the media reflect a violent world.
6. Individuals, not the government, bear responsibility for determining what materials are appropriate for themselves and their children. (ALA 2001)

3. Offensive Language

Language used in print, AV materials, and music has become progressively more "colorful" over the years. Today, explicit sexual slang and profanity are commonplace in many works. Many fear that language influences subsequent behavior, especially for young people, and like violence, there is concern that we become used to profane language in everyday speech.

4. Concern with Formats

Although print materials have been censored for thousands of years, a particular concern today is audiovisual materials. Visually oriented media are particularly powerful as people's visual senses are among the strongest. Therefore, people are more deeply and immediately affected by what they see on a screen than by what they read in a book. Audio materials have also come under attack. Lyrics from rap music have been particularly subject to requests for limitation and removal. One argument used by censors is that the combination of words and music makes the message more powerful than the use of the words alone. It is hard to deny that music can intensify an experience; that is why movies have musical accompaniment at strategic moments.

5. Concern for Children

Our fear of the harmful effects of ideas on youth goes back to classical Greece—recall that Socrates was put to death for corrupting the youth of Athens. Every society seeks to protect its young from undesirable influences. The first obscenity case in English law occurred around 1860 when the English court was concerned with the effects of "obscene" materials on "vulnerable minds" including children. Interestingly, the obscene materials in this case were anti-Catholic pamphlets.

People who abhor censorship, in general, might still experience qualms when it comes to circulating materials with adult themes to the young. In fact, defending unrestricted access to such materials is probably the most difficult intellectual freedom task that LIS professionals perform, and the matter is further complicated by legal concerns. Almost all states now have "harmful to juvenile" statutes that create obscenity standards for youth that are easier to meet than those for adults. The librarian is confronted not just with people's natural concerns that certain materials might negatively affect children and adolescents, but with the real possibility that an irate citizen or public official might employ legal means to restrict or eliminate library materials. On the other hand, there is no substantive evidence that such laws actually protect children and, ironically, such laws "might have detrimental effects on their imaginations, their psychological development, and their ability to cope with various challenges in life" (Dresang 2006, p. 180).

D. The World Wide Web and the Debate over Filtering

The ubiquity of the Web and its relative ease of use permits millions of individuals, including minors, to access thousands of Web sites, some of which might be sexually explicit. There is an understandable desire to limit children's exposure to these sites. As noted earlier, federal legislation, especially the Children's Internet Protection Act (CIPA) and the subsequent Supreme Court decision upholding its constitutionality, made some type of filtering mandatory in libraries receiving federal E-rate or LSTA monies related to Internet access. Similarly, state "harmful to juvenile" laws prompted some libraries to implement filtering to protect themselves from potential liabilities. These filters, known as blocking software or content filters, prevent access to certain Internet sites, primarily in two ways:

- **Keyword or word blocking**: compares Web page content with a list of disapproved words or phrases. This type of blocking is among the easiest to implement, but also the most inexact because it tends to block many sites inappropriately.

- **Site blocking**: compares Web pages to a list of disapproved sites. For the most part, the software company creates a list of sites to be blocked, although some filters allow additional sites to be blocked and for some blocked sites to be unblocked. In general, companies do not identify which sites are blocked, arguing that it would put them at a competitive disadvantage. Because new Web sites are being created daily, filters that rely on site blocking must be constantly updated.

Blocking software, usually installed either on a local computer or on a server, relies on categories identified as "blocked" or "permitted." The categories most commonly blocked include sexuality, nudity, profanity, and violence. Some organizations have tried to help both Web site developers and users label Web sites so that filtering functions more effectively. For example, the ICRA, formerly known as the Internet Content Rating Association, is part of the Family Online Safety Institute, an international, non-profit organization working to improve Internet safety. The ICRA invites content providers to complete a questionnaire that describes their sites, especially regarding the presence or absence of profanity, nudity, and sexual content, violence, gambling, drugs, or alcohol. ICRA generates content labels based on the responses of the Web site creators. These labels can then be used by parents when setting their browsers to accept or reject access to certain sites (ICRA 2010). Although none would dispute the desirability of reducing young peoples' exposure to violent, hateful, or pornographic sites, a variety of issues make filtering problematic:

- **Overblocking**: The blocking of sites that were not intended to be blocked. Overblocking raises important issues in that it deprives individuals of access to constitutionally protected information. An example of the irony of overblocking was presented in the case of the Flesh Public Library in Ohio, whose filter blocked access to its own Web site. More seriously, educational information on human sexuality or health is frequently blocked. The Kaiser Family Foundation reported, for example, that information on diabetes, sexually transmitted diseases, depression, and suicide had been blocked (Edward 2002). Other blocked sites dealt with Georgia O'Keeffe and Vincent Van Gogh, a UN report on HIV/AIDS, and the home pages of the Traditional Values Coalition, the Wisconsin Civil Liberties Union, and the National Coalition to Prevent Censorship. Filters have also blocked the Declaration of Independence, *Moby Dick*, and "The Owl and the Pussy Cat." In a policy report reviewing the research on filters from 2001 to 2006, the Brennan Center for Justice (2006) concluded, "Although statistics and percentages in this field of research can be misleading, one conclusion is clear from all of the studies: filters continue to block large amounts of valuable information" (p. 73). Such blocking constitutes a form of prior restraint and is contrary to our constitutional traditions.

- **Underblocking**: Filters often fail to block a significant percentage of the sites they were intended to block. For example, a study by the Kaiser Family Foundation revealed that filters give parents a false sense of security; nearly 10 percent failed to block pornographic sites (Kranich 2004). Another study in *Consumer Reports* found that even the "best" sites failed to block 20–30 percent of objectionable sites, and less stringent filters failed to block 50–90 percent of objectionable sites (*American Libraries* 2001).

- **Subjective and discriminatory judgment**: The criteria used by the filter developers for blocking sites are subjective. Of particular concern is that they substitute their own judgments for those of teachers and librarians. This is problematic because the line between what is legally obscene and what might be simply offensive can be thin, and it is not clear that software developers can make such distinctions. This problem is exacerbated by the refusal of many filter manufacturers to provide information on the subjects and sites that were blocked. Kranich (2004) observed that filters could not discriminate sites that might be inappropriate for a six-year-old, but not for a sixteen-year-old.

- **Susceptibility to errors**: Producers of filtering products often rely on automated systems for making content decisions. This type of "mindless mechanical blocking" inevitably leads to many mistakes (Heins and Cho 2001). Unfortunately, artificial intelligence programs are simply not yet sufficiently refined to make the subtle distinctions necessary to screen out only the sites that were intended to be screened. The impact of these errors in some cases could be small; in others it could deprive users of important information. Filters on local computers tend to be less reliable than filters installed on servers, and they have more problems involving conflicting software.

- **Vulnerability to dismantling**: Knowledgeable users, including young people, can often bypass filtering software. The belief that filters remove or substantially reduce children's access to sexually explicit material, profanity, or violence is questionable.

- **Computer problems**: Blocking software can affect computer performance during installation, maintenance, upgrades, and removal.

- **Privacy**: Filtering software can, in some cases, track Internet use, including time, date, which computer was used, and specific sites accessed. This capability jeopardizes the confidential use of library resources by patrons.

Despite these problems, several arguments support the need for some filtering. The Internet permits access to sites that are extremely violent, hateful, or sexually explicit. Although some might argue that adults should be able to view such material freely, most would argue that such imagery is not appropriate for young people. The Supreme Court, in its ruling on CIPA (see Chapter 8), described the protection of children from such material as a compelling interest of the state.

Proponents argue that filters, although imperfect, are the most feasible way to provide such protections. It is true that libraries have for years, through their policies, explicitly or implicitly chosen not to collect pornographic materials, and it could be argued that filters are simply a logical extension of that process. Perhaps the most avid defense of filters came from David Burt, a librarian who was also working in the filtering industry. Burt (1997) expressed particular concern that the level of exposure to pornography in public libraries was significantly greater than librarians admitted. His arguments included the following:

- Although keyword blocking has its problems, the better filters can have this feature disconnected, leaving the more accurate site-blocking feature to govern access.
- Better filters are increasing in their refinement so that fewer nonpornographic sites related to sexuality are blocked.
- Libraries have always restricted the choices of patrons to some extent to material deemed appropriate. Restricting sites that are pornographic is neither new nor undesirable.
- Although filters do perform some type of preselection activity before librarians can review the material, this feature is not new; publisher approval plans have been preselecting materials for years.
- The claim that filters are unconstitutional misconstrues what filtering is; filters restrict access to materials that are not yet part of the library collection. This process is no different from deciding not to select some materials, and as such it is not ipso facto censorship or a violation of constitutional rights.

Auld (2003) observed, "Despite the onslaught of reports denying their effectiveness, filters, when managed properly, can and do achieve a virtually pornography-free online environment while only minimally affecting access to constitutionally protected speech" (p. 38). He made the following four points (Auld 2005):

1. Filtering materials on the Internet does not go against our intellectual freedom principles.
2. Filters are effective.
3. Communities, including staff and patrons, are complaining about pornography on computer screens in their public libraries.
4. The U.S. Supreme Court ruled that there are circumstances in which filtering is constitutional. (p. 197)

The ALA and other organizations did not view these arguments as compelling; rather, they recognize the Internet as another forum for speech that requires First Amendment protection. Among the pertinent resolutions and policies passed by the ALA regarding filtering were: "Resolution on Opposition to Federally Mandated Internet Filtering," "Guidelines and Considerations for Developing a Public Library Internet Use Policy," and "Resolution on the Use of Filtering Software in Libraries." Of particular concern to the ALA is that filters deprive both young people and adults of constitutionally protected speech, and that libraries have a special obligation to protect such access. Many filters were intended to reduce access to certain sites only for minors. The ALA suggested other less restrictive means for ensuring that children do not use the Internet inappropriately, in particular parents' supervision of their children's Internet use while in the library.

Possible Filtering Strategies

- Creating Internet use policies that clearly indicate appropriate and inappropriate use of library computers and establishing penalties for violations of the policy
- Installing filters on all computers
- Installing filters on some terminals, for example, in the children's area but not in the adult area
- Installing filters but setting them to the least restrictive levels
- Asking librarians to supervise Internet use and informing patrons when their use is inappropriate
- Controlling Internet access (especially on unfiltered machines) through the use of library cards or "smart cards"
- Installing privacy screens so that material considered offensive by some cannot be easily viewed accidentally
- Installing computers in locations not easily viewed by third parties, to prevent accidental exposure to offensive material

---

The Supreme Court decision supporting CIPA did not settle the issue of filtering for libraries. Although filtering was not considered an unconstitutional violation of patron rights, the Court indicated that filters must be easily disabled for adult patrons, and that if adults believed their First Amendment rights were violated as a result, they might find a sympathetic ear in the Court.

III. THE INFORMATION POLICIES OF THE AMERICAN LIBRARY ASSOCIATION

Clearly, LIS professionals frequently struggle with their perceived obligations—personal, professional, and organizational—regarding intellectual freedom and First Amendment rights. In response to these pressures, ALA has adopted a variety of policies meant to guide librarians in protecting the rights of their patrons. Most of these policies were developed by ALA's Intellectual Freedom Committee (IFC), which was created in 1940, one year after the initial passage of the Library Bill of Rights, to promote and protect its values by developing policies and written interpretations (ALA 2002). These policies provided national guidance to the library community on some of the most complicated issues facing LIS professionals. Given the burden of this responsibility, the Office of Intellectual Freedom was created in 1967 to help coordinate ALA's intellectual freedom activities. Today it is responsible for implementing the intellectual freedom policies adopted by ALA. It also presents conferences, collects data, and generally promotes the concept of intellectual freedom.

Policymaking remains in the jurisdiction of the IFC (ALA 2002). The policies and their rationale, promulgated by the IFC and passed by ALA Council, can be found in the Office of Intellectual Freedom's *Intellectual Freedom Manual* and also at the ALA Web site (www.ala.org). The following is a brief discussion of some of the major IFC policies organized into four areas: philosophical foundations, access issues, modification of materials, and administrative aspects.

A. Philosophical Foundations

1. The Library Bill of Rights

The fundamental obligations of libraries and library professionals are clearly defined by the central document of the ALA: the Library Bill of Rights (see Figure 9.1).

These obligations include selecting materials for the entire community and the rejection of censorship based on characteristics of the author (Section 1); selecting materials with a wide array of viewpoints and the rejection of censorship due to doctrinal disapproval of content (Section 2); rejecting censorship in general and cooperating with others to fight the abridgement of free speech (Sections 3 and 4); providing library materials and services to all individuals regardless of their characteristics (Section 5); and permitting equitable access to library facilities (Section 6). Upholding the Library Bill of Rights is not easy, especially when attempting to balance the entire range of obligations noted above. The ALA recognized this challenge and subsequently issued a variety of formal interpretations to assist librarians, discussed next.

Figure 9.1. The Library Bill of Rights

The American Library Association affirms that all libraries are forums for information and ideas, and that the following basic policies should guide their services.

1. Books and other library resources should be provided for the interest, information, and enlightenment of all people of the community the library serves. Materials should not be excluded because of the origin, background, or views of those contributing to their creation.

2. Libraries should provide materials and information presenting all points of view on current and historical issues. Materials should not be proscribed or removed because of partisan or doctrinal disapproval.

3. Libraries should challenge censorship in the fulfillment of their responsibility to provide information and enlightenment.

4. Libraries should cooperate with all persons and groups concerned with resisting abridgement of free expression and free access to ideas.

5. A person's right to use a library should not be denied or abridged because of origin, age, background, or views.

6. Libraries which make exhibit spaces and meeting rooms available to the public they serve should make such facilities available on an equitable basis, regardless of the beliefs or affiliations of individuals or groups requesting their use.

Adopted June 18, 1948. Amended February 2, 1961, June 27, 1967, and January 23, 1980, by the ALA Council. Reprinted with permission from the American Library Association.

2. The Freedom to Read Statement

The Freedom to Read Statement was originally adopted in 1953 and revised in 1972. It was jointly prepared by ALA and the American Book Publishers Council and directed at both publishers and librarians. It concerns the importance of reading to a democratic society and the inadvisability of suppressing of ideas due to perceived controversial or immoral content. Among the key points were that the greatest diversity of views, both unorthodox and orthodox, were in the public's interest; that the possession of materials does not constitute an endorsement of the ideas contained within them; that librarians should not permit works to be labeled as subversive or dangerous; and that it was the responsibility of publishers and librarians to protect people's freedom to read, to oppose censorship, and to provide access to a diversity of ideas. Perhaps the Freedom to Read Statement's (ALA 2004a) most notable assertion was the recognition of the importance of the freedom to read, its promise, and its dangers:

> We do not state these propositions in the comfortable belief that what people read is unimportant. We believe rather that what people read is deeply important; that ideas can be dangerous; but that the suppression of ideas is fatal to a democratic society. Freedom itself is a dangerous way of life, but it is ours. (p. 1)

3. The Intellectual Freedom Statement

The Intellectual Freedom Statement expresses the position of the ALA Council and the Freedom to Read Foundation, which is closely associated with ALA. The document closely parallels the Freedom to Read Statement, asserting the importance of our freedom of expression and, through seven propositions, asserting the need for diverse collections and the obligation to resist censorship attempts by individuals or groups. In addition, the statement expresses concern that library professionals are often subjected to threats of legal, financial, and personal pressures as part of efforts to censor materials. The statement reasserts our obligation to resist such attempts.

4. Freedom to View Statement

In response to the growing interest in AV materials, the Educational Film and Video Association adopted a statement in 1979 protecting the rights of viewers and creators of AV materials. Titled the Freedom to View Statement, this document (see Figure 9.2) parallels in many ways the Library Bill of Rights.

5. Privacy: An Interpretation of the Library Bill of Rights

The ALA has a long tradition of affirming the right to privacy of library patrons. Its statements often focus on protecting personally identifiable information, such as the

---

Figure 9.2. Freedom to View Statement

The FREEDOM TO VIEW, along with the freedom to speak, to hear, and to read, is protected by the First Amendment to the Constitution of the United States. In a free society, there is no place for censorship of any medium of expression. Therefore, we affirm these principles:

1. It is in the public interest to provide the broadest possible access to films and other audio-visual materials because they have proven to be among the most effective means for the communication of ideas. Liberty of circulation is essential to insure the constitutional guarantee of freedom of expression.

2. It is in the public interest to provide for our audiences, films and other audiovisual materials which represent a diversity of views and expression. Selection of a work does not constitute or imply agreement with or approval of the content.

3. It is our professional responsibility to resist the constraint of labeling or prejudging a film on the basis of the moral, religious, or political beliefs of the producer or film maker or on the basis of controversial content.

4. It is our professional responsibility to contest vigorously, by all lawful means, every encroachment upon the public's freedom to view.

Drafted by the Educational Film Library Association's Freedom to View Committee, and adopted by the EFLA Board of Directors in February 1979. Reprinted with permission from the American Library Association.

---

identification of a particular patron with a specific item, but it also includes resources consulted, questions asked, records of database searches, records regarding use of facilities, and interlibrary loan records.

Underlying the ALA's position is the belief that patrons will not use materials or make inquiries regarding controversial topics if they believe such actions are not free from public exposure or governmental intrusion. Such exposure and criticism create a chilling effect on First Amendment rights. Adopted in 2002, Privacy: An Interpretation of the Library Bill of Rights reaffirms that protecting the privacy rights of patrons is an ethical obligation of libraries and librarians, and that patrons have a right to be free from unreasonable intrusion or surveillance of their library use. The interpretation also emphasizes that patrons have a right to know about library policies and procedures regarding records that contain their personal information, such as circulation records. Collection of personal information should be limited to only what is necessary to accomplish the mission of the library.

Since its adoption in 2002, libraries have been visited by federal, state, and local law enforcement agencies requesting information on the library use habits of individuals. These activities prompted ALA in 2004 to revise a 1991 version of the "Policy Concerning Confidentiality of Personally Identifiable Information about Library Users" (ALA 2004b). Noting the potential threats to individuals' First Amendment rights, the policy states, "The government's interest in library use reflects a dangerous and fallacious equation of what a person reads with what that person believes or how that person is likely to behave." Recognizing that legitimate national security interests must be respected, the policy also observed that "there has been no showing of a plausible probability that national security will be compromised by any use made of unclassified information available in libraries."

The ALA privacy interpretation was further enhanced by a set of guidelines titled, "RFID in Libraries: Privacy and Confidentiality Guidelines" (ALA 2006). This policy guides librarians in selecting and implementing RFID technologies, identifies best practices, and makes suggestions regarding how to work with vendors. Key issues address educating the public and staff about RFID technologies; permitting alternatives to RFID borrowing processes if desired by patrons; ensuring that the personally identifiable information collected is protected and used appropriately; and protecting library users' privacy whenever possible.

6. Intellectual Freedom Principles for Academic Libraries: An Interpretation of the Library Bill of Rights

Although the Library Bill of Rights was written with many types of libraries in mind, it has most often been associated with public libraries. "Intellectual Freedom Principles for Academic Libraries" provides a specific application of the Library Bill of Rights to academic libraries. Among its provisions, the interpretation affirms the critical importance of intellectual freedom in the development of academic library collections and services, and emphasizes the necessity of (1) protecting patron privacy, (2) developing collections and services that meet the institutional mission, (3) preserving and replacing materials on controversial topics, and (4) providing open and unfiltered access to the collection and information.

B. Access Issues

1. Restricted Access to Library Materials

As noted above, some librarians practice censorship when they choose not to select certain materials they consider offensive. Should a library restrict access to materials it believes are problematic? The ALA interpretation, stated in "Restricted Access to Library Materials," indicates that when libraries use techniques such as closed or restricted shelving (materials available only to staff) or create "adults-only sections, it is a de facto suppression of ideas. But aren't there legitimate reasons to restrict access to some materials? The ALA recognizes that it is acceptable to restrict access to materials for special reasons, such as protection from mutilation or theft, but these should not be used as a pretense for censorship.

The interpretation also addresses the use of legally mandated electronic filters in schools. The policy notes that virtual restrictions are problematic and that school libraries must make concerted efforts to ensure that the filters do not prevent access to constitutionally protected speech. The interpretation also addresses schools that employ computerized reading management programs that assign reading levels to books and other materials, which often confines reading to the program's reading lists. The interpretation states, "Organizing collections by reading management program level, ability, grade, or age level is another example of restricted access" and fails to reflect the reading abilities of many library users.

2. Free Access to Libraries for Minors

ALA's policy "Free Access to Libraries for Minors" clearly states that library materials are not to be restricted on the basis of a patron's age. Hence reading areas restricted to adults, collections limited to adults or teachers, or restricted access to interlibrary loan all would constitute violations of the ALA Library Bill of Rights. In this interpretation, ALA also asserts a key position in regard to access for young people:

> The American Library Association opposes libraries restricting access to library materials and services for minors and hold that it is the parents—and only parents—who might restrict their children—and only their children—from access to library materials and services. (ALA 2002, p. 92)

In other words, the library (except for school libraries) does not serve in loco parentis (in the place of the parent), and the responsibility for controlling the reading, viewing, or listening habits of children is vested with the parent alone.

3. Access for Children and Young People to Videotapes and Other Nonprint Formats

Because of the growing prominence of nonprint formats, ALA established an interpretive document, "Access for Children and Young People to Videotapes and Other Nonprint Formats," in 1989 and amended it in 2004. This interpretation again noted that libraries do not serve in loco parentis and reaffirmed the association's stand that materials should not be restricted on the basis of the patron's age. It specifically rejected policies that set minimum age limits or used cost as a reason for restriction. The interpretation makes clear that the definition of materials is construed broadly to include not only print materials but sound, images, data, games, software, and other content in all formats such as tapes, CDs, DVDs, computer games, software, databases, and other emerging technologies.

Libraries were also cautioned about the inappropriateness of using Motion Picture Association of America (MPAA) or Entertainment Software Rating Board ratings as a means of restricting access to movies or games. At the same time, however, the interpretation protected the right of distributors to affix such ratings on their products and warned librarians that the removal of such ratings would constitute expurgation.

4. Economic Barriers to Information Access

Over the years, some libraries have charged minimal fees for a variety of reasons. With the increasing number of formats, expanding demands to purchase new technologies, and serious constraints on library budgets, many libraries have been tempted to charge substantial fees for their services. This interpretation affirmed that free access to information is a fundamental mission of publicly funded libraries, and that fees ipso facto create barriers to access. The policy states unequivocally that access to information in all formats should be provided equitably and that charging fees for materials, services, and programs is anathema to the concept of free and equal access. Ability to pay should not govern ability to know.

5. Access to Library Resources and Services Regardless of Gender or Sexual Orientation

The advocacy efforts of several groups representing gays, lesbians, and other sexual minorities have brought the issue of sexual orientation into the public forum. Consistent with ALA's general philosophical stand on free and equal access to libraries, the "Access to Library Resources and Services Regardless of Gender or Sexual Orientation" statement affirms these rights and explicitly rejects the nonselection of materials because of the sexual orientation of the creator.

6. Services to Persons with Disabilities

Passed in January 2009, this interpretation reemphasized the library's responsibility to provide the highest levels of service to all users to support "their full participation in society." The interpretation supports a proactive approach to individuals with disabilities and places a responsibility on LIS professionals to be aware of assistive technologies that could improve library services. In addition, libraries should train staff to ensure that individuals with disabilities are treated sensitively and should make sure that accommodations are available when requested to provide full access to library services and programs.

7. Access to Electronic Information, Services, and Networks

The potential and real problems arising from the Internet prompted ALA in 1996 to create a new interpretation of the Library Bill of Rights, which was amended in 2005. "Access to Electronic Information, Services, and Networks" reflects the consistent position of ALA regarding the right of access to information for all library users. The interpretation noted that electronic information services and networks provide extraordinary amounts of information on a global level and that the library cannot attest to the accuracy of all this information. Nonetheless, the guidance asserted that "access should not be restricted or denied for expressing or receiving constitutionally protected speech." It also asserted that access should not be limited because some content might be controversial and that minors have equal rights of access to electronic information sources. Similar to earlier interpretations, this one placed the burden of restricting access to information on the parents of minors rather than on the librarian. In addition, it reconfirmed that users of electronic information services and networks in libraries have a right to privacy and to have their confidentiality protected. The interpretation acknowledged that in some instances the law might require filtering, but in doing so, the library was to employ the "least restrictive level" to maximize access to constitutionally protected speech.

8. Minors and Internet Interactivity

As learning tools have increased in sophistication, some libraries have considered limiting students' use of interactive Web tools. This situation became sufficiently problematic that ALA passed "Minors and Internet Interactivity" in 2009. The interpretation noted that education can be promoted through Internet tools that allow students to share documents, videos, and graphic materials. If inappropriate uses are discovered, they should be dealt with as individual behaviors rather than by attempting to restrict access in a general way. Although young people's involvement in social networking raises legitimate privacy concerns, emphasis should be placed on teaching them about responsible conduct rather than on restricting access to those networks. Restricting interactive Internet tools inhibits students from being part of a community of learners and inhibits free expression and thus their First Amendment rights.

9. Access to Resources and Services in the School Library Media Program

Schools are frequently involved in censorship efforts because of their in loco parentis responsibilities. Parents expect schools to protect their children from harm; indeed, schools are legally obligated to do so. Some parents believe that this harm extends to exposure to "unhealthy" materials. Access to the Web has exacerbated the problem. The ALA recognizes the importance of specifically addressing the needs of school library media centers. "Access to Resources and Services in the School Library Media Program" notes that the underlying value of intellectual freedom should be sustained by school libraries and that the ALA Library Bill of Rights applies in these settings. ALA also affirms that school library media centers have a unique role in promoting critical thinking and problem solving in a pluralistic society. Collections should be developed broadly on the basis of educational criteria free from personal or doctrinal prejudices. Access to the collection and facilities should be free and open and attempts to restrict materials by limiting use, charging fees, or creating closed or restricted shelving should be resisted. The interpretation also notes that while English is the customary language of the United States, library collections should also recognize the "linguistic pluralism" of those the library serves. It places the responsibility for creating broad collections that reflect diverse points of view directly in the hands of the school librarian.

10. Statement on Library Use of Filtering Software

Of primary importance to the ALA is the protection of library users from violations of their First Amendment rights. Because filters can deprive both adults and young people of access to material that is constitutionally protected, the ALA opposes their use. Among their specific concerns are that filters can impose the point of view of the developer of the filtering software, that producers do not identify what sites are blocked, that the criteria used to block sites are poorly defined, and that parents, not the library, should be responsible for regulating the Internet use of their children. ALA passed the "Statement on Library Use of Filtering Software" in July 1997 and revised it in November 2000.

11. Resolution Reaffirming the Principles of Intellectual Freedom in the Aftermath of Terrorist Attacks

The shocking events of September 11, 2001, understandably disturbed and frightened people. In their aftermath, Congress passed a variety of legislation such as the U.S.A. PATRIOT Act. Although many of the provisions of these acts were important to restore confidence and security, the ALA, as well as other groups concerned about individuals' civil liberties, grew concerned that certain elements of these laws promoted potentially oppressive behavior on the part of governmental officials. The fear that the legitimate exercise of free speech might be compromised led to the passing of the "Resolution Reaffirming the Principles of Intellectual Freedom" in January 2002. In it, ALA reaffirmed its opposition to government censorship and suppression of news and government information, exhorted libraries to protect the privacy and confidentiality of their users, and affirmed the importance of dissent and timely provision of information to the citizenry.

12. Resolution on the U.S.A. PATRIOT Act and Related Measures That Infringe on the Rights of Library Users

Similar to the previous statement, this resolution, passed in January 2003, expresses concern that some of the provisions of the PATRIOT Act inappropriately expanded the authority of the federal government to investigate citizens and noncitizens. Such authority threatens the privacy rights of patrons using libraries and impedes the dissemination of knowledge. As such, ALA declared that the act is "a present danger to the constitutional rights and privacy rights of library users." Without unimpeded access to libraries and free inquiry within them, the purpose of libraries and their democratic mission cannot be fulfilled. The resolution exhorts libraries to educate patrons about the possible excesses of the PATRIOT Act and to take action to ensure that the privacy rights and the rights of inquiry of library users are not adversely affected.

C. Modification of Materials

1. Expurgation of Library Materials

Rather than restricting potentially controversial items, some librarians might attempt to alter library materials. This might include obliterating text or altering or excising a photograph. Any attempt to alter material in this manner is considered expurgation of library materials and, hence, a type of restricted access. As such, it is a violation of the ALA Library Bill of Rights.

2. Statement on Labels and Rating Systems

Libraries contain materials on many subjects, representing many points of view. The presence of these materials does not, in itself, constitute an endorsement of the contents, but the library does have to make professional judgments about how to organize them and make them available. For example, we label some books history, others as science. It is also typical to create and label sections of collections by genre, such as mystery or Western. These actions are considered by the ALA as "viewpoint-neutral directional aids" and are not a violation of the Library Bill of Rights. Insofar as labeling does not attempt to restrict access, it is acceptable. ALA's concern is with affixing prejudicial labels intended "to warn, discourage or prohibit users or certain groups of users from accessing the material." For example, labeling materials "adults only" or "teachers only" would have a tendency to restrict access. As noted previously, placing MPAA ratings on videos and DVDs, unless already provided by the distributor, is considered a violation of this policy.

Similarly, the inclusion of ratings on bibliographic records is also prohibited. In 2005, the policy was reviewed and updated to incorporate issues related to the Internet and electronic access. The policy indicates that "the ability for library users to access electronic information using library computers does not indicate endorsement or approval of that information by the library." Hitchcock (2006) suggested that this interpretation is not as helpful as it might be in relation to the enhancement of electronic bibliographic records through the use of fields that have links to external electronic files that contain evaluative information. No doubt as electronic access increases, the ALA will need to revisit this issue.

D. Administrative Aspects

1. Challenged Materials

From time to time, individuals challenge materials, insisting that they be removed or restricted. Challenges are stressful because they frequently involve political pressure and unpleasant media exposure. Censorship attempts threaten the dissemination of ideas and as such, challenge the basic principles of intellectual freedom. The statement on challenged materials asserts that libraries should have a clear materials selection and collection development policy, including criteria for the collection of Web sites. Materials that conform to that policy should not be removed simply because individuals challenge them. Rather, the library should protect such materials and insist on an adversary hearing (as a first step) so that such requests can be closely scrutinized. This is not to say that a library should never remove materials or Web sites, but doing so under pressure should be avoided.

2. Policy on the Confidentiality of Library Circulation Records

When individuals borrow something from a library, it is normally assumed that no one else has access to the circulation record. Underlying the privacy of circulation records is the belief that if individuals think that their reading, listening, or viewing habits can be scrutinized, they might feel pressure or embarrassment. Breaching the right and expectation of privacy of one's reading habits can create a chilling effect on an individual's use of the library, and essentially restricts the right to use the library and the ideas contained within.

Bowers (2006) identified a variety of situations in which the government tried to obtain library circulation records. In the 1960s and 1970s, the IRS attempted to obtain information on individuals checking out materials on explosives. Similarly, in the 1970s and 1980s the FBI's Library Awareness Program attempted to examine the reading habits of individuals thought to be security risks or from countries unfriendly to the United States. In 2004, the FBI attempted to obtain records regarding individuals checking out biographies of Osama bin Laden.

Not all attempts to obtain circulation records come from federal law enforcement agencies as local officials also make requests. ALA policy asserts that any records that associate an individual with particular materials are confidential and should be released only after the library is satisfied that a subpoena has been properly issued. This means that LIS professionals should usually insist on a court hearing to ensure that they are required to turn over the records. This policy has been quite useful.

Because of the increased attention from law enforcement agencies, the ALA in 2005 promulgated some additional guidelines, "Confidentiality and Coping with Law Enforcement Inquiries: Guidelines for the Library and Its Staff" (ALA 2005). These guidelines review the basic philosophical principles that support the need for confidentiality of library records and recommend various actions libraries can take to help protect confidentiality, such as not creating unnecessary records and destroying records in a timely and lawful manner when they are no longer needed. They also identify procedures to follow when law enforcement agents visit the library or when the library receives subpoenas or search warrants issued by a regular court or a FISA warrant.

3. Guidelines for the Development and Implementation of Policies, Regulations, and Procedures Affecting Access to Library Materials, Services, and Facilities

In the early 1990s, a homeless individual was removed from a public library for inappropriate behavior. There was much debate over this issue, which came to be known as the Kreimer case (*Kreimer v. Bureau of Police* 1991), because although the library community wanted to ensure the rights of each individual, even one who might behave differently, they also wanted to maintain control of the library environment for the safety and access of others. Because the case was so controversial, the library community looked to ALA for guidance on the development of rules and regulations regarding patron behavior. The guidelines made it clear that patron behavior rules should be no more restrictive than absolutely necessary, should be consistent with constitutional protections of citizens, and should be consistent with the ALA Library Bill of Rights and the mission of the library. The guidelines further condemned restrictions placed on specific groups of people, such as children or the homeless, and asserted that local guidelines should be clearly written including an appeal procedure.

After more than a decade, Kelly (2006) analyzed the impact of Kreimer and several other court decisions regarding hygiene and patron behavior in public libraries and concluded:

1. Libraries are considered public forums and removing individuals on the basis of a particular political message violates an individual's right to freedom of speech.
2. The First Amendment is applicable when considering an individual's right to receive information in libraries.
3. A disruptive individual can be removed.
4. Personal hygiene can be a reason for removal as long as the standards for removal are clear and reasonable.

The long-term implications of Kreimer have also been a focus of the Hunger, Homelessness, and Poverty Task Force (2005) of ALA's Social Responsibility Roundtable. The task force was particularly concerned about the growth of local library policies such as "odor policies." The task force felt that some librarians were ignoring the underlying dynamics of poverty and that homelessness and poor hygiene were being treated as forms of behavior, rather than as a symptom of extreme poverty. Consequently, the homeless were being ignored as a service population and denied access. These issues are likely to grow in intensity during periods of economic distress.

IV. AN INTERNATIONAL PERSPECTIVE ON FREEDOM OF EXPRESSION

Although the ALA Library Bill of Rights is the centerpiece that guides library practice in the United States, it is instructive to remember that the battle for freedom of expression is a concern throughout the world. In 2002, the International Federation of Library Associations celebrated its seventy-fifth anniversary. At this meeting, it passed the Glasgow Declaration (see Figure 9.3). It is a fitting expression of the universal concern for the free flow of ideas and the ability of all to express those ideas. The close kinship with the Library Bill of Rights is manifest.

Figure 9.3. The Glasgow Declaration on Libraries, Information Services, and Intellectual Freedom

Meeting in Glasgow on the occasion of the 75th anniversary of its formation, the International Federation of Library Associations and Institutions (IFLA) declares that:

IFLA proclaims the fundamental right of human beings both to access and to express information without restriction.

IFLA and its worldwide membership support, defend and promote intellectual freedom as expressed in the United Nations Universal Declaration of Human Rights. This intellectual freedom encompasses the wealth of human knowledge, opinion, creative thought and intellectual activity.

IFLA asserts that a commitment to intellectual freedom is a core responsibility of the library and information profession worldwide, expressed through codes of ethics and demonstrated through practice.

IFLA affirms that:

- Libraries and information services provide access to information, ideas and works of imagination in any medium and regardless of frontiers. They serve as gateways to knowledge, thought and culture, offering essential support for independent decision-making, cultural development, research and lifelong learning by both individuals and groups.

- Libraries and information services contribute to the development and maintenance of intellectual freedom and help to safeguard democratic values and universal civil rights. Consequently, they are committed to offering their clients access to relevant resources and services without restriction and to opposing any form of censorship.

- Libraries and information services shall acquire, preserve and make available the widest variety of materials, reflecting the plurality and diversity of society. The selection and availability of library materials and services shall be governed by professional considerations and not by political, moral and religious views.

- Libraries and information services shall make materials, facilities and services equally accessible to all users. There shall be no discrimination for any reason including race, national or ethnic origin, gender or sexual preference, age, disability, religion, or political beliefs.

- Libraries and information services shall protect each user's right to privacy and confidentiality with respect to information sought or received and resources consulted, borrowed, acquired or transmitted.

IFLA therefore calls upon libraries and information services and their staff to uphold and promote the principles of intellectual freedom and to provide uninhibited access to information.

Statement prepared by the International Federation of Library Associations and Institutions (IFLA), Free Access to Information and Freedom of Expression (FAIFE) Committee and approved by the Governing Board of IFLA 27 March 2002, The Hague, Netherlands. Proclaimed by the Council of IFLA 19 August 2002, Glasgow, Scotland. Available: www.ifla.org/en/publications/the-glasgow-declaration-on-libraries-information-services-and-intellectual-freedom. Reprinted with permission.

V. SUMMARY

LIS professionals are critical information providers, and the policies they adopt on the selection, organization, and dissemination of information determine in large part their ability to uphold their professional obligations and fulfill the library's mission. Few policies are as important as those related to intellectual freedom and resistance to censorship. Libraries represent a special forum: a place where everyone can find a broad range of points of view presented in a variety of formats on topics of interest, even if those topics might be controversial. The intellectual freedom policies adopted by the ALA serve as both a philosophical and instrumental foundation for the practices of libraries and LIS professionals.

The task of defending intellectual freedom is challenging and LIS professionals have often been subjected to intense pressures as they ensure open access to information. There is little reason to believe that these problems will dissipate. On the contrary, with the increasing use of the Web, it is likely that they will increase. Only a firm understanding of the principles of the profession can provide the necessary rationale to protect patrons' rights to read and view materials of their choosing.

REFERENCES

Aiken, Julian. 2007. "Outdated and Irrelevant? Rethinking the Library Bill of Rights—Does It Work in the Real World?" *American Libraries* 38 (September 1): 54–56.

American Libraries. 2001 (April): 23.

American Library Association. 2001. "Violence in the Media: A Joint Statement." Chicago: ALA.

———. 2002. *Intellectual Freedom Manual.* 6th ed. Chicago: ALA.

———. 2004a. "Freedom to Read Statement" Chicago: ALA.

———. 2004b. "Policy Concerning Confidentiality of Personally Identifiable Information about Library Users." Chicago: ALA.

———. 2005. "Confidentiality and Coping with Law Enforcement Inquiries: Guidelines for the Library and Its Staff." Chicago: ALA.

———. 2006. "RFID in Libraries: Privacy and Confidentiality Guidelines." Chicago: ALA.

Asheim, Lester. 1954. "The Librarian's Responsibility: Not Censorship but Selection." In *Freedom of Book Selection.* Edited by Frederic Mosher. Chicago: ALA, 95–96.

Association of American Publishers, American Library Association, and Association for Supervision and Curriculum Development. 1981. *Limiting What Students Shall Read.* Washington, DC: Association of American Publishers.

Auld, Hampton. 2003. "Filters Work: Get Over It." *American Libraries* 34 (February): 38–41.

———. 2005. "Do Internet Filters Infringe upon Access to Materials in Libraries?" *Public Libraries* (July/August): 196–198.

Bowers, Stacey L. 2006. "Privacy and Library Records." *Journal of Academic Librarianship* 32 (July): 377–383.

Brennan Center for Justice. 2006. *Internet Filters: A Public Policy Report*, 2nd ed. New York: The Brennan Center for Justice.

Burbules, Nicholas C. 2001. "Paradoxes of the Web: The Ethical Dimensions of Credibility." *Library Trends* 49 (winter): 441–453.

Burt, David. 1997. "In Defense of Filtering." *American Libraries* 28 (August): 46–48.

Busha, C. H. 1971. "The Attitudes of Midwestern Public Librarians toward Intellectual Freedom and Censorship." Unpublished dissertation. Indiana University. Cited in Serebnick (1979).

Dewey, Melvil. 1989. "The Profession." *Library Journal* (June 15): 5. Reprint of article in *American Library Journal* 1 (September 1876): 5.

Doyle, Tony, and John L. Hammond. 2006. "Net Cred: Evaluating the Internet as a Research Soucrce." *Reference Services Review* 34: 56–70.

Dresang, Eliza T. 2006. "Intellectual Freedom and Libraries: Complexity and Change in the Twenty-First Century Digital Environment." *Library Quarterly* 76: 169–192.

Eakin, M. L. 1948. "Censorship in Public High School Libraries." Master's thesis. Columbia University. Cited in Serebnick (1979).

Edward, Ellen. 2002. "Web Filters Block Health Information." *Washington Post*, December 11, A02.

Farley, J. J. 1964. "Book Censorship in the Senior High Libraries of Nassau County, N.Y." Unpublished dissertation. New York University. Cited in Serebnick (1979).

Fiske, Marjerie. 1959. *Book Selection and Censorship: A Study of School and Public Libraries in California*. Berkeley: University of California Press. Cited in Serebnick (1979).

Garrison, Dee. 1972–1973. "The Tender Technicians: The Feminization of Public Librarianship." *Journal of Social History* 6 (winter): 131–156.

Goodstein, Laurie. 2007. "Prisons Purging Books on Faith from Libraries." *New York Times*, September 10.

Heins, Marjorie, and Christina Cho. 2001. *Internet Filters: A Public Policy Report*. Free Expression Policy Project, National Coalition Against Censorship, fall.

Hitchcock, Leonard A. 2006. "A Critique of the New Statement on Labeling." *Journal of Academic Librarianship* 32 (May): 296–302.

Hopkins, Dianne McAfee. 1993. "A Conceptual Model of Factors Influencing the Outcome of Challenges to Library Materials in Secondary School Settings." *Library Quarterly* 63 (January): 40–72.

Hunger, Homelessness, and Poverty Task Force. 2005. "Are Public Libraries Criminalizing Poor People?" *Public Libraries* 44 (May/June): 175.

ICRA. 2010. "About ICRA." Available: www.fosi.org/icra (accessed February 10, 2010).

Island Trees Union Free School District v. Pico. 102 S. Ct. 2799 (1982).

Kelly, James. 2006. "Barefoot in Columbus: The Legacy of Kreimer and the Legality of Public Library Access Policies Concerning Appearance and Hygiene." *Public Libraries* 45 (May/June): 42–49.

Kranich, Nancy. 2004. "Why Filters Won't Protect Children or Adults." *Library Administration and Management* 18 (winter): 14–18.

Kreimer v. Bureau of Police for the Town of Morristown, et al. 765 F. Supp. 181 (D.N.J. 1991).

Kunkel, Dale, and Lara Zwarun. 2006. "How Real Is the Problem of TV Violence?" In *Handbook of Children, Culture and Violence*. Edited by Nancy E. Dowd, Dorothy G. Singer, and Robin Fretwell Wilson. Thousand Oaks: Sage, 203–224.

Martino, Steven C., Rebecca L. Collins, Marc N. Elliott, Amy Stachman, David E. Kanouse, and Sandra H. Berry. 2006. "Exposure to Degrading Versus Nondegrading Music Lyrics and Sexual Behavior among Youth." *Pediatrics* 118: 430–441.

Mathews, Virginia H., Judith G. Flum, and Karen A. Whitney. 1990. "Kids Need Libraries: School and Public Libraries Preparing the Youth of Today for the World of Tomorrow." *School Library Journal* 36 (April): 33–37.

Norman, Dax R. 2006. "Website You Can Trust." *American Libraries* (August): 36.

Pope, M. J. 1973. "A Comparative Study of the Opinions of School, College, and Public Librarians Concerning Certain Categories of Sexually Oriented Literature." Doctoral dissertation, Rutgers University, Rutgers, NJ.

Rieh, Soo Young, and David R. Danielson. 2007. "Credibility: A Multidisciplinary Framework." In *Annual Review of Information Science and Technology*. Vol. 41. Edited by Blaise Cronin. Medford, NJ: Information Today, 307–364.

Ross, Catherine J. 2006. "Constitutional Obstacles to Regulating Violence in the Media." In *Handbook of Children, Culture and Violence*. Edited by Nancy E. Dowd, Dorothy G. Singer, and Robin Fretwell Wilson. Thousand Oaks, CA: Sage, 291–310.

Schultz, Connie. 2007. "One Word Ignites Some Librarians' Ire." *Cleveland Plain Dealer*, February 20.

Serebnick, Judith. 1979. "A Review of Research Related to Censorship in Libraries." *Library Research* 1: 95–118.

Smith, Abby. 2007. "Valuing Preservation." *Library Trends* 56 (summer): 4-25.

Swan, John. 1986. "Untruth or Consequences." *Library Journal* 111 (July 1): 44–52.

Wilson, Barbara J., and Nicole Martins. 2006. "The Impact of Violent Music on Youth." In *Handbook of Children, Culture and Violence*. Edited by Nancy E. Dowd, Dorothy G. Singer, and Robin Fretwell Wilson. Thousand Oaks, CA: Sage, 179–202.

SELECTED READINGS: INFORMATION POLICY AND LIBRARIES

Books

Adams, Helen R., Robert F. Bocher, Carol A. Gordon, and Elizabeth Barry-Kessler. *Privacy in the 21st Century: Issues for Public, School, and Academic Libraries*. Westport, CT: Libraries Unlimited, 2005.

American Library Association. *Intellectual Freedom Manual*. 7th ed. Chicago: ALA, 2006.

Samek, Toni. *Librarianship and Human Rights: A Twenty-First Century Guide*. Oxford: Chandos, 2007.

Swan, John C., and Noel Peattie. *The Freedom to Lie: A Debate about Democracy*. Jefferson, NC: McFarland, 1989.

Woodward, Jeannette. *What Every Librarian Should Know about Electronic Privacy*. Westport, CT: Libraries Unlimited, 2007.

Articles

Bee, Robert. "The Importance of Preserving Paper-Based Artifacts in a Digital Age." *Library Quarterly* 78 (April 2008): 179–194.

Church, Jim. "Blogs, Battles, & Bees." *Library Journal* 133 (May 15, 2008): 60–66.

Cloonan, Michele Valerie. "W(h)ither Preservation?" *Library Quarterly* 71 (April 2001): 231–242.

Cloonan, Michele V., and Shelby Sanett. "The Preservation of Digital Content." *Portal: Libraries and the Academy* 5 (2005): 213–237.

Dobija, Jane. "The First Amendment Needs New Clothes." *American Libraries* 38 (September 2007): 50–53.

Hahn, Trudi Bellardo. "Impacts of Mass Digitization Projects on Libraries and Information Policy." *Bulletin of the American Society for Information Science and Technology* 33 (October/November 2006): 20–24.

Jaeger, Paul T., John Carlo Bertot, Charles R. McClure, and Lesley A. Langa. "The Policy Implications of Internet Connectivity in Public Libraries." *Government Information Quarterly* 23 (2006): 123–141.

Jaeger, Paul T., and Zheng Yan. "One Law with Two Outcomes: Comparing the Implementation of CIPA in Public Libraries and Schools." *Information Technology and Libraries* (March 2009): 6–14.

Kranich, Nancy. "Why Filters Won't Protect Children or Adults." *Library Administration and Management* 18 (winter 2004): 14–18.

Relyea, Harold C. "Access to Federal Government Information: A New Status Report." In *The Bowker Annual*. 53rd ed. Medford, NJ: Information Today, 2008, 3–27.

Schmidt, Cindy M. "Those Interfering Filters! How to Deal with the Reality of Filters in Your School Library." *Library Media Connection* (March 2008): 54–55.

Smith, Abby. "Valuing Preservation." *Library Trends* 56 (summer 2007): 4–25.

10

The Values and Ethics of Library and Information Science

But if indeed we have no philosophy, then we are depriving ourselves of the guiding light of reason, and we live only a day-to-day existence, lurching from crisis to crisis, and lacking the driving force of an inner conviction of the value of our work. (Foskett 1962)

I. THE VALUES OF LIBRARY AND INFORMATION SCIENCE

Librarians and information professionals are moral agents, responsible to themselves, others, and society as a whole. Our values and ethics provide a framework for our conduct, policies, and services. Without them, we are, as Foskett observed, merely lurching about—stumbling in the dark. Values are strongly held beliefs that serve to guide our actions. When we think of values, we associate them with words like convictions or principles more than opinions. Values structure our experience and provide insight when we must make important decisions affecting the future. Institutions and professions also have values, which provide for institutional and professional stability and consistency when important issues arise. Society and the library are constantly changing, but our values often remain the same, serving as an important compass when changes in purpose are contemplated. Let us take a look at some of the basic values that are integral to our professional work.

> **Seven Values of Library and Information Science**
>
> 1. Service
> 2. Reading and the book are important
> 3. Respect for truth and the search for truth
> 4. Tolerance
> 5. The public good
> 6. Justice
> 7. Aesthetics

A. Seven Values of Library and Information Science

1. The First Value: Service

Perhaps the most distinctive feature of library and information science, in contrast, for example, to computer science, is that the purpose of the field is to communicate knowledge to people. This is more than just "meeting an information need," which is often the common parlance for the activities of the modern library. Underlying the value of service is the betterment of the individual and the community as a whole. Bringing knowledge to people and the society is the sine qua non of the profession. Pierce Butler (1951) characterized this notion succinctly over fifty years ago:

> The cultural motivation of librarianship is the promotion of wisdom in the individual and the community... to communicate, so far as possible, the whole of scholarship to the whole community. The librarian undertakes to supply literature on any and every subject to any and every citizen, for any and every purpose.... [These actions], in the long run, will sharpen the understanding, judgment, and prudence of the readers and thus sustain and advance civilization. (pp. 246–247)

Libraries and LIS professionals are about serving people and society as a whole. Service to others has been the foundation of American librarianship for more than a hundred years, and this value applies to LIS professionals no matter what type of library or information service is involved.

> Our natural reaction to the approach of a patron is not irritation at being interrupted, but delight at another chance to help someone pick his or her way through our beloved maze. It is, we should admit, a noble urge, this altruism of ours, one that seems both morally and psychologically good. (Finks 1991, p. 353)

Librarianship emerged as one of the service-oriented professions of the nineteenth century in part as a reaction to the profit-centered, entrepreneurial excesses of the industrial revolution (Winter 1988). As such, librarianship arose from the same American wellspring as nursing, social work, teaching, medicine, law, and the clergy.

This service orientation might also be related to the fact that American libraries, at least since the latter half of the nineteenth century, have been numerically dominated by women. When women entered the workforce during this period, their activities were expected to conform to the stereotypes of appropriate behavior for their gender (Garrison 1972–1973). Women occupied professions distinguished by their nurturing characteristics, teaching, nursing, social work, and librarianship among them. Garrison (1972–1973) referred to nineteenth-century librarians as "tender technicians" (p. 131). Serving others, usually at a sacrificial wage one might add, was part and parcel of librarianship.

However, as fiscal resources dwindle in today's economy, libraries are more and more pressured to act as businesses. A business-oriented approach would emphasize concepts such as increased productivity, pricing information as a commodity, and repackaging information services to market as products for sale. Estabrook (1982) warned, however, that transforming library practice to a business model could change the very nature of library service. For example, it could lead to libraries only serving certain patrons—those who are easiest to satisfy and therefore most cost efficient—and ignoring those difficult to serve or reluctant to use library services. Fortunately, widespread adoption of many business-oriented practices does not seem to have had these deleterious effects. Many libraries do, in fact, use management techniques, technologies, and marketing strategies often borrowed directly from the private sector while continuing to provide quality service—testimony to the persistence of service as a fundamental value in most libraries—whether in the private or public sector.

Part of the reason for the tenaciousness of the service value might be because it has played such an explicit role in the philosophical foundations of librarianship for so long. Many of those tenets were articulated by one of the most notable figures in the history of librarianship, S. R. Ranganathan. Ranganathan (1892–1972) conducted much of his work and study in India, beginning its first school of library science. His contributions were international in scope, influencing librarianship in America as well as other countries. He explored a number of philosophical and theoretical issues, most notably classification theory, and developed some of the most fundamental underpinnings of libraries and librarianship.

> The vital principle of the library—which has struggled through all the stages of its evolution, is common to all its different forms and will persist to be its distinguishing feature for all time to come—is that it is an instrument of universal education, and assembles together and freely distributes all the tools of education and disseminates knowledge with their aid. (Ranganathan 1963, p. 354)

Ranganathan proposed five laws of library science that remain central to our understanding of libraries, and that reflect his deeply held conviction that the library is dedicated to the service of all people (1963). A brief review of these laws provides a surprisingly contemporary perspective on the central values of library service.

> **Ranganathan's Five Laws of Library Science**
>
> 1. Books are for use.
> 2. Books are for all.
> 3. Every book its reader.
> 4. Save the time of the reader.
> 5. The library is a growing organism.

a. Books Are for Use

Ranganathan observed that in earlier times, books were often chained to prevent their removal, and that the emphasis was on storage and preservation rather than on use. He did not reject the notion that preservation and storage were important because, before the invention of the printing press, materials were rare and difficult to produce. But he asserted that the purpose of such activities was to promote their use. If stored and preserved materials were not used, libraries had little value. By emphasizing use, Ranganathan refocused the attention of the profession on access-related issues such as the library's location, loan policies, hours and days of operation, and such mundanities as furniture, and the quality of staffing. Ranganathan's law maintains its currency, particularly as emphasis is now being placed on quality customer service and developing a customer orientation. Given contemporary attitudes about public institutions needing greater accountability, this orientation is both healthy and essential for survival.

b. Books Are for All + RA Services + follow rules/regulations

Ranganathan felt that all individuals from all social environments are entitled to library service, and that the basis of library use is education, to which all are entitled. These entitlements, however, are not without some important obligations for both libraries and patrons. Among these are that librarians should have excellent firsthand knowledge of the people served, that collections should meet the special interests of the community, and that libraries should extensively promote and advertise their services to attract a wide range of users. In addition, Ranganathan felt that library selectors should emphasize materials that are well written and well illustrated. Library users, on the other hand, should be advocates for library service, follow the rules and regulations, keep the library in good order, and take out only materials that are needed.

Ranganathan understood that to accomplish these objectives, society must contribute. For example, he argued that the state is obligated to provide financial resources through taxation and legislation so that all people can be served by libraries. In addition, the state should create a library authority, with a state librarian, whose duty it would be to ensure library service by creating institutions for that purpose. Similarly, the local library authority is obligated to provide service to all individuals in the local area.

c. Every Book Its Reader

Ranganathan argued that the library could devise many methods, such as direct access to the collection (open shelving), to ensure that each item found its appropriate reader. He saw open shelving as critical because it gave people the chance to examine the collection freely. According to Ranganathan (1963), "In an open access library, the reader is permitted to wander among the books and lay his hands on any of them at his will and pleasure" (p. 259). Another strategy for maximizing the chances of matching a reader with a book involved how the collection was arranged. Ranganathan suggested that collections should be arranged by subject for the most effective access. He was not dogmatic about this arrangement, however, and he possessed a very modern sense of the need for marketing library materials. For example, he suggested that the library set up displays that showcased certain collections, such as newly acquired materials. He also suggested special reading areas for popular materials. Other avenues for matching books with readers included using trained professional staff to survey patrons about the collections, providing reader's advisory services, conducting programs such as story hours, providing extension services, and selecting good books. Finally, the library could promote and market its services to readers through publicity, displays, publications, and public activities such as festivals.

d. Save the Time of the Reader

Ranganathan recommended the application of appropriate business methods to improve library management. He observed that centralizing a library collection in one location provided distinct advantages. He also noted that excellent staff would include those who possessed strong reference skills, as well as strong technical skills in cataloging, cross-referencing, ordering, accessioning, and circulation. All of these functions contribute to timely service to the user. In a way he anticipated, although not necessarily predicted, today's more competitive environment in which the seeker has more than one option for finding material and information.

e. The Library Is a Growing Organism

Ranganathan described this law as the fundamental principle that governs library organization: "It is an accepted biological fact that a growing organism alone will survive. An organism which ceases to grow will petrify and perish" (p. 326). Ranganathan argued that libraries must accommodate growth in staff, the physical collection, patron use, and the facility including reading areas, shelving, and space for the catalog. As collections grew, he anticipated increased need for security against theft and a need to design traffic flow to permit easy movement around the floors. He further recognized that personnel structure and decision making would also be affected by this growth. He anticipated the increased division of labor among administrative, technical, and reference staff and recommended that an administrative staff council be created to assist in the operations and organization of the library. This clearly anticipated the participatory management styles of the 1960s and beyond.

Ranganathan's laws are central to library and information science and they make explicit many of the principles that guide our practices for structuring library collections, services, and staff even today. Gorman (1995) revisited Ranganathan's work and advanced five new laws:

- **Libraries serve humanity**. This is a restatement of the service ethic that permeates librarianship, recognizing that the "dominant ethic of librarianship is service to the individual, community, and society as a whole" (p. 784).

- **Respect all forms by which knowledge is communicated**. In Ranganathan's time, print materials dominated. For this reason, his principles talk of books and readers. But today, knowledge can be found in libraries in many more forms. According to Gorman, "each new means of communication enhances and supplements the strengths of all previous means" (p. 784). This new principle suggests that library workers should not fear that new forms of communication will replace print; rather, librarians should exploit all media to advance library service.

- **Use technology intelligently to enhance service.** The obligation of library professionals is neither to resist new technologies nor to use technology uncritically. Rather, it is to recognize the potential of some technologies to help libraries accomplish their missions. To the extent that new technologies can offer advantages to library service, they should be applied in a constructive and intelligent manner.

- **Protect free access to knowledge.** The historical role of the library as one of the foundations of democratic institutions remains as important today as ever. The controls and centralization that some new technologies require can exacerbate many of the problems involved in protecting intellectual freedom. The knowledge of the world's cultures must be freely transmitted to all; otherwise freedom is threatened and tyranny promoted.

- **Honor the past and create the future.** A central value of librarianship is the recognition that the past serves as a guide to the future. The library has been a central institution for archiving humankind's cultural record. To this end the library must continue to protect the historical record and perhaps use it as a guide, while adapting to the needs of the future.

2. The Second Value: Reading and the Book Are Important

A central value of both libraries and library workers has been and continues to be a deep and abiding respect for both reading and the book:

> The first presupposition associated with the appearance of libraries is a faith in the power and use value of books, as repositories of practical, technical and theoretical knowledge, of wisdom and truth, of a particular state of the language and a social memory. (Jacob 2002, p. 42)

Consider some of the advantages that books possess:

- Are generally lightweight and very portable, easy to take to the beach or to bed
- Require no electricity (except when it's dark)
- Require no additional equipment such as video display terminals, printers, and so on
- Require little maintenance and repair, and when repair is needed it is usually quite inexpensive and can be accomplished by an individual with minimal training; no service contract is needed
- Require no diagrams or documentation to use
- Can get pretty damp and dusty and still function

- Can be dropped on the floor with little damage
- Are comparatively cheap
- Can be browsed easily and contain finding aids, such as an index, that are relatively easy to use (compared with using Boolean logic)
- Provide a large number of thoughtful and interconnected ideas in one place that can be read from start to finish or scanned in sections
- Are an excellent source for stimulating the imagination
- Store easily
- Can be written in and text can be easily underlined for emphasis during later reading and study
- Require little knowledge to operate
- Can last a very long time, especially when printed on acid-free paper

This is not to say that each of these features is unique to books, but in combination they represent a very impressive technology. It is unlikely that any electronic technology will possess this combination of advantages in the near future.

The book offers other advantages as well. For example, Neill (1992) argued that books stimulate more active intellectual involvement and diminish the passivity associated with screen time. Compared to television and movies, books can convey more complex concepts and more closely approximate real life. Thus exposure to books often leads to improved understanding, discovery, and growth in our personal lives.

> Reading is a visual, vocal and auditory process which also requires the reader's thoughts to follow the thread of an argument or meditation, to share a vision. A book is a tool of learning and stimulator of thought, a kind of cognitive prosthesis which, when consulted, provides information, ideas, coherent logic, knowledge or wisdom. (Jacob 2002, p. 43)

The strength of the profession's commitment to reading is evidenced by the library's concern for those who cannot read. Millions of U.S. adults are unable to read an eighth-grade-level book or simple but essential items such as bus schedules, newspapers, and maps. For these individuals, the world of information is dramatically inaccessible. Thus libraries continue to emphasize books and reading, even while images dominate the popular media. It is no doubt a reason why many LIS professionals feel ambivalent when they see more and more library collection expenditures for audiovisual materials and electronic technologies.

3. The Third Value: Respect for Truth and the Search for Truth

When individuals seek answers to questions, they expect the library to provide timely and accurate information. Library professionals would consider themselves remiss if they failed in that task. However, library users are sometimes investigating issues that are much more complex than simply answering a single question. Respecting the search for truth requires that librarians reduce barriers that might frustrate that search. For example, if individuals believed that their circulation records could be made public, they might not look for information considered controversial. Therefore librarians reduce this barrier by protecting individuals' privacy rights by refusing to supply information concerning circulation records to others.

4. The Fourth Value: Tolerance

Tolerance has a complementary relationship to truth; tolerance admits of the possibility that our ability to judge the truth is flawed, and that there might be many truths, or that the truth in some cases might not be known. It presumes that more than one perspective on a subject might be reasonable and that exposure to many ideas might help us understand and approach the truth. The value of tolerance thus suggests that library collections should possess a variety of perspectives on a wide array of topics. Swan (1986) argued that librarians must have the untrue on their shelves as well as the true. For example, Hitler's *Mein Kampf* contains ideas that are clearly false, but analyzing such ideas might prove quite useful in teaching individuals about the truth of our past and the dangers that might lie in the future. If such material were unavailable it might impede one's understanding of the truth. Tolerance suggests that LIS professionals should be nonjudgmental in terms of the value or direction of a library user's inquiry. Without such a value, library collections would be little more than the dogmatic assertions of the majority.

5. The Fifth Value: The Public Good

The notion of the public good is fundamental to library service and has several implications. First, it assumes that people and society as a whole are changed and, in the long run, improved by ideas. There is little reason for libraries to exist if we do not believe that they make a positive contribution to society. As noted earlier, a list of those contributions might include promoting literacy, reading, and education; preserving the cultural record; serving as a community center; and offering programs that entertain and inform. Second, the notion of the public good recognizes people's right to enjoy life and that the library has a role in promoting entertainment and pleasure. Certainly the presence of copious fiction, romance, travel, and popularized science and history attests to LIS professionals' strong feelings about this dimension of library service. It is notable that the value of the public good is sufficiently ambiguous to accommodate both "improvement" and "entertainment." The third implication of the public good is that LIS professionals place service to the community above personal interest, and that service to the community requires LIS professionals to actively reach out to those who could benefit from library services, regardless of age or economic status.

6. The Sixth Value: Justice

McCook (2001) pointed out that an underlying goal of our profession is information equity: "inherent in this goal is social justice—working for universal literacy; defending intellectual freedom; preserving and making accessible the human record to all" (p. 81). In part, this means that each individual should have equal access to library and information services and be respected as an individual. Providing inadequate service to any individual is a violation of such a value.

The philosopher John Rawls (1958) noted, however, that justice cannot be understood solely as equality; it must also include fairness. Equality implies an equal amount; fairness implies the amount that is needed or deserved. This is an important distinction for LIS professionals, because it might mean that some services provided are fair rather than equal. For example, children's services might not be equal to adults' because their needs are different. The value of justice requires LIS professionals to recognize when equality is required, such as when ensuring access, and when fairness is at issue, such as serving those with extenuating or special circumstances.

7. The Seventh Value: Aesthetics

Certain materials are collected because they possess the elements of extraordinary creativity—the works of genius that epitomize the best of our cultural achievements. The great music, art, literature, and philosophy of the past, as well as those modern works that appear to have like potential, are often prized by libraries, even when their circulation levels are low. These works often receive special consideration for preservation.

Although one might debate which of these seven values is most important, there is general agreement that they are consistent among LIS professionals around the world. Koehler (2003), for example, in an international survey of nearly 1,900 librarians, found that patron service was the highest-rated value throughout the world and that information literacy, equality of access, preservation of the intellectual record, and intellectual freedom were also among the top-rated values. These values inform the actions of LIS professionals and account for their misgivings and resistance when these values are threatened.

B. Core Values and the ALA

Although the ALA promulgated a variety of policies reflecting its values, such as policies on intellectual freedom and ethical conduct, there was no one document that clearly enunciated all the critical values of the field. The need for such a document was voiced at the ALA's first Congress on Professional Education in 1999. A Core Values Task Force was appointed to formulate the critical values and released a Statement on Core Values in 2000. These included:

- Connection of people to ideas
- Assurance of free and open access to recorded knowledge, information, and creative works
- Commitment to literacy and learning
- Respect for the individuality and the diversity of all people
- Freedom for all people to form, to hold, and to express their own beliefs
- Preservation of the human record
- Excellence in professional service to our communities
- Formation of partnerships to advance these values (ALA 2000)

Reaction was mixed; one editorial writer described it as "a bland homogenization of euphemisms" (Buschman 2000), and it was not adopted.

In the meantime, the Association of College and Research Libraries (Spaulding 2002), a division of ALA, adopted its own core values for academic libraries:

- Equitable and open access to information
- Service
- Intellectual freedom
- Cooperation, collaboration, and sharing of resources
- Commitment to the profession of librarianship
- Fair use
- Education and learning
- Commitment to the use of appropriate technology
- Knowledge as an end in itself
- Conservation and preservation of knowledge
- Diversity
- Scholarly communication and research
- Global perspective

In 2004, the ALA made another attempt to identify core values, drawing from preexisting statements already embodied in the ALA policy manual. Passed by the association, the ALA core values include the following:

- **Access**: ensuring that all information resources are provided equally regardless of format and technology.
- **Confidentiality/privacy**: ensuring that all interactions with patrons are private and confidential and that the principles of intellectual freedom are upheld.
- **Democracy**: ensuring that the First Amendment rights of users are protected so that the citizenry can be appropriately informed.

- **Diversity**: ensuring that a broad range of services are provided to all populations.
- **Education and lifelong learning**: ensuring that all types of libraries and library services support the education of users throughout their lifetime.
- **Intellectual freedom**: ensuring that the principles of intellectual freedom are upheld.
- **The public good**: ensuring that libraries support the public good and promote democratic institutions.
- **Preservation**: ensuring that all types of information are preserved.
- **Professionalism**: ensuring that library services are supported by professionally educated staff members from graduate programs in higher education.
- **Social responsibility**: ensuring that libraries participate in the amelioration of the substantive social problems of the day. (ALA 2004)

These values, although they tend to focus on public libraries, fairly represent of the values of LIS professionals in general. All information organizations, for example, must respect democratic institutions and individual rights. As a foundation for how LIS professionals should conduct themselves, these values represent a sensible and helpful framework.

II. THE ETHICS OF LIBRARY AND INFORMATION SCIENCE

Ethical deliberations are extremely complex because they deal with fundamental questions of right and wrong. Central to the issue of ethics is how people should be treated and how one should act, if one wishes to act rightly. To help make ethical decisions, people draw on philosophical, religious, and legal sources, and the divergent points of view offered in these various perspectives account for lively discussion. These debates are not explicated here as we cannot determine once and for all what is right or wrong in a given instance. Rather, my purpose is to identify some of the major principles, codes, obligations, and ethical dilemmas that accompany our professional responsibilities.

The focus of ethical debates in librarianship has varied over the years. For example, DuMont (1991) examined three historical periods and found that each dealt with different ethical issues. In the years prior to 1930, American librarianship was engaged in building and maintaining collections and the ethical questions concerned whether to include materials with potentially corrupting attributes. From 1930 to 1950, the ethical discussions focused on how people in libraries, including staff, should be treated. Debate centered on issues such as job security, safe working conditions, education, and training. Another ethical concern was related to the free access to information, perhaps due, at least in part, to the rise of fascism in Nazi Germany (Harris 1973). Since 1960, the ethical issues have centered on improving the public good, promoting social justice, and taking socially progressive political positions. Debate focused on affirmative action, the needs of the underserved, and the ethical responsibilities of the reference librarian in answering questions. In regard to the latter, for example, Hauptman (1976) questioned whether reference librarians should provide information on building a car bomb, and Dowd (1989) explored whether they should provide information on freebasing cocaine. The underlying question was whether reference librarians can be totally neutral in the performance of their duties, or whether social consequences of the information should be considered.

Almost every LIS professional at some time will be confronted with an ethical issue. For example, Hoffman (2005) surveyed Texas librarians in public libraries and schools and found that more than one-third had experienced an ethical dilemma related to censorship, copyright, or patron privacy. However, only a third of the respondents indicated that they applied the ALA Code of Ethics to their daily work situations, and school librarians were more likely to report a tension between the Code and their day-to-day responsibilities. In some circumstances, concern for ethical behavior arises, not because particular actions might be unethical, but because certain actions result in undesired outcomes or diminished productivity.

Although there have been several conferences on ethical issues, and the *Journal of Information Ethics* regularly offers thoughtful discussions, the reality is that for most LIS professionals, today's work environment allows very little time for reflection on values and ethical practice. These circumstances highlight the need for examining now, how the ethical actions of LIS professionals affect and are affected by a number of factors and stakeholders.

Froehlich (1992) identified at least seven stakeholders in the information dissemination process who might be affected by our actions, including authors, publishers, database producers, database vendors or networks, information professionals, the organization and managers, and the end users or consumers. He proposed an ethical model addressing professional conduct from three perspectives: self, organization, and environment. The self is a moral agent, the person who must act or suffer the consequences of the actions of others; the organization is the institution, also a moral agent, that acts in an autonomous manner and directs the actions of others; the environment includes the standards of the community, or professional societies, that create the ethical context in which the self and organization operate. Ethical stresses arise from the interactions and imperatives of each of these elements, which are sometimes not easily or consistently balanced. Hence, there might be a conflict between the self as an individual and the self as an employee or a member of an organization. For example, a librarian might have a personal belief that certain content is morally offensive. As an individual moral agent, the librarian might believe that such material is inappropriate for dissemination; at the same time, there are organizational and professional standards of conduct that dictate that the material should be freely disseminated. Such conflicts might be infrequent for some and commonplace for others, but they are inevitable for most. The need to discuss such ethical concerns is further highlighted by the fact that library and information science is a service-oriented profession; our most important stakeholder is our user.

A. Factors in Ethical Deliberations

Most of the time, LIS professionals do not think consciously about the ethical ramifications of what they do; our behavior follows from training and habit. It is only in special situations that ethical dissonance arises. In such situations, there is general agreement that we need standards of professional conduct to limit unethical actions. In addition, ethical constraints apply not only to individuals but to organizations. Libraries and other information organizations are not value neutral; they act, make choices, affect human beings, and receive, allocate, and disseminate resources in ways analogous to individuals. They too have ethical obligations.

In fact, there are no occupations in which ethical practices do not apply, although some professions are more likely to confront ethical issues than others. In order for LIS professionals to take informed and appropriate action, they must anticipate and understand the nature of ethical dilemmas likely to occur in libraries, be familiar with the ethical prescriptions of the field, and know the factors that should be considered when deliberating ethical issues. At least four considerations factor into ethical deliberations: social utility, survival, social responsibility, and respect for the individual. These factors are not ethical principles in themselves, but they are critical variables to consider in arriving at a decision. In fact, it is the constant attempt to balance these factors that often makes ethical decisions so difficult.

1. Social Utility

Public organizations are intended to serve important social ends. Libraries are certainly among those institutions that have a socially desirable purpose. Academic libraries advance society by educating students and producing research that will improve society; public libraries meet the educational, recreational, and informational needs of the general public; and school libraries help prepare students to enter the job market and provide them with the life skills to function effectively in society. The extent to which an organization accomplishes its social purpose is its social utility. Decisions and actions that aid the organization in accomplishing its social purpose are ethically desirable but not always easy to make. For example, suppose a supervisor needed to release a personable employee who made an earnest effort but was simply unable to meet the demands of the job. The decision to terminate might, therefore, produce considerable discomfort despite the fact that keeping the employee would impair the library's function. Another example might be that in order for one's own worthy organization to succeed, other worthy institutions might be disadvantaged. For example, the library might compete with city parks, law enforcement, or schools for a limited amount of public monies. Similarly, if the library develops DVD collections or computer games, it might have a detrimental effect on local businesses that rent or sell them.

2. Survival

Organizations, like individuals, strive to survive. When people are threatened and they act in self-defense, it is generally presumed that they are acting correctly. Libraries regularly confront issues that challenge their survival. Perhaps the most obvious example is when some members of a community object to something in the collection or when the library allows patrons to access questionable material on the Internet. In a censorship case, the need to survive might conflict with the social utility factor. Censors often threaten the library's funding. Under these circumstances, the library's leadership might consider bowing to these pressures because the continued existence of the library is considered more important than the retention of a few items in the collection. On the other hand, there seems little value in protecting the library's fiscal survival if it can no longer meet its social purpose: free access to all types of ideas, even objectionable ones.

3. Social Responsibility

Organizations have an obligation not only to survive and fulfill their specific purposes but to serve the larger society. Public organizations, in particular, must meet this obligation because their survival depends in large measure on society's fiscal support. LIS professionals recognize that they have social responsibilities to their communities as well as responsibilities to help the library survive and perform their professional functions. For example, a policy promoting equal employment opportunity ensures that all members of the society have an equal opportunity for library positions. Another example might be a policy to order as many items as possible on acid-free paper to minimize pollution. As in the previous examples, there might be conflicts with other factors.

4. Respect for the Individual

People have a right to act as they see fit, insofar as they do not violate the dignity and respect of others. LIS professionals strive to respect individuals in many ways. For example, libraries are open to all persons, and the collections are tailored to individual interests as well as for the masses. Librarians pay special attention to building collections that represent a wide range of materials, reflecting diverse perspectives. Libraries protect the privacy of patrons' circulation records, and ensure that the rules and policies treat employees fairly and respect their privacy as well.

Again, balance is important. For example, library administrators might choose to purchase more materials with broader appeal to improve the prospects of the library's survival. They might reason that the public will be more inclined to support the library and there will be less possibility of dissatisfaction with controversial selections. Such a choice puts greater emphasis on survival and less on respect for the individual. Other conflicts might occur between social responsibility and respecting the individual. For example, the former factor might be used to justify compliance with law enforcement authorities who request the circulation record of a patron who committed a serious crime.

All of the factors mentioned above are important. Nonetheless, even when LIS professionals think they have made the best decision after weighing all of the various factors, there is often a residue of dissatisfaction. This ambivalence arises, in part, because of the often-competing interests of the public, board members, administrators, and staff. Attempts to arrive at decisions that will satisfy all of these parties frequently result in frustration. Balancing them is a complex and challenging task. There is no simple formula for determining which factor weighs more heavily in a given situation. Rubin and Froehlich (1996) suggested four questions that might be helpful in these deliberations:

1. To what extent is the survival of the organization threatened?
2. To what extent will the purpose of the organization be harmed?
3. To what extent is the organization or employee socially responsible or irresponsible when acting in a particular manner?
4. To what extent are the actions of the organization or individuals acting in its behalf harming or benefiting other individuals, organizations, or the profession? (p. 41)

B. Categories of Ethical Concern

Ethical dilemmas in library and information science generally arise in relation to two issues. One area is information ethics, concerned with the use and misuse of information. Issues include the ownership of information, intellectual property rights, free or restricted access, use of government information, ensuring privacy and confidentiality, data integrity, and the international flow of information. The second area deals with professional behavior, including how we apply ethical principles to our decisions and actions as information professionals (Smith 1993a). These two areas are closely related and often overlap, more a matter of emphasis rather than unique content, and often discussion of one cannot proceed satisfactorily without discussing the other.

From these two issues arise a number of professional practice issues linked to ethical considerations, including "accuracy, comprehensiveness, obligations to the client, responsibilities to the community, and the long term commitment to preserve the record of knowledge" (Byrne 2002, p. 10). The following is a more detailed discussion of some of the many categories of ethical concern within the library and information context.

1. Free Access to Information and the Effects of Information

"The basic function of the library is to optimize the value of recorded information for humankind" (Finks 1991, p. 86). The decisions made by LIS professionals might determine who receives information and who does not. Failure to perform this function is a violation of professional ethics. Accomplishing it, however, requires a careful balancing of interests, realizing that both benefits and harms might arise.

The freedom of information tenet touches virtually all activities and policies of LIS professionals. Primary guidance comes from the ALA Code of Ethics and the American Society for Information Science and Technology's (ASIS&T) Professional Guidelines, which refer to "free and equal access" (ALA 1995; ASIS&T 1994). But we need to consider other questions as well, such as the tension that comes from the need to protect individual rights and the imperative to act in a socially responsible manner. Smith (1993b) characterized this tension as a dynamic relationship between three components: (1) freedom, meaning intellectual freedom; (2) information democracy, that is, promoting the need for social equity in information; and (3) responsibility, or the obligation to promote the social good. Some might argue that inappropriate and potentially harmful content should be restricted either by prohibiting, filtering, or monitoring such access, particularly if young people are involved. Others would argue that it is the ethical duty of LIS professionals to provide access to all, including young people, and that we should not violate patrons' privacy rights by acting as watchdogs. Internet use further complicates matters. Wyatt (2006) argued that the ethics of monitoring Internet use are a matter of degree. For example, constantly monitoring computer activities would constitute unethical conduct because it is a serious privacy intrusion, but periodically monitoring to provide assistance, which also allows a check on appropriate computer use, is not.

With the growth of the World Wide Web and the vast amount of information, some accurate, some not, that is now available, Wengert (2001) argued that librarians' responsibility to provide accurate information is greater than ever. However, a duty to provide access does not free us from assessing potential harms. Baker (1992) articulated this consideration as "Do no harm" (p. 8). She was referring specifically to the activities of library administrators, but the underlying notion applies in other instances as well. It suggests that library activities should minimize harm to others. Ethical behavior not only protects the rights of others but also considers their welfare. These issues are particularly evident in the debate over whether LIS professionals should disseminate materials about suicide to minors. Similarly, there is some evidence that exposure to violent materials might lead to levels of increased aggressive behavior; as a consequence, some librarians are concerned about the dissemination of violent materials to minors (Green and Thomas 1986). It is not being suggested here that LIS professionals should act as censors, but rather that considering the effects of information on a particular patron lies well within the domain of ethical deliberations. Intellectual freedom issues, although intimately related, do not exhaust other important considerations when making ethical decisions.

2. Selection Decisions

Selection decisions determine the nature of the library collection and there is an ethical obligation to meet the needs of the patrons, to use appropriate selection criteria, to hire qualified selectors, and to establish an efficient system for procuring items. Ethical conflicts arise when selectors choose items of particular interest to them, rather than their patrons, or acquire items simply because they are popular and increase the chance for improved funding. If they bow to pressure from administrators or powerful members of the community and select items that fail to meet the selection criteria, ethical dissonance arises. Perhaps even more common, sometimes selectors fear that a particular selection will be both popular and controversial and therefore they opt not to select it. In each of these cases, ethics are a factor.

3. Privacy

Respect for privacy is a fundamental concept in a democratic society. As the amount of personally identifiable information stored in computer networks increases, privacy issues are magnified. With the passage of the U.S.A. PATRIOT Act, the government increased its powers of surveillance to prevent terrorism (discussed in more detail in Chapter 8). Suffice it to say here that the government now has a surveillance capability that was unavailable previously and can track someone's activities on the Internet. The library has the dual responsibilities of protecting the privacy and intellectual freedom rights of patrons and ensuring that the library computers are not being used for unlawful purposes.

4. Copyright

Although copyright is fundamentally a legal concept subsumed under the broader notion of intellectual property, it is also an ethical issue. Librarians often make copies of materials or encourage others to do so without seeking copyright permission (discussed in more detail in Chapter 8). This is not with the intention of depriving copyright owners of their rights, but in fulfillment of the library's mission to provide information. The issue of copyright involves competing ethical considerations. If the library's mission is to promote the dissemination of information to all users, then aren't LIS professionals ethically bound to disseminate as much information as possible? On the other hand, don't we have an obligation to respect and protect the rights of both authors and patrons? After all, if copying reduces the incentive for authors to produce works, then the library will have nothing to disseminate. LIS professionals want authors to profit, but they do not want authors and publishers to restrict and control the flow of information.

Ethical debates over electronic information will no doubt increase. For example, as LIS professionals deal with digital rights management contracts and technologies, to what extent should they attempt to circumvent them to provide information to patrons? To what extent should they attempt to limit patrons who might be abusing copyright privileges? Should LIS professionals comply with licenses that have few or no provisions for fair use?

5. The Organization of Information

Organizing information has been a fundamental task of librarianship since its beginnings. Usually this task was considered from a strictly conceptual and procedural perspective, largely a question of techniques: which ones were best, and which were the easiest to understand and use? However, organization is not without ethical implications. For example, a cataloger might classify some materials as adult that were really aimed at young people, because the cataloger believed they were inappropriate for children. These biases, whether intentional or not, deprive or inhibit access to information, inappropriately silencing the voices of authors or producers who have a right to be heard. Such actions violate several fundamental values of librarianship, particularly excellence in service.

How knowledge is organized often reflects a society's attitudes. For example, the Dewey Decimal Classification System has been criticized for diminishing the importance of contributions from non-Western cultures. When organizing information we must consider what values, prejudices, or preconceptions we might bring to this process. Technical services play a critical role in executing professional values; too often technical services are perceived as having only an oblique relationship to the patron. But their purpose is the same as all other library functions: to provide the highest-quality service. In fact, the patron has a direct relationship with technical services, because they determine, to a considerable extent, how access is accomplished. As Bierbaum (1994) noted, "The mission of technical services is to provide bibliographical and physical access to collections and information" (p. 13). Among other things, this implies that technical services professionals have an ethical obligation to maintain high bibliographic standards, to process materials efficiently and effectively, to reduce barriers to information, to keep up with technical and professional issues in technical services, and to resist censorship.

6. Information Policy

Information policies include the international, national, state, and organizational laws and regulations governing information technologies and the ability of citizens to access information, and hence have ethical ramifications. Consider just a few examples: restricting materials to those under eighteen; failing to develop policies or practices that meet the information needs of people who are poor, disabled, or members of minority groups; and revealing circulation records to others.

7. Information Quality

Ethical obligations extend to the quality of information. To the extent that a library can ensure that the information it provides is timely and accurate, it preserves its service values. When libraries cannot ensure quality, they might well have an obligation to inform patrons that there might be deficiencies, limitations, or biases in the information provided. This obligation becomes especially relevant when people are searching automated databases and the Web. There might be a temptation to let patrons believe that these systems access all relevant information, which, as professionals, we know to be untrue. LIS professionals have ethical duties, if not legal ones, to ensure that such systems are not misrepresented.

If one assumes that information professionals are just that—professionals—then they have an ethical obligation to maintain high professional standards in their work. We certainly expect that a doctor's recommendations are based on the most scientifically accurate information and best practices; the same assumption applies to attorneys. When they fail to meet the standards of practice in their fields, they are subject to charges of malpractice. Although Diamond and Dragich (2001) pointed out that there is a potential liability for malpractice for LIS professionals, thus far there is a lack of evidence that any legal actions have occurred. Nonetheless, they suggest that LIS professionals should focus on "what constitutes good practice in librarianship" (p. 395). LIS professionals might not have the same legal obligations as some other professionals, but their ethical obligations to maintain the highest standards of service are similar to those of any profession.

Do LIS professionals provide the highest levels of service? Ulvik and Salvesen (2007) suggested that if reference librarians conducted inadequate interviews, they would not be acting in the best interest of their patrons. Other activities that would fail to meet the highest standards of practice might include the following:

1. Opening reference queries that do not help to clarify questions or obtain sufficient information to answer the question
2. Inadequate inclusion of the patron in the search process
3. Lack of empathy
4. Showing discomfort with questions of a sensitive nature
5. Using communication strategies that foreclose the process prematurely
6. Giving insufficient opportunity for young people to choose materials on their own

Isaacson (2004) suggested that sometimes reference librarians provide answers that satisfy or please a patron, but are not necessarily the best answers—ones that the patron might not want to hear. McKinzie (2002) argued that libraries fail to provide the highest quality of service when they permit paraprofessionals to perform reference services that should be the responsibility of degreed staff. All of these examples serve to highlight the need to consider our activities from the standpoint of best practice.

Ethical Issues in the Fair Treatment of Personnel

Violations of Privacy

- Revealing information about employees to individuals who do not need to know such information or revealing information that might unnecessarily damage the individual's personal or professional reputation.
- Misusing personnel records or files, including inappropriate access to computer files.
- Collecting any personal information about employees that is not related to the necessary functions of the organization.
- Conducting inappropriate investigations of an individual's personal history or using irrelevant personal information to make a personnel decision.
- Conducting drug, alcohol, HIV, or other testing unless it is essential to the safe operation of the job or is directly related to the safety of others.
- Monitoring employees with video cameras or tape recorders without their knowledge or consent, unless significant and specific job-related reasons make such monitoring necessary.
- Using a polygraph unless there is clear and substantial reason for its use (e.g., in cases of suspected theft).
- Attempting to censor the writing or speech of employees unless such speech or writing would significantly damage the institution's ability to perform its essential function.

Misuses of Authority

- Showing favoritism to friends or relatives.
- Making personnel decisions out of anger or spite.
- Writing inaccurate job references for employees to prevent them from gaining other employment or to encourage their departure.
- Collecting job-related information from employees, without informing them of the potential consequences (e.g., for disciplinary action).
- Retaliating against employees who are outspoken or who have merely exercised their legal rights.
- Withholding information from an individual to ensure or promote job failure.

Organizational Inadequacies

- Designing a system of rewards that fosters cheating, sabotaging the work of others, or withholding important information, or that places emphasis only on quantity rather than quality (e.g., providing substantial financial rewards for higher library circulation).
- Paying wages and benefits that do not give minimal protection and security to employees.
- Creating a personnel system that discriminates or is unfair in administering essential personnel functions.
- Permitting the hiring and placement of individuals with a master of library science degree in support staff positions.
- Misusing behavior modification techniques to manipulate employees.
- Knowingly allowing employees to work in unsafe or unhealthy working conditions, especially without their knowledge or consent

(*Source:* Rubin 1990, p. 39.)

---

8. Administration and Management

Among the many ethical issues in management and administration are the ethical use of consultants, obligations in business dealings with vendors or others, and the fair treatment of personnel. LIS professionals have considerable interest in the last category.

C. Professional Codes of Ethics

As noted earlier, LIS professionals seldom have the time or opportunity to think about ethics and when conflicts arise, we act almost automatically without taking much time to reflect on the implications of our acts. The fact that people generally act out of habit highlights the importance and power of our early professional training. Once the ethics of one's profession are ingrained, acting in accordance with them should follow as an integral element of our everyday behavior. This is not to say that one's personal ethics cannot vary from one's professional ethics. In most cases, however, one would hope that professional ethics can be seen as a specialized example of our personal ethical practices although from time to time, they might conflict.

Regrettably, it is not clear how the socialization of professional ethics in information professionals takes place. It is true that the basic ethical principles are often reviewed in schools of library and information science, but Buchanan (2004) reported that although topics such as privacy, censorship, and intellectual freedom are often covered, there are no standard readings or content for ethics education in LIS curricula. In fact, she noted that there is also no agreement as to the amount of theory and practical application needed, although using case studies appears to be a particularly popular method.

The primary means of communicating ethical principles in the professions appears to be through codes of ethics. Codes of ethics for librarians appeared in the mid to late twentieth century and include ALA's Code of Ethics, the Society of American Archivists' (SAA's) Code of Ethics for Archivists, and the ASIS&T Professional Guidelines. Other information-based disciplines also have codes of ethics, such as the Association for Computing Machinery's Code of Ethics and Professional Conduct, and the Society of Competitive Intelligence Professionals' Code of Ethics for CI Professionals. Professional codes are important for at least four reasons:

1. They represent a statement of the fundamental values of the profession.
2. They are useful in teaching new professionals about fundamental values.
3. Reading (and rereading) them, listening to others discuss them, and seeing them applied promotes their assimilation.
4. When particularly knotty ethical issues arise, the professional code can serve as a decision-making guide and as a jog for one's conscience.

Koehler (2002, p. 327) described most ethical codes related to the information professions as "prescriptive" and "aspirational" in that they recommend conduct and also tend to identify the greater purposes that they serve. Codes are "a way of enhancing the profession's reputation and professional trust, and of defining and sensitizing persons to their professional responsibility" (Sturgeon 2007, p. 57).

The content of codes might vary considerably, but they often are consistent in their themes. Trushina (2004) examined the ethical codes adopted by library associations in thirty countries and found the greatest emphasis placed on the importance of free access, confidentiality of users, and intellectual freedom. Koehler and Pemberton (2000) examined the ethical codes of various information organizations and identified five shared themes:

- Whenever possible, place the needs of clients above all other concerns.
- Understand the roles of the information practitioner and strive to meet them with the greatest possible skill and competence.
- Support the needs and interests of the profession and the professional associations.
- Insofar as they do not conflict with professional obligations, be sensitive and responsive to social responsibilities appropriate to the profession.
- Be aware of and responsive to the rights of users, employers, fellow practitioners, one's community, and the larger society. (p. 329)

Simply reading the codes will not inculcate them into professional practice. Because only a few people participated in the discussions that created the codes, some of the provisions might seem obscure or unnecessarily arbitrary. Failure to debate and internalize the meaning and rationale behind the codes can leave the professional ill prepared to act appropriately in a crisis. This is especially problematic when professionals must justify their actions. Unless the individual can articulate a solid understanding of the code's rationale, the explanation is likely to sound dogmatic rather than like a thoughtful justification of professional conduct. Nonetheless well-written codes "reveal the tension among the various values that the profession represents" (Sturgeon 2007, p. 57).

Obviously, an ethical code is only as good as the willingness of individuals to follow it. For the professions, such as law and medicine, violations of the codes are enforceable through loss of licensure and disciplinary actions. This type of action is certainly appropriate for professions where one's life or liberty might be affected. In other professions, including library and information science, the codes are enforced through the norms of the profession—that is, other professionals subject unethical conduct to criticism and disapproval. Professional codes establish a social expectation that they will be followed because they represent consensus on appropriate behavior.

1. ALA Code of Ethics

There was little demand for an ethical code for librarians before the twentieth century. The earliest discussions took place between 1903 and 1909. Two individuals were particularly influential and contributed significantly to these early discussions: Mary Wright Plummer, director of the Pratt Institute Library School, and Charles Knowles Bolton, librarian of the Boston Athenaeum. The ALA considered a code in 1928, but it was not formally adopted until 1938 (Lindsey and Prentice 1985) (see Figure 10.1, p. 428). The ALA Library Bill of Rights was adopted a year later. Together, these two documents form the ethical foundation for the library and information science professions.

The Code of Ethics explicitly recognizes the potential conflicts in values inherent in library and information science and establishes one overriding value: "commitment to intellectual freedom and freedom of access to information" (ALA 1995). Although not formally subdivided, the eight provisions of the code focus on three general areas: access issues, rights of authors and creators, and employment issues.

a. Access Issues

Consistent with the overriding value cited in the preamble, three of the eight provisions deal directly with the issue of access. The first provision emphasizes the obligation to treat all equally, emphasizing equal treatment and access. The second suggests that there is an obligation to promote intellectual freedom and to resist attempts to censor library materials. The third recognizes the special nature of librarian-patron interactions. It highlights the privileged character of that relationship, albeit not necessarily in the legal sense. To this end, the librarian is exhorted to protect the privacy of all patrons and to ensure that their interactions remain confidential.

b. Rights of Authors and Creators

Although the Code of Ethics places great emphasis on service to patrons, one provision recognizes that the producers or creators of information are critical participants in this process and also deserve ethical treatment. Obviously, failure to recognize this aspect of information transfer and dissemination could seriously restrict the distribution of information products to libraries, with unhappy consequences for library service. To this end, Section IV of the code recognizes that authors and creators have the right to benefit from their creativity but a balance must be respected to ensure that library users have access to those ideas.

c. Employment Issues

Employment issues comprise more provisions of the code than any other issue. Section V suggests that treating fellow employees ethically is itself part of the ethical obligation to respect the rights and welfare of all employees. Section VI recognizes the essentially altruistic nature of the professional obligation and reminds us that our personal or private interests are not to be served above the interests of patrons,

Figure 10.1. ALA Library Code of Ethics

As members of the American Library Association, we recognize the importance of codifying and making known to the profession and to the general public the ethical principles that guide the work of librarians, other professionals providing information services, library trustees and library staffs.

Ethical dilemmas occur when values are in conflict. The American Library Association Code of Ethics states the values to which we are committed, and embodies the ethical responsibilities of the profession in this changing information environment.

We significantly influence or control the selection, organization, preservation, and dissemination of information. In a political system grounded in an informed citizenry, we are members of a profession explicitly committed to intellectual freedom and the freedom of access to information. We have a special obligation to ensure the free flow of information and ideas to present and future generations.

The principles of this Code are expressed in broad statements to guide ethical decision making. These statements provide a framework; they cannot and do not dictate conduct to cover particular situations.

I. We provide the highest level of service to all library users through appropriate and usefully organized resources; equitable service policies; equitable access; and accurate, unbiased, and courteous responses to all requests.

II. We uphold the principles of intellectual freedom and resist all efforts to censor library resources.

III. We protect each library user's right to privacy and confidentiality with respect to information sought or received and resources consulted, borrowed, acquired or transmitted.

IV. We respect intellectual property rights and advocate balance between the interests of information users and rights holders.

V. We treat co-workers and other colleagues with respect, fairness, and good faith, and advocate conditions of employment that safeguard the rights and welfare of all employees of our institutions.

VI. We do not advance private interests at the expense of library users, colleagues, or our employing institutions.

VII. We distinguish between our personal convictions and professional duties and do not allow our personal beliefs to interfere with fair representation of the aims of our institutions or the provision of access to their information resources.

VIII. We strive for excellence in the profession by maintaining and enhancing our own knowledge and skills, by encouraging the professional development of co-workers, and by fostering the aspirations of potential members of the profession.

Adopted June 28, 1997, by the ALA Council; amended January 22, 2008. Reprinted with permission from the American Library Association.

the employer, or other employees. Section VII focuses on a very delicate aspect of professional work. Each of us brings to the workplace a set of values, beliefs, and moral perspectives that govern our everyday behavior, but sometimes, acting in our professional capacity, we should act in the best interests of our clients. Section VII suggests that we act to serve the patron, even if the material provided might violate our own values. Finally, Section VIII emphasizes the professional obligation to improve one's skills continually. In an increasingly complex information and technological environment, this is certainly vital. Interestingly, the obligation as set forth in this provision is broader than just self-improvement; it extends to the development of others. As such, it is especially pertinent to library decision makers and managers who have the capacity to create opportunities for training and development for their staff.

2. Society of American Archivists

Although some of the ethical issues confronted by archivists overlap with those noted above, the special function of archives—the storage and dissemination of cultural records of long-term value—has some special ethical burdens. Members of the SAA recognized this in their own Code of Ethics (see Figure 10.2), most recently revised in 2005 (SAA 2009).

Figure 10.2. Code of Ethics for Archivists

Preamble

The Code of Ethics for Archivists establishes standards for the archival profession. It introduces new members of the profession to those standards, reminds experienced archivists of their professional responsibilities, and serves as a model for institutional policies. It also is intended to inspire public confidence in the profession.

This code provides an ethical framework to guide members of the profession. It does not provide the solution to specific problems.

The term "archivist" as used in this code encompasses all those concerned with the selection, control, care, preservation, and administration of historical and documentary records of enduring value.

I. Purpose

The Society of American Archivists recognizes the importance of educating the profession and general public about archival ethics by codifying ethical principles to guide the work of archivists. This code provides a set of principles to which archivists aspire.

II. Professional Relationships

Archivists select, preserve, and make available historical and documentary records of enduring value. Archivists cooperate, collaborate, and respect each institution and its mission and collecting policy. Respect and cooperation form the basis of all professional relationships with colleagues and users.

III. Judgment

Archivists should exercise professional judgment in acquiring, appraising, and processing historical materials. They should not allow personal beliefs or perspectives to affect their decisions.

IV. Trust

Archivists should not profit or otherwise benefit from their privileged access to and control of historical records and documentary materials.

V. Authenticity and Integrity

Archivists strive to preserve and protect the authenticity of records in their holdings by documenting their creation and use in hard copy and electronic formats. They have a fundamental obligation to preserve the intellectual and physical integrity of those records.

Archivists may not alter, manipulate, or destroy data or records to conceal facts or distort evidence.

(Continued)

Figure 10.2. Code of Ethics for Archivists *(Continued)*

VI. Access

Archivists strive to promote open and equitable access to their services and the records in their care without discrimination or preferential treatment, and in accordance with legal requirements, cultural sensitivities, and institutional policies. Archivists recognize their responsibility to promote the use of records as a fundamental purpose of the keeping of archives. Archivists may place restrictions on access for the protection of privacy or confidentiality of information in the records.

VII. Privacy

Archivists protect the privacy rights of donors and individuals or groups who are the subject of records. They respect all users' right to privacy by maintaining the confidentiality of their research and protecting any personal information collected about them in accordance with the institution's security procedures.

VIII. Security/Protection

Archivists protect all documentary materials for which they are responsible and guard them against defacement, physical damage, deterioration, and theft. Archivists should cooperate with colleagues and law enforcement agencies to apprehend and prosecute thieves and vandals.

IX. Law

Archivists must uphold all federal, state, and local laws.

Approved by the SAA Council, February 5, 2005. Reprinted with permission of the Society of American Archivists.

This code deals with many issues, including ethical issues, related to the acquisition of and access to archival collections. There is an inherent tension associated with the primary purpose of archival services. The archivist is obligated to safeguard and protect materials of lasting value by applying best-practice preservation techniques. Ethical conflicts arise due to the concomitant responsibility to promote access to these materials by ensuring that only reasonable restrictions be placed on their use. It is a natural temptation for an archivist to do everything possible to preserve the human record, but archives are of little value if they cannot be consulted relatively easily. The archivist is ethically bound to minimize restrictions and to create the necessary finding aids so that the collection can be used. This tension is especially challenging when the works are rare and fragile.

Another ethical consideration in archival work is the issue of privacy related to the donation of letters and correspondence. Sometimes those who wrote the letters or who are the subject of the correspondence might not know that this material was donated. Archivists are exhorted to protect the privacy of such individuals, especially if they had no control over the provision of such records to the archives. This highlights the careful balancing of interests required of archivists who must consider both the rights of access to information and the protection of the privacy of others.

Finally, archivists often find themselves in competition with other archives to obtain certain materials. Archivists are expected to act ethically in procuring materials, accurately representing the capacity of the archive to store and maintain them.

Similarly, archivists must avoid competition that might work against preservation of the materials, and they should not attempt to appropriate records already archived in other organizations.

3. ASIS&T Guidelines for Professional Conduct

The ethical guidelines from ASIS&T are more broadly written because they are aimed at information workers in all types of occupations, not just librarianship (see Figure 10.3).

Figure 10.3. ASIS&T Professional Guidelines

Dedicated to the Memory of Diana Woodward

ASIS&T recognizes the plurality of uses and users of information technologies, services, systems and products as well as the diversity of goals or objectives, sometimes conflicting, among producers, vendors, mediators, and users of information systems.

ASIS&T urges its members to be ever aware of the social, economic, cultural, and political impacts of their actions or inaction.

ASIS&T members have obligations to employers, clients, and system users, to the profession, and to society, to use judgement and discretion in making choices, providing equitable service, and in defending the rights of open inquiry.

Responsibilities to Employers/Clients/System Users

- To act faithfully for their employers or clients in professional matters
- To uphold each user's, provider's, or employer's right to privacy and confidentiality and to respect whatever proprietary rights belong to them, by limiting access to, providing proper security for and ensuring proper disposal of data about clients, patrons or users.
- To treat all persons fairly.

Responsibility to the Profession

To truthfully represent themselves and the information systems which they utilize or which they represent, by

- not knowingly making false statements or providing erroneous or misleading information
- informing their employers, clients or sponsors of any circumstances that create a conflict of interest
- not using their position beyond their authorized limits or by not using their credentials to misrepresent themselves
- following and promoting standards of conduct in accord with the best current practices
- undertaking their research conscientiously, in gathering, tabulating or interpreting data; in following proper approval procedures for subjects; and in producing or disseminating their research results
- pursuing ongoing professional development and encouraging and assisting colleagues and others to do the same
- adhering to principles of due process and equality of opportunity.

(Continued)

Figure 10.3. ASIS&T Professional Guidelines (Continued)

Responsibility to Society

To improve the information systems with which they work or which they represent, to the best of their means and abilities by

- providing the most reliable and accurate information and acknowledging the credibility of the sources as known or unknown

- resisting all forms of censorship, inappropriate selection and acquisitions policies, and biases in information selection, provision and dissemination

- making known any biases, errors and inaccuracies found to exist and striving to correct those which can be remedied.

To promote open and equal access to information, within the scope permitted by their organizations or work, and to resist procedures that promote unlawful discriminatory practices in access to and provision of information, by

- seeking to extend public awareness and appreciation of information availability and provision as well as the role of information professionals in providing such information

- freely reporting, publishing or disseminating information subject to legal and proprietary restraints of producers, vendors and employers, and the best interests of their employers or clients.

Information professionals shall engage in principled conduct whether on their own behalf or at the request of employers, colleagues, clients, agencies or the profession.

Adopted 5/30/92. Reprinted with permission from American Society for Information Science and Technology, 1320 Fenwick Lane, Suite 510, Silver Spring, Maryland 20910, USA.

These guidelines acknowledge that some information services are part of private organizations and that the proprietary interests of employers must be taken into account in the dissemination of information. Nonetheless, many of the underlying principles are similar to the ALA Code of Ethics. The ASIS&T Code identifies three basic areas of ethical responsibility: (1) responsibilities to employers, clients, and system users; (2) responsibilities to the profession; and (3) responsibilities to society. Like the ALA code, these guidelines consider the right to privacy, confidentiality, and fair treatment of clients, users, and employers. The guidelines, under a more general notion of protecting privacy and confidentiality, also highlight a critical obligation of those who design and administer information systems—to provide security for those systems. In addition, as in the ALA code, the responsibility to the profession includes the promotion of continuing education. The guidelines add, however, the responsibility not to misrepresent one's qualifications or the information system that is being used. The responsibility to the society also echoes the ALA code in the emphasis on free and equal access to information.

D. Do Information Technologies Invite Ethical Lapses?

Today's technological environment highlights some of the deficiencies of these ethical codes. For example, Hauptman (2001) identified a variety of issues that accompany the use of computers and electronic information networks including charging fees, hacking, poor data integrity, inappropriate use of e-mail, cheating, and plagiarism. He observed that "technology changed the ways in which we create, store, and access data and information so dramatically that a real qualitative difference emerges" (p. 434). In fact, the very nature of these technologies might encourage or even promote unethical conduct (Rubin 1995). If this is true, then relying solely on ethical codes might not be sufficient. It is, therefore, worthwhile to consider some of the qualities of these new technologies that might promote unethical actions.

1. Computer Use Promotes a Sense of Anonymity

Although some computer use occurs in public areas, most people use their computers in an office or at home. Even if people are in the same room, it is relatively difficult for them to observe what someone might be doing on a computer. The feeling that one cannot be found out tends to increase one's propensity to commit unethical acts.

2. Theft Can Be Accomplished from Great Distances

Prior to the advent of computers, stealing generally required that the thief be present when an item was stolen. Computers, on the other hand, permit accessing an item through telephone or cable lines or satellite transmission. The result is that a computer file might be stolen by an individual in another city, state, or country. It is unlikely that such a thief will feel vulnerable to detection.

3. Copying Is Easy

The electronic medium is highly flexible. It is usually quite simple to download or make a copy of an electronic file while leaving the original unchanged. Under these circumstances, it is tempting to rationalize that nothing was actually taken. Electronic theft is essentially an intangible act; electronic impulses are not nearly as concrete as paper or objects. Perhaps this is why individuals seem to have fewer misgivings about copying software.

4. Potential Audiences Are Large and Easily Reached

Because of the nature of the Web, messages can now be sent quite easily to millions of individuals simultaneously, an act dubbed spamming. This capacity presents an opportunity for the unscrupulous to exploit large numbers of unwitting victims. In a world where social interaction is increasingly integrated into the digital environment, the opportunities for unethical behaviors increase. For LIS professionals, our responsibilities are not only to conduct ourselves appropriately, but to design our systems so that unethical conduct is inhibited. We must be particularly sensitive as new methods of communication attract our attention, that our excitement over their potentialities does not distract us from our obligations.

E. Organizational Approaches That Promote Ethical Behavior

Institutional approaches that can help promote ethical conduct include the following:

1. Establishing rules and regulations that clearly identify the ethical obligations of employees and management and clearly state the penalties for ethical violations
2. Developing training and education programs that sensitize information professionals to ethical issues
3. Punishing individuals for ethical violations
4. Establishing an ethics code within the organization
5. Hiring and promoting individuals who demonstrate ethical behavior and understanding
6. Developing a system of rewards that provides an incentive for ethical actions and a disincentive for unethical ones

All of these approaches are helpful. However, in the end ethical conduct rests first and foremost on individual behavior. Each of us, as professionals, is an individual moral agent, and we do not give up our ethical obligations when we become employees. The ethical codes of the profession are generally adequate, although sometimes they do fail us with their lack of specificity. Others have restated or supplemented these codes with additional principles (Baker 1992; Rubin and Froehlich 1996). For example, Froehlich (1992) offered the following five principles: minimize harm, respect the autonomy of others, act justly and fairly, seek social harmony, and comport with organizational, professional, and public trust. In general, the most basic principles for ethical conduct for LIS professionals would include the following:

1. Promote open, unbiased access to information.
2. Maintain professional skills and knowledge
3. Act honestly with colleagues and consumers of information
4. Respect the privacy and confidentiality of others.
5. Provide the best service possible.

III. SUMMARY

No matter which principles or codes we examine, it is clear that LIS professionals embrace the notion that our duties and obligations extend far beyond just doing a job. Our professional behavior follows from fundamental principles of respect for individuals and the desire to benefit both the organization and the society. These precepts are not new; on the contrary, they are quite old.

Ethical situations arise in many contexts during the execution of our professional responsibilities. The resulting ethical deliberations are complex and often require a balancing of many interests and considerations: individual, organizational, and societal. If LIS professionals abide by the fundamental ethical tenets expressed in our Code of Ethics and the ALA Bill of Rights, the mission and values that underlie American libraries can be preserved and sustained. Although it might not be possible to find one statement that encompasses all the ethical obligations of LIS professionals, the American Library Association promulgated a statement titled "Libraries: An American Value" (ALA 1999) (see Figure 10.4) that goes a good way toward accomplishing this goal and could easily be adapted to a variety of information settings.

Figure 10.4. Libraries: An American Value

Libraries in America are cornerstones of the communities they serve. Free access to the books, ideas, resources, and information in America's libraries is imperative for education, employment, enjoyment, and self-government.

Libraries are a legacy to each generation, offering the heritage of the past and the promise of the future. To ensure that libraries flourish and have the freedom to promote and protect the public good in the 21st century, we believe certain principles must be guaranteed.

To that end, we affirm this contract with the people we serve:

We defend the constitutional rights of all individuals, including children and teenagers, to use the library's resources and services;

We value our nation's diversity and strive to reflect that diversity by providing a full spectrum of resources and services to the communities we serve;

We affirm the responsibility and the right of all parents and guardians to guide their own children's use of the library and its resources and services;

We connect people and ideas by helping each person select from and effectively use the library's resources;

We protect each individual's privacy and confidentiality in the use of library resources and services;

We protect the rights of individuals to express their opinions about library resources and services;

We celebrate and preserve our democratic society by making available the widest possible range of viewpoints, opinions and ideas, so that all individuals have the opportunity to become lifelong learners-informed, literate, educated, and culturally enriched.

Change is constant, but these principles transcend change and endure in a dynamic technological, social, and political environment.

By embracing these principles, libraries in the United States can contribute to a future that values and protects freedom of speech in a world that celebrates both our similarities and our differences, respects individuals and their beliefs, and holds all persons truly equal and free.

Adopted by the Council of the American Library Association February 3, 1999. Reprinted with permission from the American Library Association.

NOTE

I am indebted to Dr. Thomas Froehlich, Kent State University, for many discussions on the ethical factors that affect deliberations in library and information science. The factors presented here were a product of those discussions.

REFERENCES

American Library Association. 1995. "Code of Ethics." Available: http://ala.org (accessed September 4, 2009).

———. 1999. "Libraries: An American Value." Available: http://ala.org (accessed September 4, 2009).

———. 2000. "Librarianship and Information Service: A Statement on Core Values." Fifth draft, April 28, 2000. Available: www.pla.org/ala/educationcareers/education/1stcongressonpro/ 1stcongressstatement.cfm (accessed February 10, 2010).

———. 2004. "Core Values of Librarianship." Available: www.ala.org/ala/aboutala/offices/oif/statementspols/corevaluesstatement/corevalues.cfm (accessed February 10, 2010).

American Society for Information Science and Technology. 1994. "ASIS&T Professional Guidelines." Available: www.asis.org/AboutASIS/professional-guidelines.html (accessed September 4, 2009).

Baker, Sharon L. 1992. "Needed: An Ethical Code for Library Administrators." *Journal of Library Administration* 16: 1–17.

Bierbaum, Esther Green. 1994. "Searching for the Human Good: Some Suggestions for a Code of Ethics for Technical Services." *Technical Services Quarterly* 11: 1–18.

Buchanan, Elizabeth A. 2004. "Ethics in Library and Information Science: What Are We Teaching?" *Journal of Information Ethics* 13 (spring): 51–60.

Buschman, John. 2000. "Editorial: Core Wars." *Progressive Librarian* 17 (summer). Available: www.libr.org/PL/17_Editorial.html (accessed February 8, 2010).

Butler, Pierce. 1951. "Librarianship as a Profession." *Library Quarterly* 21 (October): 235–247.

Byrne, Alex. 2002. "Information Ethics for a New Millenium" In *The Ethics of Librarianship: An International Survey*. Edited by Robert Vaagan. IFLA Publications 101. Munich: K.G. Saur, 8–18.

Diamond, Randy, and Martha Dragich. 2001. "Professionalism in Librarianship: Shifting the Focus from Malpractice to Good Practice." *Library Trends* 49 (winter): 395–414.

Dowd, Robert. 1989. "I Want to Find Out How to Freebase Cocaine; or Yet Another Unobtrusive Test of Reference Performance." *Reference Librarian* 25–26: 483–493.

DuMont, Rosemary. 1991. "Ethics in Librarianship: A Management Model." *Library Trends* 40 (fall): 201–215.

Estabrook, Leigh. 1982. "The Library as a Socialist Institution in a Capitalist Environment." In *The Economics of Information*. Edited by Jana Varlys. Jefferson, NC: McFarland, 3–16.

Finks, Lee W. 1991. "Librarianship Needs a New Code of Professional Ethics." *American Libraries* 22 (January): 84–92.

Foskett, D. J. 1962. "The Creed of a Librarian: No Politics, No Religion, No Morals." Paper given at North Western Group, Reference, Special, and Information Section, Manchester Literary and Philosophical Society House, Manchester, England, March 27, 1962.

Froehlich, Thomas J. 1992. "Ethical Considerations of Information Professionals." *Annual Review of Information Science and Technology (ARIST)* 27: 292.

Garrison, Dee. 1972–1973. "The Tender Technicians: The Feminization of Public Librarianship." *Journal of Social History* 6 (winter): 131–156.

Gorman, Michael. 1995. "Five New Laws of Librarianship." *American Libraries* 26 (September): 784–785.

Green, Russell G., and Susan L. Thomas. 1986. "The Immediate Effects of Media Violence on Behavior." *Journal of Social Issues* 42: 7–27.

Harris, Michael. 1973. "The Purpose of the American Public Library." *Library Journal* 98 (September 15): 2509–2514.

Hauptman, Robert. 1976. "Professionalism or Culpability? An Experiment in Ethics." *Wilson Library Bulletin* 50: 626–627.

———. 2001. "Technological Implementations and Ethical Failures." *Library Trends* 49 (winter): 433–440.

Hoffman, Kathy. 2005. "Professional Ethics and Librarianship." *Texas Library Journal* (fall): 96–98.

Isaacson, David. 2004. "Is the Correct Answer the Right One?" *Journal of Information Ethics* 13 (spring): 14–18.

Jacob, Christian. 2002. "Gathering Memory: Thoughts on the History of Libraries." *Diogenes* 49 (April): 41–57.

Koehler, Wallace. 2002. "Trends of Library Associations and Ethics in the US." In *The Ethics of Librarianship: An International Survey.* Edited by Robert Vaagan. IFLA Publications 101. Munich: K.G. Saur, 323–336.

———. 2003. "Professional Values and Ethics as Defined by 'The LIS Discipline.'" *Journal of Education for Library and Information Science* 44 (spring): 99–112.

Koehler, Wallace, and Michael Pemberton. 2000. "A Search for Core Values: Towards a Model Code of Ethics for Information Professionals." *Journal of Information Ethics* 9: 26–54.

Lindsey, Jonathan A., and Ann E. Prentice. 1985. *Professional Ethics and Librarians.* Phoenix, AZ: Oryx.

McCook, Kathleen de la Peña. 2001. "Social Justice, Personalism, and the Practice of Librarianship." *Catholic Library World* 72 (December): 80–84.

McKinzie, Steve. 2002. "For Ethical Reference, Pare the Paraprofessionals." *American Libraries* 33 (October): 42.

Neill, Sam D. 1992. "Why Books?" *Public Library Quarterly* 12: 19–28.

Ranganathan, S. R. 1963. *The Five Laws of Library Science.* New York: Asia, 1963. First published 1931.

Rawls, John. 1958. "Justice as Fairness." *Philosophical Review* 67: 164–194.

Rubin, Richard. 1990. *Human Resources Management in Libraries: Theory and Practice.* New York: Neal-Schuman.

Rubin, Richard E. 1995. "Moral Distancing and the Use of Information Technologies: The Seven Temptations." In *Proceedings of the Ethics in the Computer Age Conference, November 11–13, 1994.* New York: Association for Computing Machinery.

Rubin, Richard E., and Thomas J. Froehlich. 1996. "Ethical Aspects of Library and Information Science." *Encyclopedia of Library and Information Science.* Vol. 58 (Supplement). New York: Marcel Dekker, 33–52.

Smith, Martha M. 1993a. "Editorial." *North Carolina Libraries* 51 (spring): 4.

———. 1993b. "Information Ethics: Freedom, Democracy, Responsibility." *North Carolina Libraries* 51 (spring): 6–8.

Society of American Archivists. 2009. "Code of Ethics for Archivists." Available: www .archivists .org/governance/handbook/app_ethics.asp (accessed September 3, 2009).

Spaulding, Helen H. 2002. "New Realities, New Relationships." Available: www.ala.org/ala/ mgrps/divs/acrl/publications/crlnews/2002/sep/newrealities.cfm (accessed February 10, 2010).

Sturgeon, Roy L. 2007. "Laying Down the Law: ALA's Ethics Codes." *American Libraries* 38 (November): 56–57.

Swan, John. 1986. "Untruth or Consequences." *Library Journal* 111 (July 1): 44–52.

Trushina, Irina. 2004. "Freedom of Access: Ethical Dilemmas for Internet Librarians." *Electronic Library* 22: 416–421.

Ulvik, Synnove, and Gunhild Salvesen. 2007. "Ethical Reference Practice." *New Library World* 108: 342–353.

Wengert, Robert G. 2001. "Some Ethical Aspects of Being an Information Professional." *Library Trends* 49 (winter): 486–509.

Winter, Michael F. 1988. *The Culture and Control of Expertise: Toward a Sociological Understanding of Librarianship.* Westport, CT: Greenwood.

Wyatt, Anna May. 2006. "Do Librarians Have an Ethical Duty to Monitor Patrons' Internet Usage in the Public Library?" *Journal of Information Ethics* 15 (spring): 70–79.

SELECTED READINGS: ETHICS AND VALUES

Books

Adams, Helen. *Ensuring Intellectual Freedom and Access to Information in the School Library Media Program.* Westport, CT: Libraries Unlimited, 2008.

Buchanan, Elizabeth A., and Kathrine A. Henderson. *Case Studies in Library and Information Science Ethics.* Jefferson, NC: McFarland, 2009.

Gorman, Michael. *Our Enduring Values: Librarianship in the 21st Century.* Chicago: ALA, 2000.

McMenemy, David, Alan Poulter, and Paul F. Burton. *A Handbook of Ethical Practice: A Practical Guide to Dealing with Ethical Issues in Information and Library Work.* Oxford: Chandos Publishing, 2007.

Preer, Jean. *Library Ethics.* Westport, CT: Libraries Unlimited, 2008.

Articles

Aiken, Julian. "Outdated and Irrelevant?" *American Libraries* 38 (September 2007): 54–56.

Crowley, Bill, and Deborah Ginsberg. "Professional Values: Priceless." *American Libraries* 36 (January 2005): 52–55.

Doyle, Tony. "Should Web Sites for Bomb-Making Be Legal?" *Journal of Information Ethics* 13 (spring 2004): 34–37.

Finks, Lee W. "What Do We Stand For? Values without Shame." *American Libraries* 20 (1989): 352–356.

Fricke, Martin, Kay Mathiesen, and Don Fallis. "The Ethical Presuppositions Behind the Library Bill of Rights." *Library Quarterly* 70 (2000): 468–491.

Koehler, Wallace. "Professional Values and Ethics as Defined by 'The LIS Discipline.'" *Journal of Education for Library and Information Science* 44 (spring 2003): 99–119.

Miltenoff, Plamen, and Robert Hauptman. "Ethical Dilemmas in Libraries: An International Perspective." *Electronic Library* 23 (2005): 664–670.

Trushina, Irina. "Freedom of Access: Ethical Dilemmas for Internet Librarians." *Electronic Library* 22 (2004): 416–421.

Ulvik, Synnøve, and Gunhild Salvesen. "Ethical Reference Practice." *New Library World* 108 (2007): 342–353.

Watstein, Sarah B. "Do Libraries Matter?" *Reference Services Review* 34 (2006): 181–184.

Wengwert, Robert G. "Some Ethical Aspects of Being an Information Professional." *Library Trends* 49 (winter 2001): 486–509.

Willingham, Taylor L. "Libraries as Civic Agents." *Public Library Quarterly* 27 (2008): 97–110.

Wyatt, Anna May. "Do Librarians Have an Ethical Duty to Monitor Patrons' Internet Usage in the Public Library?" *Journal of Information Ethics* 15 (spring 2006): 70–79.

Appendix A

Summary of Major Library and Information Science Associations and List of Additional Associations

AMERICAN LIBRARY ASSOCIATION (ALA)

Founded in 1876, the American Library Association is the oldest and largest library association in the world. Any individual or organization that has an interest in libraries can join. A wide variety of types of libraries participate in ALA membership and activities, including state, public, school, and academic libraries, as well as libraries in government, commerce, the arts, the armed services, hospitals, and prisons. As of July 31, 2008, the organization had 3,373 organizational members, 265 corporate members, and 63,389 personal members for a total of 64,656. The stated mission of the organization is "to provide leadership for the development, promotion, and improvement of library and information services and the profession of librarianship in order to enhance learning and ensure access to information for all" (*ALA 2008–2009 Handbook of Organization*).

The association has identified seven key action areas to which it is devoting substantial energies:

1. Diversity
2. Equitable access to information and library services
3. Education and lifelong learning
4. Intellectual freedom
5. Advocacy for libraries and the profession
6. Literacy
7. Organizational excellence (www.ala.org)

ALA is an impressive bureaucracy with 17 round tables, 11 divisions, 57 state and regional chapters, 25 affiliated organizations, and a headquarters staff of approximately 270 employees. ALA is operated by a council, an executive director, and an executive board. A large number of committees composed primarily of ALA members play a critical role in reflecting the professional and political interests of the association. Round tables focus on such areas as continuing library education, armed forces libraries, ethnic materials, library history, and government documents. Divisions focus on services for children and adults, public libraries, and academic libraries. Standing committees include accreditation of programs of library and information studies, literacy and outreach, pay equity, diversity, development and recruitment, research and statistics, the status of women in librarianship, and membership. The primary political lobbying is effected by the Washington office of the American Library Association, which monitors political legislation and other activities that could affect the well-being of libraries and attempts to influence legislation to conform to the goals of the ALA.

The association authors many publications, including books and journals focusing on a variety of aspects of the profession. These include *Reference and User Services Quarterly*, a publication of the Reference and User Services Association (RUSA); *Public Libraries*, from the Public Library Association (PLA); *Library Administration and Management*, from the Library Leadership and Management Association (LLAMA); *Young Adult Library Services*, from the Young Adult Library Services Association (YALSA); *Children and Libraries*, from the Association for Library Service to Children (ALSC); *College and Research Libraries*, from the Association of College and Research Libraries (ACRL); and *American Libraries*, the official organ of the American Library Association. Such publications not only provide news and information on library activities, but also serve as sources for published research, analysis, and continuing education in professional practice. The association also holds two major conferences a year: the Midwinter Meeting, which is primarily devoted to committee activities, and the Annual Conference, where there are major program presentations.

AMERICAN SOCIETY FOR INFORMATION SCIENCE AND TECHNOLOGY (ASIS&T)

The American Society for Information Science and Technology was originally known as the American Documentation Institute. In 1968 its name was changed to the American Society for Information Science. In 2000 the name was again altered to its current one. ASIS&T was founded in 1937 by the Science Service and the microfilm services of the Bibliofilm Service of the U.S. Department of Agriculture. The money to finance the institute originally came from a grant from the Chemical Foundations, and the purpose of the institute was to produce scientific bibliographies, develop microphotography devices, and generally explore other mechanisms for improving the communication of recorded knowledge. Originally only institutional members were permitted, but in 1952 changes were made to the bylaws of the organization to permit individual membership. Membership consists of approximately 4,000 individuals and 300 institutional members. ASIS&T has twenty-one special interest groups (SIGs), which are designed to bring together members with common interests. For example, there are SIGs on digital libraries, bioinformatics, medical informatics, human-computer interaction, information architecture, knowledge management, and visualization, images, and sound.

Today, the focus of ASIS&T is on all aspects of the information transfer process, including organization, storage, retrieval, evaluation, and dissemination. Its stated mission is "to advance the information sciences and related applications of information technology by providing focus, opportunity, and support to information professionals and organizations" (www.asis.org). Its membership includes, but is not limited to, computer scientists, linguists, librarians, engineers, medical practitioners, chemists, and educators. The society also functions as an instrument of professional development through conferences, continuing education programs, professional development workshops, and publications. Among its major publications are *Journal of the American Society for Information Science and Technology* and *Annual Review of Information Science and Technology*. ASIS&T also publishes its conference proceedings and is cosponsor of *Information Science Abstracts*.

ASSOCIATION OF RESEARCH LIBRARIES (ARL)

The Association of Research Libraries was founded in December 1932 as a not-for-profit organization. It is governed by a board of directors, executive director, and a small headquarters staff. Unlike most other library organizations, membership is restricted to North American institutions; many of these are university libraries, although some are major public libraries, special libraries, and national libraries. There are approximately 120 members.

The mission of ARL is as follows:

> ARL influences the changing environment of scholarly communication and the public policies that affect research libraries and the diverse communities they serve. ARL pursues this mission by advancing the goals of its member research libraries, providing leadership in public and information policy to the scholarly and higher education communities, fostering the exchange of ideas and expertise, and shaping a future environment that leverages its interests with those of allied organizations. (www.arl.org)

ARL conferences provide a useful opportunity to exchange information on topics related to research libraries' survival. The organization has identified a number of key issues as well:

1. Copyright and intellectual property
2. Diversity
3. E-science
4. Leadership development
5. Legislation and appropriations
6. Library assessment
7. New models of publishing
8. Preservation
9. Special collections (www.arl.org)

In 1970 ARL created the Office of Management Services (OMS), now known as the Office of Leadership and Management Services (OLMS), which is intended to improve the leadership and management of human resources and the collections of research and academic libraries. This office collects statistics, prepares reports, and provides training and staff development in a variety of areas of management. Among the major publications of ARL are the *ARL Annual Salary Survey* and publications regarding statistics for academic law libraries, academic health service libraries, and preservation, among others.

INTERNATIONAL FEDERATION OF LIBRARY ASSOCIATIONS AND INSTITUTIONS (IFLA)

The International Federation of Library Associations and Institutions was founded in 1927, primarily to create a place for the leading librarians of Europe and America to meet and discuss contemporary issues of mutual interest. Today, IFLA is "an independent, international, non-governmental, not-for-profit organization" (www.ifla.org). Its international scope is broad, with more than 1,600 members from approximately 150 nations. It is headquartered in The Hague.

Among the mission and values of IFLA are to

> promote high standards of provision and delivery of library and information services, . . . encourage widespread understanding of the value of good library and information services, . . . represent the interests of our members throughout the world, . . . the endorsement of the principles of freedom of access to information, . . . the belief that people, communities and organizations need universal and equitable access to information, ideas and works of imagination for their social, educational, cultural, democratic and economic well-being, . . . the conviction that delivery of high quality library and information services helps guarantee that access, . . . [and] the commitment to enable all Members of the Federation to engage in, and benefit from, its activities without regard

to citizenship, disability, ethnic origin, gender, geographical location, language, political philosophy, race or religion. (www.ifla.org)

Many of the major American library associations are members, including ALA, the Association of Research Libraries, and the American Association of Law Libraries (AALL). IFLA is organized into eight divisions: General Research Libraries, Special Libraries, Libraries Serving the General Public, Bibliographic Control, Collections and Services, Management and Technology, Education and Research, and Regional Activities.

IFLA has a variety of programs that represent the main interests of the association. In partnership with the Conference of Directors of National Libraries (CDNL), the IFLA-CDNL Alliance for Digital Strategies (ICADS) was established in August 2008 to succeed the former IFLA-CDNL Alliance for Bibliographic Standards (ICABS). ICADS concentrates on the issues of "creating and building digital collections," "managing digital collections," and "accessing digital collections." Other programs include the Committee on Copyright and other Legal Matters (CLM), the Committee on Free Access to Information and Freedom of Expression (FAIFE), and committees to promote the improvement of library and information services in developing countries, the preservation and conservation of library materials, and "the development, maintenance and promotion of the UNIMARC format" (www.ifla.org).

IFLA issues a variety of monographs, professional reports, newsletters, and periodicals including *Libri*, *IFLA Journal*, and the *IFLA Directory*.

THE MEDICAL LIBRARY ASSOCIATION (MLA)

The Medical Library Association was founded in 1898 as the Association of Medical Librarians. It is the second oldest national library association in the United States and serves as the primary professional association for health sciences librarians in the United States and Canada. The purpose of the MLA is to promote the growth and development of medical libraries, to serve as an advocate for health information professionals, and to support the exchange of medical literature among its members. MLA also attempts to promote educational and professional growth among health sciences librarians and provides a considerable number of continuing education programs to meet this purpose.

There are more than 3,600 individual members, 1,100 institutional members, and a growing corporate membership. As of 2009, MLA had thirteen geographic regional chapters and eighteen special interest groups (SIGs), including those for mental health, clinical librarians, libraries in curriculum, molecular biology and genomics, pediatric librarians, and complementary and alternative medicine. (www.mlanet.org).

In contrast to most other forms of librarianship, medical librarians can be certified, and MLA adopted its first formal certification program in 1949. The credentialing criteria established by MLA stress educational qualifications, knowledge in core areas of medical information, and different levels of professional development. Recognition is provided by MLA's Academy of Health Information Professionals (AHIP). The association also produces monographic and periodical publications, including the *Journal of the Medical Library Association* (*JMLA*), *MLA News*, and *Handbook of Medical Library Practice*.

SPECIAL LIBRARIES ASSOCIATION (SLA)

The Special Libraries Association is a not-for-profit corporation founded in 1909 as a response to a growing number of special libraries. It is an international association of librarians who work in special libraries serving such areas as business, research, government, and universities. There are more than 11,000 members from more than eighty-three countries. SLA has fifty-six regional chapters and twenty-six divisions representing various subject fields and interests, and numerous caucuses, which are information groups that foster discussion and interaction among members with common interests (www.sla.org). SLA is sustained by five core values: leadership, service, innovation and continuous learning, results and accountability, and collaboration and partnering.

The association provides a variety of services, including consulting services to organizations that want to create or expand their information services and continuing education courses to advance the role of the professional librarian. Its Professional Development Center offers both distance learning and on-site learning experiences to assist in the management of special libraries.

SLA has become more politically active since the 1980s to deal with governmental policy areas that have direct effect on special libraries, such as copyright implementation and compliance, networking legislation, government information policies, and telecommunications. The monthly magazine of SLA is *Information Outlook*, which serves as a major professional continuing education tool for special librarians. The Web site is available at www.sla.org.

LIST OF ADDITIONAL LIBRARY ASSOCIATIONS OR CLOSELY RELATED ORGANIZATIONS

General

American Indian Library Association
Canadian Library Association

Council on Library Resources
Friends of Libraries USA
Information Industry Association
National Information Standards Organization
National Librarians Association

Archives/Bibliographical

Bibliographical Society of America
Society of American Archivists

Arts

American Film and Video Association (formerly the Educational Film Library
  Association)
Art Libraries Society of North America
Music Library Association
Theatre Library Association

Asian American

Asian/Pacific American Librarians Association
Chinese-American Library Association

Government/Federal

Association for Federal Information Resources Management
Chief Officers of State Library Agencies
Federal Library and Information Center Committee
National Association of Government Archives and Records Administrators

Law

American Association of Law Libraries

Library Education

Association for Library and Information Science Education

Religion

American Theological Library Association
Association of Christian Librarians
Association of Jewish Libraries
Catholic Library Association

Church and Synagogue Library Association
Lutheran Church Library Association

Business/Science

Association of Academic Health Sciences
Library Directors Patent and Trademark Depository
Library Association Society for Competitive Intelligence Professionals

Visual Images

Association for Information and Image Management
Association of Visual Science Librarians

Appendix B

Accredited Master's Programs in Library and Information Science in the United States and Canada

Alabama

University of Alabama
School of Library and Information Studies
Tuscaloosa, AL

Arizona

University of Arizona
School of Information Resources and
    Library Science
Tucson, AZ

California

San Jose State University
School of Library and Information
    Science
San Jose, CA

University of California at Los Angeles
Graduate School of Education and
    Information Studies
Department of Information Studies
Los Angeles, CA

Colorado

University of Denver
College of Education
Library and Information Science Program
Denver, CO

Connecticut

Southern Connecticut State University
School of Communication, Information
    and Library Science
Department of Information and Library
    Science
New Haven, CT

Florida

Florida State University
School of Library and Information
    Studies
Tallahassee, FL

University of South Florida
School of Library and Information
    Science
Tampa, FL

Georgia

Valdosta State University
Department of Information Studies
Valdosta, GA

Hawaii

University of Hawai'i at Manoa
Library and Information Science Program
Honolulu, HI

Illinois

Dominican University
Graduate School of Library and
    Information Science
River Forest, IL

University of Illinois at Urbana-
    Champaign
Graduate School of Library and
    Information Science
Champaign, IL

Indiana

Indiana University
School of Library and Information Science
Bloomington, IN

Iowa

University of Iowa
School of Library and Information Science
Iowa City, IA.

Kansas

Emporia State University
School of Library and Information
    Management
Emporia, KS

Kentucky

University of Kentucky
School of Library and Information Science
Lexington, KY

Louisiana

Louisiana State University
School of Library and Information Science
Baton Rouge, LA

Maryland

University of Maryland
College of Information Studies
College Park, MD

Massachusetts

Simmons College
Graduate School of Library and
    Information Science
Boston, MA

Michigan

University of Michigan
School of Information
Ann Arbor, MI

Wayne State University
School of Library and Information Science
Detroit, MI

Mississippi

University of Southern Mississippi
School of Library and Information Science
Hattiesburg, MS

Missouri

University of Missouri
School of Information Science and
    Learning Technologies
Columbia, MO

New Jersey

Rutgers University
School of Communication and
    Information
Library and Information Science
    Department
New Brunswick, NJ

New York

Long Island University
Palmer School of Library and Information
    Science
Brookville, NY

Pratt Institute
School of Information and Library Science
New York, NY

Queens College
City University of New York
Graduate School of Library and
 Information Studies
Flushing, NY

Saint John's University
Division of Library and Information Science
Queens, NY

University at Albany,
State University of New York
Department of Information Studies
Albany, NY

University at Buffalo, State University
 of New York
Graduate School of Education
Library and Information Studies
Buffalo, NY

Syracuse University
School of Information Studies
Syracuse, NY

North Carolina

North Carolina Central University
School of Library and Information
 Sciences
Durham, NC

University of North Carolina at Chapel
 Hill
School of Information and Library Science
Chapel Hill, NC

University of North Carolina at
 Greensboro
Department of Library and Information
 Studies
Greensboro, NC

Ohio

Kent State University
School of Library and Information Science
Kent, OH

Oklahoma

University of Oklahoma
School of Library and Information
 Studies
Norman, OK

Pennsylvania

Clarion University of Pennsylvania
College of Education and Human
 Services
Department of Library Science
Clarion, PA

Drexel University
College of Information Science and
 Technology
Philadelphia, PA

University of Pittsburgh
School of Information Sciences
Pittsburgh, PA

Puerto Rico

University of Puerto Rico
Escuela Graduada de Ciencia y
 Tecnologías de la Información
San Juan, PR

Rhode Island

University of Rhode Island
Graduate School of Library and
 Information Studies
Kingston, RI

South Carolina

University of South Carolina
School of Library and Information Science
Columbia, SC

Tennessee

University of Tennessee
School of Information Sciences
Knoxville, TN

Texas

Texas Woman's University
School of Library and Information
  Studies
Denton, TX

University of North Texas
Department of Library and Information
  Sciences
Denton, TX

University of Texas at Austin
School of Information
Austin, TX

Washington

University of Washington
Information School
Seattle, WA

Washington, DC

Catholic University of America
School of Library and Information
  Science
Washington, DC

Wisconsin

University of Wisconsin-Madison
School of Library and Information
  Studies
Madison, WI

University of Wisconsin-Milwaukee
School of Information Studies
Milwaukee, WI

Canada

Dalhousie University
School of Information Management
Halifax, NS

McGill University
School of Information Studies
Montreal, QC

University of Alberta
School of Library and Information
  Studies
Edmonton, AB

University of British Columbia
School of Library
Archival and Information Studies
Vancouver, BC

University of Montreal
École de Bibliothéconomie et des
  Sciences de l'Information
Montreal, QC

University of Toronto
Faculty of Information
Toronto, ON

University of Western Ontario
Faculty of Information and Media Studies
London, ON

Index

Page numbers followed by the letter "f" indicate figures and sidebars.

R

DON'T MISS THIS BOOK'S COMPANION WEB SITE!

www.neal-schuman.com/foundations

Find expanded Selected Readings lists for the major subject areas covered in this book:

> History and Mission of Libraries
> The LIS Profession
> Intellectual Organization of Libraries
> Libraries as Organizations
> Impact of Technology
> Information Science
> Information Policy
> Information Policy and Libraries
> Ethics and Values

About the Author

Richard E. Rubin is Director and Professor at the School of Library and Information Science at Kent State University, Kent, Ohio. He received his AB in Philosophy from Oberlin College, his MLS from Kent State University, and his PhD from the School of Library and Information Science at the University of Illinois. He has spoken and presented workshops throughout the United States primarily on aspects of human resource management, including hiring, performance evaluation, discipline and termination, worker motivation, and ethics in the workplace. Dr. Rubin has been active in professional associations on the national and local level, most recently serving as Chair of the ALA Committee on Accreditation.

Dr. Rubin is the author of numerous publications, including three books, *Human Resources Management in Libraries: Theory and Practice* (Neal-Schuman, 1991), *Hiring Library Employees* (Neal-Schuman, 1994), and two editions of *Foundations of Library and Information Science* (Neal-Schuman 2000, 2004). His articles have appeared in a variety of journals, including *Library Quarterly* and *Library and Information Science Research*, and he coauthored (with Thomas Froehlich) the article on ethics in library and information science for the *Encyclopedia of Library and Information Science*.